The Social History of
Crime and Punishment
in America

HV
6779
.S63

PARIS JUNIOR COLLEGE

The social history of crime and

39902000955791

3 The Social History of Crime and Punishment in America

AN ENCYCLOPEDIA

Wilbur R. Miller ■ EDITOR

State University of New York at Stony Brook

LEARNING CENTER
PARIS JR. COLLEGE

⑤SAGE reference

Los Angeles | London | New Delhi
Singapore | Washington DC

Los Angeles | London | New Delhi
Singapore | Washington DC

FOR INFORMATION:

SAGE Publications, Inc.
2455 Teller Road
Thousand Oaks, California 91320
E-mail: order@sagepub.com

SAGE Publications India Pvt. Ltd.
B 1/I 1 Mohan Cooperative Industrial Area
Mathura Road, New Delhi 110 044
India

SAGE Publications Ltd.
1 Oliver's Yard
55 City Road
London EC1Y 1SP
United Kingdom

SAGE Publications Asia-Pacific Pte. Ltd.
3 Church Street
#10-04 Samsung Hub
Singapore 049483

Vice President and Publisher: Rolf A. Janke
Senior Editor: Jim Brace-Thompson
Project Editor: Tracy Buyan
Cover Designer: Bryan Fishman
Editorial Assistant: Michele Thompson
Reference Systems Manager: Leticia Gutierrez
Reference Systems Coordinators: Laura Notton,
    Anna Villasenor
Marketing Manager: Kristi Ward

Golson Media
President and Editor: J. Geoffrey Golson
Director, Author Management: Susan Moskowitz
Production Director: Mary Jo Scibetta
Layout Editors: Kenneth Heller, Stephanie Larson,
    Oona Patrick, Lois Rainwater
Copy Editors: Mary Le Rouge, Holli Fort
Proofreader: Barbara Paris
Indexer: J S Editorial

Copyright © 2012 by SAGE Publications, Inc.

All rights reserved. No part of this book may be reproduced or utilized in any form or by any means, electronic or mechanical, including photocopying, recording, or by any information storage and retrieval system, without permission in writing from the publisher.

Library of Congress Cataloging-in-Publication Data

The social history of crime and punishment in America : an encyclopedia /
Wilbur R. Miller, general editor.
    v. cm.
 Includes bibliographical references and index.
 ISBN 978-1-4129-8876-6 (cloth)
    1. Crime--United States--History--Encyclopedias. 2. Punishment--United
States--History--Encyclopedias. I. Miller, Wilbur R., 1944-
 HV6779.S63 2012
 364.97303--dc23
                                    2012012418

12 13 14 15 16 10 9 8 7 6 5 4 3 2 1

Contents

Volume 3

List of Articles   *vii*

	Articles		
L	*975*	O	*1269*
M	*1053*	P	*1315*
N	*1175*	Q	*1475*

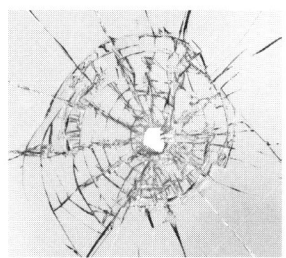

List of Articles

A
Ableman v. Booth
Abortion
Abrams v. United States
Adair v. United States
Adams, John (Administration of)
Adams, John Quincy (Administration of)
Adultery
Adversarial Justice
African Americans
Alabama
Alaska
Alcatraz Island Prison
Alien and Sedition Acts of 1798
American Bar Association
American Civil Liberties Union
American Law Institute
American Revolution and Criminal Justice
An American Tragedy
Anarchists
Anti-Federalist Papers
Antitrust Law
Appeals
Appellate Courts
Arizona
Arkansas
Arpaio, Joseph M.
Arraignment
Arthur, Chester (Administration of)
Articles of Confederation

Atlanta, Georgia
Attica
Auburn State Prison
Augustus, John
Autobiographies, Criminals'
Automobile and the Police
Aviation and Transportation Security Act of 2001

B
Bail and Bond
Bail Reform Act
Bailey, F. Lee
Bakker, Jim
Ballistics
Baltimore, Maryland
Barron v. Mayor of Baltimore
Beaumont, Gustave de
Bedford Hills Correctional Facility
Berkowitz, David
Bertillon System
Bible
Bigamy/Polygamy
Bill of Rights
Billy the Kid
Birmingham, Alabama
Black Panthers
Blackstone, William
Blood Sports
Blue Laws. *See* State Blue Laws
Bodie of Liberties

vii

Bodine, Polly
Boles, Charles
Bonnie and Clyde
Book of the General Lawes & Libertyes
Booth, John Wilkes
Bootlegging
Borden, Lizzie
Border Patrol
Boston, Massachusetts
Bounty Hunters
Bowers v. Hardwick
Brandenburg v. Ohio
Brennan, William J., Jr.
Brocius, William
Brockway, Zebulon
Brown v. Board of Education
Brown v. Mississippi
Buchanan, James (Administration of)
Buck v. Bell
Bundy, Ted
Buntline, Ned
Bureau of Alcohol, Tobacco, Firearms and Explosives
Buren, Martin Van (Administration of)
Burger, Warren
Burglary, Contemporary
Burglary, History of
Burglary, Sociology of
Bush, George H. W. (Administration of)
Bush, George W. (Administration of)
Byrnes, Thomas

C
California
Camden, New Jersey
Caminetti v. United States
Capital Punishment
Capone, Al
Carter, Jimmy (Administration of)
Chain Gangs and Prison Labor
Chandler v. Florida
Chapman, Mark David
Chicago, Illinois
Chicago Seven/Democratic National Convention of 1968
Child Abuse, Contemporary
Child Abuse, History of
Child Abuse, Sociology of
Child Murderers, History of
Children, Abandoned

Children's Rights
Chillicothe Correctional Institution
Chinese Americans
Chinese Exclusion Act of 1882
Chisholm v. Georgia
Christie, Agatha
Cincinnati, Ohio
Citizen Participation on Juries
Civil Disobedience
Civil Rights Act of 1866
Civil Rights Act of 1875
Civil Rights Laws
Clayton Anti-Trust Act of 1914
Clemency
Cleveland, Grover (Administration of)
Cleveland, Ohio
Clinton, William (Administration of)
Clinton Correctional Facility
Code of Silence
Codification of Laws
Cohens v. Virginia
Coker v. Georgia
Colonial Charters and Grants
Colonial Courts
Colorado
Common Law Origins of Criminal Law
Community Policing and Relations
Community Service
Compton, California
Computer Crime
Comstock Law
Confession
Confidence Games and Frauds
Connecticut
Constitution of the United States of America
Convention on the Rights of the Child
Convict Lease System
Coolidge, Calvin (Administration of)
Corporal Punishment
Corrections
Corruption, Contemporary
Corruption, History of
Corruption, Sociology of
Counterfeiting
Court of Common Pleas
Court of Oyer and Terminer
Court of Quarter Sessions
Courts
Courts of Indian Offenses
Coverture, Doctrine of

Crabtree v. State
Crime and Arrest Statistics Analysis
Crime in America, Causes
Crime in America, Distribution
Crime in America, Types
Crime Prevention
Crime Rates
Crime Scene Investigation
Criminalization and Decriminalization
Criminology
Critical Legal Studies Movement
Cruel and Unusual Punishment
Cruelty to Animals
Cummings, Homer
Cunningham, Emma
Customs Service as Police
Czolgosz, Leon

D
Dahmer, Jeffrey
Darrow, Clarence
Davis v. State
Dayton, Ohio
Death Row
Declaration of Independence
Defendant's Rights
Delaware
Democratic National Convention of 1968. *See* Chicago Seven/Democratic National Convention of 1968
Dennis v. United States
Deportation
DeSalvo, Albert
Detection and Detectives
Deterrence, Theory of
Detroit, Michigan
Devery, William
Dewey, Thomas E.
Dillard v. the State of Georgia
Dillinger, John
Dime Novels, Pulps, Thrillers
Discretionary Decision Making
District Attorney
Domestic Violence, Contemporary
Domestic Violence, History of
Domestic Violence, Sociology of
Douglas, William O.
Dred Scott v. Sandford
Drinking and Crime
Drug Abuse and Addiction, Contemporary

Drug Abuse and Addiction, History of
Drug Abuse and Addiction, Sociology of
Drug Enforcement Administration
Due Process
Duren v. Missouri
Dyer Act

E
Earp, Wyatt
Eastern State Penitentiary
Eddy, Thomas
Eisenhower, Dwight D. (Administration of)
Eisenstadt v. Baird
Electric Chair, History of
Electronic Surveillance
Elkins Act of 1903
Elmira Prison
Embezzlement
Emergency Quota Act of 1921
Enforcement Acts of 1870–1871
English Charter of Liberties of 1100
Enron
Entrapment
Environmental Crimes
Equality, Concept of
Espionage
Espionage Act of 1917
Estes v. Texas
Ethics in Government Act of 1978
Everleigh Sisters
Executions

F
Famous Trials
Fear of Crime
Federal Bureau of Investigation
Federal Common Law of Crime
Federal Policing
Federal Prisons
Federal Rules of Criminal Procedure
Federalist Papers
Felonies
Ferguson, Colin
Fillmore, Millard (Administration of)
Film, Crime in
Film, Police in
Film, Punishment in
Fingerprinting
Fish and Game Laws
Fletcher v. Peck

Florida
Floyd, Charles Arthur
Ford, Gerald (Administration of)
Forensic Science
Fornication Laws
Fraud
Freedom of Information Act of 1966
Frontier Crime
Frontiero v. Richardson
Fugitive Slave Act of 1793
Fugitive Slave Act of 1850
Furman v. Georgia

G

Gacy, John Wayne
Gambling
Gangs, Contemporary
Gangs, History of
Gangs, Sociology of
Gardner, Erle Stanley
Garfield, James (Administration of)
Gates v. Collier
Gender and Criminal Law
Genovese, Vito
Georgia
German Americans
Gibbons v. Ogden
Gideon v. Wainwright
Giuliani, Rudolph
Glidewell v. State
Gotti, John
Grafton, Sue
Grant, Ulysses S. (Administration of)
Great Depression
Green, Anna K.
Gregg v. Georgia
Griffin v. California
Griswold v. Connecticut
Grutter v. Bollinger
Guiteau, Charles
Gun Control
Guns and Violent Crime

H

Habeas Corpus, Writ of
Habeas Corpus Act of 1679
Habeas Corpus Act of 1863
Hamilton, Alexander
Hammett, Dashiell
Hanging
Harding, Warren G. (Administration of)
Harris, Eric. *See* Klebold, Dylan and Eric Harris
Harrison, Benjamin (Administration of)
Harrison Act of 1914
Hauptmann, Bruno
Hawai'i
Hayes, Rutherford B. (Administration of)
Hays, Jacob
Hereditary Crime
Hillerman, Tony
Hispanic Americans
History of Crime and Punishment in America: Colonial
History of Crime and Punishment in America: 1783–1850
History of Crime and Punishment in America: 1850–1900
History of Crime and Punishment in America: 1900–1950
History of Crime and Punishment in America: 1950–1970
History of Crime and Punishment in America: 1970–Present
Holden v. Hardy
Holmes, Oliver Wendell, Jr.
Holt v. Sarver
Homeland Security
Homestead Act of 1862
Hoover, Herbert (Administration of)
Hoover, J. Edgar
Hurtado v. California

I

Idaho
Identity Theft
Illinois
Immigration Crimes
Incapacitation, Theory of
Incest
Indecent Exposure
Independent Treasury Act
Indian Civil Rights Act
Indian Removal Act
Indiana
Infanticide
Insanity Defense
Internal Revenue Service
Internal Security Act of 1950
International Association of Chiefs of Police
Internment

Interrogation Practices
Interstate Commerce Act of 1887
Intolerable Acts of 1774
Iowa
Irish Americans
Italian Americans

J
Jackson, Andrew (Administration of)
Jackson, Mississippi
James, Jesse
Japanese Americans
Jefferson, Thomas
Jefferson, Thomas (Administration of)
Jewish Americans
Johnson, Andrew (Administration of)
Johnson, Lyndon B. (Administration of)
Johnson v. Avery
Judges and Magistrates
Judiciary Act of 1789
Juries
Jurisdiction
Justice, Department of
Juvenile Corrections, Contemporary
Juvenile Corrections, History of
Juvenile Corrections, Sociology of
Juvenile Courts, Contemporary
Juvenile Courts, History of
Juvenile Delinquency, History of
Juvenile Delinquency, Sociology of
Juvenile Justice, History of
Juvenile Offenders, Prevention and Education
Juvenile Offenders in Adult Courts

K
Kaczynski, Ted
Kansas
Kansas City, Missouri
Katz v. United States
Katzenbach v. McClung
Kennedy, John F. (Administration of)
Kennedy, Robert F.
Kent State Massacre
Kentucky
Kevorkian, Jack
Kidnapping
King, Martin Luther, Jr.
King, Rodney
Klebold, Dylan, and Eric Harris
Knapp Commission

Korematsu v. United States
Ku Klux Klan
Kunstler, William

L
La Guardia, Fiorello
Landrum-Griffin Act of 1859
Larceny
Las Vegas, Nevada
Law Enforcement Assistance Act
Law Enforcement Assistance Administration
Lawrence v. Texas
Laws and Liberties of Massachusetts
Lawyers Guild
Leavenworth Federal Penitentiary
Legal Counsel
Leopold and Loeb
Libertarianism
Lincoln, Abraham (Administration of)
Lindbergh Law
Lindsey, Ben
Literature and Theater, Crime in
Literature and Theater, Police in
Literature and Theater, Punishment in
Livestock and Cattle Crimes
Livingston, Edward
Lochner v. New York
Los Angeles, California
Louisiana
Loving v. Virginia
Luciano, "Lucky"
Lynchings

M
Macdonald, Ross
Madison, James (Administration of)
Madoff, Bernard
Magna Carta
Maine
Malcolm X
Mandatory Minimum Sentencing
Mann Act
Manson, Charles
Mapp v. Ohio
Marbury v. Madison
Marshall, John
Martin v. Hunter's Lessee
Maryland
Maryland Toleration Act of 1649
Massachusetts

Matteawan State Hospital
Mayflower Compact
McCarthy, Joseph
McCleskey v. Kemp
McCulloch v. Maryland
McKinley, William (Administration of)
McNabb v. United States
McVeigh, Timothy
Memoirs, Police and Prosecutors
Memphis, Tennessee
Menendez, Lyle and Erik
Miami, Florida
Michigan
Military Courts
Military Police
Minnesota
Minor v. Happersett
Miranda v. Arizona
Miranda Warnings. *See Miranda v. Arizona*
Mississippi
Mississippi v. Johnson
Missouri
M'Naghten Test
Mollen Commission
Monroe, James (Administration of)
Montana
Moonshine
Morality
MOVE
Mudgett, Herman
Mug Shots
Muhammad, John Allen
Muller v. Oregon
Munn v. Illinois
Murder, Contemporary
Murder, History of
Murder, Sociology of
Murders, Unsolved
Music and Crime

N

Narcotics Laws
National Association for the Advancement of Colored People
National Commission on Law Observance and Enforcement
National Congress on Penitentiary and Reformatory Discipline
National Organization for Women
National Police Gazette

National Prison Association
National Security Act of 1947
Native American Tribal Police
Native Americans
Nebraska
Nelson, "Baby Face"
Ness, Eliot
Neutrality Enforcement in 1793–1794
Nevada
New Hampshire
New Jersey
New Mexico
New Orleans, Louisiana
"New Punitiveness"
New York
New York City
Newark, New Jersey
News Media, Crime in
News Media, Police in
News Media, Punishment in
Nitti, Frank
Nixon, Richard (Administration of)
North Carolina
North Dakota
Northwest Ordinance of 1787

O

Oakland, California
Obama, Barack (Administration of)
Obscenity
Obscenity Laws
Ohio
Oklahoma
Oklahoma City Bombing
Olmstead v. United States
Omnibus Crime Control and Safe Streets Act of 1968
Oregon
Organized Crime, Contemporary
Organized Crime, History of
Organized Crime, Sociology of
Oswald, Lee Harvey

P

Padilla v. Kentucky
Paine, Thomas
Paretsky, Sara
Parker, Isaac
Parker, William
Parole

Peltier, Leonard
Pendleton Act of 1883
Penitentiaries
Penitentiary Study Commission
Penn, William
Pennsylvania
Pennsylvania System of Reform
People v. Pinnell
People v. Superior Court of Santa Clara County
Percival, Robert V.
Peterson, Scott
Petty Courts
Philadelphia, Pennsylvania
Pickpockets
Pierce, Franklin (Administration of)
Pittsburgh, Pennsylvania
Plea
Plessy v. Ferguson
Poe, Edgar Allen
Police, Contemporary
Police, History of
Police, Sociology of
Police, Women as
Police Abuse
Political Crimes, Contemporary
Political Crimes, History of
Political Crimes, Sociology of
Political Dissidents
Political Policing
Polk, James K. (Administration of)
Pornography
Posses
Presidential Proclamations
President's Commission on Law Enforcement and the Administration of Justice
Prison Privatization
Prison Riots
Prisoner's Rights
Private Detectives
Private Police
Private Security Services
Probation
Proclamation for Suppressing Rebellion and Sedition of 1775
Procunier v. Martinez
Professionalization of Police
Prohibition
Prostitution, Contemporary
Prostitution, History of
Prostitution, Sociology of

Punishment of Crimes Act, 1790
Punishment Within Prison
Pure Food and Drug Act of 1906
Puritans

Q
Quakers

R
Race, Class, and Criminal Law
Race-Based Crimes
Racism
Rader, Dennis
Ragen, Joseph
Ramirez, Richard
Rape, Contemporary
Rape, History of
Rape, Sociology of
Ray, James Earl
Reagan, Ronald (Administration of)
Reform, Police and Enforcement
Reform Movements in Justice
Rehabilitation
Religion and Crime, Contemporary
Religion and Crime, History of
Religion and Crime, Sociology of
Reports on Prison Conditions
Retributivism
Reynolds v. United States
Rhode Island
Ricci v. DeStefano
Riots
Robbery, Contemporary
Robbery, History of
Robbery, Sociology of
Roberts v. Louisiana
Rockefeller, Nelson
Roe v. Wade
Romer v. Evans
Roosevelt, Franklin D. (Administration of)
Roosevelt, Theodore (Administration of)
Roth v. United States
Rothstein, Arnold
Ruby Ridge Standoff
Rule of Law
Rural Police

S
Sacco and Vanzetti
Salem Witch Trials

San Francisco, California
San Quentin State Prison
Santobello v. New York
Schenck v. United States
School Shootings
Schultz, "Dutch"
Scopes Monkey Trial
Scottsboro Boys Cases
Secret Service
Securities and Exchange Commission
Sedition Act of 1918
Segregation Laws
Selective Service Act of 1967
Sentencing
Sentencing: Indeterminate Versus Fixed
Serial and Mass Killers
Sex Offender Laws
Sex Offenders
Sexual Harassment
Shaming and Shunning
Sheppard, Sam
Sheppard v. Maxwell
Sheriffs
Sherman Anti-Trust Act of 1890
Simpson, O. J.
Sin
Sing Sing Correctional Facility
Sirhan Sirhan
Slave Patrols
Slavery
Slavery, Law of
Smith, Susan
Smith Act
Smuggling
Snyder, Ruth
Sodomy
South Carolina
South Dakota
Spillane, Mickey
St. Louis, Missouri
Stamp Act of 1765
Standard Oil Co. of New Jersey v. United States
State Blue Laws
State Police
State Slave Codes
State v. Heitman
Steenburgh, Sam
Strauder v. West Virginia
Strikes

Students for a Democratic Society and the Weathermen
Supermax Prisons
Supreme Court, U.S.
Suspect's Rights
Sutherland, Edwin

T

Taft, William Howard (Administration of)
Tax Crimes
Taylor, Zachary (Administration of)
Taylor v. State
Tea Act of 1773
Technology, Police
Television, Crime in
Television, Police in
Television, Punishment in
Tennessee
Terrorism
Terry v. Ohio
Texas
Texas Rangers
Texas v. White
Thaw, Harry K.
Theories of Crime
Thoreau, Henry David
Three Strikes Law
To Kill a Mockingbird
Tocqueville, Alexis de
Torrio, John
Torture
Townshend Acts of 1767
Traffic Crimes
Training Police
Trials
Truman, Harry S. (Administration of)
Twining v. New Jersey
Tyler, John (Administration of)

U

Uniform Crime Reporting Program
United States Attorneys
United States v. Ballard
United States v. E. C. Knight Company
United States v. Hudson and Goodwin
United States v. Nixon
United States v. One Book Called Ulysses
Urbanization
USA PATRIOT Act of 2001
Utah

V

Vagrancy
Vermont
Vice Commission
Vice Reformers
Victim Rights and Restitution
Victimless Crime
Victorian Compromise
Vigilantism
Violence Against Women Act of 1994
Violent Crimes
Virginia
Vollmer, August
Volstead Act

W

Waco Siege
Walling, George
Walnut Street Jail
Wambaugh, Joseph
Warren, Earl
Washington
Washington, D.C.
Washington, George (Administration of)
Watergate
Weathermen, The. *See* Students for a Democratic Society and the Weathermen
Webb v. United States
Weeks v. United States
West Virginia
White-Collar Crime, Contemporary
White-Collar Crime, History of
White-Collar Crime, Sociology of
Whitney v. California
Wickersham, George
Wickersham Commission
Wilson, James Q.
Wilson, O. W.
Wilson, Woodrow (Administration of)
Wisconsin
Witness Testimony
Wolf v. Colorado
Women Criminals, Contemporary
Women Criminals, History of
Women Criminals, Sociology of
Women in Prison
Wuornos, Aileen
Wyoming

X

Xenophobia

Y

Yates, Andrea
Yates v. United States

Z

Zeisel, Hans
Zodiac Killer

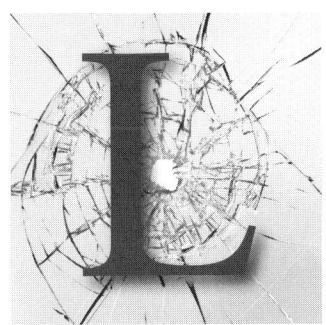

La Guardia, Fiorello

Fiorello Henry La Guardia (1882–1947) was the 99th mayor of New York City (1934–45). He reorganized the police force and restored trust in a municipal government that had been perceived as patronage laden and corrupt during the mayoralty of James J. Walker (1926–32).

La Guardia was born Fiorello Enrico La Guardia in New York's Greenwich Village. His father was Achille La Guardia, a lapsed Roman Catholic who was a bandmaster in the United States Army, and his mother, Irene Coen Luzzato, was Jewish. La Guardia was raised an Episcopalian. His middle name "Enrico" was changed to "Henry" (the English form of Enrico) when he was a child. He grew up in Prescott, Arizona, attending public school and high school there, where his father was posted. When his father became ill during the Spanish–American War, he was discharged from the army, and the family moved to Europe. They lived in Trieste, Austria, his mother's hometown.

La Guardia joined the U.S. State Department's Consulate Service at the age of 17 and served in American consulates in Budapest and Trieste between 1901 and 1904. From 1904 to 1906, he was the American consular agent in Fiume, Hungary. He returned to the United States to study law at New York University, graduating in 1910. While in law school he was an interpreter for the U.S. Bureau of Immigration at Ellis Island.

Political Career

In 1915, La Guardia entered public service as a deputy attorney general in the New York State attorney general's office. An unsuccessful Republican congressional candidate in 1914, he was elected to the U.S. House of Representatives two years later. Shortly after taking office, La Guardia joined the U.S. Army Air Service in August 1917 as a lieutenant. He commanded a bomber unit on the Italian-Austrian front during World War I in a plane named the *Congressional Limited*. He left the service as a major at the end of the war.

In 1919 Congressman La Guardia was elected president of the New York City Board of Aldermen (the local legislative body), defeating the Democratic incumbent, Robert L. Moran, by 1,300 votes. Defeated for re-election in 1921, La Guardia was elected again to the House of Representatives in 1922, where he served until March 3, 1933. His major legislative achievement was the Norris-La Guardia Act, which he cosponsored with Senator George W. Norris. The 1932 law stripped federal courts of their jurisdiction over the enforcement of "yellow-dog contracts," which prohibited employees from joining labor unions. The act permitted employees to form unions without employer interference and denied the courts jurisdiction to issue injunctions in nonviolent labor disputes. In 1929 La Guardia challenged Mayor Jimmy Walker, losing by more than 500,000 votes. La Guardia charged the Walker administration with corruption but was overwhelmed by the Democratic Party's "Tammany Hall" machine. In 1932 La Guardia lost his congressional seat in the Roosevelt landslide.

Mayor of New York

Walker resigned in 1932 after an investigation conducted by Samuel Seabury found that many of La Guardia's charges against the mayor and his administration were true. La Guardia ran again, this time as a Republican-fusion candidate, making corruption his main issue. La Guardia was elected in a three-way race. Taking office January 1, 1934, La Guardia made ending corruption in government and racketeering in business a top priority. La Guardia's first action as mayor was to order the police to arrest mobster Charlie "Lucky" Luciano. In a radio address, La Guardia declared war on gangsters, saying, "Let's drive the bums out of town." La Guardia attacked Frank Costello's slot machine empire and had thousands of the machines confiscated by the police. In a media event, the mayor took a sledgehammer to some of the "one-armed bandits" and had them dumped off a barge into the East River. Relying on a provision of the New York City charter that designated the mayor as a "magistrate," La Guardia occasionally heard criminal cases in the magistrate's court, which had jurisdiction over petty crimes. La Guardia also succeeded in shutting down the burlesque theaters, whose risqué shows offended him.

La Guardia's war against Luciano eventually succeeded as Thomas E. Dewey, the special investigator for organized crime, was able to convict the first boss of the Genovese crime family of heading a prostitution ring. Luciano was

At a special session of the executive committee of the U.S. Conference of Mayors in Washington, D.C., on July 14, 1939, Mayor Fiorello La Guardia, the conference's president, sits at a table flanked by the mayors of Cleveland, Ohio, and Milwaukee, Wisconsin, while the mayors of other major cities stand behind him. They were discussing a strike by Works Projects Administration employees.

sentenced to a 30-to-50-year term (he would be paroled in 1946, with the stipulation that he leave the United States for Sicily).

However, despite the mayor's bluster against organized crime, biographer Thomas Kessner observed in 1989 that

> incantations against punks and tinhorns won headlines, and La Guardia's support for abusing known criminals encouraged the police, but the fireworks did not significantly impede the growth of underworld racketeering.

La Guardia was re-elected in 1937 and 1941. In 1945, he decided not to seek a fourth term. La Guardia served as president of the U.S. Conference of Mayors (1936–45), U.S. director of the Office of Civilian Defense (1941–42), chairman of the U.S. section of the Permanent Joint Board on Defense (1940–46), special U.S. ambassador to Brazil (1946), and director general of the United Nations Relief and Rehabilitation Administration (1946). La Guardia died of pancreatic cancer at his home in the Riverdale neighborhood of the Bronx on September 20, 1947.

Jeffrey Kraus
Wagner College

See Also: *Adair v. United States*; Corruption, History of; Dewey, Thomas E.; Gambling; Luciano, "Lucky"; New York; New York City; Organized Crime, History of.

Further Readings
Bayor, Ronald H. *Fiorello La Guardia: Ethnicity and Reform*. Arlington Heights, IL: Harlan Davidson, 1993.
Brodsky, Alyn. *The Great Mayor: Fiorello La Guardia and the Making of the City of New York*. New York: St. Martin's Press, 2003.
Garrett, Charles. *The La Guardia Years: Machine and Reform Politics in New York City*. New Brunswick, NJ: Rutgers University Press, 1961.
Hecksher, August III. *When La Guardia Was Mayor: New York's Legendary Years*. New York: W. W. Norton, 1978.
Jeffers, H. Paul. *The Napoleon of New York: Mayor Fiorello La Guardia*. Hoboken, NJ: John Wiley & Sons, 2002.

Kamen, Gloria. *Fiorello: His Honor, the Little Flower*. New York: Atheneum, 1981.
Kessner, Thomas. *Fiorello H. La Guardia and the Making of Modern New York*. New York: McGraw-Hill, 1989.

Landrum-Griffin Act of 1959

The Landrum-Griffin Act of 1959, officially called the Labor-Management Reporting and Disclosure Act of 1959 (LMRDA), became law on September 14, 1959. The purpose of the law is to protect the rights of workers, regulate union finances and activities, and offer some protections for employers.

The corruption in trade unions in the United States was common knowledge from the early 1900s. Congressional investigations by the McClellan Committee, chaired by Arkansas Senator John L. McClellan during the 1950s, examined the practices of labor unions in the United States, particularly those that fell under the umbrella of the American Federation of Labor and the Congress of Industrial Organizations (AFL-CIO). The committee primarily focused on the president-elect of the Teamsters Union, James R. Hoffa, and practices used by the Teamsters. Investigators uncovered both embezzlement of union treasury funds and the violation of the legal rights of some union members. In response, the AFL-CIO dropped the Teamsters and other investigated groups from its ranks in an effort to improve its reputation.

Origin and Passage
Congressional sponsors of the Landrum-Griffin Act included Congressmen Philip M. Landrum (D-GA) and Robert P. Griffin (R-MI), who took the recommendations of the McClellan Committee, as did Senators John F. Kennedy (D-MA) and Barry Goldwater (R-AZ). Various bills were introduced during the 1959 session to address the union issues, including Landrum-Griffin, Kennedy-Ervin, and the Goldwater bills. Each bill had similar provisions but not everyone supported one version.

The Kennedy-Ervin bill and the Goldwater bill contained the regulation of unions and the requirement to disclose financial information to prevent trustees from embezzling monies from union funds. The AFL-CIO supported Kennedy's bill; however, other groups did not like the pro-union stance of the proposed law. Goldwater's bill reflected the interests of the Eisenhower administration. The Kennedy bill was amended to include the bill of rights proposed by McClellan, which led to its passage in the Senate. The Landrum-Griffin bill was introduced after the Kennedy bill vote, and it had the support of the administration and the management groups who questioned the pro-union Kennedy proposal. The Landrum-Griffin Act contained stronger wording than the Kennedy version on picketing, secondary boycotts, and "hot cargo" clauses, which allowed union workers the right to refuse handling goods from companies under a strike. The final conference version of the bill sought to end corruption in unions and placed them under federal regulation, and amended the Taft-Hartley Act of 1947 to strengthen the wording about secondary boycotts.

In its final version, the law set out to protect the rights and interests of union members. The law included a bill of rights for individuals who belonged to unions. Financial issues were resolved by requiring unions to account for all monies in disclosure statements. The procedure for union election of officers was established in the law as well to prevent the shady election practices of union leaders. The final law included civil and criminal penalties for union leaders who violated the finance laws set out in this act. The rights provided for union members did not extend to all union members; public-sector employees, who worked for the government, did not come under this law.

The act also contained amendments to existing labor legislation. The National Labor Relations Act was amended to protect the rights of employers. Labor unions could no longer use secondary boycotts and also lost the right to picket employers to gain representation rights.

The Landrum-Griffin Act passed Congress and became law on October 14, 1959, when signed by President Dwight Eisenhower. The unions, 54 in all, had to revise their constitutions to comply with the law. Over time, the Department of Labor and its Office of Labor Management, which oversaw the implementation and regulations of the law, saw an increase in the number of complaints against unions. The valid complaints often led to indictments on charges of embezzlement and other illegal acts. The federal government finally reined in the Teamsters in the late 1980s. Union membership and power has been in a state of steady decline since the Federal Aviation Administration strike in 1981, when Ronald Reagan fired the striking workers. Private-sector companies began the same practice of firing union members versus negotiating with the unions. Increasingly global markets and trade agreements have led companies to relocate to other countries rather than pay the higher wages demanded by unions..

Theresa S. Hefner-Babb
Lamar University

See Also: Corruption, History of; Eisenhower, Dwight D. (Administration of); Organized Crime, History of.

Further Readings
Ballace, Janice R. *The Landrum-Griffin Act: Twenty Years of Federal Protection of Union Members Rights*. Philadelphia: Industrial Research Unit, Wharton School, University of Pennsylvania, 1979.
"Labor Management Reporting and Disclosure Act of 1959." 73 Stat. 519 (September 14, 1959).
Laughlin, Doris B. and Anita L. W. Schoomaker. *The Landrum-Griffin Act and Union Democracy*. Ann Arbor: University of Michigan Press, 1979.

Larceny

Also referred to as "larceny-theft," larceny deals with the carrying away of a person's property without his/her consent for the purposes of permanently depriving the owner of that property or the benefits of its ownership. Larceny has historically carried connotations of nonviolence. In many jurisdictions, larceny differs from embezzlement in that it must occur without the owner's consent in an illegal manner. In embezzlement cases, the owner of a company or firm and the criminal may be one and the same. Larceny is distinct from burglary in that it generally does not involve unlawful breaking and entering, and it is considered separate from robbery, which often denotes that property has been stolen by violence. During the 20th century, most states rejected pure larceny statutes in favor of including larceny under general theft statutes because it was considered much easier to win convictions using more specific theft laws. Massachusetts alone retained its separate larceny laws and continues to charge criminals under a number of separate larceny laws that include larceny with intent to defraud, larceny by false pretense, and larceny by embezzlement.

Each state determines for itself whether a particular crime is grand or petty larceny, depending on the value attached to the property. The value assigned to the misdemeanor charge of petty larceny is generally somewhere between $200 and $1,000. Other factors may also be taken into account. Virginia, for instance, differentiates between items stolen from a person who is not present and those taken directly from an individual. A perpetrator may be charged with grand larceny for stealing money or any item of value totaling $5 or more if it is taken directly from a person or when a firearm is stolen, regardless of whether it is taken directly from a person. Grand larceny is a felony rather than a misdemeanor. Grand larceny generally carries a state prison term, while petty larceny convictions may result in a brief stay in a local or county jail.

Some states use the term *felonious larceny*. In North Carolina, for instance, it is felonious larceny to steal items whose value is $1,000 or more or to knowingly receive such items. It is also felonious larceny to steal firearms, explosives, and incendiary devices, regardless of the value involved in the theft. Michigan also has a felonious larceny statute; and individuals who steal items from residences, offices, stores, gas stations, shops, warehouses, mills, factories, hotels, schools, barns, granaries, ships, places of worship, locker rooms, or any public building may be charged with "larceny in a building." New York's larceny statutes encompass trickery, embezzlement, false pretenses, and acquiring stolen property in addition to the traditional definition of larceny. Felony larceny in New York involves items valued at more than $1,000, but there are varying degrees of felony larceny according to values involved and the circumstances of the theft.

Criminals engage in larceny for a number of reasons varying from a perceived need for the item(s) involved or the cash value received from the stolen property to peer pressure or to money to buy alcohol or drugs or to maintain a lavish lifestyle. The typical larcenist plans out a crime beforehand to the point that he/she knows exactly when a homeowner is likely to be away from home or what kind of protection is in place in public buildings. At the domestic level, perpetrators of larceny are more likely to strike when no one is at home, but those who rob public places such as museums have become so brazen that they often commit their crimes in broad daylight when a building is full of visitors. Professional larcenists often have "inside help" when committing their crimes. That help may sometimes be inadvertent, as when a would-be perpetrator strikes up a friendly conversation with a maid, gardener, or chauffer in order to gather valuable information about a potential target's home and schedules. Homes with alarm systems that ring directly at the local police station are considered somewhat safer than those that notify security companies because security companies are required to follow an established protocol, giving a criminal additional time to complete a theft. Both dogs and dead bolts have also proved effective in deterring would-be thieves.

Larceny at the Federal Level

While the FBI is not usually concerned with misdemeanors, the Uniform Crime Reports specify that larceny theft is defined as "the unlawful taking, carrying, leading, or riding away of property from the possession or constructive possession of another." The term *larceny* does not encompass all thefts. For instance, motor vehicle theft is not generally identified as larceny because of the value involved in the crime and the tendency for such crimes to include violence. Neither does larceny encompass thefts that occur in conjunction with robberies or burglaries, embezzlement, confidence games, forgery, or check fraud. However, larceny may occur in conjunction with these crimes. When considering occupational crime, larceny encompasses obtaining ownership of another's property through trickery or fraud.

According the FBI, criminal actions classified as larceny include the following: pickpocketing, purse snatching, shoplifting, bicycle theft, theft of items from motor vehicles, theft of automobile parts and accessories, theft of items from buildings that are open to the public, and theft from coin-operated devices or machines. According to the Uniform Crime Reports, throughout the United States, some 6,327,230 larcenies occurred in 2004. That figure was a decline of 4 percent from the previous year. Overall, larceny thefts comprised 67.9 percent of all property crimes in 2009, and most of these crimes involved items stolen from motor vehicles, including parts and accessories. More than 27 percent of larceny cases involved items stolen from vehicles with the exclusion of accessories. Shoplifting accounted for another 18.1 percent, and items taken from public buildings amounted to 11.1 percent. Crimes classified under the "other" label comprised 29.8 percent of total larceny crimes committed in 2009. The average loss suffered was reported at $864, totaling approximately $5.5 billion in overall value. When larceny is considered in combination with other property crimes such as burglary and motor vehicle theft, property crimes account for 90 percent of crimes reported in the United States.

Historical Aspects

From a historical perspective, the most frequent crime committed in the United States has been larceny by stealth. American common law, which evolved from English common law, is used by the federal legal system and by all states except Louisiana, which uses the Civil Code. The concept of larceny was developed not by the British parliament but by the British courts in the 17th century to describe theft of property by nonviolent means. The courts subsequently identified the offenses of larceny by trickery to describe stealing property through fraud or deceit and larceny by false pretenses to connote occasions when a title to property was transferred from one owner to another based on false information. Grand larceny in England carried a sentence of death, and those convicted of the lesser offense of petit larceny were forced to surrender their property to the Crown. Under common law, the implementation of larceny laws has sometimes been characterized by what some scholars have labeled "fuzziness," which had led to difficulties in convicting those charged with larceny.

Dating back to ancient Greece and Rome, implementation was sometimes used for political purposes. Following the Civil War, Congress passed the First Reconstruction Act of 1867, requiring southern states reentering the Union to revise their constitutions to prevent criminal convictions from interfering with the right to vote. As power gradually returned to the hands of the same men who had led the southern states in the glory days of the south, southern states began reenacting laws such as those making even petty larceny convictions grounds for keeping former slaves from exercising the right to vote. This practice had two goals: keeping African Americans out of the political system and blocking the rise of the Republican Party in the "solid south."

Early in the 20th century, the code of New York State specified that larceny involved the intention to deprive or defraud an owner of his/her property or benefits from said property for the benefit of the larcenist. The code was challenged in 1906 in the case of an executive who had allegedly taken money out of a company account. He claimed the money was legitimately taken in order to reimburse him for an authorized contribution to the Republican National Committee. His acquittal clarified the interpretation of larceny, stipulating that intention was a major element in determining whether larceny had been committed. The courts held that the executive had not demonstrated a desire to remove company funds for his own use. In 1916, the United Kingdom tried to clarify its own larceny laws with a new Larceny Act. By 1968, however, larceny was eradicated from the English legal system through the enactment of the Theft Act. Larceny statutes were also abolished in Wales and Ireland.

Throughout American history, incidences of larceny have been tied to the social fabric of the period. In the last half of the 19th century, rapid industrialization produced a culture of street children who were some of the most accomplished larcenists of the period. Nowhere was this more evident than in New York City, where large numbers of children known as "rats," "gamins," "Arabs," "urchins," and "gutter-snipes" peopled

Boys stealing coal from a railroad coal yard in Boston, Massachusetts, in January 1917. In the late 19th century, street children may have numbered as many as 10,000–50,000 in New York City alone. After laws were strengthened in 1875, many more of those children involved in pickpocketing and other types of larceny were convicted—as many as 1,500–2,000 a year.

the underworld of pickpocketing. Most of them stole money rather than other items of value. Estimates of their number varied between 10,000 and 50,000. New York's street children were predominantly male (95 percent), between the ages of 14 and 17 (84 percent), and native born (82 percent). Only 15 percent of them lived entirely on the streets. In the absence of child labor laws, many of these children worked at jobs that presented them with a plethora of opportunities to ply their illegal trade. Some of them blacked boots, sold newspapers, or swept sidewalks. Others became expert at salvaging.

While some street children learned their skills at "professional" thief schools, most of them honed their skills by working with other street children through informal apprenticeships. Originally, these young larcenists were rarely caught because they were so expert at their crime and because they could move extremely quickly. Even those who were caught were generally released for lack of evidence.

Certain areas were known to be the hangouts of the young pickpockets, particularly the Bowery, lower Broadway, and Park Row. They also hung out at post offices, hotels, elevated railroad stations, and ferries. By the 1840s, pickpocketing was rapidly becoming the venue of professional thieves. Between 1859 and 1876, the number of pickpocketing convictions among street children rose from 52 to 242. A toughening of the laws in 1875 significantly increased subsequent conviction rates. Thereafter, from 1,500 to 2,000 youths were convicted of larceny each year.

The 1960s and Beyond

The drug culture that developed in the United States in the 1960s and continued into the 21st century has often been linked to crimes such as larceny. The same can be said of the gang culture that developed during that same period. Before 1961, there were only 64 cities that reported significant gang activity, and most of them were large cities such as New York, Los Angeles, Boston, and Chicago. By 1980, gang activity had spread to more than 170 American cities, and by 1992, gangs were creating major problems in 766 cities. In some areas, gang members specialized in larceny.

Some historians of criminal behavior believe that larceny was the crime that characterized much of 20th-century America because it occurred at such high levels throughout the century. Some 4.3 million cases of larceny were reported in the United States in the 1970s. By 2002, the rate had risen to 7.1 million. Predictably, attitudes toward larceny and other crimes also shifted during the 20th century. In 1968, for the first time in American history, a Gallup poll revealed that concern over the soaring crime rate was the top domestic issue among respondents. The following year, larceny rates increased 240 percent. As large numbers of larcenists moved to the suburbs, crime rates rose accordingly.

Despite this phenomenon, overall crimes rates have been declining in the United States since the early 1990s, when larceny theft was recorded at a rate of 3,185.1 per 100,000 inhabitants. By 2,000, the rate had dropped to 2,477.3 per 100,000/population; it declined even further to 2,060.9 per 100,000 in 2009. Geographic area may have a significant impact on larceny rates in a given area. In the 1990s, for instance, individuals living in New York City were 10 times more likely to be the victim of thieves than individuals living on Long Island and were six times more likely to be victimized than those living in Westchester County.

For most of the 20th century, personal and business cash and property were likely to appear in physical form and were generally located on the owner's premises or in a local bank or a safety deposit box. By the early 21st century, fraud had replaced larceny as the most prevalent crime in the United States. This shift from the prominence of larceny to fraud was due in large part to a radical transformation in the ways in which property is owned as a result of the technology and communication explosions. Financial transactions are now more likely to involve credit and debit transactions than cash. Additionally, high-priced items such as automobiles, jewelry, or artwork may be leased or borrowed rather than being owned by the person physically possessing them. Large sums of money and ownership of property are now easily transferred from one owner to the other with a few clicks of a computer mouse over the Internet. Paychecks are digitally deposited, reducing the chances that individuals keep large sums of money on their persons or in their homes. As a result of technological changes, criminals find it much easier than in the past to convert cash to property and vice versa. Unlike the petty larcenist of the past, the present perpetrator of fraud is more likely to be involved with organized crime. Stolen goods are now quickly converted to collateral for drugs or even for illegal arms. Additionally, the returns from fraud are generally much higher than returns on items taken during the course of larceny.

In cities throughout the United States, so-called retail theft gangs are in operation. Professional criminals recruit members to engage in shoplifting. They then provide them with lists of desirable low-volume goods that bring in high value, sending them out to local retail stores to steal such items as razor blades, batteries, over-the-counter drugs, infant formula, and designer clothing. If the thief is caught, he/she is assumed to be acting alone and is likely to be treated leniently by storeowners and the courts.

Notorious Cases

The media can be counted on to keep high-profile or unusual cases of larceny in the public eye. This was true in a recent Texas larceny case that certainly qualified as "unusual." The cattle rustling that was common in the Old West was often prosecuted under larceny laws. A new twist on this practice surfaced in 2004 when it was revealed that Roddy Dean Pippin, a quiet, clean-cut 20-year-old, had been rustling castle for the previous 18 months. Like the rustlers of the Old West, Pippin, who has been dubbed the "last rustler," covered his tracks with broken tree limbs. In all, Pippin stole 130 head of cattle, quickly loading them into his pick-up truck and immediately branding them with a modernized version of the old west branding iron.

While many modern corporate crimes are prosecuted under fraud laws, circumstances may dictate that certain criminals have violated larceny laws instead. In 2004, publishing conglomerate Hollinger, Inc., the owner of newspapers that include the *Chicago Sun-Times*, was faced with the theft of $400 million over a six-year period by former CEO Conrad Black. The amount stolen roughly equaled the company's entire assets amassed between 1997 and 2003. There was ample proof of Black's crimes. He had spent $1.4 million on chefs, maids, and butlers to work at his four homes. He also laid out $39,000 for upkeep on automobiles that included a Rolls-Royce and spent $39,000 in company funds on a birthday party for his wife.

In 2009, New York executives Mark Focht and Gary Katcher were charged with grand larceny in Greenwich, Connecticut, in connection with the misappropriation of some $8.8 million from hedge funds controlled by Stagg Capital. While initial withdrawals had been made for the purpose of keeping a second company, afloat, Focht was charged with stealing $840,000 for his personal use. He had attempted to cover his tracks through the purchase of securities that turned out to be bogus.

Some of the most brazen cases of larceny in the United States have dealt with the theft of art objects. This crime is ranked third in black market items stolen, outranked only by drugs and illicit arms. Some 15,000 new art objects are stolen each year, and only about 5 percent of them are ever recovered. Experts say the current upswing in such cases is partially a response to the looting of archaeological sites in Iraq. The items most often taken include paintings, icons, antiques, and rare books. While the most common targets are museums, larcenists also steal art objects from churches, libraries, and private homes. Some of the thieves are so inept that they end up damaging or even destroying art works because they do not have the knowledge to protect them properly during transport. The most notorious of all art thefts in the United States took place in Boston's Isabella Stewart Gardner Museum in 1990. Two thieves disguised as police officers were admitted by a night security guard, who was subsequently overpowered and tied up. The thieves then proceeded to steal Rembrandt's only seascape, *The Storm on the Sea of Galilee*, a Jan Vermeer oil painting, five Edgar Degas drawings, and a bronze Chinese beaker dating to the 12th or 13th century. Despite the lure of a $5 million reward, none of the items have been recovered.

Even the religious community has not been exempt from having its members identified as larcenists. In July 2010, Father Kevin Gray, the former pastor of Sacred Heart Parish in Waterbury, Connecticut, was arrested and charged with first-degree larceny. Over a seven-year period, the priest had stolen a total of $1.3 million from his church. The money was used to hire male escorts, buy expensive clothing, stay at luxury hotels, and

Rembrandt's only seascape, The Storm on the Sea of Galilee, *which has been missing since it was stolen from Boston's Isabella Stewart Gardner Museum in 1990, in one of the highest-value property thefts ever.*

dine at high-priced restaurants. Gray was subsequently suspended from the ministry.

Larceny has also tainted the entertainment industry. In December 2001, actress Winona Ryder, best known for her roles in quirky films such as *Beetlejuice* (1988) and *Edward Scissorhands* (1990), was arrested at Saks Fifth Avenue in Los Angeles and charged with shoplifting 20 items worth $4,760. Ryder could have faced a prison term of almost four years. In reality, she took a four-year hiatus from filmmaking and briefly entered rehab. In October 2009, talk show host David Letterman went public with admissions that he had engaged in sexual relations with several women on his staff after being threatened with blackmail. His blackmailer, Robert Halderman, a producer for *CBS News*, was charged with grand larceny for trying to extort $2 million from Letterman in return for keeping his sexual shenanigans out of the public eye.

Elizabeth Rholetter Purdy
Independent Scholar

See Also: 1921 to 1940 Primary Documents; 1941 to 1960 Primary Documents; Burglary, History of; Crime in America, Types; Embezzlement; Fraud; Robbery, History of.

Further Readings
Albanese, Jay. "Fraud: The Characteristic Crime of the 21st Century." *Trends in Organized Crime*, v.8/4 (Summer 2005).
Belville, Robert . *A Treatise on the Law of Homicide and of Larceny at Common Law*. London: W. Clarke and Son, 1799.
Cromwell, Paul F., et al. *Breaking and Entering: An Ethnographic Analysis of Burglary*. Newbury Park, CA: Sage, 1991.
Department of Justice. "Crime in the United States." http://www2.fbi.gov/ucr/cius2009/data/table_01 .html (Accessed October 2011).
Federal Bureau of Investigation. "Larceny-Theft." http://www2.fbi.gov/ucr/cius2009/offenses/ property_crime/larceny-theft.html (Accessed October 2011).
Fletcher, George. "The Metamorphosis of Larceny." *Harvard Law Review*, v.89 (1976).
Gifoyle, Timothy J. "Street Rats and Gutter-Snipes: Child Pickpockets and Street Culture in New York City, 1850–1900. *Journal of Social History*, v.37/4 (Summer 2004).
Holloway, Pippa. "A Chicken Stealer Shall Lose His Vote: Disenfranchisement for Larceny in the South, 1874–1890." *Journal of Southern History*, v.75/4 (November 2009).
Kaplan, John and Robert Weisberg. *Criminal Cases and Materials*. Boston: Little, Brown, 1991.
Wells, Joseph T., ed. *Corporate Fraud Handbook: Prevention and Detection*. Hoboken, NJ: Wiley, 2004.

Las Vegas, Nevada

Located in Clark County, Nevada, Las Vegas has been, since the early 1950s, the leading American casino destination. Throughout a crucial part of its history, the city's casino industry was tied to those with connections to organized crime. Founded in 1905 in a land auction conducted by the Salt Lake, Los Angeles, and San Pedro Railroad, Las Vegas was, in its earliest years, a watering stop for that railroad's route. Gambling was, at the town's inception, legal in Nevada; it had been so since 1869. When the railroad laid out the physical plan for the new city, it designated one block, Block 16, for "vice," which translates to gambling, drinking, and prostitution—classic Western saloon diversions. Off the main thoroughfare of Fremont Street yet easily accessible to visitors arriving by train, Block 16 offered relatively low-stakes, unremarkable debauchery.

When, in 1910, commercial gambling became illegal in Nevada, the popular pastime did not disappear from Las Vegas. Instead, it lingered without the sanction of law. This was small-scale and largely "disorganized" crime, and, again, not that exceptional. With the relegalization of commercial gambling in 1931 came greater opportunities for tourism, which was also spurred by the construction of nearby Hoover Dam (1930–35). It was in part because of the increased tourist traffic spurred by the dam (even after its completion, it remained a sightseeing attraction) that the area attracted interest from hotel developers. Gambling in the downtown area, chiefly on Fremont Street, remained relatively small scale. Most of the

Binion's casino, which dates back to the early 1950s, on Fremont Street, where most Las Vegas casinos clustered before the development of larger resort casinos on the Las Vegas Strip. A series of scandals during the 1950s brought to light connections between organized crime and Las Vegas casinos. In 1955, the state legislature created the Gaming Control Board in order to try to maintain a good image for what had become the state's largest business.

"gambling halls" were bars and saloons outfitted with a few gaming tables and slot machines. They were firmly rooted in the small-town milieu of that main street, and attracted mostly curiosity seekers.

El Rancho Vegas

The 1941 opening of the El Rancho Vegas, three miles from downtown and outside the city limits, set the stage for the development of a new kind of gambling tourism. Its developer, Thomas Hull, had operated El Rancho chain motels in most of the major urban centers of California, including San Francisco, Fresno, Sacramento, and Los Angeles, before being lured to Las Vegas by the local chamber of commerce, which had long been seeking a "first-class" hotel to burnish the city's tourist luster. Tellingly, however, Hull did not build his hotel on Fremont Street, or anywhere easily accessible to the tiny urban core that had developed over the previous 35 years. He built it on the Los Angeles Highway, then the city's chief auto link to southern California. Far from the train station, it was nonetheless superbly convenient for visitors driving up from Los Angeles. This was a rejection of the existing urban grid that, to an extent, foreshadowed the national postwar trend toward suburbanization and would have profound implications for the nature of casino resorts and their attractiveness to organized crime.

The El Rancho Vegas' structure was as groundbreaking as its location, and at least partially dictated by it. It was a direct contrast to the downtown gambling halls, which generally did not offer more than limited entertainment options and scant accommodations; it would have been laughable to suggest to a tourist that she spend her entire Las Vegas stay in a single such establishment. The El Rancho Vegas, however, was designed as an insular, all-in-one destination, with a hotel, restaurant, dinner theater, swimming pool, and retail shopping. The self-contained casino resort became the model for what became the Las Vegas Strip, stretching southward beyond city limits. The self-contained nature of these establishments was fueled by an appreciation of the laws of probability: The longer the casinos could keep visitors playing games with a small, but definite, bias in favor of the house, the more likely they were to perform well financially. Casinos with added attractions like hotels, dining, and entertainment were simply more likely to succeed than small, stand-alone gambling halls.

The need to build a hotel and to underwrite loss-leading restaurant and entertainment departments boosted the initial investment and continuing operating costs for casino resorts. In the immediate postwar period, with the success of the casino resort concept proven (the El Rancho Vegas was followed by the Hotel Last Frontier and the Flamingo), prospective casino owners began seeking to build. Many of them, however, ran into difficulties; banks would not lend money to projects as risky as gambling casinos, and many other lenders remained dubious. Those involved with illegal gambling operations, however, saw the possibilities, and many of them also had large amounts of undeclared income that they could invest.

Criminals and Casinos
The first coincidence of underworld capital and resort development came with the Flamingo, which had been started by Los Angeles nightclub and media impresario Billy Wilkerson. After running short of construction capital, Wilkerson was amenable to the advances of a group of "eastern investors" who pledged to bankroll his project but remain silent partners. The group's on-site representative, Benjamin "Bugsy" Siegel, soon proved to be anything but silent; before the resort opened, he removed Wilkerson from his leadership position on threat of violence. Wilkerson wisely took Siegel, a founding member of the Murder, Inc. hit squad, at his word. Siegel had used his connections with various organized crime figures to raise capital for the resort; following his June 1947 murder, these figures maintained a degree of involvement in the project through their sponsorship of select managers, who periodically diverted a share of the casino's proceeds back to their illicit investors, a process known as "skimming."

In the 1940s and 1950s, several men with varying connections to ongoing illicit activities moved to Las Vegas as owners, managers, and employees of casinos. Most of them had been former bootleggers who had moved into gambling with the advent of repeal in 1933. Now mostly middle-aged, they were seeking stability and respectability; Las Vegas was one of the few cities in the nation that would let them have these while practicing a craft they knew—running gambling operations. The Desert Inn was a signature example of such an operation; its ostensible impresario, the personable gambler Wilbur Clark, has his name on the marquee. A group of former bootleggers from Cleveland led by Moe Daltiz actually ran the casino; behind them, some suspected, stood even more secret investors with connections to ongoing criminal activities in the east.

Over the next decade, a slew of casino resorts opened along what became known as the Las Vegas Strip; most of them had some degree of underworld financing. The connections between organized crime and Las Vegas casinos were brought to the fore in several scandals during the 1950s, the most spectacular of which was the attempted murder of reputed Mob boss Frank Costello. Costello, gunned down in Manhattan, was discovered to have on his person a piece of paper with that month's exact take for the recently opened Tropicana casino, along with notations possibly indicating the share of the "skim" diverted to several of his associates. The Nevada Gaming Commission forced the casino's sale, but rumors of the links between casinos and unsavory characters continued to circulate.

To combat such threats (and to forestall federal action), in 1955, the state legislature created the Gaming Control Board, which was tasked with eliminating undesirables from the gaming industry and maintaining the good image of what had become the state's largest business. During the early 1960s, the Gaming Control Board and the Justice Department under Attorneys General Robert F. Kennedy and Nicholas Katzenbach clashed over the extent of skimming in Las Vegas casinos; Kennedy at one point was prevented from conducting a city-wide raid only by the intervention of Nevada Governor Grant Sawyer.

Regulatory and police actions aside, the 1950s and early 1960s saw the maturation of the casino industry on the Las Vegas Strip. As late as 1952, it was believed that federal action might cause the closure of the Nevada casino industry. The Kefauver Committee had focused public attention on organized gambling nationwide in 1950–51, and for a time it appeared that Congress might pass a ruinous excise tax on casino gambling, as it had done to bookmaking. The state of Nevada's greater financial reliance on gambling, however, made it a very interested guarantor of the industry's continued well-being. With the Gaming Control Board forcing the more flagrant "undesirables" out of the industry, casinos in Las Vegas were free to grow.

Growth of Legitimate Industry
Ultimately, that growth would prove the undoing of organized crime in the Nevada gaming industry. Both a generational shift and the shifting nature of organized crime, as well as deeper structural changes in Las Vegas casinos, ultimately drove those with organized crime affiliations from direct involvement in Nevada's gaming industry. Generally speaking, the former bootleggers who provided the human and financial capital to build up the casinos of the Las Vegas Strip in the 1940s and 1950s were, by the 1960s, in their 60s and either retiring or passing away. Their children had, for the most part, not followed them into organized crime, and those who went into the gaming industry largely did so from a business school background, not one in "the rackets."

At the same time, organized crime was changing throughout the nation. Gambling, though still a source of revenue, became less important than narcotics smuggling, labor racketeering, prostitution, and loan-sharking. Those involved with organized crime, therefore, had fewer connections to the business of gambling than the former bootleggers who had made their livings from gambling-related enterprises in the 1930s. The leadership for the next generation of casino managers and owners would not come from organized crime.

The state legislature, sensing the changes in the industry, responded to the need for new investment. In 1967 and 1969, Nevada amended its gaming laws to permit for the first time ownership of casinos by publicly traded corporations. This, it was hoped, would spur the entrance of new capital into the industry and foster its growing respectability. It largely worked. Following the passage of the Corporate Gaming Acts, some casino companies, like Harrah's in northern Nevada, took themselves public, raising money for improvements and expansions. Other companies, such as Lum's, came from outside the state and purchased existing casinos, like Caesars Palace. Soon, the traditional syndicates, run by those with ties to former bootleggers and reputedly financed by mobsters, were becoming scarcer.

Meanwhile, changes in how casino resorts operated essentially priced organized crime out of their financing. In the late 1950s, the industry, following overbuilding in the middle of the decade, turned to business travel to supplement its existing customer base: gamblers and vacationers. With convention groups booked in the mid-week, casino resorts found they could afford to get bigger. Once, 200-room hotels were the norm. By 1969, hotels had become much larger; in that year, Kirk Kerkorian's International (today the Las Vegas Hilton) opened with 1,500 rooms, making it the largest hotel in the world at the time. With new resorts soon passing the 2,000-room mark, they simply became too expensive for the traditional syndicates of investors to afford. As the International's 1971 purchase by Hilton Hotels demonstrates, large hotel operators began to apply their hospitality management expertise and name-brand identities—two areas in which the older syndicates had no special proficiency—to the casino industry.

There remained isolated incidents of skimming and mob penetration of Las Vegas casinos. In the late 1970s and early 1980s, state and federal investigations uncovered skimming at the Aladdin and Stardust casinos. The 1985 state-mandated sale of the Stardust from its owners, who had been implicated in a Mob-related skimming operation, to the Boyd Group, symbolizes the ultimate passing of the torch. By 1999, the National Gambling Impact Study Commission concluded that organized crime was no longer actively involved in the ownership of casino resorts.

Since then, the casino industry in Las Vegas has grown astronomically. In 1970, Clark County, Nevada, had annual gaming revenues of approximately $369 million. By 1980, that number had soared to $1.6 billion; a decade later, it stood at

The Las Vegas Strip in 2009. Because of the ongoing recession that year, a number of construction projects were stalled, leaving idle cranes hovering above the city. Logos for some of the publicly traded corporations that now dominate the city's casino industry, such as MGM Resorts International, and companies owned by private equity funds like Caesars Entertainment, can be seen in the photograph. In spite of the recession, in 2010 casinos in Clark County still reported nearly $9 billion in revenues.

$4.1 billion. In 2010, the county's casinos brought in nearly $9 billion in revenues, a testament to the evolution of Strip casinos from gambling dens run by former bootleggers to lavish resorts. As a result, though Las Vegas continues to host its share of crime, of both the organized and disorganized varieties, its casino industry is no longer synonymous in the public mind with organized crime. Today, the Las Vegas Strip is dominated by large, publicly traded corporations such as MGM Resorts International and companies owned by private equity funds like Caesars Entertainment. Whether a case study in the normalization of deviance or an example of the triumph of the market, Las Vegas casinos are, most observers agree, free from control by organized crime.

David G. Schwartz
University of Nevada, Las Vegas

See Also: Gambling; History of Crime and Punishment in America: 1950–1970; Luciano, "Lucky;" Nevada; Organized Crime, Contemporary; Organized Crime, History of; Organized Crime, Sociology of; Prostitution, Contemporary; Schultz, Dutch; Television, Police in.

Further Readings
Haller, Mark. "The Changing Structure of American Gambling in the Twentieth Century." *Journal of Social Issues*, v.35 (1979).
Moehring, Eugene P. *Resort City in the Sunbelt: Las Vegas, 1930–2000*, 2nd ed. Reno: University of Nevada Press, 2000.
Moehring, Eugene P. and Michael Green. *Las Vegas: A Centennial History*. Reno: University of Nevada Press, 2005.
Schwartz, David G. *Roll the Bones: The History of Gambling*. New York: Gotham Books, 2006.

Schwartz, David G. *Suburban Xanadu: The Casino Resort on the Las Vegas Strip and Beyond*. New York: Routledge, 2003.

Law Enforcement Assistance Act

President Lyndon B. Johnson signed the Law Enforcement Assistance Act of 1965 into law (Public Law 89-197) on September 22, 1965. The act authorized the attorney general to provide grants to state and local agencies for crime control research and law enforcement training. The attorney general created the Office of Law Enforcement Assistance (OLEA) to manage grants issued as part of the program. The act and the OLEA remained effective until 1968 when the program was folded into the newly formed Law Enforcement Assistance Administration. The Law Enforcement Assistance Act represented one of the first attempts by the federal government to address crime through a national program.

The act was passed because of rising fears about crime in postwar America. Federal statistics in the early 1960s showed a dramatic increase in crime, which became an important issue in the 1964 presidential election. In response, President Johnson asked Congress to encourage federal involvement in crime prevention by approving a broad crime study known as the President's Commission on Law Enforcement and the Administration of Justice. He also proposed the Law Enforcement Assistance Act to provide short-term research and funding until the President's Commission completed its full study.

The Law Enforcement Assistance Act gave the attorney general the power to offer grants to private nonprofit and public organizations interested in improving law enforcement, corrections, and criminal justice. The funds were used for demonstration programs, law enforcement training, and research into new methods of crime control at the state and local levels. During its three years of operation, the OLEA gave $20.6 million to 359 distinct projects. While a number of cities and states benefited from the funds, Washington, D.C., received the largest share. Spending under the act is credited with professionalizing law enforcement; in total, $4.4 million was granted to training programs and $1.4 million to college-level education for police officers.

While the Law Enforcement Assistance Act did represent increased federal involvement in criminal justice, it was not an attempt to federalize crime control. Congress and President Johnson explicitly stated that the act would not put state or local law enforcement under the authority of the federal government. Instead, the Attorney General's Office would simply be offering its expertise and financial support to help modernize and strengthen police forces. Despite these claims, the act did increase the visibility of federal action in the realm of criminal justice, placating those voters who called for the Johnson administration to address rising crime. More importantly, the act paved the way for later federal intervention in crime control. It also increased interest among law enforcement professionals in long-term studies and training programs.

Beyond its significance in federal crime policy, the Law Enforcement Assistance Act, one of the first block grants passed by Congress, was an important political innovation. As opposed to categorical grants, which stipulated exactly how and by whom money would be spent, block grants authorized federal agencies to give large amounts of money to local groups who could then spend it according to their own needs. The successes of the Law Enforcement Assistance Act made block grants an attractive option for lawmakers. As a result, block grants became popular in criminal justice and other areas, such as transportation, health, housing, and education.

When the President's Commission on Law Enforcement and the Administration of Justice completed its study of crime and the justice system in 1967, it supported the continuation of programs like the Law Enforcement Assistance Act. In fact, findings recommended that the federal government increase funding of law enforcement initiatives. Acting on this suggestion, Congress passed the Omnibus Crime Control and Safe Streets Act (P. L. 90-351) in 1968. Under Title I of the Safe Streets Act, Congress established the Law Enforcement Assistance Administration (LEAA) to fund future research and development projects.

The OLEA dissolved upon the creation of the LEAA, and the LEAA replaced the grant program created by the Law Enforcement Assistance Act of 1965.

Megan Stubbendeck
University of Virginia

See Also: Johnson, Lyndon B. (Administration of); Law Enforcement Assistance Administration; Omnibus Crime Control and Safe Streets Act of 1968; President's Commission on Law Enforcement and the Administration of Justice; Professionalization of Police.

Further Readings
Feeley, Malcom M. and Austin D. Sarat. *The Policy Dilemma: Federal Crime Policy and the Law Enforcement Assistance Administration, 1968–1978*. Minneapolis: University of Minnesota Press, 1980.
Johnson, Lyndon B. "Statement by the President Following the Signing of Law Enforcement Assistance Bills." http://www.presidency.ucsb.edu/ws/index.php?pid=27270 (Accessed January 2011).

Law Enforcement Assistance Administration

The Law Enforcement Assistance Administration (LEAA) was a federal agency within the U.S. Department of Justice. The LEAA was established by the Omnibus Crime Control and Safe Streets Act of 1968 and was abolished in 1982. The LEAA worked within the U.S. Department of Justice to administer federal funding to state and local law enforcement agencies and funded educational programs, research, state planning agencies, and local crime initiatives.

In 1964, Lyndon Johnson was elected president of the United States. He created the President's Commission on Law Enforcement and the Administration of Justice. In 1968, Congress passed the Omnibus Crime Control and Safe Streets Act, which then signified the most comprehensive crime legislation in the nation's history. Although some sections of the bill applied to federal policing, the real significance of this act was in its goal to better finance local law enforcement and facilitate interagency coordination for crime fighting.

States that formed state planning agencies and created comprehensive programs to improve law enforcement and the operation of the criminal justice system were allocated planning grants from the LEAA. Within each state, regional planning councils formed, and these councils submitted their proposals to LEAA, which funded them through grants. The nature of the funded programs varied and included money for cadet programs, special crime-fighting units, community relations activities, and a statewide uniform crime-reporting system.

The Office of Academic Assistance (OAA) was also established under LEAA to administer the Law Enforcement Education Program (LEEP). LEEP provided financial aid to students enrolled in colleges and universities who agreed to seek careers in criminal justice upon graduation.

Effect on Law Enforcement
In its first year, the LEAA granted $300 million, primarily to police departments for equipment purchases. The LEAA helped police departments that had wanted to professionalize but could not because they lacked funds. Over the years, the LEAA funded programs to train local bomb squads, pilot programs studying alternatives to incarceration, drug treatment programs, and state court organization and training programs. Significantly, the LEAA was responsible for developing national training programs for state and local law enforcement officers and lawyers, bringing modern techniques to many departments for the first time. In March 1973, the LEAA ordered any police department receiving federal funding to end minimum height requirements, which most women could not meet.

By 1975, the LEAA had awarded more than $4 billion to state and local governments to improve police, court, and correctional systems to combat juvenile delinquency. By 1981, the LEAA had granted more than $8 billion in funds. States adopted 70 percent of LEAA-sponsored programs in one form or another. It thus made a significant contribution to the modernization of local law enforcement.

More enduring was the act's innovation of the National Institute of Law Enforcement and Criminal Justice. The Katzenbach Commission, as it was known, issued dozens of studies on crime and criminal justice. Examining the socioeconomic roots of crime, the commission's recommendations correlated with the policy approaches of Johnson's Great Society. The commission called for more education, better training of law enforcement officers, and increased research on crime.

The National Institute of Justice (NIJ) was created under the Omnibus Crime Control and Safe Streets Act of 1968 to advance law enforcement technology and knowledge through technology and social research grants to academic institutions and other organizations, just like the LEAA. The NIJ and LEAA collectively contributed to the field of criminal justice by collaborating with state and local governments. In 1978, it was renamed the National Institute of Justice. Some functions of the LEAA were absorbed by NIJ on December 27, 1979, with passage of the Justice System Improvement Act of 1979. The act, which amended the Omnibus Crime Control and Safe Streets Act of 1968, also led to formation of the Bureau of Justice Statistics. In 1982, the LEAA was succeeded by the Office of Justice Assistance, Research, and Statistics (1982–84) and then the Office of Justice Programs in 1984.

The LEAA did receive criticisms of the manner in which financial resources and technical assistance were allocated to state and local governments. Some critics believed that its objectives were ambiguous and at times conflicting, and that the program was too broadly defined and lacked meaningful structure. Others pointed to the fact that members of state planning agencies that were to receive the federal funds and disperse them as they saw fit to local areas were dominated by law enforcement agencies and local government units and consequently did not incorporate the ideas of citizen groups or the interests of minorities. Some believed that the control of LEAA funds by law enforcement undermined the chance that other programs that community leaders proposed, such as counseling and therapy, would get funded. Others questioned the actual crime reduction that followed the implementation of LEAA-funded programs.

Liz Marie Marciniak
Nicholas A. Hall
University of Pittsburgh at Greensburg

See Also: Johnson, Lyndon B. Administration of; Law Enforcement Assistance Act; Omnibus Crime Control and Safe Streets Act of 1968; President's Commission on Law Enforcement and the Administration of Justice.

Further Readings
President's Commission on Law Enforcement and the Administration of Justice. *The Challenge of Crime in a Free Society: A Report*. Washington, DC: U.S. Government Printing Office, 1967.
Scheingold, Stuart. *The Politics of Law and Order*. New York: Longman, 1984.
Wadman, Robert C. and William T. Allison. *To Protect and Serve*. Upper Saddle River, NJ: Pearson Prentice Hall, 2004.
Walker, Samuel. "Reexamining the President's Crime Commission: The Challenge of Crime in a Free Society After Ten Years." *Crime and Delinquency*, v.24 (1978).
Wilson, James Q. *Thinking About Crime*. New York: Vintage Books, 1985.

Lawrence v. Texas

To what extent is private sexual conduct between consenting adults protected by the U.S. Constitution? The U.S. Supreme Court was forced to grapple anew with this question in the case of *Lawrence v. Texas* (2003). The case arose in 1998 when police, responding to a reported weapons disturbance, entered the private residence of John Lawrence, who was engaged in intimate sexual conduct with his male partner, Tyron Garner. Both men were arrested, charged, and convicted of violating a Texas statute prohibiting "deviate sexual intercourse with another individual of the same sex." The men appealed their conviction, claiming their rights had been violated under both the Texas and U.S. Constitutions. In upholding

The Texas State Capitol building in Austin, Texas, in 2009. The majority in Lawrence v. Texas struck down the Texas law and also overturned Bowers v. Hardwick, thereby striking down all remaining antisodomy laws, both heterosexual and homosexual.

their convictions, the Court of Appeals for the Texas Fourteenth District cited the U.S. Supreme Court's decision in *Bowers v. Hardwick* (1986), which upheld a Georgia statute criminalizing sodomy. In granting certiorari in the *Lawrence* case, the Supreme Court focused on whether the Texas law violated the petitioners' interests in liberty and privacy protected by the due process clause of the Fourteenth Amendment.

Justice Anthony Kennedy delivered the court's opinion in *Lawrence*, which was joined by Justices Stephen Breyer, Ruth Bader Ginsburg, David Souter, and John P. Stevens. Justice Sandra Day O'Connor filed a separate opinion concurring in the outcome, while Justices William Rehnquist, Antonin Scalia, and Clarence Thomas dissented. Justice Kennedy's opinion begins by stating, "Liberty presumes an autonomy of self that includes freedom of thought, belief, expression, and certain intimate conduct." The opinion then traces the relevant case law, including *Griswold v. Connecticut*, *Eisenstadt v. Baird*, and *Roe v. Wade*, noting that in these cases the Supreme Court invalidated statutes that impinged upon both individuals' and couples' rights to privacy regarding marriage, procreation, contraception, and intimate sexual conduct. Justice Kennedy therefore situates the *Lawrence* case alongside others in which the liberty and privacy interests inherent in the U.S. Constitution protect people from "unwarranted government intrusions." But in *Bowers v. Hardwick*, decided only 17 years earlier, the Supreme Court found that a similar statute did not violate the U.S. Constitution. The majority in *Lawrence* therefore revisited the *Bowers* decision, finding two central problems with its reasoning.

First, the majority opinion in *Bowers* begins by stating, "The issue presented is whether the Federal Constitution confers a fundamental right upon homosexuals to engage in sodomy...." In the *Lawrence* opinion, Justice Kennedy argues that such a narrow construction of the constitutional question fundamentally misapprehends the liberty claim at stake. The proper constitutional question is, rather, whether the Constitution confers a fundamental right upon adult persons, regardless of sexual orientation, to engage in private, consensual sexual conduct. Second, the majority in *Bowers* relied on the notion that moral disapproval and criminal prohibition of same-sex sexual conduct has deep roots in American history.

However, in the majority opinion in *Lawrence*, Justice Kennedy cites numerous scholarly contributions from history and gender and sexuality studies to show that in fact the United States has no long-standing tradition of criminalizing same-sex sexual conduct. Rather, the sodomy statutes once common throughout the United States regulated non-procreative sexual behavior of all kinds, regardless of the sexual orientation of those involved. Sodomy statutes significantly predate the notion, which emerged in the late 19th century, that homosexuals and heterosexuals are distinct. In *Bowers*, however, the history of sodomy was rewritten to be essentially and exclusively concerned with homosexuals. Thus, the majority in *Bowers* incorrectly conflated the regulation of sodomy with the criminalization of same-sex sexual conduct, thereby attributing "ancient roots" to the latter.

In an article titled "What Gay Studies Taught the Court," George Chauncey recounts how the amicus brief filed by historians in the *Lawrence* case demonstrated that the Texas statute in question, adopted in 1973, was characteristic of mid-20th-century laws that specifically targeted homosexuals in a discriminatory manner. In fact, only a year later, in 1974, the state of Texas decriminalized heterosexual sodomy, underscoring how its sodomy law singled out the intimate conduct of homosexuals.

Therefore, the problematic reasoning evident in the *Bowers* decision, combined with the fact that, by 2003, the vast majority of states had already repealed their sodomy statutes, led the majority in *Lawrence* not only to strike down the Texas law but to also overturn *Bowers v. Hardwick*, thereby striking down all remaining antisodomy laws, both heterosexual and homosexual. Citing the Supreme Court's decision in *Planned Parenthood v. Casey* (1992), Justice Kennedy concludes his majority opinion in *Lawrence v. Texas* by stating

> The petitioners are entitled to respect for their private lives. The state cannot demean their existence or control their destiny by making their private sexual conduct a crime ... It is a promise of the Constitution that there is a realm of personal liberty which the government may not enter.

Jason J. Hopkins
University of California, Santa Barbara

See Also: *Bowers v. Hardwick*; Due Process; Equality, Concept of; *Romer v. Evans*; Sodomy.

Further Readings

Anderson, Ellen Ann. *Out of the Closets and Into the Courts: Legal Opportunity Structure and Gay Rights Litigation*. Ann Arbor: University of Michigan Press, 2005.

Bernstein, Mary. "Liberalism and Social Movement Success: The Case of United States Sodomy Statutes." In *Regulating Sex: The Politics of Intimacy and Identity*, Elizabeth Bernstein and Laurie Schaffner, eds. New York: Routledge, 2005.

Bowers v. Hardwick, 478 U.S. 186 (1986).

Chauncey, George. "What Gay Studies Taught the Court: The Historians' Amicus Brief in *Lawrence v. Texas*." *Journal of Lesbian and Gay Studies*, v.10/3 (2004).

Eskridge, William N. *Dishonorable Passions: Sodomy Laws in America, 1861–2003*. New York: Viking, 2008.

Lawrence v. Texas, 539 U.S. 558 (2003).

Richards, David A. J. *The Sodomy Cases:* Bowers v. Hardwick *and* Lawrence v. Texas. Lawrence: University Press of Kansas, 2009.

Laws and Liberties of Massachusetts

The Laws and Liberties of Massachusetts were adopted in 1648 to replace the provisional Bodie of Liberties of 1641. *The Laws and Liberties* did incorporate several clauses from the Bodie of Liberties but represented the first systematic attempt to construct a complete system of governance and law by an English colony in a single code. *The Laws and Liberties* represent an attempt by the leaders of the colony to harmonize the laws of men with biblical law. It also codified several protections for criminal defendants that existed by practice in the common law.

The Laws and Liberties are organized alphabetically by topic covered. They attempt to provide sections for all areas of civil and criminal law as well as establishing the structure of governance for the colony. The code did not change the existing structure of colonial governance but simply codified it. Some colonists had been pushing for a written code of laws that was in line with biblical law since the 1630s, but their request was opposed by Governor John Winthrop, who feared that a codified set of laws that did not conform to the common law of England would provide the king a cause for revoking the colony's charter. He also feared that a set code of laws would limit the discretion of magistrates to take into account the circumstances of the violation of a law that might mitigate the punishment. The deputies of the colonial towns managed to place enough pressure on the governor and his counsel to have them agree to adopt a code of laws. It was universally agreed that the laws should reflect substantive biblical law to which were added English common law procedures.

The criminal law set forth in *The Laws and Liberties* was based on biblical law and included capital punishment for witchcraft, blasphemy, bestiality, sodomy, adultery, cursing a parent or being a rebellious son, in addition to murder, rape, and treason. However, capital punishments were rarely, if ever, carried out for cursing a parent, rebelliousness, or blasphemy without another capital charge also lying against the person. In addition, there were lesser punishments contemplated by the code for first-time offenses and the capital punishment was only to be applied to repeat offenders. There were instances of capital punishment being inflicted for adultery, bestiality, sodomy, witchcraft, murder, and rape. *The Laws and Liberties* also proposed community intervention to punish wayward servants and children who were not being sufficiently disciplined by parents.

The Laws and Liberties provided defendant rights, including the right to a jury trial and a prohibition on torture to obtain a confession or information. Capital punishment was prohibited unless two witnesses or equivalent certain testimony was provided against a criminal defendant. In addition, strangers, idiots, and children were to have allowance from the court if they were to violate a law in accordance with their diminished reason or knowledge. *The Laws and Liberties* did not contain some of the more forward-looking defendant rights contained in the Body of Liberties, including the right to counsel and the right for the defendant to compel and swear witnesses on his behalf.

The Laws and Liberties have been cited as a precursor to some of the rights contained within the Bill of Rights of the United States. They governed the colony of Massachusetts Bay for nearly 40 years until the colony was collapsed into the dominion of New England by King James II in 1686. The common law of England was implemented by Governor Edmund Andros during the duration of the dominion.

John Felipe Acevedo
University of Chicago

See Also: Bible; Bodie of Liberties; Colonial Charters and Grants; Constitution of the United States of America; Massachusetts.

Further Readings
Dunn, Richard S., ed. *The Laws and Liberties of Massachusetts 1648*. Reprinted From the Unique Copy of the 1648 Edition in the Henry E. Huntington Library, With Introduction. San Marino, CA: Huntington Library, 1998.
Haskins, George Lee. *Law and Authority in Early Massachusetts: A Study in Tradition and Design*. New York: Macmillan, 1960.
Wolford, Thorp L. "The Laws and Liberties of 1648." In *Essays in the History of Early American Law*, David H. Flaherty, ed. Chapel Hill: University of North Carolina Press.

Lawyers Guild

The National Lawyers Guild (NLG) is a nonprofit legal organization that was founded in 1937. While the association has chapters throughout the nation, the national office is housed in New York City. The NLG attempts to protect the rights of workers, women, farmers, the disabled, and people of color. The NLG aims to eliminate racism, sexism, homophobia, environmental destruction, and xenophobia, and to improve upon labor issues and the rights of workers, voting rights, and people's civil rights and liberties. The NLG continues to use the law to protect the people, advance social justices, and support progressive social movements.

The mission, as stated by the preamble to the NLG constitution states, "The NLG is dedicated to the need for basic change in the structure of our political and economic system. [The NLG] seeks to unite the lawyers, law students, legal workers, and jailhouse lawyers to function as an effective force in the service of the people, to the end that human rights shall be regarded as more sacred than property interests."

Membership and Structure
When the NLG first began, membership was exclusively offered to lawyers. Now, membership

is offered to lawyers, legal workers and aides, legal investigators, and paralegals. Jailhouse lawyers (prisoners who provide legal services to other inmates) are not required to pay dues and have been eligible for membership since 1971. Additionally, law school students are eligible for membership in their school's chapter. The NLG is divided into nine geographical regions and 120 chapters that consist of at least eight members who have paid dues. A regional vice president represents each region at the National Executive Committee (NEC) conference.

The NEC oversees the NLG and meets four times per year to vote on related issues. The NEC is run by a nationally elected president, two executive vice presidents, a treasurer, two law student vice presidents, one national legal worker vice president, one national jailhouse lawyer vice president, nine regional vice presidents, an executive director, a representative of the national office staff, and representatives from 10 of the NLG projects and committees.

History

The NLG was created in 1937 as an alternative to the American Bar Association. The NLG protested against the American Bar Association's policies by allowing African American and Jewish members to join, making it the first racially integrated bar association. The NLG believes in serving the people and protecting their rights as opposed to serving other public or private organizations that may violate the rights and needs of the people. The NLG assisted in the creation of unions and organizations that supported the advancement of human and civil rights, such as the United Auto Workers and the Congress of Industrial Organizations (CIO). One of the NLG's initial causes during the Great Depression was support of President Franklin Roosevelt's economic program known as the New Deal, which focused on relief, recovery, and reform. The NLG came under attack during the 1950s by Wisconsin's Republican U.S. Senator Joseph McCarthy. He accused the NLG of being a front for a political communist organization because of what he called the group's extreme "left-wing" views. The NLG was able to endure these allegations of being a communist front by limiting the types of projects taken on by the organization. Eventually, the NLG began to shift its focus onto promoting and protecting the civil rights of African Americans.

Lawyers associated with the NLG have assisted in the prosecution of Nazis during World War II and fought racial discrimination lawsuits in cases such as *Hansberry v. Lee*, which argued against Jim Crow laws in the city of Chicago, and in well-known Supreme Court cases for civil rights such as *Dombrowski v. Pfister*, *Goldberg v. Kelly*, and *Monell v. Department of Social Services*. In 1945, the NLG was asked by the U.S. government to represent the American people at the founding of the United Nations. Members of the NLG also assisted in the drafting of the Universal Declaration of Human Rights. Members of the NLG founded the International Association of Democratic Lawyers (IADL), the American Trial Lawyers Association (ATLA), and other institutions that promote human and civil rights, such as the National Conference of Black Lawyers.

NLG members were the first lawyers to open storefront law offices, which offered community-based legal services to low-income clients. Additionally, NLG lawyers have offered support to resisters of the Vietnam War draft, antiwar activists, and Black Panther Party members; the group sued the FBI for illegal surveillance of legal activist organization activities that took place at the NLG national office and the in private offices of important NLG members. The NLG has supported the advancement of social justice internationally by encouraging Palestinian rights, opposing apartheid in South Africa, and offering support for the antinuclear movement. In 2007, the NLG supported the movement for impeachment of President George W. Bush and Vice President Dick Cheney.

The NLG comprises approximately 20 committees, projects, and task forces. They include the Anti-Racism Committee, Anti-Sexism Committee, Disability Rights Committee, Drug Policy Committee, Environmental Justice Committee, Labor and Employment Committee, Legal Workers Committee, Military Law Task Force, Prison Law Project, United People of Color Caucus (TUPOCC), and the National Immigration Project.

Carrie Wai
Kristina Wood
California School of Professional Psychology

See Also: Civil Rights Laws; McCarthy, Joseph; Roosevelt, Franklin D. (Administration of).

Further Readings

Buhle, Mari Jo, Paul Buhle, and Dan Georgakas. *Encyclopedia of the American Left.* Chicago: University of Illinois Press, 1992.

Ginger, Ann Fagan and Eugene M. Tobin, eds. *The National Lawyers Guild: From Roosevelt Through Reagan.* Philadelphia: Temple University Press, 1988.

National Lawyers Guild. http://www.nlg.org (Accessed February 2011).

Tyson, James L. *Target America.* Chicago: Regnery Gateway, 1981.

Leavenworth Federal Penitentiary

U.S. Penitentiary Leavenworth, the oldest penitentiary in the federal prison system, is located 25 miles north of Kansas City, Kansas, on State Highway 73. It sits in close proximity to the U.S. Disciplinary Barracks that serve as the sole maximum-security prison for the U.S. military. It has been called the "hothouse" and the "big top" due to its poor ventilation and the domed main building that serves as its administrative area. Prior to its construction, federal inmates were held in state prisons. The Federal Bureau of Prisons, which operates Leavenworth, was established in 1930 with the objective of providing consistent and centralized administration for the 11 federal prisons in existence at that time.

Leavenworth sprawls over 1,580 acres, of which 23 are contained inside its 35-foot-high walls. The walls are purported to extend into the ground another 35 feet to prevent escape. Approximately 12 feet in width and over 3,000 feet in length, the walls contain six gun towers. The use of concertina and electrified wire further ensure that the walls are not breached. Cables are strung between these walls and are suspended above the prison's yard and recreational areas to prevent escape by aircraft. Currently, Leavenworth houses 1,894 medium-security male inmates. Inmates are held in four housing units comprised of A, B, C, and D dorms. Dorms are of a five-tiered design—placing the roof nearly 150 feet above the floor. In the 1980s and 1990s, A, B, and C dorms underwent extensive renovation. Today, D cellblock remains the only dorm true to the original design. Complaints have circulated for years about the poor heating, air conditioning, and overall ventilation within these housing units. In 1910, the attorney general approved the construction of an additional cellblock to house female offenders; however, this plan was later abandoned.

Leavenworth was designed by St. Louis architects Eames and Young following the blueprint popularized by the Auburn Correctional Facility in New York. This design arranges cellblocks in large rectangular configurations. These cell blocks were largely self-contained units that typically served as the location for group labor. As the first federal penitentiary, construction on Leavenworth began in 1895. Military prisoners provided the labor and were marched the four miles daily to the construction site, making the return trip in the evening. They also processed and refined lumber, made bricks, and quarried stone to support construction efforts. It wasn't until 1903 that prisoners were housed in

Prisoners in striped uniforms marching to dinner at Leavenworth Federal Penitentiary in an early photograph of the prison from around 1910. The striped suits were used until 1927.

the completed facility. The construction of the prison lasted for more than 30 years, with the dome added in 1926.

Upon opening, prisoners were required to wear the traditional striped uniform now popularized by the film industry. These uniforms persisted until 1927, when they were replaced with a dark blue uniform. These uniforms were used until the conclusion of World War II, at which time inmates were provided surplus military fatigues. Today, standard uniforms include khaki shirts and pants, with older military coats used during the winter months. On September 5, 1930, Carl Panzram became the first prisoner to be executed at Leavenworth. Claiming to have killed over 21 people (including children) and having confessed to the rapes of 1,000 men, Panzram was eventually hanged for the murder of Leavenworth's laundry foreman. Records indicate that when the noose was placed around his neck, Panzram spat in the executioner's face and urged him to get on with it. Today, Leavenworth operates a large factory system that produces items for sale to government agencies. These items include printed materials, textiles, and furniture. These factories employ over half the inmate population and produce several million dollars in profit each year. Inmates that work in Leavenworth's factories earn prevailing free market wages. Factory wages exceed those paid to inmates with traditional institutional jobs that include janitorial, maintenance, and painting assignments.

In 1960, Federal Prison Camp Leavenworth was opened and houses 477 minimum-security male inmates. Located adjacent to the penitentiary, its inmates help maintain the prison grounds and provide a ready source of skilled workers who repair the prison's aging structure.

Today, Leavenworth is just one prison among 115 other institutions operated by the Federal Bureau of Prisons. In its entirety, the federal prison system is currently responsible for the care and custody of 209,000 inmates. Leavenworth was the largest maximum-security federal prison in the United States from 1903 until 2005. In 2005, Leavenworth's custody level was reduced from maximum to medium security. Its most infamous resident (and arguably the most dangerous prisoner in America) was Thomas Silverstein, who killed several fellow inmates and a correctional officer. Because of these killings, Silverstein was kept in a specially designed cell with the designation of "no human contact" status. When Leavenworth's security designation was decreased, Silverstein was transferred to ADX Florence, a super-maximum security prison located in Colorado. While most federal prisoners have never seen Leavenworth, its storied reputation persists.

Curtis R. Blakely
Truman State University

See Also: Auburn State Prison; Federal Prisons; Kansas; Penitentiaries.

Further Readings
Earley, Pete. *The Hot House: Life Inside Leavenworth Prison*. New York: Bantam Books, 1993.
LaMaster, Kenneth. *U.S. Penitentiary Leavenworth, Kansas*. Mount Pleasant, SC: Arcadia Publishing, 2008.

Legal Counsel

As stated in the familiar Miranda warning, those involved in the criminal process have a right to an attorney, also referred to as the right to legal counsel. This right is afforded to people being interrogated, accused, prosecuted, and convicted of crimes. However, the actions and protections associated with the right vary according to the stage of the criminal process, the punishment associated with the crime, and characteristics unique to the person such as mental capacity and financial situation.

The right to legal counsel is a constitutionally guaranteed federal right. A right to "Assistance of Counsel" for "all criminal prosecutions" is explicitly stated in the Sixth Amendment. The right to counsel is seen as an integral part of both the right to due process before being deprived of life or liberty and the right not to incriminate oneself afforded by the Fifth Amendment. States are also obligated to respect these rights since both amendments have been incorporated to the states through the Fourteenth Amendment.

However, until the 20th century, the right to counsel was available to only the privileged few. There were no guarantees that counsel would be appointed for those who could not afford an attorney. There were no guarantees that a person would be represented by counsel prior to appearing in court. And since people were not informed that they had a right to counsel, those who were unfamiliar with the legal system were left alone through a process that could result in their imprisonment or death.

Through the late 20th and early 21st centuries, the U.S. Supreme Court has developed extensive case law interpreting, applying, and distinguishing the Fifth and Sixth Amendment rights to counsel. The two most famous cases, *Gideon v. Wainwright* (1963) and *Miranda v. Arizona* (1966), have ensured that the indigent have access to legal representation and that those subjected to custodial interrogation are informed of their right to counsel, respectively. However, the right to legal counsel is far more nuanced than these two cases indicate.

Role and Types of Legal Counsel

The right to legal counsel is grounded in the principle of fairness and the adversarial nature of the American legal system. In America, the criminal legal process is adversarial as characterized by the presentation of opposing arguments by the prosecution and defense to an impartial jury. It is expected that the jury will be able to identify the truth and decide the guilt or innocence of the defendant. In this system, the defendant's legal counsel is to act as an advocate for the defendant, challenging the prosecution's case and ensuring that the defendant's rights are protected and the process is fair.

Representation by legal counsel is important to ensure that the criminal legal process remains fair. The criminal legal process is initiated by and driven by government, whether state or federal, action that may be inherently unfair. It is the role of legal counsel to ensure that the defendant is treated fairly throughout the process. Legal counsel is expected to understand the process itself as well as the implication of the defendant's choices and actions throughout the process. As a result, legal counsel is expected to assist and advise the defendant, thus ensuring that the government actors, such as the prosecution and police, do not take unfair advantage of the defendant or the situation. The principle of fairness also dictates that the government not restrict or impede the ability of the defendant and legal counsel to prepare and present a defense.

It is possible for a criminal defendant to waive the right to legal counsel at any point or for the entire criminal legal process. However, this is not recommended and is rarely done. Few criminal defendants have an understanding of the criminal legal system necessary to adequately protect their rights or ensure fairness. Even when the defendant has some legal training, as in *Crooker v. California* (1958), involvement in the process and lack of experience risks incriminating or detrimental actions that may have been avoided by advice from legal counsel.

Criminal defendants can be represented by either privately retained or publicly appointed legal counsel. If the defendant has the financial means, he/she can choose to retain a lawyer privately. If, however, the defendant cannot afford a lawyer and meets the state or federal considerations for indigence, the court will appoint a lawyer. Financial standards for indigence vary by state, and some states do allow for partial indigence. The financial status of those claiming indigence is verified by the court, and the defendant is required to report any changes in financial status to the court. Courts can require reimbursement for the costs of legal counsel if the defendant's financial status improves.

When appointing legal counsel, the court may appoint a public defender or a panel attorney. Some states have established an office of public defenders. These are lawyers who focus solely on representing indigent criminal defendants. Panel attorneys are lawyers who have a private practice but spend a portion of their time providing legal counsel for indigent criminal defendants. Although, in essence, a court-appointed lawyer is an employee of the government because fees are paid by the government, he/she is expected to represent and advocate for the defendant. The principle of fairness requires that the government not interfere in the defense through the manner of appointing legal counsel, including who is appointed and the time provided for preparation of the case.

Right to Counsel

As mentioned, the right to legal counsel is guaranteed in both the Fifth and Sixth Amendments. There is a difference between these two rights, and the Supreme Court has enforced that difference through its decisions. The right to legal counsel guaranteed in the Fifth Amendment is to ensure the defendant's rights as well as fairness of the process. The Fifth Amendment right to counsel is applicable in processes and procedures before the government has taken formal action to prosecute. Although a person has a right to an attorney during this period, it is not an absolute right because there must be a request for legal counsel. In other words, it is the responsibility of the person desiring legal counsel to take action.

Conversely, the Sixth Amendment right to counsel applies once the government has indicated that it will prosecute and, therefore, has begun criminal proceedings. In this situation, the right to counsel is absolute because the person must take action to waive the right. Even if the person waives the Sixth Amendment right to counsel and chooses to self-represent, the court may deny the request if it is in the best interest of either the defendant (e.g., if the defendant is illiterate or has mental issues) or justice (e.g., if self-representation would significantly impede the trial). The court also has the right to appoint a "standby" attorney in the event that the defendant has a change of mind.

Before the *Miranda* decision, exercise of the Fifth Amendment right to counsel was dependent on the person knowing the right, the police notifying the person of the right, and the person understanding that he/she could exercise the right. Even when the person chose to exercise the right, he/she was not afforded immediate protections. For example, in 1958, the Supreme Court found that there was no violation of a right when the police refused to honor the request for counsel until after a confession was made (*Cicenia v. Lagay*, 1958). On the same day, the Supreme Court found in *Crooker* that there was no violation of right to counsel when a confession was made absent counsel because the person had an understanding of the legal process and had previously refused to exercise his right to counsel. Presaging *Miranda*, the Supreme Court ruled in *Escobedo v. Illinois.* (1964) that denial of counsel during custodial questioning after counsel had been requested and without warning was a violation of the right to counsel.

By 1966, the Supreme Court realized that the variety of procedures in place to make people aware of their Fifth Amendment rights was inadequate. In the *Miranda* decision, the Supreme Court indicated a warning that is to be given before a person is questioned or interrogated or makes a statement that could be self-incriminating. The Supreme Court believed that after this warning, the person could knowingly and intelligently waive or exercise his/her rights, including the right to having legal counsel present.

During the 1970s, the Supreme Court announced two decisions that could be seen as limiting the Fifth Amendment right to counsel. In *Kirby v. Illinois* (1972), the Supreme Court refused to extend the right to counsel to identification by a victim before the prosecutorial process has begun. Reinforcing that the request for legal counsel must be specific, the court, in *Fare v. Michael C.* (1979), determined that the request by a juvenile for his probation officer was a knowing and intelligent waiver of the right to counsel.

The Supreme Court continues to require that exercise of the Fifth Amendment right to counsel requires an explicit request for counsel. For example, the right to invoke counsel could not be established when the person contradicted himself by making limited requests for counsel as well as statements of willingness to speak with authorities (*Connecticut v. Barrett,* 1987). Furthermore, merely mentioning a lawyer or making comments about a lawyer is not sufficient to exercise the right to counsel (*Davis v. United States*, 1994).

In 1981, the Supreme Court clarified and reinforced *Miranda*. In *Edwards v. Arizona,* the Supreme Court held that once a person has requested an attorney, it cannot be considered that the right was subsequently waived because he responded to continued custodial questioning unless the person initiated the communication. Because of the coercive conditions that exist when a person is in the custody of the government (including police stations and prison) there is a risk that the person will be unfairly influenced to provide information that would not be provided in other, less coercive, situations. The Supreme Court agreed to apply this ruling retroactively in

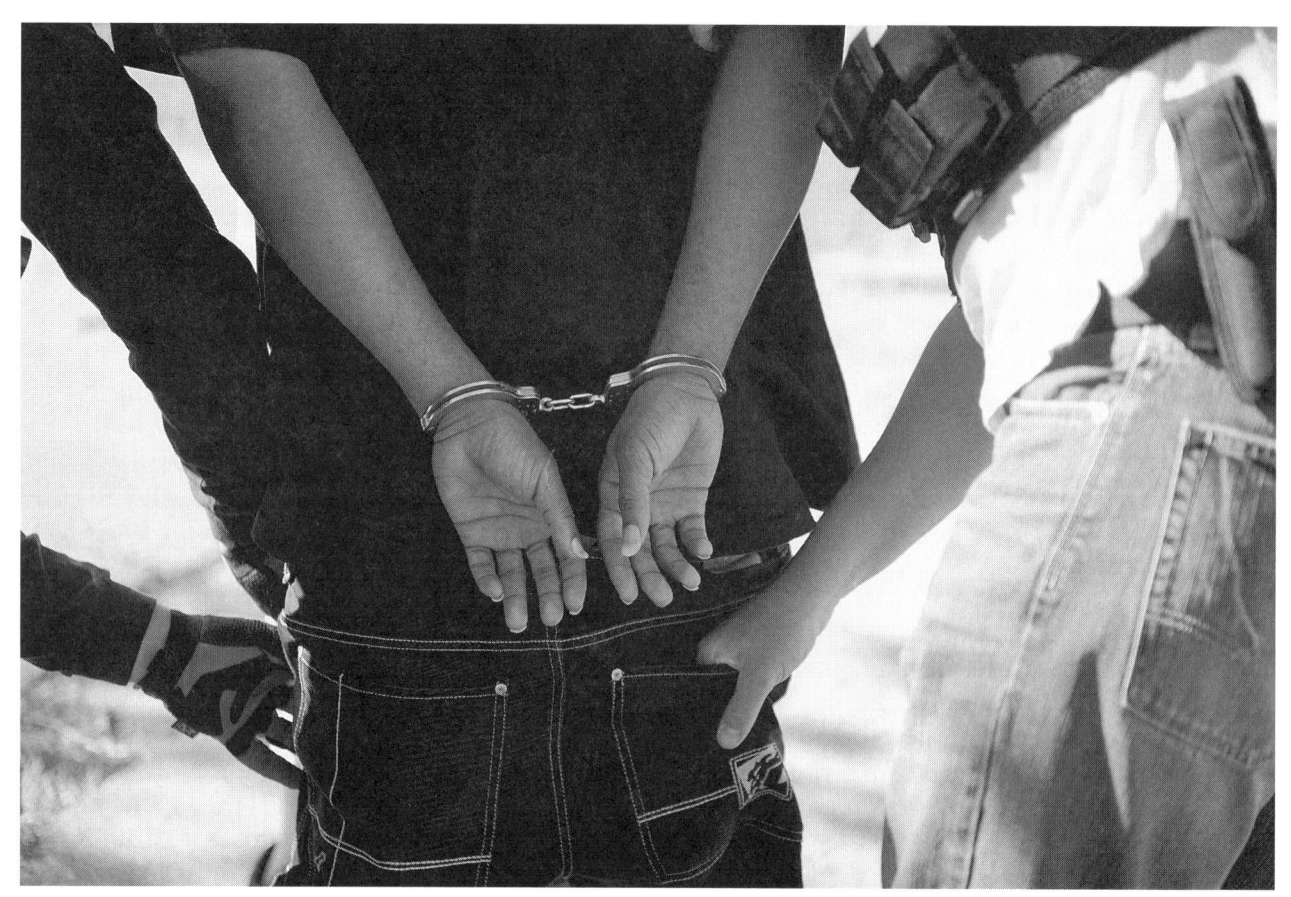

A man being searched during an arrest in Tulsa, Oklahoma, in May 2001. The Fifth Amendment right to counsel is applicable in processes and procedures before the government has taken formal action to prosecute. This means that although a person has a right to an attorney during this period, it is not an absolute right because there must be a request for legal counsel.

situations where it was decided before a direct appeal of a final conviction could be heard (*Shea v. Louisiana*, 1985).

The Supreme Court continues to refine and reinforce *Edwards*. In *Arizona v. Roberson* (1988), the Supreme Court found a violation of Fifth Amendment rights when the person invoked the right to counsel but police interrogated him regarding a separate investigation without the presence of counsel while he remained in custody. In other words, once a person in custody requests a lawyer, that right has attached for the entire time that he/she is in custody. Since the court recognizes that the mental effects of being in custody continue even after release, the right to counsel remains attached for 14 days after release (*Maryland v. Shatzer*, 2010).

However, the Supreme Court also clarified that invocation of the right to counsel is specific to the offense (*Texas v. Cobb*, 2001). As different offenses require different elements of proof, they also separate invocation of the right to counsel. Therefore, the right to counsel invoked during one custodial interrogation does not extend to another custodial interrogation even if it is on related charges.

The Supreme Court is reinforcing and refining the Miranda warnings in three general areas. First, the Supreme Court has refined what constitutes adequate warnings. In *Wyrick v. Fields* (1982), the Supreme Court explained that in order to determine whether the right to counsel has been waived, the "totality of the circumstances" must be considered. This is consistent with the rulings that clarified *Edwards* because those rulings looked at the impact of the circumstances in which the questioning occurred. Furthermore, a person can waive his/her Fifth Amendment right to counsel with knowing and understanding without having knowledge of all possible charges or having the consequences of his/her actions explained (*Colorado v. Spring*, 1987). It is also not necessary to explicitly explain that legal counsel can be present during questioning as long as there is an explanation that legal counsel can be consulted prior to questioning and the right to counsel can be invoked at any time (*Florida v. Powell*, 2010).

Second, the Supreme Court has clarified the consequences of questioning after invoking the Fifth Amendment right to counsel. If counsel is requested after the Miranda warning but the person responds to questions before counsel arrives, those responses cannot be used to question the validity of the request for counsel (*Smith v. Illinois*, 1984). In addition, the right to counsel does not end once a person has consulted with his/her legal counsel (*Minnick v. Mississippi*, 1990). Once a person has requested legal counsel, further questioning cannot occur without the presence of the legal counsel unless the person specifically initiates the communication in the absence of counsel.

Third, the Supreme Court continues to reiterate that there is a difference between Fifth and Sixth Amendment right to counsel. To illustrate, the court has ruled that invocation of the Sixth Amendment right to counsel during the first court appearance does not carry the implication that the Fifth Amendment right to counsel had been invoked (*McNeil v. Wisconsin*, 1991).

Sixth Amendment Right to Counsel

When considering the Sixth Amendment right to counsel, the Supreme Court has been concerned with identifying those parts of the criminal legal process that require the presence of counsel. In general, the Supreme Court has applied the Sixth Amendment right to counsel to proceedings associated with conviction beginning with the first judicial appearance. The intent is that the right to counsel attaches when the government has indicated its intention to prosecute. This right extends through the right of first appeal. Although a defendant is allowed to have legal counsel at any time prior to the first judicial appearance and during discretionary appeals, these actions are not covered by the Sixth Amendment right to counsel.

The importance of the Sixth Amendment right to counsel is that it prevents actions and proceedings that could harm the defendant from occurring without legal counsel's knowledge or participation. For example, once the Sixth Amendment right to counsel is in effect, government agents, including police and informants, are not allowed to solicit information or confessions from the defendant without the presence of his legal counsel.

Historically, the Supreme Court afforded defendants charged in capital offenses greater protections under the Sixth Amendment right to counsel due to the severity and irrevocability of the punishment. More recently, Supreme Court decisions have recognized the importance of legal counsel in any case where the defendant may lose his or her liberty. A "critical stage" assessment is used to determine if legal counsel is available at the points in the criminal legal process that directly impact the outcome of the process. This change toward the critical stage assessment began in *Hamilton v. Alabama* (1961). When the Supreme Court viewed the impact of the pleading at arraignment under Alabama law, it ruled that it was a critical stage in the process and, therefore, the defendant required the benefit of counsel. Two years later, the Supreme Court used this same logic to determine that preliminary hearings under Maryland law are a critical stage in the process, thus requiring counsel to ensure that the defendant can plead intelligently (*White v. Maryland*, 1963).

Beyond the critical stage assessment, the Supreme Court found other conditions under which counsel was required beyond the trial process. In *Gagnon v. Scarpelli* (1973), the Supreme Court acknowledged that legal counsel should be available when warranted by the complexity of issues. As a result, the determination of whether legal counsel is necessary should be made on a case-by-case basis. This assessment also applies to probation hearings. Unfamiliarity with the law and mental illness necessitate legal counsel to ensure that the trial process is fair (*McNeal v. Culver*, 1961).

The Supreme Court has since extended right to counsel protections to post-indictment lineups (*United States v. Wade*, 1967), preliminary hearings (*Coleman v. Alabama*, 1970), pretrial interactions with the government (*Kansas v. Ventris*, 2009), identification after initiation of adversarial proceedings (*Moore v. Illinois*, 1977), sentencing

(*Estelle v. Smith*, 1981), a psychiatric exam to determine future dangerousness (*Powell v. Texas*, 1968), suspension of a sentence that could result in loss of liberty (*Alabama v. Shelton*, 2002), a parolee's response to notification of review (*Moody v. Daggett*, 1976), and capital case clemency hearings (*Harbison v. Bell*, 2009).

The Supreme Court has also identified procedures that are not covered by the Sixth Amendment right to counsel. These include post-conviction hearings (*Pennsylvania v. Finley*, 1987), prison disciplinary hearings (*Baxter v. Palmigiano*, 1976), and summary court-martial (*Middendorf v. Henry*, 1976). In making these determinations, the Supreme Court considered such factors as the impact on loss of liberty as well as the impact on the process and its intended goals.

The Supreme Court generally affords fewer rights to prisoners than to those who have not been convicted or who are on probation. However, it also acknowledges and protects the prisoner's rights to make claims. Although prisoners do not have a protected right to counsel after the first appeal, the Supreme Court has mandated that states provide meaningful access to the courts, including stationery supplies, law libraries, and assistance with filing legal papers (*Bounds v. Smith*, 1977).

Appointment of Counsel

In order to ensure protection of the Sixth Amendment right to counsel, both the federal and state governments are required to provide legal counsel to indigent defendants. Historically, this requirement has been subject to several limitations beyond the need to prove indigence. Since the requirement to appoint counsel is grounded in the Sixth Amendment, the government is only required to appoint counsel for those portions of the criminal legal process protected by that right as described above. For example, appointment of counsel is not required for discretionary appeals.

Appointment of counsel has also been limited by the type of case. Indigent defendants charged with capital offenses have historically been appointed counsel because of the consequences of the punishment. Furthermore, the appointment of counsel was originally only available for federal crimes because the Sixth Amendment was not applicable to the states. This position was established in *Betts v. Brady* (1942) when the Supreme Court upheld Maryland's limitation on crimes eligible for appointment of counsel. The Supreme Court began to move away from this position in 1956 with the *Griffin v. Illinois* decision that indigent prisoners, even those not convicted of capital offenses, had the same right of appellate review as nonindigent prisoners.

However, it was not until *Gideon* that the Sixth Amendment right to counsel was incorporated to the states. *Gideon* specifically overruled *Betts* and found that the right to counsel is one of the fundamental rights that are applicable to the states through the due process clause of the Fourteenth Amendment. This ruling also extended the right to have counsel appointed beyond capital cases. On the same day, the Supreme Court extended the right to have counsel appointed to the first appeal in *Douglas v. California* (1963). With these rulings, the Supreme Court brought appointment of counsel in line with the Sixth Amendment right to counsel application from first judicial appearance through first appeal.

In its jurisprudence, the Supreme Court continues to grant appointment of counsel in a manner consistent with its rulings on the Sixth Amendment right to counsel. In *Mempa v. Rhay* (1967), the Supreme Court decided that counsel must be appointed for indigent defendants at all parts of the criminal legal process where the rights of the defendant could be affected. Conversely, the Supreme Court has refused appointment of counsel in post-conviction proceedings because these are not considered part of the criminal process (*Murray v. Giarratano et al.*, 1989). However, if the crime occurs in prison, the Sixth Amendment right to counsel, and therefore appointment of counsel, is not triggered until formal charges are filed (*United States v. Gouveia et al.*, 1984).

In *Argersinger v. Hamlin* (1972), the court clarified that the Sixth Amendment right to counsel is based on whether a person will be deprived of his/her liberty, not on the type of offense. Appointment of counsel for indigent defendants, therefore, should be available in all cases where there is a potential for loss of liberty. This ruling has been refined in two respects. Appointment of counsel is not required if loss of liberty is authorized for the crime charged but it will not be imposed by the court (*Scott v. Illinois*, 1979).

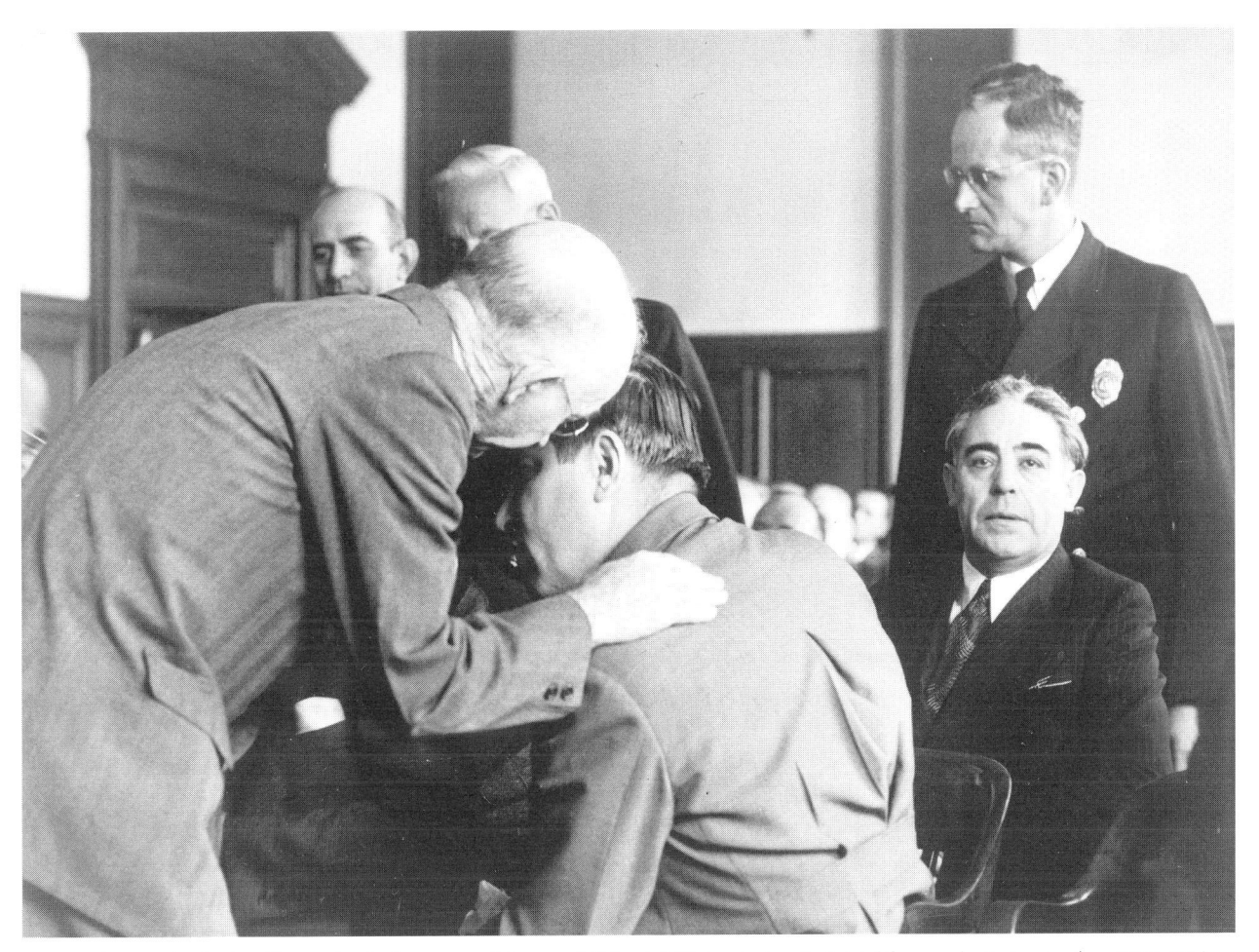

New York organized crime figures Louis Capone and Emanuel "Mendy" Weiss during their trial for murder in September 1941. Weiss is consulting with an attorney, while Capone (no relation to Al Capone) looks at the camera. Both were convicted and, after several years of appeals, executed in the electric chair at Sing Sing prison in March 1944 along with another conspirator.

However, if a defendant's charge includes additional punishment as a habitual offender, counsel is required (*Chewning v. Cunningham*, 1962).

Ineffectual Counsel
As the right to counsel and appointment of counsel have evolved to cover a greater variety of cases, concerns about ineffective counsel have been increasingly raised and addressed by the Supreme Court. These claims are based on the principle that the right to counsel implies that legal counsel will be effective. When a claim of ineffective counsel is raised, the burden of proof lies with the person raising the claim.

In 1984, the Supreme Court established the Strickland test as a guide for claiming ineffective counsel (*Strickland v. Washington*, 1984). This is a two-pronged test. First, the claimant must prove that the actions of counsel fell below an objective standard of reasonableness. Second, the claimant must prove that those actions resulted in prejudice so great that there was reasonable probability that they altered the outcome of the trial.

Proving both criteria of the Strickland test is difficult for three reasons. First, the claimant must specifically state the actions that were not objectively reasonable. Second, the Supreme Court has indicated that there is a presumption that legal counsel acted reasonably. This is based on the understanding that in preparing and presenting a case, legal counsel chooses among a range of strategies and tactics. A hindsight review of these choices can unfairly find fault and impose a biased judgment of actions. Third, the claimant must prove that a reasonable probability exists that the outcome of the trial would be different if not for the actions of the legal counsel. This requires proving more than just a possibility or an expectation that the outcome would have been different.

The Supreme Court has issued two rulings that have further clarified its position on ineffective counsel. In *United States v. Cronic* (1984), the Supreme Court explained that the right to effective counsel is based on the need for the defense to provide a meaningful adversarial test of the prosecution's case. Most recently, the Supreme Court has reiterated that effective legal counsel is to ensure the fairness of the process. A fair process does not necessarily mean that the outcome will be favorable to the defendant (*Cullen v. Pinholster*, 2011).

Supreme Court decisions since *Strickland* have also provided guidance in meeting the Strickland test. To meet the reasonableness test of Strickland, the Supreme Court has explained that the circumstances of the case must be considered (*Roe v. Flores-Ortega*). In *Bell v. Cone* (2002), the Supreme Court provided three instances where the prejudice standard of *Strickland* would be met: (1) the effect of actions resulted in the complete denial of legal counsel at a critical stage, (2) counsel did not subject the prosecution's case to adversarial testing, and (3) counsel was expected to assist in a situation where competent legal counsel could not provide effective assistance.

This does not mean that the Strickland test is insurmountable. Litigants have successfully claimed ineffective counsel when no pretrial discovery was done (*Kimmelman v. Morrison*, 1986), when the case file was not appropriately reviewed (*Rompilla v. Beard*, 2005), and in cases where counsel failed to discover or present mitigating circumstances at sentencing.

Although it is the intent that the defendant and legal counsel will work together on the case, legal counsel is allowed latitude to act in the best interests of the defendant. For example, legal counsel's authorization is seen as sufficient to allow a judge to preside over voir dire (*Gonzalez v. United States*, 2008), to make trial scheduling decisions (*New York v. Hill*, 2000), and to provide assurances that the defendant was properly informed of the nature and elements of the charge (*Bradshaw v. Stumpf*, 2005).

Kathleen Barrett
Georgia State University

See Also: 1921 to 1940 Primary Documents; Adversarial Justice; Appeals; Bill of Rights; Capital Punishment; Constitution of the United States of America; Defendant's Rights; *Gideon v. Wainwright*; *Miranda v. Arizona*; Prisoner's Rights; Suspect's Rights.

Further Readings
Bacigal, Ronald J. *Criminal Law and Procedure: An Overview*. Clifton Park, NY: Delmar Cengage Learning, 2009.
Carp, Robert A. and Ronald Stidham. *Judicial Process in America*, 8th ed. Washington, DC: CQ Press, 2010.
del Carmen, Rolando V. *Criminal Procedure: Law and Practice*, 8th ed. Belmont, CA: Wadsworth, 2009.
Harr, J. Scott and Kären M. Hess. *Constitutional Law and the Criminal Justice System*, 4th ed. Belmont, CA: Wadsworth, 2008.

Leopold and Loeb

On September 10, 1924, Nathan Freudenthal Leopold, Jr. (November 19, 1904–August 29, 1971), and Richard Albert Loeb (June 11, 1905–January 28, 1936) were convicted of the kidnapping and murder of 14-year-old Robert "Bobby" Franks. Franks's death was particularly shocking, in part because of its randomness, but also because the murderers had no motive other than to satisfy their obsession with committing the "perfect crime." In light of these facts, the prosecution demanded the death penalty, which prompted the defendants' families to retain Clarence Darrow, an outspoken foe of capital punishment.

At the time of the murder, Leopold and Loeb lived in the wealthy, primarily Jewish neighborhood of Kenwood on Chicago's south side. They first met, however, while attending the University of Chicago in 1920. Both were considered child prodigies: Leopold was 16 when he began college, and Loeb was the youngest graduate of the University of Michigan. Given his intellect, Leopold believed he was a Nietzschean "superman" and convinced Loeb that their actions, the criminal nature of which notwithstanding, were beyond reproach. The two were also lovers; in exchange for his role as Loeb's partner in crime, Leopold demanded periodic sexual favors from Loeb. This arrangement led to the commission of numerous crimes, from petty theft to burglary, and eventually murder.

On the afternoon of May 21, 1924, Leopold and Loeb drove around Kenwood looking for a victim. They settled upon Bobby Franks, who had been walking home from an after-school baseball game. Loeb, whom Franks knew, offered to give Franks a ride. Though it was never proven who actually delivered the fatal blow, within seconds of driving away, one of the two repeatedly struck Franks on the head with a chisel. When Franks did not succumb quickly, they suffocated him to death. The two then drove for several hours until nightfall, whereupon they poured hydrochloric acid on Franks's face and genitals and deposited his body in a culvert by Wolf Lake.

The two had planned the murder for several months. Part of the plan involved contacting their victim's family and demanding a ransom. Immediately after leaving Franks's body, the two contacted Franks's parents; however, before they could deliver further instructions, Franks's body was discovered by a man who had been walking along the railroad tracks that passed over the culvert. Distinctive horn-rimmed, tortoiseshell eyeglasses were found near the body. Police traced the glasses to Leopold, and, after a lengthy interrogation, the two men confessed to the crime.

Contrary to popular belief, the "trial of the century" was actually a hearing that lasted several months, during which time it was the focus of intense nationwide media attention. At Darrow's behest, both men pled guilty to the charges. Darrow believed this could spare the two from an otherwise certain death sentence. Thus, Judge John Caverly heard mitigating evidence presented by both Darrow and Illinois state attorney Robert Crowe, which included unprecedented extensive psychiatric testimony. Moreover, Darrow's summation is still considered one of the most eloquent critiques of capital punishment ever given. In it, Darrow attacked the death penalty as a throwback to a less humane time when retribution was the law of "the beast and the jungle." At the conclusion of his argument, the judge and several spectators were reportedly moved to tears and a minute or two of silence. Ultimately, Judge Caverly sentenced both defendants to life in prison for murder plus 99 years for kidnapping. Caverly claimed to have been more persuaded by the defendant's youthful age and the potential contributions to criminology that studying Leopold and Loeb might offer than by any of the other mitigating evidence presented.

Leopold and Loeb were remanded to Illinois' Joliet Prison. Loeb was killed in 1936 by an inmate who slashed him with a razor, allegedly to resist Loeb's sexual advances. Leopold was released after 34 years of being a model prisoner. He went on to earn a graduate degree, teach mathematics, and author a book on ornithology. Even though Leopold eventually married, in a 1960 interview, he admitted that he was still deeply in love with Loeb.

Brian Frederick
Henry F. Fradella
California State University, Long Beach

See Also: 1921 to 1940 Primary Documents; Autobiographies, Criminals; Capital Punishment; Chicago, Illinois; Darrow, Clarence; Famous Trials; Kidnapping; Murder, History of.

Further Readings
Higdon, Hal. *Leopold & Loeb: The Crime of the Century*. Chicago: University of Illinois Press, 1999.
Leopold, Nathan F., Jr. *Life Plus 99 Years*. New York: Doubleday, 1958.
McKernan, Maureen. *The Amazing Trial and Crime of Leopold and Loeb*. New York: New American Library, 1957.

Libertarianism

On its face, libertarianism is an ideology of human freedom that promotes the ability of individuals to act and think freely to the extent that they do not infringe on the rights of others to do the same. Starting from the presumption that humans have absolute control over their own bodies and their labor, a concept known as self-ownership, libertarians conclude that the state is a primary threat to human freedom, often characterizing it as a fundamentally violent or criminal entity. For right-libertarians such as Murray Rothbard, taxation becomes "theft," conscription becomes "enslavement," and any nondefensive use of violence by the state becomes "murder." As such, libertarianism often contends that government should be either abolished (anarchism) or radically minimalized (minarchism).

There exist three major camps in libertarian thought: right-libertarianism, socialist libertarianism, and left-libertarianism; the extent to which these represent distinct ideologies as opposed to variations on a theme is contested by scholars. Regardless, these factions differ most pronouncedly with respect to private property. Right-libertarians see strong private property rights as the basis of freedom and thus are—to quote the title of Brian Doherty's text on libertarianism in the United States—"radicals for capitalism."

Meanwhile, socialist libertarians view any concentration of power into the hands of a few (whether politically or economically) as antithetical to freedom and thus advocate for the simultaneous abolition of both government *and* capitalism. Meanwhile, left-libertarians try to strike a balance by embracing self-ownership and weak property rights while arguing for egalitarian control of natural resources. While right-libertarianism has been equated with libertarianism in general in the United States, left-libertarianism has become a more predominant aspect of politics in western European democracies over the past three decades.

Right-Libertarianism

Since the 1950s, libertarianism in the United States has been associated almost exclusively with right-libertarianism, which combines an antistatist commitment to individual freedom with strong support for private property rights and free markets. At times embracing the cause of anarcho-capitalism, right-libertarians advocate little to no government control over capitalism and promote private solutions to public concerns such as health, crime, and education.

Right-libertarian thought draws from an array of political and economic thinkers, most notably Ayn Rand, Isabel Patterson, Rose Wilder Lane, Milton Friedman, Ludwig von Mises, and Friedrich Hayek; perhaps the greatest influence on popular conceptions of libertarianism in the United States, Ayn Rand inspired the Objectivist movement through her novels *Atlas Shrugged* and *The Fountainhead*. Both texts promoted capitalism as the only economic system that could be morally justified on the basis of freedom. By the 1960s, Objectivism had evolved into cultlike status, eventually providing a (albeit conflict-ridden) basis for the emergence of a libertarian movement in the 1960s and the Libertarian Party in the early 1970s. While Rand later alienated herself from popular libertarianism, her ideas continued to inform the libertarian commitment that capitalism and freedom were foundationally linked.

While maintaining their allegiance to capitalism, American libertarians of the 1960s and 1970s broke ranks with conservatives and found alliances with leftists against the Vietnam War draft and other social issues, including the legalization of marijuana and the decriminalization of alternative lifestyles. While libertarians of prior years stressed the importance of disseminating libertarian ideas and serving an educational function, the political shifts in the 1960s and 1970s found libertarians for the first time pursuing explicitly politicized ends. By 1971, the Libertarian Party was officially founded in reaction to President Richard Nixon's economic policies. Particularly significant in California and Colorado, the party enjoyed a national presence by 1980. According to Jennifer Burns, the party's shift away from a Randian subculture toward a policy focus facilitated the attraction of educated professionals, many of whom became active in the emergence of key libertarian think tanks, such as the Cato Institute (founded in 1977), the Reason Foundation (founded in 1968), and the Independence Institute (founded in 1985). However, by the early 1990s, the Libertarian Party lacked potency as a serious political force. Given the success and legitimacy of libertarian think tanks, particularly the Cato Institute, Burns suggests that the Libertarian Party had the uncanny effect of making

Right-libertarians carrying signs at a Tea Party tax day protest in St. Paul, Minnesota, on April 15, 2010. They called for smaller government and the repeal of new healthcare laws.

mainstream the libertarian movement by concentrating more extreme libertarians in the less legitimate Libertarian Party. As in the early heyday of libertarianism under Ayn Rand, the most widely influential manifestations of libertarianism today take the form of educational outreach, not politics, eventually leading Burns to conclude that libertarianism is a predominant, though not defining, sensibility within American politics. As such, right-libertarianism in the United States remains a fruitful discourse with which to articulate conservative claims, even as it lacks political efficacy as a separate ideology. However, even without its own movement, libertarian sensibility informs numerous social movements in the United States, including the U.S. patriot movement, the gun-rights movement, and the incipient Tea Party movement.

Left-Libertarianism

In contrast to the United States, where a right-libertarian sensibility dominates, western European nations with strong leftist political parties tend to see the emergence of left-libertarian parties, as detailed by Kent Redding and Jocelyn S. Viterna. According to them, these parties are united by their "critique of the statist and bureaucratic tendencies of modern welfare states … inequality and environmental degradation produced by capitalist market economies." This dual emphasis means that while many left-libertarians embrace the notion of self-ownership and agree with right-libertarians that individuals have an absolute right over their own bodies against the encroachment of the state and other social actors, they disagree with right-libertarians with respect to property rights, arguing instead that individuals have no inherent right to natural resources. Namely, these resources must be treated as collective property that is made available on an egalitarian basis. Unlike socialist libertarians, who aim to dismantle private property and the social arrangements that make private property possible, left-libertarians maintain a weak notion of private property rights while advocating for redistributive systems that equalize access to natural resources. Several significant contributions have been made by left-libertarians in detailing their maverick splicing of individualism with redistributive egalitarianism, most notably the two collections *The Origins of Left-Libertarianism: An Anthology of Historical Writings* and *Left-Libertarianism and Its Critics: The Contemporary Debate* (both edited by Peter Vallentyne and Hillel Steiner). In addition to Vallentyne and Steiner, other prominent proponents of left-libertarianism include Michael Otsuka, Allan Gibbard, Baruch Brody, James Grunebaum, Philippe Van Parijs, and Nicolaus Tideman.

The joining of radical, antistatist individualism with egalitarian redistribution of natural resources is both the promise and pitfall of left-libertarianism, accounting for its popularity in political philosophy and much of the criticism directed toward it. The most prominent critiques have either attacked left-libertarianism as an incoherent, contradictory philosophy or argued that left-libertarianism is not fundamentally new—but rather a variant on the traditional, pro-state left in libertarian garb. These objections seem to be voiced most strongly by American critics; in contrast to its political successes in much of western Europe, left-libertarianism is seen in the United States as either lacking a defensible endorsement of strong property rights (the critique from the right and right-libertarians) or "eating with the devil" (to paraphrase from Barbara Fried's influential "Left-Libertarianism: A Review Essay") by capitulating to right-wing notions of individualism.

Socialist Libertarianism

Unlike left-libertarians, who equivocate to some degree regarding the right to private property, socialist libertarians seek an abolishment of private property in addition to an abolishment of the state. Viewing both capitalism and government as modes of domination that pit a powerful elite against a weak and subordinate majority, socialist libertarians are consistent in their demand to obliterate systems of oppression on both economic and political grounds. Indeed, dissolving the state in hope of expanding human freedom would mean little if the system of private property were left untouched; if taxation is "theft," as right-libertarians would have it, then so is property, according to socialist libertarians.

Socialist libertarianism sounds like anarchy, and for good reason; in fact, anarchists began using the term *libertarian* in the mid-1800s, far before the right-wing usage in the United States that began in the 1950s. While anarchism and socialist libertarians have a rich history of revolutionary thinkers ranging from Emma Goldman to George Orwell, the best-known socialist libertarian thinker of today is probably Noam Chomsky.

Intellectual Property Rights

There is some debate among libertarians about intellectual property rights. On the one hand, some view intellectual property as yet another "product of human labor" (to quote Ayn Rand), while others recognize its distinctiveness from physical property. Those supporting the former view emphasize the role of creation in demarcating "one's property," whereas those supporting the latter view emphasize the importance of scarcity in designating property rights. Unless the object of ownership is itself scarce, so the argument against intellectual property rights goes, property rights are inconsistent with libertarianism insofar as they would infringe on the ability of individuals to exercise freedom (i.e., think).

Crime and Criminal Justice

What constitutes crime? Under libertarianism, human freedom should not be inhibited unless the exercise of freedom limits the ability of others to exercise their freedom. Crime includes any actions that violate this tenet: Stealing is no good, but lifestyle choices that affect no one but the person who practices them should not be regulated. Crime always infringes on another person or his/her property; the terms *victimless crime* and *crimes against the state* are oxymoronic to a libertarian ear. For this reason, libertarians support, for example, the decriminalization of drug use and sexual acts between consenting adults.

Libertarians blame crime on state programs that encourage dependency and discourage individual responsibility, on the one hand, and ill-fated attempts to police victimless crimes, on the other. Right-leaning libertarians in particular argue that government programs have created a culture of dependency that facilitates crime; decreasing crime, therefore, would entail ending welfare and increasing economic opportunity through free market initiatives. In addition, libertarians on both the left and right in the United States argue that the government-led "war on drugs" has been a failure, increasing violent crime by wasting valuable prison and policing resources on victimless crimes such as marijuana possession.

The libertarian approach to punishment is premised on the decriminalization of victimless crimes, on the one hand, and a heightened emphasis on victims and victim's rights, on the other. Libertarians would significantly scale back state resources spent on housing nonviolent prisoners, reserving prison space for violent offenders. Rather than providing a warehouse for prisoners, the state would generally serve as a mediating entity to ensure that victims receive full restitution for crimes committed against them, including any direct or indirect losses incurred. Libertarians are also concerned with the individual rights of the accused and convicted, opposing laws that would permanently strip rights such as voting. Because of their emphasis on victim rights, on the one hand, and the rights of the accused and convicted, on the other, libertarians have mixed feelings toward certain criminal justice issues such as the death penalty. While some view it as the highest form of victim-centered justice, others see it as an example of excessive and unnecessary (not to mention expensive) government intrusion and state-sanctioned violence.

Libertarians embrace individualistic approaches to policing. The American Libertarian Party, for example, states that expanding the right to self-defense is "the most effective crime deterrent available." Libertarians strongly believe that state institutions—particularly the police—are ineffective in protecting individuals from crime and that individuals themselves are ultimately responsible for their own protection from crime. To address these issues, some libertarians support police vouchers. A system popularized by Murray Rothbard for an array of services typically provided by the government, vouchers can be used to provide individuals with tax breaks or direct funds to hire private police forces or organize themselves into police.

In addition to emphasizing free market approaches to policing, libertarians are concerned about the abuse of power by the police and other state paramilitary institutions. The Cato Institute, for example, has published papers on the militarization of American police forces and the rapid increase in often violent "no-knock" police raids under the auspices of the U.S. war on drugs.

The Future of Libertarianism
While left-libertarianism has successfully established itself in the form of political parties in numerous western European countries, the ascendency of right-libertarianism in the United States remains unclear. While numerous developments suggest that libertarianism as a political doctrine is on the rise in the United States (including most notably the Tea Parties and initiatives such as the free state movement), there are no clear indications that these developments are more than a momentary articulation of libertarian sensibility, to use Jennifer Burns's terminology.

Jennifer D. Carlson
University of California, Berkeley

See Also: Anarchists; Douglas, William O.; Morality; Political Dissidents; Tax Crimes; Three Strikes Law.

Further Readings
Burns, Jennifer. "Oh Libertarianism, Where Is Thy Sting?" *Journal of Police History*, v.19/4 (2007).
Doherty, Brian. *Radicals for Capitalism: A Free-Wheeling History of the Modern American Libertarian Movement*. New York: PublicAffairs, 2008.
Fried, Barbara. "Left-Libertarianism: A Review Essay." *Philosophy & Public Affairs*, v.32 (2004).
Rand, Ayn. *Atlas Shrugged*. New York: Plume, 1999.
Rand, Ayn. *The Fountainhead*. New York: Signet, 1996.
Redding, Kent and Jocelyn S. Viterna. "Political Demands, Political Opportunities: Explaining the Differential Success of Left-Libertarian Parties." *Social Forces*, v.78/2 (1999).
Vallentyne, Peter and Hillel Steiner, eds. *Left-Libertarianism and Its Critics: The Contemporary Debate*. New York: Palgrave Macmillan, 2001.
Vallentyne, Peter and Hillel Steiner, eds. *The Origins of Left-Libertarianism: An Anthology of Historical Writings*. New York: Palgrave Macmillan, 2001.

Lincoln, Abraham (Administration of)

Abraham Lincoln, (1809–65) president during the American Civil War, had a deep and long-lasting interest in and impact upon crime and punishment. A self-taught lawyer, Lincoln enjoyed a brilliant legal career before ascending to the presidency, with vast experience as both a trial and appellate lawyer. Although his tenure as president saw him focused primarily upon military matters, Lincoln was forced to deal with many issues involving crime and punishment caused by the conflict facing the United States at that time. Specifically, Lincoln faced decisions related to punishing suspected Confederate sympathizers, balancing war powers with civil liberties, and maintaining stability when definitions of *property*, *citizen*, and *treason* were in flux and uncertain. Lincoln was also able to shape conceptions of crime and punishment through his appointments of justices to the U.S. Supreme

Court and his nominations for the attorney general of the United States.

Lincoln was famously born in a single-room log cabin in what is now LaRue County, Kentucky. Lincoln's father, Thomas, owned several farms at the time of his son's birth, although faulty title to this land caused the family to relocate to Indiana in 1816 to start over. After Lincoln's mother died when he was 9, Thomas Lincoln married Sarah Bush, who encouraged her stepson's educational aspirations. After the family moved to Illinois in 1831, Lincoln moved on his own to New Salem, where he was unsuccessful as a storekeeper. An interest in politics led to Lincoln's election to the Illinois state legislature in 1834 as a Whig. At this point, Lincoln decided to become a lawyer. Rather than training with a practicing attorney, Lincoln taught himself the law, reading William Blackstone's *Commentaries on the Laws of England* and being admitted to the bar in 1836. Lincoln moved to Springfield, where he entered practice with John Todd Stuart, cousin of Lincoln's future wife, Mary Todd. Stuart and Lincoln were partners until 1841, after which time Lincoln entered into a partnership with Stephen Logan from 1841 to 1844, and then with Richard Herndon beginning in 1844. As a lawyer, Lincoln had extensive trial and appellate experience, handling both civil and criminal cases. Lincoln appeared before the Illinois Supreme Court in 175 cases. Although popular legend focuses on Lincoln's log cabin roots, he enjoyed a highly lucrative practice, with

Abraham Lincoln being sworn in as president by U.S. Supreme Court Chief Justice Roger Taney. When the Civil War began, Taney issued an order holding that neither the president nor his agents could issue an order suspending the writ of habeas corpus and that the military had no right to detain an individual unless a judicial body had authorized such action. Lincoln ignored Taney's decision and continued to suspend the writ of habeas corpus on his own authority for several years.

the Illinois Central Railroad being one of his largest clients.

The Civil War President
In 1846, Lincoln was elected to the U.S. House of Representatives, but chose not to run for reelection. He made two unsuccessful runs for a seat in the U.S. Senate, falling to fellow Whig Lyman Trumball in 1854 and, running as a Republican, to Democrat Stephen A. Douglas in 1858. Despite these setbacks, Lincoln developed a national following and was elected president of the United States in 1860. Although he won a majority of the electoral votes, Lincoln only carried about 40 percent of the popular vote in a field with four candidates. Lincoln's election was highly unpopular in the south, and those in favor of secession soon began to move to leave the Union. Ultimately, 11 states seceded and formed the Confederate States of America (CSA). On February 8, 1861, Jefferson Davis was named the president of the CSA, and after the Battle of Fort Sumter, which was fought April 12–13, 1861, the American Civil War began. The ongoing war greatly shaped Lincoln's approach to crime and punishment.

Faced with a conflict involving riots, further threats of secession, and independent militias hostile to the Union cause, Lincoln suspended the use of the writ of habeas corpus. The writ of habeas corpus is an order, issued by a court, allowing a prisoner to demand that a public official take that prisoner before a court so that the court can determine if probable cause exists to detain the prisoner. In 1861, Lincoln was faced with pro-CSA mobs attacking federal troops in Maryland. Fearful that Maryland would secede, leaving Washington, D.C., cut off from the rest of the Union, Lincoln ordered increased troops to defend the capital. When Thomas Hicks, governor of Maryland, and George Brown, mayor of Baltimore, asked that the Union army be prevented from crossing the state, Lincoln declared martial law in Maryland and ordered troops to apprehend Confederate agents and others opposed to the Union cause. Lincoln faced heated opposition from a group of northern Democrats known as the Copperheads, who were called such in reference to the poisonous snakes with copper-colored heads. The Copperheads vehemently opposed the policies of the abolitionists and favored political compromise that would lead to a negotiated end to the war with the Confederate States. To that end, the Copperheads opposed the military draft and Lincoln's attempts to free the slaves or to arrest those who spoke against military policy. Although the Copperheads believed they were exercising their constitutional right to speak out against policies that they opposed, Lincoln and many of his contemporaries asserted that such opposition bordered on treason. Lincoln's actions against the Copperheads, including his attempts to suspend the writ of habeas corpus, were and remain controversial, and some historians maintain that while the Copperheads posed a serious threat to Union efforts, they were in many ways exercising types of free speech first popularized during the era of Jacksonian democracy.

In April 1861, Lincoln asked Attorney General Edward Bates for an advisory opinion regarding suspension of the right to a writ of habeas corpus. Later in that month, as tensions increased, Lincoln told General Winfield Scott, the commander in chief of the Union army, that the writ of habeas corpus was suspended, a decision that was not immediately announced. On May 24, 1861, Lieutenant John Merryman of the Maryland militia was arrested for pro-CSA beliefs and for recruiting and training Confederate troops and engaging in sabotage of telegraph lines and rail crossings. Merryman appealed for a writ of habeas corpus to the U.S. Circuit Court for the District of Maryland, where U.S. Supreme Court Chief Justice Roger Taney was sitting. Taney issued a writ of habeas corpus, but when a U.S. marshal attempted to serve this, the Union army refused to comply. In response, in *Ex parte Merryman* (1861), Taney issued an order holding that neither the president nor his agents could issue an order suspending the writ of habeas corpus and that the military had no right to detain an individual unless a judicial body had authorized such action. Lincoln ignored Taney's decision and continued to suspend the writ of habeas corpus on his own authority for several years, until the U.S. Congress authorized his action through the Habeas Corpus Act of 1863.

As president, Lincoln appointed five justices to the U.S. Supreme Court, including Noah Haynes Swayne, Samuel Freeman Miller, David Davis, Stephen Johnson Field, and, as chief justice, Salmon P. Chase. These appointments greatly changed the makeup of the court, moving it away from the pro-slavery support it had given appellants under Taney. In 1861, Lincoln appointed Edward Bates as the attorney general. Bates, who had proven instrumental in carrying out the arrests of southern sympathizers, resigned in 1864 because of disagreements with Lincoln regarding the Emancipation Proclamation and the arming of freed slaves. Bates was succeeded by James Speed, an ardent opponent of slavery, who, after Lincoln's assassination on April 14, 1865, became affiliated with the Radical Republicans. Lincoln's legacy with regard to crime and punishment is mixed, as he both worked to extend the rights of many while also suppressing the voices of those who opposed his policies.

Stephen T. Schroth
Jason A. Helfer
Jamal A. Nelson
Knox College

See Also: 1851 to 1900 Primary Documents; 1961 to 1980 Primary Documents; Booth, John Wilkes; Fugitive Slave Act of 1850; Habeas Corpus Act of 1863; History of Crime and Punishment in America: 1850–1900; Illinois.

Further Readings
Weber, J. L. *Copperheads: The Rise and Fall of Lincoln's Opponents in the North.* New York: Oxford University Press, 2006.
Wilson, D. L. *Lincoln's Sword: The Presidency and the Power of Words.* New York: Alfred A. Knopf, 2006.
Wilson, D. L. and R. O. Davis, eds. *Herndon's Informants: Letters, Interviews, and Statements About Abraham Lincoln.* Urbana: University of Illinois Press.

Lindbergh Law

"Lindbergh Law" is the name that was given to the Federal Kidnapping Act, which was passed after the kidnapping and murder of Charles Lindbergh's son in 1932. Lindbergh was an aviator and inventor who was known at the time as "Lucky Lindy" after his successful solo transatlantic crossing in a single-engine plane named the *Spirit of St. Louis*. This feat brought him fame and fortune, and ultimately the loss of his son, Charles Lindbergh, Jr.

In 1932, Charles Lindbergh, Jr., was taken from his bedroom in the family home in East Amwell, New Jersey. A ransom note was left in the room demanding a payment of $50,000. This was followed by a second ransom note demanding $70,000, and then a third letter making the same request. There were many theories as to whether the kidnapping was the act of a single person or a group of conspirators.

There were additional ransom demands from others and claims of payments, yet the baby was not returned to the Lindbergh family. Several months after the abduction, the boy's body was inadvertently discovered in a wooded area near the Lindbergh home by a truck driver. Bills from the ransom started to appear in circulation shortly after it was paid, but it was not until 1934 that police were able to identify a person with the money. Bruno Richard Hauptmann was identified as a prime suspect in the case because he passed a $20 gold note that was believed to be part of the ransom money paid by the Lindbergh family. The investigation led to additional evidence against Hauptmann, including a large portion of the ransom and a source of the wood used to build the ladder found outside the baby's room. In the end, Hauptmann was tried, convicted, and put to death for the crime.

The Federal Kidnapping Act of 1932
Representatives from the New Jersey State Police, the Jersey City Police Department, the New York City Police Department, the Internal Revenue Service Law Enforcement Division, and the Federal Bureau of Investigation (FBI) were involved in the investigation of the abduction. According to the U.S. Constitution, police power rests with the states. The authority of law enforcement officers to investigate crimes ends at their jurisdiction's borders. It has been suggested that state border limitations initially hampered the investigation. Perhaps the results may have been different if a single law enforcement entity had the authority to investigate such crime without consideration of local authorities and state borders. Federal law enforcement agents would

not have such limitations and could pursue kidnappers wherever they might run.

In response to the Lindbergh kidnapping, Congress passed the Federal Kidnapping Act of 1932. The act addresses the unlawful seizure, confinement, or kidnapping of an individual for ransom or reward—a person who was alive when the transportation began. Because the authority of the federal government rests with matters involving interstate activities, the act specifically states that an element of the offense is the willful transportation of the victim across state lines and that the failure of the kidnapper to release the victim within 24 hours of the abduction creates "a rebuttable presumption that such person has been transported to interstate of foreign commerce." This provides the FBI with the authority to investigate a kidnapping. To ensure that there is not a delay regarding the FBI's involvement, the section also states that the FBI is not precluded from initiating its investigation prior to the end of the 24 hours.

Keith Gregory Logan
Kutztown University

See Also: 1851 to 1900 Primary Documents; 1921 to 1940 Primary Documents; Famous Trials; Hauptmann, Bruno; Jurisdiction; Kidnapping.

Further Readings
Aiuto, Russell. "The Theft of the Eaglet: The Lindbergh Kidnapping." TruTv. http://www.trutv.com/library/crime/notorious_murders/famous/lindbergh/index_1.html (Accessed January 2011).
Federal Bureau of Investigation. "The Lindbergh Kidnapping." http://www.fbi.gov/libref/historic/famcases/lindber/lindbernew.htm (Accessed January 2011).
"National Affairs: 4U-13-41." *Time Magazine*. http://www.time.com/time/magazine/article/0,9171,930523,00.html?internalid=ACA (Accessed January 2011).

Lindsey, Ben

Leading American jurist, social and economic reformer, and advocate for the juvenile justice system, Benjamin Barr Lindsey (1869–1943) was born in Jackson, Tennessee, to Landy Lindsey and Leticia Anna (Barr) Lindsey. His father had served as a captain in the Confederate army and worked as a telegraph operator. In 1877, Landy Lindsey moved to Denver, Colorado, to mine, but instead found steady work as a telegraph operator with the Denver and Southern Park Railroad. Two years later, Lindsey, his mother, brother, and sister joined Landy in Colorado. In 1881, Lindsey and his brother began school in the elementary department of Notre Dame University in Indiana, but by 1885, the family had fallen on hard times and Lindsey's family was sent back to Tennessee where he attended the preparatory school at the Southwest Baptist University.

After three years in Jackson, Lindsey returned to Denver to take care of his family in the wake of Landy's death. Lindsey found a job keeping records for a real estate company, delivered newspapers, and worked as a janitor in the evenings. Eventually, he found work as an office boy in the law offices of R. D. Thompson, where Lindsey borrowed law books and prepared himself for the Colorado bar examination, which he passed in 1894. Immediately, Lindsey became involved in local Democratic politics and worked for Charles Thomas, the Democratic candidate for governor in 1898. In 1899, a successful Thomas appointed Lindsey as public administrator and guardian of the Denver County Court, an office that showed Lindsey firsthand the problems of underprivileged children. Two years later, in 1901, Lindsey was appointed judge of the Denver County Court, and he soon recognized the need for a special court that dealt solely with the issues of children. His long-time battle on behalf of children led him to create the Juvenile Court of Colorado, which in 1907 became the Juvenile and Family Relations Court.

Lindsey continued to marry his work in the law with politics and, after 1914, was assisted by his wife Henrietta (Brevoort) Lindsey. In his early career, he was instrumental in the passage of Colorado's child labor law and contributory delinquency laws that held parents and employers responsible for the delinquency of minors. He also helped establish Denver's public playgrounds, athletic teams, summer outings, and camps for the city's children, an early version of the Fresh Air Fund.

Benjamin Lindsey, leading American jurist, social and economic reformer, and advocate for the juvenile justice system, in a photograph from between 1910 and 1915.

Lindsey soon decided, however, that the underlying pressures of widespread vice, corruption, and economic injustice were the main causes of juvenile delinquency. During his tenure in Colorado, he helped pass an eight-hour work law, employer's liability law, Mother's Pension law, a new voter registration law, and liberalized the divorce laws—all addressing widespread social injustice. In 1910, he took his first steps into extralegal activity by writing *The Beast*, an exposé of the political and corporate corruption in Colorado. In 1925, Lindsey wrote *The Revolt of Modern Youth*, followed by *The Companionate Marriage* in 1927. In these two publications he presented controversial ideas, advocating such measures as legalized birth control and trial marriage. Through his books, numerous magazine and newspaper articles, and public speeches and debates, Lindsey not only attracted large numbers of supporters throughout the country but also the ire of conservative church and political leaders, especially the Ku Klux Klan, who succeeded in having him disbarred in Colorado in 1927.

The following year, Lindsey moved to Los Angeles, California, and continued his work toward social justice as a lawyer. In 1934, he was elected to the Los Angeles Superior Court and five years later became the first judge of the California Children's Court Conciliation, a court he helped create. This court not only provided a children's court but also served as the precursor to the present marital counseling agencies. Lindsey was reelected in 1940 and served as superior court judge until his death in 1943 of a heart attack. Two years earlier, in 1941, Lindsey's final book, his autobiography titled *The Dangerous Life* was published, recounting his life of public service in the pursuit of social justice.

Robin C. Henry
Wichita State University

See Also: Children's Rights; Colorado; Juvenile Courts, History of; Juvenile Justice, History of.

Further Readings
Davis, Rebecca L. "'Not Marriage at All, but Simple Harlotry': The Companionate Marriage Controversy." *Journal of American History*, v.94/4 (2008).
Larson, Charles. *The Good Fight: The Life and Times of Ben B. Lindsey*. Chicago: Quadrangle Books, 1972.
Lindsey, Ben B. and Rube Borough. *The Dangerous Life*. New York: Arno Press, 1941.

Literature and Theater, Crime in

Crime permeates much literature and theater, although any analysis is inevitably imprecise because the term applies to any work involving detection, criminal activity, or unsolved misdeeds. Crime has been a consistent theme in a variety of literary genres, including literature, detective and crime fiction, thrillers, and children's series.

Although covering similar themes, some books and plays concentrate more on the puzzle aspects of crime, while others delve into the psychological aspects of the criminal's psyche and circumstances underlying the crime. While both approaches are popular, they often attract different types of fans and as a result are frequently marketed differently.

Origins of Crime in Literature

Crime has long been a popular theme in books and plays. Authors such as Edgar Allen Poe, Charles Dickens, Fyodor Dostoyevsky, Joseph Conrad, and Wilkie Collins all used crime as a central theme in a variety of 19th-century efforts. Dickens used crime as a frequent theme in his novels, with works such as *Oliver Twist* (1837), *David Copperfield* (1849), *A Tale of Two Cities* (1859), and *The Mystery of Edwin Drood* (1870) all exploring how crime and punishment reverberate and affect many individual lives. An advocate for social reform, Dickens often addressed social issues of the time in his books and was able to help shape public opinion regarding crime, seeing a variety of law breakers as having been forced into certain behaviors because of societal problems beyond their individual control. Dostoyevsky's *Crime and Punishment* (1866) and Conrad's *The Secret Agent* (1907) are essentially crime novels, but both works focus primarily on punishment rather than crime itself. Although Raskolnikov commits a murder in *Crime and Punishment*, and Verloc plans a terrorist act in *The Secret Agent*, these crimes are little more than starting points for tales that focus on the use and abuse of power and the redemption of the human spirit.

Poe's short story "The Murders in the Rue Morgue," originally published in *Graham's Magazine* in 1841, is often referred to as the first detective story. Poe's detective, G. Auguste Dupin, is an amateur and a devotee of ratiocination, the process of reasoning using conscious and deliberate inference. In "The Murders in the Rue Morgue," Poe established many of the literary devices that would be used by subsequent authors. For example, Poe's story is narrated by the detective's friend and investigative partner, the detective himself is brilliant and eccentric, and the final revelation of the crime is made before the reasoning that supports it is provided. Both Arthur Conan Doyle and Agatha Christie adopted these devices for their creations, Sherlock Holmes and Hercule Poirot. Dupin is a model for many other fictional detectives in addition to Holmes and Poirot. Not a professional police officer, Dupin solves crimes largely for his own amusement and satisfaction, although he does exhibit a deep desire for truth and values being able to prove an accused man innocent. He has no financial interest in the case and indeed declines a reward at the case's conclusion. Finally, Dupin emphasizes the triumph of brains over brawn. Poe wrote two additional stories featuring Dupin, "The Mystery of Marie Roget," first published in 1842, and "The Purloined Letter," which first appeared in 1844.

The first novel-length work dealing with crime is generally credited to Seeley Regester, the pseudonym of Pennsylvania-born Metta Fuller Victor. Regester's *The Dead Letter* was published as a serial in *Beadle's Monthly* in 1866 and appeared in book form the following year. *The Dead Letter* focuses on the personality and methods used by her detective, Mr. Burton, portrayed as a well-adjusted, industrious, upper-class amateur investigator. Further developments in literary treatment of crime took place at the hands of Anna Katharine Green (1846–1935), a Brooklyn Heights–born author who is credited with writing the milestone novel *The Leavenworth Case: A Lawyer's Story* (1878). In this work, Green introduced such now-familiar conventions as ballistics evidence, a body in the library, a coroner's inquest, a crime-scene sketch, the incipient change in a rich man's will, a locked room, and a partially burned letter. Green wrote 36 detective novels and four collections of short stories, and her work was popular in upscale magazines such as *The Century, Ladies' Home Journal,* and *Lippincott's*. Green greatly influenced later writers, including Mary Roberts Rineheart (1876–1958) and Agatha Christie.

Growth in Popularity

In 1887, struggling physician Arthur Conan Doyle introduced the most famous fictional detective, Sherlock Holmes. Holmes's first appearance came in the story "A Study in Scarlet," which was published in *Beeton's Christmas Annual*. Modeled after one of Doyle's medical school professors, Holmes became sensationally popular. Although Doyle continued to publish Holmes stories until shortly before his death in 1930, he had mixed views about the detective's continued success, briefly killing the character off during the 1890s only to be forced by popular demand to resurrect him in 1901. The Holmes canon consists of 56 stories and four novels, although the stories tend to be more popular, both with readers and as a source for theater, film, and television adaptations. Doyle, a tremendously gifted storyteller, adapted literary devices introduced by Poe and Collins and perfected them in ways that solidified the detective genre. Holmes is portrayed as a brilliant eccentric, a master of disguise, and an able chemist. Holmes uses deductive reasoning to solve crimes, although he is an able and athletic sleuth who is more than willing to go into the field to track down criminals. The criminals Holmes faced represented either criminal masterminds, such as Professor Moriarty, or common offenders who often used supernatural trappings in their pernicious pursuit of pecuniary profit.

While the classical detective story was evolving through the exploits of such detectives as Holmes, who was frequently featured in *Collier's* magazine, other aspects of crime fiction were being developed in the genre known as dime novels. Dime novels originally contained stories related to the frontier and westerns, but after 1880 focused largely on crime, mystery, and detective tales. Unlike the stories featured in *Collier's* and other "slick" publications, which aimed at a middle-class audience, dime novels were pitched at a working-class market, especially boys and men. In such series as Street & Smith's Nick Carter stories, Munro's Old Sleuth tales, and others, many popular conceptions of how detectives operated were sown. Most criminals in dime novels were portrayed as venal, harsh, and interested in pecuniary gain, although the occasional master criminal, with hopes of world dominance, was sometimes used. In many ways, the dime novel could be seen as a harbinger of the American hard-boiled school that would develop later, as the stories dealt with a more realistic portrayal of rough streets and cold-blooded criminals.

The Golden Age

Although crime in literature and theater had been popular for decades, it exploded after 1920, based chiefly upon the work of such writers as Agatha Christie, Dorothy L. Sayers, John Dickson Carr, Raymond Chandler, Rex Stout, Ellery Queen, Dashiell Hammett, and Erle Stanley Gardner. Encompassing the years between World War I and World War II, the "golden age" saw crime fiction dramatically increase in popularity. Interestingly, the popularity of the newer golden age authors work supplemented, but did not supplant, that of earlier writers, such as Poe and Doyle, who continued to enjoy significant sales. Golden age authors depicted all crime in their work, but especially focused upon murders. Murder, and indeed all crime, was seen as an affront against the established order, and the efforts of fictional detectives helped to assure the reading public of the triumph of good over evil.

Beginning with the publication of her first novel, *The Mysterious Affair at Styles* (1920), Christie's career lasted more than 50 years and resulted in 66 novels and five collections of short stories. Her books have sold more than 4 billion copies and have been translated into more than 100 languages, making her the best-selling author of all time. Her fictional detectives include Hercule Poirot, Jane Marple, Tommy and Tuppence Beresford, Superintendent Battle, Mr. Parker Pine, investigator, and Harley Quin. Christie was also well known for her plays, including *The Mousetrap* (1952) and *Witness for the Prosecution* (1953). Among her more influential novels are *The Murder of Roger Ackroyd* (1926), *The Murder at the Vicarage* (1930), *Murder on the Orient Express* (1934), *The ABC Murders* (1936), *And Then There Were None* (1939), *The Body in the Library* (1942), *The Clocks* (1963), and *Curtain* (1975). Christie's works are almost all whodunits, plot-driven detective stories that feature a puzzle regarding who committed a crime. Usually featuring middle- and upper-class characters, Christie's books generally begin with a murder, which the detective either stumbles across or is asked by a client or old friend to solve. The detective next interrogates each suspect, assembles clues, and examines the scene of the crime. In a final denouement, the detective gathers all of the suspects and, over the course of 30 or more pages, unravels the mystery and denounces the criminal. Although some of her work did deal with "super criminals," most of Christie's novels dealt with villains who killed, stole, or blackmailed because they were evil. This theme, seemingly old-fashioned, may account for her lasting popularity and was a topic that would again become popular in works by contemporary American authors such as Patricia Cornwell and Jonathan Kellerman.

Sayers, Christie's contemporary and acquaintance, was an Oxford-educated poet, theologian, and playwright. An admirer of Collins and Doyle, Sayers is perhaps best remembered for her aristocratic sleuth, Lord Peter Wimsey, who meets, falls in love with, and eventually marries mystery novelist Harriet Vane, a character modeled on Sayers herself. Vane in many ways served as the prototype for female private investigators who became popular during the 1970s and after, such as Marcia Muller's Sharon McCone, Sue Grafton's Kinsey Millhone, and Sara Paretsky's V. I. Warshawski. Sayers's novels are considered classics, with *Unnatural Death* (1927), *Strong Poison* (1930), *Five Red Herrings* (1931), *Murder Must Advertise* (1933), *The Nine Tailors* (1934), and *Gaudy Night* (1935) being especially influential. Sayers's books dealt with criminals who upset the social order through their deeds, including murder, blackmail, extortion, graft, and poison letters. Criminals were usually portrayed as weak, desperate, and venal. Sayers's novels often explore themes unrelated to the mystery, such as the ethics of advertising or the role of women's education.

The popularity of British mystery novels during the 1930s was such that Pennsylvania-born John Dickson Carr wrote more than 70 novels that featured detectives who were English, published both under his name and the pseudonym Carter Dickson. Carr created two major detectives, Dr. Gideon Fell, a rotund cape-wearing consultant who worked with Scotland Yard, and Sir Henry Merrivale, a baronet and former head of the British Secret Service. An American who lived for many years in England, Carr was the master of the locked-room mystery, a subgenre in which a detective solves a seemingly impossible crime that takes place within a space where no murderer could have gained entry or egress. Among his books, *The Hollow Man* (1935), *The Arabian Nights Murder* (1936), and *The Crooked Hinge* (1938), are especially well regarded. Fellow American Ellery Queen, the pseudonym of two Brooklyn-born cousins, Frederic Dannay (1905–82) and Manfred Bennington

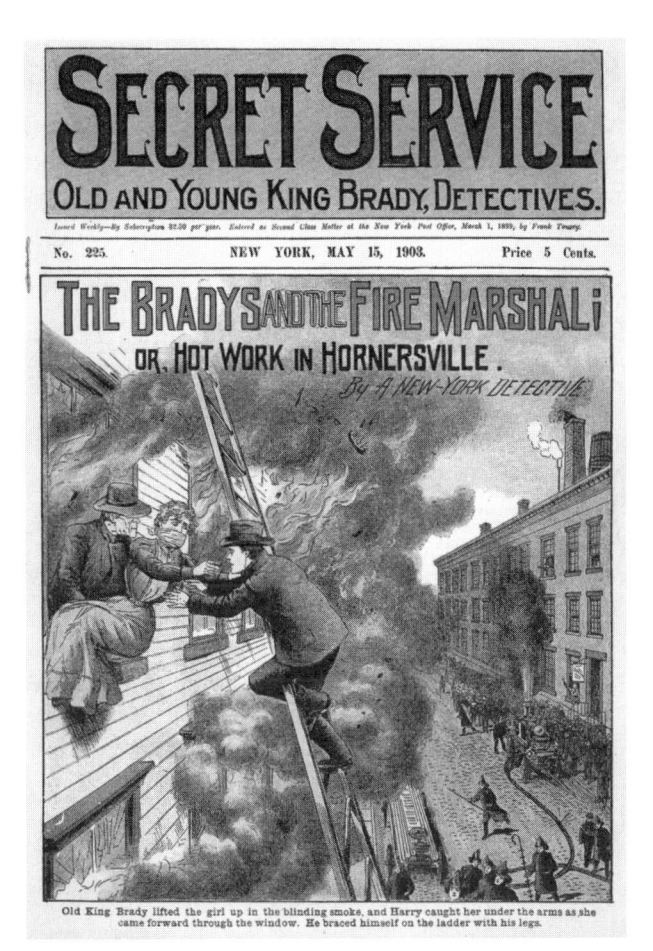

The first novel-length work was published as a serial in Beadle's Monthly *in 1866 and only later appeared in book form. This popular detective serial from 1903 featured a color cover and purported to be written by a "New York detective."*

Lee (1905–71), was one of the most popular and influential of 20th-century mystery writers, writing, editing, anthologizing, and starring in detective fiction. Using a literary convention common since the Nick Carter stories, the name "Ellery Queen" was used for both the author credits and as the name of the detective hero who was featured in a series of books, beginning with *The Roman Hat Mystery* (1929) and concluding with *A Fine and Private Place* (1971). The most popular American crime series of the 1930s and 1940s, Queen also was featured in a series of films as well as a radio program. Modeled in many ways on S. S. Van Dine's Philo Vance, Queen the character began as an Ivy League–educated scholar of private means who investigates crimes, often with his police inspector father in tow, chiefly as a means of finding intellectual stimulation. As the series progressed, Queen began to display more human emotions, sometimes becoming deeply affected by the individuals in his cases, who often pursued crime because of human frailty or personal circumstances that drove them to make bad choices. Queen the author also became highly influential as an anthologist of mystery fiction and in 1941 founded *Ellery Queen's Mystery Magazine*, a periodical that continues to publish crime-related fiction by new and well-known authors.

Pulps and the Hard-Boiled Genre

In the United States, pulp magazines, also known as "pulps," also enjoyed great popularity and often featured stories that focused upon crime. At the height of their popularity during the 1920s and 1930s, many pulp magazines sold up to a million copies per issue. Popular titles included *Adventure, Amazing Stories, Black Mask, Dime Detective, Flying Aces, Horror Stories, Marvel Tales, Oriental Stories, Planet Stories, Spicy Detective, Startling Stories, Thrilling Wonder Stories, Unknown*, and *Weird Tales*. Pulp magazines remained popular through the 1950s, when paperback books reduced their popularity. Pulps allowed many new voices to gain a following, and their lack of respect permitted many conventions to be broken. The term *pulps* derives from the cheap wood pulp paper on which the publications were printed. Unlike magazines printed on more expensive paper (known as "glossies" or "slicks"), pulps featured lurid and exploitative stories and sensational cover art. The pulps took advantage of new high-speed presses, low payments to authors, and inexpensive paper to reduce the price of the magazine to 10 cents per issue as opposed to glossies that generally sold for a quarter. Although held in low regard at the time, authors such as Raymond Chandler, Dashiell Hammett, Erle Stanley Gardner, and Rex Stout all began writing for the pulps. During the 1920s, the hard-boiled school of crime fiction originated in the American pulps, featuring as it did the loner sleuth combating violent villains in a corrupt and difficult world.

Raymond Chandler began writing in 1933, after retiring from a business career. Generally credited as a founder of the hard-boiled genre of crime fiction, Chandler wrote in an unsentimental way about violence and sex. Admired for his lyrical style, Chandler's best work includes *The Big Sleep* (1939), *Farewell, My Lovely* (1940), and *The Long Goodbye* (1953). Chandler set most of his fiction in Los Angeles, and writers such as W. H. Auden, Evelyn Waugh, and William Faulkner spoke warmly of his work. Although sometimes criticized for his portrayals of minorities and women, Chandler is generally acknowledged as one of the greatest writers of the 20th century and one who influenced the genre greatly. Chandler's villains were corrupt and venal, but no more so than the opponents in law enforcement and finance. Dashiell Hammett, a major influence of Chandler's, also contributed greatly to the hard-boiled school. Although his productivity was curtailed by alcoholism and other health conditions, Hammett is regarded as one of the greatest writers of crime fiction of all time. His more famous crime solvers include Sam Spade, Nick and Nora Charles, and the Continental Op. Hammett's novels include *Red Harvest* (1929), *The Dain Curse* (1929), *The Maltese Falcon* (1930), and *The Glass Key* (1931). Hammett also wrote many short stories that were published in the pulps.

Erle Stanley Gardner also began writing after another career, determining that he enjoyed writing more than the practice of law. Although his work never received the critical acclaim of Chandler or Hammett, Gardner was the highest-selling American author for much of the 20th century. Gardner's most famous creations, lawyer Perry Mason and his secretary Della Street, worked to assist clients who were being prosecuted for crimes and getting little assistance from the police. Mason would work to obtain evidence that he often produced in the courtroom, sometimes using illegal means to do so. Gardner was a strong storyteller, but his characters tended to be one-dimensional. Rex Stout, another author who began writing crime fiction later in life, created the nearly 300-pound detective Nero Wolfe and his assistant, Archie Goodwin. Wolfe seldom leaves his brownstone in New York City, relying on Goodwin to interview suspects he cannot get to come to his office. The ultimate armchair detective, Wolfe often seems more interested in dining and raising orchids than solving cases, for which he receives hefty fees. Important works include *The League of Frightened Men* (1935), *And Be* a Villain (1948), *In the Best Families* (1950), and *Champagne for One* (1958). The books are notable for Wolfe's disdain for the police and his support for the downtrodden.

During the golden age, crime fiction was so popular that series were developed for children. Most popular among these were the Hardy Boys and Nancy Drew books. Produced by the Stratemeyer Syndicate, with authorship attributed to Franklin W. Dixon and Carolyn Keene, respectively, the books were written by a series of ghost authors, with Leslie McFarlane writing most of the Hardy Boys stories and Mildred Wirt penning most of the Nancy Drew adventures. Although the young sleuths solved crimes, including auto thefts, kidnapping, and embezzlement, the books did not include murders, which were seen as too violent for juvenile readers. While golden age novels as a whole are often perceived as adhering to relatively conservative values, insofar as justice must prevail and protagonists work to restore order, this is even more evident in children's series books, which use mystery chiefly to heighten plot interest.

Post–Golden Age Developments

Since the end of the golden age, literature and theater involving crime have changed tremendously in some ways and not at all in others. Some of this is because of the longevity and continued success of golden age writers, many of whom lived into the 1970s and remain bestsellers and household names to this day. Many of the writers who have succeeded the golden age writers have also emphasized refining traditional genres of crime fiction, rather than creating new styles of their own. For example, Ross Macdonald, Robert B. Parker, Marcia Muller, Sara Paretsky, and Sue Grafton all have written in the hard-boiled style first pioneered by Hammett and Chandler. Macdonald's sleuth, private investigator Lew Archer, lives and works in Los Angeles, as did Chandler's Marlowe. Both Archer and Marlowe are single and live in apartments, and Macdonald uses the pithy style of Hammett and Chandler for his books. The differences, while subtle, involve the psychological depth that Macdonald uses to provide insights into his characters' motivations. Archer, much like Parker's Spenser, provides a more sensitive private investigator, one who eschews the machismo and aloof nature of his predecessors. Archer often sympathizes with the villains he pursues, seeing concepts of *right* and *wrong* as being ambiguous and indistinct in a world that is often evil and corrupt itself. Spenser in particular demonstrates a need for female companionship that is very different from the needs of Spade or Marlowe.

Post–golden age sleuths also are able to more readily embrace feminism, and one of the largest shifts is the number of female private investigators. Muller's Sharon McCone, Paretsky's V. I. Warshawski, and Grafton's Kinsey Millhone have demonstrated that women can thrive in a world corrupted and controlled by men. Moving beyond socially constructed conceptions of gender, this new generation of female private investigators has demonstrated that time can alter deeply rooted stereotypes. Equally significant are the changing roles of ethnic minorities. Golden age writers, when they wrote about non-Caucasian characters at all, tended to reinforce stereotypical prejudices. Indeed, little notice was taken of societal or institutional racism. A new generation of writers has addressed this, introducing characters who are members of ethnic minority groups, such as Walter Mosley's African American private investigator Ezekiel "Easy" Rawlins or Tony Hillerman's Navajo police officers Jim Chee and Joe Leaphorn. The representation of traditionally victimized groups has grown in other ways as well, as evidenced by Steig Larsson's Lisbeth Salander, who has suffered psychological and sexual abuse.

Non-hardboiled mysteries have also been updated. Amanda Cross's Kate Fansler worked as an English professor when not solving crimes, Patricia Cornwell's Dr. Kay Scarpetta works as a medical examiner, and Jonathan Kellerman's Alex Delaware is a child psychologist. Interestingly, the "old-fashioned" view of criminals as evil, popularized by authors such as Agatha Christie, has made a return in the work of authors such as Cornwell and Kellerman. The increasing popularity of crime fiction has led to a wider variety of subgenres, some familiar, such as legal procedurals, and some new, such as mysteries featuring a culinary theme. Even as the number of bookstores nationally has decreased, an increasing number of amateur detectives serve as owners or employees of such shops. As increased media exposure strives to make the public more aware of criminal

Mary Roberts Rinehart, author of the popular crime novel The Circular Staircase *(1908), along with hundreds of other stories, books, and plays, around 1915.*

activity, it seems likely that crime will continue to play an important role in literature and theater.

Theater

Stage productions of crime dramas during the 19th century were, for the most part, imports from Great Britain. Beginning in the 1870s, Americans such as J. J. McCloskey and Harlan Page Halsey brought their dime novel detectives Daring Dick and the Old Sleuth to the stage with some success. Anna Katharine Green also wrote a stage version of *The Leavenworth Case* in 1892, featuring her detective Ebenezer Gryce.

It was William Gillette's play *Sherlock Holmes* (1899), however, that proved to be the breakthrough hit, being revived across America and England for decades. For the first two decades of the 20th century, American stages saw many new plays with a crime focus, including Elmer Rice's *On Trial* (1914), Bayard Veiller's *The Thirteenth Chair* (1916), and Mary Roberts Rinehart's *The Bat* (1920). Beginning in the 1930s, however, imports from Britain began to crowd the American stage, including plays by A. A. Milne, Patrick Hamilton, and, especially, Agatha Christie. During the 1940s, 1950s, and 1960s, some Americans were able to find success on Broadway, including Owen Davis's *Mr. and Mrs. North* (1941), Ira Levin's *Interlock* (1958), and Frederick Knott's *Wait Until Dark* (1966). Since the 1980s, few crime dramas have been successful in the United States, even those that were popular in Britain. The few that have been successful include Warren Manzi's *The Perfect Crime* (1988) and Larry Gelbart's *City of Angels* (1989).

Stephen T. Schroth
Jason A. Helfer
Diana L. Beck
Knox College

See Also: Christie, Agatha; Detection and Detectives; Dime Novels, Pulps, Thrillers; Film, Crime in; Gardner, Erle Stanley; Grafton, Sue; Hammett, Dashiell; Hillerman, Tony; Literature and Theater, Police in; Paretzky, Sara; Poe, Edgar Allen; Television, Crime in.

Further Readings

Cohen, D. A. *Pillars of Salt, Monuments of Grace: New England Crime Literature and the Origins of American Popular Culture, 1674–1860.* New York: Oxford University Press, 1993.

Herbert, R. *The Oxford Companion to Crime and Mystery Writing.* New York: Oxford University Press, 1999.

Palmer, J. *Thrillers: Genesis and Structure of a Popular Genre.* New York: St. Martin's Press, 1979.

Rodensky, L. *The Crime in Mind: Criminal Responsibility and the Victorian Novel.* New York: Oxford University Press, 2003.

Winks, R. W., ed. *Detective Fiction: A Collection of Critical Essays.* Upper Saddle River, NJ: Prentice Hall, 1980.

Literature and Theater, Police in

Intense interest in the operations of police departments and the travails of police officers has resulted in these being popular themes in literature and theater. Unlike detective novels, which usually concentrate on a single crime and its consequences, literature that concentrates on the police often explores investigations into several unrelated crimes. The occurrence of police officers and police departments mirrors, with a short delay, the development of police and law enforcement agencies themselves. Police and law enforcement agencies became common in metropolitan areas during the mid-19th century. Books and plays containing police officers as characters became common during the latter half of that century. Initially, police officers were figures of derision, used in books and plays chiefly for comic relief or as a means to comment upon the inefficiencies of government agencies. By the mid-20th century, however, the reputation of the police had risen sufficiently for them to have become the subject of their own genre, known as police procedurals. As societal changes have affected the United States over the past 50 years, so too have these transformations been reflected in writing about the police. More recent plays and books have examined pertinent social issues, including feminism, race relations, discrimination, and police abuse. Depictions of the police in literature and theater continue to be a popular and prevalent form in which to explore these issues.

Background

Formal policing was relatively unknown at the time of the American Revolution. During the colonial period, watchmen and constables provided law enforcement in villages and towns, while rural areas relied upon sheriffs. By the early 19th century, Boston, Massachusetts, had established independent day and night watches, which constituted a series of patrols to help keep the peace and discourage crime. Only in 1845, however, did the New York legislature establish a modern police department for New York City, using the force in London as a model. The London force, known formally as the Metropolitan Police, had been formed under Sir Robert Peel in 1829 to respond to rampant crime in the British capital. In the United States, other large cities initiated their own forces shortly after New York—Chicago's police department began operation in 1851, and Boston and Philadelphia started theirs in 1854. The Metropolitan Police, often referred to as "Scotland Yard" in reference to the street abutting the rear entrance of its headquarters, although responsible only for law enforcement within Greater London, had an effect upon policing throughout the United Kingdom, as its representatives were often consulted by local authorities. The United States' vast size, as well as its tradition of local control, ensured that police procedures and practices were much more diverse. Not until the turn of the 20th century were there efforts made to professionalize urban police departments, many of which had been warrens of patronage and graft.

Changes that occurred during the first decades of the 1900s included instituting career administrators, using civil service exams for hiring and promotion decisions, and encouraging education for officers. These changes were accelerated after J. Edgar Hoover became the director of the Bureau of Investigation, now the Federal Bureau of Investigation (FBI), an agency of the U.S. Department of Justice, in 1924. Although often derided today, Hoover moved quickly to establish the FBI as the model crime-fighting organization in the United States. Hoover's FBI stressed academy training programs, data collection, and scientific analysis of evidence, services it made available to local law enforcement agencies. For this reason, the FBI was enormously influential in shaping how local and state police departments thought of themselves and their work. As the civil rights movement of the 1960s developed support from a broad array of the population, many began to criticize law enforcement agencies for violence and for hiring practices that excluded women and members of many ethnic minority groups. During this time, allegations of corruption and graft once again began to be made. A series of decisions by the U.S. Supreme Court between 1961 and 1966, including *Escobedo v. Illinois* (1964) and *Miranda v. Arizona* (1966), affirmed and expanded the constitutional rights of those accused of committing crimes, thereby altering some practices and behaviors of police officers. In response, during the 1970s, the federal government increased funding for law enforcement initiatives at the national, state, and local levels, raising the profile of police agencies while also providing monetary support for recruitment, training, education, and research. The prevalence of the police in political discussions and in the news media created a corresponding interest in the reading and theater-going public in matters related to law enforcement.

Early Appearances

Depictions of police officers in literature and theater began soon after larger municipalities began to form independent police departments. As might be expected from then-current perceptions of law enforcement, early portrayals of police officers in books and plays depicted them as bumbling, inefficient, and not especially intelligent. Arthur Conan Doyle's fictional depictions of police officers at work in the Sherlock Holmes stories are typical—police officers frequently arrested the wrong person, overlooked exculpatory evidence, and tended to resist offers of assistance. During the 1850s and 1860s, British dramatist Tom Taylor began writing plainclothes officers into many of his plays, as well as private detectives. Taylor's character Hawkshaw represented one of the first and most successful stage detectives and appeared in his highly successful work, *The Ticket of Leave Man* (1863). Scotland Yard officers were depicted on the boards for the first time in Watts Phillips's *Maude's Peril: A Drama in Four Acts* (1867). Many works of Charles Dickens and Wilkie Collins also were made into plays, with those featuring detectives and police officers being especially popular. Although many of these plays originated in the United Kingdom, they also were produced—and well received—in the United States.

During the golden age of detective fiction, which roughly spanned the period between World War I and World War II, mystery novels were extremely popular with audiences on both sides of the Atlantic. Although some of the detectives in these novels were police officers, they usually represented retired members of the force, colorful exotics, or exceptions to the rule. For example, Agatha Christie's Hercule Poirot, who first appeared in *The Mysterious Affair at Styles* (1920), was a retired Belgian police officer, but he was much more representative of an armchair detective than a member of an active police force. In a similar manner, Earl Dean Biggers's Charlie Chan first appeared in *The House Without a Key* (1925). Chan was a Chinese American who served as a lieutenant with the Honolulu Police Department; despite this, he fit the role of a private detective much more than he did a member of an organized force, often operating alone and traveling out of his jurisdiction to solve crimes. Finally, upon his first appearance in *A Man Lay Dying* (1934), Ngaio Marsh's Roderick Alleyn was a detective-inspector (later chief superintendent) in the Criminal Investigation Department (CID) at Scotland Yard. Although he began his career as a constable, Alleyn is clearly a gentleman detective, the younger son of a baronet who was educated at Oxford University. Although technically a member of the police, Alleyn represented an earlier conceptualization of law enforcement, with members of the rank and file still representing a less intelligent, lumbering, and inefficient approach to law enforcement.

Police Procedurals

In no small part because of the public relations onslaught launched by J. Edgar Hoover and the FBI during the 1920s and 1930s, public perceptions of police forces began to change radically. Under Hoover, during the 1930s, the FBI conducted a well-publicized "war on crime" that led to the capture, conviction, or death of well-known criminals such as John Dillinger, Lester "Baby Face Nelson" Gillis, Kate "Ma" Barker, and George "Machine Gun Kelly" Barnes. Lawrence Treat introduced a genre known as the police procedural to U.S. readers with his work *V as in Victim* (1945), while Maurice Procter brought it to the British with *The Chief Inspector's Statement* (1951). Police procedurals represent a type of crime fiction that attempts to concentrate on the realities of police investigation and routine, rather than merely concentrating on a puzzle to be solved as much detective fiction does. To solve a crime, the protagonists in police procedurals use modern science to gather and interpret evidence, working with other police officers as a team rather than the independent behavior demonstrated by many amateur sleuths.

Many of the advances publicized by the FBI's Scientific Crime Detection Laboratory in films and on radio programs of the 1930s began to appear in police procedurals during the 1940s and following decades. Such venues greatly increased public interest in police officers and law enforcement. These advances included such innovations as recording and matching fingerprints; analyzing chemicals, fibers, bodily fluids, ashes, and other physical evidence; interpreting blood splatter patterns; examining public and financial records; collecting and scrutinizing computer data; and identifying and using informants. These sorts of real-life components of crime solving are at the heart of police procedurals. This focus on practical and realistic procedures is unlike much of detective fiction, in which sleuths instead rely upon intuition, coincidence, and brilliance to solve puzzles. National differences in police traditions, practices, and routines have caused significant differences to exist between police procedurals from the United States, Great Britain, and elsewhere.

American Police Procedurals

Police procedurals developed differently in the United States and the United Kingdom. Lawrence Treat, one of the earliest writers of police procedurals, developed certain literary devices that define the genre. Treat's police procedurals featured three recurring characters: Lieutenant Bill Decker, Detective Job Freeman, and Detective Mitch Taylor. Treat explained and adhered to real-life law enforcement procedures and relied heavily upon Freeman's interpretations of scientific evidence that are analyzed in his police laboratory. Treat's work also emphasized the interpersonal relationships between his characters, portraying Decker's harried role as the administrator of the homicide division of the New York Police Department (NYPD) and Taylor's involvement in graft and corruption, which leads to his demotion and ultimate dismissal from the force. These literary devices greatly affected later writers such as Ed McBain, Joseph Wambaugh, Tony Hillerman, and others.

Ed McBain began his 87th Precinct series with *Cop Hater* (1956), and the series continued until his death, with the final entry being *Learning to Kill* (2006). McBain readily acknowledged his series' debt to Jack Webb's radio and television series *Dragnet*. Early on, McBain established the tone and practices that influenced his series and the work of other authors. All of the 87th Precinct books are set in Isola, a thinly veiled fictional version of Manhattan. The other New York City boroughs are also represented, with Calm's Point representing Brooklyn, Majesta standing in for Queens, Riverhead corresponding to the Bronx, and Bethtown symbolizing Staten Island. Although the entire series focused on detectives of the 87th Precinct, different detectives were featured in different novels. Almost all of the books feature a significant role for Detective 2nd Grade Stephen "Steve" Carella. Colleagues of Carella include Arthur Brown, Eileen Burke, Alex Delgado, Richard Genero, Roger Havilland, Cotton Hawes, Bert Kling, Meyer Meyer, Bob O'Brien, Andy Parker, and Hal Willis. McBain usually began books with a corpse and then shadowed the police investigation as officers attempted to find out how the murder occurred. McBain was especially good at describing the day-to-day operations of the justice system, providing details of police routine, and larding the books with visuals, such as depictions of police forms or handwritten notes. The 87th Precinct series was immensely popular, with individual novels adapted as motion pictures and the series itself running briefly as a television program in the 1960s. Other television series reflect its influence, such as the award-winning 1980s program *Hill Street Blues*.

Many of the literary devices introduced by McBain were continued by Dell Shannon, a pseudonym of Elizabeth Linington, who also wrote as Lesley Egan. Shannon wrote about Los Angeles Police Department (LAPD) central homicide Lieutenant Luis Mendoza for over a quarter of a century, beginning with *Case Pending* (1960). In her day considered the "Queen of Procedurals," Shannon was one of the first women to write police procedurals. Although somewhat out of fashion today because of Shannon's far-right-wing political ideology, her books evoke a simpler era when members of the LAPD were heroes who were determined to protect and to serve the citizens of Los Angeles. Shannon's books contained many technical inaccuracies related to police procedures, although this did not harm their popularity when written.

Other writers who followed McBain and Shannon and who wrote about law enforcement adhered to a focus on police work but augmented their novels with elements from detective fiction as well. For example, Tony Hillerman began his long-running series about Navajo Tribal Police officers Sergeant Jim Chee and Lieutenant Joe Leaphorn with *The Blessing Way* (1970). While Hillerman carefully adhered to procedures and methods officers adhered to in the field, a great deal of his works' appeal focused upon themes and elements present in Navajo culture, religion, and witchcraft. Police officers were thus portrayed much more as individuals than they had been in the past, with Chee's love of traditional Navajo practices contrasting with Leaphorn's pragmatic and cynical worldview. Joseph Wambaugh, perhaps the most prominent former police officer who writes police procedurals, is a former member of the LAPD. Wambaugh began a run of police procedurals and nonfiction works, including *The New Centurions* (1970), *The Blue Knight* (1971), and *The Onion Field* (1973), that drew great interest to the training, perceptions, and realities of police officers in the field. Wambaugh considers the most important aspect of his work to be the conversation sparked regarding how the job of policing affects and changes officers.

Patricia Cornwell, whose series featuring medical examiner Kay Scarpetta, began with *Postmortem* (1990) to explore forensic pathology, a subgenre of police work seldom before explored. In the Scarpetta series, Cornwell explores the use of forensic technology in solving crimes. In the series' beginning novels, Scarpetta serves as the chief medical examiner for the Commonwealth of Virginia, heading an agency that conducts autopsies and provides forensic services for police departments across the state. Throughout the Scarpetta novels, police are portrayed as human, with their virtues and frailties depending upon the individual. Cornwell's work has been highly influential, inspiring a variety of television programs, such as *CSI: Crime Scene Investigation*, as well as changing jury perceptions regarding the types of evidence that police teams are expected to submit at criminal trials. Other law enforcement personnel in Cornwell's work include Pete Marino, a homicide detective for the Richmond Police Department, and Benton Wesley, a profiler for the Federal Bureau of Investigation (FBI) with whom Scarpetta eventually becomes romantically involved.

This theatrical poster for The Sidewalks of New York *from 1896 features a police foot chase on Broadway in New York's Herald Square, as "Buttons" McGurk, the "King of the Bums," tries to outrun a policeman wielding a gun and a baton.*

Jonathan Kellerman, who writes about forensic psychologist Alex Delaware, also has provided a different twist on police operations in the more than 20 books he has written featuring the character. Beginning with *Bough Breaks* (1985), which was given an Edgar Award for best first novel by the Mystery Writers of America (MWA), Kellerman has explored contemporary law enforcement practices in Southern California. Delaware frequently helps his friend, Milo Sturgis, an LAPD detective, in his investigations. While Delaware is portrayed as a cool, analytical, and level-headed professional, Sturgis is a career police officer who is large, blundering, uncouth, and gay. Through Sturgis, Kellerman examines the changing face of American law enforcement, exploring how increasing diversity in police forces has caused old stereotypes to be challenged and created new problems to be addressed. Kellerman's LAPD has African American, Asian, and Latino officers, as well as Caucasians. The varied predispositions, prejudices, and preferences of these diverse individuals permit Kellerman to weave a postmodern analysis of American law enforcement, challenging many stereotypes and labels often applied to police officers.

International Police Procedurals
Although police procedurals from Great Britain and other nations developed concurrently with their American counterparts, significant and substantial differences exist between the two variations of the genre, some of which have influenced American authors and public perceptions. One of the best-regarded police procedurals was *Last Seen Wearing…* (1952), written by Hillary Waugh, who although British was living in the United States at the time. Indeed, as *Last Seen Wearing…* was set in the United States, it has been claimed by both Americans and British critics as their own. John Creasey, perhaps the most important contributor to the British police procedural, began writing crime novels during the 1930s. Beginning with *Gideon's Day* (1955), Creasey, writing using the pseudonym J. J. Marric, introduced a series that brought the British police procedural into its own. The Marric books, which featured Detective George Gideon of Scotland Yard, set new standards for accuracy and attention to detail. In the books, Gideon typically supervises his subordinates' investigations into several crimes, usually unrelated. More than any other police procedural, the Marric books began the now-common plot structure where several autonomous story lines are threaded throughout a single novel. The Marric books almost uniformly portray the police as human functionaries of a system designed to protect the common welfare. Wildly popular with the reading public, Creasey's books also garnered great critical acclaim and were largely influential with other writers, especially in the United States.

Colin Dexter also had great success writing about his Oxford-based Inspector Morse. Beginning with *Last Bus to Woodstock* (1975), Dexter wrote 13 novels about Morse, concluding the series with *The Remorseful Day* (1999). While Morse exhibits many eccentricities more common to amateur sleuths, such as his love of Wagner, beer, and crossword puzzles, Dexter's focus upon the dull work of routine places the series within the police procedural genre. Morse, together with his subordinate, Sergeant Lewis, juxtaposes qualities of the English gentleman detective with a career as a CID of the Thames Valley Police, one of the largest territorial law enforcement agencies in the United Kingdom. Morse displays many attributes common to workers in any system, including boredom, depression, and frustration with bureaucracy.

Dexter's contemporary, Reginald Hill, also shaped the British police procedural. Hill has written more than 20 novels featuring Detective Superintendent Andrew Dalziel, Detective Inspector Peter Pascoe, and Detective Sergeant Edgar Wield of the Yorkshire constabulary. Hill has introduced various structural devices that have moved the police procedural closer to other genres of literature, including presenting portions of the plot in nonchronological order and alternating sections from a book with sections from another work allegedly written by Pascoe's wife, Ellie. Among Hill's best-regarded works are *Deadheads* (1983) and *Underworld* (1988). Hill's work has been adapted successfully for television, and these programs have been aired in both the United States and the United Kingdom.

Martin Beck, of Sweden's National Homicide Squad, was created by the husband-and-wife team of Maj Sjöwall and Per Wahlöö. Inspired by McBain's 87th Precinct series, the 10 Sjöwall and Wahlöö books were preconceived as part of a 300-chapter indictment of the Swedish welfare system as seen through the eyes of a working police superintendent. Beginning with *Roseanna* (1965), the series commenced as a straightforward police procedural. Over time, however, the leftist sympathies of Sjöwall and Wahlöö emerge. While Beck continues to investigate graft and track murderers, the police work is balanced with social criticism, and Sjöwall's and Wahlöö's indictment of the Swedish welfare state of the early 1970s is fascinating and relevant to the stories. The Sjöwall and Wahlöö books often have two or more plots running concurrently, and are known for their brilliant plotting. Translated into many languages, the Sjöwall and Wahlöö books were influential across borders, helping to shape police procedurals in the United States, and selected novels were adapted for television and film.

Another Swedish author, Steig Larsson, enjoyed great success with a trio of books known as the Millennium Series, comprising *The Girl With the Dragon Tattoo* (2005), *The Girl Who Played With Fire* (2006), and *The Girl Who Kicked the Hornet's Nest* (2007). The trilogy's primary characters, Lisbeth Salander and Mikael Blomkvist, are not police officers. During the second and third books in the series, however, Jan Bublanski, Sonja Modig, and a team of other officers investigate a series of suspected crimes that are interrelated with other aspects of the plot. While some police officers are portrayed as corrupt, Bublanski and Modig are depicted as honest and human, adept at deciphering cyber information and a grand conspiracy. Originally planned as a 10-volume saga, the series was ended by Larsson's untimely death. The immense popularity of the series, however, and its immediate adaptation into film versions, suggests that the intertwining of the police procedural with other plot strands may continue to be accepted and well liked.

Theater

During the 19th century, American audiences were very keen on plays that portrayed authentic notorious cases, with works by Dion Boucicault, Watts Phillips, and Tom Taylor being especially popular. In these works, police officers were generally shown as stock characters, pursuing villains and upholding the peace. As dime novels increased in popularity, audiences clamored to see a more active sleuth, which resulted in well-liked plays such as J. J. McCloskey's *Daring Dick, the Brooklyn Detective* (1870). Although police officers appeared in other works, it was almost always in a secondary role, which changed only after American William Gillette wrote and starred in *Sherlock Holmes* (1899), which used Arthur Conan Doyle's popular character in a romantic plot that has almost nothing in common with the stories of the canon. After the turn of the 20th century, mystery farces such as Augustin McHugh's *Officer 666* (1912) were very popular, although police in these works were often shown as incompetent, corrupt, and inefficient.

During the mid-20th century, crime-based drama enjoyed a renaissance of popularity on the stage, perhaps inspired by the popularity of the genre on radio and in film. Plays such as Vera Caspary's *Laura* (1947), Alec Coppel's *The Joshua Tree* (1958), and Frederick Knott's *Write Me a Murder* (1961) were successful on Broadway and tended to portray police officers as hardworking, competent, and resourceful. During the 1970s, comedy thrillers became popular, with plays such as Ira Levin's *Deathtrap* (1979) and Rupert Holmes's *Accomplice* (1989) and *Sleight of Hand* (1992) being highly successful. Although police procedurals have been very popular on television and in films in recent decades, for the moment they seem to have disappeared from the stage, perhaps because those media are better able to show the scientific processes that modern police investigations utilize than the stage. As the genre has proven popular in other media, however, it might be premature to assert they will not reappear.

Stephen T. Schroth
Jason A. Helfer
Diana L. Beck
Knox College

See Also: Christie, Agatha; Detection and Detectives; Dime Novels, Pulps, Thrillers; Film, Police in; Hillerman, Tony; Literature and Theater, Crime in; Television, Police in.

Further Readings

Cohen, D. A. *Pillars of Salt, Monuments of Grace: New England Crime Literature and the Origins of American Popular Culture, 1674–1860.* New York: Oxford University Press, 1993.

Palmer, J. *Thrillers: Genesis and Structure of a Popular Genre.* New York: St. Martin's Press, 1979.

Rodensky, L. *The Crime in Mind: Criminal Responsibility and the Victorian Novel.* New York: Oxford University Press, 2003.

Winks, R. W., ed. *Detective Fiction: A Collection of Critical Essays.* Upper Saddle River, NJ: Prentice Hall, 1980.

Literature and Theater, Punishment in

Punishment has long been a dominant theme in literature and theater. In a literary or theatrical context, punishment often refers to a negative or unpleasant consequence imposed upon an individual or group in response to behavior those in an authoritative position deem wrong or unacceptable. The Bible deals often with conceptions of punishment, as do authors such as Plato, Dante Alighieri, Charles Dickens, Joseph Conrad, and Graham Greene. Classic and modern crime fiction also grapple with and explore punishment, although recently, ways in which this construct is presented have been changing. This change has occurred as more contemporary conceptions of crime, justice, and fairness have affected depictions of and opinion regarding punishment. Long-held opinions regarding punishment, which tended to conceive of the construct as stemming from God or social institutions, have changed so that it is often now seen as a psychological condition. Despite these transformations, punishment remains an important and vital element in much of literature and theater.

Changing Conceptions of Punishment

Human conceptions of punishment are often tied to depictions in literature. While on the one hand, these literary depictions are grounded in contemporary mores and opinions regarding penalties and justice, on the other hand, they also have a tremendous influence in shaping public opinion regarding what punishment represents. Many literary and theatrical representations of justice traditionally had a rather conservative worldview, which led to punishment of wrongdoers being the logical resolution. As time passed, those with a more radical perspective began to question many aspects of the established social order, such as the inequitable distribution of wealth, the lack of suffrage, or the role of women or ethnic minorities. As more radical themes began to be explored, a change in what constituted an appropriate punishment also occurred.

Works such as the Bible, for generations the most commonly read book, portrayed punishment in a vengeful manner, with God compensating evil deeds by chastisement and castigation. While still conservative, some increasingly diverse perspectives regarding punishment were introduced during the Renaissance. Dante Alighieri worked on *The Divine Comedy* between 1308 and his death in 1321. In this work, set in 1300, the classical Roman poet Virgil serves as a guide for Dante's journey through the inferno and then up the mountain Purgatorio.

In *The Divine Comedy*, Dante depicts Hell as a series of nine concentric rings, each leading deeper into Earth. The deeper one travels into the various rings, the more severe the punishments provided. Dante so arranged his inferno that the different rings represent different levels of infractions. The allegory Dante created suggests that different actions on Earth result in different punishments in the afterlife. Immediately popular upon its publication, *The Divine Comedy* became overlooked during the 18th century, only to enjoy a renaissance during the 19th century, serving as inspiration for a host of authors, including William Blake, Ezra Pound, T. S. Eliot, C. S. Lewis, James Joyce, Dorothy L. Sayers, Samuel Beckett, Seamus Heaney, Robert Pinsky, and John Ciardi.

Novelists such as Charles Dickens also explored themes of punishment, albeit within a more secular context than many earlier works. During the Victorian era, those with a more radical perspective, including Dickens, began to introduce themes that would greatly change perceptions of punishment. In *Great Expectations*, for example, originally published in 1860, crime and punishment are dealt with in ways that emphasize the psychological, rather than the physical, burdens of either. Punishment is meted out to various characters in the novel, as Miss Havisham dies as the result of burns suffered in a fire and Magwitch dies after being captured trying to leave England, but the real punishment suffered is the realization of the characters that they have behaved in inappropriate and self-serving ways. Miss Havisham realizes that she has harmed Pip, while Pip understands that his great ambition has cost him many real and valuable friendships. *Great Expectations* influenced later authors, such as Joseph Conrad and Graham Greene, who examined punishment as being as much a psychological condition as societal retribution. Greene was especially interested in punishment and examined throughout his work various themes related to punishment, including who determines punishment, for what reasons it is meted out, and what sorts of behaviors are to be censured or lauded. The ambiguity of punishment was examined by Greene in *The Confidential Agent* (1939), *The Ministry of Fear* (1843), and *The Third Man* (1950), all of which heavily influenced later writers, especially Ross Macdonald.

In the United States, dime novels—popular works aimed at working-class readers—began to publish a great deal of crime fiction between 1880 and 1900. In these works, popular series detectives such as Nick Carter and the Old Sleuth pursued criminals who had harmed men and women who were familiar to the readers, such as shopkeepers, widows, and peddlers. While dime novel heroes would sometimes cooperate with authorities, punishment of villains by whatever means was the primary goal. As a result, the capture and punishment of the person responsible for the crime was the primary goal, whether it occurred by turning the wrongdoer over to the police or by private means.

Borrowing from the methods employed by Pinkerton detectives, dime novel sleuths shadowed suspects, eavesdropped on conversations, and used a variety of disguises to discover the identities of criminals. Persistence and hard work were the hallmarks of dime novel detectives, rather than the rational deductions of sleuths such as Holmes, who were more popular with the middle classes. Criminal motives tended to stem from simple greed, and the dime novels helped to shape popular conceptions of detective work.

Traditional and Hard-Boiled Detective Fiction

Although punishment as a theme in literature and theater has always been popular, it is especially pertinent to mystery fiction. As a separate genre, certain elements of narrative developed through the works of many authors, which became conventions over time. Conventions serve to undergird the form and provide structure for writers' innovations. Most mystery fiction centers on the portrayal of an investigator, whether professional or amateur. Also present in most mystery fiction is the presence of a problem that the investigator seeks to solve, most often some sort of a crime, with murder, theft, or embezzlement being popular. The 19th century saw great change, much affected by the Industrial Revolution and the increasing use of technologies that altered patterns of life that had been in place for centuries. In an effort to reassure an uneasy public, mystery writers such as Edgar Allen Poe, Arthur Conan Doyle, Agatha Christie, and many others sought to create worlds in which the evil were apprehended and crimes were punished by official channels. These authors, often referred to as "traditional," developed a set of conventions by which they dealt with crime and punishment. As readers became more comfortable with many of the changes wrought by the 19th century, a new style of mystery fiction developed, known as "hard-boiled." Hard-boiled mysteries remove crime from the upper-middle-class settings favored by traditional writers, and move it instead to the realm of shady characters and urban streets. Initiating new conventions, hard-boiled authors such as Dashiell Hammett, Raymond Chandler, and Ross Macdonald set forth as protagonists practical individuals who were not surprised by crime and who were able to fight for justice using considerable firepower and determination. As hard-boiled writers created stories in which corrupt social institutions were the norm and where self-reliant individuals were able to provide the punishment that the system often could or would not, this genre has proven successful with audiences who share some of these disappointments. Punishment is dealt with differently between the traditional and hard-boiled traditions, although there are many similarities.

Agatha Christie's *The Body in the Library*, published in 1942 and featuring her elderly sleuth Miss Jane Marple, uses many traditional conventions. The setting of the book is the small rural town of St. Mary Mead, where a maid discovers the corpse of an unknown young woman in the library of the country home of staid Colonel and Mrs. Bantry. When the police do not immediately arrest someone for the murder, local gossips begin to allege that the tawdrily dressed young woman was having an affair with Colonel Bantry—and Mrs. Bantry, distressed for her husband, asks her friend and neighbor Miss Marple to assist with the investigation. When the victim is discovered to be a dancer at a nearby seaside resort, Miss Marple and Mrs. Bantry check in as guests to look into the girl's past. A second body, that of a

16-year-old missing girl guide, is discovered in a burned car. Miss Marple interviews various suspects and then unmasks the murderers, who are arrested and taken into the judicial system, where they will be put to death. Punishment is intended to restore order and to penalize wrongdoers. In many ways, *The Body in the Library* is an archetype of the traditional genre. Many of the characters are from upper-class backgrounds, and the first victim is a socially climbing interloper. While the murderers are punished at the end of the book for their crime, the victim herself is also punished for her social climbing and inability to accept the limitations of her lower-class background. At the end of the novel, the murderers are turned over to the authorities to meet their fate. Punishment is thus used by the traditional writers to maintain social order and to extract justice for criminal, and social, missteps.

This traditional approach contrasts greatly with that used by the hard-boiled writers. Hard-boiled fiction developed first in dime novels and later in pulp magazines such as *Black Mask*. Writers for the dime novels, which were highly popular during the 19th century, made popular many conceptions regarding how detectives and other crime fighters worked, combining realistic details of the cities in which their sleuths worked with criminals whose motivations and actions were familiar to readers. Becoming popular beginning in the 1920s, the pulp writers focused upon simplicity in language, similar to that employed by Ernest Hemingway and others, and plausible plots where action sprang from characteristics of the protagonist and other characters. By incorporating such techniques, pulp fiction developed an American sense of realism, including perceptions of punishment, which was very different from that of the traditional school. Writers such as Dashiell Hammett, whose Continental Op stories often appeared in *Black Mask*, opened up the style in ways that made it seem more realistic and less exaggerated. Unlike many detective heroes of the era, the Continental Op was short, overweight, and pushing 40. The employee of an established detective agency, the Continental Op balances the goals of his clients against the needs of his employer, and demonstrates the professionalism and persistence needed by a professional detective. This developed a style that was

American stages put on productions of British plays for most of the 19th century, but William Gillette's Sherlock Holmes *(1899) changed that. The play, advertised here in a poster from 1900, was a great success and played for decades.*

clearly American and modern, as opposed to the traditional detective story, which was British and romantic. Hammett viewed punishment as a result, one that might be pursued through official channels but that could also be the consequence of the Continental Op's private actions. In *Red Harvest* (1929), for example, the Continental Op faces off against both the corrupt police officers and gangsters who run Personville, pitting the two groups against each other so that they destroy each other. Punishment thus is achieved without the sanction of the authorities nominally charged with keeping the peace.

In Raymond Chandler's *The Big Sleep* (1939), in which he introduces his private investigator Philip Marlowe, a fresh perspective on punishment and society is provided. The novel begins with Marlowe visiting the palatial home of General

Sternwood, who hires him to intercede with a blackmailer, Arthur Gwynn Geiger. Geiger is attempting to extort money from Sternwood regarding promissory notes his daughter Carmen has signed. Marlowe begins his investigation and is soon embroiled in incidents involving pornography, drugs, blackmail, gambling, and murder. Although Marlowe himself kills several men, he is exonerated by the police. He also provides the police with evidence to arrest and convict several other individuals but refrains from providing evidence related to the illegal actions of the Sternwood sisters, believing he owes his loyalty to his client, their father. At the end of the novel, Marlowe's world is no safer or more orderly than it was before he took the case. Punishment is thus seen as a ramification that occurs for some but not all individuals. The streets on which most individuals live also represent a place where connections and social status play a role in the penalties one may suffer. The concept of punishment is thus represented as arbitrary and capricious, as opposed to the logical repercussion it represents in traditional mystery stories.

American Ross Macdonald, who created private investigator Lew Archer, did much to extend the hard-boiled genre's handling of constructs such as punishment and justice. Archer, who first appeared in *The Moving Target* (1949), had a more nuanced view of evil and the world in which it existed than did Hammett or Chandler. Macdonald, who held a Ph.D. in English literature from the University of Michigan, was especially influenced by Chandler and Greene. Believing that evil acts were situational—and often caused by environment, opportunity, and economic pressures—Archer often is less involved in meting out punishment than in serving as a witness to events that were set into play years before as a result of betrayal, meanness, and greed. In *The Galton Case* (1959), for example, Archer examines a case involving a young man of wealth who is kidnapped from his parents' estate when young and then raised in poverty; while he eventually returns to his family as an adult, the harm of the intervening years has taken its toll on all involved. In the series set in the mean streets of southern California, Macdonald's Archer often sympathized with both victims and wrongdoers, viewing the broken dreams of all involved as a sort of metaphor for the ecological breakdown being witnessed during the 1960s and 1970s along California's coast. Highly erudite, Macdonald, with Hammett and Chandler, can be credited with elevating hard-boiled fiction to the status of literature.

The distinction between traditional and hard-boiled treatments of justice is not always clear-cut. Christie, in many ways the doyenne of the traditional school, takes liberties with established notions of punishment and justice in several of her works. For example, in *Murder on the Orient Express*, a novel published in 1934, Christie's detective Hercule Poirot is a passenger on a trans-European train journey that gets stopped by heavy snowfall. Another passenger on the train is stabbed to death during the night, and Poirot proceeds to investigate. Discovering the victim's unsavory past, which includes kidnapping and infanticide, Poirot opts to permit the murderers to go free, feeling that the punishment the victim received was appropriate. Similarly, in her 1953 play, *Witness for the Prosecution*, Christie rejected traditional expectations regarding punishment. In the play, Sir Wilford Robarts, a leading barrister, is engaged to handle the murder defense of Leonard Vole, a working-class young man. Vole, who is married, is accused of murdering Emily French, a wealthy older woman who was infatuated with him. Although Vole's German-born wife, Romaine, claims he was with her at the time of the murder, at the time of the trial she is called as a witness for the prosecution and alleges that Vole indeed committed the crime. After a surprise witness casts doubt upon Romaine's testimony, the jury acquits Vole. A post-verdict explanation of the truth leads to Miss French's murderer being killed, which Robarts refers to as an "execution" rather than a "crime." While traditional insofar as both murders were resolved and life returned to normal, they demonstrated a developing notion of punishment that expanded upon the conception that only one resolution—the penal system—is an option. The works also explored the idea that sometimes crime is justified, or at least not completely wrong, especially when in response to evil actions of others.

Social Consciousness

As social consciousness grew during the 1960s regarding some of the harms caused by government agencies and corporations, a new type of hero emerged, one who sought retribution for clients who had nowhere else to turn. John D. MacDonald created Travis McGee, a character who appeared in 21 novels, beginning with *The Deep Blue Good-by* (1964). McGee, tall, rugged, and athletic, is neither a police officer nor a private investigator, but instead describes himself as a salvage consultant, who assists those seeking to recover property for a fee. McGee, who lives on a 52-foot houseboat docked at Slip F-18 at Bahia Mar Marina in Fort Lauderdale, Florida, takes new cases only when in need of spare cash or when his moral compass indicates that his assistance is needed, such as when one of his few friends is poorly treated or killed. MacDonald also dealt with issues involving Florida's environment, especially being wary of changes brought about by venal developers and corrupt regulatory bodies that put monetary gain over the public good. McGee seeks to punish those with little regard for the environment, working to thwart their plans in such books as *Bright Orange for the Shroud* (1965). Although MacDonald began as a pulp writer, and the McGee series began as paperback-only publications, his stature grew to the point that *The Green Ripper* (1979) was given the National Book Award.

Building upon the belief that punishment was sometimes best handled outside official channels, authors such as Robert B. Parker, Marcia Muller, Sue Grafton, and Sara Paretsky created private investigators beginning in the 1970s who built upon this theme. Parker's private investigator, Spenser, first appeared in *The Godwulf Manuscript* (1973) and often represents individuals who have nowhere else to turn. Parker, who wrote his Ph.D. dissertation on the works of Chandler, Hammett, and Ross Macdonald, expands traditional conceptions of the hard-boiled investigator when he, for example, has Spenser search for a feminist author kidnapped by right-wing extremists in *Looking for Rachel Wallace* (1980) and negotiating between warring urban gangs in *Double Deuce* (1992). Muller, who introduced female private investigator Sharon McCone in *Edwin of the Iron Shoes* (1977), further stretched stereotypes by developing the first woman who ran her own detective agency, frequently working for single mothers, ethnic minorities, and others who were unable to get a fair hearing from the system. McCone works to mete out punishment while often confronting prejudice, causing readers to question how justice is defined in an unfair world. Grafton's female investigator, Kinsey Millhone, first appeared in *A Is for Alibi* (1982). Millhone is independent, competent, and more than willing to serve as a champion for the oppressed, whose tormentors would often escape punishment without her assistance.

Although willing to cooperate with the police, Millhone also is unafraid to work independently if that is the only way she can confront criminals. Paretsky's sleuth, V. I. Warshawski, first appeared in *Indemnity Only* (1982), and in many ways adjusts the hard-boiled genre while also maintaining many of its traditions. Warshawski narrates Paretsky's novels and engages in the types of fisticuffs and gunplay that were first explored by Hammett and Chandler. Unlike the earlier exemplars of the style, however, Warshawski worries that the toughness required by her profession impedes her life and strives to maintain a small cadre of friends and intimates in Chicago, where the series is set. Since many of Warshawski's opponents are pillars of the establishment, including insurance and financial companies, organized religion, and the medical field, to obtain punishment she must often operate by stealth, and is willing to accept punishment that occurs behind closed doors.

Theater

In addition to many works of literature that are adapted for screen, stage, or television, punishment has long been a popular theme in many theater productions on both sides of the Atlantic. Ever since the plays of ancient Greece, suspense, murder, mystery, and punishment have entertained theatergoers. While William Shakespeare dealt with murder and punishment in plays such as *Macbeth* and *Hamlet*, it was during the 19th century that crime melodramas, with their focus on capturing villains so that they could receive appropriate punishment, became popular. While these plays initially focused primarily on the search for a wrongdoer, theater producers soon found that adding suspense regarding the villain's identity was a surefire way to build an audience and increase a play's popularity. As a result, playwrights such as Tom Taylor offered a variety of detectives and police officers in his plays, such as *The Ticket of Leave Man* (1863), which featured the popular detective Hawkshaw. While for most of the 19th century, American stages were happy to import British plays, William Gillette's *Sherlock Holmes* (1899) changed that, and the play enjoyed enormous success for the next three decades.

Plays originally written for the stage by popular authors such as Christie, G. K. Chesterton, and A. A. Milne continued to build interest in the theme of punishment from the 1920s and beyond. Christie especially was a powerhouse of the theater, offering a new play 11 times in 15 years and often having multiple plays running concurrently on both the West End and Broadway. This success was not without its detractors, as evidenced by Tom Stoppard's *The Real Inspector Hound* (1968), which parodied the genre while having two theater critics, Moon and Birdboot, review a ludicrous play set at a country house. The 1970s saw the beginning of increased interest in plays involving punishment, with Anthony Shaffer's *Sleuth* (1970), Ira Levin's *Deathtrap* (1979), John Pielmeier's *Sleight of Hand* (1988), and Rupert Holmes's *Solitary Confinement* (1992) enjoying great critical and box office acclaim. Punishment is and will most likely remain a popular and relevant theme in many theatrical productions.

Stephen T. Schroth
Jason A. Helfer
Diana L. Beck
Knox College

See Also: Dime Novels, Pulps, Thrillers; Film, Punishment in; Grafton, Sue; Hillerman, Tony; Literature and Theater, Crime in; Literature and Theater, Police in; Television, Punishment in.

Further Readings
Cohen, D. A. *Pillars of Salt, Monuments of Grace: New England Crime Literature and the Origins of American Popular Culture, 1674–1860.* New York: Oxford University Press, 1993.
Herbert, R. *The Oxford Companion to Crime and Mystery Writing.* New York: Oxford University Press, 1999.
Palmer, J. *Thrillers: Genesis and Structure of a Popular Genre.* New York: St. Martin's Press, 1979.
Rodensky, L. *The Crime in Mind: Criminal Responsibility and the Victorian Novel.* New York: Oxford University Press, 2003.
Stewart, G. *Death Sentences: Styles of Dying in British Fiction.* Cambridge, MA: Harvard University Press, 1984.
Winks, R. W., ed. *Detective Fiction: A Collection of Critical Essays.* Upper Saddle River, NJ: Prentice Hall, 1980.

Livestock and Cattle Crimes

Livestock and cattle crimes include specific offenses: theft, killing, bestiality, and abuse. In 17th-century New England, colonies kept cattle, oxen, sheep, and hogs. Livestock were crucial to the production of agricultural goods; without these animals, it was nearly impossible to successfully farm, sell, trade, and even survive. Livestock crimes reported during the 17th and 18th centuries included theft, killings, and bestiality.

Accusations of livestock theft in New England were brought against both neighboring colonists and Native Americans. Livestock often broke through fences and strayed onto other properties. New England towns held elections for specific offices designed to handle stray livestock. These elected positions included cattle reeve, swine/hog reeve, goat reeve, hay-ward, and pound-keeper. The duty of a reeve was to watch for stray livestock and prevent the animals from destroying crops. Hay-wards were responsible for caring for both fences and cattle. The pound-keeper caught and cared for stray livestock.

Despite the creation of these offices, not all strays were caught. In these cases, the owner of the wandering animal often claimed livestock was stolen and demanded reparation. Killing wild livestock that trespassed was considered theft because these animals were property. Native Americans killed wild and stray livestock that damaged crops and subsequently collected the remains for meat. As a result, Native Americans were often accused of livestock theft. Additionally, livestock killings were utilized by Native Americans as a retaliatory tactic against the colonists. As colonial dominion spread, Native Americans were concurrently deprived of land. Native Americans who carried out attacks on colonists often slaughtered livestock.

Incidents of bestiality in the colonies did surface in the 17th century. Cases were based upon accusations by individuals claiming to witness the act. Evidence took the form of the likeness in appearance of newborn livestock to the accused person. An individual convicted of bestiality faced a death sentence.

The Eighteenth and Nineteenth Centuries

In the 18th century, the colonies demanded independence from Great Britain. The result was the Revolutionary War. Both British and American military troops took livestock from private properties for their own supply. Theft of livestock by the militaries was a means of survival. There were incidents in which simple destruction of livestock was a tactic employed by British sympathizers. This was an effort to influence the tide of the war.

In the 19th century, theft of livestock in time of war reoccurred. One example is that of the Beefsteak Raid in 1864. The raid was led by Major General Wade Hampton of the Confederate army during the Civil War. The operation was conducted in response to the Confederate army's dwindled food supply. Major General Hampton was successful in rustling more than 2,000 head of cattle from the Union army.

Outside acts of war, the 19th century saw the rise of laws defining livestock crimes. Behaviors that included rebranding or altering the brand of another individual's animal and slaughtering livestock lacking a brand were criminalized. Such laws were enforced as an effort to foil attempts at theft.

In the 19th century, livestock crime intertwined with range wars/feuds, blood feuds, and cattle wars.

Cowboys branding calves to ensure proof of ownership in case of loss or theft in Colorado around 1900. In the 19th century, new laws were created to more clearly cover many types of livestock crimes, including rebranding or altering the brand of another individual's animal. Slaughtering livestock lacking a brand was also made a crime.

These feuds originated from disputes over ownership of land, water rights, murder, livestock theft, or a combination of these factors. Theft, mutilation, and/or killing livestock were used in retaliation. Cattle, sheep, and other livestock ranchers involved in feuds were at odds with each other, homesteaders, Native Americans, and settlers. Infamous examples include the Sutton-Taylor feud, the Pleasant Valley war, and the Graham-Tewksbury feud. Accusations of rebranding and cattle rustling were brought against those who were perceived as threats against an operation's prosperity and monopolization of the cattle/livestock trade.

Horse and cattle theft carried a death sentence. Individuals caught stealing cattle or horses were often hanged for their crimes. Horse and cattle thieves were lynched if a group of vigilantes was able to capture the accused before the authorities did. Execution for cattle and horse theft was seen as a deterrent.

The Twentieth and Twenty-First Centuries

In the 20th and 21st centuries, livestock and cattle crimes were mainly limited to theft. These latter centuries have seen a trend toward livestock theft throughout the United States. Cattle rustling in particular became problematic in the 20th century. Perpetrators of livestock theft can and do resort to strategies to facilitate the crime and elude capture. These strategies have been deemed inhumane under current law. Abusive treatments that can occur during the course of livestock theft include the use of overly aggressive dogs, inhumane slaughtering, and mutilation of the animals as a means to remove any tags, marks, brands, and other identifiers.

In response to livestock crimes and other agrarian-related offenses, jurisdictions developed law enforcement task forces that specialize in agricultural crimes. These and similar law enforcement units are tasked with investigating livestock crimes and communicating with the agricultural community on how to better protect livestock and prevent future victimization.

Rural/agricultural task forces promote target hardening strategies. Target hardening strategies are tactics employed by potential victims that make committing livestock crimes difficult for potential offenders. Emphasis is placed on marking or branding livestock, securing property enclosures, reporting crimes, and other practices.

Penalties for livestock crimes today vary by state. Fines and/or incarceration (depending on the value of livestock destroyed/damaged/stolen) are the norm. Execution for cattle theft is still on the books in many states; however, these sentences are not enforced.

Kimberly Chism
Sam Houston State University

See Also: Capital Punishment; Crime Prevention; Deterrence, Theory of; Executions; Frontier Crime; Hanging; Homestead Act of 1862; Larceny; Lynchings; Native Americans; Rural Police; Vigilantism.

Further Readings

Anderson, Virginia DeJohn. *Creatures of Empire: How Domestic Animals Transformed Early America*. New York: Oxford University Press, 2004.

Bedau, Hugo Adam. *The Death Penalty in America: Current Controversies*. New York: Oxford University Press, 1997.

Field, Ron. *Petersburg 1864–65: The Longest Siege*. New York: Osprey Publishing, 2009.

Friedman, Lawrence M. *Crime and Punishment in American History*. New York: HarperCollins, 1993.

MacLear, Anne Bush. *Early New England Towns: A Comparative Study of Their Development*. New York: Columbia University Press, 1908.

Rosa, Joseph G. *Age of the Gunfighter: Men and Weapons on the Frontier 1840–1900*. New York: Smithmark, 1993.

Sanford, Albert Hart. *The Story of Agriculture in the United States*. New York: D. C. Heath and Co., 1916.

Livingston, Edward

Edward Livingston (1764–1836) was born in Cleveland County, New York, to a prominent family. He represented New York and, later, Louisiana in Congress. From 1831 to 1833, Livingston served as the U.S. secretary of state under President Andrew Jackson. Educated at Princeton University, Livingston graduated in 1781 and was admitted to the bar in 1785. He practiced law in New York City before representing New York in the 4th, 5th, and 6th Congresses. He is well known for his outspokenness. He joined Andrew Jackson and others in a vote against Jay's Treaty, or the British Treaty. Livingston also opposed the Alien and Sedition Laws. He introduced legislation on behalf of American seamen and vehemently attacked the president when he allowed the extradition to Britain of a man claiming American citizenship who had committed murder aboard a British frigate. Livingston served as the U.S. attorney for the District of New York from 1801 to 1803. He was appointed mayor of New York for the same time period. Following an outbreak of yellow fever in the city, he was noted as performing with courage and valor, despite his own sickness with the disease. Livingston moved to New Orleans, Louisiana, in 1804. There, he practiced law, participated in the real estate business, and authored the famous legal code that bears his name.

In 1820, Livingston served as a member of the Louisiana State House of Representatives and was ultimately elected to represent Louisiana in the 18th, 19th, and 20th Congresses. He served in the House until 1829, when he was elected to the Senate. In 1821, the Louisiana legislature requested the development of a new code of criminal law and procedure. Though never adopted by Louisiana, the Livingston Code was heralded for its simplicity and vigor and focused on reform of sentences, due process, and prison discipline. The code called for the abolition of capital punishment and the application of penitentiary labor as a matter of choice and reward for good behavior, bringing with it better housing accommodations. This was a stark contradiction to the perspective that labor should be used as a punishment forced upon the inmate. This code would influence the penal reforms in many countries, including England, France, and Germany, and ultimately be adopted by Guatemala. The philosophy of the code was not retributive or vindictive but rather focused on reform and remediation. Finally completed in 1824 after accidentally being burned, the Livingston Code was not printed until 1833. Written in both English and French, it consisted of four codes—Crimes and Punishments, Procedure, Evidence in Criminal Cases, and Reform and Prison Discipline. The

Edward Livingston around 1823, when he was serving in Congress as a representative from the state of Louisiana and completing his Livingston Code, which influenced reforms to prison systems in Europe and elsewhere.

code focused on reform within the corrections system, including abolishing the death penalty. Livingston's code provided for the conversion of prison labor to a voluntary system rather than a requirement for prisoners.

In 1831, Livingston resigned from the Senate after he was appointed to the cabinet; he served as secretary of state for President Andrew Jackson until 1833. Edward Livingston died on May 23, 1836, after moving to Montgomery Place, a Hudson River estate he had inherited from his sister.

Nicole Hendrix
Radford University

See Also: Codification of Laws; Jackson, Andrew (Administration of); Reform Movements in Justice.

Further Readings
Carosso, Vincent P. and Lawrence H. Leder. "Edward Livingston and Jacksonian Diplomacy." *Louisiana History*, v.7 (Summer 1966).

Cole, Donald B. *Martin Van Buren and the American Political System.* Princeton, NJ: Princeton University Press, 1984.
Friedman, Lawrence. *A History of American Law.* New York: Simon & Schuster, 2005.
U.S. Department of State. "Secretary of State Edward Livingston." http://history.state.gov/departmenthistory/people/livingston-edward (Accessed September 2011).

Lochner v. New York

The Supreme Court struck down a New York law limiting the number of hours one could work in a bakery on the grounds that the law violated the freedom of contract implicit in the due process clause of the Fourteenth Amendment. The case became emblematic of the court's staunch resistance to governmental regulations of the economy from the late 1800s until the New Deal. In 1895, at the urging of the bakers' union, New York passed a law restricting bakers to work no more than 10 hours per day and 60 hours per week. The state claimed the regulation was aimed to protect the health and safety of bakery workers. In 1902, Joseph Lochner, a bakery owner in Utica, was fined for violating the law and appealed to the Supreme Court.

The due process clause states that "no person shall be denied life, liberty, or property without due process of law." Traditionally, the constitutional right to due process had been interpreted to guarantee fair judicial procedures, but the court during this era embraced a theory of substantive due process. Under this doctrine, courts could

New York City bakers carrying a giant loaf of bread in a Labor Day Parade on May 1, 1909, just a few years after the Lochner *decision that struck down a New York law limiting the number of hours one could work in a bakery. New York had passed the original law in 1895, restricting bakers to work no more than 10 hours per day and 60 hours per week at the urging of the bakers' union.*

nullify laws that interfered with a liberty interest, which the court had interpreted to include the right to make contracts without governmental interference. On a 5–4 vote, the Supreme Court overturned Lochner's conviction because the New York law unreasonably restricted the rights of both bakery owners and workers to negotiate terms of employment. Such a restriction amounted to a denial of the liberty of contract and therefore due process. Justice Rufus Peckham acknowledged that the state had a right to exercise its police powers, which are regulations designed to uphold the health, safety, and morals of its citizens. In this case, however, Peckham dismissed the claim that conditions in a bakery were sufficiently unhealthy to justify government regulation.

Lochner is perhaps best remembered for its two dissenting opinions. Justice John Marshall Harlan quoted at length from evidence submitted by the state describing the health risks bakers undertake at their jobs. These studies convinced Harlan that New York was not abusing its police powers in passing this regulation. Justice Oliver Wendell Holmes, Jr., went further and accused the majority of basing its decision on laissez faire economics. Holmes argued that the Constitution was not meant to embody any particular economic theory. Instead, Holmes believed that judges must defer to policy decisions made by the elected branches of government. According to Progressive critics, *Lochner* represented an abuse of judicial power for failing to allow legislatures enough discretion to address modern economic problems. After *Lochner*, states and the federal government attempted other means of economic regulation, many of which the Supreme Court struck down on freedom of contract grounds. This time period in the court's history is often referred to as the *Lochner* era. Facing entrenched judicial hostility to New Deal economic programs, President Franklin D. Roosevelt in 1937 proposed expanding the size of the Supreme Court so he could appoint justices friendly to his agenda.

Though Roosevelt's plan failed, the Supreme Court felt sufficiently threatened that it changed its course that year and overturned *Lochner* in the case *West Coast Hotel v. Parrish*. The next year in *United States v. Carolene Products*, the court announced that it would demonstrate greater deference to legislatures in judging the constitutionality of economic regulations, which formed the basis on which the current court operates. While the court no longer recognizes freedom of contract as a liberty interest under the due process clause, it does currently extend substantive due process protection to other liberty interests, such as privacy. Many legal scholars have criticized the *Lochner* Court for being out of touch with the changes to the American economy brought about during the Industrial Revolution. Recently, Howard Gillman has attempted to portray *Lochner* in a more favorable light by arguing that the decision is based on Jacksonian values of economic individualism. Paul Kens, however, maintains that the dominant concern of *Lochner* was a commitment to social Darwinism—that market forces alone should be allowed to dictate economic survival.

William D. Blake
University of Texas

See Also: Due Process; *Holden v. Hardy*; Holmes, Oliver Wendell, Jr.; *Muller v. Oregon*.

Further Readings
Gillman, Howard. *The Constitution Beseiged: The Rise and Demise of Lochner Era Police Powers Jurisprudence*. Durham, NC: Duke University Press, 1993.
Kens, Paul. *Lochner v. New York: Economic Regulation on Trial*. Lawrence: University of Kansas Press, 1998.
Lochner v. New York, 198 U.S. 45 (1905).
McCloskey, Robert G. and Sanford Levinson. *The American Supreme Court*. Chicago: University of Chicago Press, 2010.

Los Angeles, California

Twenty-first-century Los Angeles is California's most populous city (with 3.8 million in 2010) in a gigantic sprawling metropolitan area with 12 million residents in over 80 contiguous municipalities. Los Angeles city, county, and metropolitan areas have provided the locations, backdrops, and story lines for classic and contemporary works of crime fiction, including Raymond Chandler's *The Big Sleep* (1939) and James Ellroy's *The Black Dahlia* (published in 1987 but based on the unsolved murder of Elizabeth Short in January 1947), police procedural radio and television shows, including *Dragnet* and more recently *Law and Order: Los Angeles*, and numerous Hollywood and independent movies of all genres. Similarly, the city has witnessed sensational and high-profile crimes and trials throughout much of its post-1848 U.S. existence. These include William Edward Hickman's kidnap, murder, and dismemberment of a 12-year-old girl in 1927, the "Red Light Bandit" robberies and rape of Caryl Chessman in the late 1940s, serial "Lonely Hearts" killer Harvey Glatman in the 1950s, the Manson "Family" killings of August 1969, the Menendez brothers' trial in August 1989 for the murder of their parents, the 1995 trial and acquittal of former football star O. J. Simpson for the murder of his ex-wife and her friend in June 1994, and the May 2009 conviction of music producer Phil Spector for the murder of actress Lana Clarkson.

In 2010 Los Angeles experienced the lowest number of homicides since 1967, part of a downward trend since the early 2000s (the 2003 homicide rate was 8.7 percent). There were 297 murders in 2010, compared to over 600 per year during the 1990s. Many commentators attributed the decline to better policing and a more disciplined police force but complex economic, political, demographic, and cultural factors were undoubtedly also important in accounting for the decline. High homicide rates have been part of the city's history since it was a chaotic frontier town in the mid-19th century. Plagued by frontier violence, war between Mexico and the United States, political instability, racial hostilities and lethal interethnic confrontations between Anglos, Hispanics, and Native Americans, disputes over land and wealth, and high tolerance for extralegal violence, Los Angeles County was the most violent county in California from the 1830s to the 1850s. The homicide rate for the late 1830s and early 1840s may have been as high as 100 per 100,000 adults per year, rising to 198 per 100,000 in the late 1860s, linked in part to increased availability of revolvers, but then falling to 23 per 100,000 by the early 1890s.

A more diversified economy, gender-balanced population, greater political stability, and declining proportions of non-Anglos in the population seem to account for the decline. Nevertheless, Chinese and Hispanic residents of Los Angeles continued to experience greater hostility, prejudice, and discrimination and thus higher rates of interracial and intraracial homicide. The gap between Hispanic and Anglo homicide rates continued to widen in the early 20th century as Anglos "benefited from decent urban schooling, better policing, and higher-paid factory jobs and salaried work." As in San Francisco, Chinese residents were often confined to the most dangerous and crime-ridden neighborhoods with high rates of property crime, interpersonal violence, and vice-related offenses. By contrast, the city's smaller African American community, often linked to the service economy and semiskilled job opportunities, had a relatively low homicide rate but were still victims of interracial violence.

1900–1950

During the first half of the 20th century, Los Angeles became geographically more complex and demographically more diverse. As a key transportation hub with extensive rail, increasing road, and later air links, and a growing wage-labor economy, it attracted both native-born migrants and legal and illegal immigrants. The population of the city of Los Angeles had reached 500,000 by 1920. Mexican American arrivals were central to the burgeoning agricultural, manufacturing, and service sectors. The World War II years and related wartime industrial expansion were a watershed in African American migration, while the post-1960s immigration streams of Mexicans, Central Americans, Asians, and Europeans have produced a multiracial and multicultural city in every sense.

Prior to 1979, law enforcement in Los Angeles was overwhelmingly white and male. A volunteer constable force was set up in 1853 and the first paid force of six officers was established in 1869. The Los Angeles Police Department (LAPD) had 130 officers in 1903 and 544 by 1920. It now has over 10,000 officers. The LAPD is generally considered to be the first city police force to hire women, albeit in limited gender-specific duties. Alice Stebbins Wells, a white, middle-class, 37-year-old assistant pastor and social worker, was appointed in spring 1910 as a police officer assigned to the Juvenile Bureau. In 1914 the LAPD set up a City Mother's Bureau in which female officers specialized in crime prevention, for example, through street patrols and vice investigations, and were central in the protection of adolescent girls and vulnerable children. Wells inspired many female recruits across the country and in 1915 became founder and president of the International Association of Policewomen.

August Vollmer, leading police reformer and advocate of scientific policing and enhanced professionalism during the Progressive Era, became Los Angeles police chief 1923–24 at the behest of the Citizens Anti-Crime Commission, which sought to reorganize a police department that was riddled with corruption and ineffectual at controlling crime, particularly gambling, illegal liquor, and prostitution during the national Prohibition period, and to improve the city's squalid and overcrowded jail system. Vollmer's reorganization of the force and his intelligence-gathering methods were not popular with the rank and file, but the LAPD did undergo improvements in recruitment systems, communications, and technical expertise and in detection and investigation. Its reputation for corruption, partisanship, and conservatism remained.

LAPD relations with Mexican American and Latino communities throughout the 20th century were punctuated with violent confrontations and police brutality. During the 1920s and 1930s the LAPD's long-standing policy of aiding the antilabor business establishment and protecting vice brought it into conflict with non-Anglo communities. LAPD officers generally viewed Mexican Americans with acute suspicion and believed that violence and crime were biological characteristics of this group, often with tragic consequences, as demonstrated in the 1942-43 Sleepy Lagoon case. The murder of José Díaz led to the indiscriminate roundup of 600 Mexican/Chicano youths and subsequent trial and conviction (later reversed on appeal) of 17 members of the 38th Street Gang. Wartime hysteria over a reputed wave of Mexican American juvenile delinquency, altercations between white naval personnel and Mexican American youths, and heavy-handed police tactics contributed to the June 1943 Zoot Suit Riots.

The 1950s and 1960s

Police Chief William H. Parker (1950–66) sought to transform the LAPD into the model for professional big-city police departments, but his administration was also defined by strict authoritarianism, strident anticommunism, and acute suspicion of minority civil rights. Increased heroin use in the barrios and ghettos of Los Angeles from the 1950s also shaped police attitudes and suspicions. In the years after World War II, Mexican American and African American communities grew ever more frustrated with LAPD conduct and tactics. In December 1951, over 50 LAPD officers brutally beat seven young men, five of whom were Hispanic, in their custody at the central city jail. African American residents were increasingly frustrated by poor race relations, Jim Crow discrimination, and police violence, and there were several confrontations between black civil rights protesters, Nation of Islam members, urban black residents, and the police during the 1960s. Police brutality and misconduct became a powerful political organizing focus for activists in the many social protest movements of the decade. The LAPD police infiltrators were accused of engaging in criminal activities in order to disrupt and destroy Chicano and Black protest organizations.

In August 1965, the arrest of a young African American male for drunken driving by a white highway patrolman, followed by a scuffle with arriving LAPD officers, precipitated the Watts Riot in south central Los Angeles that required National Guard intervention, left over 1,000 injured and 34 dead, and resulted in substantial property damage. Complex economic, political, and police brutality factors framed the larger context for such a serious outbreak of urban disorder and further events in 1970–71, including the Chicano Moratorium Riot and the killing of journalist Ruben Salazar. Charges of police brutality and political repression followed the LAPD into the 1970s.

The Rodney King Riots

Late-20th-century attempts to depoliticize the LAPD and improve community relations suffered a major setback in March 1991 when a bystander videotaped four white police officers beating African American resident Rodney King. Images of the officers using a stun gun on King, repeatedly kicking him, and hitting him with batons were

Los Angeles Police Department officers dressed in riot gear in preparation for an immigrant rights march for amnesty in downtown Los Angeles, California, on May 1, 2006. The department had only 130 officers in 1903 and 544 by 1920. In a measure of the city's growth and complexity in the early 21st century, the Los Angeles Police Department is now made up of over 10,000 officers.

broadcast around the world, generating acute public outrage and political denunciation. At the subsequent trial, the four officers were acquitted and the city exploded in violence. There were echoes of 1965 as 60 people died and thousands were injured, and a billion dollars of property damage resulted.

The reputation of the LAPD was tarnished again with the late 1990s Rampart CRASH (Community Resources Against Street Hoodlums) corruption scandal. Street gangs had existed in Los Angeles for much of the 20th century but grew dramatically in number and size from the late 1960s to become alliances of neighborhood gangs that were part of larger networks of Crips, Bloods, and others. Anxieties over gang warfare became more acute in the context of a more visible globalization of the drug trade, immigrant smuggling, and money laundering. CRASH was an anti-gang program implemented in the early 1990s but became synonymous with unwarranted arrests of largely Latino residents in an area to the west of central Los Angeles, drug dealing by officers, witness intimidation, planting of evidence, illegal shootings, and other problematic activities. The appointment of William J. Bratton in October 2002 as LAPD chief of police signaled a willingness to restore the department's reputation and to implement a robust crime-fighting strategy that many commentators suggest has succeeded as evidenced by the city's declining homicide rate.

Vivien Miller
University of Nottingham

See Also: 1961 to 1980 Primary Documents; African Americans; California; Hispanic Americans; King, Rodney; Police, Contemporary; Police Abuse; Reform, Police and Enforcement; Riots; Vollmer, August.

Further Readings

Appier, Janis. *Policing Women: The Sexual Politics of Law Enforcement and the LAPD.* Philadelphia: Temple University Press, 1998.

Dunn, William. *The Gangs of Los Angeles.* Lincoln, NE: iUniverse, 2007.

Escobar, Edward J. "The Dialectics of Repression: The Los Angeles Police Department and the Chicano Movement, 1969–1971." *Journal of American History,* v.79/4 (1993).

Escobar, Edward J. *Race, Police, and the Making of a Political Identity: Mexican Americans and the Los Angeles Police Department, 1900–1945.* Berkeley: University of California Press, 1999.

Monkkonen, Eric H. "Homicide in Lost Angeles, 1827–2002." *Journal of Interdisciplinary History,* v.36/2 (2005).

Odem, Mary. "Single Mothers, Delinquent Daughters, and the Juvenile Court in Early 20th Century Los Angeles." *Journal of Social History,* v.25/1 (1991).

Pagain, Eduardo Obregan. *Murder at the Sleepy Lagoon: Zoot Suits, Race, and Riot in Wartime LA.* Chapel Hill: University of North Carolina Press, 2006.

Parrish, Michael. *For the People: Inside the Los Angeles County District Attorney's Office, 1850–2000.* Los Angeles, CA: Angel City Press, 2001.

Roth, Randolph. *American Homicide.* Cambridge, MA: Harvard University Press, 2009.

Stevens, Errol Wayne. *Radical L.A.: From Coxey's Army to the Watts Riots, 1894–1965.* Norman: University of Oklahoma Press, 2005.

Louisiana

Inextricably linked with race, class, and politics, Louisiana has had a colorful and sensationalistic history of crime, police, and punishment. New Orleans has frequently ranked as the "murder capital" of the United States, and Louisiana's prison system, primarily the Louisiana State Penitentiary at Angola, generally known as Angola, has alternately been called "the worst prison in the United States," "a sewer of degradation," the "bloodiest prison in the south," and "the Alcatraz of the south." In his book *Black Rage in New Orleans,* Leonard N. Moore claims that since World War II, "The New Orleans Police Department has been one of the most brutal, corrupt and incompetent police units in the United States."

When Louisiana became a state in 1812, 66 percent of the population of New Orleans was African American (one-third were slaves). Thus, New Orleans was initially considered a tripartite society (slaves, free blacks, and whites). About 25 percent of its population was French, Irish and German immigrants. With increasing legal restrictions, the free black population decreased, making the city 33 percent black before the Civil War. Jim Crow segregation quickly changed New Orleans into a biracial city: People were categorized as either black or white, both legally and socially. Although Irish immigrants could frequently be found in the criminal courts of antebellum New Orleans, at the same time, major concerns centered on controlling the black population. Issues of race marked the development of crime, policing, and punishment in New Orleans and in Louisiana.

New Orleans maintained a population that was 33 percent black until the black rural migration to the city in the late 1940s and early 1950s. By the year 2000, the city was 66 percent black. Black rural migrants came to New Orleans for better jobs, but they were relegated to the low-paid unskilled sector of the labor force. This second migration to New Orleans, coupled with the ensuing white flight, left poor black citizens bearing the brunt of the city's increasing social problems: increasing crime, corrupt police, and harsh punishments.

Crime

Louisiana's earliest criminal code was the "Crimes and Offences" section of the Orleans Territorial Acts, 1806. Commonly known as the Code Noir, or Black Code, it defined particularly severe and unequal punishments designed to control slaves and free people of color, thereby maintaining the institution of slavery. Many of these codes were reinstated during the late 1800s and became what are commonly known as the Jim Crow laws. Louisiana did not have a codified criminal code until 1942.

New Orleans, the largest city in Louisiana, has been portrayed as a crime-ridden and violent town since before the Civil War. Antebellum visitors to New Orleans observed that crime was the "ruling element in New Orleans society," with at least 225 criminal homicides between 1857 and 1860 and a homicide rate of 35 per 100,000, making New Orleans a more dangerous city than others of its size at the time. (By comparison, Philadelphia had a homicide rate of 3.6, and Boston's rate was about 7.5 during corresponding years.) Lesser crimes also clogged the lower courts. Although prostitution was not a crime, activities surrounding it were. As a result of indirect attempts to control prostitution, women caught up in wholesale sweeps were dragged to court, charged with disorderly conduct, then usually fined and released. Gambling, duels, and vagrancy also kept the lower courts filled, and upon the eve of almost every election, the city braced itself for mob violence in support of or in opposition to the candidates.

Pervasive violence, represented by vigilantism, lynchings, and massacres, characterized Louisiana in the second half of the 19th century: The dominant (generally white) class resisted the enfranchisement of former slaves and often took the law into its own hands to undermine it. During Reconstruction, homicides occurred primarily in the rural areas of northwestern Louisiana. Furthermore, according to Gilles Vandal, Louisiana's post–Civil War homicides were not black-on-black crime but were mainly white-on-black, a preview of the state's later pattern of lynching.

Post–Civil War New Orleans also suffered riots, lynchings, and a general deterioration of law and order, especially after Reconstruction. Federal supervision and a racially integrated New Orleans police force both controlled the level of violence during Reconstruction but at the same time created a general disrespect for the law within the upper class. With the dismantling of the integrated force and dwindling funds, vigilantes combated local crime waves. At times, the community effectively reverted to a frontier level of law enforcement. Numerous murders of and by political figures occurred, with the police themselves often perpetrators of the violence. In New Orleans, disrespect for life and property was so prevalent after Reconstruction that local newspapers were nostalgic for the "safer" previous years. Culminating with the 1890 assassination of New Orleans Police Chief David C. Hennessy, and the consequent lynching of 11 Italians in retaliation in 1891, New Orleans and Louisiana became bywords for political corruption and general lawlessness.

After Reconstruction, lynching was employed as the most brutal form of social control, shaped by economic and cultural contexts in which whites lynched blacks. Louisiana's per capita lynching rate was ranked second behind Mississippi; the state had the top three lynching parishes (counties) in the United States: Quachita, Caddo, and Bossier. Consistent with the pattern of homicides during Reconstruction, all three ranking parishes were in the northern part of the state. Ending in the 1940s, lynchings did not prevent legal executions, and capital punishment laws had interesting similarities to the original pre–Civil War Black Codes. For instance, in the late 19th and early 20th centuries, the death penalty was possible for not only homicide but also for rape, poison with intent to murder, lying in wait with intent to murder, and assault with a dangerous weapon in perpetration of or attempting to perpetrate arson.

Corruption

The focus of crime in Louisiana intensified on political corruption in 1939, when Governor Richard Leache's administration was exposed as one of the most corrupt in the history of Louisiana politics. Known as the scandals of 1939—the Louisiana Hayride—Governor Leache, along with scores of lesser government officials, was convicted of a variety of federal crimes such as income tax evasion, embezzlement and using the mail to defraud. The federal government, which led the investigation, also revealed that Leache, along with New Orleans Mayor Robert Maestri and Lt. Governor Earl Long, encouraged the Mafia to continue to expand its illegal activities in Louisiana, mainly in the area of gambling. One of the most shocking revelations of the scandal centered on Louisiana State University (LSU). The university's president, James Monroe Smith, among other university officials, was found to have illegally used millions of dollars of the university's funds. President Smith, the only one of the group to be convicted of state offenses, was sentenced to 8–24 years of hard labor in the Louisiana State Penitentiary at Angola. For his infamy, the former LSU president appeared on the cover of the December 11, 1939, issue of *Life* magazine, garbed in the convict's black and white striped uniform. Despite such sensationalized corruption, Smith later held the position of superintendant of vocational rehabilitation at Angola, where he died in June 1949.

With the exception of an increase from 1989 to 1993, since the 1970s, national crime rates have generally decreased. Louisiana's crime rates have followed the same general pattern. Yet even as Louisiana's murder/nonnegligent manslaughter rate has continued to decrease along with the rest of the nation (from 32.7 in 1995 to 11.8 in 2009 according to the Federal Bureau of Investigation's Uniform Crime Report), New Orleans managed to maintain the dubious distinction of being named the murder capital of the United States at least three times, in 1994, 2000, and 2008.

Police

Policing in Louisiana has always been connected to issues of race, ethnicity, politics, and corruption. One of the earliest policing activities in Louisiana was performed by the members of the slave patrols, designed to control slaves in the rural areas through the use of local ordinances and the directives of the Black Code of 1806. After Reconstruction and during the Jim Crow period, one of Louisiana's main policing functions was to maintain segregation, formally and informally, as depicted in lynchings and in the refusal of the police to support school integration through the 1950s and 1960s.

According to Dennis Rousey, the development of paramilitary municipal police forces in the south predated those of the north (with New Orleans unique in initiating a military-style police force in 1805). Shreveport, situated in Reconstruction's northern "Bloody Caddo" Parish, followed with the establishment of its force in 1839. Baton Rouge, Louisiana's capital, did not create its force until just after the Civil War, with the appointment of its first chief of police in 1865. The Louisiana State Police was created in 1936.

From their inception, Louisiana's police departments were white institutions. Although during Reconstruction the New Orleans Metropolitan Police Department had a proportionate number of black police with full powers, integration ended with cessation of federal supervision and Republican control of the city in 1877. The decreasing numbers of New Orleans' black police officers led to abusive practices in the African American community by a dominant white police force. By the late 19th century, the New Orleans police force had deteriorated into a notoriously corrupt, undersized, and underfunded organization. Its reputation for brutality against African Americans flourished and was sustained through the 20th century.

New Orleans did not integrate its force again until the 1950s, when two officers were assigned to patrol African American neighborhoods. By 1965, only 3 percent of Louisiana police were African American, and none were in supervisory positions. The New Orleans Police Department was arguably one of the most brutal, corrupt, and incompetent police units in the United States in the postwar period. Reform was a top priority in 1995 when Mayor Marc Morial appointed Richard Pennington of Washington, D.C., as the police chief of New Orleans. Pennington instituted various policies that resulted in a striking decrease in the overall homicide rate, from 363 in 1995 to 158 in 1999.

After a failed mayoral campaign, Pennington left in 2002, and the city's murder rate has escalated ever since. The inefficient, illegal, and corrupt behaviors of the New Orleans police in the aftermath of Hurricane Katrina, coupled with recent convictions of a number of police officers, have not changed the public's impression of this force.

Punishment

Researchers claim that current mass imprisonment in Louisiana is a backlash against the civil rights movement. With respect to the racial proportion of the prison population, the Civil War was the most decisive event for the south in the history of penology because it changed the racial composition of prisons from primarily white to primarily black males. Yet Louisiana was unique. While it is commonly believed that slaves were not found in southern prisons before the Civil War, they made up one-third of the population in Louisiana's first

Prisoners loading lumber onto a riverboat at the Angola State Penitentiary landing on the Mississippi River in Louisiana around 1900. Angola has at times been called the worst prison in the United States. Today it covers 18,000 acres and houses 5,000 prisoners, 90 percent of whom are serving life sentences and will likely die there.

penitentiary at Baton Rouge. As Louisiana turned to imprisonment to control newly freed slaves after the Civil War, the racial distribution of prisoners soon reversed; the population became almost 90 percent black by the 1890s.

In 1835, a penitentiary was built in Baton Rouge for the purpose of saving money that the state had previously paid to Orleans Parish for housing state convicted felons in the parish prison, the local jail in New Orleans. Not realizing the anticipated savings or profit, Louisiana began leasing its prisoners in 1844, a practice that continued until December 31, 1900, with a short interruption during the Civil War. After the war, prisoners were subcontracted by the lessee, Samuel L. James, to railroads, former plantations, and back to the state to rebuild the levees and the roads that had suffered wartime destruction. Brutality and high death rates were a constant under the lease.

Leased prisoners first appeared at Angola, the location of the future state penitentiary, in 1880; James purchased the former plantation and brought convict women to work in his household, and some men to work the plantation. The state purchased the James plantation at Angola when it resumed control of the prisoners on January 1, 1901. Angola was then a complex of approximately 8,000 acres. When the state was able to purchase 10,000 more acres in 1922, Angola became the largest prison in the United States. Angola then became the only penitentiary in the state when the Baton Rouge facility closed in 1917. A facility for first offenders was opened in 1957 at DeQuincy in western Louisiana; it was also used to relieve the overcrowding from Angola.

Women were incarcerated at Angola in a camp separate from the men. They were eventually transferred to a women's facility in St. Gabriel, approximately 40 miles southeast of Angola, in 1961; they remained under the administrative control of Angola for another decade, until a brand-new facility was built for them at St. Gabriel.

Because of segregation, the first institutions for juveniles that opened in 1904 and 1926 were for white boys and white girls, respectively. Dependent African American children were found in local jails and the state penitentiary until 1948, when the State Industrial School for Colored Youth opened. This facility became coed in 1956 and desegregated in 1969, when the U.S. District Court ordered desegregation of juvenile facilities.

In 1995, Human Rights Watch issued a critical report of Louisiana's secure juvenile facilities. After a Department of Justice lawsuit in 1998, Louisiana separated the juvenile system from the adult system in 2004, by establishing Youth Services for the state's Office of Juvenile Justice. Youth Services set a goal of decreasing the number of juveniles in custodial facilities, and the result has been a 77 percent reduction in the custodial youth population over the past 10 years. Three secure facilities for boys in different parts of the state and one for girls presently hold a total population of 496 juveniles.

Louisiana Prisons Today

The 18,000 acres that comprise today's Louisiana State Penitentiary at Angola actually consist of multiple plantations, some of which were originally owned by one of the largest slave traders in the south, Isaac Franklin. Angola is considered a model of plantation imprisonment because the work is primarily agricultural. Similar to slaves, prisoners were classified according to their physical abilities and were worked from sunup to sundown. Angola prison laborers grow most of the vegetables for the prisoners living there and for a number of other penal institutions in the state. A series of investigative reports throughout the 20th century revealed such brutality at Angola that it was labeled the worst prison in the United States. Attempts at penal reform throughout the 1900s were short-lived because the state legislature provided only sporadic financial support for the penitentiary, wrongly believing that it should be self-supporting. In 1974, when Judge E. Gordon West observed that the conditions at Angola "would shock the conscience of a civilized society," the legislature was finally forced to financially support the prison system under federal court order, and meaningful penal reform in Louisiana began. The Louisiana Department of Corrections was the only statewide system accredited by the American Corrections Association in 1996. Angola is known for having the award-winning prison news magazine *The Angolite* and one of the best prison hospice programs in the United States. Angola also has a Bible College that awards associate and bachelor's degrees in Christian ministry.

As of 2010, the Louisiana Department of Corrections consists of 12 adult facilities that hold more than 40,000 prisoners, 70 percent of whom are African American. Women comprise 6.4 percent (2,630) of the total population; half of them are African American. Unique among state correctional systems, Louisiana houses half of its population in local jails throughout the state, under contract with local sheriffs. Louisiana has ranked in the top three for incarceration rates since 1987 and took the lead in 1998 with a per capita incarceration rate of 709 per 100,000. By 2009, Louisiana had the highest incarceration rate (881) in the Western world.

The get-tough movement of the United States has affected Louisiana with the passage of truth in sentencing laws and the elimination of the 10–6 rule in 1974, which had allowed life-sentenced prisoners to be considered for parole after they served 10 years and six months. In fact, it was an almost automatic release. Now, almost 25 percent of Louisiana prisoners serve natural life sentences (without parole). As most of the natural life and virtual life prisoners are housed at Angola, 90 percent of Angola's 5,000-prisoner population is predicted to die there. Meanwhile, recommendations for pardon and parole for the majority of offenders have almost come to a halt compared to previous eras. The percentage of parole board—recommended releases has decreased from 15.4 percent in 1994 to 4 percent in 2010. A proposed 2009 bill that would have eliminated the pardon and parole boards failed to pass the state legislature. Recognizing the financial costs of such an imprisonment rate, Louisiana has recommended and implemented various corrective actions. However, even the Department of Corrections notes in its 2009 internal analysis that none of the proposed changes that affect prisoner populations at the entry point will have an immediate impact on reducing the current prison population.

With a budget shortfall for the past two years, and facing what legislators have called an "over-the-cliff" budget year 2010–11, the governor recommended that Louisiana sell three of its adult prison facilities to help alleviate financial troubles. After strong opposition by prison employees, this proposal failed. Recommendations by professional corrections administrators and outside experts historically have gone unheeded. Whether Louisiana will implement the most recent penal reform recommendations of national think-tanks such as PEW, the Vera Institute, and the JFA Institute of Washington, D.C., is anyone's guess.

Marianne Fisher-Giorlando
Grambling State University

See Also: 1851 to 1900 Primary Documents; 1961 to 1980 Primary Documents; 1921 to 1940 Primary Documents; African Americans; Corrections; Lynchings; New Orleans, Louisiana; Prison Privatization; *Roberts v. Louisiana*.

Further Readings
Carleton, Mark T. *Politics and Punishment: The History of Louisiana State Penal System*. Baton Rouge: Louisiana State University Press, 1971.
Louisiana Department of Public Safety and Corrections. "Monthly Statistical Performance Report: Briefing Book." http://www.corrections.state.la.us/quicklinks/statistics/statistics-briefing-book (Accessed February 2011).
Louisiana Office of Juvenile Justice. "Demographic Profiles of Youth in Custody." http://ojj.la.gov/ojj/files/Demographic%20Profiles%20for%20Secure_9.pdf (Accessed February 2011).

Moore, Leonard N. *Black Rage in New Orleans: Police Brutality and African American Activism From World War II to Hurricane Katrina*. Baton Rouge: Louisiana State University Press, 2010.
Pfeifer, Michael J. *Rough Justice: Lynching and American Society 1874–1947*. Urbana: University of Illinois Press, 2006.
Rousey, Dennis C. *Policing the Southern City: New Orleans 1805–1889*. Baton Rouge: Louisiana State University Press, 1996.
U.S. Department of Justice. *Prisoners in State and Federal Institutions on December 31, 1971, 1972, and 1973*. Washington, DC: U.S. Government Printing Office, 1975.
Vandal, Gilles. *Rethinking Southern Violence: Homicides in Post–Civil War Louisiana, 1866–1884*. Columbus: Ohio State University Press, 2000.

Loving v. Virginia

Loving v. Virginia was a 1967 U.S. Supreme Court decision striking down Virginia's anti-miscegenation statutory scheme that banned marriages between white and nonwhite people. The court held that the racial classifications of certain Virginia statutes restricted the freedom to marry and violated the equal protection clause and the due process clause of the Fourteenth Amendment. The racial classifications constituted arbitrary and invidious discrimination because marriage is a fundamental right upon which the state cannot infringe. The case established marriage as a category requiring the highest standard of judicial review.

Richard Loving, a white man, and Mildred Jeter, a black woman, were residents of Virginia who legally married in the District of Columbia. The couple returned to Virginia and resided in Caroline County. A grand jury indicted them in 1958 because of Virginia's restrictions on interracial marriage. The couple pleaded guilty. The trial judge suspended the couple's sentence of one year of jail time, provided that they leave Virginia for 25 years. The couple moved to Washington, D.C., where, with the help of the American Civil Liberties Union (ACLU), they sued to set aside the sentence as offending the Fourteenth Amendment. After procedural delays in state court, the couple instituted a class action suit in federal court, and eventually their case reached the Supreme Court of Appeals of Virginia, which upheld the antimiscegenation statutes. The couple appealed to the U.S. Supreme Court.

Two Virginia statutes were at stake in the holding. The first voided all marriages between a white person and a "colored person." The second prohibited white people from marrying a person of any race that was not white. Section 1-14 of the Virginia Code defined a colored person as "every person in whom there is ascertainable any Negro blood." It defined American Indians as "every person not a colored person having one fourth or more of American Indian blood." The case was argued before the court in April 1967. Chief Justice Earl Warren, writing for a unanimous court in June 1967, reasoned that the Fourteenth Amendment, as one of three Civil War Amendments—the other two being the Thirteenth and Fifteenth Amendments—sought to eliminate state-sanctioned racial discrimination. The Equal Protection Clause of the Fourteenth Amendment therefore demanded strict judicial scrutiny of any statutory racial classification. Thus, to be valid, such a racial classification had to be necessary to achieve a permissible state objective besides racial discrimination.

The Virginia statutes were not necessary to achieve a valid state objective. The purpose of the Virginia statutes was solely to prohibit and punish interracial marriage. Therefore, the statutes were invalidated as unconstitutional pursuant to the Fourteenth Amendment. When the case was decided, 16 states had antimiscegenation statutes on their books. Antimiscegenation statutes were common in America from the colonial period until this court decision. The Warren Court established that although states had rights to regulate marriage under their police power, state power over marriage was not unlimited. The fact that the Virginia statutes applied equally to whites and nonwhites was irrelevant because the statutes contained racial classifications that triggered high levels of judicial scrutiny. The court would not entertain the argument of equal application of the laws because states could not be permitted to equally apply that which violated the U.S. Constitution. Equal application, in other words, could not immunize statutes from the critical scrutiny of federal judges. Justice Warren found that no overriding purpose justified the Virginia statutes, which were designed to maintain white supremacy. This case is significant because of its effect on the civil rights movement and its interpretation of the Fourteenth Amendment. After this decision, no state could forbid a person from marrying a person of another race.

Allen Mendenhall
Auburn University

See Also: Civil Rights Laws; Constitution of the United States of America; Race, Class, and Criminal Law; Race-Based Crimes; Racism.

Further Readings
Alonso, Karen. *Loving v. Virginia: Interracial Marriage.* Berkeley Heights, NJ: Enslow, 2000.
Gold, Susan Dudley. *Lifting the Ban Against Interracial Marriage.* Tarrytown, NJ: Marshall Cavendish, 2008.
Newbeck, Phyl. *Virginia Hasn't Always Been for Lovers: Interracial Marriage Bans and the Case of Richard and Mildred Loving.* Carbondale: Southern Illinois University Press, 2004.

Luciano, "Lucky"

American organized crime figure "Lucky" Luciano (1897–1962) was born Salvatore Lucania in Lercara Friddi, Sicily, near Palermo, and immigrated to the United States with his family in 1906. Lucania quickly became enmeshed with the criminal underworld of New York City's Lower East Side, notching his first arrest (for shoplifting) a year after his arrival. As he reached his teen years, Luciano graduated to shakedown antics and, through physical intimidation, assumed a position of leadership in the junior gangland of his neighborhood. As a teenager, he was imprisoned for six months for selling narcotics; upon his release, he resumed his criminal career. With the advent of Prohibition in 1920, Luciano's horizons broadened. He was at the near-midpoint of the ambitious cohort of criminals born between 1892 and 1900 that historian Mark Haller identifies as ascending in power during Prohibition. Within this group of predominantly Italian and Jewish immigrants and first-generation American slum dwellers, Luciano distinguished himself quite early. Associating himself with several groups involved with importing—and hijacking—shipments of illegal spirits, Luciano became a rising star in the bootlegging world, associating with notables like Meyer Lansky, Frank Costello, Benjamin "Bugsy" Siegel, Vito Genovese, "Legs" Diamond, "Lepke" Buchalter, Jacob "Gurrah" Shapiro, and Arthur Flegenheimer ("Dutch" Schultz).

In 1927, mob boss Joe Masseria enlisted Luciano as his chief assistant, largely due to his genius for organization. By 1931, however, Massiera, realizing perhaps Luciano's ambitions to be more than a lieutenant, became dissatisfied with Luciano. Learning of his boss's displeasure, Luciano worked with rival gang leader Salvatore Maranzano to engineer Massiera's execution-style murder, clearing the way for Maranzano to assume the top position in New York's tenuous criminal hierarchy. Later that year, Luciano arranged Maranzano's murder, effectively eliminating the last of the old-guard "Mustache Pete" mobsters from leadership and marking the final step in his cohort's assumption of control over New York City's organized crime. For the next five years, Luciano reigned as a power broker in New York's criminal underworld, allegedly earning a fortune, first in bootlegged liquor and, after the repeal of Prohibition in 1933, from narcotics smuggling and wholesaling, illegal gambling, and prostitution. Reportedly, one of Luciano's lieutenants had taken over the "combination" of bookers who controlled much of the city's prostitution under orders from Lucky himself.

In early 1936, a strike force under the aegis of special prosecutor Thomas E. Dewey conducted citywide raids that netted prostitutes, madams, and others associated with the sex trade. Ultimately, Dewey used the testimony of those arrested in the raids to win a conviction against Luciano for a variety of prostitution-related violations. His conviction was upheld on appeal, and he was sentenced to 35 years in prison. After 10 years in prison, Luciano saw his sentence commuted by now Governor Dewey, on grounds of his wartime service to national security, which likely meant guaranteeing labor peace and security along New York's docks. He was immediately deported to Italy, where, it was alleged, he continued to exercise influence over American organized crime and may even have escalated his narcotics smuggling. Wishing to return to the United States, he settled for a move to Fulgencio Batista's Cuba, but U.S. government pressure forced his speedy return to Italy.

In Italy, Luciano continued to work for a return to the country he claimed as his true home, but police believed he continued to mastermind a global narcotics-smuggling network. His attempts to return to the United States failed; as his health deteriorated in his later years, he became less close-mouthed about his earlier criminal activities, speaking to reporters and even dictating notes that became the basis of a biography. In January 1962, while meeting with American film producer and subsequent biographer Martin Gosch about a prospective movie project, Luciano suffered a heart attack at Naples' Capodichino Airport and died. At the time, police believed the 65-year-old to still be actively involved in the international narcotics trade. His body was subsequently interred at St. John's Cemetery in Queens, New York.

David G. Schwartz
University of Nevada, Las Vegas

See Also: 1941 to 1960 Primary Documents; 1961 to 1980 Primary Documents; Gambling; Genovese, Vito; Italian Americans; Organized Crime, History of; Rothstein, Arnold; Schultz, Dutch.

Further Readings
Gosch, Martin and Richard Hammer. *The Last Testament of Lucky Luciano*. Boston: Little, Brown, 1975.
Haller, Mark. "The Changing Structure of American Gambling in the Twentieth Century." *Journal of Social Issues,* v.35 (1979).
Peterson, Virgil. *The Mob: 200 Years of Organized Crime in New York*. Ottawa, IL: Green Hill Publishers, 1983.
Schwartz, David G. *Cutting the Wire: Gaming Prohibition and the Internet*. Reno: University of Nevada Press, 2005.

Lynchings

A lynching is a form of extralegal violence carried out by a mob. The earliest use of the term in colonial America seems to have been during the Revolutionary War as "lynch law" or "Lynch's law" to refer to the punishment of British loyalists by Charles Lynch, a Virginia planter and justice of the peace. During the westward movement, vigilantes carried out lynchings, which increasingly involved lethal violence, with Mexicans, Native Americans, Chinese laborers, and white outlaws among the victims.

However, from the Revolutionary era onward, mob violence was also a law enforcement problem in cities. During the Civil War, in 1863, the "draft riots" occurred in New York City. Protesting conscription into the military by the federal government, mobs that included many Irish immigrants engaged in several days of violence, rampaging through the city, destroying property, and setting upon and killing several African American men. Black children were forced to flee when an orphanage was burned down. This violence, which targeted blacks as scapegoats, was a prelude to the racialized violence that became identified with the Deep South.

Between 1889 and 1932, approximately 3,745 people were lynched in the United States. The majority of these lynchings occurred in the southern states that formed the so-called Black Belt rather than in the border states of the upper south. The majority of the victims of these lynchings were African American. Because of their value as property, slaves in the south had been provided some protection from mob violence. In the post–Civil War era, freed blacks were the targets of lethal violence by both mobs and vigilante groups.

Post–Civil War Era

The end of the Civil War saw the rise of white vigilante groups such as the Ku Klux Klan (KKK). Often clad in robes and other regalia, these groups sought to terrorize blacks in the south. The punishment carried out by these groups was directed not only against accused criminals but against blacks who violated established racial etiquette or who challenged white supremacy through attempted social, economic, or political mobility. The propaganda of these vigilante groups focused on the alleged rise of the "new Negro criminal" who was free to prey on whites because he was no longer controlled by the system of slavery. In this scenario, white vigilantes who enforced traditional southern racial patterns were portrayed as heroes, fighting to preserve the southern way of life that had been disrupted by the Civil War and was now threatened by blacks. Although there was little evidence to support the allegations, the articles and editorials that appeared in southern newspapers depicted lustful black men ("fiends") preying on white girls and women. This myth of the black rapist spread beyond the region as northerners read accounts of lynchings in the south. The threat of the black rapist was used as a rationale for keeping black men in their "place." The southern "code of honor" was evoked to justify the use of mob violence in the alleged defense of white womanhood.

As vigilante violence against blacks increased, with the number of lynchings peaking in the 1890s, the ritual characteristics of these events also began to take shape. Lynchings involved the shooting, hanging and/or burning and often the mutilation of the victim. In one such case, widely covered by newspapers, a black man named Sam Hose was lynched in Newman, Georgia, on April 2, 1899. Before he was burned alive, his ears, fingers, and genitals were cut off. After he was dead, his body was allowed to cool and then was crushed to secure pieces of bones and liver, which were sold as souvenirs.

The image of blacks as "beasts" and of "Negro regression" in the aftermath of slavery served as justification for the violence directed against African Americans in the south. Early social science supported rather than refuted images of black savagery. Cesare Lombroso, the "father of positivist criminology," described Africans as less evolved physically and mentally than Europeans. Social Darwinists echoed this assertion of white superiority.

Twentieth-Century Lynchings

Vigilante violence against blacks had surged in the south during a period when such mob violence was diminishing in other regions of the country. At the same time, southern historians eulogized the happy slaves of the old south. Director D. W.

This photograph of the aftermath of the June 15, 1920, triple lynching of Elias Clayton, Elmer Jackson, and Isaac McGhie, who had been accused of raping a white woman in Duluth, Minnesota, was made into a postcard, as were many other such photos. Between 1889 and 1932, approximately 3,745 people were lynched in the United States, and the majority were African American.

Griffith's *The Birth of a Nation* brought this old south perspective to movie audiences. Acclaimed by critics for its technical achievements, the film was the first Hollywood blockbuster. Based on *The Clansman* (1905) by former minister Thomas Dixon, the film presented a distorted account of federal occupation of the south after the Civil War. Using white actors in "blackface" (theatrical makeup), the film presented black and mulatto characters as villains. In a famous scene, a black soldier, who has been lusting after the white hero's young sister, pursues her through the woods. Fearing rape ("a fate worse than death" for a white woman), she jumps from a precipice before her brother can arrive to save her. Heartbroken, the white hero turns to the white vigilante group that he has formed, the KKK, to free the oppressed whites.

As these lynchings continued into the 20th century, the coverage by newspapers outside the south reinforced negative perceptions of the region. Aside from African American press, the *New York Times* and the *Chicago Tribune* were among the first newspapers to describe vigilante violence in the south as barbarism. This stigma that was perceived as hindering social and economic progress in the south as well as the fact that large numbers of blacks were migrating north, creating a labor shortage, led some white southerners to advocate the suppression of lynching. Some southerners also feared the federal government might intervene on the side of blacks.

African American activists had been engaged in a campaign against lynching since the last decades of the 19th century. Founded in 1909, the National Association for the Advancement of

Colored People (NAACP) documented lynching events, often sending undercover investigators to the scenes. Crusading journalists and editors such as Ida B. Wells (later Wells-Barnett) also reported on the violence of southern mobs. Forced to flee Memphis, Wells later published *Southern Horrors: Lynch Law in All Its Phases*.

African American women, known as "Negro clubwomen" also organized to resist lynching in the south. By the 1920s, they had been joined in their antilynching stance by organizations of white southern women who objected to lynchings allegedly carried out as acts of chivalry for the protection of white womanhood.

Lynching and Legal Action

Over the years, activists attempted to obtain legislation that would make lynching a federal offense. The Dyer Anti-Lynching Bill proposed by Representative Leonidas Dyer (R-Missouri) was defeated by political maneuvering in Congress in 1922 and 1923. In spite of this defeat, the number of lynchings continued to decline each year. However, there were still sensational events such as the lynching of Claude Neal in Jackson County, Florida, in 1934.

Neal had been accused of the rape and murder of a white neighbor. His abduction from the police and the announcement of the time and place of his lynching were reported in newspapers in the north. With no request for help from local authorities, the governor did not intervene by sending militia. An audience of white men, women, and children, some of whom had come from surrounding counties and even other states, witnessed Neal's lynching.

The execution of Neal in Florida came several years after mob violence had been averted in Scottsboro, Alabama, when nine young black men were accused by two white women of raping them. The accusations in the "Scottsboro Boys" case are now generally recognized as a racial hoax (a false accusation that depends for its credibility on racial stereotypes). The two young women and the nine black youths, ranging in age from 13 to 21, had been "riding the rails" (riding illegally on the train), a practice common during the Great Depression as the unemployed poor moved from place to place seeking work. When the train stopped in Scottsboro, the two young women were discovered and made their claim that they had been raped.

The Scottsboro Boys case is relevant in a discussion of lynching because during this era, rape was a capital offense. One factor in the decrease of mob violence in the south seems to have been the increase in the number of legal executions of black males accused of crimes against whites. In this case, the Scottsboro Boys were saved from death because the case became an international cause célèbre when the Communist Party and the NAACP intervened, vying for the right to provide a defense team.

By the 1930s, lynchings were viewed as symbolic of biased southerner justice and black oppression. As recent historians have noted, the occurrence of racial violence in other regions of the country was often ignored in this critique of the south. In the aftermath of World War I, during the "Red Summer" of 1919, race riots occurred in cities across the country. The movement of black migrants out of the south placed increasing demographic pressure on established black communities in the north and midwest, and more conflicts along the borders between blacks and whites occurred.

In the 1940s and 1950s, legal action produced some gains for African Americans. In 1954, in *Brown v. Board of Education*, the Supreme Court struck down the doctrine of "separate but equal" and directed the south to dismantle its system of legal segregation. A year later, the case of Emmett Till, a 14-year-old boy from Chicago who was killed in Money, Mississippi, in an act of private vigilantism, brought renewed attention to the south. Although the two white men who were suspected of killing Till were placed on trial, they were acquitted by an all-white jury. They later admitted in a magazine interview that they had killed the boy for showing disrespect to the wife of one of them while visiting their store. The Till case attracted national attention when Till's mother chose to have her son's coffin open, displaying his battered and mutilated body to mourners. The photo of Till in his coffin became iconic when it appeared on the cover of an African American magazine. Till's murder was perceived as a lynching by many of the young activists who would take part in the civil rights movement.

Depictions in Media

In 1960, Harper Lee's novel *To Kill a Mockingbird* was published. As had the "lynching plays" and novels written by African American authors during the late 19th and early 20th centuries, the novel examined the impact of racial prejudice and racial violence on the lives of southerners. However, Lee's novel, set in the 1930s and written as the memoir of a young girl's coming of age, reached a far wider audience. The 1962 film based on the novel starred Gregory Peck as Atticus Finch, the white attorney who takes on the defense of a black laborer accused of raping a young white woman. Before he can defend his client in court, Finch must spend the night at the jail helping the sheriff to protect his client from the mob of white men who come to break him out of jail and lynch him.

In 2000, *Without Sanctuary*, an exhibition of photographs and picture postcards that were souvenirs of lynchings, opened in New York City and later traveled to Pittsburgh, Atlanta, and Chicago. Collected by an antique dealer from flea markets and private sellers, this exhibit highlighted the fact that lynchings were communal events that attracted a cross-section of whites, including women and children. Fearing no legal consequences, members of these mobs had posed with the bodies of their victims. The picture postcards of hanging, burned, and mutilated bodies often carried cheerful messages from the sender to the recipient about the lynching event.

Conclusion

Social scientists and historians have offered a variety of explanations of lynchings in the south and elsewhere, considering factors such as economic conditions and demographics. The striking aspect of these events is that rather than being spontaneous eruptions of violence, the most horrendous of these lynchings were often planned, announced, and staged as spectacle. The symbolic message of the lynchings was powerful warning to the groups from whom the victims were drawn. The failure of federal, state, and local criminal justice systems to intervene reflected the lack of status of the victims and prevailing racial/ethnic attitudes.

Frankie Y. Bailey
State University of New York, Albany

See Also: 1901 to 1920 Primary Documents; African Americans; Hanging; History of Crime and Punishment in America: 1850–1900; Ku Klux Klan; National Association for the Advancement of Colored People; Race-Based Crimes; Riots; Segregation Laws; *To Kill a Mockingbird*; Torture; Vigilantism; Violent Crimes.

Further Readings

Clarke, James W. "Without Fear or Shame: Lynching, Capital Punishment and the Subculture of Violence in the American South." *British Journal of Political Science*, v.28/2 (1998).

Tolnay, Stewart E. and E. M. Beck. *A Festival of Violence: An Analysis of Southern Lynchings, 1882–1930*. Urbana: University of Illinois Press, 1995.

Waldrep, Christopher. "National Policing, Lynching, and Constitutional Change." *Journal of Southern History*, v.74/3 (2008).

Macdonald, Ross

Ross Macdonald is one of the pen names of Kenneth Millar (1915–83), a novelist whose specialty was crime fiction. He is best known for his Lew Archer detective novels and is regarded as the successor to Raymond Chandler and Dashiell Hammett in the evolution of the private detective novel.

Millar was born December 13, 1915, in Los Gatos, California, to Jack and Annie (née Moyer) Millar, who took their young son to Vancouver, British Columbia. Millar had a difficult childhood. His parents separated when he was 4, and his mother took him to her hometown of Kichener, Ontario, where they lived with his maternal grandmother for a year. He was sent to live with various relatives (occasionally spending time with his parents, who attempted to reconcile on two occasions) and returned to Kitchener to finish high school at the Kitchener-Waterloo Collegiate and Vocational School. It was during this time that he began reading Dashiell Hammett's work, which inspired him to become a writer.

In 1932, Millar entered Waterloo College, transferring to the University of Western Ontario the following year. In 1938, after graduating from college, he married Margaret Strum, who also became a crime novelist, writing 16 books between 1947 and 1987. Their daughter, Linda, was born in June 1939 (she died in 1970). He also obtained a teaching certificate and took a job at the Kitchener high school he had attended.

While working on a doctorate at the University of Michigan (he defended his dissertation in 1951), Millar published his first novel, *The Dark Tunnel* (1944). Millar's second novel, *Trouble Follows Me* (1946), was written during his service in the U.S. Navy (1944–46). *Blue City* (1947) and *The Three Roads* (1948) followed.

During this period, Millar created a character who later appeared in a series of novels (like Chandler's Philip Marlowe and Hammett's Sam Spade): Los Angeles–based Lew Archer, whom he named after Sam Spade's murdered partner in *The Maltese Falcon* (Miles Archer) and the author Lew Wallace. He first introduced the character in the 1946 short story "Find the Woman." Archer appeared in a novel for the first time in *The Moving Target* (1949). Millar decided to use the pseudonym of "John Macdonald." His publisher, Knopf, came up with the idea of an author's photo that depicted a trench coat–wearing Millar in silhouette, smoking a cigarette, in order to generate publicity. There were 17 more novels, the last of which, *The Blue Hammer*, appeared in 1976. Most of the novels were set in Southern California with "Santa Teresa" serving as the pseudonym for Santa Barbara, where Millar and his wife lived for many years.

With *The Drowning Pool* (1950), Millar adopted the pen name "John Ross Macdonald" (to avoid confusion with John D. MacDonald, who created Florida detective Travis McGee). The pseudonym "Ross Macdonald" was introduced with the publication of *The Barbarous Coast* (1955). *The Goodbye Look* (1969) was his first best seller. The 1966 film *Harper*, starring Paul Newman, was based on *The Moving Target*. *The Drowning Pool* became a movie in 1975, also starring Paul Newman as Lew Archer (Newman had used the name "Harper" for the lead character in the earlier film because his two previous films, *Hud*, and *The Hustler*, had started with an H). *The Underground Man* (1971) was made into a 1974 television movie starring Peter Graves.

In 1960, a non-Archer novel, *The Ferguson Affair*, appeared. The protagonist was Bill Gunnarson, a young lawyer. In 1973, Millar published a nonfiction work, *On Crime Writing*, in which he analyzed the genre and offered insight into his own writing. In describing the detective story, he wrote

> The nightmare can't be explained away, and persists in the teeth of reason. An unstable balance between reason and more primitive human qualities is characteristic of the detective story. For both writer and reader it is an imaginative arena where such conflicts can be worked out safely, under artistic controls.

The Mystery Writers of America gave Millar their Grand Master Award in 1974 (he and his wife are the only husband and wife to receive this award). The *New York Times* described his Lew Archer novels as "the finest series of detective stories ever written by an American." In 1981, he was diagnosed with Alzheimer's disease. He died in a nursing home in Santa Barbara at age 67 on July 11, 1983.

Jeffrey Kraus
Wagner College

See Also: Dime Novels, Pulps, Thrillers; Grafton, Sue; Hammett, Dashiell; Literature and Theater, Crime in; Literature and Theater, Police in; Literature and Theater, Punishment in; Private Detectives; Spillane, Mickey.

Further Readings
Bruccoli, Matthew J. *Ross Macdonald*. San Diego, CA: Harcourt Brace Jovanovich, 1984.
Macdonald, Ross. *On Crime Writing*. Santa Barbara, CA: Capra Press, 1973.
Nolan, Tom. *Ross Macdonald: A Biography*. New York: Scribner, 1999.
Sipper, Ralph B. *Inward Journey: Ross Macdonald*. Santa Barbara, CA: Cordelia Editions, 1984.

Madison, James (Administration of)

James Madison (1751–1836) began his political career and influence on American history as an early Virginian politician, having represented Virginia as a delegate to the Constitutional Convention in 1787. Madison, author of the *Federalist Papers*, was an advocate of a strong national government. In debates, he emphasized that the Constitution's protections, particularly government as a system of checks, balances, and separated powers, would prevent tyrannical government and maintain order. While he is most widely famed for his substantial contributions to the framing of the U.S. Constitution, whether through his written work or the offices he held, the significance of James Madison on the political and legal structures of the United States is enduring.

Supreme Court Developments

As secretary of state, James Madison was a party in the landmark case *Marbury v. Madison* argued before the Supreme Court. At the end of his presidency, John Adams appointed William Marbury to serve as a justice of the peace. Yet Marbury's commission paperwork had not been officially delivered to him by John Marshall, then secretary of state, before the Adams presidency culminated. When Madison assumed the office of secretary of state, he did not deliver the commission paperwork to Marbury, which resulted in the lawsuit initiated by Marbury. Ultimately, the unanimous ruling established the power of the Supreme Court to exercise judicial review, which authorizes the Supreme Court to review

S. W. Fores's 1814 cartoon, The Fall of Washington, depicts President James Madison and likely John Armstrong, his secretary of war, fleeing the White House, the only president to do so because of a foreign invasion. Early in his presidency, Madison was in constant dispute with other nations over trade and territory. The discord eventually culminated in a formal declaration of war against Britain in 1812; during the Battle of Blandesburg, British soldiers invaded Washington, D.C., overcame its forces, and set fire to public buildings.

the federal constitutionality of laws related to the cases it hears.

A few years after the *Marbury v. Madison* decision, Madison was selected by President Thomas Jefferson to be his successor and to run for president in the election of 1808. The Democratic-Republican ticket ran Madison with George Clinton for vice president against Federalists Charles Pinckney and Rufus King. The primary issue that characterized the election was Federalist opposition to the Embargo Act of 1807. The contentious act, passed under the Jefferson administration while Madison was secretary of state, ultimately did not ruin Madison's opportunity to become president. In fact, James Madison was inaugurated as the fourth president of the United States in 1809.

As secretary of state during the Jefferson administration, Madison was involved in the case that established judicial review, and later, during Madison's administration, the Supreme Court utilized the newly established power. The decision in *Fletcher v. Peck* declared an act of the Georgia state legislature inconsistent with the provision of the Constitution (Article 1, Section 9) that prohibits bills of attainder and ex post facto laws. Also in his first term, President Madison used the veto to reject two bills that he deemed to be unconstitutional. One bill sought to incorporate an Episcopal church outside Washington, D.C., into the territory of the city. The other vetoed bill would have granted public lands as relief to members of a Baptist church in the Mississippi Territory. For Madison, each of the bills violated the nonestablishment clause in the First Amendment to the U.S. Constitution. Contentions over land continued to define the major events of James Madison's presidency.

Foreign Engagements

The opposition to the Embargo Act that Madison faced in his first presidential campaign argued that the limitations the act placed on trade with foreign nations damaged the shipping and transportation industries that would otherwise benefit from trade exchanges. Within the first few months of his presidency, Madison addressed the issue. He announced that the United States would rescind the embargo placed on Britain with the understanding that Britain would act similarly. The accord, called the Erskine Agreement, fell through after Madison learned that it had been cancelled by the British; he followed suit weeks later.

In the years that followed, the Madison administration was in constant dispute with Britain, France, Spain, and various Native American nations over trade policy and territory. Accordingly, throughout his presidency Madison called for the expansion of American territory and the military. The engagements with Spain, Britain, and Native Americans spanned numerous territories. The disputes led many to call for war against France while a formal declaration of war against Britain was proclaimed in 1812. Later that year, British soldiers invaded and defeated American soldiers in Washington, D.C., during the Battle of Blandesburg. The British set fire to public buildings and forced Madison to be the only president to flee the White House because of a foreign invasion.

In an extremely competitive election, Madison won reelection to the presidency in 1812 against Federalist DeWitt Clinton. With news of Napoleon Bonaparte's failed invasion of Russia and the unraveling of the French Empire, Madison removed the trade embargo with neutral countries. Finally, in 1814, Britain and the United States negotiated and signed the Treaty of Ghent that ended the War of 1812. The First Bank of the United States lost its charter in 1811 under the Madison administration as many Congress members were concerned about British interest in the private bank.

In 1816, the United States chartered a new national bank, the Second Bank of the United States, to deal with war debt placed on the national treasury. President James Madison was succeeded by Democratic-Republican James Monroe, who was elected in 1816 and inaugurated in 1817.

Sierra J. Powell
University of California, Irvine

See Also: Bill of Rights; Constitution of the United States of America; Federalist Papers; *Fletcher v. Peck*; *Marbury v. Madison*.

Further Readings
Brant, Irving. *James Madison: The Nationalist, 1780–1787*. Indianapolis, IN: Bobbs-Merrill Company, 1948.
Ketcham, Ralph. *James Madison: A Biography*. Newton, CT: American Political Biography Press, 2003.
Wills, Gary. *James Madison*. New York: Henry Holt and Company, 2002.

Madoff, Bernard

Bernard "Bernie" Lawrence Madoff (1938–) is believed to have operated the largest Ponzi scheme in history, totaling some $65 billion (estimates vary). A Ponzi scheme is a type of fraud in which investors are paid returns based on income provided by the investments of subsequent investors and generally attracts new investors by paying returns higher than those provided by more orthodox types of investment. A Ponzi scheme can continue as long as there is sufficient new investment to pay off those already in the scheme, requiring both a steady influx of new cash and the willingness of most of the investors to defer taking cash out of the scheme (e.g., by demanding payment of interest rather than reinvesting it).

Madoff graduated from Hofstra University in 1960. That same year, he founded the Wall Street trading firm Bernard L. Madoff Investment Securities, which became, by the early 1980s, one of the largest independent trading operations in the securities industry. Madoff built this volume in part through the practice of paying for order flow, a controversial but legal practice in which he paid brokerage firms a few cents per order to send orders through his firm, which he could afford due to the large spread of 12.5 cents between the buy and sell price on each trade (this spread would drop to 6.5 cents in 1997 and to one cent in 2001). By 1989, Madoff's firm handled over 5 percent of the trading volume on the New York Stock Exchange and Madoff was one of the highest-paid individuals working on Wall Street. Not all Madoff investors knew they were investing their money with him: some were invested in "feeder funds" whose assets were invested with Madoff without the knowledge of the individuals whose money was involved. In 1990, Madoff became nonexecutive chairman of NASDAQ, an electronic stock market operated by the National Association of Securities Dealers.

Madoff came under suspicion as early as 1992, when federal investigators suspected he was connected to a Ponzi scheme run by Frank Avellino and Michael Bienes (Avellino had funneled investors to Madoff since the 1960s). However, Avellino and Bienes shut down their firm and no further investigation was directed at Madoff's activities. In May 2000, Harry Markopolos, a private fraud investigator in Boston who had been asked to reverse-engineer Madoff's returns (which were consistently high regardless of the general performance of the stock market), concluded that Madoff was running a Ponzi scheme and sent an eight-page memo regarding this to the Securities and Exchange Commission (SEC) office in Boston. Nothing came from this communication, and in 2005, Markopolos again communicated his suspicions to the SEC, sending a 21-page memo stating in even greater detail why he believed Madoff was running a fraudulent operation. However, the SEC made only minimal investigations and decided there was no evidence to conclude Madoff was guilty of fraud. Madoff's scheme was brought down in part by the financial slowdown in 2008, because his investors started making withdrawals from his fund in large numbers, and he was not able to bring in enough new cash to pay them off. On December 11, 2008, Madoff was arrested, and on June 29, 2009, he was sentenced to 150 years for numerous crimes, including international money laundering, securities fraud, mail fraud, wire fraud, money laundering, and perjury.

Besides being a Ponzi scheme, Madoff's fraud qualifies as an affinity scam because most of his investors were, like himself, Jewish. Madoff was a well-known philanthropist and served on the boards of numerous nonprofit organizations, many of which invested funds with him. Some major Madoff investors, including well-known figures such as Nobel Prize–winner Elie Wiesel, were members of the Fifth Avenue Synagogue in New York City. Their investments were funneled to Madoff through J. Ezra Merkin, who until 2009, served as president of this synagogue. Wiesel's charity, the Elie Wiesel Foundation for Humanity, also lost almost all of its assets through Madoff's fraud. Other Jewish organizations with major investments with Madoff included Yeshiva University, the Carl & Ruth Shapiro Family Foundation, Hadassah, the Jewish Community Foundation of Los Angeles, and the Picower Foundation.

Sarah Boslaugh
Kennesaw State University

See Also: Confidence Games and Frauds; Jewish Americans; Securities and Exchange Commission; White Collar Crime, Contemporary; White-Collar Crime, Sociology of.

Further Readings
Lipner, Seth E. "Madoff Feeder Funds Lose Their Immunity." *Forbes* (December 16, 2010).
"The Madoff Affair." Public Broadcasting System. http://www.pbs.org/wgbh/pages/frontline/madoff (Accessed June 8, 2011).
Markopolos, Harry. *No One Would Listen: A True Financial Thriller*. Hoboken, NJ: Wiley & Sons, 2010.
"Times Topics: Bernard L. Madoff." *New York Times*. http://topics.nytimes.com/top/reference/timestopics/people/m/bernard_l_madoff/index.html?scp=1-spot&sq=madoff&st=cse (Accessed June 8, 2011).

Magna Carta

Many people in America hold the opinion that the political concepts of liberty and freedom originated with the American colonists and the Declaration of Independence. In fact, these concepts came to the forefront during the Enlightenment, which was a period of time during the 18th century in Europe when numerous philosophers began to seriously present the idea of a free and democratic society as an alternative to the monarchies that were prevalent in Europe at that time. These philosophers included such luminaries as John Locke, Baron Montesquieu, Immanuel Kant, and Jean-Jacques Rousseau. However, even the philosophers of the Enlightenment were influenced by previous writings and political events. One of the more important events was the Magna Carta.

During the 13th century in England, governments was based on the feudal system. The feudal system consisted of a number of lesser nobles, such as barons, counts, and dukes, who owned land and swore fealty to a king. As feudal lords, these lesser nobles ruled over their serfs and peasants, who were legally bound to that noble—to work for the noble, pay taxes, and perform military service when required. The nobles, in turn, owed their loyalty to the king and had to pay taxes and provide troops in time of war.

In the 13th century, King John ruled England. King John was not a popular king because of the high taxes he leveled against his lesser nobles, his arbitrary treatment of his lesser nobles, and the unsuccessful wars he had conducted. A number of King John's nobles began to conspire against him because of his oppression. On June 15, 1215, at Runnymede, to prevent open rebellion, King John agreed to what is now known as the Magna Carta. At that time, it was called the Great Charter. In exchange, the lesser nobles renewed their oaths of loyalty to King John. The Magna Carta was not the first attempt at liberty and freedom in England. In 1100, the English Charter of Liberties was created and was an influence on the nobles who forced King John to place his seal upon the Magna Carta.

The Magna Carta contained a number of provisions that were remarkable for their time. Although there were over 60 provisions, a few are considered of high importance. First, it mandated that the court be fixed in a particular place. Previously, court had been held where the king was present, which made it difficult to have a case heard when the king was traveling. Second, trials should be held in the district where the dispute occurred. The first and second requirements foreshadowed the Sixth Amendment requirement of the U.S. Constitution to hold criminal trials in the district where the crime occurred. Third, any punishments meted out had to fit the crime and could not be excessive, which provides the historical basis for the Eighth Amendment to the U.S. Constitution prohibiting cruel and usual punishments or excessive fines. Fourth, no freeman could be punished or imprisoned except by a judgment of his peers, which is guaranteed by the Sixth Amendment and foreshadowed the concept of due process in the Fifth Amendment and the right to trial by one's peers in the Sixth Amendment. Fifth, justice could not be bought or delayed, which foreshadowed the requirement for a fair trial. Sixth, corruption by local officials was

The Magna Carta, 1297, is widely viewed as one of the most important legal documents in the history of democracy. At the time of its writing, it was called the Great Charter.

prohibited and just compensation for property seized by the government had to be given, foreshadowing the Fifth Amendment to the U.S. Constitution. And seventh, the Magna Carta provided that if the king did not adhere to the provisions of the Magna Carta, his nobles could revolt and remove him, which is echoed in the U.S. Declaration of Independence and the Second Amendment. However, the most important principle advanced by the Magna Carta was that the ruler (the king) was not above the law.

Even though it was an English document that predated the American Revolution by 500 years, it was a significant influence on the Founding Fathers. Thus, its historical importance and effect on the American criminal justice system cannot be overstated. Although the original Magna Carta was only in effect for a short time, because King John repudiated it shortly after placing his seal on it, leading to his downfall, it was rewritten several times. It was not until the 16th century that it acquired its current name of Magna Carta. Although many parts of it were later repealed, the basic rights it expressed remained in the legal philosophy of England and were carried forth to the U.S. Declaration of Independence, the Constitution, and the Bill of Rights.

Wm. C. Plouffe, Jr.
Independent Scholar

See Also: 1600 to 1776 Primary Documents; Bill of Rights; Civil Rights Laws; Declaration of Independence; Due Process; English Charter of Liberties of 1100; Rule of Law.

Further Readings
Holt, James C., ed. *Magna Carta and the Idea of Liberty*. Hoboken, NJ: Wiley, 1972.
Howard, A. E. Dick. *Magna Carta: Text & Commentary*. Charlottesville: University of Virginia Press, 1998.

Maine

The northeasternmost state, Maine has been settled since the early 17th century but was part of Massachusetts until 1820, when it was made an independent state as part of the Missouri Compromise. Today, it is one of the 16 states without a capital punishment statute. During its colonial, Massachusetts, and early statehood periods, a total of 21 executions were carried out, all but one of them for murder (the exception was a 1780 treason case). The last executed criminal in Maine was Daniel Wilkinson, who had murdered a police officer during an 1883 burglary. When he was executed by hanging in 1885, he died slowly by strangulation instead of the swift death intended; his suffering helped death penalty opponents successfully abolish capital punishment in 1887.

Law Enforcement
There was no separate Maine prison when it was part of Massachusetts; convicts were sent south to the prisons on Castle Island in Boston Harbor and in Charlestown. As in many areas in the early 19th century, enough crimes were handled through punitive measures like flogging or fines that discussion of a Maine state prison does not seem to have begun until a full two years into statehood, despite what might be considered an inevitable need for such.

The Maine legislature passed an act in 1823 to create a state prison, and the Maine State Prison opened the following year. It was located in Thomaston because, as the halfway point between Kittery and Eastpoint, it was more or less the center of population at the time. The original prison design kept the inmates in underground cells and put them to work in the stone quarry. When a fire destroyed much of the building in 1923, the new prison that replaced it was exceptionally modern for the time, making use of recent technological innovations. In 2002, prison overpopulation led to the construction of a larger prison in Warren, replacing the Thomaston facility.

In the early decades of statehood, town police forces were formed to supplement the county sheriffs that had been founded in the colonial era. Over time, an important part of the duties of sheriffs as a result became the provision of law enforcement to rural parts of their counties; Maine has always had numerous small towns and unincorporated areas. The state police helped fill this gap as well when it was founded in 1921, originally as highway police whose duties were expanded several times in the pre–World War II years.

Crime

Maine was one of the first states to pass prohibition laws, as part of the 19th-century temperance movement that eventually led to federal Prohibition. Commonly called the Maine Law, the statute was passed in 1851 and sponsored by Neal Dow, the mayor of Portland and "Napoleon of Temperance." The law prohibited the sale of all alcoholic beverages, except for "medicinal, mechanical, or manufacturing purposes." Additionally, the general public was encouraged and empowered to help enforce this prohibition: Any three voters could appear before a judge and request that a search warrant be issued if they suspected someone of selling illegal liquor.

The Maine Law gained international infamy almost immediately. Even decades later, a Manchester, England, street was named Maine Road in honor of the law and its role in the temperance movement. Its reception in Maine, of course, was rather less favorable, and complaints of the working class and the state's Irish immigrants culminated in the Maine Law Riot, or Portland Rum Riot, on June 2, 1855. Fueled by rumors that the Dow company was storing a large amount of rum (for medicinal uses, to be distributed to pharmacists) and the widespread sentiment that the law had anti-immigrant motives, the riot began with three men exploiting the search warrant component of Maine's law and applying for a search warrant for the building where the rum was held. Within hours, the crowd grew to at least 1,000—some contemporary accounts claim 3,000 people surrounded the building by the evening. The militia was called to deal with the crowd, and eventually fired upon them, resulting in one death and seven injuries. Dow was in fact prosecuted for improperly acquiring the rum, and although he was acquitted, the law was repealed the following year.

The violent crime rate in Maine is low—122 crimes per 100,000 inhabitants in 2010—but has gradually risen since 2004, after a period of steady decline since a late 1970s peak (224.7 per 100,000 in 1977). Unlike the national crime rate, the Maine crime rate did not rise in the 1990s, at which time it had declined to almost half of that peak. Most of the decline is owed to the steep decline in burglaries and assaults; the murder rate has remained constant (and low), while rape has actually climbed sharply and steadily (less than 10 per 100,000 in 1976; 29.3 in 2010). Some part of the increase in rape statistics may be because of an increase in victims, reporting their rape, but the statistic should not be blithely overlooked.

During the 1970s (when crime was on the rise), there was a general tendency across the country to enact penal reforms. In 1976, as part of that trend, Maine abolished its parole board, introduced flat sentencing (sentences without minimums or maximums), and split most criminal offenses into multiple categories of seriousness. The overall effect has been that offenders since have served longer sentences on average, with no demonstrable effect on recidivism. Further, an unusually high percentage of Maine inmates are incarcerated for probation violations that in other states would not result in jail time. This has led to prison overcrowding, causing activists and legislators in the 21st century to call for new reforms—in particular, the reinstatement of a parole program and the greater usage of home arrest programs for nonviolent offenders. Some of those calling for prison reform have included former guards and prison chaplains. A number of deaths of inmates in the 21st century stoked the fires of reform activism, as activists claimed the living conditions of overcrowded prisons were creating an unsafe environment.

One small gain in sentencing reform has been the decriminalization of small amounts of marijuana, which is punishable as a violation carrying a fine and no jail time. Despite decriminalization, drug-related crimes, including burglaries and theft, increased from 2009 to 2010, which authorities attributed to rural drug users stealing to fund their habits. Similar spikes had been seen in the previous year. In 2011, 12 years after approving medical marijuana, Maine became the first east coast state to open a medical marijuana dispensary. The first was opened in Frenchville, on the Canadian border, followed by dispensaries in Biddeford, Ellsworth, and Auburn.

Bill Kte'pi
Independent Scholar

See Also: Penitentiaries; Prohibition; Rape, Contemporary; Riots.

Further Readings
Galaway, Burt. "Crime Victim and Offender Mediation as a Social Work Strategy." *Social Service Review*, v.62/4 (December 1988).
Littlefoot, Elizabeth and Mark Umbreit. "An Analysis of State Statutory Provisions for Victim-Offender Mediation." *Criminal Justice Policy Review*, v.15/4 (December 2004).

Malcolm X

Malcolm X (1925–65) was a Black Muslim leader. Though he was born Malcolm Little in Omaha, Nebraska, Malcolm X used several aliases, including Jack Carlton, Detroit Red, Big Red, Malachi Shabazz, and El-Hajj Malik El-Shabazz. His father, Earl Little, was a Baptist minister, born in Jamaica, and a follower of the black nationalist leader Marcus Garvey. In 1931, when Malcolm X was 6 years old, his father was killed. His mother, Louise Norton Little, struggled to raise her eight children but was committed to a psychiatric institution, at which point Malcolm X was placed in a foster home.

At age 13, he was charged with delinquency and was sent to a juvenile detention home. He dropped out of school in the eighth grade and went to live with a sister in Boston, Massachusetts; he became involved in various criminal activities in Roxbury, Massachusetts, including burglary, selling drugs, pimping, and gambling. He also acquired a serious cocaine habit. In 1942, he moved to Harlem in New York City and became more involved in a criminal lifestyle.

In 1946, when he was 20 years old, Malcolm X was sentenced to 10 years in prison for burglary. While incarcerated in Charlestown, Massachusetts, he became an avid reader and expanded his vocabulary. His brother, Reginald, visited him in prison and told him about the Black Muslims, whom he had joined. While incarcerated, Malcolm X converted to the Nation of Islam led by the Honorable Elijah Muhammad. He dropped "Little," which he referred to as his slave name, and replaced it with "X," symbolizing that he was an ex-slave, as well as an ex-Christian, ex–pork eater, ex-drinker, and ex-smoker.

Involvement in Black Muslims

Malcolm X was paroled in 1952 after serving seven years. After he was released from prison, he went to Chicago, Illinois, to meet Elijah Muhammad; a close relationship was established between the two. Malcolm X became an assistant minister at the Black Muslim mosque in Detroit, Michigan. After studying personally under Elijah Muhammad, Malcolm X was charged with helping organize a mosque in Philadelphia, Pennsylvania. In 1954, he became a leader of the Harlem mosque. In May 1960, he was appointed minister of Temple No. 7 in Harlem.

In 1957, Malcolm met Betty Jean Sanders, a student nurse. They were married the next year; she changed her name to Betty Shabazz, and they eventually had six daughters. Their second daughter, Qubilah, was arrested in 1995 for hiring someone to kill Louis Farrakhan.

Malcolm X waits at Martin Luther King, Jr., press conference, March 26, 1964, during the Senate debate on the civil rights bill. It was the only time the two men ever met.

Malcolm X served as a charismatic spokesman for the Nation of Islam. He was an articulate speaker and an accomplished debater. He called for black nationalist separation; he spoke out against the prevailing trend of racial integration, criticizing most of the civil rights movement as well as its use of nonviolent civil disobedience. He advocated the use of more aggressive techniques, which he asserted were justified self-defense in response to institutionalized violence by white society against blacks. In 1961, Malcolm X helped create *Muhammad Speaks*, the official newspaper of the Nation of Islam. In 1963, he was appointed national minister of the Nation of Islam. However, Malcolm came to question the integrity of Elijah Muhammad. As a result, on March 23, 1963, Malcolm was placed on a 90-day suspension and could not publicly speak for the Nation of Islam.

Split With the Nation of Islam
On March 8, 1964, Malcolm X, after learning of indiscretions by Elijah Muhammad, announced that he was separating from the Nation of Islam. After his departure, Louis Farrakhan was appointed to his position at Temple No. 7; Farrakhan also assumed the role of national spokesman.

Malcolm X established two new organizations, first the Muslim Mosque, Inc., and then on June 28, 1964, the Organization of Afro-American Unity. He then made several trips to Europe and Africa and in 1964 he went to Mecca, Saudi Arabia, as a pilgrim, where he discovered white Muslims worshipping side by side with members of all races. This moving experience led him to renounce the black separatist ideology and to call for integrated civil rights efforts. After completing his pilgrimage, he changed his name to El-Hajj Malik El-Shabazz.

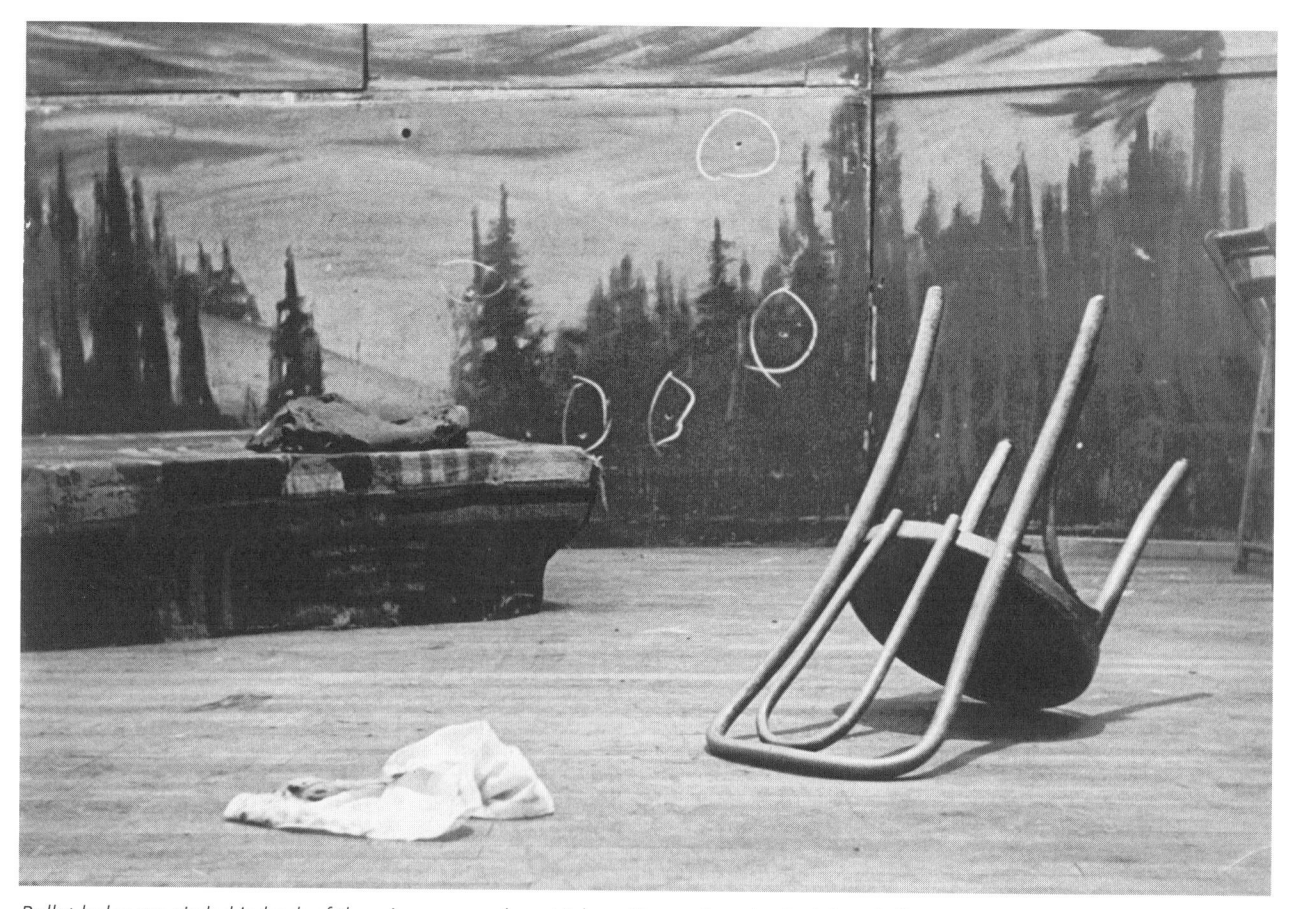

Bullet holes are circled in back of the crime scene where Malcom X was shot: the Audubon Ballroom stage in Manhattan, where he was speaking on February 21, 1965. Three gunmen rushed the stage and he was shot at least 15 times at close range; he was pronounced dead on arrival at Columbia Presbyterian Hospital. Police intelligence warned Malcom X of the threat, but he ignored it.

The Federal Bureau of Investigation (FBI) infiltrated the Nation of Islam and used an array of surveillance techniques, including wiretaps, audio bugs, and cameras, to monitor the group's activities. There had been well-known death threats against Malcolm X. On February 14, 1965, Malcolm and Betty's home in East Elmhurst, New York, was firebombed, but no one was hurt. On February 21, 1965, while Malcolm X was onstage for a speaking engagement at the Audubon Ballroom on West 166th Street in Manhattan, three gunmen rushed the stage. He was shot at least 15 times at close range and was pronounced dead on arrival at Columbia Presbyterian Hospital. He was buried at Ferncliff Cemetery in Hartsdale, New York. In March 1966, Norman 3X Butler, Talmadge Hayer, and Thomas 15X Johnson, all members of the Nation of Islam, were convicted of first-degree murder. It has been rumored that Elijah Muhammad and Louis Farrakhan ordered the assassination.

The 1965 assassination of Malcolm X illustrates how potentially effective criminal justice intelligence can be, as police intelligence indirectly warned Malcolm X of the impending threat, but he chose to ignore the warning. Some have criticized law enforcement officials for not more directly warning him of the impending danger, but this is difficult to fairly evaluate in retrospect. At any rate, his trusted confidant, Bouza, who was at Malcolm X's side giving first aid, was actually an undercover agent.

Victor B. Stolberg
Essex County College

See Also: African Americans; Civil Rights Laws; Racism.

Further Readings

DeCaro, Louis A. *On the Side of My People: A Religious Life of Malcolm X*. New York: New York University Press, 1996.

Magida, Arthur J. *Prophet of Rage*. New York: Basic Books, 1996.

Marable, Manning. *Malcolm X: A Life of Reinvention*. New York: Viking, 2011.

X, Malcolm. *The Autobiography of Malcolm X: As Told to Alex Haley*. New York: Penguin Books, 2007.

Mandatory Minimum Sentencing

Mandatory minimum sentencing is a determinate sentencing structure that requires judges to sentence offenders to specific sentence lengths for particular crimes. All states and the federal government of the United States use some form of mandatory minimum sentencing, usually for offenses that involve violence, drugs, guns, drunk driving, and/or repeat offenders. Mandatory minimum sentencing has come with benefits and costs for the court and correctional systems. Current efforts exist to research and examine mandatory minimum sentencing in various states to determine if such laws should be kept or repealed.

Legislative efforts of mandatory minimum sentencing began in the 1970s and 1980s alongside the push for government and the criminal justice system to be tougher on crime and the war on drugs. During this time, the public demanded that judges should have less discretion in their sentencing decisions. In the 1980s and 1990s, many states began shifting from indeterminate sentencing (i.e., loose sentencing structures that allow high amounts of discretion) to determinate or fixed sentencing (i.e., sentencing structures that limit judicial discretion and provide guidelines for sentencing lengths). Mandatory minimums were created with the purpose of being tough on crime, while ensuring that offenders went to prison for specified amounts of times, effectively to reach the goals of deterrence and incapacitation.

All states and the federal government had some type of mandatory minimum sentencing provision by the mid-1990s. Typically, the crimes with mandatory minimum sentences are considered by the public and legislators to be offenses that have the most negative impact on society, victims, and the criminal justice system. Crimes that involve violence, drugs, guns and other weapons, drunk driving, and habitual offenders most often have mandatory penalties. Two of the most used types of mandatory minimum sentencing are three strikes laws and truth-in-sentencing. Three strikes laws require judges to sentence individuals to lengthy prison sentences (e.g., 25 years to life in prison) due to the offender's habitual offender status with a conviction of a third felony offense.

Truth-in-sentencing statutes state that convicted offenders must serve the prison sentence they are assigned without chance of parole; states differ in execution of this law and some state laws require that only 85 percent of the time be served.

Criticisms have abounded about mandatory minimum sentencing structures that include concerns with severe penalties, discriminatory practices, increased prosecutorial power, and increased incarceration rates. Research has suggested that mandatory minimum sentencing has increased the severity of prison sentences, which means that more offenders are in prison for longer sentences, and thus mandatory sentences have been declared a contributing cause to prison overcrowding. Other research has demonstrated that racial and ethnic minorities are more apt to receive mandatory minimums, whereas majorities are more likely to receive reduced charges from prosecutorial discretion. This means that more minorities obtain longer and harsher sentences, and majorities receive shorter prison sentences, reduced charges, and less serious criminal histories. In addition, mandatory minimum sentencing has reduced the discretion and power bestowed to judges during sentencing and displaced it to prosecutors in the charging and plea negotiation stages of trial.

In addition, findings have suggested that the original goals have not been met; mandatory minimum sentencing laws are not deterring individuals from engaging in criminal behavior, however, they work well in incapacitation efforts. In addition, other unintended consequences, such as increased budgets for the courts and correctional systems, have started new arguments over the acceptable use of mandatory minimum sentencing practices. In light of these criticisms, some states and the federal government have begun examining their use of mandatory minimums. States such as Delaware, Maryland, Nevada, and Rhode Island have repealed certain provisions of mandatory minimum sentencing as connected to specific laws. Others, such as Pennsylvania and the federal government, have created task forces to examine mandatory minimum sentencing to determine effectiveness and ways to lower unintended consequences (e.g., increased prison rates and budget expenses). Yet, most states and the federal government do not have plans to repeal mandatory minimum sentencing laws, but want to ensure these laws are constitutional and beneficial to the system.

Jennifer L. Huck
Indiana University of Pennsylvania

See Also: Discretionary Decision Making; Sentencing; Sentencing: Indeterminate Versus Fixed; Three Strikes Law.

Further Readings

King, R. S. "The State of Sentencing 2007: Developments in Policy and Practice." The Sentencing Project. (2008). http://sentencing project.org/Admin/Documents/publications/sl_statesentencingreport2007.pdf (Accessed December 2011).

National Council on Crime and Delinquency. "National Assessment of Structured Sentencing." Bureau of Justice Assistance. (1996). http://www.ncjrs.gov/pdffiles/strsent.pdf (Accessed December 2011).

Parent, Dale, Terence Dunworth, Douglas McDonald, and William Rhodes. "Key Legislative Issues in Criminal Justice: Mandatory Sentencing." National Institute of Justice (1997). http://www.ncjrs.gov/pdffiles/161839.pdf (Accessed December 2011).

Spohn, Cassia. *How Do Judges Decide? The Search for Fairness and Justice in Punishment*. Thousand Oaks, CA: Sage, 2009.

Walker, Samuel. *Sense and Nonsense About Crime and Drugs: A Policy Guide*, 5th ed. Belmont, CA: Wadsworth, 2001.

Mann Act

Also known as the White Slave Traffic Act of 1910, the Mann Act is a federal statute that addresses the interstate and foreign transportation of crimes involving prostitution and human trafficking. The 61st Congress of the United States of America passed the Mann Act on June 25, 1910. Authored and sponsored by Illinois congressman James Robert Mann in 1909, under the direction of federal prosecutors from Chicago, this multi-sectioned federal statute was originally designed to regulate interstate and foreign commerce and prohibit the transportation of women for any and all "immoral purposes," with an emphasis on prostitution. Chicago prosecutors believed that women, including underage girls, were being forced into prostitution. The Mann Act stated that any person who knowingly transported or caused to be transported, or aided or assisted in obtaining transportation, and/or knowingly persuaded, induced, enticed, or coerced any woman, including girls under the age of 18, to go from one place to another in interstate or foreign commerce, or in any territory or the District of Columbia, for the purpose of prostitution or debauchery, or for any other immoral purposes, whether with or without her consent, would be guilty of a felony criminal offense and face imprisonment for a term of 5–10 years. President William Taft later signed the bill into law.

In its early stages, the Mann Act was also used as an institutional tool for racial segregation under Jim Crow. In its first-ever application, Jack Johnson, the first African American boxer to hold the world heavyweight title, was arrested for violating the Mann Act. Johnson was charged in Chicago with transporting a woman whom federal prosecutors described as a prostitute over state lines for "immoral" purposes. In court, federal prosecutors argued that Johnson committed a "crime against nature" for engaging in sexual intercourse with a Caucasian woman. Johnson was later convicted and was sentenced to imprisonment at Fort Leavenworth.

Clarifications and Amendments

The U.S. Supreme Court upheld the constitutionality of the Mann Act in *Hoke v. United States*. In November 1910, Effie Hoke arranged for another female, Annette Baden, to travel from New Orleans, Louisiana, to Beaumont, Texas, for the purpose of prostitution. Both women

This Illustration in the January 1912 edition of Puck *depicts the vices of illicit activities, which were addressed by the Mann Act. A woman holding a "red light" lantern with her dogs, all representing death, disease, suicide, and insanity, lurk underneath a business used as a front for tawdry activities. Men and women spill over the edge near a waiting patrol wagon and form a human river of misery.*

were tried and found guilty. Upon appeal, the Supreme Court held that although the U.S. government could not regulate prostitution because the court felt prostitution was an issue for each state to decide, the federal government could regulate travel for "immoral purposes" or purposes of prostitution.

The Supreme Court broadened the scope of the Mann Act in *Caminetti v. United States*. In March 1913, Drew Caminetti and his friend Maury Diggs, both of whom were married and having affairs, took their mistresses by train from Sacramento, California, to Reno, Nevada. Their wives tipped off the police, and both men were arrested upon their arrival in Reno. Caminetti and Diggs were tried and found guilty of violating the Mann Act. Upon appeal, the Supreme Court held that noncommercial and/or consensual extramarital sex acts fall under the broad scope of "immoral purposes."

Throughout the past 100 years, although various changes have been made, the U.S. Supreme Court has repeatedly ruled that prosecution under the Mann Act is constitutional. In 1978 and 1986, the Mann Act was amended to (1) update the definition of "transportation," (2) include gender-neutral (male or female) protections against sexual exploitation and child pornography, and (3) replace the terms *debauchery* and *immoral purposes* with the phrase *any sexual activity for which any person can be charged with a criminal offense*. This provided the framework for allowing the U.S. government to remove itself from legislating morality while retaining and strengthening the foundation of the Mann Act as a prosecutorial weapon in the fight against human trafficking.

In one of its most recent and highly publicized applications, in 2008, the Mann Act was used by federal prosecutors out of New York as an investigative tool regarding the criminal activities of an organized prostitution ring, directed at the Emperors Club VIP; the investigation included in its focus then New York Governor Elliot Spitzer.

Tony Gaskew
University of Pittsburgh at Bradford

See Also: Nevada; Prostitution, History of; Sex Offender Laws.

Further Readings
Caminetti v. United States, 242 U.S. 470, 37 S. Ct. 192, 61 L. Ed. 442 (1917).
Grittner, F. K. *White Slavery: Myth, Ideology, and American Law*. New York: Garland, 1990.
Hoke v. United States, 227 U.S. 308, 33 S. Ct. 281, 57 L. Ed. 523 (1913).
Langum, D. *Crossing Over the Line: Legislating Morality and the Mann Act*. Chicago: University of Chicago Press, 1994.
"White-Slave Traffic Act of 1910." *United States Statutes at Large*. Washington, DC: Government Printing Office, 1911.

Manson, Charles

Charles Manson (1934–) was an illegitimate, unplanned child, born to a 16-year-old mother. His mother was irresponsible, into drugs and criminal activity, and utterly unable to care for a child. She reportedly sold him when he was a young child for a pitcher of beer. As a result, Manson bounced from relative to relative and eventually began practicing the same behavior as his mother. He was first caught stealing at age 9, and his crimes got progressively worse as he was transferred from one "school for boys" to another across the nation. He was found to be emotionally needy, criminally sophisticated, and moderately intelligent, with an IQ of 106. Although eventually he was released from the juvenile placement centers, his patterns of behavior did not change, even after the 1955 birth of his child, Charles Manson, Jr. His offenses ranged from pimping and the theft of government checks to grand theft auto and rape. He was in and out of jails and prisons through March 21, 1967, when he was released and put on a bus to San Francisco.

The "Family"
Proficient with a guitar, Manson was soon able not only to blend into the hippie lifestyle but to collect followers. He kept these individuals, mostly emotionally battered young women, under control by twisting their notions of good and evil and plying them with LSD and other amphetamines. The main idea behind Manson's infamous Helter

Skelter, named after the Beatles song of the same name, was that Armageddon was soon going to occur: The black populations of the world were going to rise up against the whites and kill and enslave them; however, according to Manson, they would be unable to retain their power, so he and his followers would hide out in a hole in the desert until they had amassed a population of 144,000, at which time they would come out of hiding into a world that was now theirs. Charles Manson was the fifth angel, also known as Jesus Christ. The Beatles were the other four.

Manson decided that he needed to jump-start Helter Skelter and sent his "Family" out on separate occasions to brutally murder high-profile individuals, crimes they hoped would be blamed on the blacks. The most notorious of these was actress Sharon Tate. Tate was eight months pregnant with her husband Roman Polanski's child. She and her group of friends (Abigail Folger and her boyfriend Voytek Frykowski, and Jay Sebring) were gathered together in a gated ranch house off Cielo Drive, above Beverly Hills. They, along with Tate's unborn child and Steve Parent, a young man who came to visit the caretaker, were all stabbed, beaten, or shot to death August 9, 1969. When the police arrived, they found "PIGS" hand-painted in blood on the wall. The next night, Manson's followers murdered Leno and Rosemary LaBianca in much the same way: shooting, then multiple stabbings (approximately 42 to Rosemary, alone). This time, they left a misspelled "HEALTHER SKELTER" and "DEATH TO PIGS" in blood.

Within a month after the LaBianca murders, a gun matching ballistics was found and turned in to the Los Angeles Police Department (LAPD), and tips had come in from several different sources. However, the entire truth was still unknown until Susan Atkins disclosed a detailed description of both series of murders to two inmates, Virginia Graham and Ronnie Howard. Both inmates managed to inform the proper authorities, and in conjunction with several outside reports about the Manson family, the LAPD felt they finally had a solid case and made the arrests. It took the grand jury only 20 minutes to hand down the final indictments: Charles Manson, Charles "Tex" Watson, Patricia Krenwinkel, Susan Atkins, and Linda Kasabian were each charged with seven counts of murder and one count of conspiracy to commit murder; Leslie van Houten was charged with two counts of murder and one count of conspiracy to commit murder. On January 15, 1971, after a long, drawn-out trial, during which a lawyer and a witness had been murdered and the judge was violently threatened by Manson himself, the verdict was guilty on all counts.

On March 29, the death penalty was imposed for all the defendants. In 1972, the California Supreme Court abolished the death penalty in the state; all of the defendants are now serving life sentences. Manson has been a relatively unruly prisoner since incarceration, ending up in the Secure Housing Unit (SHU) several times, and always for offenses such as distributing drugs or threatening prison staff. He had been eligible for parole every five years but did not show up for his hearings in 2007 or 2012. The denial of his 2012 bid likely means that he will never be granted parole as he will not be eligible again until 2027, when he would be 92.

Brandy B. Henderson
University of South Florida

See Also: 1961 to 1980 Primary Documents; California; Capital Punishment; Serial and Mass Killers.

Further Readings
Bugliosi, V. and C. Gentry. *Helter Skelter: The True Story of the Manson Murders*. New York: Bantam, 1982.
Crime Library. "Charles Manson and the Manson Family." http://www.trutv.com/library/crime/serial_killers/notorious/manson/murder_1.html (Accessed December 2010).
Hickey, Eric. *Serial Murderers and Their Victims*. Belmont, CA: Wadsworth, 2010.

Mapp v. Ohio

In *Mapp v. Ohio* (1961), the Supreme Court extended its decision on the federal exclusionary rule from *Weeks v. United States* (1914) and overruled the precedent of *Wolf v. Colorado* (1949).

In *Weeks*, the court held that evidence obtained without a search warrant, and, therefore, in violation of Fourth Amendment protections against "unlawful search and seizure," could not be used in federal criminal prosecutions. The court, however, did not specify whether the exclusionary rule applied to state criminal prosecutions. In *Wolf*, the court held that state courts were bound by the Fourth Amendment and were required to obtain warrants for searches, but, nevertheless, stopped short of extending the exclusionary rule to state courts.

In *Mapp*, the court overruled *Wolf* and held that the exclusionary rule did apply to state criminal prosecutions. This important legal decision firmly established the exclusionary rule in criminal procedure and disallowed the use of unlawfully obtained evidence in criminal prosecutions in the United States. By extending the exclusionary rule to state courts, the court strengthened the Fourth Amendment's protections of personal privacy and security from official lawlessness. Furthermore, *Mapp* was the first of several cases in which the court re-evaluated the role of the due process clause of the Fourteenth Amendment as it applied to the states. *Mapp* marked a period of change in the court toward greater judicial activism on behalf of civil rights and liberties.

On May 23, 1957, police officers from the Cleveland Police Department received a tip from an informant that a suspect in a bombing case was hiding in the home of Dollree Mapp. The officers also suspected that Mapp was in possession of illegal gambling equipment in her home. Three officers arrived on the scene and demanded entrance into Mapp's home, but she called her attorney and refused to let them enter without a search warrant. More officers arrived on the scene and then, a few hours later, the officers forcibly entered her home. When Mapp demanded to see the warrant, one officer waved a piece of paper in front of her. She grabbed the paper and a struggle ensued as the officers rescued the "warrant." The police officers handcuffed Mapp for being belligerent and proceeded to search her home.

Meanwhile, Mapp's attorney arrived, but the officers refused to let him enter the home or see his client. During the search, the officers did not find the suspect or any illegal gambling equipment;

A 1957 mug shot of Dollree Mapp in Cleveland, Ohio. After police failed to present an authentic search warrant at her home, Mapp's appeal eventually reached the Ohio Supreme Court.

however, in her basement, they found a trunk that contained sexually explicit books, pictures, and photographs. The officers arrested Mapp for possession of documents that were illegal under Ohio's obscenity law prohibiting "lewd, lascivious, and obscene material." At her trial, Mapp's attorney asked about the search warrant, but the police failed to present a copy of the warrant. Nevertheless, Mapp was convicted of violating Ohio's obscenity law.

Mapp appealed to the Ohio Court of Appeals, and subsequently to the Ohio Supreme Court, on the basis that Ohio's obscenity law violated her First Amendment right to freedom of expression and that the police's warrantless search of her home violated her Fourth Amendment right to privacy and security from police harassment. Her attorney argued that the illegally obtained evidence should not have been admissible at trial. The Ohio courts were not convinced that Mapp's First Amendment rights had been violated and they used *Wolf* as a precedent to uphold the admissibility of illegally obtained evidence at trial in state criminal prosecutions. Her appeals were denied.

Mapp appealed her case to the U.S. Supreme Court. The case was argued on March 29, 1961, and after deliberations, on June 19, 1961, the court held that the exclusionary rule did apply to state courts. The court held that the due process clause of the Fourteenth Amendment extended the Fourth Amendment's protections of privacy to the states. Therefore, the exclusionary rule should also be enforceable against the states. Furthermore, the exclusionary rule was necessary to discourage law enforcement from violating the protections of the Fourth Amendment. Subsequent court decisions in *Nix v. Williams* (1984) and *United States v. Leon* (1984), however, have modified the exclusionary rule by creating the "inevitable discovery" and "good faith" exceptions.

Julie Ahmad Siddique
City University of New York Graduate Center

See Also: Federal Rules of Criminal Procedure; Police Abuse; Reform, Police and Enforcement; *Weeks v. United States*; *Wolf v. Colorado*.

Further Readings

Long, Carolyn. Mapp v. Ohio: *Guarding Against Unreasonable Searches and Seizures.* Lawrence: University Press of Kansas, 2006.

Zotti, Priscilla. *Injustice for All*: Mapp v. Ohio *and the Fourth Amendment*. New York: Peter Lang, 2005.

Marbury v. Madison

Marbury v. Madison (1803) was a case decided by the U.S. Supreme Court, and Chief Justice John Marshall's opinion established judicial review. Judicial review is the power of the Supreme Court to review any statute for its adherence to the United States Constitution. Although important in retrospect, the Supreme Court did not use judicial review to strike down a congressional statute again until *Scott v. Sandford* (1857). In the wake of the presidential election of 1800, in which President John Adams was defeated by Thomas Jefferson, the Federalists in the national elected branches took steps to minimize their losses. With the aid of Congress, President Adams offered more than 200 federal court nominations. Most importantly, Chief Justice Oliver Ellsworth stepped aside, which allowed the president to nominate John Marshall, then secretary of state, to become the nation's fourth chief justice.

Additionally, President Adams nominated several justices of the peace for the District of Columbia. Although the Senate voted to confirm the nominees for these positions, Secretary of State John Marshall forgot to deliver the commissions. James Madison, secretary of state under newly elected President Jefferson, refused to deliver the commissions. William Marbury, whose nomination had been confirmed by the Senate, asked the Supreme Court to issue a writ of mandamus in an effort to receive his commission as justice of the peace. This action was possible under the Judiciary Act of 1789, which allowed the high bench to issue such a writ to anyone holding federal office. In a carefully crafted opinion, Chief Justice Marshall suggested that the court ask itself three questions. First, did Marbury have the right to receive the commission as justice of the peace? Marshall answers affirmatively that Marbury does have such a right. Second, Marshall asks if U.S. law affords Marbury a remedy to having not received his rightful commission. Marshall again answers affirmatively, stating that U.S. law does, indeed, afford him these protections.

Finally, Marshall asks if the correct remedy is "a *mandamus* issuing from this court?" It is the answer to this question, answered negatively, that provides the heart of this opinion. Marshall declared that "[i]f congress remains at liberty to give this court appellate jurisdiction, where the constitution has declared their jurisdiction to be original; and original jurisdiction where the constitution has declared it to be appellate; the distribution of jurisdiction, made in the constitution, is form without substance." In other words, as Article III, Section 2, of the Constitution defines when the Supreme Court will have original jurisdiction, Congress's efforts to expand the court's original jurisdiction under the Judiciary Act, which Marbury used to take his case directly to the Supreme Court, is contradictory to the Constitution. As such, Marshall continues, "that an act of the legislature, repugnant to the constitution, is void." And, whose job is it to decide if a law is "repugnant to the constitution?" According to the Chief Justice, the answer is clear. The apex of Marshall's opinion comes when he announces that "[i]t is emphatically the province and duty of the judicial department to say what the law is."

Marshall's opinion does two things. First, it helps to establish the Supreme Court as a co-equal branch of the national government. While this position is taken for granted today, the court did not always enjoy such prestige. For example, before Chief Justice Marshall established the Supreme Court's legitimacy, some Supreme Court justices retired for what was then considered "higher office," including Chief Justice John Jay, who resigned to become governor of New York, and Justice John Rutledge, who resigned to become the chief justice for the South Carolina Supreme Court. Another, more important, example of the Supreme Court's lack of institutional legitimacy was the reaction of President Thomas Jefferson when the court agreed to take Marbury's case. First, Jefferson supporters in Congress began to consider impeaching two sitting justices. Additionally, Congress and the president acted to abolish the 1802 Supreme Court term rather than allow the court to hear the case.

Although not used again against acts of Congress until 1857 in *Scott v. Sandford*, the power of judicial review is a cornerstone power that the Supreme Court has over the elected branches of the national and state governments. Its reach has extended into nearly all areas of national policy, including criminal law and punishment. By the 1990s, the Supreme Court had declared about 150 federal laws and 1,200 state laws unconstitutional. Areas of particular interest include state laws about the civil rights and liberties found in the Bill of Rights and legislation. Recent examples of the use of judicial review to overturn local or state laws are the gun rights case from Chicago, *McDonald v. Chicago*, in which the Supreme Court said that an absolute ban on firearms violates the Second Amendment, and *Lawrence v. Texas*, in which the Supreme Court overturned a Texas state law forbidding homosexual acts, on the grounds that the law violated the due process clause of the Fifth and Fourteenth Amendments.

Marbury is arguably the most important case the Supreme Court has ever heard. It provided the court with its most important check on its co-equal branches at the national level and gave it a tool to keep the states in check. Importantly, the case has allowed the Supreme Court to have an incredible impact in areas of crime and punishment throughout American history.

Tobias T. Gibson
Westminster College

See Also: *Cohens v. Virginia*; Marshall, John; *Martin v. Hunter's Lessee*.

Further Readings
Howard, Robert M. and Jeffrey A. Segal. "A Preference for Deference? The Supreme Court and Judicial Review." *Political Research Quarterly*, v.57/1 (2004).
Marbury v. Madison, 1. CR.(5 U.S.) 137 (1803).
Murphy, Walter F., C. Herman Pritchett, Lee Epstein, and Jack Knight. *Courts, Judges, and Politics: An Introduction to the Judicial Process*. New York: McGraw-Hill, 2006.
Rose, Winfield H. "Further Thoughts on 'Marbury v. Madison.'" *PS: Politcal Science and Politics*, v.37/3 (2004).

Marshall, John

John Marshall (1755–1835) was the chief justice of the U.S. Supreme Court between 1801 and 1835. His court opinions during this period provided the foundation for constitutional law in the United States and helped move the U.S. Supreme Court into the center of power in the American criminal justice system, making it capable of overruling Congress. Marshall remains the longest-serving chief justice and is known for reinforcing the principle that federal courts are obligated to exercise judicial review and must examine laws purported by citizens to violate the U.S. Constitution. During his service, he helped establish the Supreme Court as the final authority on determining the meaning of the Constitution in cases and controversies that must be decided by the federal courts.

Marshall is credited with essentially solidifying the third branch of the federal government, the judiciary branch. In doing this, he focused on developing the nation's federal power in the name of the Constitution and the rule of law. These efforts were unpopular to many and brought about great opposition from those who wanted stronger state governments and state control. His tenure in office covered the span of six U.S. presidents (John Adams, Thomas Jefferson, James Madison, James Monroe, John Quincy Adams, and Andrew Jackson). Thomas Jefferson (and the Jeffersonians) disagreed with Marshall's reasoning in many of his cases, arguing that if his growing view of judicial power became common practice, it would be "placing us under the despotism of an oligarchy."

One of the most important impacts Marshall had on the internal operations of the Supreme Court was in changing how decisions were handed down and announced. Prior to his service, each justice would write his own separate opinion (also known as *Seriatim Opinion*). He changed the process into the practice of having the court hand down a single opinion (the opinion of the court), thus allowing a clear and concise ruling.

The three previous chief justices (John Jay, John Rutledge, and Oliver Ellsworth) are not perceived as having had the impact that Marshall had on the evolving court. He is credited with giving the U.S. Supreme Court the presence, power, and dignity that would allow it to take an equal place against the other branches of government (executive and legislative). To do this, Marshall used federalist approaches to build a strong federal government over the opposition of the Jeffersonian Democrats, who wanted stronger state governments. By doing this, he established the Supreme Court as the final arbiter of constitutional interpretation. This placed the court as a power that could overrule the Congress, the president, the states, and all lower courts if that is what a fair reading of the Constitution required.

Significant Rulings

While Marshall decided 44 cases in total dealing with constitutional questions, legal scholars argue that four had the most significant impact during his service. In *Marbury v. Madison* (1803), he guided the decision that it was the duty of the court to disregard any act of Congress that the court thought contrary to the Constitution. In *Cohens v. Virginia* (1821), his court held that Congress could lawfully pass an act that permitted a person who was convicted in a state court to appeal to the Supreme Court of the United States, if he alleged that the state act under which he was convicted conflicted with the Constitution or with an act of Congress. Through this case, Marshall asserted the power of the U.S. Supreme Court to review state supreme court decisions in criminal matters when individuals claim their constitutional rights have been violated.

In *McCulloch v. Maryland* (1819), the court decided that Congress, in the exercise of a delegated power, has wide latitude in the choice of means, not being confined in its choice of means to those that must be used if the power is to be exercised at all. Finally, in *Gibbons v. Ogden* (1824), the Marshall Court held that when the power to regulate interstate and foreign commerce was conferred by the Constitution on the federal government, the word *commerce* included not

John Marshall was the Supreme Court chief justice from 1801 to 1835. He is credited with solidifying the third branch of the federal government: the judiciary branch.

only the exchange of commodities, but the means by which interstate and foreign intercourse was carried out. As a result, Congress had the power to license vessels to carry goods and passengers between the states, and an act of one of the states making a regulation that interfered with such regulation of Congress was, *pro tanto*, of no effect. These cases essentially established the Supreme Court as the final interpreter of the Constitution.

Marshall had the ability to be a judge more than simply a statesman. He felt that his responsibility was not only to decide many historical constitutional questions properly but also to ensure that the people of the United States should be convinced of the correctness of his interpretation of the Constitution. His opinions, therefore, had to carry to those who studied them a conviction that the Constitution, as written, had been interpreted according to its evident meaning. When discussing his rulings, he stated that he simply used logic in making his determinations. He believed that one should look at the question at issue, the guarantees of the U.S. Constitution, and allow the inexorable rules of logic to do the rest. In doing so, he delivered decisions that were simple, clear, and dignified.

Life Outside the Court

Being an author and family man were two other activities on which he worked equally hard. Being an admirer of President George Washington, he published a five-volume biography titled *Life of Washington*. Marshall used this biography of Washington to discuss the history of the American colonies and to reiterate his federalist ideals. His home and family were in Richmond, Virginia. While he was never viewed as being religious and never joined a church, he did help several churches in his hometown build several memorials to lost members. Given his professional responsibilities, he was required to live in Washington, D.C., for a three-month annual term and additional weeks while serving as a circuit court judge in Raleigh, North Carolina.

In 1923, Marshall's outside interests led him to become the first president of the Richmond branch of the American Colonization Society, which was dedicated to resettling freed American slaves in Liberia, on the west coast of Africa. In 1829, he was a delegate to the state constitutional convention. During his service as a delegate, he spoke strongly to promote the necessity of an independent judiciary. Mary Willis Ambler, his wife of 49 years, died on December 25, 1831. Marshall's ailing health was exacerbated by the stress of this event, and he died in July 1835 at the age of 79, having served as the chief justice of the U.S. Supreme Court for more than 34 years.

Gordon A. Crews
Marshall University

See Also: *Cohens v. Virginia*; *Gibbons v. Ogden*; *Marbury v. Madison*; *McCulloch v. Maryland*; Supreme Court, U.S.

Further Readings
Abraham, H. J. *Justices and Presidents: A Political History of Appointments to the Supreme Court*, 3rd ed. New York: Oxford University Press, 1992.
Beveridge, A. *The Life of John Marshall, in 4 Volumes*. Boston: Houghton Mifflin, 1919.
Corwin, E. W. *John Marshall and the Constitution: A Chronicle of the Supreme Court*. New Haven, CT: Yale University Press, 1919.
Johnson, H. A. *The Chief Justiceship of John Marshall From 1801 to 1835*. Columbia: University of South Carolina Press, 1998.

Martin v. Hunter's Lessee

Martin v. Hunter's Lessee was an 1816 case brought before the U.S. Supreme Court in which the court ordered a state, Virginia, to follow its decrees. In the early years of the republic, during which the fledgling national government was struggling to assert its authority over the established state governments, this case was one of a few seen as having decisive legal authority toward stabilizing the relationship between the federal and state governments in a manner consistent with federal superiority. This case began when a British loyalist, Lord Fairfax, inherited land in Virginia. When the Revolutionary War began, the elderly Fairfax remained in Virginia. When he died in 1781, he left the land to his nephew, a British subject who lived in England. The inheritance was not allowed by Virginia law, however, because the state said that no "enemy" could be left land in an inheritance. The state confiscated the land, and assigned a portion of property to David Hunter, who began to sell tracts. Denny Martin, Fairfax's nephew, believing he had inherited the land, began to sell it as well, and Supreme Court Chief Justice John Marshall was among those who purchased land from the inheritance. Because of this transaction, Justice Marshall recused himself from the Supreme Court's decision, meaning that he did not participate in the proceedings of the court. The case came to the Supreme Court, and the court found that the Virginia law was in violation of the provision in the 1783 Treaty of Paris, which states that the United States would prevent the confiscation of land from British loyalists.

Decision

This case, although related, begs a different question than the one raised in *Marbury v. Madison*, a case in which the question was the expansion of the court's original jurisdiction by Congress. In *Marbury*, the Supreme Court's answer was that tampering with original jurisdiction was unconstitutional. In *Martin*, the court, in a decision penned by Justice Joseph Story, allowed that Congress could alter its appellate jurisdiction.

The Virginia Supreme Court declined to follow the U.S. Supreme Court's order and issued a decision that stated that the state court was not subject to the U.S. Supreme Court's appellate jurisdiction. Furthermore, according the state court, the Judiciary Act of 1789 was unconstitutional to the extent that it extended the Supreme Court's appellate jurisdiction over the state court's decisions. The Virginia Supreme Court's decision was appealed to the Supreme Court, which decided that Congress could expand its appellate jurisdiction, such as it had in Section 25 of the Judiciary Act, to review state court decisions that related to federal law.

According to Justice Story, the national judicial branch can serve to overturn presidential or congressional actions, and such a check on state courts should not be considered dangerous to the republic's system of government. Moreover, with the Supreme Court's power of judicial review over state tribunals, it can act to ensure a uniform system of law within the constitutional system.

Ramifications

Martin v. Hunter's Lessee is a foundational case for substantiating the claim that the Supreme Court has jurisdiction over state courts. Although the court was not fully solidified until 1821, when it decided *Cohens v. Virginia*, the *Martin* case was instrumental in impacting the role that the Supreme Court has in its relationship with state judicial systems. The Supreme Court has played major roles in many state cases, including the criminalization of segregation and increases in the protections afforded by the Constitution's warrant clause.

Some commentators opine that Story was strongly influenced by Chief Justice Marshall, although Marshall had recused himself. No matter which member of the Supreme Court was primarily responsible for the opinion, it is a landmark in American constitutional law. *Martin* played a major role in establishing the federal government's—and the Supreme Court's—primacy over state governments. Although the Supreme Court's appellate role and its ability to exercise judicial review over state judiciaries were not firmly established until 1821 in *Cohens v. Virginia*, the Supreme Court laid its foundations in *Martin*.

Tobias T. Gibson
Westminster College

See Also: *Cohens v. Virginia*; *Marbury v. Madison*; Marshall, John.

Further Readings

Epstein, Lee and Thomas G. Walker. *Constitutional Law for a Changing America*, 6th ed. Washington, DC: CQ Press, 2007.

Randall, Richard S. *American Constitutional Development*. New York: Longman, 2002.

Schwartz, Bernard. *A History of the Supreme Court*. New York: Oxford University Press, 1993.

Maryland

The fifth most populous state in the Union, Maryland was one of the original Thirteen Colonies, having been founded by royal charter as a haven for Catholics by Lord Baltimore. Though other states have since become more predominantly Catholic, Maryland is unique among the original colonies in its Catholic origins. In later years, Maryland was famous as the site of Fort McHenry, the bombardment of which during the War of 1812 was the basis for the lyrics of "The Star-Spangled Banner."

The first prisons in Maryland—the Maryland Penitentiary and the Maryland House of Correction—were built in the 19th century and operated autonomously until 1916, when they were reorganized under the State Board of Prison Control (superseded by the Board of Welfare in 1922 and the Department of Correction in 1939). The Maryland Penitentiary was built in 1811 and was intended to house a small number of prisoners who would be used as work gangs during the day and kept in solitary confinement at night. Prior to the building of the penitentiary, convicts were kept in county jails for short periods of time or used in work gangs, spending their nights in guarded workhouses. After the Civil War, the penitentiary was criticized for its working and living conditions, resulting in reformations that included a prison library, night school for illiterate convicts, and the building of the Maryland House of Correction in Anne Arundel County, designed for inmates serving less than three years. From 1921 to 1940, the facility served as Maryland's women's prison, until a new women's prison was opened. For most of Maryland's history, inmates were used as contract laborers in a wide variety of industries. Contract labor was restricted after World War I and eventually eliminated in 1937.

Police and Punishment

The earliest law enforcement in Maryland was handled by town constables and county sheriffs, and as towns grew larger, the constabulary was transformed into a professional police force. The modern Baltimore Police Department was established in 1845 by act of the state legislature. The difference between constable and police officer was not merely semantic: constables were neither trained nor paid as professionals and often held other jobs, especially in small towns or early decades. Further, it was the professional police departments that introduced modern police procedures and technology, like police call boxes and fingerprinting.

Maryland has had a capital punishment statute since the colonial era, and until the latter half of

An 1888 issue of Frank Leslie's Illustrated Newspaper *shows a state police steamer overhauling a pirate boat on Chesapeake Bay. After the Civil War, the growing oyster-harvesting industry sparked "oyster wars," clashes between pirates and lawmen.*

the 20th century, nearly every execution had been by hanging in public in the county of the crime's occurrence; the exceptions were a female slave burned at the stake, and a soldier shot for desertion. From 1808 (when first-degree murder was statutorily defined) until 1908, death was always the penalty for first-degree murder; after that time, the sentencing judge was given the option of life imprisonment, and beginning in 1916, juries were given the option of returning a sentence of "guilty without capital punishment." The public outdoor hangings of Maryland's early days were eliminated in 1922, which sought to eliminate the unsavory specter of large crowds by moving hangings indoors to the Maryland State Penitentiary. Beginning in 1955, the method of execution changed to a lethal gas chamber. This was changed again in 1994 to lethal injection.

Like the rest of the country, Maryland's death penalty was suspended after the Supreme Court's 1972 *Furman v. Georgia* decision, which required capital punishment statutes to be redrafted in order to ensure consistency in their application. In Maryland's case, this led to the death penalty again being the mandatory sentence for first-degree murder, and the Maryland legislature adopted the method introduced in Georgia and affirmed in its constitutionality by the 1976 *Gregg v. Georgia* decision, that of bifurcated trials, in which the jury first decides guilt, and then punishment, with a review of aggravating and mitigating circumstances, and a mandatory appellate review. In the late 1980s, Maryland's death penalty law was amended to exclude the mentally disabled and juveniles from execution.

In 2002, executions in Maryland were halted by executive order until a University of Maryland–College Park study could be conducted to examine the fairness of the application of the death penalty. The study eventually found both racial and geographic disparities, implying that the statute as applied did not fulfill the requirements for constitutionality established in *Furman*. However, the next governor, Robert Ehrlich, ended his predecessor's moratorium in 2004. Executions were subsequently suspended again in 2006 when the Maryland Court of Appeals found in its *Evans v. Maryland* decision that the protocol for lethal injections had not been adopted via the process mandated by the state's Administrative Procedures Act. This suspension was unexpectedly extended in 2011 when Hospira, the company manufacturing the sodium thiopental used in Maryland's lethal injections, announced it was ending distribution, which required the state to draft new regulations. Governor Martin O'Malley has attempted to use the suspension as an opportunity to end capital punishment in the state, but the legislature has not been amenable; meanwhile, five inmates await eventual execution on death row.

Crime
Maryland's Criminal Injuries Compensation Board (CICB), run by the Department of Public Safety and Correctional Services, is a payer of last resort for financial assistance to the victims of violent crime, including medical and mental health expenses, lost wages, crime scene cleanup expenses, and funerals. Claims must be filed and are examined for eligibility, particularly including contributory misconduct on the part of the victim. All other means of payment must have been exhausted, and there is a total cap of $45,000 including category-specific caps. The money paid out to victims is generated by fees collected from criminal offenders, not the state's tax budget. A 2003 internal review of the CICB found that it worked well for those who filed, but only about a quarter of crime victims were familiar with the program, while at least two-thirds had injuries or expenses that seemed to meet eligibility requirements. Further, a quarter of victims elected not to pursue a needed service because of cost concerns that the program might have been able to alleviate.

Maryland is one of the states that has adopted a victim-offender dialogue program, since 2005. Intended to serve the needs of victims, the program arranges mediated encounters between victims and their incarcerated offenders in carefully controlled environments, in order to help victims with the healing process. Only certain types of crime victims are eligible, and the program involves counseling in preparation for the dialogue. Because of the care with which the encounters are handled, less than 10 dialogues have been arranged each year since the program's inception.

Following the national trend, the violent crime rate in Maryland rose steadily after World War II, doubled from 1960 to 1966, again in 1968, and peaked in the 1990s (1,000 violent crimes per 100,000 inhabitants, up from 151 in 1960) before declining again (547 in 2010). The rate remains high relative to the national average (403.6 in 2010); Maryland's violent crime rate exceeded the national average in 1964 and has remained above average since.

Bill Kte'pi
Independent Scholar

See Also: 1600 to 1776 Primary Documents; Baltimore, Maryland; Capital Punishment; Victim Rights and Restitution.

Further Readings
Baltimore County Public Library. "Maryland History." http://www.bcplonline.org/info/history/maryland.html (Accessed September 2011).

Lane, Charles. *Stay of Execution*. Lanham, MD: Rowman & Littlefield, 2010.
Okonowicz, Ed. *True Crime: Maryland*. Mechanicsburg, PA: Stackpole Books, 2009.

Maryland Toleration Act of 1649

Charles I granted Cecilius (Cecil) Calvert, second Lord Baltimore, the proprietary charter for a "palatinate" (feudal government) called Maryland in April 1632. The charter application and settlement plans originated with his father George Calvert, but he died. The charter's controversy was over George's earlier conversion to Roman Catholicism and consequent resignation as a royal minister. Protestant opponents thought that Maryland would become a Catholic colony with residents loyal to the pope instead of to the king. Two ships, the *Ark* and the *Dove*, including Jesuit priests, made landfall in March 1634. Most of the 20 gentlemen aboard were Catholic, but the majority of the 200 servants and craftsmen were Protestant. Cecil Calvert left instructions with his brother Leonard, the governor, that Catholics should conduct privately their observances and avoid religious discussions. Cecil Calvert, as lord proprietor, had the power to lay taxes, provide landed estates, designate officials, and set up churches. Early Protestant and Catholic settlers shared a church structure in St. Mary's, the original capital. Religious liberty and relative tranquility was the norm in Maryland. Puritans fleeing religious persecution in Virginia settled in Maryland and actively participated in political life. This was contemporaneous with the English Civil War (1642–51), when Puritans under Oliver Cromwell beheaded Charles I. English religious and political strife would affect events in Maryland throughout the 1600s.

The Maryland legislature, or General Assembly, formed in 1634, and four years later Cecil Calvert acceded to settler demands to instigate bills. In 1647, there was an unsuccessful Protestant rebellion against the government. In 1648, Cecil appointed as governor a Protestant Virginian, William Stone. The April 21, 1649, Acts of Assembly contain "An Act concerning Religion," which later on became popularly known as the Maryland Toleration Act. The act covers four pages and is not subdivided in the modern style, but there are two distinct preambles and two sets of proscriptions subject to punishment. Carl Everstine, Maryland's legislative reference director, set out the accepted view that the act's first part originated with the Puritan-led assembly, while the second part was written by Cecil Calvert, reflecting his pragmatic religious toleration. Dr. Everstine's modern spellings are used in the following statutory quotations.

The first preamble states, "In a well governed and Christian commonwealth, matters concerning religion and the honor of God ought in the first place to be taken into serious consideration and endeavored to be settled." The act sets out the death penalty and confiscation of lands to the lord proprietary for blaspheming God, cursing or denying "Jesus Christ to be the son of God," or denying or using "reproachful speeches words or language concerning" the Holy Trinity. There were fines or whipping or jailing for non-payment, for such language regarding the Virgin Mary, the holy Apostles, or Evangelists, or for calling "in a reproachful manner" any person in the Maryland "Province a heretick, Scismatick, Idolator, puritan, Independent, Presbiterian, popish priest, Jesuite, … Lutheran, Calvinist, Anabaptist, Brownist, Antinomian, Roundhead, Separatist, or [other religious name]." Profaning the Sabbath by intoxication, disorderly recreation, or unnecessary work was fined. The only recorded case of a person capitally charged was Jacob Lumbrozo, a Jewish Portuguese doctor who immigrated to Maryland and became a prominent landholder. In 1658, he allegedly challenged Jesus's divinity. Before trial, Lord Protector Richard Cromwell provided an amnesty for England and the colonies, possibly sparing Lumbrozo his neck.

The second preamble states, "whereas the enforcing of the conscience in matters of religion hath frequently fallen out to be of dangerous consequence in those commonwealths where it hath been practiced, and for the more quiet and peaceable government of this Province and the better to preserve mutual love and amity among the inhabitants," followed by the proscriptions "no person

... professing to believe in Jesus Christ shall ... be any ways troubled, molested [i.e., disturbed] or discountenanced for or in respect of his or her religion nor in the free exercise thereof within this Province ... nor any way compelled to the belief or exercise of any other religion against his or her consent, so as they be not unfaithful to the Lord Proprietary, or molest or conspire against the civil government." This was subject to fine and damages to the wronged party, with whipping and imprisonment for nonpayment. The act was repealed by the 1654 legislature, a pro–English Commonwealth body. This repeal was undone when Lord Baltimore reestablished control in 1658. Following England's Glorious Revolution, a Protestant rebellion took over Maryland in 1689, passing anti-Catholic laws and attempting to establish the Church of England.

Nigel J. Cohen
Independent Scholar

See Also: 1600 to 1776 Primary Documents; Colonial Courts; Maryland; Religion and Crime, History of.

Further Readings
Everstine, Carl N. "Maryland's Toleration Act: An Appraisal." *Maryland Historical Magazine*, v.79/2 (1984).
Maryland State Archives. "Proceedings and Acts of the General Assembly January 1637/8–September 1664." http://www.msa.md.gov (Accessed May 2011).

In this 1793 engraving, Lycurgus looks at the equal laws of religious and civil liberty as placed in the hands of Cacilius Calvert Baron of Baltimore, who was the original establisher in his colony of Maryland many years before William Penn.

Massachusetts

One of the original thirteen colonies and among the oldest settlements in the United States, the Commonwealth of Massachusetts has long enjoyed cultural and political significance. As the "Cradle of Liberty," Boston was home of many of the agitators who presaged the Revolutionary War; the Industrial Revolution in the United States began in Lowell and Springfield; the transcendentalist and abolitionist movements of the 19th century centered around Massachusetts; and the Pioneer Valley was home not only to the Reformed Puritan pastor Jonathan Edwards, who catalyzed the first Great Awakening, but is now home to the Five College system, which is considered a bastion of liberal education.

Crime
Massachusetts is one of the states with a number of "blue laws" grounded in religious proscriptions, many of them dating from the Puritan period. For instance, until 1990, off-premises alcohol sales (that is, bottles or cans, as opposed to beverages served in an establishment) were universally banned on Sundays. In 1990, an exception was made for towns within 10 miles of the New Hampshire or Vermont borders. In

1992, Sunday sales were permitted from the Sunday before Thanksgiving until New Year's Day. Since 2004, alcohol sales have been legal on all days except Thanksgiving, Christmas, and Memorial Day.

Organized crime in Massachusetts is dominated by the Boston-based Winter Hill Gang and the Patriarca crime family. The Winter Hill Gang, named for the neighborhood in Somerville (north of Boston), has been active since the 1950s and has included many prominent Boston gangsters. The gang first came to national attention during the Irish Gang War of the 1960s, waged against the McLaughlin Gang of Charlestown, and was at its greatest influence in the 1960s and 1970s. In time, the gang's ability to acquire territory proved superior to its ability to make use of that territory and effectively generate revenues, and by the end of the 1970s, gang leaders were forced to borrow money from the Angiulo brothers. The activities of the Winter Hill Gang have inspired movies like *The Departed* and TV series like *Brotherhood*.

The Angiulo brothers—Donato, Francesco, Gennaro, and James—were associates of the Patriarca crime family and represented Patriarca interests in Boston's North End and the northern New England states from the 1950s to about the 1980s, when their power waned as a result of Winter Hill Gang members "Whitey" Bulger and Stephen Flemmi informing on them to the FBI, leading to Gennaro's arrest. Bulger, after being tipped off by his Federal Bureau of Investigation (FBI) handler about a pending indictment, later went into hiding, and was a fugitive at large from 1994 to 2011, when he was apprehended in Santa Monica, California, and extradited to Massachusetts. The 48 charges for which he awaits trial include 19 counts of murder, multiple conspiracy charges, narcotics distribution, and extortion. The Bulger trial is expected to bring to light many specifics about corruption in Massachusetts.

The Patriarcas began with the criminal organization of Gaspare Messina, a Sicilian immigrant, in Boston in 1916. His successor, Phil Buccola, ran the family from 1924 to 1954, expanding its bootlegging, gambling, and loan shark operations before retiring to Sicily. It was under Buccola's successor, Raymond "Il Patrone" Patriarca, that the family acquired its current name and relocated its base of operations to the Federal Hill neighborhood of Providence, Rhode Island, where Il Patrone ran the front operations, the National Cigarette Service Company and Coin-O-Matic Distributors.

The violent crime rate in Massachusetts is close to the national average. Once significantly lower than the national average (48.8 crimes per 100,000 people in 1960, compared to the national average of 160.9), it began to catch up to the national average in the 1970s and eventually exceeded it in the 1990s, when both state and national crime rates peaked (804.9 in Massachusetts in 1993). Since that peak, the crime rate has steadily declined (466.6 in 2010), but has remained higher than the national rate.

Police

The Boston Police Department, formed in 1838, is one of the oldest police departments in the United States and was part of the growing trend of professionalization in law enforcement. Founded as the Day Police and operated independently of the night watch, which had operated since 1635, it first supplemented the night watch and then replaced it. In 1854, the Day Police were reorganized as the Boston Police Department and modeled after the Metropolitan Police Service in London.

When Massachusetts-born Robert Kennedy, brother of President John F. Kennedy, was appointed attorney general in 1961, he declared organized crime one of his top priorities, in response to the public attention to the Apalachin meeting of organized crime figures in 1957. Under Kennedy's direction, law enforcement authorities focused not only on increasing arrests but on cultivating informants within criminal groups, including Joe Barboza, a Patriarca hit man who was arrested on a concealed weapons charge in 1966 and who soon agreed to serve as a government witness in cases against many of the high-ranking members of the Patriarca family. Barboza gave false testimony against many Patriarca rivals and was killed by button men for the Angiulo brothers a few months after his 1975 release on parole.

Punishment

The first state prison in Massachusetts was Castle Island, on the shore of the Boston Harbor. First used as a fort by the English, it was converted to a prison at the end of the 18th century. Castle Island was used to house inmates from all over Massachusetts, including the northern territory that later became the separate state of Maine. The island facility was eventually replaced with more modern prisons. MCI-Concord, the Massachusetts Correctional Institution at Concord, is the oldest functioning prison in the state, having opened in 1878.

Massachusetts is one of 16 states without capital punishment, though there have been several attempts to reinstate it, the most recent by Governor Mitt Romney in 2007. The death penalty had been used in Massachusetts since the colonial era and was infamously applied to 26 people (about 8 percent of the state's total executions throughout history) convicted of witchcraft. Until 1951, first-degree murdered carried a mandatory death sentence; in that year, a new law allowed juries in cases in which murder was not committed in connection to a rape or attempted rape to recommend life imprisonment if there were mitigating circumstances. Interestingly, Romney notwithstanding, there is a long tradition in Massachusetts of gubernatorial opposition to the death penalty. The last executions in the state were of Phillip Bellino and Edward Gertson in 1947; in the decades following, six different governors routinely commuted death penalties to life sentences.

Following the 1972 Supreme Court ruling in *Furman v. Georgia*, death penalty statutes throughout the country were suspended until they could be rewritten to address the court's constitutionality concerns. For years afterward, Massachusetts death penalty advocates worked to pass a working death penalty law in the state, amending the state constitution in 1982 to state, "No provision of the Constitution ... shall be construed as prohibiting the imposition of the punishment of death," in order to help guarantee the compatibility between a death penalty statute and the state constitution. However, the statute passed inadvertently created a circumstance encouraging murder defendants to plead guilty in order to avoid a jury trial, thus avoiding the possibility of a death sentence—a violation of the right to trial by jury as well as the right to protection from self-incrimination. The statute was thus invalidated by the Massachusetts Supreme Judicial Court in 1984, and no subsequent effort to adopt a working statute has succeeded. The gubernatorial tide turned in 1991 with the election of Republican William Weld; he and every governor since have argued in favor of the death penalty.

Bill Kte'pi
Independent Scholar

See Also: 1600 to 1776 Primary Documents; 1777 to 1800 Primary Documents; Boston, Massachusetts; Kennedy, Robert F.; Rhode Island.

Further Readings
Brown, Richard D. *Massachusetts: A Concise History*. Amherst: University of Massachusetts Press, 2000.
Ethier, Eric. *True Crime Massachusetts: The State's Most Notorious Criminal Cases*. Mechanicsburg, PA: Stackpole Books, 2009.
Harshbarger, Scott. "Improving Reentry Is the Goal of Prison Reform." *CommonWealth Magazine* (Fall 2005).

Matteawan State Hospital

Matteawan, a state hospital for the criminally insane, was founded in 1893 in Fishkill, New York. The institution was representative of the new practice of creating specific facilities to house mentally ill criminals. Despite its stated goal to "cure" insane patients who had committed crimes, Matteawan suffered from many of the problems typical of late-19th-century penal institutions such as overcrowding and neglect of inmates. After several administrative changes and the creation of new facilities on the Matteawan grounds, Matteawan closed in 1977. The patients were relocated, and the institution was renamed Fishkill Correctional Facility; it presently operates as a medium-security prison.

Housing the Criminally Insane
In the colonial era, mentally ill individuals were cared for by their families or their local communities. This changed in the late 18th century. Special institutions were created to house the insane.

In this undated photograph from Bain News Service, inmates sit in the men's room at the Matteawan asylum. Opened in 1893 in Fishkill, New York, Matteawan housed mentally ill criminals, whom reformers wanted to separate from the populations of both the general prison system and traditional insane asylums. Designed to house 550 patients, it was at full capacity within two years and was overcrowded at 719 inmates six years after opening. Poor care, undertrained staff, and overcrowding led to neglect and deaths.

These were not medical facilities designed for treatment; rather, they were intended to separate those suffering from mental illness from the rest of society. By the mid-19th century, most states were operating insane asylums. However, mentally ill individuals who committed crimes were dealt with by the justice system and were incarcerated along with sane criminals.

The first institution in the United States to house the criminally insane was opened in 1859 at Auburn State Prison in New York. The founding of this facility marked a decisive shift within penal ideology in America. Reformers wanted to separate mentally ill criminals from the general prison population and from those housed in traditional insane asylums. During this era, both the legal and medical definitions of "insanity" were highly debated. The most influential Anglo-American legal guideline was the M'Naghten "right-or-wrong" test: If an individual could not recognize that the criminal act he/she committed was wrong, he/she could not be found guilty. Although the Auburn facility was originally created for convicts who were supposedly driven mad while incarcerated, by 1870, it housed criminals who were acquitted according to this insanity defense.

Almost immediately, the Auburn facility, like many penal institutions, suffered from overcrowding. The lack of sufficient provisions for inmates forced the opening of a new facility for the criminally insane, located in the town of Fishkill, New York. The location for the new institution was specifically chosen for its pastoral environment; it was a 250-acre site between the Hudson River and the Fishkill Mountains. This isolated rural setting was thought to encourage a peaceful state of mind, aiding recovery. I. G. Perry, the architect hired to design the facility, created the structure according to several provisions: provide enough windows for adequate light and ventilation (which was believed to be therapeutic), and yet place them high enough above the ground to prevent escape. The institution was named Matteawan State Hospital. It began to accept patients in 1892 and officially opened in 1893.

Matteawan was designed to house 550 patients. Two years after its opening, it was at full capacity. By 1899, the institution housed 719 inmates, which caused many of the same overcrowding problems that had contributed to its creation in the first place. There were not enough beds or chairs for the inmates, forcing many to sleep and eat on the floor. The low pay and poor training of the Matteawan staff led to misdiagnoses and neglect of the patients. Many died while incarcerated.

By this time, New York had changed its statutes regarding the discharge of criminally insane patients. Previously, if an individual had completed his sentence and either showed signs of improvement or was no longer considered dangerous, he was released. However, after 1895, New York ended this practice. Now, inmates who had completed their term were no longer discharged but instead remained at Matteawan until they were no longer considered insane by medical officials. By 1900, Matteawan continued to incarcerate almost 300 individuals who had served their time for the crime they had committed.

In 1904, Matteawan began accepting female inmates, particularly those who had been convicted of a crime and then diagnosed as insane after incarceration. Although prison officials recognized that there were individuals who may have been misdiagnosed, they also understood that in many cases inmates were indeed driven mad by long-term imprisonment.

Evolution of the System

Treatment of the inmates at Matteawan was in general accordance with the treatment of the mentally ill at noncriminal insane asylums. The only major difference was the increased security at Matteawan for patients who were prone to violence. Some of the more capable inmates were prescribed work duties: cooking, farming, making clothing, and carpentry. Others spent their time conversing with other inmates and participating in a variety of games, like cards and chess. Most were allowed daily outdoor exercise. By the mid-20th century, prescription drugs were used extensively, and the facility experimented with hypnosis and electric shock treatments.

In 1926, the New York Department of Mental Hygiene assumed control of Matteawan State Hospital. One year later, the New York Department of Corrections took over the institution. However, in 1961, Matteawan was back under the jurisdiction of the Department of Mental Hygiene. These administrative debates were representative of the indecisiveness that would eventually signal the end of Matteawan.

A new facility was added to the Matteawan grounds in 1966—the Beacon Institution for Defective Delinquents, renamed the Beacon State Institution in 1967. It was designed for mentally ill juvenile offenders who were at least 16 years old. However, just three years later, Beacon began to be closed down, and in 1974, the site was renamed Fishkill Correctional Facility. Matteawan State Hospital continued to house patients in tandem with Fishkill until 1977. In that year, Matteawan was officially closed, and the remaining patients were transferred to other institutions. Currently, Fishkill Correctional Facility operates on the original Matteawan site as a medium-security prison.

Katherine Harmer
Lehigh University

See Also: Auburn State Prison; Insanity Defense; M'Naghten Test.

Further Readings

Conrad, Peter and Joseph W. Schneider. *Deviance and Medicalization: From Badness to Sickness.* Philadelphia: Temple University Press, 1981.
Gilfoyle, Timothy. *A Pickpocket's Tale: The Underworld of Nineteenth-Century New York.* New York: W. W. Norton, 2006.
New York Correction History Society. http://www.correctionhistory.org (Accessed September 2011).
New York State Archives. http://www.archives.nysed.gov (Accessed September 2011).

Mayflower Compact

Shortly before their disembarkation in the Massachusetts Bay on November 21, 1620, the passengers of the *Mayflower* made a compact that was meant to promote a sense of unity. The document asserted the signers' commitment to establish a colony, set up a basic framework for its government, and created an important precedent for the new colony's autonomy.

A Change of Plans

The need for the compact arose after some unexpected changes in the *Mayflower*'s itinerary. Its passengers had a patent from the Virginia Company to settle near the mouth of the Hudson River, where their voyage was expected to culminate. On the way to America, however, the *Mayflower* drifted too far north and landed in what is now Massachusetts. After some efforts to sail south failed, the passengers made a decision to settle in the Massachusetts Bay. The change of plans essentially invalidated the patent they held, created a legal vacuum, and caused some tensions among the passengers. Most of them were Separatists, or Pilgrims, a closely knit group of nonconformists who came to America in search of religious freedom. But the *Mayflower* also carried a substantial contingent of non-Pilgrims, who did not share the Pilgrim's religious concerns and came to America primarily for economic reasons. Some non-Pilgrims argued that since the circumstances forced them to settle in the area not specified in the patent, they were perfectly free to conduct themselves as they saw fit.

To prevent discord, the Pilgrim leaders drew a compact. Out of 73 men on board, 41 signed the document: 37 Pilgrims and four non-Pilgrims. Among them were the first three governors of Plymouth. Most importantly, the compact was meant to emphasize the importance of laws and establish a temporary, loosely defined government. The move was important in order to dispel the notion that the lack of valid patent allowed colonists to do whatever they pleased. The compact starts with the declaration that the colonists are "loyal Subjects" of the king. To ensure their "better ordering and preservation," they pledge to establish "a civill body politike" by creating "just and equall Lawes, Ordinances, acts, constitutions, [and] offices," to which they promise "all due submission and obedience."

Although the compact asserted the signers' submission to the king's authority, it actually relied on the progressive notion that the government can operate only with the consent of the governed. The document was drawn without a consultation with the proper authorities, thus suggesting that people had the right to create laws. Furthermore, it emphasized the importance of colonists' involvement in the local government. In fact, right after the signing of the compact, the Pilgrims went on to elect their first governor. The democratic overtones in the compact reflect the Congregational principles that the Separatists embraced—and for which they were persecuted in England. They believed that people were free to separate themselves from the Church of England, the only official church in the country, and form their own congregations.

The compact was not specific enough to create a well-defined government, nor did it have any legal weight, particularly after the Plymouth colony received an official patent from London in 1621. The document, which was not even referred to as the Mayflower Compact till 1793, was hardly mentioned in early American records. Its text was not widely available until the publication of William Bradford's history *Of Plymouth Plantation* (1620–47), which was rediscovered only in the 1850s. Although some parallels can be made between the compact and the U.S. Constitution, there is no historical evidence that the authors of the latter were familiar with the compact. In the 19th century, the compact started to acquire a mythical status in American culture. John Adams, in his 1802 speech, lauded it as a distinctly American document. The compact's importance was further enhanced in the 1850s; it was included in the bas relief encircling the U.S. Capitol rotunda, which commemorates the most significant events in American history. The subject also inspired several well-known paintings, most notably by Tompkins H. Matteson and Jean Leon Gerome Ferris, which reflected the growing fascination with the Mayflower Compact.

Alexander Moudrov
Queens College, City University of New York

See Also: Bodie of Liberties; Massachusetts; Puritans.

Further Readings

Donovan, Frank R. and Hedda Johnson. *The Mayflower Compact*. New York: Grosset & Dunlap, 1968.

Langdon, George D. *Pilgrim Colony: A History of New Plymouth 1620–1691*. New Haven, CT: Yale University Press, 1966.

Lord, Arthur. *The Mayflower Compact*. Worcester, MA: Proceedings of the American Antiquarian Society, 1921.

McCarthy, Joseph

Joseph McCarthy's (1908–1957) controversial political career began with his surprising victory over Robert La Follette for the senatorial nomination; yet, he is perhaps best known for his political focus during the 1950s on the infiltration of communists in American public institutions. McCarthy's anticommunist movement was largely referred to as "McCarthyism."

Joseph McCarthy was born November 14, 1908, on a farm in Appleton, Wisconsin. He was the fifth of nine children and his parents were devout Roman Catholics. McCarthy left high school at age 14 and worked as a chicken farmer before becoming manager at a grocery store in the nearby town of Manawa. He returned to high school in 1928, and after completing the necessary qualifications, earned a place at Marquette University to study law. After graduating, McCarthy worked as a lawyer but was unsuccessful and supplemented his income by playing poker. In 1940, he became a circuit court judge but resigned when the United States entered World War II. McCarthy joined the U.S. Marines where he served in the Pacific, achieving the rank of captain.

In 1946, after the war, McCarthy defeated Robert La Follette for the Republican senatorial nomination and then defeated his Democratic opponent in the subsequent election. McCarthy had criticized La Follette for not enlisting during the war, even though La Follette was already 46 years old when Pearl Harbor was bombed and was too old to join the armed services. McCarthy spent three years in the South Pacific in World War II debriefing combat pilots, yet word got back to Wisconsin that he had fought as a tail gunner and suffered a war wound. McCarthy's experience as a tail gunner included patrols over islands already abandoned by the Japanese, and the war wound actually occurred when he broke his foot falling down a ship ladder. Nonetheless, McCarthy's victorious campaign for the Senate seat included the slogan, "Congress needs a tail gunner." McCarthy also appeared in campaign posters wearing full fighting gear, an aviator's cap, and multiple belts of machine gun ammunition wrapped around his torso. McCarthy also accused La Follette of war profiteering when his investments had actually been in a radio station. La Follette, deeply hurt by the false claims made against him, would soon retire from politics and later committed suicide.

McCarthy, the youngest member of the Senate at age 38, called a press conference on his first day to propose a solution to a coal strike. McCarthy's proposal called for the coal miners to be drafted into the military, so if they refused

Senator Joseph McCarthy in 1954. He is best known for his zealous anticommunist stance, called "McCarthyism." During the 1950s, McCarthy created committees to interview people suspected of communist sympathies and ties.

to mine coal they could be court-martialed for insubordination and shot. During his first three years, he voted along generally conservative lines, although not necessarily the Republican line; he worked against sugar rationing and fought for housing legislation.

Detractors eventually came forward, claiming that McCarthy had lied about his war record; he also was investigated for tax offenses and for taking bribes from the Pepsi-Cola Co. Fearing he would not be reelected, McCarthy held a meeting with some of his closest advisers and asked for suggestions about how he could retain his seat in the Senate. Edmund Walsh, a Roman Catholic priest, recommended a campaign against communists. In 1950, McCarthy made a speech to a Republican women's group in Wheeling, West Virginia, where he declared that communists had thoroughly infiltrated the U.S. State Department. He further stated that he had a list of 205 names; although, in the following days and weeks, the list decreased to 57 and then increased back to 81. Before the speech that day in Wheeling, McCarthy was still primarily known as the man who had defeated La Follette. Afterward, became daily television viewing.

McCarthyism

During the 1950s, McCarthy created committees to interview people suspected of communist leanings. Many were accused of being disloyal to the United States or spying for communist countries, and those who spoke out against the government were viewed as threats to society. McCarthy's efforts were viewed as indiscriminate and were widely attacked by American liberals and the American political left. He was accused of using sensationalist tactics and unsubstantiated accusations, which gave rise to the term *McCarthyism*. McCarthy was further described as a demagogue, mocked as an offensive example of fascism, and accused of persecuting good, patriotic Americans. A Senate investigation committee under Millard Tydings exonerated the U.S. State Department and labeled the charges a hoax. Pressured to produce evidence, McCarthy refused and continued to make accusations.

McCarthy was reelected in 1952 and continued to exploit the public's fear of communism as he became chairman of the Senate Permanent Investigation Subcommittee. In April 1954, he accused Secretary of the Army Robert T. Stevens and his aides of attempting to conceal evidence of espionage activities that McCarthy and his staff had allegedly uncovered at Fort Monmouth, New Jersey. The army, in turn, accused McCarthy, his chief counsel, and a staff member of seeking to obtain preferential treatment through improper means for a former consultant to the subcommittee. President Dwight D. Eisenhower persuaded the Senate to censure McCarthy's abuse of power, and though he remained in the Senate, he was ignored by the government and the media and died of acute alcoholism in 1957.

Michael Bush
Northern Kentucky University

See Also: 1941 to 1960 Primary Documents; Eisenhower, Dwight D. (Administration of); Espionage.

Further Readings
Achter, Paul. "TV, Technology, and McCarthyism: Crafting the Democratic Renaissance in an Age of Fear." *Quarterly Journal of Speech*, v.90/3 (2004).
Fried, Richard. "'Operation Polecat': Thomas E. Dewey, the 1948 Election, and the Origins of McCarthyism." *Journal of Political History*, v.22/1 (2010).
Morgan, Ted. *Reds: McCarthyism in Twentieth-Century America*. New York: Random House, 2004.
Schrecker, Ellen. *Many Are the Crimes: McCarthyism in America*. Boston: Little, Brown, 1998.

McCleskey v. Kemp

McCleskey v. Kemp was a Supreme Court decision in 1987 that upheld the use of the death penalty, which was challenged by Warren McCleskey (who was black) as unconstitutional due to racial biases in sentencing and in the administration of capital punishment in Georgia. It is one of the most controversial decisions on the use of capital punishment following the Supreme Court's reinstatement of capital punishment in *Gregg v. Georgia* in 1976.

McCleskey and three other accomplices entered a furniture store, tied up the customers, and robbed the manager. In response to a silent alarm, a police officer entered the front door of the store and was shot and killed. McCleskey was later apprehended for an unrelated offense and admitted he had participated in the furniture store robbery, although he denied having shot the police officer. At trial, McCleskey was found guilty of two counts of robbery and murder of a peace officer, which made him eligible for a capital sentence under Georgia law. The jury recommended the death sentence for the murder, and the court followed the jury's recommendation.

McCleskey subsequently filed several state-level appeals, all of which were denied. He then appealed to a federal district court. Included in his 18 claims was the argument that the capital sentencing process used in Georgia was administered in a racially discriminatory manner that violated the equal protection clause of the Fourteenth Amendment. Moreover, McCleskey argued, the increased risk of capital punishment on the basis of race also constituted an arbitrary use of this punishment, in violation of the Eighth Amendment.

The basis of these arguments came from research by David Baldus and his colleagues (referred to as the Baldus study) that demonstrated a statistically significant disparity in the application of capital punishment in Georgia based on the race of the victim and, to a lesser degree, on the race of the offender. Baldus and his colleagues analyzed over 2,000 murder cases in Georgia in the 1970s and found that defendants charged with killing white persons received the death penalty 11 percent of the time, while those charged with killing black persons received it only 1 percent of the time. They also found that blacks received the death penalty in 4 percent of cases, while whites received it in 7 percent of cases, which constituted a significant overrepresentation in the racial application of capital punishment.

The district court concluded that there was no prima facia case to support McCleskey's argument that his race, or the race of the victim, played a role in the imposition of the death penalty. It also found that there were substantial methodological errors in the Baldus Study and, on these grounds, rejected McCleskey's Eighth and Fourteenth Amendment arguments. This finding was upheld by the Eleventh Circuit Court, at which point McCleskey appealed to the Supreme Court.

The Court's Opinion

In its opinion, the court ruled against McCleskey 5–4. Delivering the opinion, Justice Lewis Powell noted that McCleskey's appeal under the equal protection clause did not establish that racially unequal application of capital punishment in Georgia specifically impacted McCleskey's sentencing. Even assuming the Baldus study was correct, the court argued, it failed to sufficiently demonstrate discriminatory intent on the part of the prosecutor, judge, or jury. Second, the majority found that McCleskey's appeal on Eighth Amendment grounds of "disparate impact" (as demonstrated by the Baldus study) was permissible in other venues such as jury venires but was not applicable to capital cases. Rather, the court argued, the differing composition of decision makers in individual capital cases made it impossible to know how individual juries might reach such decisions. In this regard, without evidence that established discriminatory intent, the opinion of the court was that juries should be given latitude to bring to their deliberations "qualities of human nature" and "varieties of human experience" that may result in disparities in sentences.

The impact of *McCleskey v. Kemp* was substantial. It was, and arguably remains, the last substantive challenge to *Gregg v. Georgia*. Following the ruling, several legal scholars likened it to earlier Supreme Court rulings such as *Dred Scott v. Sandford* and *Plessy v. Ferguson* for its upholding of racially discriminatory practices. Moreover, in ruling that the aggregate racial effects of capital punishment in Georgia were alone not sufficient to overturn the use of capital punishment, the court's ruling has restricted challenges to this punishment to cases that can show discriminatory intent.

William R. Wood
University of Auckland

See Also: African Americans; Appeals; Capital Punishment; Cruel and Unusual Punishment; *Dred*

Scott v. Sandford; Georgia; *Gregg v. Georgia*; Juries; *Plessy v. Ferguson*; Racism; Sentencing; Supreme Court, U.S.; Trials.

Further Readings
Baldus, D., C. Pulaski, and G. Woodworth. "Comparative Review of Death Sentences: An Empirical Study of the Georgia Experience." *Journal of Criminal Law & Criminology*, v.74/3 (1983).
Kennedy, R. L. "*McCleskey v. Kemp*: Race, Capital Punishment and the Supreme Court." *Harvard Law Review*, v.101/7 (1988).
McCleskey v. Kemp, 481 U.S. 279 (1987).

McCulloch v. Maryland

In 1819, the U.S. Supreme Court heard the case *McCulloch v. Maryland*, which focused on whether the state of Maryland had the right to tax the notes of the Second Bank of the United States branch in the state per the requirement of state law. The court ultimately concluded that the Constitution does not expressly give Congress the power to create a bank but it does award it the power to tax and spend. As such, the creation of a national bank is an implied power necessary to carry out the ability to tax and spend. Since federal laws have clear superiority over state laws when the two conflict, the state of Maryland had no power to tax the national bank. The previous decision of the Maryland Court of Appeals was reversed.

The debate over whether the national government should create corporations began in 1791 as a battle between Alexander Hamilton and Thomas Jefferson. In 1816, Congress decided to create the Second Bank of the United States to be headquartered in Philadelphia. A year later, the Second Bank opened a branch in Baltimore, where it issued notes, discounted promissory notes, and performed other banking tasks. Maryland then attempted to impede the business of the Maryland branch of the Second Bank of the United States by imposing a special tax on all notes of banks that were not chartered in Maryland. The act was titled "An Act to Impose a Tax on All Banks, or Branches Thereof, in the State of Maryland, Not Chartered by the Legislature." While the law was potentially generalizable to any bank, the Second Bank of the United States was the only one not chartered in Maryland at the time of the ruling. It required banks to use a special stamped paper for all notes and to pay 2 percent of the value of the notes as a tax—or a general tax of $15,000 annually.

At that time, James McCulloch was the head of the Baltimore branch of the Second Bank of the United States, and he refused to pay the tax to Maryland. John James—who was an informer who aimed to collect fines for the state—brought the suit to the court's attention. Maryland argued that the Constitution of the United States is "silent on the subject of banks." As a result, the Maryland Appellate Court sided with the state, and a writ of certiorari was issued to bring the case before John Marshall's Supreme Court.

The Supreme Court unanimously sided with the Second Bank of the United States and deemed Maryland's law to be unconstitutional. To start, Marshall—writing for the court—reminded the country that the Constitution was a social contract whereby government binds the state sovereignties. He stated there could be no doubt "that the government of the Union, though limited in its powers, is supreme within its sphere of action."

The Second Bank of the United States, founded in 1816 in Philadelphia. James McCulloch, head of the Baltimore branch that opened the following year, refused to pay the special tax on notes of banks that were not chartered in Maryland.

Hence, national law is supreme to state law when in conflict. Second, Marshall pointed out that it would not be pragmatic, or wise, to list every power Congress has. Just because the word *bank* is not found in the Constitution does not mean that Congress does not have an implied right to create a bank in order to carry out its duty to tax and spend. Lastly, Marshall highlighted the necessary and proper clause and reminded the state of Maryland that this power allows Congress to create the bank to begin with.

The fundamental case established two principles: (1) the Constitution grants to Congress implied powers that are necessary and proper for creating a functional national government, and (2) state action cannot impede valid constitutional exercises of power by the federal government. It was a key moment in the history of federalism, as it began the long process of forming a balance between state and federal power. The decision was controversial in its time as opponents of the bank remained angry, and citizens of Maryland worried that the unwillingness of the federal government to pay the tax demonstrated an attempt to gain too much power over the states—much like the British had previously. The case further served as a clear indication that the Marshall Court would side with federal government in cases against the states so long as the Constitution could be interpreted in an appropriate way. It is important to note that the ruling made in this case has had a tangible impact on crime and criminal justice, particularly since the late 1950s, because it permits the federal government to impose criminal laws on states that are deemed necessary and proper for fulfilling their role.

William J. Miller
Southeast Missouri State University

See Also: Constitution of the United States of America; Maryland; Supreme Court, U.S.

Further Readings
Gunther, Gerald, ed. *John Marshall's Defense of McCulloch v. Maryland.* Palo Alto, CA: Stanford University Press, 1969.
Hammond, Bray. "Bank Cases." In *Quarrels That Have Shaped the Constitution*, John A. Garraty, ed. New York: Harper & Row, 1987.
Plous, Harold J. and Gordon E. Baker. "*McCulloch v. Maryland*: Right Principle, Wrong Case." *Stanford Law Review*, v.9 (1957).
Smith, Jean Edward. *John Marshall: Definer of a Nation.* New York: Henry Holt & Co., 1996.

McKinley, William (Administration of)

William McKinley is more associated with economic and military measures than with important reforms of American legal institutions, although juvenile courts were created during his administration. In spite of this record, McKinley trained as a lawyer, and his political career was launched thanks to the cases that he defended and that allowed him to show a commitment to workers' rights. Yet, McKinley's determined, bold presidential style began to alert many Americans that the president was increasing the authority of his office at the expense of citizens' rights. Although as a young Republican McKinley had campaigned for the enfranchisement of blacks, in the matter of race relation, his administration was unable to challenge the "separate but equal" doctrine that found its first application in the Supreme Court ruling in *Cummins v. County Board of Education* (1899). In addition, his aggressive foreign policy greatly conditioned the lives of people outside American borders. These factors generated a climate of suspicion against the president among radical and anarchist groups that made McKinley the most infamous crime case during his presidency: his own assassination at the hands of Polish American anarchist Leon Czolgosz.

Born on January 29, 1843, in Niles, Ohio, William McKinley fought the Civil War in the Union army, where he eventually became a brevet major of volunteers. After the war, he began working for Charles Giddens, who had one of the most famous legal studies in Poland, Ohio. In 1866, McKinley went to the state of New York to study law at the renowned Albany Law School. He was admitted to the bar in Warren, Ohio, in March 1867 and opened his own practice in Canton, which, with its promising industrial prospects, seemed the perfect center to launch a political career. McKinley soon became the associate of prominent attorney Judge George W. Belden, and the cases that he discussed gave him the reputation of a calm and rational lawyer and a skillful orator. In 1870, he was elected prosecuting attorney for Stark County, a position that gave him increased visibility and a larger audience, although, for a slim margin, he was not re-elected for a second term. While in charge, McKinley was coherent with his increasing activism in the temperance movement, vigorously prosecuting the illegal sale of liquor to Mount Union College.

The Striking Mine Workers' Case

McKinley had his most famous case as a lawyer in the spring of 1876 when the economic depression engineered by the Panic of 1873 led to labor troubles in the Tuscarawas Valley. The workers in the coal mines in the valley went on strike, demanding better wages and improved working conditions. The mine operators decided to use strikebreakers to continue production, but their presence led to violent clashes with the strikers, and Governor Rutherford B. Hayes was forced to send troops to reestablish order. The strike was quickly terminated by military intervention, and a group of strikers were arrested for disorderly conduct. Although public opinion was strongly unsympathetic to the strikers' case, hearing that no lawyer had accepted it, McKinley took it. He successfully demonstrated that the violent events surrounding the strikes could have been avoided had the mine operators been more sensible. McKinley managed to have all workers but one acquitted and refused to accept a fee for his services.

This case paved the way for McKinley's political career, as even his opponent and mine owner Marcus Alonzo Hanna appreciated the lawyer's thorough approach. A leading Republican, Hanna became one of McKinley's staunchest supporters throughout all his political campaigns. When he became president in 1896, McKinley even offered Hanna a cabinet post, but Hanna refused it. As Ohio governor, McKinley promoted legislation to prevent labor disputes and violent events like those in the Tuscarawas Valley. He sponsored laws to improve the security of dangerous workplaces and created an arbitration system to prevent the exacerbation of strikes.

During McKinley's administration, in 1899, the first juvenile courts were established. Until then, in most states, there was no difference in the prosecution and punishment of adults and children. The establishment of the juvenile court gave the opportunity to begin developing a modern juvenile justice system. Although the first juvenile court was established in Illinois, when McKinley served as Ohio governor, he explicitly demanded from the legislature further appropriations for reform schools and for the creation of a specific penal system for young offenders that could rehabilitate rather than simply punish them.

McKinley was elected president just after the Supreme Court upheld the "separate but equal" doctrine with the ruling in *Plessy v Ferguson*, which was further confirmed by the court with *Cummins v. County Board of Education* (1899). McKinley had been raised an abolitionist and promoted several African Americans to appointed offices. Yet, for fear of alienating southern voters, his administration did not challenge either the rulings or the segregation laws (commonly known as Jim Crow laws) that quickly proliferated throughout the American south to make African Americans inferior citizens to whites. Although sympathetic to the African Americans' fate in a segregated society, McKinley did not exercise federal power to enforce the Fifteenth Amendment. This state of affairs meant that African Americans' legal rights did not significantly improve until the 1960s.

McKinley was assassinated on September 6, 1901, in Buffalo, New York, while in the city to deliver a speech at the Pan-American Exposition the previous day. His murderer was the deranged anarchist Leon Czolgosz. Although Czolgosz was an assassin acting alone, the murder provoked a national hysteria against immigrants and leftists who became potential terrorists and threats to national security. The perception that Italians and eastern European Jews had radical ideas led nativist groups to campaign to bar them from American soil.

Luca Prono
Independent Scholar

See Also: African Americans; Czolgosz, Leon; Juvenile Courts, History of; Strikes.

Further Readings

Miller, Scott. *The President and the Assassin: McKinley, Terror, and the Empire at the Dawn of the American Century.* New York: Random House, 2011.

Morgan, Howard W. *William McKinley and His America.* Kent, OH: Kent State University Press, 2003.

McNabb v. United States

McNabb v. United States is a 1943 U.S. Supreme Court ruling that requires all persons arrested under federal criminal violations to be brought promptly before a committing federal magistrate for an initial appearance. This decision, along with the U.S. Supreme Court rulings in *Upshaw v. United States* (1948) and *Mallory v. United States* (1957), led to the McNabb-Mallory doctrine, which excludes from federal criminal proceedings confessions obtained after an "unnecessary delay" in presenting a person arrested before a federal magistrate. Although the McNabb-Mallory doctrine is still applied in various jurisdictions, in 1968, Congress passed the Omnibus Crime Control and Safe Streets Act, which allowed the admission of a confession at trial as long as the confession was "voluntary," making the requirement for persons arrested under federal criminal violations to be brought promptly before a federal magistrate just one element in determining the admissibility of a confession.

Additionally, Title 18 U.S.C. A. § 3501 et seq. provides specific guidelines for the admissibility of confessions in criminal proceedings: In any criminal prosecution brought by the United States or by the District of Columbia, a confession shall be admissible in evidence if it is voluntarily given. Before such confession is received in evidence, the trial judge shall determine any issue as to voluntariness. The trial judge, in determining the issue of voluntariness, shall take into consideration all of the circumstances surrounding the giving of the confession, including (1) the time elapsed between arrest and arraignment of the defendant making the confession, if it was made after arrest and before arraignment; (2) whether such defendant knew the nature of the offense with which he was charged or of which he was suspected at the time of making the confession; (3) whether such defendant was advised or knew that he was not required to make any statement and that any such statement could be used against him; (4) whether such defendant had been advised prior to questioning of his right to the assistance of counsel; and (5) whether such defendant was without the assistance of counsel when questioned and when giving such confession.

Untaxed Whiskey

On July 31, 1940, the Chattanooga office of the Alcoholic Tax Unit received information from several informants that members of the McNabb family, a clan of Tennessee mountaineers, were selling whiskey on which federal taxes had not been paid. Federal agents devised a plan in which the informants would meet with members of the McNabb family and obtain an amount of the untaxed alcohol, and agents would then make arrests on the spot. While four agents conducted visual surveillance, the government informants met five members of the McNabb family (Emuil, Barney, Freeman, Raymond, and Benjamin McNabb) and obtained a quantity of untaxed alcohol. As agents moved in and attempted to effect arrests, the McNabbs fled the area; agents decided not to pursue them and instead secured the confiscated untaxed alcohol. Shortly afterward, a gunshot was heard, and federal agents discovered that one of their fellow law enforcement agents had been fatally wounded.

Later the same evening, federal agents entered the McNabb settlement, arresting Freeman, Raymond, and Emuil McNabb. All three were immediately placed in a holding cell in the Federal Building in Chattanooga for more than 14 hours, from 3:00 Thursday morning until 5:00 that afternoon. Benjamin McNabb surrendered to federal agents and was also placed in a detention cell. The McNabbs were never brought before a U.S. commissioner or judge for arraignment. They were provided with food but were not permitted to have visits from family or friends or to seek legal advice from attorneys. Over the 48 hours that followed, federal agents interrogated the McNabbs, obtaining confessions from Freeman, Raymond, and Benjamin. Based primarily on these confessions, Freeman, Raymond, and Benjamin were convicted of second-degree murder and sentenced to a 45-year term of imprisonment. Emuil and Barney McNabb, who made no incriminating admissions, were acquitted during the criminal trial.

On appeal, the U.S. Supreme Court ruled that the confessions of Freeman, Raymond, and Benjamin McNabb should have been excluded from trial because federal agents of the Alcoholic Tax Unit had improperly obtained the confessions by delaying the defendants' appearance before a federal judicial officer. In fact, a federal procedural law (later enacted in the Federal Rules of Criminal Procedure, Rule 5) during this time period required all federal law enforcement officers to take any person charged with any federal crime before the nearest U.S. commissioner or judicial officer for an initial appearance or arraignment. Based upon this procedure, the Supreme Court ruled that the confessions of the McNabbs should have been excluded from evidence at criminal trial. The court noted in its ruling that the arresting federal law enforcement officers had subjected the accused to the pressures of a procedure that is wholly incompatible with the vital but very restricted duties of the investigating and arresting officers of the federal government, which tends to undermine the integrity of the criminal proceeding.

Tony Gaskew
University of Pittsburgh at Bradford

See Also: Bureau of Alcohol, Tobacco, Firearms and Explosives; *Miranda v. Arizona*; Prohibition; Supreme Court, U.S.

Further Readings
Admissibility of Confessions, 18 U.S.C. A. § 3501 et seq.
Mallory v. United States, 354 U.S. 449, 77 S. Ct. 1356 (1957).
McNabb v. United States, 318 U.S. 332, 63 S. Ct. 608 (1943).
Miranda v. Arizona, 384 U.S. 436, S. Ct. (1966).
Omnibus Crime Control and Safe Streets Act of 1968, 42 U.S.C. A. § 3701 et seq.
Upshaw v. United States, 335 U.S. 410, 69 S. Ct. 170, 93 L. Ed. 100 (1948).

McVeigh, Timothy

Timothy James McVeigh (1968–2001), an American terrorist and mass murderer who sympathized with the militia movement, was responsible for the Oklahoma City bombing on April 19, 1995, an act that killed 168 people, including 19 children, and injured more than 680 others.

Before his execution by lethal injection in 2001, McVeigh was incarcerated in the U.S. Penitentiary Administrative Maximum Facility—the "Supermax"—in Fremont County, Colorado. McVeigh was born in Lockport, New York, to William and Mildred McVeigh. Those who knew him said McVeigh was withdrawn but showed an interest in computer hacking and firearms. McVeigh joined the U.S. Army in 1988, served in the first Gulf War and was given an honorable discharge in 1992. Shortly thereafter, McVeigh became more and more interested in gun rights and antigovernment literature.

Following the confrontation at Ruby Ridge and especially the Waco siege, where he protested the actions of the federal government, McVeigh traveled the country while working at gun shows. Durin this time, McVeigh became convinced America was on the brink of collapse; this led him to seek out safe areas of the country in which to live as well as to stockpile firearms and other items for survival.

Federal Target
In 1991, McVeigh reconnected with his former army acquaintance and future co-conspirator, Terry Nichols. McVeigh visited Nichols in Michigan and over the following three years they lived and worked gun shows together intermittently. During these years, McVeigh grew increasingly radical and learned from Nichols how to fashion explosives. Initially, McVeigh's anger was directed primarily at specific government officials and he contemplated a series of individual assassinations. He soon decided, however, to target a federal building for the reasons that it would be easier, more effective, and generate immediate attention from the public.

McVeigh and Nichols assembled a bomb composed of 5,000 pounds of nitromethane and ammonium nitrate in the back of a moving truck. On the morning of April 19, 1995, McVeigh parked the truck in front of the Alfred P. Murrah Building in downtown Oklahoma City and detonated the bomb. In addition to the human victims, the explosion harmed more than 300 buildings in the vicinity and caused over $650 million in damages. The bombing was the most devastating act of terrorism in American history before the events of September 11, 2001. From a scrap found in the debris, the Federal Bureau of Investigation (FBI) was able to trace the vehicle identification number of the rental truck and create a sketch of McVeigh, who had used an alias when renting the truck in Junction City, Kansas. Soon after, McVeigh was pulled over and arrested by a state trooper for driving without a license plate and illegal firearm possession. Days later, the authorities identified their inmate as the suspected perpetrator of the bombing.

In August 1995, McVeigh was charged with 11 federal counts, including use of a weapon of mass destruction and first-degree murder. He was found guilty on each count in June 1997. McVeigh asked for a necessity defense, claiming he was in imminent danger from the government, but his defense lawyers did not ultimately seek this plea. The U.S. Department of Justice requested and the jury recommended the death penalty. McVeigh's death sentence was delayed pending appeals and on June 11, 2001, he was executed by lethal injection. Nichols received 161 consecutive life sentences without parole because the jury deadlocked on the matter of the death penalty. Accomplice Michael Fortier, who aided McVeigh and Nichols in preparing the attack and who had also served previously with them in the same army company, testified as part of a plea bargain and in exchange received a prison sentence of 12 years and a $200,000 fine. Fortier's wife, Lori, was granted immunity. Upon his release in 2006, Michael Fortier entered into the Witness Protection Program.

Daniel C. Dillard
Florida State University

See Also: 2001 to 2012 Primary Documents; Gun Control; Kaczynski, Ted; Oklahoma; Oklahoma City Bombing; Ruby Ridge Standoff; Terrorism; Violent Crimes; Waco Siege; Witness Testimony.

Further Readings
Jones, Stephen and Peter Israel. *Others Unknown: Timothy McVeigh and the Oklahoma Bombing Conspiracy*. New York: PublicAffairs, 2001.
Michel, Lou and Dan Herbeck. *American Terrorist: Timothy McVeigh and the Oklahoma City Bombing*. New York: HarperCollins, 2001.
Wright, Stuart A. *Patriots, Politics, and the Oklahoma City Bombing*. New York: Cambridge University Press, 2007.

On April 26, 1995, crews search for victims following the bombing of the Alfred P. Murrah building in Oklahoma City, which killed 168 people. Timothy McVeigh was charged with 11 federal counts and executed by lethal injection in 2001.

Memoirs, Police and Prosecutors

Memoirs written by police officers and prosecutors have a long history in Europe and the United States. In the United States, the rise of the modern city created an environment in which the memoirs of tough, crusading criminal justice professionals echoed the narratives in the mass media about crime and crime fighters. Such early literary offerings include books written by George S. McWatters, the New York City policeman who was the author of a number of books about detective work. McWatters's books include *Knots Untied: or, Ways and By-Ways in the Hidden Life of American Detectives* (1871) and *Detectives of Europe and America, or, Life in the Secret Service* (1879). In *Police Records and Recollections of Boston by Daylight and Gaslight* (1873), Boston Police Chief Edward S. Savage examined 240 years of crime and justice in the city, moving from a chronology to episodes in his own career. In a memoir covering the early decades of the 20th century, Arthur A. Carey, chief of the New York Police Department (NYPD) Homicide Bureau, described his 33 years spent investigating suspicious deaths in *Memoirs of a Murder Man* (1930) and his goal not only to detect and apprehend murderers but to engage in the systematic study of homicides. At the same time, small-town police officers and prosecutors, local heroes, wrote their memoirs. These memoirs by police and prosecutors offer a view of the social worlds in which they function—that is, the cop culture or the courtroom work group.

Although the memoirs of the 19th century and early 20th century may seem dated in language and tone to the modern reader, what they share in common with the memoirs of the modern era is the author's attempt to provide the reader with a sense of the challenges faced by criminal justice professionals. This often involves recounting episodes in the career of the cop or prosecutor. In the modern era, when the author is a woman or a racial/ethnic minority, the memoir often offers insight into the issues facing police officers and prosecutors who were often excluded from such positions until the feminist and civil rights movements of the 1960s and resulting equal employment legislation.

Female Officers

In *Armed and Dangerous: Memoirs of a Chicago Policewoman* (2001), Gina Gallo writes about the years she spent on the force. A cop's daughter, Gallo had grown up witnessing the toll his job took both on her father and their family. She had not intended to become a police officer herself. But when her master's degree in psychology turned out not to provide the kind of job security she had hoped for, Gallo ended up taking a friend's suggestion and applying to the police department. The memoir follows Gallo from the academy, where she makes friends that she will have for the rest of her career, through her indoctrination as a rookie cop. As she becomes a veteran policewoman, patrolling some of the toughest neighborhoods in the city, Gallo experiences the emotional toll that dealing not only with people who commit crimes but with their victims can take on a police officer.

Gallo's memoir is one of a number of such works by female officers in the past decade. *Detective: The Inspirational Story of the Trailblazing Woman Cop Who Wouldn't Quit* (2006) is the story of Kathy Burke, who joined the NYPD in 1968, when there were only 10 women in her academy class of 950. Gallo came onto the force at a time when the public, male police officers, and social scientists were wondering if women could do the job. This was a time when women who had formerly been police matrons assigned to work with women and children were moving into the street as patrol officers. By the 1970s, Burke herself had attracted media attention with her exploits as an undercover cop. Writing with journalist Neal Hirschfeld, Burke begins her narrative with her experiences as a rookie cop, struggling to earn the respect of her male colleagues. As an undercover cop, she is involved in drug and extortion cases. She eventually becomes a detective assigned to elite NYPD units and receives an award for heroism before retiring from the force in 1991. In her memoir, Burke looks at the issues of leadership and corruption and at the emotional and physical toll of policing on officers.

In *No Backup: My Life as a Female FBI Special Agent* (2004), former agent Rosemary Dew (writing with Pat Pope) offers a rare view of women in this elite federal law enforcement agency. As the title would suggest, Dew's memoir deals with discrimination and sexual harassment in the FBI. During her 13 years as an agent, Dew concluded that corruption and the failure of leadership to deal with discrimination made the agency ineffective in responding to problems within the agency.

Memoirs of Administrators

In contrast, in *My FBI: Bringing Down the Mafia, Investigating Bill Clinton, and Fighting the War on Terror* (2005), former FBI director Louis J. Freeh (writing with Howard Means) offers a much more positive view of the FBI. A former New Jersey dockworker, Freeh attended law school and the FBI academy before becoming a U.S. prosecutor and then a federal judge. As a prosecutor, Freeh was involved in the Donnie Brasco case, in which an undercover cop infiltrated and then testified against the Bonanno crime family. Freeh took over as director of the FBI in 1993, shortly after the Branch Davidian standoff near Waco, Texas. He oversaw the investigation of the Oklahoma City domestic terrorist attack on the Alfred P. Murrah Federal Building. In the preface to his memoir, Freeh expresses his pride in the fact that during his tenure, he did nothing to bring disgrace or harm to the FBI or the country. He also notes that he was the only director in 80 years to voluntarily leave a position of such power.

Memoirs by big-city police chiefs examine the role of the police administrator at the municipal level. *Commissioner: A View From the Top of American Law Enforcement* (1977), written by Patrick V. Murphy (and Thomas Plate) is about Murphy's tenure as police commissioner of the NYPD. Murphy, who was born into a family of cops, decided to become a cop rather than a priest. Coming out of the navy after World War II, he found the NYPD offered employment and job security. He retired from the force in 1973 after serving as the commissioner. Murphy notes the bravery and sacrifice of police officers but also bemoans police corruption and rejects the use of "a repressive law-and-order approach to crime." As a former police administrator, Murphy discusses police management and the future of policing.

In a similar vein, in *Beat Cop to Top Cop: A Tale of Three Cities* (2010), John F. Timoney recalls his career. An Irish immigrant, Timoney advanced from a rookie cop to the youngest four-star chief in the NYPD. He was among those involved in police innovations under Police Commissioner Bill Bratton before moving to Philadelphia to serve as police commissioner there. In his next career move, Timoney went to Miami, where he served as police chief from 2003 to 2010. In his moves from New York to Philadelphia to Miami, Timoney had the opportunity to apply his policing strategies to cities dealing with serious crime problems.

During the same era, Daryl Gates was moving up through the ranks. In *Chief: My Life in the LAPD* (1992), former Los Angeles Police Chief Gates traces his path from the U.S. Navy to college on the GI Bill and then into the Los Angeles Police Department (LAPD). His account of his career covers the Watts riot, a shootout with the Black Panthers, and the deaths of Marilyn Monroe and Robert F. Kennedy. He discusses his apprenticeship with Chief William Parker and the policing tactics of the LAPD. He offers his perspective on the riots that shook the city after the acquittal of the police officers charged in the beating of Rodney King.

Movie Adaptations

Other memoirs have been written by former police officers whose stories have been told by Hollywood. Robert Leuci, whose career inspired the film *Prince of the City* (1981), recalls his 20 years with the NYPD in his memoir titled *All The Centurions* (2004). Serving from 1961 to 1981, Leuci spent much of that time in the Narcotics Division. His career overlapped with that of other well-known NYPD detectives, including Frank Serpico (*Serpico*) and Sonny Grosso and Eddie Egan (*The French Connection*). As Leuci looks back on his life from the vantage point of someone who has become a writer/adjunct professor, he concludes he is a different person now, someone who has learned to live with guilt and regret. *Donnie Brasco: My Undercover Life in the Mafia* (1997), written by Joseph D. Pistone (with Richard Woodley), also inspired a film. "Donnie Brasco" was the name used by former FBI agent Pistone when he was deep undercover in the Mafia. During the six-year-long sting operation, he assumed the identity of a jewel thief and won the trust of high-level mobsters. During the trial, which received intense media coverage, he was threatened with revenge and had his credibility questioned because he had spent years living a lie. Pistone discusses the impact of going deep undercover on the lives of his wife and children.

Other Subgenres
In another memoir about going undercover, William Queen, an Alcohol, Tobacco, and Firearm (ATF) special agent, tells of infiltrating the Mongols Motorcycle Club (Mongol Nation), a California-based motorcycle club. Titled *Under and Alone: The True Story of the Undercover Agent Who Infiltrated America's Most Violent Outlaw Gang* (2007), Queen's memoir recounts the 28 months that he spent as a bearded biker named "Billy St. John." Queen, who spent 20 years as an ATF agent, went undercover in 1998, gaining access to the biker gang through an informant. He eventually won the trust of gang members and even came to think of some of them as friends. His investigation led to the convictions of 50 Mongols. A few memoirs deal with the less sensational but still heroic lives of decorated urban cops. *The Soul of a Cop* (1992) by Paul Ragonese (with Berry Stainback) is an account of Ragonese's 17 years in the NYPD. During those years, he became one of the most decorated police officers in the country, earning five medals of valor, the 1986 cop of the year award, a letter of appreciation award, two hero of the month awards, and three commendations for saving lives.

Prosecutors
If the memoirs of police officers present them as heroic, if sometimes flawed, humans doing a tough job, the memoirs of prosecutors tend to present them much the same. *Twenty Against the Underworld: An Autobiography of a District Attorney and His Fight Against Organized Crime* (1974) is the autobiography that former New York City district attorney Thomas Dewey was working on at the time of his death. It was edited by Robert Campbell and published in 1974. Dewey was district attorney during Prohibition and went after gangsters, including Charles "Lucky" Luciano and "Dutch" Schultz. The "20 against the underworld" in the title was Dewey's name for his team of prosecutors.

In *Relentless Pursuit: A True Story of Family, Murder, and the Prosecutor Who Wouldn't Quit* (2007), Kevin Flynn, a former prosecutor in the Washington, D.C., U.S. Attorney's office,

Thomas E. Dewey, while governor of New York, leaves the White House after meeting with President Harry S. Truman. Dewey wrote a memoir about his experiences with organized crime while he was New York district attorney during Prohibition (1938–41).

recalls his effort to find justice for a mother and her 13-year-old daughter who were murdered. Flynn's prime suspect is the mother's former boyfriend, with whom she was embroiled in a custody battle for their son. As Flynn is taking the case to trial, he is also dealing with his own father's lung cancer diagnosis. He comes to see that he and the defendant have similar loner personalities, but the defendant is seriously disturbed. Flynn takes the reader through the process of building the case and going to trial and discusses his relationship with the victim's family. Similarly, in *Convictions: A Prosecutor's Battles Against Mafia Killers, Drug Kingpins, and Enron Thieves* (2009) Assistant U.S. Attorney John Kroger discusses his career path from rookie to confident prosecutor. He discusses the process of building and winning high-profile cases. He also considers some ethical dilemmas faced by prosecutors.

Former Oklahoma County district attorney Wes Lane's memoir, *Amazingly Graced: A Prosecutor's Journey Through Faith, Murder, and the Oklahoma City Bombing* (2010), is somewhat different than most memoirs by prosecutors. Although he discusses his career and the cases he has been involved in, the book is also a meditation on faith. As a lapsed Christian who had become a skeptic about God, Lane found himself going through experiences in his life that brought him back to his faith. He recounts a murder case in the late 1990s when he decided to go forward even though he did not have the victim's body, and how he began to feel God's presence in the workplace.

High-profile cases often produce books by the participants. Often these books are written by the defense attorneys in the case. In the double-murder trial of O. J. Simpson for the murders of his ex-wife Nicole Brown and a young man named Ron Goldman, both of the prosecutors on the case wrote memoirs. *In Contempt* (1996) is by Christopher Darden (and Jess Walter). Darden was a prosecutor who was African American in a murder trial in which the defense attorneys were alleging racism and corruption by the prosecution and the police. In his memoir, he looks at the Simpson trial in the context of the criminal justice system and high-profile media trials. Darden also discusses what he perceived as the mishandling of the trial by Judge Lance Ito and Darden's relationship with the defense team and his coprosecutor, Marcia Clark. In *Without a Doubt* (1998), Marcia Clark (with Teresa Carpenter), the lead prosecutor in the Simpson case, offers her own perspective on the trial proceedings. She concludes that the prosecution's case was strong enough for a conviction; however, the case was tainted by the allegations of racism and the jury's hostile response to the prosecution. However, she does discuss the errors made by the prosecution. On a personal note, Clark discusses the impact of being involved in a "crime of the century" on her personal life as she too achieved celebrity status and had to deal with the tabloid stories. The memoirs by these two Simpson prosecutors might well be read in conjunction with the memoir by the lead defense attorney Johnnie Cochran (*A Lawyer's Life*, 2004). Particularly in high-profile cases, these differing perspectives provide the reader with a fuller sense of the criminal process.

By the same token, the memoirs of police officers provide the reader with a sense of the "front end" of the criminal justice process as viewed by criminal justice professionals who often share common goals with prosecutors and work closely with them.

Frankie Y. Bailey
State University of New York, Albany

See Also: Adversarial Justice; African Americans; Police, Women as; Simpson, O. J.

Further Readings
Burke, Kathy and Neil Hirschfeld. *Detective: The Inspirational Story of the Trailblazing Woman Cop Who Wouldn't Quit*. New York: Scribner, 2006.
Dew, Rosemary and Pat Pape. *No Backup: My Life as a Female FBI Special Agent*. New York: Carrol & Graf, 2004.
Gallo, Gina. *Armed and Dangerous: Memoirs of a Chicago Policewoman*. New York: Forge Books, 2001.
Howe, Nick, David Wilson and Diane Kemp. "Police Disclosures: A Critical Analysis of Some Recent Police Autobiographies." *Howard Journal*, v.49/3 (2010).

Memphis, Tennessee

Memphis is a city in Shelby County, Tennessee, located on a bluff overlooking the Mississippi River. With a 2006 population of 670,902, Memphis is the largest city in Tennessee. The population is 61.4 percent African American and 34.4 percent white with smaller numbers of other ethnic groups. Thanks to its strategic riverside location and the construction of three railroad lines leading to the city in the 19th century, Memphis was an important commercial city in the 19th and early 20th centuries (and was a center of the U.S. slave trade in the 1850s, following repeal of a Tennessee law banning the internal slave trade); in the 20th century, it played an important role in the civil rights movement.

Memphis was incorporated in 1826, and that year a sheriff was appointed for Shelby County. In 1848, Memphis was granted a charter making it a city, and the police force was expanded: The office of city marshal was created, and a police station and jail were constructed. The city continued to grow in size and in 1850, 26 men served on the police force, including the city marshal (a title changed to "chief of police" in 1860). Memphis was placed under Union military occupation for three years during the Civil War (beginning in June 1862), which encouraged the growth of smuggling and profiteering. However, the fact that the Memphis police force was populated during these years by men loyal to the Union made Memphis an attractive residence for African Americans, and the African American population of the city quadrupled between 1860 and 1870. Memphis experienced several yellow fever epidemics in the 1870s, and the police department was honored by the city government for remaining on patrol while many other citizens left the city (the epidemics of 1878 and 1879 caused the deaths of about 40 percent of the force).

Crump Machine
Edward Crump ("Boss Crump") was mayor of Memphis in 1910–15 and created a political machine that controlled much of Memphis politics until his death in 1954. The Crump machine was noted for its willingness to overlook vices such as gambling and prostitution and for its disinclination to enforce Prohibition, but it was efficient in providing essential services such as garbage collection and street cleaning and in obtaining New Deal funds for public buildings and infrastructure improvements. Memphis acquired a reputation for violent crime in this period and in 1932 was described as the "murder capital of the world," as 102 homicides were committed in the city that year. The famous criminal George "Machine Gun" Kelly was a native of Memphis and was arrested there in 1933.

Police Force
After World War II, civil service exams for policemen were reimplemented, and several African Americans were appointed to the force (the department had included African American members as early as 1878, but only sporadically). In 1958, 10 women joined the force, though these commissioned officers were not armed: Women did not begin training in the same classes as men at the police academy until 1970 and were not assigned to patrol cars with male officers until 1973. One of the first women who joined the force in 1958 was Julia Clare Lester, who was promoted to lieutenant in July 1979 and to captain in 1988. The first female African American officer in Memphis was Claudine Penn, hired in 1968; Penn became the first female African American sergeant and then the first African American female captain.

In February 1968, Echol Cole and Robert Walker, sanitation workers in Memphis, were crushed to death by a truck. When the city failed to respond satisfactorily to this incident in the view of African American employees who saw it as part of a long-standing pattern of abuse and neglect, 1,300 African American men employed by the Department of Public Works went on strike, demanding better safety standards, higher wages, and recognition of their union. The strike garnered considerable public support and also drew the attention of national civil rights leaders, including Martin Luther King, Jr., who was shot and killed on April 4, 1968, while in Memphis to address the striking workers. James Earl Ray was convicted of King's murder and died in prison in 1998.

In the riots following the assassination of King, the National Guard and Tennessee Highway Patrol were called in to assist the Memphis and Shelby County forces. Several reforms were made in the police department after the King assassination: A 60-man Special Services Unit was created, a Crime Scene Squad was created to gather scientific evidence, and five four-man Sniper Squads began training. As the department was largely white and male at this time, two predominantly African American recruit classes were put through

Tennessee law was revised to authorize the use of deadly force to carry out an arrest only if all other means of arrest were exhausted, a warning was given, there was probable cause of a felony involving serious physical harm, and the suspect was believed to pose serious physical harm to the officers or others unless immediately apprehended.

According to the CQ Press rankings, based on Federal Bureau of Investigation (FBI) statistics from 2009, in 2010, Memphis had the 12th-highest crime rate in the country with a score of 236.32 (where 0 would indicate an average crime rate and a positive number a higher than average rate). In 2009, 12,055 violent crimes were reported in Memphis, including 132 murder or nonnegligent manslaughters, 382 forcible rapes, 4,139 robberies, and 7,402 aggravated assaults. In that year, 47,195 property crimes were reported, including 13,943 burglaries, 29,059 larceny-thefts, 4,193 motor vehicle thefts, and 333 cases of arson.

Sarah Boslaugh
Kennesaw State University

See Also: African Americans; Civil Rights Laws; Racism; Strikes.

Further Readings
Ashmore, Eddie M. "The History of the Memphis Police Department." http://www.memphispolice.org/Memphis%20PD%20History.pdf (Accessed June 2011).
CQ Press. "City Crime Rankings 2010–2011." http://os.cqpress.com/citycrime/2010/citycrime2010-2011.htm (Accessed June 2011).
Stanford University. "Martin Luther King, Jr., and the Global Freedom Struggle." http://mlk-kpp01.stanford.edu (Accessed June 2011).
Tennessee Historical Society. "The Tennessee Encyclopedia of History and Culture Version 2.0." http://tennesseeencyclopedia.net (Accessed June 2011).

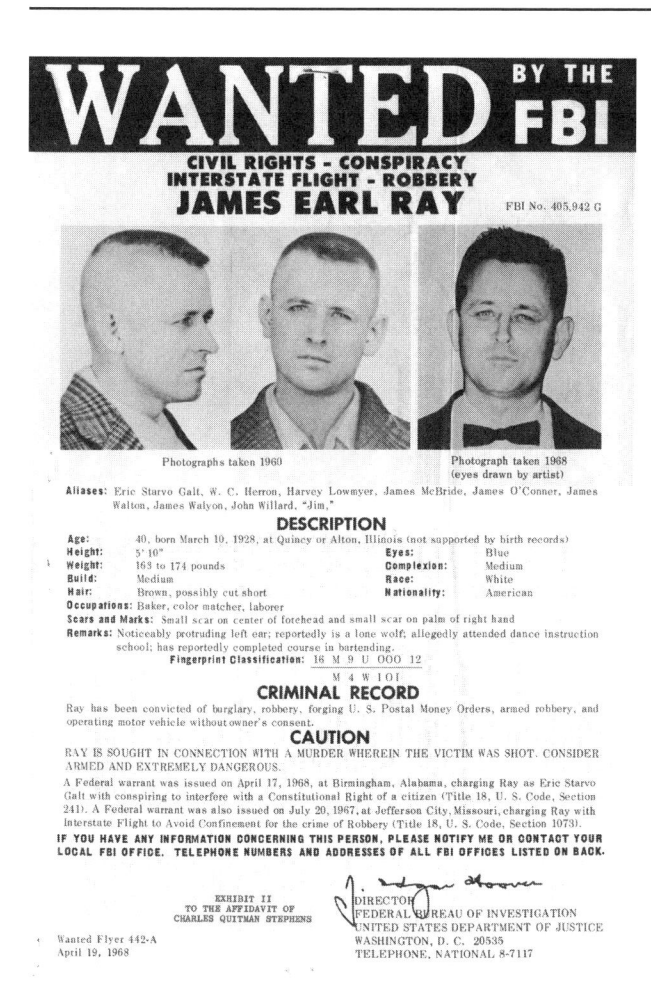

This FBI Wanted poster, dated April 19, 1968, seeks the capture of James Earl Ray, who was ultimately convicted of murdering Martin Luther King, Jr., in Memphis, Tennessee. After the assassination, riots prompted police reforms in the city.

the police academy in an attempt to correct this in balance. In 1978, the Memphis police went on strike for eight days after contract negotiations failed, and law enforcement was temporarily provided by the Highway Patrol, the Shelby County Sheriff's Department, and the National Guard.

Punishment and Crime
The 1985 U.S. Supreme Court decision *Tennessee v. Garner* required Tennessee to revise its state law concerning the use of deadly force. The suit referenced a case in Memphis in 1974 in which police, responding to a report of a prowler, shot at a fleeing suspect (in accordance with Tennessee law and police department policy at the time) and killed him. After the Supreme Court decision,

Menendez, Lyle and Erik

Lyle and Erik Menendez were convicted of murdering their parents, Jose and Kitty Menendez, in 1996, after two trials. Their parents had been murdered on August 20, 1989, and had received several close-range shotgun wounds. Although the brothers were questioned at the beginning of the investigation, it was only later that they were considered suspects in the crime. After the second trial, the young men were convicted and sentenced to life in prison.

Lyle and Erik Menendez were 21 and 18 at the time of their parents' death. Jose and Kitty were only 40 and 44. Jose was the president of LIVE Entertainment, a video-distribution company partly owned by a movie-production company. Their marriage had not always been ideal, with Jose admitting to having several affairs and sending his wife into serious depression. Jose was adamant that his sons be successful and well rounded. Lyle attended Princeton until he was found guilty of committing plagiarism and was requested to take a year off by the president of the university. Erik often emulated the behaviors of his older brother. Both sons felt extreme pressure to succeed in all aspects of their lives.

From Burglary to Murder
In 1988, the boys began burglarizing homes in Calabasas, California, many of which were owned by their parents' friends. It was estimated that they stole over $100,000. Their father was outraged, and shortly after the parents learned about the burglaries, Jose moved his family to Beverly Hills, citing harassment by residents in Calabasas due to his sons' transgressions. On August 20, 1989, the Beverly Hills Police Department received a 911 call from Lyle Menendez, claiming that he and his brother had just discovered their parents lying in pools of blood on the floor of their home. Police arrived to find the bodies and took the sons into custody for questioning, although not as suspects. Questioning lasted approximately 20 minutes and was discontinued because Erik was uncontrollably sobbing. They provided police with a timeline of their activity for that evening, establishing an alibi.

The boys began spending their inheritance only four days after the death of their parents. By the end of 1989, they had spent more than $1 million, thus arousing suspicion from the police. The police discovered that they had hired a computer expert to erase their mother's hard drive almost two weeks after her murder. On October 31, Erik confessed to the murder of his parents to his psychotherapist, Jerome Oziel, who would become a key witness during the trials of the young men. Lyle was arrested on March 8, 1990, and Erik, who was in Israel at the time, was arrested on March 11, 1990. Erik hired Leslie Abramson as his attorney. Both young men pleaded not guilty and were held without bail on first-degree murder charges. Eventually, Jill Lansing was hired to defend Lyle.

The first trial, which was joined for both defendants for expedience, began on July 20, 1993. Lyle and Erik spent over three years in jail before the beginning of the trial. The prosecution called Dr. Oziel to testify, who spent six days re-creating the murder in the alleged words of the young men who had confessed to him previously. During Erik's testimony, allegations of sexual and physical abuse by both parents surfaced. The jury, after 16 days of deliberation, was deadlocked, thus resulting in a mistrial. The retrial began in August 1995. The prosecution used different attorneys, while Abramson was still the lawyer for Erik. Lyle was represented by the public defender. Again, claims of sexual and physical abuse against the boys surfaced, but this time the jury made a decision within four days. Both were found guilty of two counts of first-degree murder and conspiracy to commit murder. During the sentencing phase, 18 witnesses were called by the defense to testify on behalf of the brothers. On July 2, 1996, both men were sentenced to life in prison without the possibility of parole. They were separated in September of that year and have not seen each other since.

Jeanne Subjack
Sam Houston State University

See Also: Murder, Contemporary; Violent Crimes.

Further Readings
Dunne, Dominick. *Justice: Crimes, Trials, and Punishments*. New York: Three Rivers Press, 2002.
Pergament, Rachel. "The Menendez Brothers." http://www.trutv.com/library/crime/notorious_murders/famous/menendez/index_1.html (Accessed November 2010).
Soble, Ron and John H. Johnson. *Blood Brothers: The Inside Story of the Menendez Murders*. Memphis, TN: Onyx Publishing, 1994.

Miami, Florida

Miami, incorporated in 1896, was always a multiethnic city with large numbers of Cuban, Italian, and Bahamian immigrants and a small Chinese population in the early 20th century, but it was also a southern city that was segmented by race and wealth. African American residents were effectively confined to "Colored Town" or the Central Negro District (later Overtown) by restrictive clauses in land deeds. White immigrants settled in adjoining neighborhoods, while wealthy, usually native-born, white residents lived closest to Biscayne Bay, Miami Beach, and Coral Gables. The City of Miami Police, established as the city was being incorporated, had jurisdiction over Colored Town, but also came into contact with blacks in northern Miami's unincorporated areas with saloons, gambling dens, and brothels. Black arrests on vice-related, gambling, and drunkenness charges increased sharply in the 1910s and were accompanied by accusations of police brutality. The city had a dual system of justice in which police arrested African Americans but ignored many offenses committed by whites, the courts frequently issued harsher sentences to black offenders, and juries usually exonerated police officers and other whites in black homicides. Beginning in the 1900s, black residents sought unsuccessfully the appointment of black police officers to provide protection in the nonwhite districts.

The summer of 1920 was marked by a series of violent conflicts between black and white Miamians following threats of lynching, bombings of black residences, and the murder of a respectable black business owner by a drunken white resident, who was acquitted. In the nativist climate of the 1920s, the Ku Klux Klan established itself as an organization defending law and order in Miami. The city was also enjoying a spectacular real estate boom and thousands arrived, eager to make their fortune—along with grifters, pickpockets, and thieves—but many became victims of fraudulent land and real estate scams. The Miami city police force grew from 40 officers in 1921 to 350 in 1926 but struggled to keep pace with the growing population and rising liquor-related offenses, including smuggling and bootlegging during Prohibition. Greater Miami became increasingly economically dependent on tourism, and so gambling, drinking, and sex were tolerated. Grand jury reports found the Miami police force was cutting in on the profits of many criminal enterprises. However, the city was also linked to organized crime, including vacationing gangsters (Al Capone bought a house on Star Island in 1927), and as a stopover for those traveling between northern cities and Havana.

The collapse of the boom in 1926 coincided with an increase in homicides in the city, while the death and destruction wrought by the hurricanes of September 1926 and 1928 and the worsening economic situation further exacerbated racial tensions. Harry Kier, a young African American bellboy, was beaten to death by the city's police chief in March 1928. Kier had been arrested for speaking directly to a white woman who was staying at the hotel where he worked. This was one of several incidents of police brutality and murder involving black citizens, and where police officers were deemed to have acted in self-defense. Black residents continued to bear the brunt of police brutality in the 1930s. The July 1937 murder of 19-year-old Stafford Dames, Jr., by three policemen, who were acquitted of any wrongdoing by an all-white jury, spurred Dames's father and others to form a local branch of the National Association for the Advancement of Colored People (NAACP).

The first five African American Miami police officers were appointed in 1944 to protect and serve the black communities and were effective despite having more limited powers and restricted assignments than white officers. The establishment of the Miami Colored Police Benevolent Association in 1946 brought a key protagonist to the fight to end segregation within the police.

Post–World War II Miami

Public anxieties over the infiltration of labor unions, hotels and nightclubs, casinos, and other gambling outlets by gangsters linked to northern syndicates rose after World War II. Miami gained the reputation of a wide-open city, and corruption of police, sheriffs, and local officials reached major proportions. This situation threatened to discourage desirable tourists and settlers. In early 1948, six community leaders, who were instrumental in the formation of the Crime Commission of Greater Miami, hired Daniel P. Sullivan, a former Federal Bureau of Investigation (FBI) agent, as director. The commission conducted well-publicized

An officer with Miami's Special Investigation Section Narcotics Unit watches U.S. Navy sailors, Coast Guardsmen, and agents unload nine tons of cocaine onto a pier at Naval Air Station Key West. Drug trafficking is an ongoing problem for Miami.

investigations into the activities of major crime syndicate figures and the extent of local corruption. Its work was given national exposure in July 1950 when Senator Estes Kefauver, chair of the U.S. Senate Crime Investigating Commission, held hearings in Miami that revealed the wide extent of corruption. This led to the immediate suspension of Dade County sheriff James "Jimmy" Sullivan and other local officials (later reinstated by the governor).

The city was also rocked by bombings in 1951 and 1958 aimed at African American homes and Jewish synagogues that arose partly in response to threats to dismantle residential segregation but were linked more widely to white racism, anti-Semitism, anticommunism, and the arrival of increasing numbers of Puerto Ricans. These events undermined the city's image as being more progressive than others in the south, as did the 1954 moral panic over homosexuals. Between 1945 and 1955, the greater Miami population grew 126 percent to more than 700,000. The sheriff of Dade County had approximately 11 white deputies and two "colored" deputies to handle all crimes except capital cases, which were sent to the Criminal Investigation Bureau, and traffic cases, handled by the Dade County Road Patrol (with more than 50 traffic officers). There were approximately 700 police officers to serve the Miami and Miami Beach areas. The establishment of a unique "Negro police station and court" between 1950 and 1963, with a black police station, separate detention cells, and a black judge and bailiff in a special municipal court, improved police protection for black residents and ensured the hiring of black officers. However, black officers were denied the same training and promotion opportunities as whites, and this reinforced their secondary status.

In the 1950s and 1960s, threats, intimidation, economic reprisals, and violence were deployed against black civil rights protesters and their Latino, white, and Jewish allies. The Miami Police Department, through intimidation and terror, played a powerful role in maintaining white supremacy and the color line into the 1960s. Miami's black neighborhoods were still characterized by unpaved roads, homes without indoor plumbing, infrequent garbage collections, bars and gambling often situated next to schools and homes, and overcrowding. The immigration of tens of thousands of Cuban refugees after 1959 also increased economic competition between African Americans and Latinos. The 1965 destruction of parts of Overtown to make way for I-95 and the forced removal of many black residents to other segregated districts, anger over white commercial dominance and police brutality, and frustration over slumlords and the paucity of black-owned businesses provided the backdrop to a major disturbance three years later. In August 1968, as the Republican National Convention took place in Miami Beach, the black community of Liberty City erupted into several days of rioting.

Continuing Tensions

Black fears of economic displacement continued to grow in the 1970s and 1980s as Miami underwent dramatic economic and demographic growth. Between 1960 and 1990, the population of Dade County more than doubled to 2 million people, and Miami became a Caribbean American city because of the large numbers of Latino and Caribbean arrivals. It handled more than a third of U.S. trade with Latin America and more than half of U.S. trade with the Caribbean and Central America and was a major banking center. However, Miami's reputation in the early 1980s was as the crime and murder capital of the United States and as the major entry point for drug traffic from South America and the Caribbean; its banking sector was associated with money laundering. Riots in the 1980s damaged the city's reputation further.

The convergence of the acquittal of four Miami police officers of shooting a black male, renewed waves of Cuban immigration and the Mariel boatlift, and the influx of Haitian refugees led to an explosion of black violence in Overtown and Liberty City, which spread to other areas and continued for several days. December 1982 saw three days of rioting in Overtown after a Hispanic policeman shot a black youth; when the officer was acquitted by an all-white jury in March 1984, another outbreak of looting and property destruction took place. In January 1989, a fourth major riot erupted after another Hispanic officer shot and killed a black motorcyclist. By this time, the sheriff's department had become the Metro-Dade County Police Department (1981–97), now called the Miami-Dade County Police Department (MDPD). The Miami City Police remains a separate force.

It took more than a decade after the riots for Miami to begin to shed its image as a high-crime city and for its police forces to begin to rebuild relations with the city's different ethnic and racial communities. As that process continued, crime, policing, and forensic investigations in Miami were the centerpieces of slick television productions *Miami Vice* (1984–90) and *CSI: Miami* (2002–), although very little of the latter is actually filmed in south Florida. Nevertheless, the street gang situation in Miami continues to generate community and law enforcement concern. Miami-Dade County has 230 documented gangs. Estimates of membership numbers range from less than 2,000 to more than 5,000.

Vivien Miller
University of Nottingham

See Also: 1961 to 1980 Primary Documents; African Americans; Capone, Al; Florida; Ku Klux Klan; Riots.

Further Readings
Dulaney, W. Marvin. *Black Police in America*. Bloomington: Indiana University Press, 1996.
Dunn, Marvin. *Black Miami in the Twentieth Century*. Gainesville: University Press of Florida, 1997.
Fejes, Fred. "Murder, Perversion, and Moral Panic: The 1954 Media Campaign Against Miami's Homosexuals and the Discourse of Civic Betterment." *Journal of the History of Sexuality*, v.9 (2000).
George, Paul S. "Policing Miami's Black Community, 1896–1930." *Florida Historical Quarterly*, v.57 (1979).
Tscheschlok, Eric. "Long Time Coming: Miami's Liberty City Riot of 1968." *Florida Historical Quarterly*, v.74 (1996).
Wilbanks, William. *Murder in Miami: An Analysis of Homicide Patterns and Trends in Dade County (Miami) Florida, 1917–1983*. Lanham, MD: University Press of America, 1984.

Michigan

Michigan was originally home to various Native American tribes; in the 1600s, French fur traders began settling the state, founding Detroit in 1701. After passing between the French, British, and Americans, and then becoming embroiled in a dispute with Ohio commonly referred to as the Toledo War, the territory now known as Michigan became a U.S. state in 1837. Waves of immigration from Europe (starting in the mid-1800s) and the American south (starting in the 1910s) have marked the development of crime, police, and punishment in the state. Today, Michigan faces problems not of immigration but of population decline; as the only state to depopulate since 2000, Michigan has lost a seat in Congress and finds itself with fewer public funds with which to provide core services. Michigan is a large but unevenly unpopulated state; more than half of its population of just under 10 million live in the southeastern metro Detroit region.

Crime

Michigan's first criminal code was published in 1846, and was limitedly revised in 1931. As noted by legal scholar Ronald J. Bretz, the code is simply a list of crimes with corresponding punishments and is highly dependent on common law; criminal offenses have been historically defined by state courts rather than by the criminal code itself, although the 1974 Criminal Sexual Conduct Act does explicitly define sexual crimes.

The constitution of crime as a social problem in Michigan can be linked to broad social trends facing the state. The mid-1800s saw a rapid increase in the state's European working-class population, particularly in Detroit. As detailed in John Schneider's *Detroit and the Problem of Order*, working-class ethnic enclaves were viewed as suspicious centers of vices such as gambling and prostitution, with police departments in Detroit (1865) and Ann Arbor (1871), for example, founded at the behest of local citizens concerned about so-called "dangerous classes."

While the annual average number of homicide arrests in Detroit rarely exceeded 10 before the turn of the 20th century, new crime trends began emerging in the late 1910s, with as many as 237 homicide arrests in Detroit in 1918. Detroit stood at the epicenter of these criminal changes. As a convenient entry point for bootleggers from Canada who were headed to Chicago, Detroit became home to crime rings such as the infamous Purple Gang, which trafficked illegal liquor into the United States. White and African American migrants from the American south strained Detroit's resources, particularly its housing market. Paired with racist housing practices, many African American newcomers lived in dilapidated conditions, living life on the social and economic margins. These conditions were exacerbated by white-on-black violence as well as policing practices that disproportionately victimized and criminalized African Americans.

Whites began leaving Detroit in the 1920s and then practically evacuated the city after the 1967 riot. This urban exodus of whites to the suburbs created a dynamic of divestment and deindustrialization in which Detroit's relatively low-crime white suburbs were de facto segregated from high-crime African American Detroit. The city soon acquired its reputation as a "murder capital" with more than 700 murders in 1974 alone.

In the 1970s, murder rates peaked in Michigan, with not less than 831 murders per year during that decade (or 9.1 murders per 100,000), and violent crimes remained at alarmingly high levels throughout the 1970s and into the 1980s. While crime has significantly declined starting in the 1990s, Michigan's state-level murder and nonnegligent manslaughter rate of 6.3 per 100,000 is still heavily skewed by Detroit's 40.2 rate per 100,000 (based on 2009 Federal Bureau of Investigation [FBI] data), with more than half of all Michigan murders occurring in Detroit. Though relatively low in population, Flint and Saginaw also exhibit high violent-crime rates. And while data from the past five years shows that crime rates have generally gone down in Detroit and in the state at large, some of the city's predominantly white suburbs have again experienced increases in crime.

Police

As in the rest of the country, local police departments in Michigan were founded in the mid- to late 1800s in growing cities such as Detroit (1865), Ann Arbor (1871), Grand Rapids (1871), and Lansing (1893).

The Michigan State Police (MSP) was founded in 1917 as an emergency replacement for the National Guard; today, the MSP oversees policing protocols throughout the state, provides auxiliary services to areas with limited local police patrol, and maintains state records on firearms, sex offenders, and criminal history.

Upon their founding, Michigan's police departments were predominantly white institutions; as southern African Americans began migrating to Michigan from 1910 to 1930, police departments, particularly the Detroit Police Department (DPD), were tasked with managing not only crime but also racial tensions. This often resulted in clear patterns of police brutality against African Americans by the 1920s. In addition, the DPD also suffered from racial segregation. Even by the late 1960s, only 5 percent of the DPD was nonwhite. By the 1970s, trust between the department and Detroit residents had all but eroded in the face of flagrant police brutality experienced leading up to and during the 1967 riot together with the notoriously bloody STRESS (Stop the Robberies, Enjoy Safe Streets) program implemented thereafter. The Malice Green beating of

1992 together with rather regular reports undermining the DPD's public legitimacy (for example, the force was first in the United States in citizen deaths, according to 2000 FBI statistics) have also marred the department. Nevertheless, the force has made efforts to address these issues; today, it has one of the highest proportions of nonwhite officers among U.S. police departments, and like other forces throughout the state, the DPD has increasingly adopted a community policing approach over the past three decades. As Michigan police departments pare down their services due to diminished public funding, community policing initiatives are likely to play an increasingly important role in police departments throughout the state.

Punishment

Michigan has experienced a dramatic increase in prison facilities and inmate population since 1970. With only 9,079 prisoners in 1970, Michigan's inmate population reached an all-time high of 51,554 in 2007. According to legal scholar Ronald J. Bretz, changes in Michigan's parole system in the early 1990s that lowered parole rates together with ramped-up sentences for drug violations under the 1978 Michigan Controlled Substances Act are credited for prison population growth during the 1990s.

Moreover, the 1998 truth-in-sentencing law now requires that all inmates serve their minimum sentences and, for inmates convicted of certain crimes, removes the possibility of early release for good behavior while incarcerated. The prison population declined to 45,478 by 2010 after a decrease of 3,260 prisoners in 2008–09, and the prison population is second only to California's. The Michigan Prisoner Reentry Initiative (MPRI), a program aimed at supporting prisoner reentry into society, is in part credited with this reduction, having successfully lowered parole revocation rates over the past five years.

In May 2010, U.S. Immigration and Customs Enforcement and the Wayne County, Michigan, Sheriff's Office seized nine weapons, 70 grams of cocaine, 145 grams of marijuana, and 150 marijuana plants as part of a suspected drug-growing operation in Detroit. Michigan's reputation as one of the nation's toughest states on drugs includes its lowering of parole rates along with ramped-up sentences for drug violations in the early 1990s and its contentious mandatory life sentence for certain repeat offenders.

Today, Michigan prisoners reside at 34 facilities; as late as 1970, only four prisons were in operation. The state's first prison in Jackson, Michigan, opened in 1839 and expanded until 1924, when it was replaced by another Jackson prison. With a capacity of 5,000 inmates, the new facility became the world's largest walled prison. The renovated facility continues to operate as the Southern Michigan Correctional Facility. The second facility, the Detroit House of Correction, opened in 1860 and moved location in 1920. Female prisoners, along with convicted bootleggers who slept in outdoor tents, were housed at the facility. The Detroit House of Correction was abandoned in 1986, and female inmates are now incarcerated at the Huron Valley Correctional Complex. According to a report from the Institute on Women and Criminal Justice, 4.3 percent of all prisoners in Michigan in 2004 were women, representing a growth rate of 293 percent since 1977.

Juvenile inmates were first held at the Jackson facility in the 1850s; the House of Correction for Juvenile Offenders in Lansing was built in the mid-1850s, followed by the subsequent construction of various facilities aimed specifically at juvenile offenders. Michigan's juvenile justice system was reformed in 1996 through a series of new laws that called for the creation of new juvenile facilities and dramatically modified how juvenile offenders are processed by the criminal justice system. Today, juveniles in various stages of Michigan's criminal justice system are housed at the Bay Pines Center, the Maxey Training School, and the Shawono Center.

As legal Bretz notes, while the state generally follows national trends in terms of prison population changes, various aspects of Michigan's penal system are noteworthy. The state abolished the death penalty with its revised penal code of 1846, and its probation and parole systems were instituted relatively early, in 1885. Other aspects of Michigan's criminal justice system have raised serious concerns regarding the administration of punishment. For example, in the mid-1990s, the state passed a law removing the minimum age for a juvenile to be tried as an adult and required that juveniles as young as 14 years old must be tried and sentenced as adults for certain offenses. Michigan soon thereafter made international headlines when Pontiac native Nathaniel Abraham was tried and convicted for murder at the age of 11. Another noteworthy aspect of Michigan's criminal justice system is its long-standing prison industries, which began in the mid-1850s. After the end of the contract labor system by the early 1900s, Michigan began operating prison-based factories that continue to operate today. Under the 1980 Correctional Industries Act, the self-sufficient Michigan State Industries uses prison labor to produce goods for governmental and nonprofit organizations.

Looking Ahead

Given Michigan's population decline and poor economy, the public funds available for policing and punishment remain lacking. In the summer of 2009 alone, 100 MSP officers were let go, dwindling the MSP's force to its smallest size in 40 years; similar reductions in police resources have been seen throughout the state. As Michigan explores cost-effective ways of administering these core public services, changes in crime, punishment, and policing are likely to follow.

Jennifer D. Carlson
University of California, Berkeley

See Also: Capital Punishment; Detroit, Michigan; Juvenile Offenders in Adult Courts; Race, Class, and Criminal Law; Race-Based Crimes; Racism.

Further Readings
Boyle, Kevin. *Arc of Justice: A Saga of Race, Civil Rights, and Murder in the Jazz Age.* New York: Henry Holt & Co., 2005.
Disaster Center. "Michigan Crime Rates 1960–2009." http://www.disastercenter.com/crime/micrime.htm (Accessed August 2011).
Fine, Sidney. *Violence in the Model City: The Cavanagh Administration, Race Relations, and the Detroit Riot of 1967.* Detroit, MI: Wayne State University Press, 2007.
Finkleman, Paul and Martin J. Hershock, eds. *The History of Michigan Law.* Athens: Ohio University Press, 2006.
Schneider, John. *Detroit and the Problem of Order, 1830–1880: A Geography of Crime, Riot, and Policing.* Lincoln: University of Nebraska Press, 1980.

Military Courts

In the United States, the military is often regarded as a separate society, one that operates within a unique context and with unique demands. As a result, crime and punishment in the military differ in important ways from civilian courts. Two types of military courts exist: courts-martial and military tribunals. The first represents the criminal justice arm of the U.S. military forces. These courts are charged with maintaining and enforcing criminal law among service members. These bodies try military offenses and have broad jurisdiction over service members as well as civilians attached to the military during times of war and, to a lesser degree, enemy prisoners of war. The second type of military court employed by the United States is the military tribunal (sometimes also known as a military commission). While courts-martial are generally used against service members for criminal offenses and breaches of military regulations, military tribunals are often temporary bodies typically reserved for prosecuting spies, saboteurs, and other nonuniformed combatants.

Courts-Martial

American courts-martial are an outgrowth of the British Articles of War, and the creation of these courts by the Continental Congress predates the writing of the Constitution. However, the American system differs from the British system in one important respect: The creation and revision of the rules regarding military justice were the purview of Congress, while they were to be administered by the executive. During the 19th and 20th centuries, there was a slow but steady growth in the number and types of procedural protections afforded to defendants. Courts-martial derive authority from two sources. The first source is the Uniform Code of Military Justice (UCMJ), the code of military laws legislated by Congress through its constitutional powers to raise, support, and maintain armies and navies and to provide for their organization and discipline. It was created in 1951 in order to provide a greater degree of uniformity in military law among the different branches of the military service. The second source is presidential implementation of the UCMJ through Executive Order 12743, the Manual for Courts-Martial (MCM). As commander in chief of the military, it is the duty of the president to implement the UCMJ. The MCM not only includes the UCMJ but also establishes rules for courts-martial and rules of evidence for the military. Each military branch has also developed supplemental rules to the MCM that meet its unique needs.

The basic structure of the military criminal justice system would be familiar to most civilians. Courts-martial are capable of trying both civilian offenses, should the military decline to turn the accused over to civilian authorities, and uniquely military offenses such as dereliction of duty or failure to report. Depending on the severity of the offense and the nature of the charges, offenders may be referred to one of three types of courts-martial: summary, special, or general. Summary courts-martial deal with minor offenses and have limited punitive powers. Special courts-martial handle both capital and noncapital offenses, afford the accused access to an attorney, and have broader punitive powers. General courts-martial concern themselves with the most severe offenses and have the broadest punitive powers (including the death sentence).

It should also be noted that courts-martial are not considered to be part of the federal judiciary. While their appellate structure leads to the U.S. Court of Military Appeals and, ultimately, the U.S. Supreme Court, they are more subject to control by political and bureaucratic forces than the Article III judiciary.

Military Tribunals

While courts-martial can be used against prisoners of war, military tribunals are typically reserved for prosecuting spies, saboteurs, and other unlawful combatants. Used with less frequency than courts-martial, such tribunals have recently come under public scrutiny as a result of the wars in Afghanistan and Iraq and the broader war on terror carried out by the United States in the wake of the September 11, 2001, attacks.

Military tribunals have existed in various forms since the American Revolution, when they were used by both American and British forces to mete out justice to spies and prisoners of war. Throughout the 19th century, military tribunals were used in the prosecution of individuals deemed enemies of the state. During the War of 1812, General Andrew Jackson declared martial law in New

The Nazi saboteur trial in the fifth-floor courtroom of the Department of Justice building, Washington, D.C., July 1942, in its third day of proceedings in the trial of eight Nazi agents accused of engaging in sabotage against American war industries. President Roosevelt issued an order creating the special seven-member military commission (back row) because the more politically desirable death penalty would not have been allowable in civilian courts. The tribunal quickly reached a conclusion and issued the death penalty.

Orleans. When a local author suggested this was not appropriate and asserted that civil judges, rather than military tribunals, should hear accusations against citizens, Jackson ordered his arrest. When his arrest was appealed via a writ of habeas corpus, a local judge ordered his release and was subsequently arrested himself. Military tribunals were also used throughout the first half of the 19th century to prosecute British subjects during the War of 1812, combatants on both sides during the Mexican–American War, and Native Americans during the Indian wars. Both Congress and the Supreme Court authorized, reviewed, and occasionally limited the use of military tribunals during this time, considering them primarily within the scope of executive power. It was during the Civil War, however, that military tribunals first became an issue of national importance.

In a famous move during the Civil War, President Abraham Lincoln suspended habeas corpus rights and declared martial law in multiple areas. The presidential suspension of habeas corpus (an action subsequently approved by Congress) allowed the military detention of citizens without immediate recourse to civilian courts, an act of questionable legality that would come before the Supreme Court in several important cases. The ensuing military trials of civilians and prisoners of war moved suspects out of the civilian criminal justice system and denied them the protections it affords defendants and the principle of trial by jury. The tribunals were challenged before the Supreme Court, but decisions were not issued until after the war. In *Ex parte Milligan* (1866), the justices held that the trial of citizens in military courts was explicitly unconstitutional when civilian courts were still operating, even in areas of martial law. According to *Milligan*, only when the military is the sole remaining authority within an area may military tribunals be used to try civilians.

Tribunals were little used in the period between the end of the Civil War and World War II. One significant episode occurred in 1942 in a controversial incident commonly called the "Nazi Saboteur case." Eight German agents, two of whom were American citizens, traveled from Germany to the United States in order to engage in sabotage against American war-building industries and infrastructure. They were quickly apprehended after their arrival, and President Franklin Roosevelt issued an order creating a military tribunal to try the men. He chose to use a tribunal rather than a civil court because the politically desirable penalty—death—would not have been allowable in civilian courts. The tribunal reached a conclusion quickly, issuing death sentences for all eight men. Roosevelt commuted the sentences of the two men to prison terms. Habeas corpus requests were filed with the Supreme Court, which ultimately issued an opinion in support of the military tribunal. Writing in *Ex parte Quirin* (1942), the court declined to issue any writ of habeas corpus, ruling that the military tribunals were a legitimate exercise of both legislative and executive power. Importantly, the court both upheld the precedent of *Milligan* and distinguished between lawful and unlawful combatants. Uniformed soldiers are considered lawful combatants and must be treated as prisoners of war; soldiers and agents of enemy powers who act outside of uniform (e.g., spies and saboteurs) are unlawful combatants and are subject to military tribunals. Other tribunals were also used during World War II, and their use was largely upheld in the immediate postwar era.

Modern Military Tribunals

After the September 11, 2001, attacks, the ensuing war on terror, and wars in Afghanistan and Iraq, a new chapter in the use of military tribunals began. Shortly after the events of 9/11, the Bush administration issued a military order creating a military tribunal system for use against persons designated as "enemy combatants" under the rules of war (i.e., nonuniformed belligerent agents). These tribunals proceeded for some time, but their use was unwieldy and controversial. They were attacked in some quarters as violating basic civil liberties and the humanitarian protections found in the Geneva Conventions. The Bush administration maintained the position that they were a necessary tool in the war on terror. These issues were taken to the civil courts of the United States, and the Supreme Court responded to these cases with its decision in *Hamdan v. Rumsfeld* (2006).

Salim Hamdan, a former driver for Osama bin Laden, had been designated an enemy combatant by the government and was set to be tried for war crimes by the Bush administration's new military tribunal system. Hamdan challenged the constitutionality of the tribunal system, a challenge that eventually made its way before the Supreme Court. The court faced two questions: First, could federal courts enforce Geneva Convention protections through writs of habeas corpus? And second, were the type of military tribunals then in use authorized by congressional legislation or the president's executive powers? The court's majority found that federal courts could enforce Geneva Convention protections as part of the laws of war; further, the majority also found that military tribunals must obey the laws of the United States and the laws of war, and that the type of tribunal at question was authorized by neither congressional legislation nor executive power. As a result of the *Hamdan* decision, Congress passed the Military Commissions Act (MCA) of 2006, giving the Bush administration the power to reconstitute a new military tribunal system. The new law also limited the ability of federal courts to enforce the Geneva Convention's through writs of habeas corpus.

The Obama administration continued the use of military tribunals. Some changes have been made to the system in response to the continuing concerns of civil libertarians, but the tribunal system continues to be unwieldy in the face of challenges and changing circumstances. There is an express goal on the part of the Obama administration to close the Guantanamo facility, transferring the enemy combatants there to other facilities or nations. This continues to be an issue of contention, as does the conduct of military tribunals themselves. One example of this continued debate is the Military Commissions Act of 2009, which sought to amend the previous MCA to provide more protections for the accused in military tribunals. It is likely that this debate will continue to be shaped by both domestic political pressures and the course of the war on terror in coming years.

The Judge Advocate General's Corps (JAG) serves as the legal entity for all branches of the U.S.

armed forces. Though different branches of the armed forces organize their respective JAGs differently, they usually perform similar duties. JAG officers also issue legal advice in any number of substantive areas, including military law, environmental law, administrative law, government contracting, and international relations. JAG members also serve as prosecutors for the military in courts-martial and sit as judges in various military courts.

Darren A. Wheeler
Eric van der Vort
Ball State University

See Also: 1851 to 1900 Primary Documents; 1941 to 1960 Primary Documents; Bush, George W. (Administration of); Terrorism.

Further Readings
Fidell, Eugene and Dwight Sullivan, eds. *Evolving Military Justice*. Annapolis, MD: U.S. Naval Institute Press, 2002.
Fisher, Louis. *Military Tribunals and Presidential Power: American Revolution to the War on Terrorism*. Kansas City: University Press of Kansas, 2005.
Schueter, David. *Military Criminal Justice: Practice and Procedure*. New York: LexisNexis, 2008.

Military Police

The military police is the police force under the jurisdiction of the U.S. military. Each branch of the military has a separate military police force: The U.S. Army has the Military Police Corps, the U.S. Marine Corps has the Provost Marshal's Office, the U.S. Navy has the Masters-at-Arms, and the U.S. Air Force has the Air Force Security Force (formerly known as the Security Police and the Air Police). The Army Military Police Corps is the oldest and largest of the U.S. military police forces. It can trace its lineage back to the Marechaussee Corps, a special unit created by General George Washington on June 1, 1778. The term *Marechaussee* was adopted from the French term *Marecheaux*, which were the French provost marshal units dating back to the 12th century. The Marechaussee Corps was a mounted unit whose primary mission was to apprehend deserters, rioters, and stragglers. In cases of high crimes and desertion, the unit carried out executions. During battle, the unit guarded rear areas, protected baggage and supply lines, and guarded prisoners of war (POWs). At the Battle of Yorktown, the Marechaussee Corps acted as a security detail for General Washington and his headquarters, but at the conclusion of the Revolutionary War, the corps was disbanded. The Marechaussee Corps was the first MP-like organization in the United States, and it performed many duties much like the Army Military Police Corps of today.

Discipline on Continental navy ships during the Revolutionary War was the responsibility of each ship's master-at-arms. The master-at-arms ensured that discipline was maintained on the ship; ensured that no sailors deserted or left the ship without authorization; inspected any and all things that were brought aboard; took care of all prisoners, either naval or POWs; and made sure that the ship's company was familiar with the use of small arms and basic infantry tactics. The master-at-arms tradition dates back to the time of Charles I of England and even today, sailors with the master-at-arms designation continue to serve as military police on U.S. Navy ships and installations.

From the end of the Revolutionary War until the outbreak of the Civil War, there were no formally organized military police units in the U.S. Army. Military commanders were responsible for maintaining discipline and order within their own units. Oftentimes, commanders would detail certain officers and men to perform law enforcement functions within their units; however, this practice proved unsatisfactory during the Civil War. Disciplinary problems within the Union army led to the establishment of the Provost Marshal Corps. These military police units enforced curfews, tracked deserters, protected civilian property from plundering, and when necessary joined in battle. The provost marshal units' jurisdiction was later expanded to include the authority to search citizens, seize weapons and contraband, and make arrests.

During the latter part of the Civil War, the Veteran Reserve Corps (VRC) was established to augment the provost marshal units. The VRC was comprised of wounded Union veteran soldiers who were unable to serve in a line unit because of injury or illness. The VRC protected commissaries and quartermaster and transportation depots. They also escorted POWs to the prisons in the north. One of the VRC's most significant responsibilities was to guard draft offices. Oversight responsibility of the military police and VRC units was given to the Office of the Provost Marshal General (PMG). At the end of the Civil War, Congress dissolved the Office of the PMG as well as the VRC and other military police units.

Military Police in the World Wars

In 1917, as the United States entered World War I, military commanders again recognized the need for military police units. Military police personnel performed the same duties as they had in previous wars but with a few significant additions. Military police were responsible for helping move men and equipment from the rear area to the front lines. They made sure that main supply routes were open, and they conducted reconnaissance of alternate routes in the event that the main routes became blocked. Military police personnel conducted rear area security and checked all individuals traveling in leave areas, major cities, and examining points in rear army areas. As in earlier conflicts, military police personnel were responsible for taking control of POWs from forward troops and escorting them to the rear; however, for the first time, POWs were confined for extended periods of time, and military police personnel were needed to provide security at these facilities. Also for the first time, military police were called upon to investigate serious crimes.

Company D, 10th U.S. Veteran Reserve Corps (VRC), in Washington, D.C., in April 1865. During the latter part of the Civil War, the VRC, comprised of wounded Union veteran soldiers unable to serve in a line unit because of injury or illness, was established to bolster the provost marshal units. The VRC served as security guards for railroads and draft offices, provost guards in large towns, and escorts for prisoners of war. They also performed all types of garrison duty. The Office of the Provost Marshal General oversaw the VRC units.

Traditionally, Pinkerton detectives were tasked with investigating serious crimes that occurred among the troops; however, these detectives could not accompany the soldiers to France, so a special group of military police personnel were needed to assume this responsibility. In May 1918, the Army Criminal Investigations Division (CID) was established to fulfill this mandate. Just a few months after approving the establishment of the CID, Congress denied a request from the army to make the military police a permanent branch. World War I ended, and military police units were again disbanded.

On September 26, 1941, shortly before the U.S. entry into World War II, the Military Police (MP) Corps was finally established as a separate branch within the U.S. Army. According to an initial MP field manual, personnel assigned to the branch were responsible for investigating all crimes and offenses committed by persons who were subject to the Uniform Code of Military Justice (UCMJ), enforcing police regulations, reporting violations of lawfully given orders, and preventing the commission of acts that were subversive to discipline or that discredited the U.S. Army in any way. In addition to their law and order duties, military police personnel during the war were expected to perform their traditional support duties: controlling the movement of traffic in the battlefield area as well as in the military installations, relieving combat organizations of custody of prisoners of war, and operating the POW system. After the war, military police personnel remained in Germany as part of the occupying forces. They guarded Nazi prisoners at the Nuremberg Trials and executed condemned Germans.

In October 1945, General Dwight D. Eisenhower established a special constabulary of 38,000 military soldiers to control the U.S. Zone of Occupation in Germany. The new organization, known as the U.S. Constabulary, was tasked with maintaining general military and civil security, assisting in accomplishing the American government's objectives, and controlling the borders of the U.S. Zone of Occupation. The Constabulary was expected to cooperate with local German police forces hunting black marketers and former Nazi leaders and to conduct general law enforcement and traffic control. The U.S. Constabulary was a new type of unit, designed specifically for policing postwar Germany and guarding the border with the adjoining zones of occupation. It was the primary police authority in postwar Germany until 1952, when it was disbanded.

During World War II, the air corps was still part of the army. Army military police assigned to the air force performed many of the same wartime duties as their counterparts who were assigned to army units. On September 18, 1947, the U.S. Army Air Force became the U.S. Air Force. On that same day, assigned army military police became air police. Later while fighting in Vietnam, the air police had the critical mission of securing air force bases against Viet Cong attack. The name *Air Police* was changed to *Security Police* (SP). After the war, the SP branch was divided into two primary functional areas, law enforcement and base security. In their law enforcement role, SPs perform duties equivalent to a civilian police department. In their base security role, SPs perform limited combat support operations. Other current miscellaneous SP duties are missile security, convoy actions, and the capture and recovery of nuclear weapons. Recently, SPs have augmented army military police personnel in securing prisons and enemy detainees in Iraq and Afghanistan.

Vietnam and Beyond

The Vietnam War brought army military police personnel into direct combat with the enemy. MP corps personnel executed their traditional duties of maintaining good order and discipline but also were called upon to provide dog teams for scout dog duties, to man checkpoints at traffic control points, to provide convoy security, to investigate motor vehicle accidents, to patrol off-limits areas, to protect critical facilities, and to investigate serious criminal offenses involving black market operations, drug offenses, and war crimes.

Following the Vietnam War, the MP corps branch designation was changed from combat service support to a combat support. This redesignation meant that not only did MP corps units receive specialized law enforcement training, but they were also equipped and trained to fight as infantry when required. The dual functionality of the MP corps made it the force of choice for military commanders in contingency and low-intensity conflict operations. The role of the army military police was again expanded—rather than war operations, their primary focus was the restoration of civil authority, humanitarian assistance, disaster relief, and other similar peacekeeping operations. During the later part of the 20th century, MP corps personnel were employed in a variety of missions throughout the world. Examples include inter alia military police support in Grenada (1983); support of Operation Just Cause in Panama (1989); Haitian refugee support in Guantanamo Bay, Cuba; and peacekeeping operations in Haiti, Somalia, and Kosovo.

The MP corps again assumed its wartime mission during Operation Desert Shield/Desert Storm (1990–91). For the first time, the army had to rely primarily on reserve and National Guard military police personnel to conduct wartime law enforcement and combat support operations. Military police personnel also coordinated defensive support with Arab host nations and other service military police and security elements.

Military Police Today

Since the terrorist attacks on September 11, 2001, military police have played a vital part in wartime operations in the Middle East. Their combat support missions have included protection of ground convoys, area security operations, personal security missions, and the maintenance and administration of detainee internment facilities. In 2004, military police personnel were accused of mistreatment of enemy detainees at the Abu Ghraib prison outside Baghdad, Iraq. International condemnation of the detainee maltreatment forced the army to review relevant doctrine and institute a major overhaul of military police training in that critical area.

The Posse Comitatus Act (PCA) has historically restricted the use of military police in domestic law enforcement. The PCA does not apply where Congress has expressly authorized use of the military to execute the law. Beginning in the early 1980s, drug enforcement concerns led to legal changes that opened a new chapter in U.S. law; military police were allowed to provide a vast array of support for civilian police. The Military Cooperation with Civilian Law Enforcement Agencies Act, enacted in 1981, opened the door for military police to cooperate with civilian police officers.

Military police personnel have been called on to assist domestic law enforcement in counter-drug operations, civil disturbances, counterterrorism actions, and special security operations. Examples include inter alia military police helping civil authorities with disaster relief after the San Francisco earthquake in 1989; riot and looting control in Los Angeles following the controversial Rodney King court ruling in 1992; and providing search and rescue, evacuation, humanitarian assistance, and presence patrols to New Orleans city residents after Hurricane Katrina in 2005.

In recent years, there has been an initiative among military branches to divorce their military police personnel from their historical garrison law enforcement role and to civilianize certain installation security functions. At a growing number of military installations in the United States, civilian contractors have assumed a number of responsibilities previously retained by military police such as pass and ID issuance and gate sentry duty.

Deborah A. Sibila
Sam Houston State University

See Also: 1851 to 1900 Primary Documents; 1941 to 1960 Primary Documents; Eisenhower, Dwight D. (Administration of); Military Courts; Police, History of.

Further Readings
Cucullu, Gordon and Chris Fontana. *Warrior Police: Rolling With America's Military Police in the World's Trouble Spots*. New York: St. Martin's Press, 2011.
Falerios, Kenton J. *"Give Me Something I Can't Do:" The History of the 82nd Military Police Company From WWI to the Iraq War*. Bloomington, IN: AuthorHouse, 2007.
Young, R. *Combat Police: U.S. Army Military Police in Vietnam*. Bloomington, IN: AuthorHouse, 2003.

Minnesota

Minnesota is known for progressive politics, civic involvement, and moderate social policies. Crime control programs developed in Minnesota have been emulated in various other jurisdictions around the country and even to some degree around the globe. Crime in Minnesota is regulated by Minnesota Statute 609, which explains the purpose of the code as follows:

1. To protect the public safety and welfare by preventing the commission of crime through the deterring effect of the sentences authorized, the rehabilitation of those convicted, and their confinement when the public safety and interest requires; and
2. To protect the individual against the misuse of the criminal law by fairly defining the acts and omissions prohibited, authorizing sentences reasonably related to the conduct and character of the convicted person, and prescribing fair and reasonable postconviction procedures.

During the 1934 Teamster strike in Minneapolis, police battle with striking truck drivers. The deadly clash lasted for four months and ended in recognition of the union.

This statute has grounded Minnesota's history of crime prevention and reflects the state's historical commitment to rehabilitation as a goal of criminal justice. The state legislature has produced model crime victim policies and domestic abuse intervention strategies. In 1974, Minnesota enacted the Crime Victims Reparations Act, which offered for the first time financial reparations to crime victims. This is considered an important expression by the legislature that not only is criminal prosecution an important aspect of crime policy, but the well-being of victims is a high priority. The Crime Victims Bill of Rights was passed in 1983, offering another significant legislative act that recognized the nature of crime and the victim's interests in the outcome of the case. In 1997, the Commissioner of Corrections implemented a victim notification system to allow victims the ability to check on the status of the offender. The 1998 legislature authorized restorative justice programs and gave community-based organizations, in collaboration with local governmental units, authority to implement and promote them.

Crime

Minnesota is a statistically "safe" state. Violent crime rates and property crime rates consistently fall below the national average. This may be predictable because research has shown that the nation's wealthier states, including midwestern states such as Minnesota, generally have crime rates below national averages. While the cause is not certain, and there are multiple variables, this fact remains true over time based on Uniform Crime Reports. In 2010 in Minnesota, violent crime decreased by 2.9 percent, and property crime decreased by 2.5 percent. However, the rates of decline for Minnesota have fallen below the rate of decline for the nation, where violent crime decreased by 5.5 percent and property crime decreased by 2.8 percent that same year. Like much of the nation, Minnesota's violent crime peaked in 1994 and then dropped to a low point in 2008.

In 2010, there were 112 homicides reported in Minnesota. Homicide offenses in Minnesota represented 0.7 percent of the total violent crimes, with an averaged occurrence of one every four days. Of these, at least 63 percent were homicide by someone known to the victim. The age, sex, and race of victims of homicide are most often represented as teens (15–19) at 19 percent, male at 77 percent, and African American at 47 percent. Likewise, the age, sex, and race of offenders is most often represented as young (15–24) at 32 percent, male at 75 percent, and African American at 39 percent. The most famous murder in Minnesota history is the Glensheen murder, named for the mansion in Duluth where it was committed. This 1977 homicide of the heiress Elizabeth Congdon and her nurse, Velma Pietila, has captured the imaginations of crime watchers for several decades.

Police

Minnesota's law enforcement is under the administration of the Department of Public Safety. The urban centers Minneapolis and St. Paul (known as the Twin Cities) were the first to establish police departments. The state's earliest police department was formed in St. Paul in 1854. Minneapolis established a police unit in 1867. These police departments grew quickly and by 1909, they were adding such technologies as motorcycles, fingerprinting, and telephones. During the 1920s, there was notorious corruption in the police department of St. Paul. During that time, high-profile criminals such as "Machine Gun" Kelly, John Dillinger, and "Baby Face" Nelson were protected by St. Paul police while committing crimes in nearby towns. During the Great Depression, the police functioned to fight gangsters, enforce Prohibition, and quell labor disputes. The 1934 Teamster strike in Minneapolis had the police in a deadly four-month clash with the labor union, ending in recognition of the union. The 1950s postwar politics left the police to deal with the aftermath of urban renewal projects that heavily impacted poorer neighborhoods. The 1960s counterculture revolution posed policing challenges of social unrest in Minneapolis and St. Paul similar to those of other urban centers. The Plymouth Avenue riots in Minneapolis left the police with tarnished community relations and a lack of public trust.

Police efforts in Minnesota, particularly in urban centers, have continued to focus on community relations. Throughout the 1990s, there was increasing demand for police accountability and awareness of racial profiling. A Civilian Review Authority (CRA) was created after public outrage about cases of racism and excessive use of force by police. Many police units, including Minneapolis, voluntarily participated in a statewide study on racial profiling, finding it to be a pervasive policing problem. In 1992, Minneapolis experienced what has been called the "darkest hour" of police-community relations when 30-year veteran cop Jerry Haaf died after being shot in the back. The shooting followed the Rodney King beating in Los Angeles and the acquittal of police officers in that trial. This gang-related incident, and the larger context of the national debate about police conduct, left not only a legacy of racial tension but also a deeper commitment to renewing community relations.

Minnesota is well known for a 1981 study of police response to domestic violence. The study, called "the Minneapolis Experiment," was conducted by criminological researcher Lawrence Sherman. This research lead to widespread changes in police response policies and practices, not only in Minnesota, but also across the nation and even to some degree internationally. In this study, arrest by police was shown to be the most effective deterrent to future domestic assault against the same victim. Subsequently, numerous law enforcement agencies across the country moved to "mandatory arrest" policies, omitting the requirements for warrant. While the Minneapolis Experiment had a massive impact on police response to domestic abuse, it was never scientifically validated through replication and as such has been criticized as shortsighted and unreliable. The debate about the deterrent effect of police intervention and arrest continues.

Punishment

Minnesota's penal system at one time included capital punishment, but it was abolished in 1911. The state's death penalty came under public scrutiny in 1906 when William Williams was set to be executed for the murder of his lover, Johnny Keller. The execution became a public spectacle when the technology of trapdoors and ropes failed. The sheriff had miscalculated the defendant's height, and Williams's feet hit the gallows floor when the trapdoor opened. The subsequent media reports of the deputies' exhausting effort to hold the rope up with their hands to strangle Williams were too much for the Minnesota public to bear. The botched execution of Williams led to success for anti–death penalty advocates in their legislative efforts to end this form of punishment. Minnesota has not reinstated the death penalty despite growing efforts to bring it back.

Minnesota's prison system has been administered by the Department of Corrections since 1959. However, the prison system precedes the state itself. In 1853, five years before statehood, a territorial prison was established in Stillwater; originally funded through a $20,000 congressional appropriation, it later became the first state prison. Soon after that time, juvenile detention centers opened, such as the State Reform School and the Orphan Asylum. Over the years, Minnesota's juvenile justice system has become increasingly punitive. During the 1980s and 1990s, Minnesota saw a drastic increase in the number of juveniles tried and punished as adults. For adults and juveniles alike, the state has shifted from a rehabilitative to a "just deserts" approach, and the rates of imprisonment have risen steadily. According to the Department of Corrections, the state's prison population has increased from 1,214 in 1957 to 8,964 in 2007. Changes in drug policies, treatment options, sentencing guidelines, welfare disbursements, and media influence all contribute to the trend. Despite the increase in prisoners, Minnesota has won national recognition for having a cost-effective correctional system.

Minnesota continues to reflect on causes and consequences of crime. Recent studies, particularly by the Minnesota Council of Crime and Justice, show that the increasing focus on criminalization and incarceration has had a disproportionate effect on Minnesota's communities of color. African American men are especially overrepresented in Minnesota's judicial system. According to the reports, the ratio of African Americans to whites in state prisons is roughly 25 to 1, leaving Minnesota with the greatest disparities in black-to-white rates of imprisonment. This fact remains a great challenge to Minnesota's citizens, legislature, and judiciary.

Mary Jo Wiatrak-Uhlenkott
University of Minnesota

See Also: 1851 to 1900 Primary Documents; Capital Punishment; Lynchings; Murder, History of.

Further Readings

Bessler, John D. *Legacy of Violence: Lynch Mobs and Executions in Minnesota*. Minneapolis: University of Minnesota Press, 2003.

Bureau of Criminal Apprehension. "Minnesota Uniform Crime Reports." http://www.bca.state.mn.us/cjis (Accessed September 2011).

Minnesota Council on Crime and Justice. Research Reports. http://www.crimeandjustice.org/council info.cfm?pID=33 (Accessed September 2011).

Minnesota Department of Corrections. "History of the Minnesota Department of Corrections." http://www.doc.state.mn.us/aboutdoc/history/1853-1889.htm (Accessed September 2011).

Minnesota Legislature. "Resources on Minnesota Issues: Crime & Corrections in Minnesota." http://www.leg.state.mn.us/lrl/issues/crime.asp (Accessed September 2011).

Minor v. Happersett

On October 6, 1869, Virginia Louise Minor, the president of the a Woman's Suffrage Association of Missouri, presented a new approach to women's suffrage at the association's first convention. She argued that the U.S. Constitution gave all native-born citizens, including women, the full rights and privileges of citizenship. Her husband, attorney Francis Minor, presented six resolutions that supported Virginia's argument that the original federal Constitution already enfranchised women. The Minors' arguments relied on the Preamble, Articles One, Four, and Six of the original Constitution, as well as section one of the newly adopted Fourteenth Amendment. Moreover, they argued that citizenship included voting rights. Though this argument had been used to support African American enfranchisement, this was the first time it was used to support women's suffrage.

In 1870, Susan B. Anthony printed "The Minor Resolutions" in the National Woman Suffrage Association's (NWSA) newspaper, *The Revolution*. Approximately 10,000 copies of this edition circulated around the country, and later that same year, the NWSA adopted the Minor Resolutions as their official strategy. These resolutions provided the rhetorical backbone to the large scale, direct-action campaign women around the country waged between 1870 and 1872, known as "The New Departure." In 1872, women showed up at registry offices and polling places around the country and demanded the right to register and vote. Though Susan B. Anthony was the most famous woman arrested and charged under this method, Virginia Minor initiated the case that made it to the U.S. Supreme Court.

On October 15, 1872, Virginia Minor appeared before St. Louis registrar Reese Happersett and requested to be registered to vote. Happersett refused, stating, "she was not a 'male' citizen, but a woman." Since Minor was a woman, she could not sue Happersett in her own right, and therefore, her husband sued on her behalf for denying her one of the basic citizenship rights, the franchise. The Minors' case was first heard in the St. Louis Circuit Court, the same location as the *Dred Scott* case in 1850. The circuit court denied the Minors' petition in 1872, and the Missouri State Supreme Court upheld the circuit court's decision in 1873. The following year, the Minors' case reached the docket of the U.S. Supreme Court. On March 29, 1875, Chief Justice Morrison R. Waite delivered the unanimous opinion that upheld both the circuit court and the Missouri Supreme Court's decisions. In his opinion, Waite stated that the court accepted that women were citizens of the United States, but that the franchise was not immediately vested to citizens. Therefore, women could be citizens, but they were disconnected from the franchise. Further, he maintained that it was up to the individual states to grant or deny voting rights. This decision not only separated the franchise from citizenship, but also ensured the need for a federal amendment.

The Minors based their arguments on the belief that state and federal citizenship could not be separated. They believed that custom and tradition, not law, were the only reasons that women were denied the franchise. They argued that at the heart of these customs lay a misunderstanding of the general characteristics of state and federal citizenship. Because Virginia Minor had been denied the right to register to vote in the state of Missouri on the grounds that she was a female, she was subject to a state prohibition to her rights in a federal election. Under Waite's dual-citizenship theory, she should have been able to register because states had the right to regulate, but not prohibit, the rights granted natural citizens under the Constitution. As federal citizens, women, just like men, were "entitled to all the rights and privileges and immunities of citizenship, chief among which is the one elective franchise." Instead of securing the franchise for women citizens, however, *Minor v. Happersett* validated the exclusionary voting practices of states and legally endorsed unequal citizenship on the basis of sex until the Nineteenth Amendment in 1920. Set in context with cases such as the *Slaughterhouse Cases* (1873) and *Bradwell v. Illinois* (1873), *Minor* signaled the court's readiness to significantly limit the legal protections offered by federal citizenship as well as the emancipatory potential of the Fourteenth Amendment.

Robin C. Henry
Wichita State University

The 1873 petition to Congress from the National Woman Suffrage Association requesting legislation granting women—who were legal U.S. citizens—the right to vote. It failed, as did Virginia Louise Minor's Supreme Court appeal two years later.

See Also: *Dred Scott v. Sandford*; Gender and Criminal Law; Missouri, *Plessy v. Ferguson*.

Further Readings
Basch, Norma. "Reconstructions: History, Gender, and the Fourteenth Amendment." In *The*

Constitutional Bases of Political and Social Change in the United States, Donald G. Nieman, ed. Athens: University of Georgia Press, 1990.

DuBois, Ellen Carol. "Taking the Law Into Our Own Hands: *Bradwell*, *Minor*, and the Suffrage Militance in the 1870s." In *Visible Women: New Essays on American Activism*, Nancy A. Hewitt and Suzanne Lebstock, eds. Urbana: University of Illinois Press, 1993.

Ray, Angela G. and Cindy Koenig Richards. "Inventing Citizens, Imagining Gender Justice: The Suffrage Rhetoric of Virginia and Francis Minor." *Quarterly Journal of Speech*, v.93/4 (2007).

Miranda v. Arizona

In 1966, the U.S. Supreme Court, in a split 5–4 decision, ruled that the Fifth Amendment privilege against self-incrimination requires law enforcement officials to explain a suspect's legal and constitutional rights once they have been charged. In particular, the court found that a suspect must be told they have the right to remain silent and the right to an attorney for any statements they make to be admissible before a court of law.

This decision spurred much public debate, with many arguing that this decision would make it so defendants were never willing to speak to police regarding crimes and would make the already taxing job of police officers even more difficult. Ultimately, the case has stood the test of time, and this did not occur. Most Americans are familiar with the case—even unknowingly—due to the reading of Miranda rights at the time of arrest.

Miranda's Case

The *Miranda* case stemmed from the arrest of Ernesto Miranda for the kidnapping and rape of an 18-year-old woman in 1965. The evidence against him at the time was circumstantial at best. Miranda was taken to the police station, interrogated for two hours, and then signed a confession statement saying that he had kidnapped and raped the young woman. The statement read: "I do hereby swear that I make this statement voluntarily and of my own free will, with no threats, coercion, or promises of immunity, and with full knowledge of my legal rights, understanding any statement that I make may be used against me." While the statement itself indicates a clear waiver of his constitutional rights, Miranda had never been informed of the rights he was choosing to forfeit. At trial, the prosecution offered the written confession into evidence, but Miranda's court-appointed lawyer objected. His argument was that since Miranda was never made aware of his rights, he could not voluntarily waive them. The judged overruled the argument and Miranda was sentenced to 20–30 years in prison.

Upon his conviction, Miranda filed an appeal with the Arizona Supreme Court stating again that his confession had not been fully voluntary because he was never informed of what the rights actually were. The Arizona Supreme Court affirmed the decision of the trial court, however. In its eyes, the fact that Miranda did not ever ask for an attorney led the court to believe he was not concerned about the proceedings and was simply making his confession. Further, the Arizona Supreme Court found that Miranda should have known his written confession could be used against him in future proceedings, and if he was worried, should not have signed the document.

The Outcome

Given the path the U.S. Supreme Court seemed to be taking under Earl Warren, a former prosecutor, most expected a favorable outcome for Miranda. In a 5–4 decision, the court ruled the confession was obtained outside constitutional parameters and should not have been admissible at trial. A dividing topic, the case saw four opinions written on it. Warren wrote for the majority and found that custodial interrogations by police officers are so coercive that no confession should be admitted unless a suspect has been made fully aware of his or her Fifth and Sixth Amendment rights. As Warren stated: "the person in custody must, prior to interrogation, be clearly informed that he has the right to remain silent, and that anything he says will be used against him in court; he must be clearly informed that he has the right to consult with a lawyer and to have the lawyer with him during interrogation, and that, if he is indigent, a lawyer will be appointed to represent him." Warren, on behalf of the court, went even further to say that "if the individual indicates in any manner, at any time prior to or during questioning, that he wishes to remain silent, the interrogation must cease ... if the individual states that he wants an attorney, the interrogation must cease until an attorney is present."

Miranda Regulations

While many criticized the decision, following *Miranda v. Arizona*, police departments across the country were required to inform suspected individuals of their rights at the time of arrest if they wanted to ensure that any statements they made would be admissible in proceedings against them later on. Many departments responded by having printed forms that must be signed and dated by a suspect after having their rights explained to them. Any waiver, however, must be knowing, intelligent, and voluntary. For the *Miranda* rule to apply, six criteria must be met. First, there must be evidence. Second, said evidence has to be testimonial in nature. Third, the suspect must be in custody at the time the testimony is taken. Fourth, the evidence has to stem from an interrogation. Fifth, the interrogation has to involve agents of the state. And last, the evidence has to be offered by the prosecution during criminal proceedings. As a result of these rules, spontaneous statements are not protected by *Miranda*. If you are picked up by the police for questioning (but not put under arrest) and claim to have killed eight people, you cannot use the fact that you were not Mirandized as a reason for your confession to be inadmissible. Once a suspect asserts any *Miranda* right, the interrogation must cease until the police have "scrupulously honored" the suspect's wishes.

Studies of *Miranda*'s impacts have found that there has been little to no effect on whether suspects agree to speak with the police, whether an attorney is present or not. One study has found that approximately 3 to 4 percent of criminal suspects walk away due to defective warnings or defective waivers. Overall, those who argued against *Miranda* have not seen their fears come true, and instead, an additional layer of protection for suspects from potential police misconduct has been added. As for Ernesto Miranda, he was consequently retried without the confession being admitted to evidence and reconvicted. He was paroled after five years and made a modest living till his death, autographing Miranda cards.

William J. Miller
Southeast Missouri State University

See Also: Constitution of the United States of America; Interrogation Practices; Police Abuse; Supreme Court, U.S.

Further Readings
Baker, Liva. *Miranda*: *Crime, Law, and Politics*. New York: Athenaeum, 1983.
Stuart, Gary L. *Miranda*: *The Story of America's Right to Remain Silent*. Tucson: University of Arizona Press, 2004.

Miranda Warnings

See Miranda v. Arizona.

Mississippi

A heavily forested southern state, Mississippi was formed from territory ceded from Georgia and South Carolina and was admitted to the Union as a state in 1817. Once a wealthy state because of the prominence of its cotton plantations, Mississippi has never fully recovered from the end of slavery and the plantation economy. Until the 1930s, when great numbers of African Americans left Mississippi for northern industrial cities, the state was predominantly black. It has historically suffered from severe race relations problems, occasionally motivating bursts of crime, as with the reactions against the civil rights movement of the 1950s and 1960s.

Police and Punishment

The first modern police department in Mississippi was established in 1822 in Jackson and answered to the city marshal. Professionalization was slow, but the work was full-time—seven 12-hour shifts a week, 365 days a year. The 1870s saw the rise of specialization in Mississippi police as in much of the Western world; police officers were issued uniforms, badges, and night sticks, and the rank of police detective was introduced. Desk sergeants and mounted police followed at the turn of the century, followed by the Mississippi Highway Patrol in 1938, which has since become the state-level police agency.

The first Mississippi State Prison was built in Jackson in 1843 to hold inmates who were incarcerated for longer terms than the inmates of county jails and whose offenses could not be punished merely with fines, corporal punishment, or other measures. When the Jackson prison was destroyed during the Civil War, Mississippi used the convict leasing system rather than add the cost of a new prison to its already considerable postwar expenses. Under that system, prisoners were leased to private sector businesses or individuals as laborers and were housed on work sites. Convict leasing ended in 1895, and new correctional facilities were built on farms in Rankin and Hinds counties. The current Mississippi State Penitentiary was built in Sunflower County in 1901.

Mississippi's occasionally harsh sentences came under fire in the odd Scott sisters case, the story of which stretches from 1993 to 2011. The Scott sisters, Jamie (23 at the time of the crime) and Gladys (19), were convicted of the armed robbery of a mini-mart with the assistance of three teenage boys. Despite the robbery netting only a few hundred dollars and a lack of previous criminal records, they both received double life sentences. The conviction was upheld by the appellate court, and the Supreme Court denied the petition for appeal in 1997 and the petition to vacate the conviction in 1998.

In 2010, however Governor Haley Barbour—who had previous denied a petition for clemency—suspended the sisters' sentences on the condition that Gladys donate a kidney to Jamie, whose dialysis was a substantial expense for the cash-strapped state. The sisters agreed and were released in 2011. The requirement of organ donation, particularly

The noncontact visitation center in Unit 32 of the Mississippi State Penitentiary in Parchman. It is the state's oldest institution, opening in 1901. The penitentiary has a capacity of approximately 4,500 in seven different housing units and houses male offenders classified to all custody levels, including long-term segregation and death row. Inmates provide more than 100,000 hours of free inmate labor each year to adjacent municipalities and counties and state agencies.

coupled with the financial motive of the state rather than some motive grounded in principles of criminal justice, has drawn heavy criticism of the state's handling of the case.

Crime

During Reconstruction, as federal authorities forced legal reforms through the formerly Confederate states, the Tennessee-based Ku Klux Klan spread to Mississippi. The first Klan—20th-century groups simply adopted the name in homage—was a vigilante gang whose members concealed their identities while enacting vengeance against Republicans, African Americans, and northern carpetbaggers. The first Mississippi Klan "den" was founded in 1866 and quickly developed into a paramilitary group, a guerrilla force determined to expel northerners and their allies and to punish blacks. The ties between the Klan and the Democratic Party were strong, both groups sharing many of the same goals pursued with different means. Lucius Q. C. Lamar, a former Confederate diplomat and later senator for Mississippi, secretary of the interior, and Supreme Court justice, was one of the Klan's supporters. Klan violence was generally very deliberately directed but could include seemingly random targets for the simple purpose of striking fear into the enemy community. The first Klan eventually died off as federal authorities began taking stronger action against it.

The second Klan, founded in Georgia in 1915, also quickly spread to Mississippi. Though called the "Invisible Empire," in most communities, the second Klan was less secretive than the first or the modern Klan; often treated as a Protestant fraternal organization, this new Klan recruited from churches and religious fraternities, redistributed some of its cash to Mississippi churches, and maintained that it was a peaceful patriotic group. In reality, its sometimes extreme violence—the burning cross was introduced by the second Klan—targeted not only blacks but Jews, Catholics, and non-Anglo immigrants. Like the first Klan, it often benefited from strong political ties and well-coordinated direction.

Though it is common to speak of "the Klan" in the 1950s through the present, since the dissolution of the second Klan in the World War II era there has been no single hierarchical Klan group, but rather numerous groups—sometimes coexisting in the same region, sometimes even sharing members—using Klan references in their names, and "the Klan" in this era refers to a Klan movement rather than a single group. The Klan resurgence in 1960s Mississippi was a powerful one, following—or responsible for—a series of violent episodes after the desegregation of Ole Miss (the state university) in 1962. Sympathy for Klan groups in Mississippi was strong, but there was a reluctance to join it that Federal Bureau of Investigation (FBI) investigators found puzzling, which may have evinced a self-consciousness or awareness of a taboo surrounding the group—or even a suspicion that in the long run, Mississippi's efforts to resist desegregation and the other aims of the civil rights movement would be fruitless.

Klan violence in the 1960s exceeded that of the 1920s and rivaled that of Reconstruction, but public sentiment turned against the Klan after the 1967 bombing of a synagogue. Those who considered themselves moderates withdrew their support from the Klan, which quickly lost its footing in the state, dying off almost completely by the end of the decade. Though Klan groups persist in the state as in much of the country, they are small, marginalized groups with none of the political sway or financial resources of previous groups.

Violence in the civil rights era wasn't confined to the Klan. Numerous racially motivated murders occurred in Mississippi in 1955, including that of black voter registration organizer Lamar Smith (shot to death in broad daylight in front of the courthouse, with no witnesses willing to come forward and no one convicted for his murder), civil rights leader George Lee (shot to death while driving his car), and 14-year-old Emmitt Till (beaten to death by a group of men for flirting with the wife of one of them). One of the activists involved both in the attempt to overturn segregation and in the investigation several of the 1955 deaths was Medgar Evers, the National Association for the Advancement of Colored People's (NAACP's) Mississippi field secretary. Evers's increasing prominence, especially after the desegregation of Ole Miss, made him a target for violence, and after at least two failed attempts to kill him in the space of two weeks, he was shot from behind on June 12, 1963, upon returning home from a meeting with NAACP lawyers. Byron de la Beckwith, a salesman and member of the white supremacist group

White Citizens' Council, was arrested for the murder, but sufficient evidence to convict him was not found until 1994, when he was finally convicted.

Mississippi's crime rate is and has generally been well below the national average. Although it followed the national trend of rising after World War II with considerable increases in the 1970s and 1990s before declining, that trend wasn't as smooth in Mississippi as in the nation as a whole. Crime temporarily fell in the mid-1970s, for instance, as well as in the mid-1980s, before climbing to a 1995 peak of 502.8 violent crimes per 100,000 inhabitants. It has tended to fall since then—and in 2010 had fallen to 269.7—with a few temporary rises, notably one coinciding with the 2008 economic collapse.

Bill Kte'pi
Independent Scholar

See Also: 1981 to 2000 Primary Documents; African Americans; Civil Rights Laws; *Mississippi v. Johnson*; Racism.

Further Readings
Ball, Howard. *Murder in Mississippi*: United States v. Price *and the Struggle for Civil Rights*. Lawrence: University Press of Kansas, 2004.
Currie, James T. "From Slavery to Freedom in Mississippi's Legal System." *Journal of Negro History*, v.65/2 (Spring 1980).
MacLean, Harry N. *The Past Is Never Dead*: *The Trial of James Ford Seale and Mississippi's Struggle for Redemption*. New York: Basic Civitas Books, 2009.
Newton, M. *The Ku Klux Klan in Mississippi*. Jefferson, NC: McFarland and Co., 2010.
Waldrep, Christopher. *Jury Discrimination*: *The Supreme Court, Public Opinion, and a Grassroots Fight for Racial Equality in Mississippi*. Atlanta: University of Georgia Press, 2010.

Mississippi v. Johnson

Mississippi v. Johnson is significant because it was the first lawsuit brought against a sitting president of the United States (Andrew Johnson) in the U.S. Supreme Court. The case was one of a series of Reconstruction era cases that came before the Supreme Court in the years after the American Civil War. In this case, the state of Mississippi sought an injunction against the president's enforcement of the laws. The case was argued before the court on April 12, 1867, and was decided three days later. The opinion was written by Chief Justice Salmon P. Chase.

In March 1867, Congress, over President Andrew Johnson's veto, enacted the Reconstruction Acts. These were four separate laws that were passed by the Republican Congress. The law disbanded the state governments established immediately after the Civil War and organized the former Confederate states (with the exception of Tennessee, which had ratified the Fourteenth Amendment and was readmitted to the Union) into five military districts. The president was empowered to appoint a military governor and place troops in the states of the former Confederacy to maintain public order. The states were required to draft new state constitutions granting African American men the right to vote as a condition for readmission to the Union.

An Attempt to Restrain the President
The lawsuit, brought by the state of Mississippi, sought "perpetually to enjoin and restrain" President Andrew Johnson and his officers and agents appointed for that purpose, especially Edward Ord, the military commander of the Fourth Military District (which included the state of Mississippi) from carrying out the Reconstruction Acts. Although President Johnson had vetoed the laws, stating in his veto message to Congress that the "power thus given to the commanding officer over all the people of each district is that of an absolute monarch," he viewed the lawsuit as a challenge to presidential authority. Johnson ordered Attorney General Henry Stanberry to challenge Mississippi's request for an injunction.

The court, in a unanimous decision, held that it could not block the president from using his authority as chief executive to enforce a statute that may be unconstitutional, stating that it had "no jurisdiction of a bill to enjoin the President in the performance of his official duties ...." The Chase Court relied on the Marshall Court's ruling in *Marbury v. Madison*, 5 U.S. (1 Cranch)

137 (1803). In that case, the Supreme Court had written that the president has two kinds of tasks: ministerial and discretionary. Ministerial tasks are those required of the office, and by failing to perform those tasks, the president could be seen as violating the Constitution. As for discretionary tasks, these were tasks where the president had latitude as to whether or not to act.

In his opinion, Chase wrote that while the court had the authority to command executive branch officials to act, this power only extended to ministerial functions, where the president had no discretion. In this case, Chase concluded that the president's task, the enforcement of the Reconstruction Acts, was "in no sense ministerial." Chase went on to write that if the court attempted to interfere with the president's performance of his discretionary tasks, that such action would be "an absurd and excessive extravagance," since the judiciary lacked the ability to enforce such an order. This became known as "executive immunity," which is based on the Constitution's separation of powers.

While the court could not stop the president from carrying out this responsibility (enforcement of the Reconstruction Acts), once he did, his actions could be challenged on Constitutional grounds in the courts.

Jeffrey Kraus
Wagner College

See Also: 1981 to 2000 Primary Documents; African Americans; Enforcement Acts 1870–71; Johnson, Andrew (Administration of); Mississippi; Presidential Proclamations.

Further Readings
Butler, Lynda Lee and David Bearinger. *The Bill of Rights, the Courts and the Law: The Landmark Cases That Have Shaped American Society*. Charlottesville: Virginia Foundation for the Humanities and Public Policy, 1999.
Foner, Eric. *Reconstruction: America's Unfinished Revolution: 1863–1877*. New York: HarperCollins, 2005.
Mississippi v. Johnson, 71 U.S. 475 (1867).
Swinney, Everette. "Enforcing the Fifteenth Amendment, 1870–1877." *Journal of Southern History*, v.28/2 (May 1962).

Missouri

Originally acquired as part of the Louisiana Purchase, Missouri was admitted as the 24th state in 1821 as part of the Missouri Compromise. A border state with significant southern and midwestern influences, it has long been the symbolic center of the United States; both the Pony Express routes and the Oregon Trail set out from Missouri, which was the gateway to the western frontier in the 19th century. Today, it is both the mean center of the American population and the most famous bellwether state, considered a microcosm of the country as a whole because of its similar demographic makeup and mix of urban and rural communities.

Police and Punishment

The new state legislature soon voted to construct the Missouri State Penitentiary to incarcerate criminals who were serving terms longer than those accommodated by town jails. It was built in Jefferson City in 1836, then the capital of the state. Prisoners were employed as brick-makers to offset the cost of their incarceration. In 2004, the penitentiary, long known as "the Walls," was replaced with the Jefferson City Correctional Center.

Early Missouri settlements had town constables or were served by county sheriffs. Formal police departments, originally overseen by city marshals, were formed as towns grew bigger; Jefferson City established its police department in 1836, and Springfield's followed in 1858.

Missouri is a capital punishment state. Like other states, following the 1972 and 1976 *Furman v. Georgia* and *Gregg v. Georgia* rulings by the Supreme Court, it was forced to rewrite its death penalty statute in order to ensure that it would be applied consistently. Further, the use of the death penalty for crimes other than murder has been suspended; the last execution for a non-homicide crime in Missouri was that of convicted rapist Ronald Wolfe in 1964. The state's post-*Gregg* death penalty statute was passed into law on May 26, 1977, based on laws already upheld as constitutional in other states, and requires at least one of 14 aggravating circumstances in order to apply the death penalty: prior capital murder conviction or multiple serious assault convictions; a second capital murder committed at the same time; use of a device in a public place that endangered persons other than the victim; a murder committed for pay (considered a separate aggravating circumstance for the defendant hiring the killer); the murder of a judicial officer or prosecutor, motivated by the exercise of their duties; torture and other "outrageously or wantonly vile" circumstances; the murder of a working police officer, corrections officer, or firefighter; a murder committed while the accused is in custody; a murder committed in order to avoid or prevent an arrest; a murder committed during the commission of a felony; the murder of a witness or potential witness in any investigation or prosecution; the murder of a correctional employee or inmate; a murder committed as the result of transit hijacking.

Since 1988, Missouri executions have been carried out by lethal injection. From 1937 to 1988, the gas chamber had been used, located at the Jefferson City Correctional Center, and before that executions had been public hangings conducted by the sheriff of the county where the crime had transpired.

Missouri's current death penalty statute has been criticized on the same grounds that caused the Massachusetts Supreme Judicial Court to find that state's 1982 death penalty statute unconstitutional: because only a jury trial can result in a death sentence, defendants are in a position in which they can take that risk or they can plead guilty, bypass jury sentencing, and accept a life sentence, possibly with parole. In Massachusetts, this circumstance was grounds for nullifying the statute, the court ruling that it violated both the right to a trial by jury and the right to protection from self-incrimination. The Missouri Supreme Court has gone in the other direction: when Patrick Nunley and Michael Anthony Taylor pleaded guilty to kidnapping, rape, and murder, the judge imposed the death sentence, acting on the assumption that the defendants had pleaded guilty only to avoid it. In appeals, defense argued that this was unconstitutional, since a jury must recommend the death sentence. The Missouri Supreme Court's ruling in 2011 was that the defendants had waived their rights to the jury sentencing, and the death sentence was upheld.

Executions, though, are on hold in Missouri as of 2011. Hospira, the company manufacturing sodium thiopental, one of the drugs used in the lethal injections in Missouri and many other states, discontinued the drug, and existing supplies expired in March 2011. An alternate source may be found, or a new drug may need to replace it; in some states, using a new drug has required legislation, but it isn't yet clear whether the Department of Corrections will need legislative cooperation in Missouri.

Crime

At the edge of the frontier, Missouri was home to a number of outlaws and bandits. Springfield has claimed to be the home of the first high noon shoot-out, when Wild Bill Hickok and Dave Tutt drew pistols in the public square, resulting in Tutt's death, for which Hickok was later acquitted. Marion Hedgepeth, born in Prairie Home in 1856, was better known as the Handsome Bandit or the Derby Kid; by age 20, he was an accomplished train robber and multiple murderer, and after serving a seven-year sentence for larceny, he became a prominent member of the Slye-Wilson Gang of highwaymen, train robbers, and safe crackers. Hedgepeth was eventually apprehended by the Pinkertons and sentenced in 1893 to 25 years in prison—a sentence that was commuted after 14 years when Hedgepeth informed on a cellmate who turned out to be H. H. Holmes (Herman Mudgett), one of the first American serial killers.

More famously, the James-Younger Gang was based out of Missouri, named for Cole Younger and his brothers (Jim, John, and Bob) and Frank and Jesse James. The gang began its criminal activity in 1866, immediately after the Civil War, which had made Missouri a site of guerrilla violence as partisanship was strong for both sides. The original core of the gang, Cole and the James brothers, had fought for the Confederacy in the war. Both were slave-owning families with southern origins; Frank James and Cole Younger fought under bushwhacker William Quantrill until Cole enlisted in the regular Confederate army, and Jesse James joined the fight in 1864 at age 16. The February after the war ended, they began robbing banks, turning their skill for violence into profit. Train robberies followed, and the gang was pursued by the Pinkertons for most of the 1870s before the gang finally fell apart in 1879, though individual criminal careers continued for years to come.

J. B. "Wild Bill" Hickok became engraved in Missouri legend when he shot poker rival David Tutt in Springfield, Missouri, in 1865. This first recorded example of a two-man, quick-draw duel cast the mold for the classic western gunfight story.

During Reconstruction in the former Confederate states, a number of veterans of the guerrilla wars fought in Missouri during the Civil War assisted the Ku Klux Klan of North Carolina. Having originated in Tennessee, the Klan had quickly spread throughout the reconstructed south in an attempt to expel Republicans, blacks, northerners, and their allies. When the war stopped, those who had been engaged in fighting it in Missouri traveled to North Carolina to help their friends and relatives there. Coincidentally, Klansmen fleeing the later federal crackdown on the Klan around 1870 fled from North Carolina to Missouri. Some of them may have been involved in the revival of the Klan in Missouri in the 20th century; the new Klan was a fraternal organization founded in Georgia in 1915, using violence to target blacks, Jews, Catholics, and immigrants.

The modern Klan in Missouri has no formal connection to the first two Klans, the second Klan having been dissolved in the World War II era. A white supremacist group, the Missouri Klan has made headlines for its attempts to "adopt" a stretch of Interstate 55, south of St. Louis. When the Department of Transportation rejected the application, a U.S. District Court judge found that the refusal was unconstitutional. The state was forced to erect signs announcing the Klan's sponsorship but countered by renaming that stretch of highway the Rosa Parks Highway.

The violent crime rate in Missouri is slightly higher than the national average: 455 violent crimes per 100,000 inhabitants in 2010 (when the national average was 403). It has followed the general national trend of rising steadily from World War II until the 1990s and then falling again, but with some deviations along the way. Crime fell in the early 1980s, for instance, only to rise to a peak of 744.4 in 1993. Before 2010, the post-1993 low was 490, reached in 2000 before rising to 540 in 2001, and then hitting 490 again in both 2003 and 2004 before again rising to 545 in 2006.

Bill Kte'pi
Independent Scholar

See Also: 1851 to 1900 Primary Documents; Capital Punishment; Frontier Crime; Kansas City, Missouri; Mudgett, Herman; St. Louis, Missouri.

Further Readings
Fellman, Michael. *Inside War: The Guerrilla Conflict in Missouri During the American Civil War.* New York: Oxford University Press, 1989.
Leslie, Edward E. *The Devil Knows How to Ride.* New York: Da Capo Press, 1998.
Stiles, T. J. *Jesse James: Last Rebel of the Civil War.* New York: Vintage, 2003.

M'Naghten Test

Through the criminal law, society attempts to develop standards of acceptable behavior that protect its citizens from harm in a manner that is consistent with its fundamental values. American societal values are based in large part on Judeo-Christian beliefs. Justice and fairness are embedded in this framework. The belief that only the culpable should be held responsible for their wrongful acts is at the core of this belief in justice and fairness. In criminal law, this means that wrongful conduct that is the product of knowledge and intent deserves punishment. Those who are incapable of truly understanding what they are doing are not culpable for their actions. Children and those without sufficient mental faculties, such as those who are mentally retarded or mentally ill, are examples of those who should not be held criminally responsible for their misdeeds. The M'Naghten test was an attempt to create a test to determine when someone should not be held criminally responsible for his or her actions.

Early Cases

The belief that some people should not be held responsible for their harmful acts has existed for well over 2,000 years. One of the earliest examples of this is seen in scholarly commentary on the Torah, dating back to the 6th century B.C.E.

A sketch of Daniel M'Naghten at trial and an engraving of his signature, published in the March 4, 1843, edition of the Scottish Reformer's Gazette. The creation of the standard of insanity in criminal proceedings is based on his murder case.

These scholars divided wrongful acts into two categories, one for actions that occur with fault, and another for those wrongs that occur without fault. Those whose actions were considered to be without fault included children and the mentally disabled. These groups were considered to lack the capacity to weigh the moral implications of their wrongful conduct.

In *Beverley's Case*, a 1603 English court decision, the court held that a "madman" could not be held criminally responsible. The court defined a "madman" as "one who does not know what he is doing, who lacks in mind and reason and is not far removed from brutes." Similarly, in a 1724 English court decision, *Rex v. Arnold*, the court ruled that one who is "totally deprived of his understanding and memory, and doth not know what he is doing, no more than an infant, than a brute, or a wild beast" shall not be held responsible for his wrongful conduct. It was not until 1843 that a standard and clearly articulated rule for determining criminal responsibility was developed.

Daniel M'Naghten

The creation of this standard resulted from public outrage over the acquittal by reason of insanity of Daniel M'Naghten, the man who, in an attempt to assassinate the prime minister, of England, Sir Robert Peel, shot and killed Edward Drummond, secretary to the prime minister in January 1843. Descriptions of M'Naghten indicate that he was likely suffering from paranoid schizophrenia, a major mental disorder in which the person's ability to distinguish reality from what is not real is severely impaired. Common symptoms of schizophrenia include hallucinations and delusions. Hallucinations, in which the patient perceives something when no external stimuli exists, can occur in any of the senses, that is, hallucinations can consist of hearing, seeing, smelling, tasting, or feeling a sensation when there is nothing to hear, see, smell, taste, or feel. The most common hallucinations are auditory, in which the patient hears voices or other sounds when those sounds do not exist.

Following the outrage from the acquittal, the English House of Lords established the set of criteria that must be met for a defendant to be found not guilty by reason of insanity. This became known as the M'Naghten test. The standard established by the House of Lords states that "to establish a defense on the ground of insanity, it must be clearly proved that, at the time of the committing of the act, the party accused was laboring under such a defect of reason, from disease of the mind, as not know the nature and quality of the act he was doing, or if he did know it, he did not know that he was doing what was wrong."

The M'Naghten test is a vast improvement over the "wild beast" standard for legal insanity. The wild beast test called for a purely subjective determination of whether the defendant should not be held criminally responsible for his or her actions. With no objective standard to follow, each juror was free to use his idiosyncratic image of a wild beast when asked to decide this issue. Given the same set of facts, such a standard could result in inconsistent verdicts depending on the makeup of the jury.

Definition of the M'Naghten Test

The M'Naghten test provides jurors with a clear standard for reaching their verdict. For the first time, a universal standard would be used by all English courts to determine whether the accused should be found not guilty by reason of insanity, a standard with clear and coherent requirements. Such a standard better serves the goal that the criminal law should be fair and just. The M'Naghten test has several important components. First, the test requires that the defendant's culpability be determined by his or her mental status "at the time of the committing of the act." Although a defendant's mental state before and/or after the commission of the act may be relevant to proving his or her mental status at the time of the act, they are not dispositive of the ultimate issue. This requirement has been a consistent key element of every version of the insanity defense.

The M'Naghten test states that it must be shown that the defendant was "laboring under (a) defect of reason, from disease of the mind." The term *disease of the mind* is no longer used by modern psychology and psychiatry. It has been replaced by "psychological disorder," "psychiatric disorder," or "mental disorder." The current formal nomenclature for mental disorders comes from the *Diagnostic and Statistical Manual of Mental Disorders, Fourth Edition: Text Revision* (*DSM-IV-TR*) published in 2000 by the American Psychiatric Association. A *DSM-IV-TR* "mental disorder" is the modern equivalent to the archaic terminology "disease of the mind."

The M'Naghten test makes clear that simply having a "disease of the mind" is not a sufficient basis for a finding that the accused shall not be held culpable for his or her wrongful acts. The accused's mental disorder must result in a "defect of reason." The requirement that the mental disorder cause a cognitive defect significantly narrows the type of mental disorder that can serve as a basis for a defense based on insanity. Mental disorders that could serve as a basis for the use of the insanity defense include, but are not limited to, psychotic disorders and disorders that can result in psychotic symptoms, dementia, and mental retardation. A psychotic disorder is one in which there is a loss of contact with reality, usually including fixed false ideas about what is taking place or who one is (delusions) and seeing or hearing things that do not exist (hallucinations).

The most common psychotic disorder used in insanity defense cases is schizophrenia. This mental disorder significantly impairs the individual's ability to distinguish between real and unreal experiences, to think logically and coherently, to have normal emotional responses, and to behave normally in social situations. While all subtypes of schizophrenia share these characteristics, the subtypes differ as to the prominence and quality of specific characteristics. For example, in schizophrenia, paranoid type, the dominant theme of the delusions and hallucinations is paranoia. Individuals with this mental disorder tend to believe that specific people or entities are out to harm them or someone they care about and often include the belief that they are the object of a conspiracy.

Another element of M'Naghten requires that the person committing the act must "not know the nature or quality of the act he was doing." This type of cognitive impairment is characteristic of dementia, mental retardation, psychotic disorders, and disorders with psychotic symptoms. However, some disorders, such as schizophrenia, are cyclic. Most people diagnosed with schizophrenia have periods of lucidity. An act done during such a period of lucidity would not fit this criterion, as the relevant time in determining criminal culpability is "at the time of the committing of the act." The final element of the M'Naghten test states that "if (the accused) did know (the nature and quality of the act he was doing), he did not know that he was doing what was wrong." As with the previous element, this type of cognitive impairment is characteristic of dementia, mental retardation, psychotic disorders, and disorders with psychotic symptoms.

The M'Naghten test has been criticized for focusing exclusively on the ability to think, to reason. The rule requires that the accused have a mental disorder that results in a "defect of reason" such that the person does not "know the nature and quality" of their actions or does not "know" that their actions were wrong. Mental disorders can cause serious impairment in a person's ability to reason. They also can substantially impair one's ability to control one's behavior.

One Example

John, a person suffering from paranoid schizophrenia, hears the voice of his deceased great grandfather warn him that students at the local high school have conspired to kill him. Living in constant fear, John keeps a loaded semiautomatic handgun with him at all times. A group of seniors from the high school is selling magazines door-to-door to raise money for their senior trip. He sees a group of high school students approach his door. When one knocks, John believes his death is imminent. He shakily draws his gun and shoots at the door until he is out of bullets. When the police arrive, they discover the bodies of five students, three dead and two wounded. John could not distinguish what was real from what was not real, believed that his deceased great grandfather spoke to him (auditory hallucination), and labored under the false belief that students from the high school were going to kill him (paranoid delusion). He emptied his gun to kill the students before they could kill him. Although he had a defect of reason (delusional; out of contact with reality) from a disease of the mind (paranoid schizophrenia), he knew the nature and quality of his actions (that he was shooting and killing the students at the door). Therefore, John does not meet the M'Naghten test, despite committing his actions because of his mental illness.

The M'Naghten test was a major step in the evolution of the defense of insanity. The principle that only those who are culpable for their actions should be held criminally responsible can be traced back to the 6th century B.C. The M'Naghten test was the first formulation of that principle in Western jurisprudence that provided jurors with a clear and coherent standard for determining whether a person should be held criminally responsible for his or her actions. Despite being criticized for its exclusive focus on the cognitive abilities of the accused, it has been adopted as the legal standard for the defense of insanity by a plurality of American states.

Allen J. Brown
Anna Maria College

See Also: Famous Trials; Insanity Defense; Sentencing.

Further Readings

American Psychiatric Association. *Diagnostic and Statistical Manual of Mental Disorders—IV-TR*. Washington, DC: American Psychiatric Association, 2000.
Beverley's Case, 76 Eng. Rep. 1118 (1603).
Huss, M. T. *Forensic Psychology: Research, Clinical Practice, and Applications*. West Sussex, UK: Wiley-Blackwell, 2009.
Melton, G., J. Petrila, N. Poythress, and C. Slobogin. *Psychological Evaluations for the Courts: A Handbook for Mental Health Professionals and Lawyers*, 3rd ed. New York: Guilford Press, 2007.
M'Naghten's Case, 8 Eng. Rep. 718 (1843).
Moran, R. *Knowing Right From Wrong: The Insanity Defense of Daniel M'Naghten*. New York: Free Press, 1981.
Rex v. Arnold, 16 How. St. Tr. 695 (1724).

Mollen Commission

British historian Lord Acton is known for his famous quote concerning government, politics, and integrity: power corrupts and absolute power corrupts absolutely. Police officers are members of the government, whether municipal, state, or federal. And police officers have enormous power, which includes the power and authority to legally kill a human being. Police corruption tends to be widespread in large municipal departments that employ hundreds or thousands of police officers. It has been suggested that the size and bureaucratic nature of large police departments inherently fosters police corruption, but there are many other causes besides just departmental size. New York City, which has the largest municipal police department in the United States, is no exception.

Frank Serpico and the Knapp Commission
In the early 1970s, the Knapp Commission was formed in New York City to investigation allegations of widespread corruption in the New York Police Department. The actions of Frank Serpico, a New York police officer who attempted to expose the corruption and who was subsequently shot for his efforts because his fellow officers failed to back him up in a drug raid, were instrumental in the success of the Knapp Commission. The Knapp Commission asked in its final report if history would repeat itself. Sadly, that comment was prophetic. Twenty years later, in 1992, the Mollen Commission was formed to investigate corruption in the New York Police Department (NYPD). On May 7, 1992, New York City police officer Michael Dowd and five other New York police officers were arrested by the Suffolk County police (not the New York police) for trafficking in cocaine. Despite 16 previous internal investigations of Michael Dowd by the New York police, no charges were ever brought against Dowd, and he was never disciplined. Further, Dowd was given superb evaluations and noted to have good career potential. Dowd had been pursued for years by New York City internal affairs investigator Joseph Trimboli, who had been ignored, delayed, harassed, and sabotaged in his investigation of Dowd by the NYPD command. As a result of ensuing scandal, New York City Mayor David Dinkins appointed the Mollen Commission to investigate the situation.

The Mollen Commission, after its creation, began an extended investigation into police corruption. What they discovered was astounding. The commission found that the Internal Affairs Division engaged in willful misconduct to cover up police corruption, including withholding vital information to protect corrupt police officers under investigation. This finding supported the allegations made by Trimboli. What was extremely disturbing was that the Internal Affairs Division was found to have kept "tickler files" on their own investigating officers without charging them, so that they could be blackmailed at a later date. The commission found that, although the majority of officers in the New York Police Department were honest, there were well-organized groups of rogue officers. These officers skimmed money from crime scenes, dealt drugs, brutalized citizens, and regularly engaged in such crimes as robbery and burglary. New police cadets were taught the "Code of Silence" and that they were not supposed to "rat" on fellow police officers. Like the Knapp Commission, the Mollen Commission also found perjury to be widespread. The police union notified officers when they were placed under investigation so that they could avoid being caught. Essentially, the Mollen Commission found that there was a pervasive attitude in the New York Police Department that valued loyalty to fellow officers over integrity and loyalty to the law. The police commanders were found to have abdicated their responsibilities, engaged in willful blindness to corruption, and were incompetent to police themselves.

Final Report
During the investigation by the Mollen Commission, Police Commissioner Raymond Kelly announced that he would upgrade the Internal Affairs Division to a separate bureau and start holding officers accountable for their investigations. The proposal was viewed as an attempt to stop the investigation and prevent external investigation of the police. The Mollen Commission rejected the change as insufficient. The Mollen Commission issued its final report on July 6, 1994. As a result of the Mollen Commission Report, in 1995, New York City created the Commission to Combat Police Corruption. The entity was permanent and independent of the NYPD and was authorized to conduct its own investigations. Some police officers, including Michael Dowd, were arrested, prosecuted, and convicted. However, there were some criticisms of the Mollen Commission that some top police leaders were protected from the inquiry.

Following the Mollen Commission Report, a new police commissioner, William Bratton, was appointed. In November 1995, Commissioner Bratton announced a plan in which police officers would be trained to tell the truth. Not a few people were stunned that New York City police officers had to be trained in such a basic ethical concept and essential requirement of the criminal justice system. Unfortunately, the Knapp Commission was correct—history repeated itself and 20 years later, the Mollen Commission had to be created to address police corruption, which the New York Police Department was incapable of doing itself.

Wm. C. Plouffe, Jr.
Independent Scholar

See Also: Code of Silence; Knapp Commission; New York City; Police, History of.

Further Readings
Baer, Harold, Jr., and Joseph Armao. "The Mollen Commission Report: An Overview." *New York Law School Law Review*, v.40/73 (1995).
Chin, Gabriel, ed. *New York City Police Corruption Investigation Commissions 1894–1994*. Buffalo, NY: William S. Hein, 1997.
Kleinig, John. *The Ethics of Policing*. Cambridge: Cambridge University Press, 1996.
McAlary, Mike. *Good Cop, Bad Cop: Joseph Trimboli v. Michael Dowd and the NY Police Department*. New York: Pocket Books, 1996.

Monroe, James (Administration of)

James Monroe (1758–1831), fifth president of the United States, distinguished himself through both military and political accomplishments. Born into a modest Virginia farming family in 1758, he led the United States during a time of expansion and prosperity. His administration is best known for setting the Monroe Doctrine, an international policy that has been applied by presidents even in modern times. Despite all of his political and military successes, financial problems and large debts haunted him most of his life, even after leaving the White House.

Monroe began college at William and Mary in Williamsburg, Virginia but did not immediately finish because of the outbreak of war with Great Britain. He volunteered with the Continental army while attending college. Monroe was involved in early open engagements with British soldiers and suffered a near-life-ending wound. He is credited with being the last president to fight in the Revolutionary War. Following the war, Monroe studied law under Virginia Governor Thomas Jefferson. Monroe was elected to the Virginia General Assembly in 1782. He also served in the Continental Congress from 1783 to 1786. Running out of money, Monroe resigned from Congress in order to practice law. Shortly after returning to practice law, he again was elected to the Virginia General Assembly. Although he did not attend the Constitutional Convention, he spoke out in Virginia on behalf of the Anti-Federalists and voted against ratification. Monroe was elected to the U.S. Senate in 1790, served as an ambassador to France and Great Britain, as governor of Virginia, as secretary of state, and as secretary of war during the War of 1812. After leading the war effort, Monroe received national acclaim and won the presidential election of 1816 without campaigning; he won reelection in 1820, running unopposed.

Era of Good Feelings
Monroe's administration served during what has been called the "Era of Good Feelings," a time of limited politically partisan conflict. He began his presidency with a tour of every state, full of pageantry and well-wishes. Monroe was the first president to conduct such a ceremonial trip since George Washington. The early part of Monroe's presidency witnessed expansion of the nation's boundaries, reduction of the national debt stemming from the War of 1812, vast improvements in transportation, and expansion of industry and agriculture. However, controversies did arise, particularly with an economic depression in 1819. National debt accumulated during Monroe's second term, political infighting occurred among his administration and conflicts arose with Russia over lands in the Oregon Territory. On the international stage, Monroe laid the foundation for the Monroe Doctrine in 1823. This policy stated that the United States would not interfere

James Monroe, lawyer and fifth president of the United States. His administration is marked by many Supreme Court rulings that increased federal powers.

with European affairs, including a potential war between France and Great Britain, but that the United States would also not allow further colonization by European or Asian nations in North or South America. While Monroe stated that the United States would not interfere with existing colonies, he clearly signaled to other nations that the Americas were exclusively within the U.S. sphere of influence.

Slavery became a major controversial issue during the administration as well. Monroe held slaves throughout his life, but he strongly supported efforts to settle emancipated slaves on the west coast of Africa in current-day Liberia. The Liberian capital, Monrovia, is named in James Monroe's honor. Disputes arose in Congress over the slavery status of new states admitted to the Union. This led to the Missouri Compromise of 1820, which allowed new southern states to be admitted as slave-holding jurisdictions but banned slavery in new northern states.

This era was also marked by many Supreme Court rulings that enhanced the power of the national government. Monroe's longtime friend, John Marshall, a persistent supporter of a strong central government, led the Supreme Court in a string of pro–national government decisions, including *McCulloch v. Maryland* (1819) and *Gibbons v. Ogden* (1824). In the case of *Cohens v. Virginia* (1821), the court ruled that it possessed the power to review and overturn a state's proceedings in a criminal case. The opinion, authored by Chief Justice Marshall, opened the door for judicial review of state criminal laws. While Monroe originally supported the Anti-Federalist ideals and espoused a weaker federal government, he nevertheless did not oppose the Supreme Court's pro–national government rulings as he looked to expand his executive powers.

In the years following his presidency, Monroe kept a low profile, declining the invitation to run for governor of Virginia and rejecting the invitation to be part of the presidential nominating convention in 1827. He remained largely out of the political limelight, never publicly voicing his opinion on political matters. He continued to struggle with debt, much of which he incurred during his public service. After being forced to sell his Virginia property to pay his debts, he died nearly destitute on July 4, 1831, in New York.

Todd A. Collins
Western Carolina University

See Also: *Cohens v. Virginia*; *Gibbons v. Ogden*; *McCulloch v. Maryland*; Slavery.

Further Readings
Brown, Stuart G., ed. *The Autobiography of James Monroe*. Syracuse, NY: Syracuse University Press, 1959.
Cunningham, Nobel E., Jr. *The Presidency of James Monroe*. Lawrence: University Press of Kansas, 1996.
Unger, Harlow Giles. *The Last Founding Father*. Philadelphia: Da Capo Press, 2009.

Montana

The fourth-largest state in the Union and one of the most sparsely populated, Montana attained statehood in 1889 after 25 years as a U.S. territory and about 50 years of white settlement before that. Its sparseness and remoteness contributed to the prevalence of outlaws, both before and after statehood.

Police and Punishment
Early law enforcement was handled by federal marshals, private security forces (especially in mining settlements during and after the gold rush), town marshals, constables, and night watchmen. Formal police departments, modeled after the city police departments elsewhere in the country (which in turn were largely modeled after the London police), barely preceded statehood and initially consisted of a police chief or city marshal overseeing plainclothes patrolmen. Uniforms were introduced around the turn of the century, and full professionalization, including mandatory certification and a six-month trial period for new patrolmen, followed in the first years of the 20th century.

The "Old Prison," today a registered historic site, was Montana's territorial prison when it was built by convict labor in 1871, became the Montana State Prison upon statehood, and remained the primary penitentiary until 1979. The building of a prison before statehood is unusual—even in early years of statehood, many states relied on county jails and cheaper nonincarcerating forms of punishment like corporal punishment and fines—and reflects both the era (Montana, becoming a state relatively late in American history, joined a union already rather mature and sophisticated) and the problems of outlawry and vigilantism. The prison suffered many problems of overcrowding and underfunding and was replaced by a new Montana State Prison in 1979.

Montana is a capital punishment state. As in other states following the Supreme Court decisions of the 1970s, homicide is one of the only crimes for which the death penalty may be used. The exception is aggravated assault or kidnapping while incarcerated in a state prison, if the offender is a persistent felony offender or has been previously convicted of murder. Death sentences are suspended in the case of mental unfitness or pregnancy.

Crime
During the territory's gold rush period of the 1860s, a gang of outlaws called the Innocents arose, focusing their efforts on robbing gold while it was being transported. The leader appears to have been Henry Plummer, the sheriff of Bannack. The brief-lived town of Hell Gate was settled in 1856 and abandoned as a viable settlement in 1865, though some settlers continued to live in the area for some time after that. During that short period, members of Plummer's gang settled in the town—probably around 1863, when Plummer's associate Cyrus Skinner purchased a saloon—and made a show of throwing their weight around. Plummer himself would use a store safe, containing $65,000 in gold dust, as his seat, leading to the rumor that the gang intended to crack the safe. It's not clear if the gang actually committed any serious crimes against town residents, but their fear of the gang grew sufficiently that a group of vigilantes was hired in 1864. They were a small portion of the Montana Vigilantes, a vigilante justice group formed the previous year in response to the territory's rampant crime and at their height included at least 500 men. Thousands more gathered to watch the Vigilantes execute Plummer, while several members of his gang were hanged from trees around town.

In Virginia City, the Vigilantes used the code 3-7-77 to notify individuals whom they would target if they didn't leave town. The origins of the code are unknown; the oldest known theory is that the criminal was given 3 hours, 7 minutes, and 77 seconds to leave town, while other theories have suggested the dimensions of a grave or a Masonic origin. Today, the Montana Highway Patrol, founded in 1935 (after a two-year period in which Montana led the nation in highway fatalities), long after the heyday of the Vigilantes, includes the code on its uniform patch.

Butte, Montana, experienced rapid growth and prosperity during the heyday of its copper mines in the 1880s, which led to the opening of numerous saloons and gambling halls. The decade also saw the establishment of Venus Alley, Butte's red-light district, which until 1917 was one of the last openly tolerated (but technically illegal) prostitution districts in a western city. A block-long brick alley in the center of town, Venus Alley included numerous "cribs" and "double deckers," rooms for prostitutes to conduct their business in, with call boxes connected to the bars and noodle houses nearby. It's no coincidence that Venus Alley, like many red-light districts, operated during one of the most sexually repressed periods in Anglo-American history; the prostitutes of Venus Alley were the mirror image of Victorian women in polite society, sexually aggressive, foul-mouthed, sharp-tongued, often drinkers. Hundreds, possibly thousands, of prostitutes of all ages and races worked in Venus Alley.

Madams operating brothels tended to hire white women and expected a greater degree of refinement from them. The most famous brothel in Montana was the Dumas Hotel, which opened in 1890. The three-story building was equipped with skylights and large parlor rooms, in addition to its many basement cribs and tunnels to other buildings in town so that the richer clientele could attend without being seen entering the premises. While most of Venus Alley was closed down in 1917, the Dumas Hotel was influential enough and wealthy enough to persist in its business, largely overlooked by law enforcement until 1982, when income tax violations shut the business down. It was later turned into a museum by new owners and is listed on the National Register of Historic Places.

Montana's crime rate is considerably lower than the national average, at 272 violent crimes per 100,000 inhabitants in 2010. Aggravated assault constitutes most of those crimes (221) with rape (32) a distant second. While in most of the country crime rates climbed steadily after World War II, soaring to a peak in the 1990s before falling, Montana's experience has differed. Montana actually reached its violent crime peak in 2001 (352) and has experienced a series of ups and downs rather than the steady slope of the national crime rate. Crime rose steadily until 1978 (237) before falling to a low of 116 in 1989, climbing somewhat until 1995 (177), falling until 1998 (138), and then accelerating rapidly to the 2001 peak.

Bill Kte'pi
Independent Scholar

See Also: Frontier Crime; Lynchings; Prostitution, History of.

Further Readings
Allen, Frederick. *A Decent, Orderly Lynching: The Montana Vigilantes*. Tulsa: University of Oklahoma Press, 2009.

Baumler, Ellen. *Dark Spaces: Montana's Historic Penitentiary at Deer Lodge*. Santa Fe: University of New Mexico Press, 2008.
Murphy, Mary. "The Private Lives of Public Women: Prostitution in Butte, Montana, 1878–1917." *Frontiers: A Journal of Women Studies*, v.7/3 (1984).
Wilson, Gary. *Outlaw Tales of Montana*. Augusta, GA: TwoDot, 2003.

Moonshine

Hooch, shine, mountain dew, or white lightning—the names change but one thing has remained constant throughout American history: Moonshine is untaxed and therefore illegal liquor. The history of moonshine predates America and continues to be written. A social history of crime and punishment in America flows through the mountains and rebellions to the speakeasies and gin joints of Prohibition and beyond into moonshine's current commodification for a consumer culture.

Whiskey Rebellion
In America's infancy, distillation of alcohol was widely practiced. As medicine, disinfectant, drink, and even currency, moonshine formed an important part of early American life. Farmers could transport more corn to market in the form of liquor; therefore, the economic aspect of distillation was significant. Shortly after the Revolutionary War, in 1791, moonshine had its first run-in with the law. An excise tax was levied against whiskey in order to help pay for the national debt incurred by the war. Those who resisted the taxes on whiskey referred to themselves as "blockaders." In some mountainous areas, tax collectors were tarred, feathered, and otherwise attacked in response to the "whiskey tax." George Washington raised a militia in Pennsylvania to quell this rebellion, which became the first official test of federal power in the United States. Not long after, as a debated political platform, the Jefferson administration repealed the tax on whiskey.

For nearly a century, aside from a short stint during the War of 1812, whiskey making was legal throughout the expanding United States—

until the Civil War. In 1862, President Abraham Lincoln formed the Internal Revenue Service. Again there was resistance, this time mostly in the form of tax evasion by the continued illicit manufacturing of alcohol. The 1870s and 1890s were periods of increased moonshining activity due to economic depression. Since this practice often occurred under the cover of darkness, it is thought that this is where the term *moonshining* originated. Stories of moonshiners and revenuers have become a large part of mountain lore, and in the early 20th century, moonshining became much bigger business. Organized crime figures like Al Capone became interested in the mountain spirits with the passage of the Volstead Act in 1919.

Prohibition

Deemed "the noble experiment," alcohol prohibition in the United States provides a strong example of unintended consequences. Distillation of intoxicating beverages was outlawed as the Volstead Act provided a definition of "intoxicating liquors," putting the Eighteenth Amendment into effect. The new law did nothing to quell the demand for alcohol, however, and continuing the supply opened opportunities for organized

On April 25, 1923, Prohibition Bureau agents and police conduct a raid on Carl Hammel's lunchroom in Washington, D.C., seizing barrels of liquor stored in the basement, where he conducted his trade in a back room. The 1919 Volstead Act had some unintended consequences. Prohibiting alcohol had little effect on demand and instead opened up opportunities for organized crime, black markets, speakeasies, gin joints, underground clubs—and moonshining, which supplied these operations.

crime in the United States through such figures as Capone. Speakeasies and gin joints, illegally operated bars, and underground clubs conducted business in spite of Prohibition, and moonshiners provided the necessary ingredient for their continued operation. Those who delivered the prohibited product were known as bootleggers or rumrunners, and these drivers built extraordinarily fast cars in order to outrun the police, if necessary, on such deliveries.

From this phenomenon was born the sporting event now known as NASCAR racing. The inability to stop production, distribution, and sale of alcohol spawned not only a black market and organized crime but also significant disrespect for the law. The success of the underground clubs and more social acceptance of alcohol, particularly during the Great Depression, combined with increased violence (culminating in the St. Valentine's Day Massacre in 1929), signaled the beginning of the end for Prohibition. In 1933, the Twenty-First Amendment repealed the Eighteenth Amendment. However, to date, the distillation of spirits is still heavily regulated and economically impractical for most. Therefore, distillation for personal beverage production remains effectively illegal.

Moonshine in the New Millennium
However, as with the rest of American history, this prohibition is widely ignored. Moonshine is still very much a part of the landscape and has even begun to be seen in an entirely new light. Manufacturers of stills for producing alcohol claim they cannot meet demand, and a quick Internet search provides a wealth of information and contacts for those interested in distilling. Even "legal moonshine" has made an impact recently, as the outlaw history of this illicit spirit has been used to commodify, market, and sell the white whiskey legitimately. Despite the changing nature of laws, social norms, crime, and punishment, moonshine remains a part of American history, past and present.

Carl Root
University of South Florida
Edward Green
Eastern Kentucky University

See Also: Bootlegging; Drinking and Crime; Internal Revenue Service; Prohibition; Volstead Act.

Further Readings
Dabney, Joseph E. *Mountain Spirits: A Chronicle of Corn Whiskey From King James' Ulster Plantation to America's Appalachians and the Moonshine Life*. Fairview, NC: Bright Mountain Books, 1984.
Miller, Wilbur R. *Revenuers and Moonshiners: Enforcing Federal Liquor Law in the Mountain South, 1865–1900*. Chapel Hill: University of North Carolina Press, 1991.
Rowley, Matthew. *Moonshine!* New York: Lark Books, 2007.

Morality

Holding offenders accountable for their behavior is a moral responsibility charged to the criminal justice system. From the earliest history of the United States, religious idealism held individuals personally accountable for criminal and deviant behavior. Even as early as the late 18th century and into the mid-19th century, nonreligious idealism altered the nature of the relationship between God and man and used new methods to hold criminals responsible. By the mid-19th century, positivists viewed the world as having influence over individual behavior in an attempt to explain criminal behavior in terms other than free will.

In the late 19th century, pragmatists and psychologists introduced psychological explanations for behavior. Pragmatists altered the concept of humanity, adding the concept of treatment to the concept of punishment. In the first half of the 20th century, existentialists again changed the concept of humanity. The existentialists claimed that every individual has the ability to make meaning of his or her own life. Each person could also determine the meaning of other people, determine the meaning of the universe, and determine the meaning of God. Accordingly, one is primarily responsible to self, but this freedom also comes with responsibility to others. Formal changes in criminal justice made throughout the history of the United States can be linked to these changing concepts of morality.

Informal changes have been influenced by popular ideas, such as social contract theory and utilitarianism. Idealists came in many forms, but each believed the world of ideas to be more real than the physical world. Positivists also came in many forms, including social positivists, biological positivists, and legal positivists. Some pragmatists emphasize sociological explanations of behavior while others are more closely associated with psychology and education. A wide variety of existentialists also exists with focuses ranging from religion to nihilism. Postmodernists have not formed a united front other than to be analytical and critical. An examination of these formal theories provides myriad explanations about the meaning of morality.

The Meaning of Morality

Morality, defined as a set of normative rules, has controlled undesirable behavior for centuries. Morality, defined as a unique set of principles, has also founded societies for centuries. In both cases, the term *morality* afforded humanity a distinct aura of authority in human development. Initially, moral responsibility linked personal responsibility to religion. Religion provided the authority required for moral certainty. Some still cling to these "original" ideas, believing they are the true foundation of this nation. For some nonreligious people, moral responsibility has evolved into ambiguity. Moral uncertainty may produce a lack of clear direction for criminal justice policy. Criminal justice policy and practice may reflect moral controversy in a society. The criminal justice system has always had the responsibility of holding offenders personally responsible for their behavior. How offenders are to be held responsible is a moral issue.

Criminal justice policy makers and practitioners do not always agree upon the meaning of morality. Reasons for adhering to any particular moral rule or moral principle may not be shared by all criminal justice professionals. Yet throughout American history, the connection of morality to the rule of law emphasizes just compensation for victims and fair and equal treatment of offenders. In every case, morality is an overarching concept, with each theory of morality containing similar components: (1) a concept of humanity, (2) a concept of the universe/environment in which humanity exists, and (3) a concept of God. For centuries, the determination of morality has been linked to the perception of reality. The imperative nature of moral values logically requires no less a base than ultimate reality, that is, God or empiricism. How one recognizes ultimate reality is the process of validating one's moral position.

Because defining morality is difficult, some have sought easy answers. Others have sought elaborate explanations. Social philosophers endeavor to validate their positions in an attempt to bring about a form of moral certainty. Each of these attempts to validate morality is unique. Consequently, each philosophy bears separate tenets for a societal response to crime and deviance.

Religious Idealism

Religious idealism depends chiefly on the concept of God and God's relationship to humanity to determine the nature of morality. During the inception of the United States and in the prior colonial period, idealism was the prominent philosophical norm. Idealism, often religious idealism, influenced definitions of deviance and criminal behavior. Idealism also affected the manner in which offenders were treated and shaped the purpose of the courts. Idealism holds that there is a prescribed purpose and intent for humanity. Not all idealistic beliefs are the same. In the early days of the United States, religious ideas dominated specific concepts that affected the concept of morality. Specifically, religious idealism developed the prominent concept of humanity as a creation of a supreme being. Behaviors contrary to the perceived nature of the creatures of God were considered to be either criminal or deviant. Consequently, offenses of witchcraft, drunkenness, or poverty may have met a community's definition of criminal behavior.

The moral imperative for the religious idealists was to behave in a manner consistent with teachings of God, and with the influence of Puritans and Quakers, the teachings reflected Christianity. Humanity was not only considered to be intelligent animals but also possessors of souls that would be judged ultimately by the Creator. The essence of humanity is the soul. Because impurity in one's soul justified punishment of wrongdoing, and as God would punish for sins, men on earth could punish wrongdoers for crimes. Through religious idealism, not only was the concept of humanity shaped, but it also formed a teleological purpose of the universe. Religious idealism also developed the concept of a deity in relation to humanity. Of course, these ideas were not unique to the United States, nor were they original; however, the influence of Puritan beliefs and Quaker theology has had an impact on the necessity of a criminal justice system and its administration.

Some considered the Christian god a vengeful god and consequently they sought revenge for wrongdoing. Many also saw the Christian god as just and fair, and therefore sought to seek retribution in a just and fair manner. The purposes of the punishment were to demonstrate to the wrongdoer that God's order had been violated. The Puritans used forms of public humiliation to shame the offender for the violation of God's order. The Quakers used reform as a method of bringing the wicked closer to God.

The influence of Quakers in the establishment of prisons in the early 19th century is an example of religious idealism's sway on criminal justice. Under this influence, prisons were designed to house convicts in isolated cells. Offenders were not allowed any personal items. They were expected to work, because Quakers prized the work ethic as a process to bring the offenders closer to God's intended purpose for them. Other than materials needed for their work, the only item an inmate could possess was a Bible. A critical disciplinary rule in the prison was silence. The notion was that the inmate would be contemplative if provided the opportunity. Religious beliefs that God has a purpose for humanity validated prisons. They also supported the notion that every individual could discover this purpose if given sufficient time to contemplate.

The consequences were disastrous for the offenders. Because of the silence and lack of human contact, the sanity of offenders was

Prisoners in the southern United States break up rocks for road construction, circa 1934–50. By the mid-19th century, one of the "cures" for crime and deviance was hard labor, which taught prisoners that crime does not pay and that honest work has value. The "congregant system" of hard labor, work, and a code of silence originated in the Auburn State Prison in New York, constructed in 1816. A portion of the profit from prisoner labor helped to support the prison.

affected. The Quakers, to their credit, recognized the failure of their method and prompted reforms of the prison system. The conditions created in the prison and their unintended consequences shocked the religious idealists. Their sense of morality provided the incentive to proceed in another direction to obtain their goal of moving criminals closer to God.

Religious idealistic morality created ideals for what a human being should be. Additionally, it provided a purpose for what the universe ought to be and an idea of the nature of God. These ideas influenced moral imperatives. Religious idealism remains in American society, and it still influences what many people believe to be moral. Influenced by their religious idealism, these people also believe that this morality should influence policy and practice in criminal justice.

Nonreligious Idealism

Nonreligious idealism was also a prominent factor in early American culture. Nonreligious idealism depended on the development of an ideal society or ideal world as a basis for moral thinking. After the Great Awakening in the mid-18th century, nonreligious idealists took on an influential role in moral development. These idealists believed concepts of justice, equality, and freedom to be more real than the lives and property these ideals defended. Included in this reality were other ideas of the American work ethic and manifest destiny. Certainly, these ideas may have originated with religious figures, but the wide acceptance of these ideas was not dependent upon accepting the Protestant Reformation as sacred. Even nonreligious people accepted the values of these concepts.

As it was for the religious idealists, ultimate reality for nonreligious idealism was not located in the physical world but in the world of ideas. However, for some idealists, material gain validated their beliefs. The importance of the work ethic and a belief in manifest destiny contributed to the richness of the American ideal, and many believed that these concepts would lead to justice, equality, and freedom. In the early years of American culture, criminal behavior and deviant behavior were considered to move America away from its aspirations.

By the middle of the 19th century, one of the "cures" for crime and deviance was hard labor. Sentencing offenders to prison at hard labor was to teach them lessons: (1) crime does not pay, and (2) honest work has value. Adopting hard labor and silence as standards of the Auburn prison in New York reflects nonreligious ideals replacing the penitence model promoted through religious idealism. In fact, the term *prison* was used to describe Auburn, rather than *penitentiary*. In this time period, morality was more of an overarching idea of society rather than a set of moral dictates. These idealistic concepts of morality influenced the criminal justice system in a more passive manner. The public accepted the criminal justice response to crime as a mechanical process of arrest and incarceration, with the belief that a better society would result. The society was willing to accept the idealism of human beings living in a purposeful universe created by God, even though a specific religious influence had abated.

Other idealistic concepts include the social contract theorists of the 18th and 19th centuries. These idealists argued that humanity is in need of a social contract. The social contract is an agreement to allow government to rule over humanity. Some social contracts claimed to move society toward a natural peaceful state. Other social contracts desired to move society away from a natural warlike stage. This popular idea appealed to Americans of this era because of the dualism and the apparent commonsense applicability. If one could know the true state of nature, then one could create a society that would morally address issues of crime and deviance. The contract denotes social obligations, and one is obligated to obey for the betterment of society.

Utilitarianism applied to crime was another form of idealism. Supporters of this approach did not empirically verify the idea that severe, certain, and swift punishment would deter criminal behavior, but they encouraged the practice of measures that were compatible with the utilitarian ideal of "the greatest good for the greatest number." Both the social contract theory of the 19th century and utilitarianism remain popular ideas in American society. A criticism of idealism is that the idealist method of validation is sufficient for the individual idealist. However, those who choose not to validate ultimate reality on faith may feel as oppressed by the religious as the religious Puritans felt oppressed by England.

Idealism works in a society where everybody agrees. Faith can bring about such agreement. Those who validate reality on something other than faith will be critical of idealism.

Positivism

Positivism of the mid-19th century altered the concept of morality by challenging the idealistic conception of God, which in turn challenged the idealist conception of humanity and the world. Positivism came from Europe and approached social conditions from a scientific perspective rather than a religious or metaphysical perspective. Positivism is a philosophy that asserts that all problems can be resolved through logic alone. Positivism rejects religious idealism and other metaphysically based ideologies. Human beings are not seen as spiritual beings but as thinking creatures often influenced by their environment in ways not previously considered. For the positivists, personal responsibility for behavior was not a failure to adhere to religious doctrine but rather a failure to understand the logical purpose for orderly behavior.

Perhaps the greatest contribution of the positivists was the development of the scientific study of society. Social situations and conditions could account for individual behavior. This perspective shifted a moral interpretation of the offender's personal responsibility. Instead of the offender making a choice to be evil or unlawful, positivism takes into account the situations in which the offender lived. Hence, criminal behavior may not be just the result of a misguided soul but the result of a reasonable person living in an adverse situation.

From a moralistic point of view, the significance of positivism was its attempt to explain deviant behavior in an objective and nonjudgmental manner. Acting scientifically, positivists attempted to explain in cause-and-effect terms that criminal behavior did not rely on adherence to a nonempirical belief system or evidence based on faith. However, this scientific method produced quasi-scientific explanations for criminal behavior. In some cases such as phrenology, it was simply a misunderstanding of the scientific method, and in other cases like atavism, it was a vain attempt to associate physical characteristics with deviant and criminal behavior. The consistency was that positivists believed human behavior could be explained scientifically and be held accountable with empirical standards.

Later criticisms of positivism noted that life is complex. Reducing life to logical considerations alone fails to account for the intricacies of human existence. Religious idealists, who remained steadfast in their ideas of humanity and the universe being divinely connected, assailed positivism. However, from positivism, sociology emerged as a field of study. Sociological studies altered the diagnosis and the treatment of offenders. The influence of positivism continued in America, affecting legal theory and philosophical phenomenology. Positivism advanced in areas of biology, sociology, and law. All these areas influenced society's moral response to crime. Offender behavior could be assessed on the basis of social conditions, including economics, geography, or social status. Biological positivists posed issues of heredity, genetics, and physical characteristics. Legal positivists used logic as the primary determiner in resolving legal conflicts. The influence of positivism remains in America's moral response to crime. The problem for the positivists has been and remains that although the process of validation may be understood, there is no singular definer of a "good" person.

Pragmatism

Pragmatism in the latter portion of the 19th century was yet another philosophical development. Again, the influence of a new philosophy altered the concepts of humanity, universe, and God. Pragmatism, a philosophy developed by Americans Charles Sanders Peirce and William James, among others, altered the course of morality by considering that every individual experiences his or her environment uniquely. The universe was not a purposeful entity. Rather, the universe was something that confounded and confronted problem-solving human beings. The view of God was altered too. God may be relevant for an individual, but pragmatism's concept of God could not endure a God that provided purpose and meaning to all of humanity. Application of the scientific process was also critical to this philosophy, but the importance was not because there was a presumption that all problems could be resolved logically but rather that logic would provide the

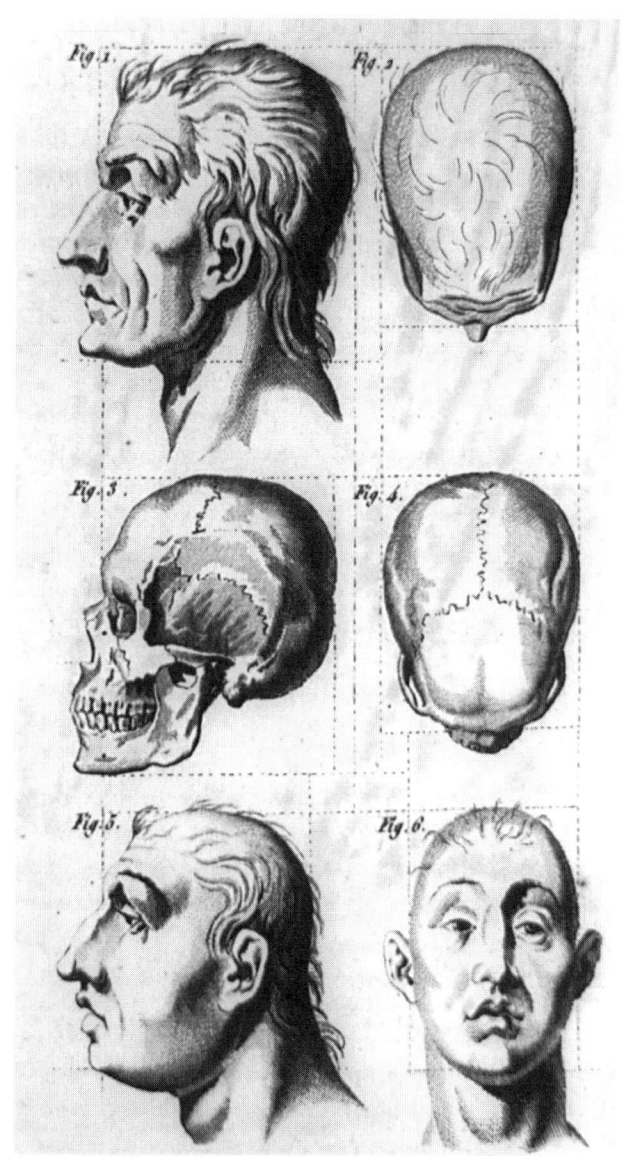

Positivism was an attempt to explain deviant behavior in an objective and nonjudgmental manner. To show that explanations for criminal behavior did not rely on a belief system, positivists adopted some dubious scientific approaches, such as phrenology.

most objective possibility in providing insight into a problem. Insight into the problem, however, could not guarantee resolution to every situation.

Pragmatists altered the concept of the individual to that of a problem solver. Unlike religious idealists seeking perfection, and unlike the positivists being benignly logical, the pragmatist lives in a confounding universe. In this confusing world, it is the responsibility of the individual to find answers. Morality for the pragmatist has the universe as the center of humanity's attention, not humanity as the center of the universe. Yet the world is a confusing place, according to the pragmatist, a place of which the individual must make sense. Compounding this perspective was the notion that individuals do not appear in the universe as mature subjects but develop into mature beings as they experience the universe in a manner unique to them.

From this pragmatic perspective, William James introduced psychology as a developing field of study. Pragmatism embraced the embryonic forms of sociology and tried to explain human behavior from a psychological and sociological point of view. To understand failure of individual moral responsibility, one must understand the psychological development of the individual and the influence of the individual's environment. To understand is not to excuse. From this pragmatic position, criminal behavior was not a condition reflecting flaws in the soul but rather flaws in thinking. If human beings are above all else problem solvers, then criminal behavior is failure to consider all possibilities or the consequences on others. Pragmatism holds to the concept of individual rights consistent with American tradition. Violating another's rights is not excusable, but it can be understood from a sociological and psychological perspective. Incarceration and hard labor provide insufficient treatment of offenders, though imprisonment remained widely used. The criticism of pragmatism for not developing the concept of humanity beyond that of a problem solver surfaced in the early 20th century.

Existentialism

Existentialism, which many scholars believe has roots similar to postmodernism, alters the concept of morality by challenging the role of humanity in the universe. In the late 19th century to the mid-20th century, existentialism rose as an alternative to previous modes of thinking. Existentialism surfaced shortly after pragmatism, again altering the basic components of morality. Existentialists believed that human beings were more than logical problem solvers, and that the universe was not merely discoverable but was open to interpretation by humanity. Existentialists placed importance on the individual. Not only is the individual a problem solver, but the individual gives meaning to his or her entire existence. The existentialists cannot deny personal responsibility for one's experience. Rather than deciding what God's plan for humanity is, an existentialist asks, "Why would an individual create a concept of God that gives God such power?" Moral responsibility is no longer an externally mandated responsibility. Moral responsibility includes adherence to principles extracted through the experience of human beings living in relation to one another. Understanding morality for the existentialist is not memorizing a set of rules but rather a complex intellectualized process in which the individual is ultimately responsible for behaving reasonably toward others. How existentialists hold one criminally responsible is unclear. They seem to borrow ideas from the pragmatists and positivists. Existentialism, though valued for its criticism of the existing social institutions, offers little in the form of concrete suggestions in asserting the need for personal responsibility in a criminal situation. Existentialism suggests alternatives to criminal justice from an intellectual perspective. However, practical applications of these ideas also suggest new criminal justice institutions. Unfortunately, there is no clear picture of how these institutions would operate.

Postmodernism

Postmodernism, like existentialism, criticizes previous philosophical and moral positions. The criticisms challenge how the individual experiences and interprets the world. Postmodernism also challenges whether one can actually experience reality or whether science can provide a certainty. The concept of reality for the postmodernist challenges other philosophical notions of reality. Rather than knowing reality through experience, postmodernists believe that reality is an interpretation of signs and images and not necessarily external to the mind of the interpreter. These and other challenges posed by the postmodernists have caused stirrings in the intellectual community about what can be claimed as a valid experience. Through rhetoric and other strategies, some postmodernists believe their claim verifies that nothing can be known. Others seem to take this opportunity to revitalize idealism. Perhaps because postmodernism criticizes moral positions better than it creates them, the impact of postmodernism on criminal justice practice and policy remains unclear. However, if taken seriously, postmodernism may push the next generation of social change in a particular direction. It may also help focus a debate on what value modernity has had for social institutions, including criminal justice.

Twentieth-Century Social Contract Theory

Though utilitarians effectively countered many of the idealistic concepts of the social contract, the social contract resurfaced in the 20th century with the work of John Rawls. Focusing on the concept of justice as fairness, Rawls introduced a method for making moral decisions based on the "veil of ignorance." Moral dilemmas can be addressed in a problematic approach even by those affected by the final decision. In effect, what a person does is to create a state of mind in which one makes a decision without considering how one will be affected. This objectivity should lead to fair decision making. This theory reinforces the notion that anyone is capable of making a meaningful moral decision, if one is able to put aside one's own interest. Rawls encourages the idea of fairness in the concept of justice. Perhaps the most important aspect of Rawls's theory is that it expands the discussion of morality to a discussion of justice.

From this theory of justice comes the question of the purpose of law in socially contractualized society. If the purpose of law is to enforce the agreement, and one does not like the consequence of the decision, why would one agree to it? If the purpose of the law is to enforce the rights of individuals, then what is the source of these rights? Why is the social contract necessary? In spite of criticisms, modern social contract theory requires that criminal justice focus on justice as fairness. Some criticism of Rawls's social contract theory stems from his idea of fairness. The social contract may provide agreement, but the question remains whether the agreement results in fairness. The importance of morality then is the role it plays in understanding justice. This may be Rawls's most important contribution.

Conclusion

Since the mid-20th century, a debate has been raging about how to connect morality and the law, with no final answer. There is no consensus as to what is moral, nor is there a final solution to how criminal justice should account for personal responsibility of offenders. From the 19th century to the 20th century, law evolved from an entity into a concept. Richard Posner suggests that law is neither, but that in a democracy, law is a human activity requiring participation from the public. If law and morality are related, perhaps morality is an activity as well. The result will be a democracy from civic discourse.

Jerry Joplin
Guilford College

See Also: 1600 to 1776 Primary Documents; 1941 to 1960 Primary Documents; 1981 to 2000 Primary Documents; Auburn State Prison; Prisoner's Rights; Punishment Within Prison; Puritans; Quakers.

Further Readings
Dworkin, Ronald. *Philosophy of Law* (*Oxford Readings in Philosophy*). New York: Oxford University Press, 1977.
Foucault, Michel. *Discipline and Punish*: *The Birth of Prison*. New York: Vintage Books, 1979.
Friedman, Lawrence. *A History of American Law*. New York: Touchstone, 2005.
Hart, H. L. A. *Law, Liberty, and Morality*. Palo Alto, CA: Stanford University Press, 1963.
Posner, Richard. *Law, Pragmatism, Democracy*. Cambridge, MA: Harvard University Press, 2005.
Souryal, Sam. *Ethics in Criminal Justice*: *In Search of Truth*, 5th ed. Burlington, MA: Anderson Publishing, 2005.
Tamanaha, B. Z. *A General Theory of Jurisprudence*. New York: Oxford University Press, 2001.

MOVE

On May 13, 1985, the Philadelphia Police Department ended a day-long siege of a row house occupied by members of the radical group MOVE by dropping a bomb on the roof of the house from a helicopter. The ensuing fire destroyed 6221 Osage Avenue and more than 60 surrounding West Philadelphia homes. During the siege and fire, six MOVE members and five of their children died; only one woman and one child escaped alive.

John Africa's Commune
Vincent Leaphart, operating under the name of John Africa, created the small group that members described as a religion, and detractors described as a back-to-nature cult, in the early 1970s. MOVE sought total transformation of its members. Members adopted the surname Africa, wore dreadlocks, refused to wash with soap, sucked on raw garlic, and limited themselves to raw food (including raw meat). The group surrounded its communal property at 309 North 33rd Street with a high fence and built a six-foot-high platform from which members frequently broadcast missives through a bullhorn. Neighbors complained that MOVE kept 50 dogs, fed rats raw meat, and disposed of garbage and human feces in the yard.

Existing conflicts metastasized when 18 MOVE members appeared brandishing weapons on their platform on May 20, 1977, to protest their treatment by the Philadelphia Police Department and Mayor Frank L. Rizzo. The city passively cordoned the home and eventually tried to "starve out" its residents (Leaphart was not among them) when negotiations over criminal warrants and health code violations failed. After more than a year of haggling, the police besieged the home on August 8, 1978. The resulting shoot-out left Officer James Ramp dead and eight uniformed services personnel injured. Eleven MOVE members eventually were convicted of murder. The events reinforced Leaphart's belief that the Philadelphia Police would stop at nothing to eliminate his organization.

Sometime in 1982, MOVE reappeared at 6221 Osage Avenue (and two other homes in West Philadelphia). Rather than assisting Osage Avenue-neighbors in dealing with the health and sanitation issues, threats and harangues broadcast over loudspeakers, or physical confrontations that MOVE induced over the next two years, the city pursued a policy of nonengagement. However, worried that MOVE might provoke a confrontation on the sixth anniversary of the August 8 raid, the police formulated a plan to force MOVE out of the house if necessary. The day passed without incident.

The city's inaction over the ensuing months allowed the situation to deteriorate. By the spring of 1985, Osage Avenue's increasingly embattled residents ratcheted up public pressure for action. MOVE used the interlude to reinforce the basement walls with tree trunks and to create a bunker on the roof that provided a secure position to observe and command the block. On May 7, Mayor W. Wilson Goode authorized the police, under the supervision of his primary deputy, Managing Director Leo Brooks, to prepare a plan to serve criminal warrants on MOVE members. Police Commissioner Gregore Sambor selected an arbitrary date—May 13—for its execution, leaving limited time for preparation.

Action began on May 12, when police evacuated the residents of the 6200 block. Early the next morning, MOVE members rejected an ultimatum to surrender. Two police teams entered neighboring houses around 6:00 A.M. under cover of water hoses, smoke projectiles, and tear gas and MOVE members responded with gunfire. For 90 minutes, police used their vastly superior firepower to engage in an intermittent gun battle with the men and women barricaded in the house. The tactical teams failed to execute the impractical and unpracticed plan to blow holes in the outer walls of 6221 Osage in order to insert tear gas. They did blow off the porch of 6221 Osage, possibly killing Vincent Leaphart in the process.

Working without a backup plan, the police persisted in trying to drive MOVE out of the house. Because the roof bunker complicated all approaches, Commissioner Sambor (in the presence of the managing director and with the mayor's approval) decided to bomb it. Rather than neutralizing the bunker and opening a hole to insert tear grass as intended, the explosion ignited gas on the roof and started a fire. Once 6221 Osage was lit, the police and fire commissioners agreed to let it strategically burn. Firefighters turned on their hoses an hour later to an out-of-control blaze. Two city blocks burned over the next six hours, leaving more than 250 people homeless.

Public Scrutiny

The bombing led to considerable public scrutiny. Reports produced by a special investigating commission convened by Mayor Goode and the county investigating grand jury highlighted the gross inadequacies of police planning, as well as hasty and ill-informed decision making during the day's action. At the heart of these failures was a leadership void at the top of the city and police hierarchies. Among the most controversial issues were the city's total failure to safeguard the children, the scale of firepower used, and the decision to use fire as a weapon. But although the city did pay significant settlements in response to lawsuits, there were few consequences for the officials who participated or directed the operation. Only the lone MOVE adult who survived, Ramona Africa, was indicted or convicted of a crime.

Peter Constantine Pihos
University of Pennsylvania

See Also: Pennsylvania; Philadelphia, Pennsylvania; Texas.

Further Readings

Anderson, J. and H. Hevenor. *Burning Down the House: MOVE and the Tragedy of Philadelphia*. New York: W. W. Norton & Co., 1987.

Philadelphia Special Investigations Commission. "The Findings, Conclusions, and Recommendations of the Philadelphia Investigating Commission." March 6, 1986.

"Report of the County Investigating Grand Jury of May 15, 1986." Court of Common Pleas of Philadelphia County, No. 86-007363 (May 15, 1986).

Mudgett, Herman

Herman Mudgett, widely considered America's first serial killer, was born in 1861 to Levi and Theodate Mudgett in Gilmanton, New Hampshire. Mudgett developed an interest in medicine at an early age and as a young boy reportedly trapped animals in order to perform surgery on them. Mudgett later married Clara Lovering at the age of 18 and had a son named Robert. Mudgett later left his family after performing an experimental surgery on his son that ended up leaving him disfigured. Mudgett attended medical school at the University of Michigan until he was expelled for stealing corpses in order to experiment on the bodies and file false insurance claims. In 1886, Mudgett took a pharmacist position in Chicago under the alias Dr. Henry H. Holmes. Although still legally married, Mudgett later married Myrta Belknap while managing a Chicago drugstore owned by the Horton family. In addition to managing the store, Mudgett also assisted Mrs. Horton in caring for her ailing husband. After the death of Dr. Horton, Mrs. Horton sold the store to Mudgett. However, Mrs. Horton eventually filed a lawsuit against Mudgett for failing to make payments on the store. Mrs. Horton vanished under mysterious circumstances shortly thereafter. Mudgett claimed she left him the store because she decided to move out west. In 1890, Mudgett hired a watchmaker and jeweler named Ned Connor. Shortly after, Connor ended up leaving his wife Julia and daughter Pearl after suspecting Mudgett and Julia of having an affair. Mudgett took out life insurance policies on both Julia and Pearl shortly before both of them went missing.

The Murder Castle

Mudgett lured many unsuspecting women from the World's Fair in Chicago to his infamous home dubbed "the Murder Castle." Mudgett hired numerous young women to work in the store and hotel section of his castle. All of the employees were required to name him as the beneficiary on their life insurance policies and, along with several customers, eventually disappeared under mysterious circumstances. Although built on the premise that it would be used for tourists coming to Chicago to visit the World's Fair, it was in reality a murder labyrinth full of elaborate trapdoors, secret passages, and sealed rooms used for torturing and killing. Chicago police discovered many of the rooms contained gas pipes and alarms that would signal when occupants tried to escape. Mudgett kept acid and other chemicals in the castle basement for dissolving the remains of his victims. He would then sell many of the skeletons to local medical schools as a way to earn additional money.

Mudgett's friend Benjamin Pitezel helped him build his castle and was his accomplice in filing fraudulent insurance claims around the country. The two devised a plan for Pitezel to fake his own death in order for Mudgett to obtain the insurance money. Pitezel would then go into hiding until Mudgett had secured the money for the both of them to split. The two later met up and traveled to various states committing fraud. Mudgett was arrested in Texas for attempting to defraud a drug company and was briefly jailed before continuing his crimes elsewhere. While serving time in Texas, Mudgett met fellow criminal Marion Hedgepeth. Mudgett convinced Hedgepeth to join him in his scheme to defraud an insurance company with his accomplice Pitezel. Mudgett later decided to murder Pitezel before the scheme came to fruition. Police detective Frank Geyer later discovered that Mudgett had also murdered Pitezel's three children: Nellie, Alice, and Howard. The autopsy of Pitezel revealed that he died of chloroform exposure prior to being found at the scene of an explosion and subsequent fire.

Herman Mudgett, also known as Henry H. Holmes, is generally considered America's first serial killer. He murdered some of his victims, primarily to collect their life insurance, within a complex labyrinth in Chicago that was dubbed "the Murder Castle."

Mudgett was sentenced to death by hanging in 1896 after being found guilty of murdering Benjamin Pitezel. Prison officials misjudged Mudgett's weight, which resulted in a botched hanging. Therefore, instead of Mudgett's neck being broken, he was left jerking and writing for 15 minutes at the gallows before strangling to death. Although Mudgett confessed to being a serial killer, the true extent of his murder trail remains unknown. It is speculated that the murder toll may have been anywhere from 30 to 300 people. Although Mudgett confessed to multiple killings, he maintained it was not really his fault because the devil made him do it.

Jacqueline Chavez
Mississippi State University

See Also: Chicago, Illinois; Murder, History of; Serial and Mass Killers.

Further Readings
Goldman, David. "Castle of Horror: The Gruesome Story of H. H. Holmes." *Biography*, v.7/5 (2003).
Jones, Phill. "The Crimes of the Mysterious Mr. Mudgett." *History Magazine*, v.12 (2010).

Mug Shots

A mug shot is a photograph taken by the police of someone arrested on suspicion of criminal behavior. Usually the picture is of the suspect's head and shoulders ("mug" being slang for "face") and often two pictures are taken, one from the front (full face) and one from the side (profile). These photographs are used to identify the suspect, to show to crime witnesses, and so on. A collection or array of mug shots is sometimes called a rogues' gallery and may include only known criminals or may also include suspects (the latter is a more controversial practice).

Modern photography was developed in the 1820s and 1830s in several countries, including France and England, but it was not until the late 19th century that photography was used systematically in police work. Alphonse Bertillon, working in the police department of Paris, France, is credited with being the first to develop a system of criminal identification that included front and side photographs similar to today's mug shots, as well as detailed anthropometric measurements, records of tattoos and scars, and notes of personality characteristics. This information was recorded on cards, which were filed and cross-indexed so they could easily be retrieved. In the United States, Alan Pinkerton and the Pinkerton National Detective Agency pioneered the use of mug shots in criminology and kept files, including photographs and newspaper clippings, on active criminals. The Irish-born policeman Thomas F. Byrnes joined the New York City Police Department in 1863 and served as head of the Detective Bureau for the years 1880–95. Among Byrnes's pioneering techniques in criminology was the compilation of a book of criminal's photographs, which he called the "Rogue's Gallery," to present to crime victims and eyewitnesses to aid in identifying perpetrators. One of the most common uses of mug shots is in the initial phase of investigating a crime. Eyewitnesses may be shown photographs of potential suspects and asked to indicate if any of them is the perpetrator of the crime in question. Mug shots may be presented singly or in groups to witnesses, and research has produced conflicting results on which method produces the most accurate identification. In physical photo spreads (the presentation of actual photographs), the one-at-a-time method of presentation has been shown to produce lower rates of false positives (e.g., falsely identifying an innocent person as the perpetrator), while with computerized mug books, the presentation of groups of photos produced more accurate results.

Mug shots are also used in "Wanted" posters to help identify a suspected criminal whom authorities want to apprehend; for instance, in the United States, such posters are often seen on bulletin boards at post offices, and in some cities they are also posted on billboards in public locations. Germany pioneered the use of television as an adjunct to wanted posters, giving out details of unsolved crimes, including photographs of suspects, with the program *Aktenzeichen XY ... ungelöst* (*File XY ... unsolved*), which began broadcasting in 1967. Similar programs have been produced in other countries, including Great Britain (*Crimewatch*), Ireland (*Crimecall*), and the United States

(*America's Most Wanted*). Mug shots of famous individuals have been printed in tabloid newspapers and are available on Websites such as The Smoking Gun, and have also been used educationally, for instance, to demonstrate the toll of drug use to audiences of students.

Eyewitness Accuracy

Although it is a common belief that "seeing is believing" and that eyewitness identification of a subject is a strong indication of guilt, in fact, eyewitnesses are far from infallible. Being a victim or eyewitness to a crime is a stressful and confusing experience that makes it difficult to form clear and detailed memories of any persons seen. The face of the suspect may also have been obscured during the alleged crime, and the criminal may have changed aspects of his or her appearance (e.g., growing or shaving facial hair) since the mug shot was taken, further complicating identification from photographs. When the practice of taking mug shots was relatively new, some criminals attempted to complicate the identification process by contorting their faces (again, so their appearance during commission of a crime would not match that of the mug shot) but this is less of a problem today. A review of wrongful convictions discovered through postconviction DNA testing found that more than 80 percent of those wrongfully convicted had been identified by one or more eyewitnesses as the perpetrator of the crime. Even in relatively simple tasks such as matching a live actor to a photograph, under relatively ideal conditions (good lighting, no delay, no interference from the emotional upset of being a crime victim or witness), people have proven to be remarkably unreliable. A series of experiments by A. M. Megreya and A. M. Burton found that accuracy of choosing the correct photograph (from a group of 10) of a live actor was roughly 70 percent, whether the identification was conducted after seeing the live actor or simultaneously. Even when test subjects were asked to match a live person to only one or two photographs, accuracy

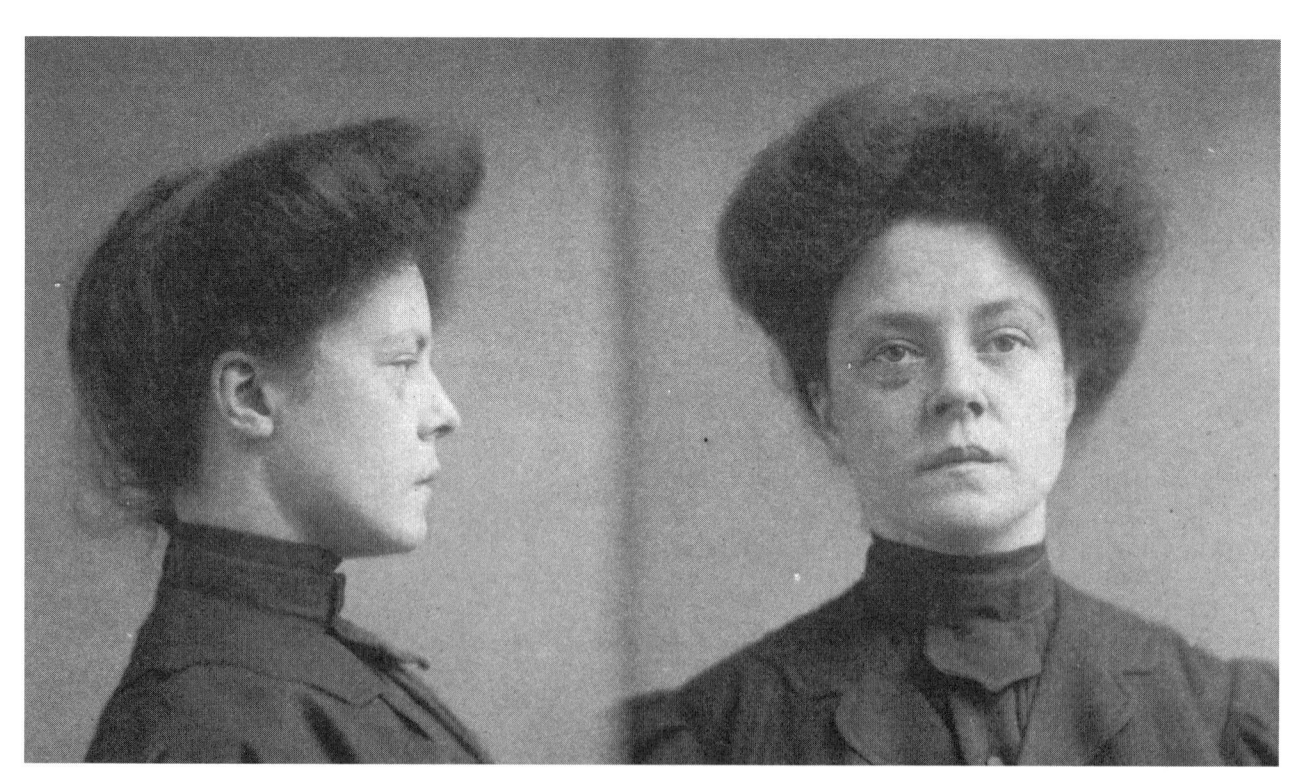

An early mug shot of a woman identified as Catherine O'Neill from the Detective Bureau of the New York City Police Department, 1906. The mug shot was part of records kept by the Pinkerton National Detective Agency, which pioneered the use of mug shots in criminology in the United States. Similar to the 19th-century method developed by Alphonse Bertillon in the Paris police department, Pinkerton's cards detailed body measurements, records of tattoos and scars, and notes of personality characteristics.

was only about 85 percent. These results suggest that difficulties in eyewitness identification may reflect difficulties in encoding unfamiliar faces, as well as in recalling those faces later.

The process of memory acquisition, storage, and retrieval is complex, and police procedures may induce a witness to falsely identify someone as the criminal being sought. It is common practice for the police to first show photographs of potential suspects (and others) to an eyewitness to a crime. If someone in the photograph is identified as the criminal, a lineup follows in which the suspect and several people similar in appearance are shown to the eyewitness, who is again asked to identify the criminal. The problem with this procedure is that seeing a person's photograph fixes his/her image in the witness's memory, and it is unlikely that anyone other than that person will be chosen from the lineup. A 1977 study by E. L. Brown and colleagues found that the rate of false identification in a lineup, if the witness had previously seen the suspect's mug shot, was 20 percent. In a second experiment, the false positive rate under these conditions rose to 29 percent, hence the term *photo-biased lineup* is sometimes applied to this method of identifying criminal suspects.

The psychological process at work is that of unconscious transference: A suspect previously seen in a mug shot will be familiar to the witness, and he or she may by mistake relate this familiarity to the crime rather than to the array of mug shots he/she was asked to review. A recent survey by S. M. Kassin and colleagues found that almost all (95 percent) of 64 psychologists known as experts in eyewitness testimony stated that they would be willing to testify in court that witnesses exposed to mug shots of a suspect are more likely to identify that suspect in a lineup. Unconscious transference may also lead an eyewitness to identify an innocent bystander as a perpetrator. Although, in general, accuracy of eyewitness identification has not been shown to be associated with factors such as gender, intelligence, or personality type, an experiment by T. J. Perfect and colleagues found that older witnesses were more likely to incorrectly identify bystanders as perpetrators when young people were involved but to not make similar mistakes when the bystanders and perpetrators were older. For young adults, no difference in accuracy was found with either older or younger perpetrators and bystanders. Other studies have found that older witnesses are particularly sensitive to the length of time they see the perpetrator's face, and that the greatest deficit in accuracy was in those age 69 and older (as compared to witnesses age 60 to 68).

Identification of suspects from mug shots is also subject to many other variables, including the interval between the crime and viewing the photographs, the amount of stress suffered by the eyewitness, the amount and quality of light at the crime scene, the length of time the suspect was seen, and whether the witness's vision was obstructed. It has been noted that people are generally less accurate in identifying individuals of a different race than their own. The use or presence of a weapon during the commission of a crime also lowers accuracy of identification as the witness's attention is likely to be drawn to the weapon (so-called weapon focus) and away from the perpetrator's face.

Another problem with asking an eyewitness to identify a suspect from photographs is what is known as the problem of relative judgment. Although eyewitnesses should be told that the perpetrator is not necessarily included within the photographs he or she will be viewing, this does not totally counteract the problem that witnesses will often select the best match to the perpetrator from the photographs presented—the person who most closely resembles the eyewitness's memory of the person he/she saw committing the crime. This also speaks to the importance of having photos of people of similar appearance to the description of the suspect (same race, general age, etc.) in the photo lineup.

Sarah Boslaugh
Kennesaw State University

See Also: Detection and Detectives; Police, Contemporary; Suspect's Rights.

Further Readings
Kassin, S. M., V. A. Tubb, H. M. Hosch and A. Memon. "On the 'General Acceptance' of Eyewitness Testimony Research." *American Psychologist*, v.56 (2001).
Loftus, Elizabeth. *Eyewitness Testimony*. Cambridge, MA: Harvard University Press, 1979.

Megreya, A. M. and A. M. Burton. "Matching Faces to Photographs: Poor Performance in Eyewitness Memory (Without the Memory)." *Journal of Experimental Psychology Applied*, v.14/4 (December 2008).

Siegel, Nina. "Ganging Up on Civil Liberties." *The Progressive* (Oct. 1997). http://findarticles.com/p/articles/mi_m1295/is_n10_v61/ai_19841065 (Accessed June 2011).

Stewart, H. A. and H. A. McAllister. "One at a Time Versus Grouped Presentation of Mug Book Pictures: Some Surprising Results." *Journal of Applied Psychology*, v.86/6 (December 2001).

U.S. National Library of Medicine. "Alphonse Bertillon (1853–1914)." http://www.nlm.nih.gov/visibleproofs/galleries/biographies/bertillon.html (Accessed June 2011).

Wilcock, Rachel, Ray Bull, and Rebecca Milne. *Witness Identification in Criminal Cases: Psychology and Practice*. Oxford: Oxford University Press, 2008.

Muhammad, John Allen

John Allen Muhammad was born John Allen Williams on December 31, 1960, in Baton Rouge, Louisiana. Perhaps one of the United States' most notorious criminals, Muhammad has been dubbed the "D.C. Sniper" for his role as the mastermind in a string of sniper-style shootings in the Washington, D.C., metropolitan area during October 2002. While Muhammad never admitted to being guilty of the crimes for which he was charged, he was convicted of two counts of capital murder in Virginia and was sentenced to death. Muhammad was executed by lethal injection on November 10, 2009, at Greensville Correctional Center in Jarratt, Virginia. While some have recognized Muhammad's execution as a loss for his family, including his four children, others consider Muhammad's actions to be the very type of crime for which capital punishment is necessary.

John Allen Muhammad was raised in Baton Rouge, Louisiana, by his aunt, who took him in at the age of 4 when his mother passed away. Muhammad fathered four children during two failed marriages and spent nine years in the U.S. Army. Muhammad had a fairly productive military career, serving in Germany and the Middle East during the Persian Gulf War, but he ended his time with the military in 1994, trying and failing twice to start his own business. After receiving divorce papers from his second wife, Mildred Green, in 1999, Muhammad fled to Antigua with the couple's three children. While in Antigua, Muhammad met Lee Boyd Malvo, who would later become his accomplice in the D.C. sniper killings. When Muhammad and his children were located in Antigua, the children were returned to the United States, and Green and the children moved to Maryland.

Muhammad reconnected with Malvo when Malvo and his mother moved to Washington State. Muhammad and Malvo formed a tight bond, and Muhammad eventually taught Malvo how to shoot a gun. Initially, the pair used tree stumps for target practice, but eventually moved on to targeting people. Before beginning their assault on the Washington, D.C., area, the pair were involved in at least one shooting in Alabama and had also been linked to shootings in several other states including Washington, Louisiana, and Arizona.

While a precise motive for Muhammad's D.C. shootings is unclear, some say that Muhammad chose the area because he planned to kill Green, his ex-wife and the mother of three of his children, citing the random sniper-style killings as a means of making Green's death appear random. Others claim that Muhammad's crimes were terroristic and based upon sympathy for Al Qaeda. Whatever the motive for his crimes, Muhammad and his accomplice committed the first of 13 shootings in the D.C. area on October 2, 2002. The shootings began as a spree, with six fatalities occurring in 30 hours. The pair shot and killed 10 and wounded three in Maryland and Virginia. Authorities had a difficult time profiling Muhammad, initially disclosing that he was likely a young, white man. Muhammad and Malvo were arrested on October 24, 2002, when a call to the sniper task force's tip line linked them to a liquor store shooting in Alabama. Fingerprints on a brochure found at the scene were found to match those of Malvo, leading to the pair's apprehension.

Virginia was chosen as the venue for Muhammad's first trial. The choice of Virginia is notable because, in 2004, the state was second only to Texas in the number of death row inmates executed since 1976. A capital conviction in Virginia would likely mean a quicker appeals process and a faster imposition of the punishment. On November 24, 2003, Muhammad was convicted of two counts of capital murder in the death of Dean H. Meyers, and a sentence of death was recommended by the jury. On March 4, 2004, Judge LeRoy Millett agreed with the jury's recommendation and sentenced Muhammad to death. Due to his young age at the time of the crimes, Malvo, Muhammad's accomplice, was sentenced to life without the possibility of parole in separate proceedings. After his sentencing, Muhammad spent the majority of his time at Sussex I State Prison in Waverly, Virginia, before being transferred to Greensville Correctional Center where he was executed by lethal injection at 9:00 P.M. on November 10, 2009, hours after Virginia Governor Tim Kaine denied his last-minute petition for clemency.

Amanda K. Cox
Pennsylvania State University, Altoona

See Also: Capital Punishment; Guns and Violent Crime; Serial and Mass Killers; Terrorism; Violent Crimes; Virginia.

Further Readings
Horwitz, S. and M. E. Ruane. *Sniper: Inside the Hunt for the Killers Who Terrorized the Nation*. New York: Random House, 2003.
Moose, C. A. and C. Fleming. *Three Weeks in October: The Manhunt for the Serial Sniper*. New York: New American Library, 2003.
Muhammad, M. *Scared Silent: A Memoir*. Largo, MD: Strebor Books, 2009.

Muller v. Oregon

Muller v. Oregon, 1908, served as a landmark decision in U.S. labor law. In its decision, the U.S. Supreme Court unanimously upheld Oregon State law restricting women's working hours to 10 per a day. The case itself stemmed from Curt Muller, a laundry owner, who appealed his local

Women work in a the shipping department of a salmon canning factory, Astoria, Oregon, circa 1904. The U.S. Supreme Court's 1908 Muller v. Oregon *decision restricting women's working hours to 10 per day was praised by traditionalists and criticized by feminists.*

court's ruling that he violated state law by having a female employee work more than 10 hours.

The Muller case came just three years after the court overturned a New York State law restricting working hours for bakers in *Lochner v. New York* (1905). One of the key factors in deciding the case was the work of Louis Brandeis, additional counsel for Oregon. He gathered data from hundreds of sources supporting the need to restrict the labor hours of women, for which most of the evidence centered upon the need of a woman's role within the home and family. The brief, later dubbed the Brandeis Brief, not only sealed the case as a victory for Oregon, but it also became a landmark in legal debate. This was the first time social science evidence had changed a court's decision.

The Muller case also stood as a watershed for labor and women's rights. Labor organizations gained more recognition with Oregon's gender-based labor code, and even though labor organizations would have to continue to fight for a standardized eight-hour work day, the framework for future debates had been established. On the other side of the aisle, women's organizations applauded the decision for its support of the woman's traditional role. Yet, the rise of First Wave Feminism criticized the law, saying that it continued to regulate women as second-rate citizens.

Annessa A. Babic
New York Institute of Technology

See Also: *Lochner v. New York*; National Organization for Women; Oregon.

Further Readings
Baer, Judith A. *The Chains of Protection: The Judicial Response to Women's Labor Legislation*. Westport, CT: Greenwood Press, 1978.
Woloch, Nancy. *Muller v. Oregon*. New York: Bedford Books of St. Martin's Press, 1996.

Munn v. Illinois

Munn v. Illinois, one of several pieces of litigation collectively known as the Granger Cases, was a decision announced by the U.S. Supreme Court in 1877. At issue was an Illinois law, enacted in 1871 under power granted by the Illinois constitution, which fixed the maximum price that could be charged by warehouses and grain elevators in Chicago and other Illinois cities with a population exceeding 100,000 residents. Enactment of this and similar legislation came at the insistence of the National Grange of the Order of Patrons of Husbandry, or the Grange, a nonpartisan agricultural interest group formed in the years immediately following the American Civil War. The organization sought to promote the interests of farm families and communities and encourage the development of agricultural industry. In less than a decade after its founding, the Grange had succeeded in lobbying for significant regulation of industries, like the railroads, that had a direct impact on the economic vitality of producers of agricultural commodities.

The case arrived at the Supreme Court on appeal from the Illinois Supreme Court, which had affirmed the decision of the Criminal Court of Cook County fining the Munn & Scott Company $100 for failing to secure a warehouse operator's license from the county and also charging rates in excess of those set by the state Grain Act. Munn and his partner argued that the law violated Article I, Sections 8 and 9 of the federal Constitution as well as the due process clause of both the Fifth and Fourteenth Amendments. The court disagreed. Chief Justice Morrison Waite penned an opinion that helped define one side of the late-19th century debate regarding the power of government to regulate the use of private property. Writing for a seven-member majority, Waite distinguished between the regulation of rights that are wholly and exclusively private, an area off limits to the state, and those private rights that, through their relation to the common and public good, may by necessity be controlled by the majority through regulation. An examination of the common law led Waite to conclude, "that when private property is affected with a public interest, it ceases to be *juris privati* [of private right] only." The doctrine established by the court extended the police power of the state to a broad array of public interests in the private sector, greatly expanding the reach of government into the vastly expanding industrial sector of the American economy.

Justice Stephen Field offered a notable dissent that came to the defense of private property and its abuse by government, extending an argument he presented earlier in the *Slaughterhouse Cases*. Field's opinion provided a recitation of the opposing side of the debate regarding private property initiated by Waite, supporting a laissez-faire model for economic regulation. This approach argued that the due process clauses of the Fifth and Fourteenth Amendment, provided a substantive right to property founded in natural law. The interpretation offered by Field defended market capitalism and the wealth earned by entrepreneurs who risked and created fortunes through their own ingenuity and effort. The power of the government to regulate business and industry, and to regulate the use of private property, not only violated economic principles, but also eroded the vested rights of property owners. To protect the due process rights and personal freedoms of the owners of capital, Field argued that the regulatory power of government must be curtailed to ensure against the redistribution of wealth.

Although Field and his allies, both on and off the court, lost in *Munn*, the idea promulgated in dissent eventually won the day. By the early decades of the 20th century, the theory of laissez faire held sway over economic thought as well as Supreme Court opinions. Field's view was articulated most clearly by the justices in the 1905 case of *Lochner v. New York*, in which the court overturned state laws that attempted to regulate the wages and hours of workers.

Charles F. Jacobs
St. Norbert College

See Also: Antitrust Law; Chicago, Illinois; *Lochner v. New York*; Supreme Court, U.S.

Further Readings
Fiss, Owen M. *The Oliver Wendell Holmes Devise History of the Supreme Court of the United States: Troubled Beginnings of the Modern State, 1888–1910: Volume III*. Toronto: Cambridge University Press, 2006.
McCloskey, Robert G. *The American Supreme Court, Second Edition*. Chicago: University of Chicago Press, 1994.
Munn v. Illinois, 94 U.S. 113 (1877).
Schwartz, Bernard. *Main Currents in American Legal Thought*. Durham, NC: Carolina Academic Press, 1993.
The Slaughterhouse Cases, 83 U.S. 36 (1873).

Murder, Contemporary

Homicide is generally considered the most serious of all crimes. In addition, it is often used by researchers as a proxy measure for other forms of violent crime because it is measured more precisely and reliably than other types of crime. The study of homicide is an ongoing criminological endeavor as its nature and magnitude change over time. The empirical examination of homicide is more useful than relying on media depictions of the crime, which may be somewhat distorted. The media tends to concentrate on specific victim types, which may not be reflective of the true nature of contemporary homicide. For example, the murder of the very young, the very old, females, and those with high socioeconomic standing receive a disproportionate amount of coverage when compared to those who are more often the victims of murder. Despite the fact that the number of homicides has decreased since the early 1990s, the public still exhibits a great deal of emotion about this crime. As de Tocqueville wrote, "the more something unpleasant diminishes, that which remains of it becomes unbearable."

Homicide Measurement
In 1961, the Federal Bureau of Investigation (FBI) began to collect nationwide homicide data, known as the Supplemental Homicide Report (SHR). Originally, it collected only victim demographics, information on the weapon used, and circumstances related to the homicide. Since then, it has increased the amount of information it includes for each homicide. It is estimated that about 90 percent of the nation's homicides are reported through this system. A recent improvement on SHR measures of homicide is the National Violent Death Reporting System (NVDRS), which collects data on all violent deaths in 17 states. The NVDRS collects data from many sources such as the state's health department, the medical examiner, the coroner's office, and the crime lab. It provides a more detailed picture of violent deaths than the SHR alone.

In the 1970s and 1980s, the United States experienced a surge in the homicide rate. In the 1970s the average rate was 9.1 (per 100,000) and 8.7 in the 1980s. The 1990s saw a decline in the U.S. homicide rate from 9.8 in 1991 to 5.7 in 1999; this mirrored the overall crime drop experienced in the United States during the 1990s. Since 2000, the homicide rate has leveled out at a range from 5.5 to 5.7 per 100,000, which is the lowest rate since the late 1960s. For the nation as a whole, rates of homicide have been relatively stable since 2000. This is also the case for whites, black females, and adult black males over the age of 25; however, this is not the case for young black males. This is also not the experience of those living in poor neighborhoods, where homicides are often increasing. The raw data may be obscuring a bifurcation of crime rates: between prosperous and poverty-stricken areas. Homicides in low-income areas are higher than rates in more prosperous communities. This also includes sharp differences in the demographic characteristics of those involved and in the relationship between the victim and offender.

Race

Homicide rates in the United States have remained relatively stable since 2000; however, the rates involving youth, as both offender and victim, have increased. This increase is especially marked in young black males. The number of homicides involving black male juveniles rose by a third. This is even more dramatic when one considers that the rate for white youths as offenders and victims has declined since 2000. The data show that blacks of all ages are disproportionately represented as both homicide victims and offenders. Blacks are about six times more likely to be victimized than whites and seven times more likely to be offenders. Racial distribution also changes by the nature of the homicide. Black victims are overrepresented in drug-related homicide at 61.6 percent of the total number of drug-related murders; however, blacks are less often the victims of sex-related homicides and workplace killings than whites. There is little difference in the rate of gang-related, felony, or gun homicides between whites and blacks as either victims or perpetrators. Most murders are, and have been, intraracial; however, this has been slowly becoming less so over the course of the last 10 years. If the perpetrator was a friend or acquaintance of the victim, then only one-twelfth were interracial. If the perpetrator was a stranger, 25 percent of the incidents were interracial.

The reasons for this racial disparity are not fully understood; however, some studies have posited various possible reasons. One factor that has been posited is differential exposure to lead, as such exposure has been linked with an increase in violent behavior. This hypothesis has been tested repeatedly and correlations have been found across time, place, neurological testing, and a series of studies controlling for several confounding variables. The group with the largest increase in homicide perpetration (black males) also had the highest lead exposure during adolescence. Linked to this hypothesis is the possible covariance of lead exposure and criminogenic neighborhoods.

Another hypothesis for this disparity is the effect of incarceration. There is some evidence to suggest that tougher sentencing laws (such as three strikes laws) did have an effect on reducing homicide initially; however, those prisoners being released seem to be committing further homicides upon their release. Upon further examination, the prisoners who do reoffend are those most likely to have returned to areas of socioeconomic disadvantage. This observation leads to policy implications such as supplying released individuals with education, drug programs, and vocational training. Despite the increases in homicide rates among young black males, the rate is still much lower than the rate during the 1980s and early 1990s during the crack epidemic that occurred in many urban areas. Some have made the point that were it not for the crime drop in the 1990s, these increases would not seem as stark or concerning.

New Orleans citizens organized a march against violent crime in January 2006 in response to multiple recent murders. The poster shows two locally well-known murder victims: musician and educator Dinneral Shavers and filmmaker and activist Helen Hill.

Age

Age is also an important differentiating factor in the study of homicide. About one third of all victims and half the offenders are aged less than 25. The victimization of children aged less than 14 years has declined to its lowest recorded level and has remained stable throughout the 2000s; however, the victimization rate of those aged 18–24 has not experienced a similar decline but has remained stable, as has the victimization of those in the over 35 age group. In 2000, the victimization rate of those aged 25–34 was at its lowest recorded level; however, since then, this rate has increased. The victimization of children aged less than 5 years (infanticide) has declined since 2000; however, the rate of infanticide has remained relatively stable across all races over the same period, except those for blacks, which reached its lowest recorded level in 2004. The most likely perpetrator of infanticide is a parent of the victim. Most parent perpetrators are male, as are their victims; and the younger the infant, the greater the risk of victimization. With regard to those more than 65 years of age, the rates of both offending and victimization have declined since 2000. Despite their overall lower level of homicide victimization, however, this group was more likely to be killed in a felony-homicide, as compared to a non-felony homicide, than those aged less than 65 years. Whites are more than twice as likely to be the victims of eldercide as blacks.

Gender

Males are disproportionately represented in both offenders and victims, accounting for about 80 percent of the victims and 90 percent of the offenders. Males killing males make up 65.3 percent of the total number of homicides, males killing females 22.7 percent, females killing males 9.6 percent, and females killing females 2.4 percent. Although the rate of victimization for both sexes has fallen since 2000, males are still four times more likely to be murdered than females. In 2005, the victimization rate for females fell to its lowest recorded level. The recorded level of male victimization reached its nadir in 2000, but has increased slightly over the 2000s. The gender distribution of homicide victimization also is dependent upon the nature of the homicide. For example, women are more than four times as likely to be the victim of a sex-related homicide and nearly twice as likely to be murdered by an intimate as males. Men are about eight times more likely to be the victim of a felony-murder and more than nine times more likely to be the perpetrator of a felony-murder than females. The gender disparity is perhaps most evident in the area of gang-related homicides. Men are about 18 times more likely to be the victim of this type of homicide and nearly 60 times more likely to be the perpetrator. Men are also nearly two times more likely to be murdered by a stranger than are women. The victimization rate of both black and white females has decreased in the 2000s, as has the offending rate for black females. White females of all ages had the lowest rates of offending.

Victim–Offender Relationship

The victim and the offender are strangers in 14–20 percent of homicides. This is approximately the same percentage as spouses and other family members. In about one-third of the cases, the victim was a friend or acquaintance of the perpetrator, and in another third of the cases the victim/offender relationship was not known. A recent study has raised an interesting point concerning acquaintance homicides. It found that, in most of these cases, the people involved knew each other through prior illegal transactions. As such, the term *acquaintance homicide* may include situations such as rival gang killings or disputes between drug dealers. Another difference in the nature of the homicide and the victim/offender relationship is that guns are more likely to be used by strangers and friends/acquaintances than they are in homicides occurring between intimates.

On the whole, intimate homicide has been on the decrease across all races, and the level for women victims reached its lowest level in 2004. The number of white females killed by intimates reached its lowest level in 2002. However, across all age groups, female victims are still more likely than male victims to be killed by an intimate. About one-third of all female victims were killed by an intimate, which is a rate 10 times higher than that for men. In the late 2000s, the percentage of intimate homicides where the weapon used was a gun has decreased, while homicides not involving a gun increased in intimate homicides with a male offender and female victim. Spousal/ex-spousal homicides have been decreasing over the last few years; however, they still remain the most common form of homicide within a family. Fathers are more likely than mothers to be killed by their children, with teenage sons being the most frequent offender in such homicides. Males who kill their sisters are usually younger than those who kill their brothers; sisters very rarely kill siblings of either sex.

Since 2000, the circumstances surrounding homicide have undergone a change. The largest category within this subset is "unknown." Of the known circumstances, arguments are the most prevalent, although this has been a declining factor in recent years. The rate of felony-homicide has continued its decrease from the 1990s, but gang-related homicides have increased since 2000 after undergoing a decrease at the end of the 1990s. After a brief spike at the start of the 2000s, the rate of murdered law enforcement officers is declining. Of the identified assailants in these cases, over 50 percent had a prior criminal record and about 40 percent had a prior record for a violent crime. The most common weapon used in the killing of a law enforcement officer is a firearm; of these homicides, 75 percent used a handgun as the murder weapon.

Gun-Related Homicide

After a dramatic decrease in firearm homicide in the 1990s, the percentage of homicides that involve a gun has increased since 2000 across all demographic groups. Homicide rates in large cities have fallen since 2000, reaching their lowest levels since the 1960s. Homicide rates in cities with populations of 250,000 to 499,999 and cities with a population between 500,000 to 999,999 have remained stable.

True to most other time periods, most homicides are carried out with firearms, 75 percent with handguns. The number of firearm homicides carried out by those aged 14–24 has increased, and youths in this age group are also the most likely to be the victim of a firearm homicide. Although the problem of homicide has decreased since the early 1990s, and has held steady since the year 2000, homicide is still a problem in the United States. Because the problem largely affects a certain section of the population, a more targeted social response may help reduce the homicide rate.

Gavin Lee
University of Arkansas at Little Rock

See Also: 1941 to 1960 Primary Documents; 1961 to 1980 Primary Documents; 1981 to 2000 Primary Documents; 2001 to 2012 Primary Documents; Gangs, Contemporary; Guns and Violent Crime; Murder, History of; Murder, Sociology of.

Further Readings

Alvarez, Alex and Ronet Bachman. *Murder American Style*. Florence, KY: Cengage Learning, 2002.

Centers for Disease Control and Prevention. "Fast Stats." http://www.cdc.gov/nchs/fastats/homicide.htm (Accessed March 2011).

Federal Bureau of Investigation. "Uniform Crime Reports." http://www.fbi.gov/about-us/cjis/ucr/ucr (Accessed March 2011).

Zimring, F. *The Great American Crime Decline*. New York: Oxford University Press, 2008.

Murder, History of

For more than two centuries, observers ranging from visitors to scholars have debated the notion of "American exceptionalism," the idea that the United States, with its traditions of democracy, liberty, social mobility, and tolerance, stands apart from other countries. While commentators disagree about the virtues of American society, the nation's levels of murder are, and long have been, truly exceptional, at least by comparison with other democratic, industrialized nations. At the start of the 21st century, the U.S. murder rate was approximately four times that of Canada, six times that of Italy, eight times that of Germany, and 11 times Japan's rate. Nor is this gap a recent creation. For more than 150 years, Americans have slaughtered one another at rates far above those of western European nations, and over the past two centuries, New York City's homicide rate was roughly 15 times London's rate. Thus, murder in America has a long and distinctive history, one bound up in broader social changes tied to race, ethnic, and gender relations and linked to shifting population currents and political and economic transformations. While scholars dispute the nation's record for equal opportunity, civil liberties, and democracy, there is no denying America's remarkable, hard-fought record for lethal violence.

Murder, or, to be more precise, homicide (the umbrella legal category that includes both intentional, premeditated "murder" and unlawful but nonpremeditated "manslaughter"), is a uniquely measurable crime. While some illegal acts such as gambling may be victimless and hence underreported, and many violent acts such as rape require victims to report the crime or law enforcers to record and investigate the offense, homicides are visible, obvious crimes that are difficult to overlook, typically featuring a corpse covered with blood and disfigured by knife or bullet wounds. Moreover, the legal definition of "homicide" has changed only modestly over the centuries and has varied little from place to place, and although many societies are purposefully oblivious to prostitution, gambling, and even—nonlethal—spousal abuse, murder is seldom ignored. Therefore, using surviving legal records and other sources, scholars can, with considerable accuracy, measure the homicide rate, defined as the number of such crimes per 100,000 people, enabling historians to compare levels of homicide over time and across space. Because homicide is the least socially constructed violent crime, historians and criminologists also frequently use the homicide rate as a proxy for levels of overall violence in society.

While it is uncertain whether tracking patterns of lethal violence also measures trends in assault or child abuse, scholars of homicide rely on these statistics to chart the history of aggressive, coercive, and pathological behavior. Furthermore, based on this technique of calculating and comparing rates, historians have argued that violent conduct has varied dramatically from place to place, era to era, and group to group. Some of these patterns reinforce our understanding of the American past, such as the long-standing trend of slaveholding and former slaveholding states having high rates of murder, while other patterns run counter to the received wisdom, such as the finding that for most of American history, large cities experienced lower homicide rates than the nation as a whole.

But studies of the history of murder extend beyond statistical comparisons. Recent scholarship has also demonstrated that the character or form of lethal violence has varied as much as the level of homicide. Weapon use has changed markedly, just as the relationships between killers and victims have shifted over the centuries. Killers, for example, mainly targeted friends and acquaintances in particular times but more often preyed on strangers or butchered spouses in other eras. By exploring the history of murder, historians can also analyze changes in culture and family life as well as class, ethnic, and race relations.

Colonial America

During the early stages of European settlement, colonial America suffered from skyrocketing levels of homicide, far in excess of the rate in 17th-century western Europe. A wide range of factors contributed to this meteoric level of bloodshed. Young men predominated in the populations of new settlements, as impoverished, unmarried indentured servants poured into Maryland, Virginia, and other colonies. A surfeit of bachelors has nearly always fueled high rates of interpersonal conflict, for aggressive young men engage in raucous activities, jostle for status, and compete for power and resources, leaving a trail of carnage in their wake. High rates of mortality from disease also likely contributed to the thrall of bloodletting, cheapening life and inuring the newcomers to death. Conflict with Native Americans added to the toll. Furthermore, at least during the early decades of settlement, legal institutions in many colonies remained underdeveloped and barely capable of mediating disputes, encouraging footloose and often besotted young men to resolve disagreements themselves. These factors, however, differed from colony to colony, and hence levels of murder varied. Homicide rates in 17th-century southern colonies—where sex ratios were especially uneven; where young, single indentured servants predominated; where relations with Native Americans were particularly acrimonious; and where malaria made life fleeting—towered over levels in northern colonies. During the middle decades of the century, for example, Virginia's homicide rate was approximately quadruple that of New England.

Homicide levels fell gradually and unevenly over the remainder of the colonial era, reflecting the balancing of sex ratios, the development of more stable legal and political institutions, and a host of other social changes. Still, lethal violence occasionally flared at the local level. When migration, racial conflict, political turmoil, or war disrupted social life, murder rates often ballooned.

Regional variations became more pronounced over time even while lethal violence dropped, with rates of homicide in New England tumbling to levels roughly comparable to those in England but slaveholding colonies experiencing significantly higher homicide rates. By the mid-18th century, Virginia's murder rate was nearly eight times that of New England. Slavery contributed to this widening gulf. Although interracial killings accounted for a portion of the regional difference, white-on-white violence generated the lion's share of the southern death toll. Slavery exerted a deeper influence on social life and dispute resolution, conditioning white southerners to rely on coercion, stunting the development of legal institutions in order to bolster the authority of white men, and eventually forging a culture of honor in which public displays of aggression became both normative and valorized.

It is neither surprising nor coincidental that slaveholding areas would suffer from elevated levels of murder or that eye gouging, nose biting, and dueling became accepted rituals for resolving disputes and establishing authority in the south. Nor it is surprising that higher rates of lethal violence in the south outlived slavery and, in fact, persist at the start of the 21st century.

The Nineteenth Century

This regional gap expanded during the early 19th century. Southern homicide rates rose, doubling between the mid-18th century and the 1820s. By contrast, northern homicide rates remained low. Even as the populations of New York City and Philadelphia ballooned and impoverished newcomers crowded into densely packed neighborhoods, the northern urban homicide rate was modest.

During the 1820s, New York City's population rose by 64 percent, and during the 1830s, it jumped by another 54 percent; ethnic and religious tensions flared, and the early stages of industrialization sparked economic dislocation, class conflict, and a series of acrimonious strikes and riots. Yet this was one of the least murderous eras in New York City's history.

The northern pattern, however, changed abruptly during the middle decades of the 19th century. Homicide rates spiked, more than doubling in many places, and the northern United States became significantly more homicidal than western Europe, producing the sizable gap in violence that persists to this day. Antebellum urban conditions fueled much of the increase as the arrival of millions of Irish and German immigrants and displaced native-born farmers, many of them poor, young, single men, contributed to searing class, ethnic, and religious tensions. Bloody riots exploded throughout the region and culminated in the 1863 New York City draft riots, in which thousands of working-class, foreign-born men violently resisted efforts to conscript them into the Union army, attacked law enforcers, vented their rage against African American residents, and killed more than 100 people in the process. But more prosaic disputes generated the majority of the murders during this era. As poor, young, working-class men crowded into cities and became concentrated in particular neighborhoods, they forged a plebeian culture that rejected the polite sensibilities, emotional restraint, and moral reforms of the middle class. Instead, working-class men created an autonomous culture, one that celebrated toughness, venerated ferocity, and glorified brutality. The bachelors who gathered in rough saloons reveled in drunkenness, gleefully watched and participated in bare-knuckle boxing matches, and affirmed their camaraderie with recreational violence, battering and bludgeoning one another to establish both their individual status among peers and a collective oppositional identity.

While the wave of violence was most pronounced and most visible in the working-class neighborhoods of cities, the surge in murder extended beyond the tough sections of major cities, such as the Five Points neighborhood of New York City. In fact, the explosion in lethal violence crossed the nation. Rates of homicide, for example, swelled in the northern countryside and in western boom towns.

Some scholars have linked the mid-century increase in violence to the American state-building process. According to this view, at both the local and the national levels, American government expanded during this era with the formation of the municipal police, the invention of the prison, and the powerful centralizing pressures unleashed by the Civil War. Because core state formation in the United States occurred at a violent time, such disorder became institutionally ingrained as the norm, in stark contrast to the state-building process in western Europe, where low levels of violence were the norm at the peak of state formation and hence aggressive behavior became more systematically regulated and criminalized. Furthermore, American federalism divided legal responsibilities for maintaining order among the local, state, and federal governments, limiting the development of more powerful and centralized legal practices, standards, and institutions. Similarly, the collapse of the second-party system, driven by the sectional crisis and ethnic divisions, no doubt weakened both formal and informal mechanisms of social control. Regardless of the precise explanation, during the mid-19th century, American violence began to assume its modern form, with rates of murder consistently higher than those of western European nations.

At the same time that the U.S. trend deviated from the European trajectory, regional differences expanded. During the final third of the 19th century, the south became even more murderous, particularly at the close of the century, when racial violence, including lynching, reached its highwater mark. More than ever before, southern whites relied on lethal violence, much of it ritualized, sadistic, and public, to bolster a racial hierarchy seemingly imperiled by the abolition of slavery, by increasing African American autonomy, and by the growing impoverishment of the region. Southern mobs, sometimes with thousands of participants and spectators, lynched approximately 800 African Americans during the 1890s. During the late 19th century, South Carolina and Louisiana had homicide rates more than 20 times that of heavily urban, industrialized Massachusetts.

The American west presented a more complicated pattern, though this region also experienced high levels of homicide. In mining camps and cattle towns, men often outnumbered women by enormous margins, political and legal institutions remained ineffective, and homicide rates sometimes mushroomed to 40 or 50 times those of northeastern urban centers. Even western cities experienced high levels of lethal violence; late-19th-century Omaha, for example, was twice as homicidal as Philadelphia or Boston. Settled agricultural areas, however, tended to be considerably less violent than frontier regions or mining camps, and the level of murders in boom towns quickly peaked and then dropped precipitously.

As murder rates rose in the south and spiked in the west during the late 19th century, lethal violence in the northeast and the midwest fell sharply. Class, ethnic, religious, and racial tensions worsened during this era, and urban population densities reached unprecedented levels. Moreover, for the first time in American history, inexpensive revolvers became widely available; the proportion of homicides committed with firearms doubled during the second half of the century. Thus, fights that had earlier produced bruised cheekbones, fractured jaws, and cracked ribs now ended with fatal bullet wounds. In short, the technology of killing improved dramatically. And yet northern society became less violent. During the final quarter of the century, Philadelphia's murder rate dropped by half, and Boston, New York City, and other major urban centers experienced similar decreases.

In the 19th century, rates of homicide swelled in areas like the northern countryside. This Henry Robinson & Company print depicts the sensational murder of Sarah Maria Cornell, a pregnant factory worker, by Ephraim K. Avery in May 1833.

Contrary to the conventional wisdom about cities, urban industrial life helped to reduce lethal violence during the late 19th century. The regimen of the assembly line and the school appears to have inculcated discipline and self-control in factory workers and children, who, in turn, became less impulsive, less inclined to engage in recreational fighting, and hence less likely to kill or be killed. In Chicago, the proportion of homicides resulting from drunken brawls fell by one-third during the closing decades of the century. Paralleling the drop in homicide—and reflecting a similar increase in self-discipline—was a sharp decline in accidental death, as city dwellers drank less, fell into machinery less, drowned less, and stumbled off roofs and into busy traffic at plummeting levels. Simply put, industrialization made urban life more orderly and less deadly, even though social tensions flared, guns became readily available, and dangers abounded in mechanized workplaces and crowded streets.

But not all forms of lethal violence decreased during this era. Public murders such as saloon fights fell most sharply. Domestic homicide, however, increased at the end of the nineteenth century, though not enough to offset the drop in public violence. In Chicago, the spousal homicide rate tripled during the final quarter of the 19th century. Cultural changes fueled this spiral, for new gender ideals encouraged men to derive status and fulfillment from family life, and those who struggled to do so sometimes reacted to these pressures by lashing out, slaughtering their wives and children—and frequently committing suicide as well. Therefore, changing cultural values transformed patterns of lethal conduct, producing an overall drop in murder, sparking shifts in the character of homicidal behavior, and making streets less violent but homes more violent.

The Twentieth Century

Over the course of the twentieth century, levels of homicide fluctuated wildly, and forms of murder varied, though the core pattern of American lethal violence was already well established. First, American homicide rates towered over those of western Europe. Early 20th-century New York, Boston, Cleveland, and Providence, for example, were each roughly 10 times more homicidal than London. Second, within the United States, regional differences persisted in the new century.

Although southern lynching peaked during the 1890s, racial violence continued. Furthermore, the south remained violent overall, even if the gap began to narrow. During the early 1910s, for example, New Orleans, Charleston, and Savannah had homicide rates three times that of Chicago and five times that of New York City, and during the late 1910s, Mississippi was more than four times more murderous than New Jersey, more than six times more homicidal than Minnesota, and seven times more murderous than Massachusetts. Third, domestic homicide continued to increase, while drunken-brawl homicide, the leading source of mid-century northern deaths, decreased. Nonetheless, both rates and patterns of murder remained fluid.

During the first three decades of the 20th century, northern violence rose once again. Nationally, the homicide rate increased by nearly one-third. Locally, the surge was often still greater. In Chicago, for example, the homicide rate ballooned, jumping almost 250 percent between 1900 and 1930. A series of celebrated murders—including the Sacco and Vanzetti robbery-murder in 1920, Nathan Leopold and Richard Loeb's thrill killing of 14-year-old Bobby Franks in 1924, and the St. Valentine's Day Massacre in 1929—made the era seemed even more murderous.

No single factor accounted for this surge. Rather, a confluence of demographic, social, and institutional forces reversed the late-19th-century pattern and sparked a jump in murder. Nearly 19 million immigrants arrived in the United States between 1900 and 1930, with more than half coming between 1905 and 1914, when World War I began in Europe and choked off the flow of travelers. The majority of the newcomers hailed from southern and eastern Europe. As a result, the United States abruptly became more ethnically and religiously diverse. Some of the immigrants hailed from parts of Europe experiencing unusually high levels of violence such as Italy and Greece, and many more confronted fierce discrimination from their new neighbors, potential employers, and local policemen and judges. Struggling against poverty and alienated from legal institutions, immigrants, at least for a short period, often experienced higher rates of violence, though such elevated levels of homicide typically lasted only a few years. During the 1910s, for example, Italian

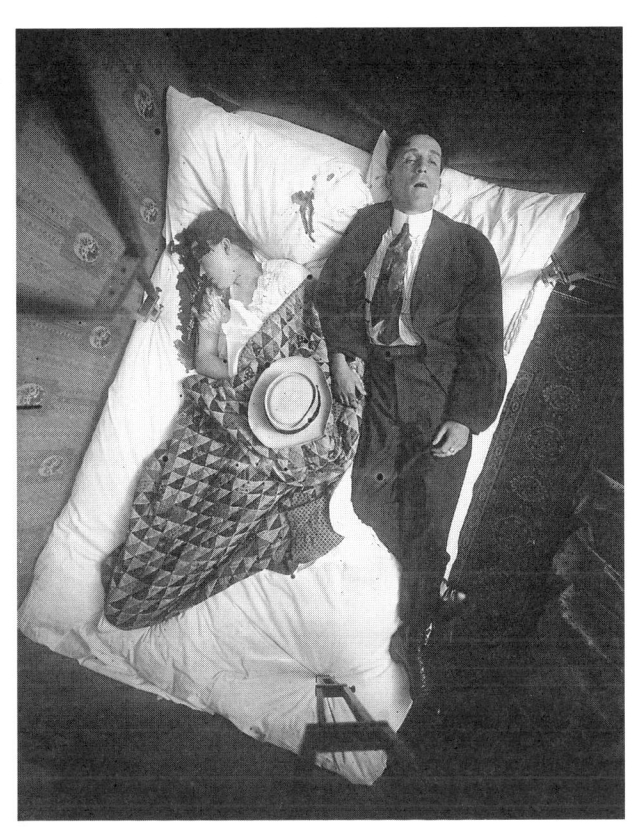

An unidentified New York City crime scene, early 1900s, from the New York City Municipal Archives. In the 20th century, American homicide rates were well above those of Europe; New York was 10 times more homicidal than London.

immigrants in Chicago suffered from a homicide rate seven times the overall level for the city.

The enormous flow of African Americans from the Deep South to the industrial cities of the north—the Great Migration—also contributed to the rising tide of lethal violence, particularly in the urban north. Approximately 1.5 million African Americans left the violent south and resettled in areas where they faced intense discrimination, were packed into emerging ghettos, received scant protection from law enforcers, and endured still higher levels of homicide. During the early 1920s, African American Cincinnatians were murdered at 13 times the overall rate for the city and 27 times the white rate. Furthermore, they died from lethal violence at nearly double the rate of African American residents in Atlanta, Dallas, and Birmingham. In the urban industrial north, poverty, racial discrimination, and isolation combined to fuel soaring homicide rates, adding to the death toll from lethal violence during the early 20th century.

Overlapping cultural and economic pressures contributed to the spike in violence as well. The commercialization of leisure, the rationalization of the marketplace, and the general prosperity of the era concentrated wealth, expanded access to consumer and luxury goods, and generated new opportunities for those willing to commit robbery, many of whom used lethal violence in the process. Newly available automobiles, by providing speedy, effective getaway vehicles, also helped to launch an explosion in payroll and bank robberies. In 1918, Chicago, by itself, had 14 times as many robberies as England and Wales, and the city's robbery-homicide rate quadrupled between 1900 and 1920. This trend continued into the 1930s and made murderous bank robbers, including John Dillinger, Charles "Pretty Boy" Floyd, and Bonnie Parker and Clyde Barrow national celebrities.

Prohibition also buoyed the early-20th-century murder rate. By creating unimaginable opportunities for those willing to manufacture, smuggle, and distribute illegal alcohol, Prohibition sparked a rapid expansion of criminal networks, most notably organized crime, and triggered unstable market conditions and turf wars among gangsters such as Al Capone. In northern cities, Prohibition-related violence accounted for 10 percent to 20 percent of local homicides during the 1920s and thus contributed to the increase in violence.

By the 1930s, however, the American murder rates began to tumble once again. Even as the Great Depression produced widespread impoverishment, homicide dropped by roughly 30 percent during this decade, providing still more evidence that poverty, by itself, does not generate violence. Chicago's homicide rate plunged by 51 percent; New Orleans's rate contracted by 39 percent; and Miami's rate fell by 38 percent during the 1930s. Moreover, regional patterns started to converge during this period, and the murder rate dropped throughout the nation, including the south.

The low levels of violence continued until the early 1960s. Nationally, the homicide rate decreased by 16 percent during the 1940s and by an additional 11 percent during the 1950s. During the mid-1950s, when homicide hit its lowest levels, the murder rate was roughly half the

1920s level. Neither World War II and the cold war nor the postwar demographic changes such as the second phase of the Great Migration or the early flow of migrants to the Sunbelt disrupted the larger trend. The overall decrease in American murder during the mid-20th century paralleled changes in western Europe, where homicide rates also plunged during the Great Depression and remained low for the next two decades.

Despite the broader convergence of regional and even international trends, some long-established patterns in American murder persisted. The south, for example, continued to experience higher rates of homicide than the northeast or the midwest. Furthermore, African Americans still suffered from elevated levels of murder. In 1940 and 1950, the African American homicide rate was 11 times the white rate, and the gap narrowed slightly—to a ninefold differential—in 1960. Nonetheless, the larger trend was toward national and international convergence, as improved transportation and communications gradually winnowed away at local and regional distinctiveness, even in murderous behavior.

This mid-century ebb, however, proved to be short-lived, both in the United States and in Europe. Violence soared during the late 1960s, and the epidemic of crime ravaged American society until the early 1990s. Between 1963 and 1973, for instance, the national homicide rate nearly doubled. Major urban centers were hit particularly hard, becoming, for the first time in American history, significantly more violent than the nation as whole, though no part of the United States was spared from this wave of murder. From the early 19th century until 1958, New York had a lower homicide rate than the United States. By 1980, the city's murder rate was 2.5 times the national rate,

A New York Police Deparment officer confronts an angry group at Seventh Avenue and 126th Street during the Harlem Riot of 1964. The riots of 1964 were the first in a series of violent race-related riots across American cities between 1964 and 1965, incited by the shooting of a 15-year-old African American by a white off-duty police officer on July 18, 1964.

and in 1991, New York City, by itself, accounted for 9 percent of all U.S. homicides—the seven largest cities produced 25 percent of the nation's murders in 1991. More visible and more shocking crimes underscored this trend of skyrocketing urban violence, including race riots and political assassinations (John F. Kennedy in Dallas in 1963, and Martin Luther King, Jr., in Memphis and Robert Kennedy in Los Angeles in 1968). The rise of violence during this period was even greater than homicide figures indicate, for dramatic improvement in trauma care enabled many badly injured crime victims to survive injuries that would have been fatal just decades earlier, complicating comparisons of late-20th-century murder rates with those of earlier eras and masking the level of serious violence in society.

Numerous factors fueled this explosion of violence. The baby boom played a particularly important role. By the early 1960s, the first wave of baby boomers, those born during the late 1940s, had reached their teenage years and thus entered the peak period of the life cycle for engaging in violent behavior. Even a small increase in the number of teenagers in a society typically triggers a rise in crime, but the coming of age of the baby boomers produced an enormous bulge in the proportion of young adults and thus a surge in violence. Scholars have estimated that this demographic imbalance accounted for more than half of the homicide increase between the early 1960s and the mid-1980s. The disorder of the 1960s and the 1970s probably added to the combustible mixture, eroding faith in the legal system and encouraging people to resolve disputes through aggressive self-help.

Likewise, the disintegration of the industrial economy and increasing African American poverty and racial segregation isolated and alienated many Americans, as jobs disappeared, inner-city schools crumbled, and the urban infrastructure collapsed. If the regimen of the workplace and the respectability and long-term opportunities promised by education inculcated restraint, then the deepening poverty and institutional problems of this period contributed to the crime wave. Finally, the introduction of crack cocaine increased violence during the late 1980s.

By the mid-1990s, the U.S. homicide rate began to fall, tumbling by 42 percent in the last five years of the century and dropping to a 30-year low. A cluster of overlapping shifts produced this decrease: handgun violence, homicide by youths, and inner-city murder dropped dramatically during this period, as did both domestic and African American homicide. The number of murders committed with handguns, for example, went down by 37 percent between 1993 and 1998, and the rate of lethal violence committed by African American men between ages 14 and 17 plunged by 67 percent. New York City's plummeting count accounted for more than 25 percent of the nation's mid-1990s decrease in homicide and 10 percent of the late 1990s drop. Levels of lethal violence have remained largely steady through the opening decade of the new century.

Criminologists and sociologists offer a variety of explanations for the recent ebbing of American murder rates. As family size has decreased, the number of young adults has fallen, accounting for approximately 10 percent of the 1990s drop. More effective policing strategies, enhanced protection and services for battered women and children, stronger gun-control laws, changes in drug markets, and increased economic opportunities for inner-city residents have all contributed to the recent trend, though policy makers and politicians fiercely debate the sources of the drop. Despite this decrease, the United States remains extremely violent by international standards, with an early-21st-century homicide rate hovering in the same range as Angola, Haiti, and Argentina.

Conclusion

Macro-level and mono-causal theories for the history of American murder offer, at best, partial explanations for the nation's long, enduring history of violence, failing to account completely for variations over time, across space, and between groups. Southern honor, for example, helps to account for regional differences but does not explain elevated levels of violence in, for example, Michigan or California. Likewise, the proliferation of handguns in the United States has contributed to the death toll from violence, but the nation was more murderous than western Europe before firearms became readily available. Demographic factors such as the surfeit of young men or the arrival of immigrants help to explain frontier violence, yet do not account for the south's consistently high levels of violence. Theories that emphasize the impact of the state-formation process or that focus on the role of trust in political institutions are suggestive, though they stop short of explaining the variability that has defined patterns of American violence. Nor is it surprising, given the size and diversity of the nation, that a complex, rapidly changing blend of social, cultural, demographic, and institutional factors has contributed to the waxing and waning of lethal violence. The one constant, however, is America's long, "exceptional" record for horrific levels of murder.

Jeffrey S. Adler
University of Florida

See Also: 1851 to 1900 Primary Documents; 1901 to 1920 Primary Documents; 1941 to 1960 Primary Documents; 1961 to 1980 Primary Documents; Crime in America, Types; Guns and Violent Crime; Violent Crimes.

Further Readings
Adler, Jeffrey S. *First in Violence, Deepest in Dirt: Homicide in Chicago, 1875-1920*. Cambridge, MA: Harvard University Press, 2006.
Beeghley, L. *Homicide: A Sociological Explanation*. Lanham, MD: Rowman & Littlefield, 2003.
Courtwright, David T. *Violent Land: Single Men and Social Disorder From the Frontier to the Inner City*. Cambridge, MA: Harvard University Press, 1996.
Lane, Roger. *Murder in America: A History*. Columbus: Ohio State University Press, 1997.
Lane, Roger. *Violent Death in the City: Suicide, Accident, and Murder in Nineteenth-Century Philadelphia*. Cambridge, MA: Harvard University Press, 1979.
Monkkonen, Eric H. *Murder in New York City*. Berkeley: University of California Press, 2001.
Roth, Randolph. *American Homicide*. Cambridge, MA: Harvard University Press Press, 2009.

Murder, Sociology of

At its simplest, murder is the illegally sanctioned termination of a human life by another person. While the Federal Bureau of Investigation's (FBI's) Uniform Crime Reporting (UCR) program designates murder as the willful, nonnegligent killing of one human being by another, this does not include justifiable homicides, accidents, or deaths as a result of negligence. According to the UCR, justifiable homicides include the killing of a felon either by peace officers in the line of duty or by private citizens when a felon is in the process of committing a felony.

The UCR data indicate that the murder rate has decreased substantially over the past two decades, from a high of 9.8 murders per 100,000 inhabitants to a low in 2009 of 5 murders per 100,000 inhabitants. This is a vast improvement, though more than 12,000 people were arrested in 2009 on murder charges. Males are much more likely to be perpetrators (nearly 90 percent) as well as victims (77 percent). Further, of the single-victim, single-offender statistics, African American offenders comprised 47 percent of 2009 offenders and 53 percent of male victims. On the other hand, white females were more likely to be victims (62 percent) than were black females. The known circumstances under which murder is most likely to occur are non-felony-related, with many of these being the outcome of an argument between acquaintances.

With the exception of female victims, murder is not likely to cross race and gender lines. In other words, 84 percent of the time, the offender is the same race as the victim. Males are murdered by other males 88 percent of the time. However, only 9 percent of offenders who kill females are also female. Of those cases in which the relationship between the victim and offender is known, nearly 35 percent of murdered females are murdered by their spouse or boyfriend.

While murder is legally defined as the purposeful termination of one life by another, sociologists argue that the violation is not about action per se. Rather, murder is an issue of class, social power, and resources (or lack thereof). Characteristics commonly attributed to the likelihood to commit murder, such as sex and race, do not by themselves indicate a propensity for murder. Rather, structural forces surrounding the individual influence the likelihood of becoming a perpetrator or victim. The sociological understanding of why murder occurs may be explained by four sociological perspectives: functionalist, conflict, social disorganization, and symbolic interactionist.

Functionalist Perspective

The functionalist view of crime, as espoused by Emile Durkheim, posits that a certain amount of crime is necessary for the continuation of social life. Excessive deviance, of course, is deemed pathological, but some level of deviant behavior—including murder—is a necessary part of the social fabric in ways that are both obvious and subtle. It is important to note that while functionalists view crime as a social good, an event that occurs with some frequency over time and is thus serving some function in the society, it is not necessarily a moral one. Functional theorists believe that any behavior that does not benefit the society or its members, for example, the functions of setting boundaries, establishing group solidarity, or serving as an instrument of innovative adaptation or tension reduction, will eventually become extinct.

When murder occurs in a society and is punished appropriately, boundaries are set for societal members. The action of sanctioning serves to remind members of the society that some behaviors are sanctioned, while others are condoned; this offers a means through which to continually verify the boundaries of the society. Further, group cohesion is reinforced because when a social member violates the social norms, the community tends to bond together, creating a band of support for either the victim or the accused.

Because of the need to be able to prosecute murderers, new technologies are created to verify the guilt or innocence of perpetrators. For example, DNA evidence can now be used to clear or convict an accused murderer. Further, rather than focusing on the breakdown of society in an increasingly violent culture, a focus on the prosecution of a murderer allows the society to direct its attention squarely toward the individual problem with a ready solution, thus reducing societal tensions. In other words, the appointment of a scapegoat allows the members of a society to believe that the cause of murderer is a lack of personal control on the part of the murderer, rather than a reflection of a systemic societal or economic problem.

Not so obvious are the latent or subtle social goods that can result from a crime such as murder. While murder is manifestly not a moral good, it does serve as a justification of the social services a culture must employ in its reduction. A direct resulting social good in this case would be the job-creating effects of hiring people to fill various roles in the criminal justice system, including patrol officers, lawyers, judges, prison guards, and parole officers. If all crime were to suddenly cease, society would have no need for this industry, and vast swathes of the population would become unemployed.

Robert Merton's strain theory elaborates that deviance is the result of a discrepancy between socially engendered goals and the legitimate means to achieve those goals. Conformists, or nondeviants, accept the notion of social boundaries and have the means to work within those boundaries. Merton's typology contains four types of deviants, including the innovator, the retreatist, the ritualist, and the rebel. In the application of this theory, a murderer would be an example of an innovator. Using the scenario of murder occurring as a result of an argument given the prevalence according to the UCR, an innovator may be unable to settle the argument through legitimate means such as reasoning and compromise. This same individual may then resort to illegitimate means to settle an argument and ensure social power over another, killing his opponent to "win" the argument.

While murder and other crimes are obviously not moral goods for society, according to the functionalist perspective, they nonetheless provide social goods, both manifest and latent, and are necessary for the successful continuation of the society. Thus, even though murder is an overwhelmingly negative aspect of society, the very existence of such crimes can result in some social goods, specifically the maintenance of social order.

Conflict Perspective

The conflict perspective posits that deviance is the result of an unequal society. Murder, then, can be seen as the manifestation of the struggle between the powerful and the powerless. Within such a general perspective are two more specific theories: pluralistic conflict theory and radical Marxist conflict theory. Pluralistic conflict theorists view murder as the result of a universal battle over scarce resources, while Marxist theorists espouse the view that murder is a structural issue that is the logical conclusion of the inequality inherent in a capitalist system.

Pluralistic conflict theorists propose that deviance such as murder is a cultural response to

The body of Orlie Comeau was found in an investigation in 1941 on the Standing Rock Indian Reservation near Cannonball, North Dakota. Today, in the face of soaring poverty, substance abuse, unemployment, disease, and high incidence of suicide, crime rates on reservations are very high and few crimes are solved. Confusing jurisdictions, insufficient FBI training in Native American culture, and distrust between federal and tribal investigators have complicated this sociological problem, hindering justice on reservations.

particular situations or events that bring to light competition for social or economic advantage. Thus, conflict is the inevitable result of distinctions between those in authority and those subject to authority. Richard Quinney's *Social Reality of Crime* (1970) articulates the following five propositions, with a sixth proposition being a composite statement, resulting in the social reality of crime:

1. *Crime is a definition of human conduct that is created by authorized agents in a politically organized society.* Murder is itself a definition of behavior that is projected on some persons by others. Political agents have the authority to deem some forms of killing, such as the killing of felons by peace officers, justifiable homicide rather than murder.

2. *Criminal definitions describe behaviors that conflict with the interests of the segments of society that have the power to shape public policy.* Those who have the power to have their interests represented in public policy, generally white upper-class males, regulate the definition of murder and victimization.

3. *Criminal definitions are applied by the segments of society that have the power to shape the enforcement and administration of criminal law.* Those who have the power to determine the definitions of murder and victimization, generally white upper-class males, also have the power to enforce the definitions (or not).

4. *Behavior patterns are structured in segmentally organized society in relation to criminal definitions, and within this context,*

persons engage in actions that have relative probabilities of being defined as criminal. The acceptance and continuation of a violent culture is learned in social and cultural settings. If a perpetrator is socialized such that murderers are not prosecuted, such as gang-on-gang violence, then the perpetrator is not likely to perceive the behavior as criminal.
5. *Conceptions of crime are constructed and diffused in the segments of society by various means of communication.* Definitions of who should be labeled as murderers are socially constructed. As such, anecdotal evidence suggests that certain segments of the population, such as felons and child predators, are categorically denied protection due to their social ostracism and status as social pariahs.

Radical Marxist conflict theorists view social conflict as the result of the ongoing social struggle between those who profit and those who suffer so that others may profit. There are two predominant conditions of conflict. First, the greater the difference between those in authority and the subjects of that authority, the more significant the conflict. Second, those subjected to authority must be organized to a degree that allows for authority to be resisted. Conflict increases when legal norms reflect the cultural norms. When the culture and laws coincide, there is a greater likelihood that a murderer will be prosecuted. If, on the other hand, there is little sympathy for the victim, there may be less likelihood that the murderer will be prosecuted. Conflict also increases when subjects have little power; if the definition and enforcement are likely to meet with little resistance, prosecution is more likely. In other words, if society's perception is that the murderer is a person of importance, he or she is less likely to be prosecuted.

Whether the inequality exists between groups over perceived scarcity of resources or between classes over structural inequality, conflict theorists would concur that murder occurs when there is an imbalance. When the individual with power seeks to maintain or gain power, the most effective way to do this is to subjugate the other, and the most effective way to subvert that power is through deviant behavior such as murder.

Social Disorganization Perspective

Deviance, according to proponents of the social disorganization perspective, is a natural by-product of social change, and while it has negative impacts on society, this disorganization is a necessary step toward reorganization. Rapid social change can result in high rates of nonconformity, disrupting the normative order. Key characteristics of social disorganization include normative competition, conflict, or lack of consensus often caused by changes in technology, urbanization, and immigration.

W. Thomas and F. Znaniecki, of the Chicago School, proposed an ecological perspective, suggesting that deviance was the result of place over person. Areas where poverty is rampant and job opportunities are scarce tend to lack social organization; thus, deviance is more likely to occur. Lacking strong societal boundaries, the people in these areas tend to develop laissez-faire attitudes and simply drift into deviant behaviors.

Consistently, the murder rate as reported in the UCR report is highest in the most populated areas. Cities exceeding 250,000 people experienced a murder rate of 10.2 per 100,000 in 2009. During that same time, cities with populations under 100,000 experienced a substantially lower murder rate (4.1) and those cities with a population less than 10,000 were only 2.8. Suburban areas experienced a murder rate of 3.0 per 100,000.

Robert Ezra Park and Ernest W. Burgess contend that areas away from the urban core that have greater uniformity, consistency, and universality of conventional values tend to have lower rates of deviancy. The corollary to this notion is, of course, that areas that are characterized by overcrowding, low rents, low rates of owner occupancy, and lower educational levels tend to have much more deviant behavior. Consider, then, who is likely to occupy this area originally emanating from the city center immediately outside the central business district, which Park and Burgess term the *transition zone*. This area of high population concentration, low education levels, and low housing values tends to be occupied by the lower class. People living in these areas often have a sense of being trapped in their social class, hopeless, with little means to escape the grasp of devastation, thus exacerbating the conflict that accompanies social disorganization. The problem is particularly acute for adolescents trapped in the transition zone—this segment of the population has even fewer resources than adults of the same area and perhaps a greater sense of being trapped by their social and physical circumstances.

Chicago's Cabrini Green, perhaps the most famous and notorious of America's housing projects, serves as a prime example of the volatile mix of a high concentration of what was once as many as 15,000 people and severely limited resources. Cabrini Green was built after World War II in reaction to a government mandate for low-income housing. Cheaply constructed with little to no upkeep, Cabrini Green's appeal as a solution declined, and those with meager resources fled, leaving behind those who had no choice but to stay. Gangs and violence moved in, increasing deviance and violence. Violence in the 1990s was so bad that police officers reportedly refused to go to the center of the Cabrini Green complex for fear for their own safety. Since that time, due to destitution and skyrocketing crime, Cabrini Green has been demolished, replaced by mixed-income housing. An important note with regard to the social disorganization perspective is that being in compressed urban areas does not *cause* deviance. Rather, deviance is more likely to occur in these areas because of the structural challenges that residents of these areas encounter.

Symbolic Interactionist Perspective

Deviance is a matter of labeling and social construction, according to symbolic interactionists. J. L. Simmons noted that deviance, like beauty, is in the eye of the beholder. Specifically, murder is only deviant and criminal where and when it is so labeled. While this may seem contrary when considering the personal devastation that results from murder, consider the issue of self-defense whereby, in this case, an individual kills another in what he or she believes to be a justifiable action in the face of a lack of available government intervention. Murder for the sake of self-preservation is often not labeled as murder as long as the killing was a justifiable reaction to the expected likelihood of the initial offense. In other words, killing someone in reaction to having been kicked would not likely be considered justifiable self-defense. However, in some cases, such as those suffering from spousal battery, ongoing abuse and fear that brings about murder in self-defense may be deemed justifiable even if the action immediately preceding the self-defense killing was not an immediate risk to life.

Howard Becker suggests that labels are created as a result of powerful "moral entrepreneurs." This labeling occurs in an orderly process: initial recruitment, role imprisonment, and entrance into sustaining subcultures. The initial recruitment phase might include coercion by peers to commit an offense. Role imprisonment takes place once the perpetrator has accepted the mantle of murderer; he or she has been labeled such by society and has accepted that label, along with the resulting social stigma. The murderer is ostracized by society and thus must seek out a sustaining subculture, a place in society in which he or she is accepted in spite of, or perhaps because of, his or her status as social pariah. It is important to note that this progression occurs only as societal labels are applied and accepted; in cases where society does not consider the perpetrator to be deviant, or even considers the murderer to be sympathetic, as in the case of a battered wife who murders her husband, the same labeling process will not occur. Indeed, the perpetrator in such a case will often not be imprisoned in the role of murderer.

Deviant behavior is learned rather than innate; socialization experiences and surroundings play an integral role in determining one's likelihood of becoming an offender. Edwin Sutherland's theory of differential association asserts that people have differential access to social resources and dominant social norms, offering an explanation of differential rates of deviant behavior. In other words, deviants are not born but develop as the result of a learning process that they see as normal, but that others view as deviant. With this assertion comes the assumption that people will behave in deviant ways when they determine the situation is appropriate for deviation with respect to their past experiences and associations with others.

The learning process of developing deviancy follows a continuum, with three modes expressing the most to least direct paths to deviance: formal, informal, and indirect-imitative. In formal instruction, deviance is taught as if through step-by-step instruction. In this case, the perpetrator is specifically taught how to load a gun, where to aim, and when to pull the trigger. In informal instruction, the perpetrator learns from another but through observation rather than through individualized instruction. For example, the perpetrator might watch another perpetrator plan and execute a murder. Finally, indirect-imitative learning involves the perpetrator learning how to commit the offense from a third-party source, such as the computer, television, or print media, rather than through direct observation or interaction.

Thus, the proponents of symbolic interactionism find that deviance is fluid; it can change in form and function over time and place. Even within set parameters, there is a wide variance in the perception of deviant behaviors, including the degree to which the behavior is perceived as variant and whether it should be sanctioned. Further, through interactions with others, society is socialized, learning how, when, and whether to behave in conjunction with the socially prescribed norms or to react in a deviant way.

Conclusion
Sociologists do not function as arbiters of the quality of social acts and actors; rather, they offer objective explanations for general social behaviors. While murder can generally be explained by the four different social behavior theories, its sanction continues the ongoing process of building social stability, maintaining power differentials, and serving as a barometer of society's relative perceptions of murder across time and place.

Leslie Elrod
University of Cincinnati

See Also: 1851 to 1900 Primary Documents; 1961 to 1980 Primary Documents; Criminology; Discretionary Decision Making; Forensic Science; Murder, Contemporary; Murder, History of; Uniform Crime Reporting Program; Urbanization; Vigilantism.

Further Readings
Becker, Howard S. *Outsiders: Studies in the Sociology of Deviance*. New York: Free Press, 1963.
Black History. "Cabrini Green." http://www.black history.com/cgi-bin/blog.cgi?blog_id=62103&cid =53 (Accessed February 2011).
Durkheim, Emile. *The Rules of the Sociological Method*. New York: Macmillan, 1964.
Federal Bureau of Investigation. "Crime in the United States: Murder." http://www2.fbi.gov/ucr/cius2009/offenses/violent_crime/murder_homicide.html (Accessed February 2011).
National Center for Victims of Crime. "Spousal Murder Laws: 20 Years Later." http://www.ncvc.org/ncvc/main.aspx?dbName=DocumentViewer& DocumentID=32701. (Accessed January 2011).
Pfohl, Stephen J. *Images of Deviance and Social Control*. New York: McGraw-Hill, 1994.
Quinney, Richard. *Social Reality of Crime*. Boston: Little, Brown, 1970.
Simmons, J. L. *Deviants*. San Francisco, CA: Boyd & Fraser, 1969.
Turk, Austin. *Criminality and the Legal Order*. Chicago: Rand McNally, 1969.

Murders, Unsolved

Americans have long had a fascination with crime, particularly with murder. While modern journalism and the 24-hour news cycle provide ample opportunity for Americans to dissect every covered murder, even in previous decades there has been a fascination with murders—particularly those that remain unsolved.

Television shows like *Unsolved Mysteries*, *America's Most Wanted*, *The First 48*, and *Criminal Minds* help make murder a topic of consideration and discussion for many as citizens become able to watch mystery stories acted out. Add in media coverage of murders, missing people, and other crimes, and citizens almost become amateur detectives. Yet most Americans are unaware of the vast number of unsolved murders in American history or the number of suspected serial killers yet to come to justice.

Early America
Given the primitive nature of policing and relative dearth of evidence-collecting techniques in early America, it should be noted that there are considerably more high-profile unsolved murders today than there were in the 18th or even early 19th century. One of the most famous unsolved murders occurred in 1843 when Emeline Houseman and her 20-month-old daughter, Anna Eliza, were brutally murdered and then burned on Christmas night in Staten Island. Their bones were broken

and their skulls shattered before the house was set on fire to hide the crime. Polly Bodine, Houseman's sister-in-law, was immediately named as the main suspect. However, there were numerous inconsistencies: Namely, that the motive was theft yet, very little was taken, and Bodine was a woman of considerable means herself. Yet Bodine had many suspicious characteristics for 1840s New York: She had separated from her husband and was sleeping with another man. She had undergone abortions. Ultimately, she was arrested and tried three times but never served time for the murders. In the second trial, she was convicted, but the jury's verdict was overturned on appeal. Despite Bodine being labeled the Witch of Staten Island, the murder remains unsolved.

Another case that created a media circus during its era was the trial of Emma Cunningham regarding the death of her husband Dr. Harvey Burdell, a prosperous dentist, in New York City. Burdell had a less than glowing public reputation as he was accused of being abusive and also embezzling. On January 31, 1857, his servants discovered his body in his office. He had been stabbed and strangled. In total, there were 15 stab wounds inflicted by a left-handed assailant. Given that Emma was left-handed, she was an immediate suspect and was quickly arrested. Despite strong suspicions that she was guilty, the jury acquitted her.

Two of the oldest unsolved murders in the United States had their roots in Arkansas politics. In 1868, Thomas Hindman was killed when he was shot through his parlor window while reading the newspaper with his children. Some 21 years later, John Clayton met a similar fate after starting an investigation into election regularities in a race in which he was posthumously declared the winner.

In 1892, in Fall River, Massachusetts, Lizzie Borden "took an axe and gave her mother 40 whacks." And when that job was neatly done, "she gave her father 41." Or did she? Despite being the only person home at the time of the murders except a maid, a rocky relationship with her parents—Andrew and Abby—and much evidence against her, Lizzie was found not guilty amid most public speculation. The crime was particularly heinous in nature: Andrew had his skull crushed and his eyeball split from the force of the blows from the hatchet raised by the assailant. The Lizzie Borden case is remembered as one of America's most famous trials, and the home in Fall River has been a robust attraction, even allowing guests to stay in the rooms where Abby and Andrew met their deaths.

Early Twentieth Century

The first half of the 20th century was marked by a series of unsolved murders throughout the United States. In 1900, William Goebel was shot by an unknown assassin the morning before he was to be sworn in as governor of Kentucky. Although he survived long enough to be sworn in, he died three days later. To this day, he is the only state governor in American history to be assassinated. Twelve years later, in Villisca, Iowa, one of the deadliest unsolved murders in U.S. history occurred when J. B. Moore, his wife, four children, and two guests were killed by an axe murderer in their home.

On May 23, 1918, New Orleans grocer Joseph Maggio and his wife were butchered while sleeping above their store. Nothing was stolen, and the ax was left in the apartment, still covered with fresh blood. Despite money and valuables being in plain sight, the killer simply left a message in chalk about the victims without taking any goods. Despite having a suspect, no evidence was ever available to link him to the murder.

In 1944, the first unsolved Hollywood murder occurred when Georgette Bauerdorf was found dead in her bathtub. A 20-year-old heiress, she was strangled and had a piece of towel stuffed in her throat. A large roll of $2 bills, thousands of dollars' worth of silver jewelry and many other valuables were left in the home. The police were able to clearly state that the murderer had a motive beyond robbery but were never able to advance the case past determining the assailant unscrewed a light bulb on her front porch and patiently awaited her arrival.

Three years later, Elizabeth Short, age 22, was found in Leimert Park in Los Angeles, mutilated and cut in half. She became known as the Black Dahlia, and her case has been the basis for many books, television episodes, and films as police and members of the public continue to try to bring her killer to justice. In 1922, an Episcopal priest and a member of the church choir (with

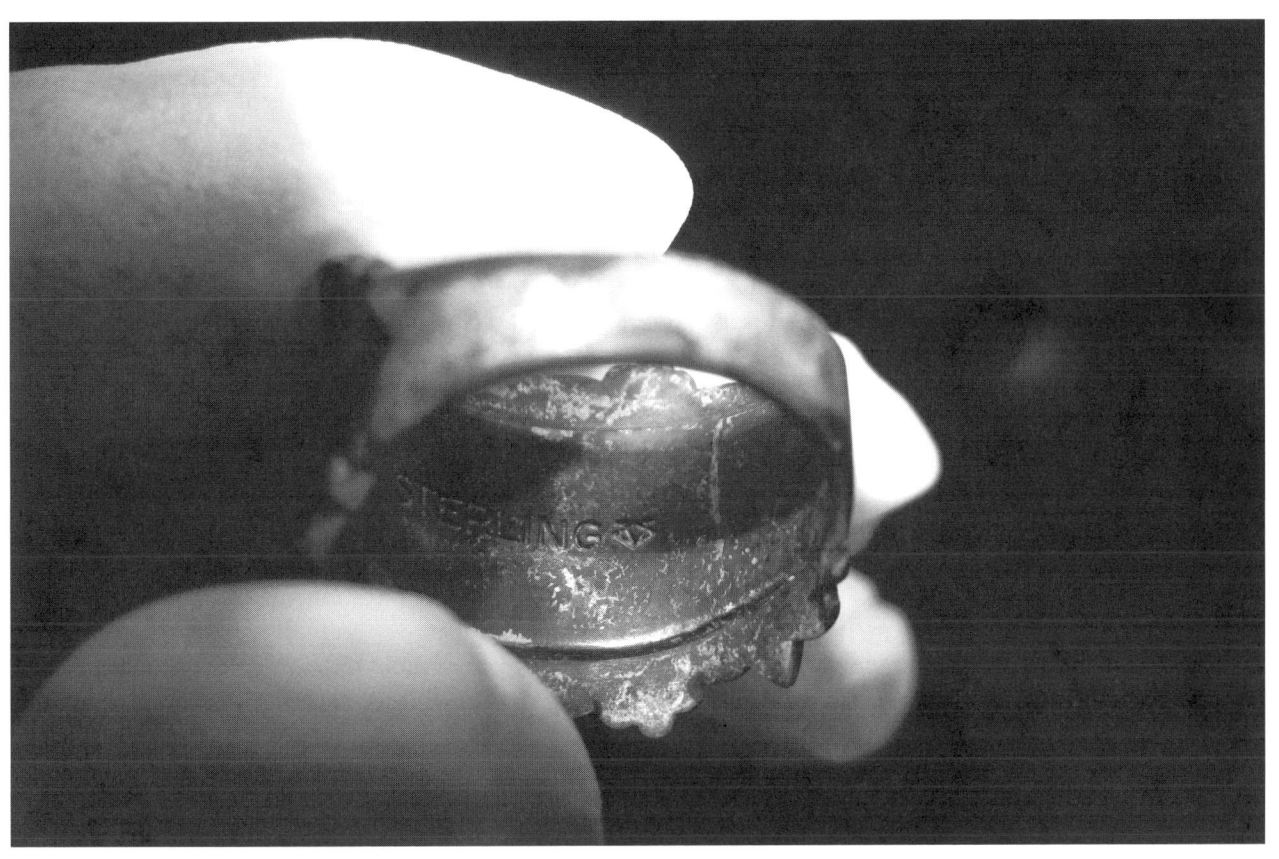

A clue to a modern unsolved murder in Kentucky: one of two rings found on a white female whose body was discovered on October 9, 2001, near Interstate 65 in Simpson County. One was a gold band and the other was a silver band with blue painted enamel flowers and leaves. New technology is used to help bring killers to justice; in this case, the state forensic anthropologist was able to create, based on scientific guidelines, a three-dimensional facial reconstruction on the victim's skull.

whom he was having an affair) were found dead in New Jersey. The priest's wife and her brothers were charged and later acquitted. While the case—commonly referred to as the "Minister and Choir Singer"—is still unsolved, it is best remembered for the sensational coverage it received from the media.

Mid- and Late Twentieth Century

In the second half of the 20th century, the number of unsolved murders in the United States increased. Pregnant Marilyn Sheppard was murdered in her home on Lake Erie in 1954. Sheppard's husband—Samuel—was tried and convicted of her murder in a trial that many compare to the O. J. Simpson murder in terms of media coverage and outrage. After having his conviction overturned as a result of media bias, the carnival atmosphere, and potential judicial improprieties, Sheppard was found innocent in his second trial. He died claiming that a bushy-haired man killed his wife and knocked him unconscious twice. No further suspects were ever brought to trial.

The 1956 murder of the Grimes sisters, who were last seen at an Elvis Presley movie at the Brighton Theater in Chicago, is another prominent unsolved murder from the era. Their disappearance led to one of the largest missing persons hunts in the United States, but eventually their bodies were found off a country road, covered in bruises and marks. Little has ever appeared in terms of solid evidence despite three or four suspects being named and one false confession, except that puncture wounds in the chests of both women suggest an ice pick may have been the weapon of choice for their killer.

In 1957, a young boy was found beaten and naked inside a cardboard box in Philadelphia. The boy, who was estimated to be between 4 and 6 years of age, was never identified. After the discovery of his body, every gas bill in the city came with a picture of the young victim. Despite widespread attention, the boy was never identified and his killer was never brought to justice. Just over a year later, another young murder victim was discovered in Springfield, Illinois. Sixteen-year-old Mary Jane Hanselman was found in the woods, bound by her own stockings and wearing her uniform from her job as a waitress. While a dishwasher from the restaurant was arrested, he was later released because of a lack of sufficient evidence, and no further arrests were ever made in the case.

A close friend of President John F. Kennedy, Mary Meyer was shot and killed in 1964 after going for a walk. A mechanic working nearby heard her cries for help and arrived in time to hear two gunshots and to see a man standing over her. Raymond Crump was ultimately tried and acquitted of the crime. Much speculation has been raised regarding potential links between Meyer's murder and the assassination of Kennedy.

In 1969, Betsy Aardsma was stabbed through the heart in broad daylight among the books of Penn State University's library. Two men came to the information desk and told a worker that "somebody better help that girl." Unfortunately, Betsy was wearing a red dress and as a result, for several minutes no one realized she had been stabbed. She died at the hospital, and the two men were never identified. Between 1970 and 1973, three younger victims were found in Rochester, New York. Now known as the Alphabet Murders, the victims (ranging from 10 to 11 years old) were kidnapped from different areas, raped, strangled, and then dumped in suburbs that started with the same letter as their name. All three victims had the same first initial in their first and last names. The case is still open and comparatively more active than most unsolved murder cases from the 1970s. In 1974, Henry Bedard was found covered in leaves in the woods in Swampscott, Massachusetts. He was returning home from Christmas shopping when he was beaten to death with a baseball bat. The case remains open.

In 1975, American actress Barbara Colby was shot to death along with a colleague while walking to a car in a parking lot. While Colby died immediately, her colleague was able to describe what happened before succumbing to his injuries. He claimed that there was no provocation and two perpetrators were present. He did not recognize either. Both were left with money and valuables, so robbery was not the motive. As of 2011, there has still been no determination made regarding the motive for the murders. Another American actor, Bob Crane, was beaten to death with a camera tripod in his apartment in Scottsdale, Arizona, in 1978. Famous for his work on *Hogan's Heroes*, Crane had allegedly called longtime friend John Carpenter the night before he was murdered to tell him their friendship was over. Carpenter had helped Crane in his activities in the underground sex scene of the late 1970s. Police found blood smears in Carpenter's carpet that matched Crane's blood type, but no charges were filed until 1994. Carpenter was acquitted, and the case has since been cold.

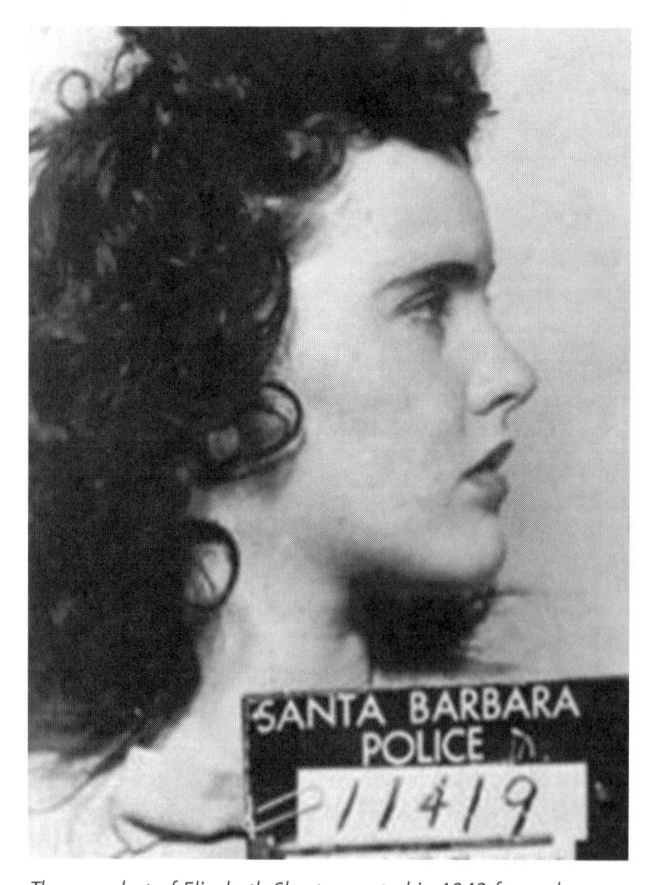

The mugshot of Elizabeth Short, arrested in 1943 for underage drinking in Santa Barbara, California. Her sensational, unsolved murder became known as the Black Dahlia after her mutilated body was discovered in Los Angeles on January 15, 1947.

Raymond Washington, founder of the Crips, was killed in 1979 while walking the streets of Los Angeles. By this time, Washington had little authority over the gang he had started and was actually attempting to unite rival gangs in peace. Always opposed to guns, Washington was wary about approaching unknown cars. He feared being the victim of a drive-by shooting. While no one was ever charged with Washington's murder, most believe he knew his killer. Washington willingly approached the car the killer was in and was shot in the stomach by a passenger. If he had not known the individuals, he would not have gotten that close.

In 1980, 14-year-old Ronda Blaylock was discovered stabbed and left for dead near the Surry-Stokes county line outside Winston-Salem, North Carolina. Ronda had gone to school, taken the bus home to a friend's house, walked back to her own house, and was walking back to her friend's house when they were picked up by a young man driving a blue pickup with a camper. The friend was dropped off at home alive, but Ronda was not seen again until her body was discovered. The friend was never able to identify the man who gave them the ride or explain why Ronda stayed in the truck with him.

In 1995, 17-year-old Deanna Cremin was found strangled behind a senior center in Somerville, Massachusetts. Cremin was walking home with her boyfriend. Her boyfriend only walked her halfway to her door and allowed her to walk to her unknowing death. As of 2005, the police had started to focus on three individuals: her boyfriend, an older admirer, and another adult man. Without witnesses coming forth, however, the crime is not likely to be solved soon. In 1996, Amber Hagerman, age 9, was found with her throat cut in a creek bed by a man walking his dog. Hagerman had been riding her bike near her grandparents' home in Texas. She was kidnapped and held for two days before being murdered. Although significant reward money was offered, no information on her killer has ever been found. Her death was not for nothing, however, as Hagerman inspired the creation of the AMBER Alert System. The day after Christmas in 1996, 6-year-old JonBenet Ramsey's body was discovered in the basement of her home in Colorado—dead from strangulation. The media coverage of Ramsey's death lasted for many years and regularly pointed an accusatory eye at her parents. Despite making it to a grand jury on multiple occasions, there have never been larger developments.

The latter half of the 1990s saw the murder of three rappers. In 1996 Tupac Shakur was killed in a drive-by shooting in Las Vegas, Nevada. A year later, Notorious B.I.G. was gunned down at a red light while driving back to his hotel in Los Angeles. Lastly, Big L. Harlem was killed near his home in Harlem. All three cases remain unsolved. Some Americans still argue that Shakur is alive. There was a composite sketch of a potential person of interest in Notorious B.I.G.'s murder, but no one was ever taken into custody. For many music fans, these three unsolved murders will remain relevant until answers appear.

The Twenty-First Century

The 21st century has brought with it a new wave of unsolved murders. Given the shorter time frame authorities have had to conduct these investigations, there is still hope they will be solved. For people like Jill-Lyn Euto (a 19-year-old stabbed to death in Syracuse in 2000), Evelyn and Alex Hernandez (a mother and son who disappeared in 2002; only Evelyn's torso was ever found), Rashawn Brezell (whose dismembered body was found in garbage bags in Brooklyn), Gail DeLay (who was beaten to death in Dallas in 2005), and Robert Wone (murdered in Washington, D.C., in 2006 while his three roommates were home), the hope is that new technology and public awareness will help bring their killers to justice.

William J. Miller
Southeast Missouri State University

See Also: 2001 to 2012 Primary Documents; Bodine, Polly; Borden, Lizzie; Cunningham, Emma; Serial and Mass Killers; Sheppard, Sam; Simpson, O. J.

Further Readings
Douglas, John and Mark Olshaker. *The Cases That Haunt Us*. New York: Scribner, 2000.
Katz, Helena. *Cold Cases: Famous Unsolved Mysteries, Crimes, and Disappearances in America*. Westport, CT: Greenwood Press, 2010.
Wilkes, Roger. *The Mammoth Book of Unsolved Crime*. New York: Running Press, 2005.

Music and Crime

Music has played an integral role in the life of mankind since recorded history. It has been used for ceremonial purposes, rallying cries, and serves as a cultural identifier for many people. Music as a creative form of expression and method of identification for individuals is evident in modern society. As a result, much debate and concern has been generated concerning the relationship between music and crime. Thus, it is vital that this connection be explored, at the very least, in a general sense.

Because the term *music and crime* conjures a number of different thoughts, there are several avenues to explore. The first is the relationship between violent criminal acts and music as the cause of those crimes, specifically, the outcry that certain forms of music may cause individuals to commit heinous acts against others. A second exploration of music and crime looks at criminal activity in songs. The third aspect of music and crime is the role that organized crime figures played in the music industry from the 1950s through the mid- to late 1980s. Music piracy, the current criminal threat to the music industry, is not a recent phenomenon. Instead, as the fourth examination of music and crime shows, the current form of music piracy is simply a technologically advanced way of engaging in copyright infringement.

Music as the Cause of Crime

Similar to other forms of media, music has, throughout history, been blamed for the ills of society. Newer forms of music and the subculture that develops as a part of the musical genre have been regarded with suspicion by older generations for many years. Musical genres such as heavy metal, rap (primarily gangsta rap), and early forms of jazz were, during their infancy, considered to be gateways to delinquent behavior by youth. This phenomenon did not develop and just begin with rock and roll of the 1950s or with rap and heavy metal in the late 1980s; however, it is these forms of music that the public, media, and authority figures began to take interest in. Early jazz, the blues, and R&B have been criticized as being the cause of youthful displays of negative attitudes, delinquent and antisocial behavior, all of which lead to criminal activity. Mankind's use of the argument "The music made me do it" goes as far back as biblical accounts, Homer's use of the sirens in the recounting of Ulysses's journey home, and the story of the Lorelei, whose voices drove listeners to suicide. Thus, one must consider and understand that although discussions regarding the relationship between violence, crime, and music are a more contemporary undertaking, the subject itself predates contemporary society.

Currently, the debate regarding musical influence on criminal behavior has focused on the affect that rap and heavy metal have on youth. Mainstream media has, in the past few decades, reported several instances in which offenders and critics of popular music have blamed each genre for some sensationalized crime committed by a juvenile offender. During the late 1980s and throughout the 1990s gangsta rap (a subgenre of rap) artists such as Tupac (2Pac) Shakur, Ice-T, N.W.A (Niggaz With Attitude), and 2 Live Crew were named as instigators of various crimes that range from assault and murder of a police officer to domestic abuse and rape. The group 2 Live Crew, whose lyrical content is considered to be lewd, degrading, and violent toward women, had their song (*As Nasty as They Wanna Be*) declared criminally obscene by a federal judge. Ice-T's *Cop Killer* was boycotted by politicians and law enforcement. Both Tupac Shakur and N.W.A have had offenders declare that their songs, which were playing at or before the time of the criminal act, made them assault or kill a police officer. Similar to rap and its subgenre gangsta rap, heavy metal and its many subcategories have been cited as the cause for various violent criminal acts by youth. Artists such as Ozzy Ozbourne, Judas Priest, Deicide, and Cannibal Corpse have been named in lawsuits that allege their music led to violence and criminal activity that led to the death of the complainants loved ones. One of the more notable references toward the link between heavy metal and criminal activity is that of the Columbine High School tragedy. Alternative rocker Marilyn Manson was pointed to as a catalyst for the two shooters' actions, which led to the deaths of 12 other students and one teacher, while 24 others were wounded. Manson was also blamed in the Santana High School shooting, which was regarded as a Columbine copycat killing.

Critics of gangsta rap and heavy metal have used these incidents to link crime to music and push to see these forms of music banned or, at the very least, censored. Despite these incidents and claims by critics, there has been no strong support or clear indication that music (specifically rap and heavy metal) leads to violence or criminal behavior. Despite much theoretical debate concerning the effect of violent music on criminal behavior, the amount of research and subsequent empirical support for one side or the other is seriously lacking. Data concerning the link between violent music and criminal activity is mixed at best. On one hand, some studies indicate that violent music (i.e., heavy metal and rap) has an effect on mood alteration but that there are no direct links between the music and an individual's decision to commit a violent criminal act. On the other hand, several studies demonstrate that exposure to violent, sexually aggressive music facilitates sexually aggressive behavior. One should note that many of these studies have limitations and the findings are questionable. Thus, strong empirical data is limited in regard to proving or disproving the idea that violent music causes certain individuals to commit violent criminal acts.

Criminal Activity in Music

From country to rap, crime and criminals have been a focal point in music dating back at least to the 19th century. Much of current music uses crime and criminals as a focal point. For instance, rap is known to tout and in some cases glamorize drug use and trafficking, assault, and a gangster lifestyle. Although some critics of popular music claim that crime in music is a recent occurrence that is unique to more aggressive styles of music (i.e., rap, heavy metal), criminality has been the subject of ballads, songs, and musical lyrics for a considerable period of time. Stagger Lee, possibly one of the better known criminal figures in music, has been the subject of more than 150 songs

Marilyn Manson playing on the Rape of the World 2007 Tour in Belfort, France, June 29, 2007. Manson's music has been considered a catalyst for the actions of several youth crimes, most notably that of senior students Eric Harris and Dylan Klebold, who killed 12 students and a teacher and wounded 24 others during a suicidal shooting spree at Columbine High School on April 20, 1999. Manson's music was also blamed for inciting Charles Andrew Williams to copycat the Columbine shootings at Santana High School on March 5, 2001.

since 1897, which is when the ballad's unknown authors wrote about events surrounding the murder of a man in a St. Louis saloon.

Crime has been the subject of a variety of other music genres as well. Blues singers have sung about a number of crimes since the genre's introduction to the music scene. Most notably, during the Depression era, many blues singers, usually poor African Americans from crime-ridden neighborhoods, sang about muggings, lover's quarrels, and murder. Rap, similar to blues, originated among African Americans as a reflection and commentary on their urban environments. Specifically, gangsta rap made its mark on the music scene with songs like N.W.A.'s *Fuck Tha Police* and Ice-T's *Cop Killer*, to name a few. The various forms of rock and roll have lauded drug abuse, underage drinking, and sex with minors. The Guns n' Roses song *Mr. Brownstone* chronicles heroin addiction, Mötley Crüe describes the lifestyle of a successful drug dealer in the hit *Dr. Feelgood*, and the band Skid Row tells the story of a young man who receives a life sentence for murder in *18 and Life*.

Although less recognized, another aspect of criminal activity in music is that of female crimes against men. A number of female artists and female groups have generated popularity and press based on songs that focused on the death of an abusive or cheating lover. Country music has led the charge with songs like the Dixie Chicks *Goodbye Earl* and Martina McBride's *Independence Day*. Both songs describe situations in which a woman who was severely beaten by her husband later killed him. The primary difference between the two is that the female in McBride's song kills herself and her abuser, whereas the Dixie Chicks female and her best friend kill the abuser and bury him in the backyard. *Miss Otis Regrets*, originally penned as a blues song of the 1930s, tells the story of a polite society lady who kills the man who seduced and then abandoned her.

Organized Crime in the Music Industry

Another aspect of the relationship between music and crime is that of criminal activity within the music industry; such crimes include illegal downloads (music piracy), organized crime, and copyright infringement. Since the days of famous Rat Pack members Frank Sinatra, Dean Martin, Sammy Davis, Jr., and Joey Bishop, the Federal Bureau of Investigation (FBI) has kept extensive files on musicians and music executives because of alleged ties to criminal organizations or, in some cases, because of criminal involvement of the artists themselves. Although the association between members of the Mafia and musicians can be traced back to the early days of jazz, it is the period between the late 1950s and the 1980s that warrants the most attention. It was during this time that mobsters saw the financial benefits of illicit involvement with the music industry.

Music distribution has, it seems, been problematic for the music industry and musicians since well before the onslaught of music piracy and illegal downloads. Since the 1950s, Morris Levy, a formidable record industry titan with alleged connections to the Genovese crime family, controlled various aspects of the record industry. His peak period of influence was from the 1950s through the 1970s, but he continued to utilize his illicit connections well into the 1980s. Levy, whose businesses included record pressing plants, distribution companies, record store chains, and record labels, printed extra or counterfeit copies of popular records and sold them on the black market in order to circumvent taxes and royalties owed to artists. He also assigned authorship of early rock and roll hits to himself in order to defraud powerless black artists of their royalties.

During the 1980s, Salvatore Pisello, an alleged drug trafficker, soldier in the Gambino crime family, and business partner to Levy, worked for MCA Records as a consultant. At this time, Pisello along with Levy swindled millions of dollars from the company in a series of questionable distribution deals. In a deal to sell $1.25 million in cutouts (copies of albums record companies are no longer selling and have cut out from their catalog) to John LaMonte, a small-time wholesaler who was connected to a New Jersey crime family, Pisello and Levy intended to rip LaMonte off. However, after being roughed up and extorted because he refused to pay for the merchandise, LaMonte turned FBI informant and exposed the Mafia's ties to the music industry.

Illegal Music Distribution (Music Piracy)

As the black market distribution deals engaged in by mob-connected record industry moguls like

Levy demonstrates illegal distribution of popular music has been taking place for decades and is not a new phenomenon that started with the technological age. Music piracy, which is still a mob-backed endeavor, has taken shape in the form of illegal digital downloads.

Music piracy is described as the unauthorized duplication and distribution of music, and it comes in two forms: physical and digital. Physical music piracy involves the unlawful duplication and distribution of music using some physical medium such as cassette tapes or compact discs. Digital music piracy is similar to physical music piracy but it includes downloading and file sharing.

Technological advancements such as the cassette tape in the 1960s, home cassette recording device in the 1970s, and the compact disc in the 1980s made duplication of music easier. The advent of the compact disc and digitally encoded music heralded a new era in music piracy. A 2006 Recording Industry Association of America (RIAA) report indicates that one in every three CDs sold worldwide is counterfeit. As of 2005, the manufacture and international traffic of illegally obtained music has netted an estimated $4 billion to $5 billion in sales.

While physical musical piracy has been a bane to the music industry, illegal digital downloading has garnered the most media and legislative attention. The era of digital downloads and file sharing began with the launch of Shawn Fanning's company Napster in 1999. Napster, which was in service from 1999 to 2001 (before legal injunctions caused it to be shut down), allowed users to share mp3 files of music and film in a manner that circumvented paying markets. This was seen as a direct violation of copyright infringement laws. Although Napster was shut down and file sharing was declared illegal, the road to massive illegal digital downloads was paved.

Groups involved in the organized distribution of illegal music both domestically and internationally range from hierarchical organized crime groups such as the Mafia to terrorist groups. Much of the money earned from music piracy goes to support illegal activities like drug trafficking, terrorism, and other organized crime endeavors.

Robin D. Jackson
Sam Houston State University

See Also: Compton, California; Computer Crime; Klebold, Dylan, and Eric Harris.

Further Readings
Gentile, Douglas. *Media Violence and Children: A Complete Guide for Parents and Professionals*. Westport, CT: Praeger, 2003.
Ingram, Jason R. and Sameer Hinduja. "Neutralizing Music Piracy: An Empirical Examination." *Deviant Behavior*, v.29/4 (2008).
Johnson, Bruce and Martin Cloonan. *Dark Side of the Tune: Popular Music and Violence*. London: Ashgate, 2009.
Tatum, Becky L. "The Link Between Rap Music and Youth Crime and Violence: A Review of the Literature and Issues for Future Research." *The Justice Professional*, v.11 (1999).
Wyman, Howard. "The Mafia and the Music Industry." http://www.crawdaddy.com/index.php/2009/01/21/the-mafia-and-the-music-industry (Accessed December 2010).

Narcotics Laws

From the Greek *narke*, meaning "numbness" or "stupor," narcotics are technically any class of drugs that induce sleep. But that narrow definition does not align with either the medical meaning of the word or the meaning ascribed to it in the law regulating narcotics. In medical parlance, "narcotics" generally refers to the opioid analgesics—a class of natural, semisynthetic, and synthetic painkillers derived from or structurally similar to opium. True opiates are derived from opium—a resinous, milky fluid produced by the opium poppy (*Papaver somniferum*). Opium contains both morphine (approximately 10 percent) and codeine (approximately 1–2 percent).

It has been used for thousands of years around the globe as a medicine for pain relief and for pleasure since it produces euphoria in the absence of pain. Semisynthetic narcotics do not exist in nature but are synthesized by altering a naturally occurring substance, such as heroin from morphine or oxycodone from thebaine, a nonnarcotic found in opium. Synthetic narcotics such as methadone and Demerol are completely synthesized in a laboratory. In moderate doses, narcotics dull the senses, relieve pain, and induce sleep. In higher doses, narcotics cause stupor, coma, convulsions, or even death caused by respiratory depression.

Morphine was first isolated in 1803 and was named after Morpheus, the Greek god of dreams. The German pharmaceutical corporation E. Merck & Company began commercially manufacturing morphine in 1827. In 1832, codeine was isolated from the poppy and, shortly thereafter, semisynthetic and synthetic narcotics began to be created. In 1898, heroin was developed as an allegedly nonaddictive opioid analgesic. Of course, heroin turned out to be much more addictive than either morphine or codeine.

Laws designed to control narcotic use are a relatively recent phenomenon, historically speaking, because until the 18th century, abuse of narcotics was not perceived as a major social problem. One of the earliest known narcotics laws was a Chinese edict issued in 1729 prohibiting the smoking of opium and its domestic sale, except under license for use as medicine. The edict, however, did little to curb the use of the drug in China, as opium addiction established itself as a major public health threat in China during the 1800s, prompting the Manchu dynasty to restrict opium use through legislation focusing on trade, primarily with Great Britain since British control over the East India Company had given the British a virtual monopoly on the opium trade. In 1799, Chinese emperor Kia King banned opium completely, making poppy cultivation, use, and trade illegal. Illicit smuggling, however, kept opium flowing into China, primarily from Turkey, leading the British and Chinese to fight two Opium Wars. Not only did China lose the wars, but it paid large indemnities, including the ceding of Hong Kong to the British. Moreover, the British victories allowed them to increase the opium trade from other areas of Asia until the turn of the 20th century.

Early U.S. Narcotics Laws

The first major concern about narcotic use in the United States occurred during the Civil War as a function of physicians using the relatively new drug morphine to treat battlefield injuries, resulting in hundreds of thousands of morphine addicts. Morphine addiction, however, was seen almost exclusively as a medical issue. It was not until 1890 that the U.S. Congress imposed a tax on opium and morphine; in 1905, Congress banned opium completely. Racism, not public health concerns, was largely responsible for these laws. Chinese immigration into the western United States spurred concern over cheap immigrant labor, as well as exaggerated fears that Chinese men were luring white women into opium dens for sexual purposes. As a result, San Francisco banned opium smoking in 1875 because that practice was associated with the Chinese. In 1883, the U.S. government began taxing opium imports. California criminalized selling opiates or cocaine without a prescription in 1907 and banned the possession of opium in 1909, the same year that the federal government banned the importation of opium.

Joseph Basile, hiding his face with his coat, under arrest in connection with the seizure of $25 million worth of narcotics in February 1949. Chief of Detectives William T. Whalen stands over some of the confiscated drugs. The Boggs Act was passed shortly afterward in 1951 to create uniform penalties and minimum sentences for federal narcotics law violations.

The Pure Food and Drugs Act of 1906 banned the interstate transportation of adulterated or mislabeled food and drugs. Requiring the labeling of ingredients in over-the-counter items had the practical effect of decreasing the availability of opioids and cocaine, the latter of which had begun to cause its own social problems.

Cocaine was isolated from the coca plant (*Erythroxylum coca*) around 1860. Within a few years, it was found in everything from toothpaste and nasal sprays to cigarettes and Coca-Cola. As a result, from the mid-1880s through the 1920s, the United States faced a major cocaine epidemic. Again racism contributed to attempts to control the drug. Contractors were alleged to be providing cocaine to African American employees to get more work out of them, and media reports of "cocaine-crazed Negroes" killing white women in the south caused a panic about the substance. These concerns led Congress to pass the Harrison Act of 1914. The law required registration and payment of a tax by all who imported, produced, or distributed opium, cocaine, or their derivatives. The act limited the availability of these substances, as well as marijuana and chloral hydrate, substances that the act classified together under the moniker *narcotics*. In 1922, Congress enacted the Jones-Miller Act, providing fines and prison sentences for those convicted of the unlawful importation of narcotics. It did little to curb the illicit drug trade other than to increase the price of opioids and cocaine. In 1932, the National Conference of Commissioners adopted the Uniform Narcotics Drug Act to achieve uniformity in state drug laws regulating narcotics, focusing primarily on opioids, cocaine, and marijuana.

Marijuana use had increased significantly during the late 1910s through the 1930s, partly as a function of the high cost of opioids and cocaine in the wake of the Harrison and Jones-Miller acts and partly because of the growth of the American jazz scene. Racism played a role in the inclusion of marijuana in the Harrison Act, largely as a function of the perceived crumbling of racial barriers when blacks and whites interacted as equals while smoking marijuana in jazz clubs. Racism against Mexican immigrants, who were perceived to be vying with unemployed Americans for limited jobs during the Great Depression, similarly prompted concerns about marijuana. Mexicans were painted as marijuana users who used violence against Americans when high, leading to the passage of the Marihuana Tax Act of 1937, the first piece of federal legislation specifically targeted at marijuana. Although the act did not prohibit marijuana use, it taxed anyone who cultivated, distributed, or used the substance, effectively placing marijuana on par with cocaine and opioids.

Narcotics Laws in the Modern Era

World War II focused attention away from drugs. International trafficking was practically eliminated. In the 1950s, amphetamines, which were originally prescribed to curb obesity and depression, became popular among students, professionals, and even homemakers. Additionally, LSD (lysergic acid diethylamide) grew in popularity in certain communities during the 1950s and 1960s. Collectively, these changes prompted federal legislation that altered the ways in which the United States dealt with illicit drugs, nearly all of which were lumped together under the term *narcotics*. The Boggs Act, passed in 1951, established uniform penalties and minimum sentences for those who violated federal narcotics laws. These penalties were increased and expanded by the Narcotic Control Act of 1956. By the mid-1960s, federal control over amphetamines, barbiturates, and LSD (none of which are true narcotics, pharmacologically speaking), expanded with the passage of the Drug Abuse Control Amendments to earlier laws.

In 1970, Congress repealed the hodgepodge of drug laws and enacted the Comprehensive Drug Abuse Prevention and Control Act of 1970. Critics of the law argued that it was passed as a punitive response to the prevailing counterculture of the time. For example, the 1960s saw major social unrest as a result of unpopular foreign policies and the slow pace of civil rights legislation. At the same time, crime was constructed as a major social problem, especially in urban areas in which minorities were viewed as the perpetrators of violence and the distributors of illegal drugs. Collectively, these reasons prompted President Richard Nixon to reinvigorate the "war on drugs" in a manner that targeted two groups critical of his administration: minorities and youth.

Title II of The Comprehensive Drug Abuse Prevention and Control Act of 1970 is commonly referred to as the Controlled Substances Act (CSA). The CSA organized all federally regulated drugs into five "schedules" of drugs based on the substance's alleged potential for abuse and its accepted medical uses. Schedule I lists substances that have a high potential for abuse and no accepted medical uses in the United States, including heroin, MDMA (ecstasy), hallucinogens such as peyote and LSD, and, controversially, marijuana. Schedule II also contains drugs with a high potential for abuse, but these drugs have accepted medical uses, including many of the opioid analgesics, stimulants such as cocaine and Ritalin, and some short- and intermediate-acting barbiturates such as pentobarbital and secobarbital. Schedule III drugs have moderate potential for abuse and a variety of accepted medical treatments, such as anabolic steroids, Ketamine, and some intermediate-acting barbiturates. Schedule IV drugs have even lower abuse potential, including the benzodiazepines/major tranquilizers, such as Xanax and Valium, long-acting barbiturates used for sleep and seizure disorders, opioids used for antidiarrheal purposes, and non-benzodiazepine sleeping pills such as Ambien and Lunesta. Finally, Schedule V drugs have the lowest potential for abuse, such as cough suppressants containing small amounts of codeine and stimulants used to treat chronic fatigue or to suppress appetite.

The CSA has been amended numerous times since 1970 but remains the primary federal law for the formal social control of drugs of abuse in the United States. Yet there have been numerous criticisms of the CSA. First, the CSA discouraged the psychopharmacological advances of the 1950s and 1960s—innovations the National Institute of Mental Health was designed, in large part, to foster. Second, by lumping tight control of drugs of abuse without significant medical uses with true narcotics, people suffering from severe chronic pain sometimes find it difficult to obtain relief because physicians often fear prescribing opioid analgesics for long-term use. Third, a criminal justice focus on controlling drugs of abuse has significantly overshadowed public health approaches, resulting not only in the underfunding of drug treatment programs but also in the spread of diseases such as hepatitis and human immunodeficiency virus and acquired immune deficiency syndrome (HIV/AIDS) as a function of the refusal to adopt policies like needle-distribution programs, which some consider to promote intravenous drug use. Fourth, federal drug interdiction efforts cost more than $19 billion a year. The money and the law enforcement efforts expended reduce the amounts of both resources that can be devoted to other priorities, from education and social services to other forms of crime control, including counterterrorism. Fifth, the continued classification of marijuana as a Schedule I substance is dubious, especially in light of the fact that since 1996, 15 U.S. states and the District of Columbia have legalized the cultivation, possession, and/or use of marijuana for medicinal purposes.

Drug Testing

Drug testing emerged as drug control efforts increased. The National Institute for Drug Abuse originally developed drug tests for military use. But other forms of drug testing became commonplace in the mid- to late 1980s, largely in response to executive orders and legislation signed by President Ronald Reagan. Originally, governmental efforts to create a "drug-free workplace" via drug testing were aimed at federal transportation employees. In 1989, over Fourth Amendment challenges, the U.S. Supreme Court decided *Skinner v. Railway Labor Executives Association*, upholding drug tests of railroad employees who were involved in accidents, and *National Treasury Employees Union v. Von Raab*, upholding suspicionless drug testing of U.S. Customs Service agents who were involved in drug interdiction efforts or who had access to classified information.

The practice eventually spread to private-sector employees and to students. Most common law challenges to private-sector drug testing were unsuccessful. Constitutional challenges to random drug testing in schools fared no better. In *Vernonia School District v. Acton* (1995), the Supreme Court upheld random drug testing of student athletes, and in 2002, it extended that holding to students who participate in competitive extracurricular activities in *Board of Education v. Earls*. Some states, however, have invalidated suspicionless testing of students on state constitutional grounds.

The ever-increasing focus on penal social control of drugs of abuse has had serious consequences for the justice system. The incarceration rate in the United States has quadrupled since

1970, largely as a function of drug-related crime. Some argue that this has created a permanent underclass in America in which convicted drug offenders find themselves closed off from educational and employment opportunities, as well as from full participation in the democratic political process because of voting disenfranchisement laws. Moreover, drug prohibition has created a criminal subculture, especially in inner cities, in which $40 billion per year in profits from the illicit drug trade are paid for in violence and fear.

Samuel G. Vickovic
Henry F. Fradella
California State University, Long Beach

See Also: 1921 to 1940 Primary Documents; 1941 to 1960 Primary Documents; 1961 to 1980 Primary Documents; Drug Enforcement Administration; Harrison Act of 1914; Pure Food and Drug Act of 1906.

Further Readings
Bonnie, R. J. and C. H. Whitebread. "The Forbidden Fruit and the Tree of Knowledge: An Inquiry Into the Legal History of American Marijuana Prohibition." *Virginia Law Review*, v.56/6 (1970).
U.S. Drug Enforcement Administration. "Drug Scheduling." http://www.justice.gov/dea/pubs/abuse/1-csa.htm (Accessed December 2010).

National Association for the Advancement of Colored People

The National Association for the Advancement of Colored People (NAACP) was founded on February 12, 1909. It is the oldest, largest, and most recognized grassroots civil rights organization in the United States. The NAACP has more than 500,000 members and supporters in the United States and other nations, who serve as civil rights leaders in their communities, campaign for equal opportunity, and conduct voter mobilization. The NAACP has championed several civil rights issues, with numerous national and state victories. In the 21st century, the NAACP continues to fight for equality in economics, healthcare, education, voter empowerment, and the criminal justice system, alongside advocating for civil rights issues in the legal arena.

Formation
The NAACP was formed in part as a response to the ongoing monstrous lynchings and the 1908 race riot in Springfield, the capital of Illinois and burial site of President Abraham Lincoln. A group of white liberals, who were dismayed by the violence against blacks, called for a meeting to discuss racial justice. The group members included Mary White Ovington, Oswald Garrison, William English Walling, and Dr. Henry Moscowitz. Around 60 persons signed the call, with seven of them being African Americans, including W. E. B. Du Bois, Ida B. Wells-Barnett, and Mary Church Terrell. The call was released on the centennial of Lincoln's birth.

The other members of the initial group included Joel and Arthur Spingarn, Josephine Ruffin, Mary Talbert, Inez Milholland, Jane Addams, Florence Kelley, Sophonisba Breckinridge, John Haynes Holmes, Mary McLeod Bethune, George Henry White, Charles Edward Russell, John Dewey, William Dean Howells, Lillian Wald, Charles Darrow, Lincoln Steffens, Ray Stannard Baker, Fanny Garrison Villard, and Walter Sachs.

The NAACP's mission echoed the focus of Du Bois's Niagara movement begun in 1905. The mission was to secure for all people the rights stated in the Thirteenth, Fourteenth, and Fifteenth Amendments to the U.S. Constitution, which promised to end slavery, equal protection under the law, and universal adult male suffrage. As such, the NAACP's main goal is to ensure the political, educational, social, and economic equality of minority group citizens of the United States and to purge racial prejudice. The NAACP seeks to bring down all barriers of racial discrimination through the democratic processes.

The NAACP emphasized local organizing. Therefore, by 1913, it had set up branch offices in Boston, Massachusetts; Baltimore, Maryland; Kansas City, Missouri; Washington, D.C.; Detroit, Michigan; and St. Louis, Missouri. Because of the pivotal role of founding member and 1929–39 president Joel Spingarn, the

Four of the most active leaders in the National Association for the Advancement of Colored People (NAACP) movement hold a 1956 poster reading "Stamp out Mississippi-ism! Join NAACP." They are, from left, Henry L. Moon, director of public relations; Roy Wilkins, executive secretary; Herbert Hill, labor secretary, and Thurgood Marshall, special counsel.

NAACP experienced rapid growth. The membership grew exponentially from 9,000 in 1917 to around 90,000 in only two years with more than 300 local branches. The organization started to see more African Americans in its leadership roles, with writer and diplomat James Weldon Johnson as its first black secretary in 1920 and Louis T. Wright, a surgeon, as its first black chairman of its board of directors in 1934.

The NAACP named its first president, Moorfield Storey, a white constitutional lawyer and former president of the American Bar Association, and established its national office in New York City in 1910. Du Bois, its only African American executive, was made director of publications and research. In 1910, the official journal of the NAACP, *The Crisis*, was founded by Du Bois.

The Crisis magazine was established as a premier crusading voice for civil rights. As one of the oldest black periodicals in the United States, *The Crisis* carries on its mission into the third millennium. The magazine is respected for its thought-provoking content, opinion, and analysis, and serves as the official voice of the NAACP in the fight for human rights for people of color. During the Harlem Renaissance, *The Crisis* also published works by Langston Hughes, Countee Cullen, and other African American literary figures. Because of Du Bois's decision to do so, the publication's prominence would rise.

The magazine is published quarterly at present (2012), forging an engaging and candid forum for important issues pertaining to people of color, the American society, and the world at large. The publication also features relevant historical and cultural achievements. In writings that address past and present racial issues, the magazine explores their impact on educational, economic, political, social, moral, and ethical matters. The quarterly also provides updates on NAACP activities at the national and local levels.

Early Advocacy Efforts

The most strenuous and central campaign in the history of the NAACP must have been the decades-long battle against lynching, spanning more than 30 years. Though expressing initial concerns about its constitutionality, the NAACP endorsed the federal Dyer Bill, which would have punished those who took part in or failed to prosecute lynch mobs. The U.S. House of Representatives passed the bill, but the Senate never did, as was the case with other antilynching legislation. It was observed that because of the NAACP report *Thirty Years of Lynching in the United States, 1889–1919*, a public debate was started and drastic drops in the incidence of lynching followed.

The NAACP's most productive period of legal advocacy was established in the 1930s. With Walter F. White as president, the association commissioned the Margold Report, which laid the ground for the triumphant reversal of the separate but equal doctrine. This doctrine had been in effect in public facilities since the 1896 decision in *Plessy v. Ferguson*. White then recruited Charles H. Houston as NAACP chief counsel in 1935. Houston's protégé Thurgood Marshall was instrumental in reversing *Plessy* in the 1954 case *Brown v. Board of Education*.

As the United States entered the Great Depression during the 1930s, the NAACP shifted its focus to economic justice, given the disproportionate toll that African Americans faced. Despite the initial years of tension with the white labor unions, the NAACP was able to partner with the emerging Congress of Industrial Organizations to secure jobs for black Americans.

White continued to play an important role in this area, especially through his mobilization with First Lady Eleanor Roosevelt, also an NAACP national member. As a friend and adviser to the first lady, White met with her on a regular basis to persuade President Franklin D. Roosevelt to proscribe job discrimination in the armed forces, defense industries, and the agencies created by Roosevelt's New Deal.

In 1941, thousands of jobs for black workers came about when Roosevelt received a threat of a national march in Washington, D.C., from labor leader A. Philip Randolph, in collaboration with the NAACP. The president also consented to a Fair Employment Practices Committee (FEPC) to ensure compliance. This focus on economic justice was a pivotal turn and continues to be a crucial part of the NAACP's work, because the effects of economic disparities are continued to be felt today for blacks and other people of color.

The NAACP continued to expand as its membership increased throughout the 1940s, reaching 600,000 members by 1946. The association remained steadfast in its legislative and legal mission to advocate a federal antilynching law and an end to state-mandated segregation. This growth in numbers was the impetus for the formation and sustenance of the civil rights movement in the 1950s.

Civil Rights Era

The civil rights era marked another breakthrough in the struggles for racial equality. In 1954, *Brown v. Board of Education* achieved the removal of segregation in public schools, owing in great part to the leadership of Marshall and the NAACP Legal Defense and Educational Fund. Lobbyist Clarence M. Mitchell, Jr., heading the NAACP's Washington, D.C., bureau, helped achieve integration of the armed forces in 1948 and the passage of the Civil Rights Acts of 1957, 1964, and 1968, as well as the Voting Rights Act of 1965.

While hard-earned racial justice legislations took nearly half a century to come about, the implementation of civil rights took even greater efforts and more extended time. Violence continued to face people of color, especially NAACP administrators and activists. Jim Crow segregation continued to persist throughout the south, and black children faced violent discrimination when they attempted to enter previously segregated schools in Little Rock, Arkansas, and other southern cities. In the south, many African Americans were still denied the right to register and vote.

The NAACP realized the importance of working within the system to effect change, but it also made rigorous grassroots outreach, such as posting bail for hundreds of Freedom Riders in the 1960s who traveled to Mississippi to register black voters and to challenge Jim Crow segregation. In 1963, Roy Wilkins, the secretary succeeding Walter White in 1955, worked with other leaders and national organizations to plan the march on Washington. In 1964, major civil rights legislation was passed, affirming the laudable achievement that the NAACP had obtained.

Given its gravity and the service of prominent leaders, the NAACP has triumphed over several injustices against people of color, at both the national and state levels. The organization's early court battles helped confirm its role as a legal advocate. An important court case at the NAACP's conception was the victorious 1910 *Guinn v. United States*, which fought against a discriminatory Oklahoma law that regulated voting by means of a grandfather clause. Five years later, the NAACP also engaged in an important battle fighting D. W. Griffith's inflammatory film *Birth of a Nation*, a motion picture that invested in the perpetuation of demeaning stereotypes of African Americans and glorified the Ku Klux Klan.

Contemporary Issues

Through its most recent campaign, "Fighting for Health Care as a Civil Right," the NAACP established an unprecedented Civil Rights Health Care War Room in Washington, D.C., along with the National Urban League and Black Leadership Forum. Together, they generated tens of thousands of phone calls to Congress, thousands of letters, and more than a dozen visits from state NAACP leadership to congressional leaders in Washington. As a result, the Patient Protection and Affordable Care Act and Health Care & Education Reconciliation Act of 2010 were passed to extend health insurance coverage to 32 million Americans and will outlaw discrimination against patients with pre-existing medical conditions.

Another prominent victory came with the "Strengthening Hate Crimes Enforcement" campaign, in which NAACP supporters sent hundreds of letters and made phone calls to Congress demanding tougher measures against hate crimes. After a 13-year campaign, the Mathew Shepard, James Byrd Jr. Hate Crimes Prevention Act was passed, allowing the federal government to prevent, investigate, and prosecute hate crimes.

The NAACP also launched the campaign "Protecting the Working Poor" through calls and letters to Congress, in which NAACP members and supporters demanded action for families struggling with unemployment in difficult financial times. Through this project, the Continuing Extension Act of 2010 was approved, extending federal unemployment benefits to those whose state-paid benefits have expired.

Another campaign aimed at upholding justice for all, the NAACP's "I Am Troy Campaign," made Troy Davis a representative of racial disparities that are still present in the criminal justice system. Davis, a former sports coach, was on death row for decades for the murder of an officer, even after seven of the nine witnesses in the original trial had recanted their testimony. This campaign culminated in a rare Supreme Court decision, in which evidence against Troy Davis was ordered to be reheard. Though Davis was executed in 2011, his case focused attention on the continuing plight of people of color in the U.S. justice system.

The NAACP's "Combating Employment Discrimination" campaign succeeded with the Lilly Ledbetter Fair Pay Act, the first act of Congress signed by President Barack Obama after taking office. This act combats discrimination in employment wages in response to the demand made in letters and faxes to Congress from NAACP supporters, insisting that equal work for equal pay become the law of the land.

The NAACP also worked on "Protecting Vulnerable Populations," a campaign that started in the days following the devastating earthquake in Haiti. Thousands of Haitian travelers and immigrants in the United States were facing deportation to their destroyed homeland. The NAACP leaders lobbied White House officials and acquired Temporary Protected Status (TPS) for Haitian nationals living in the United States.

As part of its efforts to fight for economic equality, the NAACP launched the "Curbing Predatory Lending" campaign, demanding stronger consumer protections against credit card companies. As a result, the Credit Cardholders' Bill of Rights of 2009 was passed, curbing predatory lending practices by credit card companies and benefiting Americans across all socioeconomic levels.

As an organization committed to advocating for the underserved, the NAACP launched the national campaign "Protecting Children's Health" after President George W. Bush had twice vetoed legislation to extend health coverage to working-class children. The organization gathered letters and generated calls to Congress for the sake of these children. As a result, the Children's Health Insurance Reauthorization Act of 2009 was passed, expanding health insurance coverage to 4.1 million children.

The NAACP also achieved local victories that address issues at the state level. In March 2009, the NAACP had worked diligently to get the New York legislature to repeal many of the state's Rockefeller drug laws, which had imprisoned thousands for low-level offenses. In the same month and year, the NAACP succeeded in repealing the death penalty in New Mexico. In August 2009, the state of North Carolina successfully passed the Racial Justice Act, allowing a defendant facing a capital trial or an inmate sentenced to death to use evidence showing a pattern of racial disparity as a way to challenge racial injustice in the death penalty. In 2008, the Ohio legislature passed to cap interest rates on short-term payday loans that law targeted low-income communities.

The NAACP believes in building a better America together and works to reduce the world's largest prison population. As racial profiling continues to plague law enforcement practices, eradicating racialized imprisonment will remain an ongoing goal for the NAACP. In recent years, a large number of nonviolent offenders were incarcerated with no accompanying improvement in neighborhood safety. In its efforts to keep communities safe, the NAACP advocates policies that are results based, focusing on treatment for addiction, mental healthcare, judicial discretion in sentencing, and ending racial disparities in the criminal justice system.

For instance, the NAACP endorsed H. R. 4080, the Criminal Justice Reinvestment Act, which would help states develop incarceration reduction strategies and reinvest money saved. As a country, the United States has the largest incarcerated population in the world with 2.3 million people behind bars, a 500 percent increase over the past 30 years. As a result, prisons are becoming increasingly overcrowded, leading to state governments facing the burden of expanding costs. Still, public safety has not been better because of this large-scale imprisonment. The racial and gender disproportion of inmates also reflect dire sociocultural impact. Up to 88 percent of the incarcerated are male, and 57 percent are ethnic minorities. In 2009, for instance, 42 percent of all incarcerated inmates were white, almost 40 percent were African American, and 16 percent were Hispanics.

This disproportion negatively affects particular communities of color, and the incarcerated ratio 1:31 adults in America speaks of both the detrimental human toll and staggering financial costs. Less than three decades ago, the ratio was 1:77.

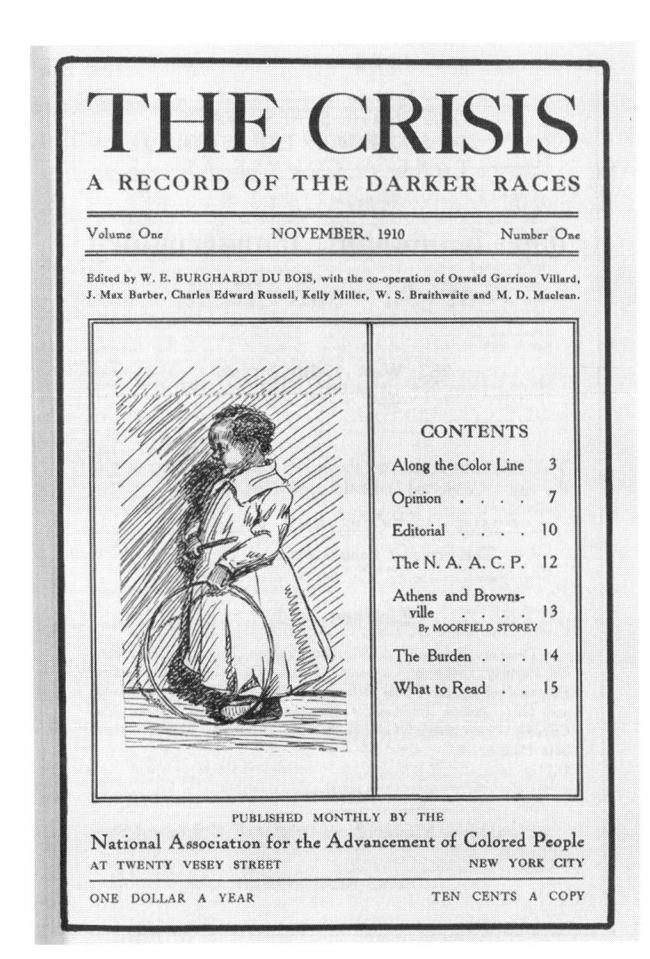

The first issue of The Crisis, the official publication of the National Association for the Advancement of Colored People (NAACP), was published in New York City in November 1910 and sold for $0.10 a copy.

In terms of financial costs, the National Association of State Budget Officers estimated in fiscal year 2008 a record spending of $51.7 billion on corrections, and $68 billion if adding costs at the local levels. The United States would benefit if such money were spent on education, health, transportation, or the like.

The need to effectively reduce the incarcerated population is still a challenge, as it requires local adaptations and flexible implementation. The NAACP believes that the one common denominator across the 50 states is the struggle in human and financial resources, the corollary of a dysfunctional criminal justice system. In this context, H. R. 4080/S. 2772, the Criminal Justice Reinvestment Act, was introduced by Congressmen Adam Schiff (California) and Dan Lungren (California), along with Senators Sheldon Whitehouse (Rhode Island) and John Cornyn (Texas). This legislation would devote grant funding for intensive analysis of criminal justice data, policies, and the cost-effectiveness of current spending on corrections in order to develop data-driven policy options that can address this. The NAACP strongly supported H. R. 4080/S. 2772 and urged its immediate enactment. Nonetheless, the bill has not become law. It will be reintroduced in the next congressional session because of its importance in the NAACP's advocacy for racial justice in the criminal justice system.

Trangdai Glassey-Tranguyen
Stanford University

See Also: Civil Rights Act of 1866; Civil Rights Act of 1875; Civil Rights Laws; Race, Class, and Criminal Law; Race-Based Crimes; Racism.

Further Readings

Hughes, Langston. *Fight for Freedom: The Story of the NAACP.* New York: Norton, 1962.

Jonas, Gilbert S. *Freedom's Sword: The NAACP and the Struggle Against Racism in America 1909–1969.* New York: Routledge, 2005.

National Association for the Advancement of Colored People. http://www.naacp.org (Accessed November 2011).

Sullivan, Patricia. *Lift Every Voice: The NAACP and the Making of the Civil Rights Movement.* New York: New Press, 2010.

Zangrando, Robert L. *The NAACP Crusade Against Lynching, 1909–1950.* Philadelphia: Temple University Press, 1980.

National Commission on Law Observance and Enforcement

The National Commission on Law Observance and Enforcement was a government commission charged with examining a variety of issues pertaining to the American system of criminal justice. The commission is more commonly referred to as the Wickersham Commission in recognition of its chairman, George Wickersham. Wickersham was an attorney and public servant who had previously served as the U.S. attorney general and had become known for his willingness to prosecute corporations under the Sherman Anti-Trust Act. The commission was made up of 11 members, who came from a variety of backgrounds. There were several prominent individuals on the commission, including Roscoe Pound, who was the former dean of Harvard Law School, and Newton Baker, who was the former U.S. secretary of war. The commission was appointed in 1929 by President Herbert Hoover through an act of Congress and was charged with gathering information regarding the scope, role, purpose, and influence of the criminal justice system.

The committee was established when Prohibition, as established by the Eighteenth Amendment, was still law. The widespread public disagreement concerning Prohibition and its effect on American society made it a particularly important social concern when the commission was appointed. As a result, the commission examined the issue of Prohibition at length and may be best known for this role. However, the scope of the commission was actually much wider than any one issue and included an overview of the nation's law enforcement, prosecutorial, and correctional functions and an assessment of the extent and causes of crime. The commission's final report was published in 14 volumes between 1931 and 1932, containing the commission's findings and recommendations:

1. Preliminary Report on Observance and Enforcement of Prohibition
2. Report on the Enforcement of the Prohibition Laws of the United States
3. Report on Criminal Statistics
4. Report on Prosecution
5. Report on the Enforcement of Deportation Laws of the United States
6. Report on the Child Offender in the Federal System of Justice
7. Progress Report on the Study of the Federal Courts
8. Report on Criminal Procedure
9. Report on Penal Institutions, Probation, and Parole
10. Report on Crime and the Foreign Born
11. Report on Lawlessness in Law Enforcement
12. Report on the Cost of Crime.
13. Report on the Causes of Crime, Volume I
14. Report on the Causes of Crime, Volume II

The commission was divided on the issue of Prohibition and its future as a viable part of American society. Evidence of this division is provided by the optional individual opinions that most commission members decided to issue. Some members argued that existing enforcement efforts should be continued in an attempt to determine if Prohibition could become a practicable public policy in American society. Other members argued that efforts to enforce Prohibition had proven their futility and that prohibition should be repealed because it was unenforceable and incompatible with public sentiment. Still, other members argued that existing efforts at enforcing Prohibition, while lacking in some respects, did not necessarily indicate a need for outright repeal. Instead, these members advocated the reform of existing policies and an accompanying revision of enforcement efforts. In spite of the differences of opinion, the commission was able to reach a consensus regarding the issue of Prohibition, which was reflected in their final report.

The commission's final report recommended against repealing Prohibition and restoring legalized saloons. Additionally, the commission's final report recommended against altering existing legislation to allow the sale of certain types of alcohol as some members had suggested as a compromise measure. At the same time, the commission's findings underscored the difficulties associated with governmental attempts to enforce Prohibition. The commission's final report noted that existing enforcement efforts and mechanisms were deficient and needed to be expanded and that increased levels of both public and state support would be necessary if ongoing enforcement efforts were to be successful. In recognition of the political realities associated with Prohibition, the commission also made a number of suggestions for change in the event that policy makers decided to revise existing legislation. Ultimately, the commission's recommendations regarding Prohibition were largely ignored by policy makers, who in 1933 enacted the Twenty-First Amendment, resulting in the repeal of Prohibition.

While the committee's findings regarding Prohibition may have dominated the public imagination, other findings may have been just as significant for the American criminal justice system. The commission noted that graft and corruption were commonplace, that plea bargaining processes were increasingly replacing jury trials, and that social factors influenced criminal propensity. Some of the commission's most sensational findings were contained in the volume on lawlessness in law enforcement. In this volume, the commission acknowledged the existence of police brutality and corruption and noted that American police officers relied on entrapment, coercion, threats, and evidence falsification during the course of their duties.

These revelations resulted in both social and political calls for the reform of the American criminal justice system. It is difficult to determine the extent to which the commission had a lasting impact on the criminal justice system. However, it appears likely that, at a minimum, the commission's findings altered the way in which the public viewed the criminal justice system and its place and purpose within larger society.

Jason R. Jolicoeur
Cincinnati State Technical and Community College

See Also: Corruption, History of; Hoover, Herbert (Administration of); Police Abuse; Prohibition; Sherman Anti-Trust Act of 1890; Wickersham, George.

Further Readings

Deakin, Thomas. *Police Professionalism: The Renaissance of American Law Enforcement.* Springfield, IL: C. C. Thomas, 1988.

Johnson, Herbert, et al. *History of Criminal Justice*, 4th ed. Cincinnati, OH: Anderson Publishing, 2008.

National Commission on Law Observance and Enforcement. *Report on Lawlessness in Law Enforcement.* Washington, DC: U.S. Government Printing Office, 1931.

National Commission on Law Observance and Enforcement. *Report on the Enforcement of the Prohibition Laws of the United States.* Washington, DC: U.S. Government Printing Office, 1931.

Walker, Samuel. *A Critical History of Police Reform: The Emergence of Professionalism.* Lexington, MA: Lexington Books, 1977.

National Congress on Penitentiary and Reformatory Discipline

The National Congress on Penitentiary and Reformatory Discipline was a meeting of prison reformers in the United States held in Cincinnati, Ohio, from October 12 to October 18, 1870. Marking the inception of the National Prison Association, the congress represented the culmination of years of efforts by reformers toward the creation of a national prison congress. It would be followed by the International Penitentiary Congress in 1872. Principles adopted by the congress advocated a number of reforms that later became central elements of prison systems in the United States, including indeterminate sentences and the progressive classification of inmates.

Reformers Congregate

The congress attracted reformers concerned with prison and penitentiary discipline from across the United States, and congressional attendees represented a broad spectrum of interests and occupations. Among those in attendance were state administrators and institutional commissioners, judges, wardens of several state penitentiaries, prison chaplains, directors of houses of refuge, institutional matrons, and members of charitable societies. The geographic distribution of attendees was uneven, and states from the midwest and northeast had the largest contingents of members present. The single largest group came from Ohio, the host state of the congress, with more than 100 members. Attendees from southern states were far less numerous and, among former Confederate states, North Carolina and Tennessee each had a sole attendee at the congress, while two attendees came from South Carolina.

Many notable American prison reformers attended the congress. Enoch Cobb Wines, advocate for penitentiary reform and secretary of the New York Prison Association, served as a vice president of the congress. Zebulon Brockway, future

The outside of an original cell door from a 1767 Burlington County Prison in Mount Holly, New Jersey. This solidly built prison, originally designed to house approximately 40 prisoners, was in constant use until November 1965.

warden of the model reformatory at Elmira, New York, served as one of the secretaries to the congress. Most prominent among politicians in attendance was the congress's president, Rutherford B. Hayes, then governor of Ohio and future president of the United States. Other notable politicians in attendance were Frederick Smyth, the former governor of New Hampshire; Daniel Haines, the former governor of New Jersey; and Conrad Baker, then governor of Indiana.

Over the course of the congress, papers by authors, both in attendance and corresponding, were presented for consideration by congressional members. Authors addressed a broad range of topics related to prison and penitentiary reform. Following the presentation of individual papers, members of the congress were given opportunities to question presenters and discuss the merits of ideas presented.

Methods of Investigation

Congressional members explored ideas such as a scientific approach to crime and punishment; the causes of crime, including intemperance and vice; and the nature of criminal populations, including the nationality of offenders. Domestic and foreign authors provided accounts of institutional practices from both the United States and abroad, ranging from prison discipline in Denmark to the Port Blair penal settlement in India to the Ohio reform farm school. Though its author was not in attendance, a notable paper by Sir Walter Crofton was read describing the Irish system—which served as the base model for the system of inmate classification that the congress advocated in its principles. The congress deliberated methods of fostering inmate reformation, with consideration devoted to education and religious training for inmates. Members of the congress took critical stances against many of the practices that characterized prisons and penitentiaries of mid-19th-century America, notably, political influence in the administration of prisons and determinate sentences for crimes.

The congress was not entirely without conflict or dissent. In an example of a minor disagreement, responses of both "no" and "yes" were given by congressional members to a question asking whether the sexes could be kept separate and reformed at the same institution. A more significant disagreement arose in which several members of the congress, including Enoch Cobb Wines, differed as to whether the highest financial results obtainable through prison labor were compatible with the highest moral results in reforming prisoners. Similarly, during the discussion of Zebulon Brockway's paper outlining the ideal prison system, A. G. W. Carter of Cincinnati argued that the nation's penitentiaries were unsuccessful at reformation—and that the nation would be better served by banishment or transportation of offenders.

Principles of the Congress

As a statement of its ideals, the National Congress on Penitentiary and Reformatory Discipline adopted 37 principles that defined the congress's stance on the nature of imprisonment, the objectives of punishment, and the methods to be employed by penal institutions. Foremost, congressional principles defined the objective of prison discipline in the United States as reformation. Principles indicated that inmate reformation was to be achieved through the use of education and religious instruction, through discipline inculcated in inmate labor, and by avoiding the use of physical force on inmates. A number of the principles adopted by the congress addressed inmate sentencing, notably, advocating for indeterminate sentences, in which sentences were not to be fixed in length but rather extend until inmates exhibited proof of reformation. Principles also advocated ensuring that sentences be of sufficient length to allow for inmate reformation, reducing the usage of gubernatorial pardons, and eliminating inequities in the length of sentences for like offenses. The principles of the congress contained provisions for changing current organizational practices within prison systems, including the centralization of prison administration and the use of progressive classification of inmates based on a system of marks. The congress also endorsed new penal management practices, including eliminating political appointments of prison administrators and requiring specialized training for reformatory officers.

Many of the reforms advocated at the National Congress on Penitentiary and Reformatory Discipline were adopted by prisons in the United States following 1870. New York's Elmira Reformatory, the model institution opened in 1876 under Zebulon Brockway, incorporated a version of the mark system, inmate classification, inmate vocational and religious training, and indeterminate sentences. Later, in the Progressive Era, both indeterminate sentences and inmate classification became central elements of prisons in the United States. Prison systems of the Progressive Era also endorsed a concept similar to reformation, termed *rehabilitation*, as the primary goal of incarceration.

Stephen E. Tillotson
Indiana University

See Also: Brockway, Zebulon; Elmira Prison; History of Crime and Punishment in America: 1850–1900; National Prison Association.

Further Readings
McKelvey, Blake. *American Prisons: A History of Good Intentions*. Montclair, NJ: Patterson Smith, 1977.
Rothman, David J. *Conscience and Convenience: The Asylum and its Alternatives in Progressive America*. Boston: Little, Brown, and Company, 1980.
Wines, Enoch Cobb, ed. *Transactions of the National Congress on Penitentiary and Reformatory Discipline*. Albany, NY: National Prison Association, 1871.

National Organization for Women

The National Organization for Women (NOW) was founded in 1966 after the Equal Employment Opportunity Commission (EEOC) decided, in 1965, not to include gender as one of the categories for which employment discrimination was not permitted. The Civil Rights Act of 1964 included, in Title VII, a prohibition against employment discrimination based on gender, but the EEOC essentially decided that this provision would not be enforced. One month after the EEOC determined that gender segregation in job posting was permissible, a conference on Title VII and the EEOC was held, where founding members of NOW met and established that they had common goals and determined to take action.

Formation and Early Years

Betty Friedan, author of *The Feminine Mystique*, attended the conference and invited several other participants to gather after the proceedings to discuss what action could be taken. EEOC officials had been recommending the formation of a private organization to see to the interests of women, just as civil rights groups had done for African Americans. Twenty-eight women came together to form NOW with the intent of ending gender-based employment discrimination. Within a few months, the organization had grown to more than 300 women and men. (It is important to note that NOW is the National Organization *for* Women, not the National Organization *of* Women, as it is often incorrectly called; the group's members are of both genders and are organized to advocate for women.) During NOW's first national conference, a written

Betty Friedan, author and feminist, was one of 29 founding members of the National Organization for Women (NOW) and was elected NOW's first president in October 1966.

statement of purpose was developed, which went far beyond employment discrimination. At the time, the stated purpose of the organization was to work toward "a fully equal partnership of the sexes" and to promote equality for women in all spheres of life.

During NOW's second annual meeting in 1967, members created a "Bill of Rights for Women" and added the passage of the Equal Rights Amendment, the repeal of antiabortion laws, and public funding for child care to its stated goals. NOW went about achieving these goals by organizing rallies and demonstrations and using the legal system. Several landmark cases in women's rights history can be traced back to the involvement of NOW. Notably, it was a NOW attorney who argued the first gender discrimination case appealed under Title VII, *Weeks v. Southern Bell*, argued in the U.S. Fifth Circuit Court of Appeals.

The plaintiff, Lorena Weeks, had been barred from advancing to a higher-paid job, that of switchman, by her employer, Southern Bell, because it was a man's job requiring the ability to lift more than 30 pounds. At the time, the company prohibited women from entering such a job because of that requirement. Somewhat theatrically, Weeks entered the courtroom carrying the typewriter she was regularly required to carry in the course of her job at Southern Bell. The typewriter weighed more than 30 pounds. The court ruled that prohibiting women from entering this job on the grounds of the 30-pound requirement violated Title VII of the Civil Rights Act.

Despite its formation as a result of employment discrimination, and frequent public demonstrations regarding that issue, NOW's early years also saw it add other women's issues to the agenda. In 1973, NOW established a task force on rape and a task force on sexuality and lesbianism. Not simply a political organization, NOW began using its members to make a difference in the everyday lives of those affected by "women's issues." NOW members were instrumental in setting up some of the first rape crisis centers and hotlines. During the same time period, after *Roe v. Wade* legalized abortion, NOW members organized to escort women into abortion clinics to protect them from protesters outside the clinics.

Recent Activism

In 1998, at NOW's annual meeting, the delegates put together a "Declaration of Sentiments" that summarized their visions, history, and methods. NOW takes pride in being a grassroots organization, despite its current size and success. The delegates wrote how they "have sued, boycotted, picketed, lobbied, demonstrated, marched, and engaged in nonviolent civil disobedience" throughout the group's 32-year history and how they had seen enormous change, but that they were not done yet. They noted that women still did not have equal decision-making power in all areas of society and that, somewhat due to gender inequality, there is still violence, poverty, and need of all kinds in American society. The visions for change have gone considerably past a desire for equal employment opportunity.

NOW continues to work on behalf of many women's issues, the most prominent of them being abortion and reproductive rights; economic justice and ending sex discrimination; lesbian rights; promoting diversity and ending racism; and stopping violence against women. Each of these issues is approached from the perspective that women are equal to men, and the law should reflect and protect this equality while taking into account the reality of men's and women's lives.

For an example of the types of ideology NOW supports, in the abortion and reproductive rights area, NOW opposes restrictions on the availability of abortion or of any reproductive healthcare service. It takes the position that funding for these services should be available just as it would be for any nonreproductive healthcare service. It is not just the availability of abortion that concerns NOW in the reproductive rights sphere. The George W. Bush administration supported legislation that would restrict access to contraceptive pills and other forms of legal birth control. NOW vigorously opposed this legislation and a similar proposal that pharmacists be allowed to choose not to dispense birth control prescriptions for moral or religious reasons. NOW also supports comprehensive, medically accurate sex education and opposes abstinence-only programs.

Most relevant to the history of crime and criminal justice is NOW's organization to support the prevention of violence against women. After being involved in establishing rape crisis centers in the early 1970s, NOW engaged in activism to change the way sexual assault and domestic violence are perceived by the public and handled by the legal system. For instance, NOW is behind efforts to make people aware that sexual assault is most often committed by someone known to the victim rather than by a stranger, and to end the distinction between forcible ("real") rape and non-forcible rape. The group works to raise awareness of the prevalence of intimate partner or domestic violence. The belief that this is a private matter and that it does not occur very frequently is an unrealistic means of dealing with the problem and can be damaging to victims. In addition to supporting efforts to prevent violence against women, NOW wants to ensure that women who have been victimized receive appropriate services and are not mistreated by the legal system. For instance, NOW supports making emergency contraceptives available to victims of sexual assault and having this service covered by public funds. NOW was also instrumental in the implementation of rape shield laws. These laws limit the admissibility of a victim's prior sexual history in a sexual assault trial, with the intent of reducing the potential for reporting a sexual assault to be a humiliating examination of the victim. NOW is a strong supporter of the Violence Against Women Act (VAWA) and its continued reauthorization.

It should be noted that, in addition to NOW's direct involvement with attempting to reduce violence against women, the social conditions that NOW represents may be associated with levels of violence against women. NOW membership may be representative of the level of organization within a community and the degree to which gender equality is supported. Both these concepts have been shown to be related to levels of sexual violence. In a 2007 study, the level of NOW membership in a state is statistically significantly negatively associated with the level of acquaintance rape. That is, in states where more people are motivated to join a feminist organization, there are lower levels of sexual assaults committed by acquaintances. In most analyses, NOW membership was unrelated to sexual assaults committed by strangers; however, one analysis showed that increased NOW membership was associated with an *increase* in sexual assault committed by strangers. A possible explanation for that finding is the backlash theory:

As gender equality increases, males may feel the need to fight back to keep women in their place, and one method of doing so is sexually assaulting them. The findings for acquaintance rape were much more consistent and support the hypothesis that gender equality is associated with reduced violence against women. Consistent with that theory, the number of female representatives in Congress for a particular state was also significantly negatively associated with acquaintance rape.

Lynn Pazzani
University of Arkansas at Little Rock

See Also: 1851 to 1900 Primary Documents; Civil Rights Laws; Equality, Concept of; Gender and Criminal Law.

Further Readings
Barakso, Maryann. *Governing NOW: Grassroots Activism in the National Organization for Women*. Ithaca, NY: Cornell University Press, 2004.
National Organization for Women. http://www.now.org (Accessed September 2011).
Parry, M. "Betty Friedan: Feminist Icon and Founder of the National Organization for Women." *American Journal of Public Health*, v.100/9 (July 2010).
Pedriana, Nicholas. "Help Wanted NOW: Legal Resources, the Women's Movement, and the Battle Over Sex-Segregated Job Advertisements." *Social Problems*, v.51/2 (May 2004).
Reger, J. "Organizational Dynamics and Construction of Multiple Feminist Identities in the National Organization for Women." *Gender & Society*, v.16/5 (October 2002).
Reger, Jo and Suzanne Staggenborg. "Patterns of Mobilization in Local Movement Organizations: Leadership and Strategy in Four National Organization for Women Chapters." *Sociological Perspectives*, v.49/3 (September 2006).

National Police Gazette

The *National Police Gazette* was a tabloid newspaper aimed at lower- and middle-class American men. From the late 19th century through the

A copy of a 1922 edition of the popular tabloid the National Police Gazette, *which was published for more than 130 years and influenced magazines like* Sports Illustrated *and* Playboy.

early 20th century, the *Gazette* exerted a huge influence on American popular culture, titillating readers with scandalous news of sex, crime, politics, and illegal sporting events. The *Gazette* began publication in 1845 and ceased in 1977, but its years of greatest influence were in the decades immediately before the turn of the 20th century, under the editorship of Richard Fox. By 1895, it was selling more than 2 million copies every week.

The American press of the early national era was not above reporting on sex scandals, and not above using such scandals to embarrass the powerful and wealthy. Accusations of sexual impropriety became a relatively common strategy of partisan politics. Perhaps the best-remembered example today remains the early journalistic sallies against Thomas Jefferson's relationship with his slave, Sally Hemings, his wife's mulatto half-sister. However, by the mid-19th century, such opportunistic smut became detached from politics, as publishers discovered it worked on its own as a useful strategy for increasing circulation. Gossip and outright fabrication became a staple of tabloid journalism.

During the early 1840s, George Wilkes—the man who would go on to found the *Gazette*—worked at the *Subterranean*, which routinely vilified the New York City police and political opponents for allegedly frequenting bordellos and engaging in various crimes. When Wilkes founded the *National Police Gazette* in 1845, he modeled his new publication on the English police gazettes that emerged in the late 1700s to chronicle crime and police activity in London. The *Gazette* covered murder more than any other crime, especially those that involved sex scandals or high society. Its stock-in-trade was detailed descriptions of interpersonal violence—women fighting men, women fighting women, or women drinking and carousing—nearly always accompanied by salacious images featuring bared limbs and ruffled petticoats, blood, and gore.

The *Gazette* ran regular columns with titles such as "Murder and Suicide," "Vice's Varieties," and "This Wicked World." It thrived on stories about sex and prostitution. The sexual indiscretions of the wealthy or pious were routinely featured. By the late 1800s, the *Gazette* was publicizing prize fighting at a time when boxing was still illegal, even awarding its own championships and prizes. The *Gazette* continued to highlight its crime coverage well into the 1870s. After the turn of the 20th century, the *Gazette*'s focus shifted to sex and sports. Even as crime became less central to the paper, sensationalist crime reporting remained a staple throughout the *Gazette*'s run. The *Gazette* engaged in primitive criminological research and theorizing. In 1846, the *Gazette* published a series of case studies of criminal careers, titled "Lives of the Felons." Included in the series were the quantitative results of a survey of criminals, reporting on the causes of their criminal activities—causes such as evil associations, intemperance, weak principles, and sudden temptations.

The *Gazette* also influenced scholarly criminologists during the 19th century. For example, the *Gazette's* publisher, Richard Fox, released a biography of Belle Starr, a consort of various men in midwestern criminal gangs. The biography was more myth-making than objective reporting.

It contained a great deal of factual embellishment and outright fabrication. An Italian reporter plagiarized the Starr biography and published the stories in Italian. Cesare Lombroso, the central figure in the Positivist school of criminology, used the Belle Starr stories. In his book *The Female Offender*, Lombroso repeated Fox's mythical version of Belle Starr's life to justify his theoretical assertions that deviant women are atavistic throwbacks to an earlier stage in human evolution.

In exposing, categorizing, ridiculing, and condemning all manner of fraud, crime, and hypocrisy—while simultaneously glorifying certain outlaws—the *National Police Gazette* delineated and clarified the boundaries between deviant behavior and acceptable behavior for generations of American men. The *Gazette* constitutes one of the richest data sources for cultural criminologists studying the late-19th-century United States and its influence on contemporary mores.

Thomas F. Brown
Virginia Wesleyan College

See Also: Literature and Theater, Crime in; New York; New York City: News Media, Crime in.

Further Readings

Cohen, Patricia, Timothy Gilfoyle, and Helen Horowitz. *The Flash Press: Sporting Male Weeklies in 1840s New York*. Chicago: University of Chicago Press, 2008.

Gorn, Elliott. "The Wicked World: The National Police Gazette and Gilded-Age America." *Media Studies Journal*, v.15 (1992).

Reel, Guy. *The National Police Gazette and the Making of the Modern American Man, 1879–1906*. New York: Palgrave Macmillan, 2006.

Schiller, Dan. *Objectivity and the News: The Public and the Rise of Commercial Journalism*. Philadelphia: University of Pennsylvania Press, 1981.

National Prison Association

The National Prison Association (NPA) was founded in Cincinnati, Ohio, in 1870 during a meeting of domestic and international prison leaders. Founding members included such correctional luminaries as Enoch Wines (New York Prison Association), Zebulon Brockway (superintendent of the Detroit House of Correction), and Franklin Sanborn (Massachusetts Board of State Charities). Early members, many of whom were actively involved in the antislavery movement, sought to improve the plight of prisoners worldwide. Of particular interest to the association were corporal punishments, forced servitude, and the use of long-term segregation, all of which were practiced widely in the 19th and early 20th centuries. Advances in offender classification and the implementation of humane disciplinary practices were sought. Members also desired to see improvement in dietary and educational provisions. Association founders authored a "Declaration of Principles" that set forth the values of the organization. These principles were later ratified by the membership. These principles quickly gained international support, giving the NPA a great deal of influence over legislative processes related to prison operations and offender treatment. Eventually, NPA was renamed the American Prison Association (1907) as a way to distinguish itself internationally. To better reflect its growing interest in rehabilitation, its name was changed yet again in 1954 to the American Correctional Association (ACA). This change also acknowledged the increasing importance of probation and parole in offender supervision and treatment efforts. Rutherford B. Hayes, then governor of Ohio and future president of the United States, was elected as the association's first president.

The "Declaration of Principles," upon which the association was founded, has guided its operations since its inception. These principles have, however, evolved and were revised at the 1930, 1960, 1982, and 2002 national meetings. Even though revisions have been made, core philosophies have remained intact. The ACA adheres to seven basic principles. These principles include recognition of the rights and dignity of offenders, a concern for

The Bergen County Jail facility in New Jersey has state-of-the-art technology featuring computer control of all inmate housing areas, an integrated perimeter security system, a sitewide duress/panic alarm system, and a computerized center control. The facility is designed and operated to meet accreditation set by the American Correctional Association (ACA).

public safety, a desire to assist offenders in becoming responsible citizens, continual assessment and improvement, the promotion of professional standards, the effective management and treatment of offenders, and serving as an advocate for crime victims. According to the association, its overall mission is to "provide a professional organization for all individuals and groups, both public and private, that share a common goal of improving the justice system."

Structure and Function

The ACA's Government and Public Affairs Department is responsible for determining the association's position on policy issues and representing it before the U.S. Congress, state and local governments, special interest and advocacy groups, and the media. The department also monitors legal and legislative activity and distributes information to its membership. To do this, the association issues the *ACA Federal Alert,* which informs members about legislation that may affect the profession. The association holds two annual conferences and publishes *Corrections Compendium* (a research-based journal published four times a year) and *Corrections Today* (a highly stylized magazine that is published six times a year). It also publishes an annual directory of all U.S. institutions and agencies that handle juvenile and adult offenders.

The ACA operates the Correctional Certification Program (CCP). The program is intended to professionalize corrections through continuing education and training. It also seeks to improve the public image of corrections and to serve as a recruitment tool. The CCP provides individuals with the opportunity to gain recognition as qualified practitioners. Participants can obtain certification as an executive, manager, or supervisor in either juvenile or adult corrections. Certification is also available in correctional healthcare and security.

The association remains the only body to grant accreditation to correctional institutions. For an institution to gain accreditation, it must submit to a rigorous process in which it develops extensive policies and procedures relating to all aspects of correctional operations. Furthermore, evidence must be presented to verify agency compliance with these operational mandates. This process generally takes about 18 months, concluding with an on-site assessment by ACA-trained auditors. Correctional accreditation signifies a dedication to continual evaluation and improvement, education and training, and a professional orientation. Once achieved, accreditation becomes a source of institutional pride and provides some protection against lawsuits. Once an institution is accredited, the process of staying accredited is continual, with reaccreditation occurring every three years.

In recent years, the ACA has reached out to students interested in corrections. For college students wanting to learn more about the correctional profession, the ACA offers opportunities to complete internships in a variety of areas. Students may choose to work in Standards and Accreditation, Professional Development, Publications and Communications, Government and Public Affairs, Information Technology, Conventions and Corporate Relations, or Membership and Finance.

The American Correctional Association is headquartered in Alexandria, Virginia, and has more than 20,000 active members. Since its creation nearly 150 years ago, the association has effectively served as an advocate for the professionalization of corrections and the humane treatment of offenders. Its influence over corrections continues to be felt on both a domestic and international basis.

Caroline Forsythe
Curtis R. Blakely
Truman State University

See Also: Brockway, Zebulon; Hayes, Rutherford B. (Administration of); Prisoner's Rights.

Further Readings

Abadinsky, H. *Probation and Parole: Theory and Practice*. Upper Saddle River, NJ: Prentice Hall, 1997.

American Correctional Association. http://aca.org (Accessed September 2011).

Pisciotta, A. W. *Benevolent Repression: Social Control and the American Reformatory-Prison Movement*. New York: New York University Press, 1994.

National Security Act of 1947

The National Security Act of 1947 (Public Law 80-235, 61 Stat. 496, 50 U.S.C. ch. 15) created the national security structure of the United States. It was signed on July 26, 1947, and affected the defense, intelligence, and executive activities of the government. The introduction notes that it is "An act to promote the national security by providing for a Secretary of Defense; for a National Military Establishment; for a Department of the Army, a Department of the Navy, and a Department of the Air Force; and for the coordination of the activities of the National Military Establishment with other departments and agencies of the Government concerned with the national security." The National Military Establishment (renamed the Department of Defense in 1949) merged the Department of War and the Department of the Navy. The secretary of defense position was created to provide civilian control over the armed forces. The three current branches of the armed forces were created when the Air Force was separated from the Army and the Marines remained with the Navy. A Joint Chiefs of Staff (JCS) was formed to provide advice to the president on military matters, but the act clearly stated it was not "establish[ing] a single Chief of Staff over the armed forces nor an overall armed forces general staff."

The backbone of the current intelligence structure was also created by the act. The Central Intelligence Agency (CIA), the first peacetime intelligence agency, was created to replace the Office of Strategic Services (OSS) that organized intelligence efforts during World War II. In addition to the CIA, the director of central intelligence position was established to oversee the entire intelligence community. The last major component was the National Security Council (NSC). The NSC's function was "to advise the President to the integration of domestic, foreign, and military policies relating to the national security." It is located in the executive branch and consists of the president, vice president, the national security adviser (position created in 1953), secretary of state, secretary of defense, and political appointees.

The need to reorganize the nation's defense and intelligence structure was clear after the experiences of World War II. During the war, there were difficulties with collaboration between civilian and military policy bodies, interservice squabbles between the army and navy; and intelligence challenges due to the ad hoc nature of the OSS. Given the postwar status of the United States and the impending cold war, it was imperative that a permanent national security structure be created. During the congressional debate on the national security structure, one of the main concerns was the role of the defense and intelligence bodies in the internal security of the country. There were repeated references to the threat of an American Gestapo.

Specific references are made in the act curtailing the role of the CIA in law enforcement and other internal security matters. It states that the director of the CIA shall "collect intelligence through human sources and by other appropriate means, except that the Director of the Central Intelligence Agency shall have no police, subpoena, or law enforcement powers or internal security functions. ... [and] provide overall direction for and coordination of the collection of national intelligence *outside* the United States" [*emphasis added*]. The act also carefully limits the role of Department of Defense intelligence agencies, noting they could "collect information *outside* the United States about individuals who are *not* United States persons" [*emphasis added*] and clearly states "[a]ssistance ... may not include the direct participation of a member of the Army, Navy, Air Force, or Marine Corps in an arrest or similar activity."

It also describes the process by which foreign intelligence, gathered by law enforcement agencies, will be shared with the director of national intelligence. The attorney general was given the power to withhold information if it "would jeopardize an ongoing law enforcement investigation or impair other significant law enforcement interests." Later amendments to the act have blurred the lines between intelligence and law enforcement agencies, such as the post–9/11 National Counterterrorism Center, established in 2004.

Chad M. Kahl
Illinois State University

See Also: Homeland Security; Terrorism; Truman, Harry S. (Administration of).

Further Readings
Hogan, Michael J. *A Cross of Iron: Harry S. Truman and the Origins of the National Security State, 1945–1954*. New York: Cambridge University Press, 1998.
Stuart, Douglas T. *Creating the National Security State: A History of the Law That Transformed America*. Princeton, NJ: Princeton University Press, 2008.
Zegart, Amy B. *Flawed by Design: The Evolution of the CIA, JCS, and NSC*. Palo Alto, CA: Stanford University Press, 1999.

Native American Tribal Police

The term *Native American* is a late-20th-century descriptor used to identify the indigenous peoples of North America that is now the United States. The term *Indian* is the descriptor used by the federal government as a matter of federal law. There is no federal statute that defines the status of Indian, although the U.S. Supreme Court has handed down decisions that do. There are currently more than 550 federally recognized Indian tribes in the United States. Each tribe is responsible for setting its enrollment criteria. Some tribes have a blood quantum requirement, while others have enrollment based on their ancestors appearing on a particular historical list of tribal members such as the Dawes Act.

The term *Indian Country* is ubiquitous; there are several types of Indian Country that are recognized by U.S. law. Reservations are a type of Indian country established by U.S. law. Early reservations were established when a tribe would sign a treaty with the United States. Each treaty signed would yield to the signing peoples the promise of protection, education, healthcare, and hunting and fishing rights. In exchange, tribe members would surrender all ancestral lands to the U.S. government. There are about 310 Indian reservations in the United States. Informal reservations are lands that once were reservations and have been disestablished, or that have unclear status but remain as trust land. Land that has/had been set aside for Indians legally retains the title of Indian Country. Dependent Indian communities have been interpreted by the U.S. Supreme Court in several tribal cases to be land federally supervised, which has been set aside for the use of Indians. A fourth type of Indian Country was created through the Dawes Act and Allotments. From 1887 until 1934, the federal government ran programs that took parcels of tract land and allotted or assigned these parcels to particular Indians or to Indian families. The fifth and final type of Indian County is listed as "special designation." Congress can designate certain lands as Indian Country for jurisdictional purposes even if these lands do not fall within the aforementioned types of Indian Country.

Before the U.S. Indian Police Academy was established at Roswell, New Mexico, in 1968, training for tribal officers was extremely limited. The program was designed to train Bureau of Indian Affairs and tribal law enforcement officers.

Policing Indian Country

There were more than 200 tribal police departments operating in Indian Country under the direction of the Bureau of Indian Affairs Division of Law Enforcement Services as of 2011. These tribal police departments serve a wide range of geographic locations ranging from small communities to very large nations, such as the Navajo Nation, which has a population of more than 250,000 members and covers 26,000 square miles, occupying parts of Arizona, New Mexico, and Utah.

The concept of tribal police can be traced back to the 1880s when John Q. Tufts was Indian commissioner of the Five Civilized Tribes, which consisted of the Choctaw, Cherokee, Chickasaw, Creek, and Seminole. Commissioner Tufts organized the first U.S. Indian Police force that would operate under the direction of the Indian agent assigned to the Union Agency. Many of the U.S. Indian police officers were given deputy U.S. marshal commissions that allowed them to cross jurisdictional boundaries and arrest non-Indians. These early commissions laid the foundation for the idea of cross-deputization.

Many of these early tribal police were recruited from the Indian Light Horsemen, a band of men who operated in enforcing the laws of the individual tribes throughout the vast lawless territories. These units were known as the Cherokee Light Horsemen, Choctaw Light Horsemen, Chickasaw Light Horsemen, and Seminole Light Horsemen. This early form of frontier police officers can be traced back to "Light-Horse Harry," a nickname given to General Henry Lee III, because of his rapid cavalry readiness during the American Revolution. During the American Revolution, Lee served as a cavalry officer in the

Continental army; he is the father of Confederate general Robert E. Lee. A light horseman is a soldier of the light cavalry, which was lightly armed, equipped, or horsed and so was especially mobile. The light horsemen were given considerable latitude when enforcing the judgments of the court. Much reliance was placed upon their on-the-spot discretion while enforcing the law, which many times gave rise to individual interpretation as to how the law would be enforced.

American Indian tribal governments were spawned from the rights of inherent sovereignty, not from the U.S. Constitution. Moreover, the creation of tribal police and tribal courts were by the U.S. Department of Interior's Bureau of Indian Affairs in the 1900s, which focused on controlling Indians and breaking up tribal leadership and tribal governments. One of the most famous encounters between tribal police and resistant Indians was when officers confronted a Hunkpapa Sioux holy man in 1890 that resulted in the killing of Sitting Bull. The arrest of Sitting Bull came under the direction of U.S. Indian agent James McLaughlin, who ordered the arrest of Sitting Bull based on his fear that Sitting Bull was preparing to flee the reservation because of the Sioux Indian belief in the Ghost Dance.

Modern Tribal Police

Tribal police are responsible for large tracts of land and operate with minimum resources. Police training is often limited and receives little to no federal help. A 2003 report produced by the U.S. Civil Rights Commission found that per capita spending on law enforcement in Indian communities was roughly 60 percent of the U.S. average, while the U.S. Department of Justice reports that crime victimization rates in Indian communities are significantly higher than in the U.S. population at large and more than twice as high as in African American communities. The structuring of tribal police departments in Indian Country can be founded in Public Law 93-638. Under this framework of law, tribes have the opportunity to establish traditional functioning governments contracting with the Bureau of Indian Affairs (BIA). Typically, the contract establishes the department's organizational framework and performance standards and provides basic funding for police operations. Officers and staff of these departments are tribal employees. This relationship with the federal government makes all officers and staff federal employees. According to the National Congress of American Indians (NCAI), tribal police departments are faced with a litany of obstacles such as complicated jurisdictional networks answering to multiple authorities, operating with limited resources, and patrolling some of the most desolate territory in the United States, often without assistance from partner law enforcement agencies.

At present, there are approximately 3,000 BIA and tribal uniformed officers available to serve an estimated 20 million Indians covering more than 56 million acres of tribal lands in the contiguous 48 states. In the United States and in Indian Country, tribes may be getting new officers, without hiring any new ones as part of a cross-deputization agreement. Historically, the relationship between tribes and the United States has been strained. Tribes do not have criminal jurisdiction over non–tribal members, and the state does not have criminal jurisdiction over tribal members. The heart of the cross-deputization agreement provides the ability for officers, both tribal and nontribal, to make arrests and sort out any jurisdictional issues later. Moreover, cooperative agreements surrounding jurisdiction are not new. Deputization and mutual aid agreements have been used and proved to be instrumental in exercising law enforcement in Indian Country.

Tribal relations in the United States have greatly improved over the past couple of decades. The need for better government-to-government relations is paramount. As trust and understanding build between tribal, state, and local governments, cooperation agreements will become more in demand. The use of cooperative law enforcement agreements, especially at a time when states are faced with huge economic deficits, becomes a win-win situation for all parties concerned.

Despite the benefits of these special arrangements, situations still exist that may serve to stall cooperative law enforcement efforts in Indian Country. The local sheriff is under no obligation to deputize tribal officers. Thus, the deputization is at the sheriff's pleasure, and a change of office, general dislike, or distrust may impair the ability of tribal law enforcement officers to receive special deputy status. For these and other reasons, a statewide solution or a state police agreement might be a better option to pursue, to reinforce tribal law enforcement authority to enforce state laws against nonnatives on reservation land.

Conclusion

Native American tribal police have a very long and well-documented past. Tribal police first operated in the post–Revolutionary War period, where early light horsemen worked to provide law and order in a vast lawless land with few resources available to them, and have continued to the 21st century, where Native American tribal police still attempt to provide law and order in vast areas with little resources. Cross-deputization has afforded some nations the cooperation and additional resources to join together with nonnative police departments to provide a broader net of services and protection.

William T. Jones
State University of New York, Canton

See Also: Frontier Crime; Native Americans; Peltier, Leonard.

Further Readings

Blurton, David M. "*John v. Baker* and the Jurisdiction of Tribal Sovereigns Without Territorial Reach." *Alaska Law Review* (June 2003).

Bobee, Hannah, Allison Boisvenu, Anderson Duff, Kathryn E. Fort, and Weona T. Singel. "Criminal Jurisdiction in Indian Country: The Solution of Cross Deputization." Michigan State University College of Law. http://www.law.msu.edu/indigenous/papers/2008-01.pdf (Accessed September 2011).

Luna-Firebaugh, Eileen. "Tribal Policing: Asserting Sovereignty, Seeking Justice." http://www.bsos.umd.edu/gvpt/lpbr/subpages/reviews/luna-firebaugh0707.htm (Accessed September 2011).

Native Americans

The term *Native American* is clouded with controversy. The *Oxford Dictionary* defines "Native American" as "a member of any of the indigenous peoples of the Americas." Therefore, any culture or race of people that existed prior to the "discovery" of American in 1492 would be classified as Native American.

Historically, Native American tribal members were governed more by societal taboos and traditions than by rules and laws. Ceremonies would be held to try to "heal" those who went against these norms. This entry will focus on the experience of Native Americans living in the United States after the arrival of explorers and colonists.

In the 1970s, the academic world began promoting the term *Native American* as a politically correct alternative to Indian. The term *Indian* was the most used and recognized label when referring to indigenous peoples of the United States. Historically, the creation of the word *Indian* is credited to Christopher Columbus, an Italian-Spanish navigator who sailed from Spain searching for a route to Asia. After 36 days at sea, Columbus's little flotilla reached land. It is still disputed today as to where Columbus actually landed, but the little island called Guanghani by its inhabitants seems to be the most favored by historians. Columbus renamed this island San Salvador. Columbus's voyage, although courageous in nature, has a very dark religious side that has been suppressed from traditional history books used to educate American students. When Columbus landed on Guanghan Island, he performed a ceremony to take possession of the land in the name of Spain. Columbus was acting under the international laws of Western Christendom. These are based on religious doctrines. These doctrines today are referred to as the Doctrine of Discovery. This archaic Judeo-Christian doctrine is still employed by the U.S. government to deny the rights of Native American Indians.

In 1452, Pope Nicholas V presented King Alfonso V of Portugal the bull Romanus Pontifex, which officially declared war against all non-Christians throughout the world and sanctioned and promoted exploration of new lands of these non-Christian nations. Theological and legal doctrines drafted during the time of the Crusades set forth a clear message that non-Christians were enemies of the Catholic faith and were identified as less than human. In the bull of 1452, Pope Nicholas ordered King Alfonso to "capture, vanquish, and subdue the saracens, pagans, and other enemies of Christ"; to "put them into perpetual slavery"; and to "take all their possessions and property."

Iroquois tribe members pose for a portrait in Buffalo, New York, in 1914. The Iroquois lived in the upper and central area of the Mohawk Valley and the lake region of central New York. Some historians believe that the Iroquois Confederacy of the people of the Five Nations, the oldest known participatory democracy, influenced the U.S. Constitution.

Columbus set sail in 1492 armed with the understanding that he was authorized to take control of and possess any land he discovered if that land was not occupied by a Christian ruler. After Columbus returned from his voyage, Pope Alexander VI issued an additional papal document, the bull Inter Cetera of May 3, 1493, which granted to Spain the right to conquer the lands that Columbus had already found or that would be discovered in the future.

What can be learned at this point is that the papal bulls of 1452 and 1493 provided the authority sanctioned by the church that Christian power could and would serve as a weapon of mass destruction involving indigenous people, thereby creating a divine fight based on the Bible to conquer and claim absolute title to and ultimate authority over newly discovered non-Christian habitants and their lands.

Doctrine of Discovery
In 1823 Chief Justice John Marshall, writing for the U.S. Supreme Court in *Johnson v. McIntosh*, in a unanimous decision pontificated that Christian European nations had assumed "ultimate dominion" over the lands of America during the Age of Discovery and that the early inhabitants upon discovery had "surrendered any fights to complete sovereignty, as independent peoples or nations." Chief Justice Marshall clearly articulated that Indians only retained a right of "occupancy" in their lands. Moreover, Marshall outlined that the United States upon victory for independence in 1776 had acquired the power of dominion from Great Britain, which set up the passing of the right of discovery to the United States.

It is important to note that a long, tremulous battle has raged in government addressing the church and state separation. The framers of the Constitution saw the need to keep the two separated. However, Chief Justice Marshall's decision in *McIntosh v. Johnson* laid the foundation for making the Christian Doctrine of Discovery for U.S. Indian policy into U.S. law that is still viable today.

Indian tribes have been an important part of American history. The U.S. Constitution makes a direct reference to Indian tribes in Article I Section 8 Clause 3, more commonly referred to as the commerce clause, stating "Congress shall have the power to regulate commerce with foreign nations, and among the several states, and with the Indian tribes." During this early time, it has been estimated that approximately 35 million people lived in North America, which included Mexico and Canada. Native governments were in full political operation, controlling the day-to-day activities within each nation's territory. Benjamin Franklin, one of the most famous framers of the U.S. Constitution, documented his observations of the Haudenosaunee government in 1783, just four years before the 1787 Philadelphia Convention began to draft the new constitution. Franklin was fascinated with the five nations (Mohawk, Oneida, Onondaga, Seneca, and Cayuga) method of government. The people of the Five Nations, also known by the

French term *Iroquois Confederacy*, comprised the oldest participatory democracy on Earth. In the early 18th century, a sixth nation was added. The Tuscaroras became part of the Haudenosaunee, which when translated means "People Building Long House."

On June 11, 1776, Iroquois chiefs were invited to speak at the meeting hall of the Continental Congress. During this meeting one, of the chiefs addressing the members stated that "we are all brothers" and that "the friendship between them would continue as long as the sun shall shine and the waters run." It was at this time that Acting President Hancock was given an Indian name by an Onondaga chief. The president's name would be "Karanduawn" or "the Great Tree." Iroquois ideas had a major impact on the founders. The European countries that colonized North America negotiated with Indian tribes through official government-to-government council sessions and by entering treaties, which recognized tribal governmental control over the territory of this emerging world. The underlying motive behind these early European encounters with natives was to procure their land in what would appear to be legitimate land transactions. Thus, the creation of treaties with Indian tribes would provide an official and legal document giving force to the land acquisition and provide a way of demonstrating a relationship between the two parties if any European country would contest or object to these land sales.

The United States for the most part adopted this traditional treaty process with Indian tribes. The method recognized the tribes as sovereign governments not aligned or affiliated with any European powers. The power of Indian tribes in the 1700s and 1800s was a power that the U.S. government realized could be a serious threat. The U.S. government negotiated and signed approximately 385 treaties with a variety of Indian tribes. These early treaties between the U.S. government and the Indian Nation had the force of a legal binding contract between "two sovereign nations."

Constitutional Rights and Laws

The first U.S. Congress, formed under a new constitution in 1789–91, enacted four statutes concerning Indian affairs. In 1789, Congress established a Department of War with responsibility over Indian affairs, which in turn set monies aside to negotiate Indian treaties and appointed federal commissioners to oversee the treaty process. By July 1790, Congress passed a law that forbid states (13 at the time) and individuals from dealing with Indians and tribes over land sales. This law is still in effect today.

The Constitution makes reference to Indian tribes but it is not expressly designated as it is in Article VI, where it is made clear that all treaties entered into by the United States "shall be the supreme law of the land." Thereby a strict interpretation of Article VI would yield that the federal government's treaties with Indian tribes are the supreme law of the United States. The exclusion of American Indians can be seen in the Constitution's method of counting the population of a state to determine how many representatives a state can have in Congress. Indians were expressly not to be counted unless they paid taxes. Conversely, Indians were not considered to be federal or state citizens unless they paid taxes. There were three "Civil War Amendments Passed by Congress" at the end of the Civil War: the Thirteenth, Fourteenth, and Fifteenth Amendments. These new amendments were put in place to handle citizenship rights. The Fourteenth Amendment extended citizen rights to ex-slaves and "[a]ll persons born or naturalized in the United States." That amendment still excluded individual Indians from U.S. citizenship rights; additionally, it excluded all Indians from being counted toward congressional representation with the caveat of taxpaying Indians. This exclusion clearly demonstrated Congress's position that Indians, unless taxpaying, were considered citizens of other sovereign governments in the year 1868 when the Fourteenth Amendment was ratified. Moreover, in 1897, Massachusetts Senator Henry L. Dawes put forth a comprehensive piece of legislation designed to put an end to the "Indian problem" in the United States. Congress passed the General Allotment Act, which was designed to impose private property ownership on Indians by dividing their reservations into individual farms. The General Allotment Act soon became known as the Dawes Act. The act was part of a broader federal policy designed to assimilate Indians into mainstream America and was coupled with government-sponsored education programs and Christian mission work. Under the Dawes Act's terms, the president used his discretion to indentify which reservations would undergo allotment in severalty. Scholars generally agree that the Dawes Act was poorly implemented and that it failed to achieve its assimilationist goals. Congress officially overturned the act in 1934 and indefinitely extended the trust period on existing allotments. Although the Dawes Act was intended to be the solution to the "Indian problem," it has instead generated more ongoing court battles that are still in existence today. The relationship between Indians and the U.S. government continued to escalate. The question on the lips of politicians and citizens was: What are we going do to with those Indians? They are not citizens of the United States, and they cannot be a foreign nation within the U.S. borders.

For the next 56 years, this view would resound in U.S. government, with a few exceptions. However, the defining moment came in 1924 when Congress passed the Indian Citizenship Act, also known as the Snyder Act. New York State representative Homer P. Snyder proposed granting full U.S. citizenship to Indians who had not already become citizens through entering the armed forces, giving up tribal affiliations, and assimilating into mainstream American society. The 1924 act was not a panacea for Native Americans. Many obstacles still remained in place. The Indian Citizenship Act provided only a quasi-citizenship for Native Americans, although more than 10,000 Indians from many different nations had served in the military and fought in World War I. The passage of the 1924 Indian Citizenship Act should have guaranteed Indians the same constitutional rights that were afforded to U.S. citizens. However, the First Amendment, which provides for freedom of religion, was not realized for Native Americans for another 50 years.

In 1934, two major pieces of legislation were enacted that affected Native Americans: the Indian Reorganization Act and the Johnson-O'Malley Act. John Collier, commissioner of Indian affairs from 1933 to 1945, brought the plight and struggles of native peoples to the forefront of the political environment. In 1926, the Institute for Government Research (IGR) authorized the Meriam Report, which served as a survey on Indian affairs in the United States. Lewis Meriam had been appointed to oversee the survey teams that were responsible for collecting information regarding the conditions of American Indians. Meriam's 847-page report served as the first major study on the status on Indians in the United States. This report was the catalyst for the 1934 Indian Reorganization Act with the exposing of the government's failure to meet its goal of protecting Native Americans, their land, and their resources. The Meriam Report emphasized the need for education in Indian country. However, the survey teams expressed that education should stress assimilation of Indian children into civilization rather than separating them from other white children as previous education policies had stressed. The report was extremely critical of Indian boarding schools. Native American boarding schools were created by the U.S. government as a means to force assimilation on Indian children.

Indian Boarding Schools

One of the most famous Indian boarding schools was founded in 1897 in Carlisle, Pennsylvania, by Captain Richard Henry Pratt. The school was the first off-reservation boarding school, which became a model for Indian boarding schools. Captain Pratt analogized Indian education with that of raising wild turkeys, stating that if the eggs are taken from the nest where they would be raised and placed in a nest of a domesticated turkey, the fledglings would then grow to be domesticated. Conversely, remove the Indian child, earlier in life the better, put him/her in an environment with kind treatment, and a domestic civilized child will emerge. The root of Pratt's ideology was to remove or erase as much as possible any trace of Native American customs, culture, language, and religion from the children at the school. Pratt's most notable statement was "kill the Indian, save the man." The Carlisle School was just one of as many as 26 Indian boarding schools across the country that operated under the direction of the Bureau of Indian Affairs (BIA). In addition, there were more than 450 Christian missionary schools that were in operation.

Indian boarding schools have a mixed legacy. Proponents point to the positive accomplishments that were gained from these forced assimilation academies. Detractors point to the thousands of

Indian children who died of infectious diseases that were common during the early 20th century. Beatings were a common form of punishment for students grieving or speaking their natural language. It was common practice to wash the mouths of Indian children with lye soap for speaking their tribal languages.

Although the United States wears a black eye from the early operation of Carlisle Indian School under the direction of Captain Pratt, Pratt also authorized a second school for Native American children, Chemawa Indian School located in Salem, Oregon. Opened on February 25, 1880, as an elementary school, the Chemawa Indian School is the oldest continuously operating Native American boarding school in the United States. In 2005, Chemawa Indian School formed a partnership with Willamette University, a private liberal arts college in Salem. While the government and religious schools aggressively sought to wipe out Indian culture, their attempts generally met with failure. Indian students refused to assimilate then, and for the most part now, into white society.

Native American Sovereignty

The United States struggled deeply with the idea of multiple sovereign dependent tribes existing within its boundaries. Although these tribes retained their quasi-independence gained through the treaty process, many political voices proclaimed a need to abolish federal supervision over tribal residents and subject the Indians to the same laws, privileges, and responsibilities as other U.S. citizens. On August 1, 1953, the U.S. Congress passed House Concurrent Resolution 108 (HCR-108), which declared that the United States had abolished federal supervision over Indian tribes. HCR-108 was passed concurrently with Public Law 280, which granted state jurisdiction over civil and criminal offenses committed by or upon Native Americans in Indian Territory

The Albuquerque Indian School was established in 1881 to provide an off-reservation primary school education to Native Americans from the southwestern United States, eventually housing 800 students through 12th grade. In 1886, the Bureau of Indian Affairs assumed control of the school from the the Presbyterian Home Mission Board. The Albuquerque Indian School operated until 1982, when its program was transferred to the Santa Fe Indian School.

in the states of Nebraska, Oregon, Wisconsin, Minnesota, and California, all states with large Indian populations. Public Law 280 is a federal law establishing a mandate that transfers federal law enforcement authority within certain tribal nations. Other states were allowed to elect similar transfer of power if the Indian tribes affected gave their consent.

From 1953 to 1964, the U.S. government terminated a total of 109 tribes as bands of sovereign dependent nations. The terminations of tribes extinguished their ancestral rights to land, hunting, and fishing as well as ended their tribal rights as sovereign nations. It also terminated all federal support to healthcare, education programs, and police and fire departments that existed on Indian lands. The tribes initially selected for termination had been considered to be groups who were the most successful in the self-determination process. Tribes did not favor Public Law 280, and scholars have written volumes stating that the termination policy had devastating effects on tribal autonomy, culture, and economic welfare. Lands rich in resources were taken over by the federal government and stripped of any value. By 1972, termination clearly had destroyed any educational system that had been put in place earlier. States were expected to assume the role of educating Indian children, and it was all too clear that the state educational systems were struggling to meet current demands without the added number of Indian children who had never been inside a public school.

Indian tribes spent the next decades repealing the effects that termination had placed on their society. By the 1960s, federal leaders began opposing the implementation of termination. Presidents Lyndon B. Johnson and Richard Nixon encouraged Indian self-determination instead of termination.

Indian Bill of Rights Act

The U.S. Supreme Court held in *Talton v. Mayes* (1896) that Indian tribal governments were not subject to restraints placed on the federal and state governments by the Constitution and the Bill of Rights. The Indian Bill of Rights extends 10 restrictions derived from the U.S. Bill of Rights and other parts of the U.S. Constitution. These comprise freedoms of speech, press, assembly, petition, religion, and security against unreasonable searches and seizures, accompanied by the requirement of a search warrant; freedom from double jeopardy; guarantees against self-incrimination, excessive bail and fines, and cruel and unusual punishment; prohibition of taking private property without just compensation; in modified form, the criminal procedure protections of the Sixth Amendment; the due process and equal protection clauses; prohibition of bills of attainder and ex post facto laws; and guarantee of a six-person criminal jury trial. Congress chose to limit its intrusion into tribal sovereignty by omitting certain other securities such as the right to be a republican form of government, the ban on religious establishments, the requirement of free counsel for indigent criminal defendants, the right to jury trial in civil cases, and the immunities clauses.

The Indian Civil Rights Act is best known for extending part of the Bill of Rights to individual Indians against tribal governments. Moreover, the Indian Civil Rights Act goes further than the language of the Bill of Rights in that it guarantees "equal protection of the law," something absent from the U.S. Constitution before the ratification of the Fourteenth Amendment. It also denies tribal governments the power to pass ex post facto laws and bills of attainder, provisions that have the power to imprison tribal members for a term greater than six months. Traditional governments did not practice imprisonment at all, supporting the idea of restorative justice; Native American justice is based on healing along with reintegrating individuals into their community. Native American justice involves bringing together victims, offenders, and their supporters to resolve a problem. Restorative justice looks beyond retribution to find deeper solutions that heal broken relationships.

Clashes With Federal Government

Richard Oakes, a Mohawk native, is credited with organizing a group of students and Indian supporters setting sail on November 20, 1969, in a chartered boat, the *Monte Cristo*, to symbolically claim Alcatraz Island in the name of all Indian people. The symbolic occupation lasted for 19 months, ending June 11, 1971. President Nixon ordered federal marshals, Federal Bureau of Investigation (FBI) agents, and Special Forces to retake the island from the remaining occupiers. Approximately 15 people were removed on that day. As a result of the occupation, the American public was reawakened to the plight of American Indians, giving birth to a political movement that continues today.

Native American clashes with state and federal government officials have continued throughout the 20th century, including the siege at Wounded Knee in 1973, which has roots in the original massacre that took place on December 29, 1890, at Wounded Knee Creek located on the Lakota Pine Ridge Indian Reservation in South Dakota. The events that occurred on December 29, 1890, are well documented in military dispatches, photographs, and eyewitness accounts. Scholars have questioned if this was a historical battle or a well-planned massacre to avenge the earlier demise of General Armstrong Custer and his 7th Cavalry. In February 1973, the American Indian movement and the Lakota Nation made a final stand for Indian rights with a siege at Wounded Knee that lasted 71 days. The foundation for the siege grew when American Indians stood against the U.S. government, which ended in an armed battle with U.S. troops. Corruption within the Bureau of Indian Affairs and Tribal Council was at an all-time high. Tension on Pine Ridge Indian Reservation was on the increase and quickly became out of control. The creation of the American Indian Movement (AIM) was instrumental in shaping the path of American Indians across the country, and the eyes of the world followed AIM protests through the occupation at Alcatraz Island to the 71-day standoff at Wounded Knee, which was sparked by the exploitation of more than 100 years of racial tension and U.S. government mishandling of relations with Native Americans. The siege at Wounded Knee was followed by what historians call the "Reign of Terror" from the U.S. government instigated by the FBI and the BIA. During the three years that followed, 64 tribal members were killed, hundreds were harassed and beaten, and more than 562 arrests were made, with only 15 people actually being convicted of any crime. A large price was paid for those 71 days of sovereignty on the land of the Lakota ancestors.

On March 30, 1990, at the Ganienkeh Reservation in Altona, New York, a rural community located about 500 miles north of New York City, as a medivac helicopter operated by the Vermont Army National Guard flew over the Indian territory, shots were fired by a tribal member using a hunting rifle at a civilian doctor, forcing the aircraft to land in a field on Ganienkeh property. After a 10-day siege, the governor was able to negotiate an agreement, releasing the helicopter and crew with no additional injuries.

Contemporary Native Americans

In recent times, Indian tribes have consistently engaged in business enterprises as a means of generating revenue for the operation of their tribal governments. Gambling, in a variety of forms, has traditionally been part of the culture of Native Americans. Today, gambling provides many nations with the much-needed revenue to meet their infrastructural needs. The Indian Gaming Regulatory Act (IGRA), passed by Congress in 1988, provided the gateway to self-determination. The IGRA represents an attempt by Congress to balance the rights of tribes engaging in activities generally free of state jurisdiction and the interests of states in regulating gaming activities within the tribe's territory. It can be argued that the balance was not struck. The U.S. Supreme Court in a case between California and the Cabazon Band of Mission Indians disagreed with California's argument. The court's decision turned on the fact that the civil part of Public Law 280 did not grant states jurisdiction to regulate Indian activities on reservations. It granted state courts the jurisdiction to hear and decide cases involving Indian parties in states that generally prohibited gambling but allowed some forms of gambling for charitable organizations or state lotteries. Indian tribes could also engage in these forms of gaming.

The decision in *Cabazon* set the stage for the IGRA. As stated, Indian gaming has become an important means of support for tribal governments; however, this has come with a cost and division of traditional and progressive members of tribal communities. Indian gaming law specifically will continue to grow and evolve in years to come. At present, there are Indian casinos operating in 28 states by 233 different nations. There are currently more than 400 Indian gaming facilities generating almost $30 billion and providing over 1 million jobs for native and nonnative people.

In 1990, Congress passed the Native American Grave Protection and Repatriation Act (NAGPRA). This act provides a process for museums and federal agencies to return certain Native American cultural items, human remains, funeral objects, sacred objects, or objects of cultural patrimony. Moreover, NAGPRA authorizes federal grants to Indian tribes, Native Hawai'ian organizations, and museums to assist with the documentation and repatriation of Native American cultural items. With the passage of NAGPRA, Indian nation burial sites are now protected, making it a crime to disturb present and ancestral burial sites.

Conclusion
The history of Native Americans has generated a plethora of political and scholarly discourse. At the time of discovery, Native Americans numbered between 20 million and 30 million; today, there are an estimated 2.5 million documented Native Americans living in and around reservation land. The framework of this tapestry is determination. Native Americans are proud people who have endured diseases, removal, termination, and assimilation into white society. Today, Indian numbers are growing; the idea of self-determination has taken hold, giving rise to a growing number of nations that now provide industry, education, healthcare, housing, and an infrastructure that can support the needs of the community.

William T. Jones
State University of New York, Canton

See Also: 1600 to 1776 Primary Documents; 1801 to 1850 Primary Documents; 1851 to 1900 Primary Documents; 1921 to 1940 Primary Documents; Constitution of the United States of America; Native American Tribal Police; Peltier, Leonard; Supreme Court, U.S.

Further Readings
Deloria, Vine, Jr., and Daniel R. Wildcat. *Power and Place: Indian Education in America*. Golden, CO: Fulcrum Publishing, 2001.
Miller, Robert J. *Native America Discovered and Conquered: Thomas Jefferson, Lewis and Clark, and Manifest Destiny*. Winnipeg, Canada: Bison Books, 2008.
Wilkins, David E. and Tsianian Lomawaima. *Uneven Ground: American Indian Sovereignty and Federal Law*. Norman: University of Oklahoma Press, 2002.

Nebraska

A Great Plains state, Nebraska is one of the country's leading agricultural producers and was initially settled primarily by homesteaders claiming free land granted in the 1860s. When the territory was first organized, there were few laws governing it, and "claim clubs" were organized by those who had land claims in any given area. The Omaha Claim Club, organized by settlers around what would become Nebraska's biggest city, first met in 1854 and appointed R. B. Whitted the city's first sheriff, as well as designating a number of other city officials. The primary goal of the claim clubs initially was to protect against illegal claim jumpers, which was the biggest concern for the first settlers. The territorial legislature was comprised mainly of claim club members, and the concerns of claims clubs and town government soon broadened. By the 1860s, Omaha police were directed to wear uniforms, and the department gradually became more organized and professionalized. In 1923, Omaha organized a separate motor force unit, installed call boxes throughout the city (many of which remain in service), and created the first American safety patrol, to protect children walking to school.

Crime
Omaha has experienced a range of crime trends over its history, with gambling and prostitution rampant in its early days as a frontier town. The Burnt District was the city's red-light district in the late 19th century and was home to about 100 brothels and saloons—many of them little more than shacks with mattresses—employing sex workers. At one point, about a third of the adult male population was estimated to have a sexually transmitted disease, which contributed to the district finally being shut down around the turn of the century. It was succeeded by the Sporting District, overseen by political boss Tom Dennison.

A Nebraska family in front of their sod house in 1886. The state was settled in large part by homesteaders claiming free land grants. The Omaha Claim Club was organized in 1854 to protect members' claims in the Nebraska Territory.

Dennison ran the city's brothels, gambling houses, and—once Prohibition began—bootlegging. He may have been responsible for inciting the Omaha Race Riot of 1919, though he was never found guilty of this.

The 1919 riots preceded by two years the establishment of the second Ku Klux Klan in Omaha but were the latest in a long history of incidents sparked by racial tensions. The African American population had doubled in the previous decade, and white workers were angry at having to compete with them for jobs, and especially at the use of African Americans as strikebreakers by the local meatpackers. When the local paper (controlled by Dennison) reported the rape of a 19-year-old white girl by a 40-year-old black man, Will Brown—though later reports by the police department said she had not positively identified him as her attacker—and presented it as merely the latest in a series of attacks that the newly elected mayor was unable to prevent, a riot was stirred up, culminating in Brown's lynching and numerous intentional and accidental killings and assaults, as well as a siege of the courthouse.

Nebraska's crime rate, at 279 violent crimes per 100,000 inhabitants in 2010, is well below the national average. While the national crime rate climbed sharply in the 1970s and 1990s before falling, Nebraska's has remained somewhat steady since an initial climb from the mid-1960s to the mid-1970s (rising from 64 to 239 from 1966 to 1974). While it rose over the course of the 1990s, it didn't rise as high as in many other states; the decline since then has been gradual, with an uptick (281 to 310) corresponding to the 2007–08 financial crisis, during which Nebraska suffered from rising fuel costs and commodity crop price volatility.

Punishment

Nebraska is a capital punishment state and has executed a total of 37 people, three of them since the rewriting of death penalty statutes after the 1970s Supreme Court rulings. Public hanging was the method of execution until 1913, when use of the electric chair was mandated. Since 2009, when the Nebraska Supreme Court declared electrocution cruel and unusual punishment, lethal injection has been the state's method of execution. Juries decide whether a case of murder in the first degree will be classed as a Class I felony, carrying the death penalty, or a Class IA felony, punished by a life sentence without possibility of parole. Juveniles and the mentally unfit are exempt from execution.

The most famous execution in Nebraska was that of Charles Starkweather, whose killing spree with his girlfriend in 1958 captured the public imagination and inspired the movies *Badlands*, *True Romance*, *Natural Born Killers*, and *The Frighteners*, as well as the Bruce Springsteen song *Nebraska* and elements of Stephen King's work. An 18-year-old high school dropout fascinated by James Dean in the movie *Rebel Without a Cause*, Starkweather took a job at a newspaper warehouse because it was near Whittier Junior High School in Lincoln, where 13-year-old Caril Ann Fugate was a student. Starkweather had just met Fugate and the two soon began a relationship. When he lost his job at the warehouse, he began working as a garbage collector and spent time plotting bank robberies. His first known act of serious violence seems almost random—on December 1, 1957, he shot to death a gas station attendant for having refused to accept credit the previous day when Starkweather tried to buy Fugate a stuffed dog.

Weeks later, an argument with Fugate's parents ended with their ordering Starkweather to stay away from their daughter; Starkweather fatally shot both of them and stabbed to death their 2-year-old daughter, Fugate's half-sister. He confessed to Fugate when she came home from school, and they hid the bodies and remained in the house for a week until relatives became suspicious. Fleeing when the police arrived, Starkweather and Fugate took to the road to evade capture, killing numerous people they encountered. Starkweather's account of events after the fact changed many times; at first, both he and Fugate insisted he had held her hostage, but at her trial he testified that she had been a willing participant and multiple murderer. Starkweather was tried for only one of the murders but received the death penalty; Fugate received a life sentence and was paroled in 1976.

While still a territory, the Nebraska government addressed the issue of constructing a prison, relying on county jails until the need could be met. A plan to house inmates in other states' prisons was explored but never implemented, and the costs of the Civil War made it impossible to receive federal money to construct a penitentiary, despite repeated requests. A temporary prison was finally built in 1870 on land appropriated south of the capital of Lincoln. The first permanent prison, the West Cell House, was built in 1876, and remained in operation until 1980.

Since the 1980s, Nebraska prisons have been over capacity and are projected to be 55 percent over capacity in 2015. More than half of Nebraska's inmates are incarcerated for nonviolent crimes. Advocates have been calling for prison reforms for years, and have received support from the federally funded Vera Institute of Justice, which found Nebraska's criminal law reforms of the 1980s and 1990s to be at fault. During that period, influenced by the war on drugs and nationwide concerns over crime, limits were placed on parole, and mandatory minimum sentencing was enacted for many crimes, among other changes. While crime rates fell—as they did nationwide—prison populations and expenses soared. From 1990 to 2005, the cost of Nebraska incarcerations more than quadrupled, and the prison population grew 3.5 times as fast as the state population. The first steps in reducing prison overpopulation came in 2003, when voluntary sentencing guidelines—eliminating many mandatory minimums—were adopted, with the stated goal of keeping Nebraska's crowded prisons a place for the violent offenders who posed the greatest risk to public safety and emphasizing community-based sanctions for nonviolent offenders, especially first-time offenders. Drug laws were reformed first, because of drug offenders' disproportionate representation in prison. New laws also emphasized rehabilitation in order to avoid recidivism.

Nebraska is one of only six states to operate a prison nursery. The nursery at the Nebraska Correctional Center for Women opened in 1994, and inmates whose release date comes before their child turns 18 months old are allowed to have that child reside with them, in recognition of the critical bond that forms between mother and child in infancy.

Bill Kte'pi
Independent Scholar

See Also: Capital Punishment; Frontier Crime; Race-Based Crimes.

Further Readings

Gless, Alan G. *The History of Nebraska Law*. Athens: Ohio University Press, 2008.

Griffith, T. D. *Outlaw Tales of Nebraska: True Stories of the Cornhusker State's Most Infamous Crooks, Culprits, and Cutthroats*. Guilford, CT: Morris Book Publishing, 2010.

Luebke, F. C. *Nebraska: An Illustrated History*, 2nd ed. Winnipeg, Canada: Bison Books, 2005.

Nelson, "Baby Face"

Infamous car thief, bootlegger, and bank robber, George "Baby Face" Nelson was born under the name Lester Joseph Gillis in Chicago, Illinois, on December 6, 1908, to Joseph and Mary Gillis. Nelson lived in a neighborhood in Chicago's Near West Side, referred to as the Patch. At a young age, he engaged in various crimes, but most notable was the stealing of car parts and cars. By the early 1930s, Nelson elevated his criminal aspirations to bank robbery, and soon he became acquainted with many rising members of the Chicago mob, who may have employed Nelson as a syndicate gunman and chauffeur. Nelson, who also operated under the alias Jimmy Williams, gained some notoriety after he escaped from a train en route to the state prison at Joliet, Illinois, where he was intended to serve time for his second bank robbery conviction. The attention that his early criminal exploits drew from the American media was minor compared to the attention the press gave Nelson once John Dillinger joined his fledgling gang and enabled them to successfully pull off numerous bank robberies across several states. During his criminal career, Nelson killed several men, including three Federal Bureau of Investigation (FBI) agents, which made him one of the most notorious gangsters during the public enemy era of the 1930s.

On March 3, 1934, John Dillinger reportedly used a wooden pistol that was smuggled in to him so he could escape from the Crown Point jail with two hostages in Sheriff Lillian Holley's V-8 Ford. It was suspected that "Baby Face" Nelson, along with Homer Van Meter, fronted the bribe money necessary for Dillinger's successful escape. On the day following the escape, Dillinger joined up with Nelson's gang in Minneapolis, Minnesota. On the same day, Nelson murdered Theodore H. Kidder, which was supposedly the result of a minor car accident in St. Paul, Minnesota. Later information revealed that Kidder sold guns and ammunition illegally through his sporting goods store, so his death may have been the result of an arms transaction gone awry.

The Federal Bureau of Investigation's (FBI's) 1931 mug shot of Lester Gillis ("Baby Face" Nelson). The criminal killed more on-duty FBI agents than any other American citizen.

As a new member of Nelson's gang, Dillinger gladly accepted a secondary role. However, after the robbery of the Security National Bank in Sioux Falls, South Dakota, where the gang made off with $49,500 and Nelson wounded a policeman, the press referred to them as the second Dillinger gang. Dillinger's distinction in the newspapers angered an envious Nelson, whose ego was greatly injured by this snub. Nelson's hot-tempered nature often led Nelson to willingly shoot police and civilians, and he frequently threatened the lives of other members in the gang. Regardless of the difficulty Nelson presented to the gang, they were able to continue to rob banks and evade capture in several states, including Illinois, Iowa, Indiana, and Wisconsin.

After Dillinger was killed by federal agents on July 22, 1934, Nelson gathered his wife, Helen, and his son, Ronald, and fled to California. In November, Nelson returned with Helen to Lake Geneva, Wisconsin, to stay with a young bootlegger named John Paul Chase at Lake Como Hotel, which was operated by Hobart Hermanson. The FBI was tipped off about Nelson's intention to spend the winter there, and agents convinced Hermanson to allow them to use his house in an attempt to ambush Nelson. On November 27, 1934, a Ford, which the FBI mistook as Hermanson's, pulled into the driveway where the trap was being laid, but instead, it was manned by Nelson. Nelson fled the scene but soon encountered a carload of agents near the town of Fox River Grove, where Nelson turned around to chase the agents. Nelson's car was disabled by a shot to the radiator. A second FBI car closed up on Nelson's car at Barrington, Illinois, but both agents Samuel Cowley and Herman Hollis were killed by Nelson, even though he sustained 17 gunshot wounds from agents. Nelson managed to escape with his wife and Chase and found refuge at a friend's house in Skokie, Illinois. Nelson died, and his body was discovered the next day, wrapped in a blanket on the northeast corner of St. Paul's cemetery.

Brian G. Sellers
University of South Florida

See Also: Bootlegging; Dillinger, John; Federal Bureau of Investigation; Gangs, History of; Guns and Violent Crime.

Further Readings

Burrough, Bryan. *Public Enemies: America's Greatest Crime Wave and the Birth of the FBI, 1933–1934.* New York: Penguin Press, 2004.

Helmer, William and Rick Mattix. *Public Enemies: America's Criminal Past, 1919–1940.* New York: Facts on File, 1998.

Ness, Eliot

Eliot Ness (1903–57) was a Prohibition and Treasury Department agent; Cleveland, Ohio, public safety director; and leader of the famed Untouchables, upon which two TV series and the 1987 movie of the same name were based. Ness was born in Chicago to Peter and Emma Ness, Norwegian immigrants. Ness was a studious boy who grew up reading Arthur Conan Doyle's Sherlock Holmes books while working in his father's bakery. Ness attended the University of Chicago, where he played tennis and earned a degree in business. After graduation, he remained at the University of Chicago and earned his Ph.D. in 1925.

Ness's first job was at the Retail Credit Company, where for two years he investigated insurance claims and verified credit ratings. Inspired by his boyhood hero Sherlock Holmes and his Prohibition agent brother-in-law, Alexander Jaime, Ness later worked for the U.S. Treasury Department before transferring to the Department of Justice's Chicago Office as a Prohibition Agent.

Tracking Al Capone

In 1929, President Herbert Hoover instructed Secretary of the Treasury Andrew Mellon to bring gangster Al Capone's reign as king of the underworld to an end. The government launched a two-pronged attack against Capone. One strategy was to investigate Capone for failure to pay income taxes; the other was to bring him down for violations of the Volstead Act.

At the time, Prohibition agents at the Department of Justice had a dubious reputation as dishonest law enforcement officers. The agents were known as corrupt and easy to bribe, and Ness became frustrated with both the reputation and the inability of his fellow agents to effectively uphold the law and shut down the openly operating vice industry in Chicago. Through the efforts of his brother-in-law Jaime, Ness eventually gained an interview with U.S. District Attorney George E. Johnson, during which he attempted to sell his idea for enforcing Prohibition laws and cleaning up the Windy City. His idea was a simple one: Organize a small, hand-picked, elite squad of agents who possessed the necessary law enforcement and other skills to accomplish the job, along with one important qualification. Ness knew, more than anything else, this squad would have to be completely and unequivocally honest, unable to be bribed.

Ness's plan was approved, and he was put in charge of the unit. He poured through the records of all agents intently, eliminating those who did not fit his criteria and eventually narrowing the list down to nine. These nine, along with Ness as their leader, began their task of bringing down Capone, perhaps the nation's most infamous gangster.

Several successful raids against Capone breweries and distilleries brought a predictable reaction from Capone: buy off the $2,800-a-year agents who were attempting to shut down his empire. Capone made several attempts, with the amount of the bribe growing larger as Ness and his men declined Capone's offers. After one incident in which Ness and two of his men turned down $2,000 bribes, Ness, always on the lookout for positive publicity, called a press conference. He reported the bribe attempts and publicly vowed that they would topple the Capone empire. The Chicago press reported on the incidents and deemed Ness and his men "the Untouchables," honest agents who could not be bought. When bribery did not work, Capone tried violence, and various attempts were made on Ness and his men, also unsuccessful. Ness and his men continued on, conducting several successful raids and confiscating trucks, stills, brewing vats, and other equipment.

While Ness and his men's efforts were successful at hurting Capone's bootlegging operations, the income tax charges took precedence, and Capone was convicted for tax evasion in 1931 and sent to the federal prison in Atlanta, and later transferred to Alcatraz. The indictments returned that

A photographer captures truckloads of beer en route to Chicago being captured and destroyed in Zion City, Illinois, circa 1920. Prohibition (a U.S. ban on selling, manufacturing, or transporting alcohol) lasted from 1920 to 1933. Eliot Ness joined the Bureau of Prohibition in Chicago in 1926 and became the chief investigator of the Prohibition Bureau for Chicago.

were based on Prohibition violations were held in abeyance in case there were problems with the tax charges, but in the end were never used. After Capone's imprisonment, Ness was promoted to chief investigator of Prohibition Forces for the Chicago Division in 1932.

Service in Cleveland
In 1933, Ness was sent to Cincinnati as a revenue agent, charged with seeking out and destroying moonshine stills in the hills of Ohio, Kentucky, and Tennessee. From there, he became the investigator in charge of the Treasury Department's Alcoholic Tax Unit for the Northern District of Ohio. In November 1935, Harold Burton was elected mayor of Cleveland, running on a reform platform and promising to clean up corruption in the Cleveland Police Department. In early 1936, Ness was tapped by Burton for the task and was appointed Cleveland's public safety director. In Cleveland, Ness made considerable progress in reforming the police, modernizing the department's policies, personnel, equipment, and methods. He also made progress in cleaning up Cleveland's criminal element, especially in the organized crime district, the notorious Mayfield Road Mob, based in Cleveland's Little Italy. Ness's reputation with the public, however, began to suffer on two fronts, professional and personal.

Cleveland was plagued by a series of gruesome murders between 1935 and 1938 in what came to be known as the Cleveland Torso Murders or the Mad Butcher of Kingsbury Run, in which a dozen or so homeless transients had been found murdered, dismembered, and decapitated. There were two prime suspects in the case, one a former World War I surgeon who was said to have been skilled at amputation. Although the suspect failed two polygraph tests and was questioned by Ness personally, Ness claimed that there was not sufficient evidence to hold him on the charge, and he was released. The suspect was a cousin of one of Ness's and mayor Burton's prime political enemies, and his release prompted speculation of political corruption and possible blackmail. Although the murders eventually stopped, Ness did not catch his man in this case.

Ness's personal reputation began to suffer with his divorce from his first wife, Edna, and subsequent marriage to Evaline McAndrew, a Cleveland socialite originally from Chicago who was 10 years Ness's junior. Ness had buried himself in his work and neglected Edna, who finally left him and moved back to Chicago, something that did not seem to sit well with Cleveland's working class and largely ethnic population of the 1930s. When Ness and McAndrew married, however, they were often seen among the city's social elite in Cleveland's best restaurants and nightclubs. Ironically, the man who claimed the reputation of drying up Chicago during Prohibition had the reputation of being a regular and frequent drinker of alcohol in Cleveland. Ness had reportedly been drinking in the early morning hours on March 5, 1942, when he was involved in an automobile accident in which 21-year-old Robert Sims was injured. The accident was portrayed as a hit-and-run in the newspapers, although Ness said that he was concerned with his wife's well-being and he had spoken to Sims about following him in his car to the hospital. When he noticed that Sims was not behind him, Ness said that he returned to the scene, but Sims had been taken to the hospital by a passing motorist.

Ness's political enemies made the most of the accident, and Ness' reputation began to suffer. According to his friends, he had lost his enthusiasm for his job and his heart was no longer in his work. Soon after the accident, he resigned and left Cleveland. Ness later worked as director of social protection for the Federal Security Agency, and then entered the private sector as president of the Guaranty Paper Corporation and the Fidelity Check Corporation.

The Untouchables

In 1957, Ness teamed up with author and sportswriter Oscar Fraley to publish his memoirs, appropriately called *The Untouchables*. Eliot Ness died suddenly of a heart attack on May 16, 1957, shortly after approving the final galleys for the book, which became a best seller. *The Untouchables* also became a prime time TV series running on ABC from 1959 until 1963. Starring Robert Stack as Eliot Ness and narrated by Walter Winchell, the show was nominated for several awards and proved popular with viewers. In 1987, *The Untouchables* was produced as a motion picture based on Ness and Fraley's book, directed by Brian DePalma and starring Robert DeNiro, Sean Connery, and Kevin Costner as Ness. Paramount Television attempted to resurrect the series in syndication in 1993–94, starring Tom Amandes and William Forsythe, but it was not as successful as the original ABC TV series.

Paul Magro
Ball State University

See Also: Bootlegging; Capone, Al; Chicago, Illinois; Cleveland, Ohio; Moonshine; Nitti, Frank; Prohibition; Television, Police in; Volstead Act.

Further Readings
Bardsley, Marilyn. "Eliot Ness: The Man Behind the Myth." http://www.trutv.com/library/crime/gangsters_outlaws/cops_others/ness/1.html (Accessed August 2011).
Federal Bureau of Investigation. "A Byte Out of History, Elliot Ness and the FBI." http://www.fbi.gov/news/stories/2007/january/ness010307/?searchterm=ness (Accessed October 2010).
Federal Bureau of Investigation. "Ness, Eliot, Freedom of Information Act Webpage." http://foia.fbi.gov/ness.htm (Accessed October 2010).
Ness, Eliot and Oscar Fraley. *The Untouchables*. New York: Popular Library, 1960.
Sifakis, Carl. *The Mafia Encyclopedia*. New York: Checkmark Books, 1999.

Neutrality Enforcement in 1793–1794

At the beginning of his second term as president, George Washington and his administration had to confront a significant foreign policy crisis. France, which had overthrown its monarchy, declared war on Great Britain. Realizing its navy was weaker than Britain's, France sought U.S. assistance. To avoid entering the war, the Washington administration proclaimed neutrality. Enforcing neutrality proved challenging, however. Lacking military strength to stop U.S. citizens from joining French naval expeditions, the administration turned to law enforcement. This marked the first effort by the United States to enforce policy through criminal law.

Washington began his second term in March 1793, having spent his first term organizing the fledgling government and establishing precedents for future presidents. Between his election and inauguration, the people of France executed their king and declared war on Great Britain. The war presented a foreign policy crisis for Washington, because France sought assistance from the United States. During the American Revolution, the Americans signed a treaty with the French obliging the United States to repay its war debt to France over a period of time and prohibiting the United States from allowing France's enemies to use United States ports to arm ships to oppose France. Now, France sought advances on its debt and the use of U.S. ports to arm French merchant ships. The war also presented a problem for Washington because the nation divided over whose side to take in the war. Many preferred the British for business reasons. Merchants conducted most of their trade with the British and wanted to continue that relationship. Many Americans identified with the French Revolution, however. They likened the French struggle to their own. Without a unified nation, Washington knew a war would make the new nation vulnerable.

Washington's desire to maintain neutrality raised several fundamental questions. Did he have the power to declare neutrality? What did neutrality mean? Did the treaty with France require the United States to permit the French to recruit ships and sailors from the American public? If so, how could the United States remain neutral? To answer these questions, Washington tasked his cabinet to work out the details. Washington's cabinet debated enforcement options. Treasury Secretary Alexander Hamilton, who favored the British, advanced a policy whereby customs officials reported violations directly to Hamilton. Hamilton would forward the relevant information to the U.S. district attorneys to prosecute the cases. Secretary of State Thomas Jefferson, a strong proponent of France, argued that grand jurors were the proper body to present allegations of neutrality violations. With Hamilton and Jefferson unable to agree, Attorney General Edmund Randolph proposed a compromise whereby customs officials would report neutrality violations directly to the district attorneys. Washington approved Randolph's proposal.

Controversy Over the Debate
While the enforcement debate was ongoing during May 1793, France forced the United States to take immediate action. French privateers, using some U.S. sailors, captured several British ships off the Atlantic coast and brought them to U.S. ports, claiming them for France. This caused British protests, forcing the United States to resolve the problem. Negotiations with France brought initial success, but the seizures continued. In June 1793, Gideon Henfield, an American sailor, was arrested by Philadelphia law enforcement authorities for serving as a prizemaster aboard a French privateer. Similar incidents followed. The arrests created the need for a special federal grand jury. Attorney General Randolph and the U.S. district attorney for Pennsylvania, William Rawle, prepared the indictment. To do this, they had to determine the law Henfield violated. Lacking a statute, Randolph and Rawle relied upon the common law. They decided that Henfield's actions, because they risked war with Britain, breached the peace of the United States. Accordingly, they drafted an indictment against Henfield and used similar versions for other indictments returned by the special grand jury in July 1793. A few weeks later, a jury acquitted Henfield. Although disappointed with the verdict, the Washington administration determined that the verdict resulted from a lack of proof rather than an improper legal theory.

After Henfield's case, the administration continued neutrality enforcement through the courts. While never gaining popular support, the government obtained some convictions. More importantly, these efforts helped keep the United States out of war. Neutrality enforcement set the precedent for using criminal law to enforce policy. Four years later, President John Adams prosecuted political opponents for sedition. Nearly 100 years later, President Ulysses S. Grant would enforce civil rights policy through prosecution. Today, nearly every social policy is supported through criminal prosecution.

Scott Ingram
High Point University

See Also: Federal Common Law of Crime; Hamilton, Alexander; History of Crime and Punishment in America: 1783–1850; Jefferson, Thomas; Washington, George (Administration of).

Further Readings
Elkins, Stanley and Eric McKittrick. *The Age of Federalism: The Early American Republic, 1788–1800*. New York: Oxford University Press, 1993.
Henfield's Case. 11 F.Cas. 1139 (1793).
Reardon, John J. *Edmund Randolph: A Biography*. New York: Macmillan, 1975.
Thomas, Charles M. *American Neutrality in 1793: A Study in Cabinet Government*. New York: Columbia University Press, 1931.

Nevada

Nevada was admitted to the Union on October 31, 1864, despite the absence of characteristics typically associated with other territories admitted into statehood. Experts speculate as to the true reason Nevada was prematurely admitted to the Union; some credit the mining of precious metals during a costly Civil War, while others credit President Abraham Lincoln's reelection campaign. The fact remains that Nevada entered the Union under unique circumstances and as such has a distinct social history of social control. Over time, Nevada's history of crime, police, and punishment have come to resemble those of other states—with notable exceptions. The state of Nevada is a 110,540-square-mile landmass divided into 17 counties occupied by approximately 2.5 million residents. Laws regulating a multitude of things (including criminal behavior) are created in a process modeled after that of the federal government, due in large part to the dependence of the state on the federal government during its early days. Laws are written and ratified by a bicameral state legislature comprising the State Senate and the State Assembly, which are currently made up of 21 and 42 members, respectively. Laws passing both bodies are signed into law by the governor and can be ruled unconstitutional by the Nevada Supreme Court. One of the unique features of the Nevada legal system is a trifurcated criminal code consisting of misdemeanors, gross misdemeanors, and felonies; most other states have a two-level system (with misdemeanors and felonies). The laws in Nevada are similar to those of other states with the exception of two important exceptions, which have been associated with infamous crime problems in Nevada history: legalized prostitution and legalized gambling.

Prostitution and Gambling

Prostitution is legal under certain circumstances in Nevada and is regulated by the state; the most important restriction on prostitution is the prohibition against licensing brothels in counties with a population base of more than 400,000. Currently, there are approximately 35 state-regulated brothels operating in nine Nevada counties. Legalized prostitution was associated with one of the most infamous criminal scandals in state history: the indictment of Joe Conforte, owner of the first

The Chicken Ranch brothel, one of 35 state-regulated houses of prostitution in Nevada. It was opened 60 miles west of Las Vegas in Pahrump, Nevada, in 1976, as close to Las Vegas as regulations would allow.

state-regulated brothel, for tax evasion in the early 1990s. Conforte fled the country prior to being tried. In late 1999, the government seized the brothel, claiming it was purchased by a Conforte-run shell company, and auctioned it off.

Additional infamous crimes in Nevada history revolve around the statewide gaming industry, which was legalized in 1931. In an effort to minimize the influence of organized crime and to restore faith in the gaming industry, the Nevada Gaming Commission (NGC) was created as a regulatory and enforcement branch in 1957. The presence of organized crime in the gaming industry reduced the amount of tax revenue, which is based on gaming revenue, by falsely reporting the amount of gaming revenue. The implementation of the NGC in 1957, along with other industry changes (e.g., the presence of corporate casino enterprises), has helped to mitigate the organized crime problem in the Nevada gaming industry.

Criminal Justice System

It is interesting to note that the NGC is one of the many agencies with law enforcement capacities in the state of Nevada. Law enforcement organizations in Nevada are regulated by the Nevada Peace Officers Standards and Training (POST) Commission, which currently recognizes approximately 140 law enforcement agencies statewide (including municipal police departments, county sheriff's offices, university police, tribal police, and other state law enforcement agencies). The first law enforcement officer in the state was the Ormsby County (now Carson County) sheriff, appointed in December 1861. Law enforcement statewide was the responsibility of the county sheriffs until the Nevada State Police organization was commissioned in 1908 to deal with civil unrest surrounding mining camp labor disputes.

The state police in Nevada no longer exist as an autonomous agency; its police function has been taken over by the Nevada Highway Patrol. The first highway patrolmen in Nevada were hired in 1923 and were responsible for collecting vehicle registration fees and enforcing motor vehicle laws throughout the state. As of 2008, there were more than 350 patrolmen responsible for enforcing traffic laws and maintaining public safety statewide. Nevada maintains an autonomous correctional system designed to confine convicted felons for the public protection. Corrections in Nevada started with the creation of the first territorial prison at the Warm Spring Hotel (near Carson City) in 1862; this facility was eventually expanded and fortified with materials from a nearby quarry to create the Nevada State Prison.

The Nevada State Prison was the only such institution statewide until the construction of other correctional facilities in the 1960s. Currently, Nevada operates eight correctional institutions and 11 minimum-security facilities, which house more than 12,000 inmates statewide. Perhaps the most famous inmate currently incarcerated in Nevada is O. J. Simpson, who was convicted of assault with a deadly weapon, kidnapping, and robbery stemming from events inside a Las Vegas hotel room in September 2007.

Nevada, like many other states, carries out the death penalty via lethal injection. Nevada was the first state to utilize lethal gas, during the execution of Gee Jon in 1924. Nevada has executed 73 persons in its history, including 12 executions performed after the death penalty was reinstated nationwide in 1976 with the Supreme Court decision in *Gregg v. Georgia*. As of 2011, there are 77 people on death row in Nevada.

Crime in Nevada has followed trends generally resembling national trends. Examining trends from 1960 through the present shows the violent crime rate peaked in Nevada in the early 1990s and has been steadily declining since. The property crime rate peaked in 1979 and has been generally declining since, although it has increased from time to time. Recently, Nevada garnered notoriety by being in the top 10 most violent states from 2005 (when it ranked ninth) through 2008 (when it ranked third), although it experienced a decline in property crime during the same period (from ninth to 18th). Nevada has steadily remained the second-highest state in the number of vehicle thefts and robberies during this four-year period. Nevada's history of crime, police, and punishment reflects the unique conditions surrounding the birth of the state; prostitution and gambling continue to set it apart from other states.

Jon Maskaly
University of South Florida

See Also: Gambling; Las Vegas, Nevada; Prostitution, History of.

Further Readings

Brents, Barbara G. and Kathryn Hausbeck. "Violence and Legalized Brothel Prostitution in Nevada: Examining Safety, Risk, and Prostitution Policy." *Journal of Interpersonal Violence*, v. 20/3 (2005).

Hulse, James W. *The Silver State*, 2nd ed. Reno: University of Nevada Press, 1998.

Nevada Department of Corrections. "Department Organization." http://www.doc.nv.gov/about/organization.php (Accessed December 2010).

Nevada Department of Public Safety. "A Brief History of the N.H.P." http://nhp.nv.gov/history.shtml (Accessed December 2010).

Nevada Gaming Commission. "Nevada Gaming Regulation." http://gaming.nv.gov/about_regulation.htm#d (Accessed December 2010).

Nevada Legislature. "Facts About the Nevada Legislature." http://www.leg.state.nv.us/General/AboutLeg/General_Short.cfm (Accessed December 2010).

Nieves, Evelyn. "Shutdown Looming at Nevada's Oldest Bordello." *New York Times* (July 19, 1999).

New Hampshire

One of the original thirteen colonies, New Hampshire's history goes back to the early 17th century. Today, it is one of the smallest and least populous states, its recent history and demographics having been greatly affected by the growth of the Boston metropolitan area in neighboring Massachusetts—and by the transformation of many former farm and orchard towns on the border into exurban bedroom communities and the cold war–fueled growth of tech sector companies like Lockheed-Martin, Raytheon, Digital, and Wang.

Police

Early law enforcement was handled by constables. In the capital of Concord, for instance, in the colonial era, the constable was an elected official who was also responsible for tax collection. Over time, the number of constables was increased. Election of constables took place at town meetings (the standard form of local government in much of New England), and anyone chosen to be constable who did not wish to serve would have to pay a fee in order to opt out of the position. In the 1830s, Concord added police officers—appointed by the town government rather than elected by the people at large—to the city police force, and the police department was formally created in 1853.

The New Hampshire State Prison was built in 1812, after being authorized by the New Hampshire General Court in 1810. An early prison industries program was begun in 1819 with the construction of a workshop in which the inmates could do hand manufacturing of various goods. For decades, there were few female inmates—never more than six at a time up until 1941, at which point the state began housing female inmates in correctional facilities in Vermont and Massachusetts. The New Hampshire Women's Prison was built in the 1980s to accommodate a growing number of female offenders. Shortly after, the state built the Northern New Hampshire Correctional Facility to deal with the growing state prison population.

Crime and Punishment

New Hampshire is a capital punishment state, and the death penalty has been used since the colonial era. Since that time, 24 people have been executed. In the colonial era, hanging was the method of execution, and the death penalty was prescribed not only for murder but for rape, abortion, burglary, counterfeiting, treason, bestiality, and homosexuality. Three of the four executions in the colonial era were for the crime of "feloniously concealing the death of a newborn," an act criminalized to such a degree out of fear that women who bore children out of wedlock or conceived by men other than their husbands would kill the child (having concealed their pregnancy) in order to maintain their secret. The fourth was Eliphas Dow, convicted for murdering Peter Clough, with whom he had been feuding for some time.

The only execution solely for rape (without subsequent murder) in New Hampshire was also its only execution of a nonwhite person, African American Thomas Powers, in 1796. All other

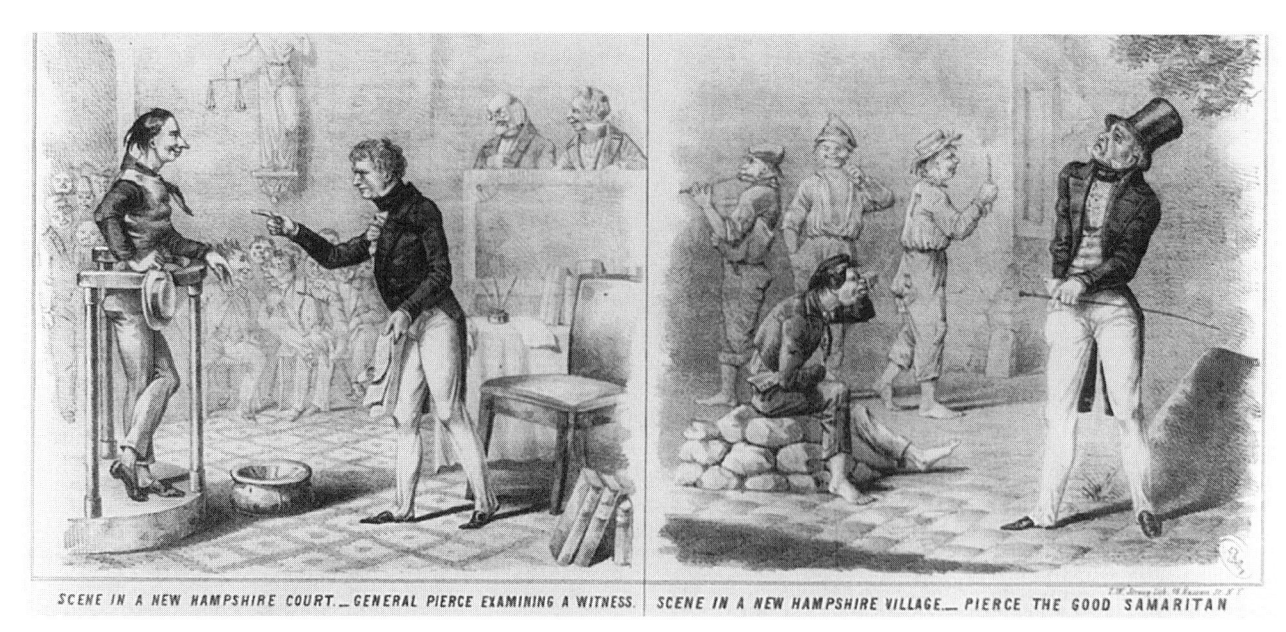

A lithograph pokes fun of General Franklin Pierce, depicting him as a trial lawyer in a New Hampshire court and giving money to the poor, saying "So, here's a cent for you, buy a stick of candy and remember to vote for Pierce, if ever he is nominated for President." Pierce was the 14th president of the United States and the only U.S. president to come from New Hampshire.

executions since statehood have been for homicide or accessory to murder. Not until 1903 was the mandatory death penalty lifted from cases of murder in the first degree, allowing juries to choose to impose a life sentence instead.

The last time an inmate was executed in New Hampshire was 1939, when Howard Long was hanged for the molestation and murder of a 10-year-old boy. Three years later, Ralph Jennings was sentenced to death for murdering a schoolteacher but committed suicide in his cell. In 1959, Frederick Martineau and Russell Nelson were convicted of murdering a man who was scheduled to testify in a Rhode Island burglary case, but they were spared the death penalty after 13 stays of execution, when the 1972 Supreme Court decision in *Furman v. Georgia* found all extant death penalties to be unconstitutional. The death penalty statute in New Hampshire was subsequently amended.

Today, although lethal injection is intended as the form of execution, New Hampshire has no execution chamber. Though hanging is legally permitted when injection is "impractical," the state's hanging gallows was dismantled in 1992. Attempts to repeal the death penalty have failed, perhaps in part because of several recent high-profile murders, such as the murder by four adolescent boys of Kimberly Cates during a home invasion in Mount Vernon in 2009. Despite the violence of the crime, it failed to fit the requirements for a capital murder under New Hampshire law, which requires that for the death penalty to be used, the murder must have been a contract killing; a murder coupled with a federal drug offense, kidnapping, or aggravated sexual assault; a murder by someone who has previously served a life sentence; or a murder of a police officer. The inability of the state to seek the death penalty in this case resulted in calls not for the repeal of the death penalty but for the rewriting of the statute in order to encompass more crimes.

There is in 2011 one inmate on death row: Michael Addison, sentenced in December 2008 for the murder of a police officer in 2006. Addison shot and killed Officer Michael Briggs when he responded to a domestic disturbance call, prompting a manhunt in the Manchester area—later expanding to Massachusetts—when Addison fled the scene.

A politically conservative state, New Hampshire has tended to be more socially liberal than mainstream American conservatives—it has one of the lowest rates of church attendance in the nation, for instance, and has legalized gay marriage—but has also attracted elements of the political fringe, including several small antigovernment groups. This was brought to national attention in 1997, when 62-year-old Carl Drega, who had a long history of arguments with state and local government over zoning and building code issues, fired shots in the air to scare off town officials when they came to his property to discuss a dispute over an assessment. He subsequently shot and killed two state troopers who were ticketing him for the rust holes in the bed of his truck, and after a circuitous evasion route, took a fortified position in a hilltop across the state line in Vermont, from which he continued firing at state troopers with an AR-15 rifle, until he was eventually killed by police gunfire.

The violent crime rate in New Hampshire has always been lower than the national average: 167 violent crimes per 100,000 inhabitants in 2010, compared to the national rate of 403. Aggravated assaults account for most of the violent crimes, but the figures for rape are slightly higher (31) than the national average (27.5) and thus constitute a significant share of violent crimes, about 18 percent. Crime has risen in recent years, having jumped from 96.5 to 175.4 from 1999 to 2000, declining slightly in the middle of the decade, and rising to present levels during the financial crisis, although New Hampshire has been less affected by the recession than most states. Rape, robbery, and murder have stayed fairly steady since the 1980s; the fluctuations have largely been in the number of aggravated assaults.

Bill Kte'pi
Independent Scholar

See Also: *Furman v. Georgia*; Massachusetts; Vermont.

Further Readings
Fassett, James H. *Colonial Life in New Hampshire.* Charleston, SC: Nabu Press, 2010.
Heffernan, N. C., et al. *New Hampshire: Crosscurrents in Its Development*, 3rd ed. Hanover, NH: University Press of New England, 2004.
Petrie, Janice S. C. *Perfection to a Fault: A Small Murder in Ossipee, New Hampshire, 1916.* Topsfield, MA: Seatales, 2000.

New Jersey

New Jersey was inhabited by Native Americans as early as 10,000 years ago. The Lenape or Lenni Lenape Indians (known as the Delaware to the English) are the aboriginal inhabitants of New Jersey who lived in small communities made up of extended family members across New Jersey, Delaware, and eastern Pennsylvania. English settlers referred to the Lenape as "Delaware Indians" after Lord De La Warr. The Lenape understood their name to connote the phrase *original people* or *genuine people*. Europeans and African slaves first entered the region during the 16th and 17th centuries. An Italian explorer sailing for the English, Giovanni de Verrazano, was the first European since Norse explorations of the region in 1000 C.E. to reach the Jersey shore, anchoring at Sandy Hook in 1524. The British explorer Henry Hudson, in service for the Netherlands, sailed through Newark Bay in 1609, claiming the land for the Dutch that was at first called New Netherlands. Trading posts began to appear in what are today the cities of Hoboken and Jersey City following the Hudson expedition. The first Europeans to build settlements in New Jersey were the Dutch, Swedes, and Finns.

The British took control from the Dutch in 1664, and the territory was subsequently divided into two proprietary colonies by 1674. Sir George Carteret took control of East Jersey and Lord John Berkeley came to administer West Jersey. The land became known as New Jersey after the Isle of Jersey in the English Channel (Carteret was formerly the governor of the Isle of Jersey). Both Carteret and Berkeley sold New Jersey lands at low prices and allowed settlers to have a measure of political and religious freedoms. This helped to facilitate the development of an ethnically diverse environment. English Quaker John Fenwick and Edward Byllinge purchased land from Lord Berkeley on the east side of the Delaware. Fenwick's allotment came to be known as the "Salem Tenth," and this comprised about 10 percent of the territory of West Jersey. John Fenwick's initial goal was to establish a colony of English Quakers. As the proprietor of Salem Tenth, Fenwick made several purchases from local Native American tribes in 1675, including land that today encompasses Salem and Cumberland counties. New Jersey became a royal British colony in 1702, effectively ending the proprietary system.

On the eve of the American Revolution, New Jersey came under direct Crown control and later declared itself to be an independent state in 1776. New Jersey was the third state to ratify the U.S. Constitution in 1787. The Industrial Revolution through the 1800s brought manufacturing industries to New Jersey and an increase in population. Historically, the state of New Jersey has been one of the most densely populated states in the Union through the 20th century. The combination of industrialization, population increase, and urbanization in New Jersey through the 20th century allows for an examination of crime and punishment in the state that reflects national trends. New Jersey contains some of the post populous crime-ridden cities in the United States, including Newark and Camden. National trends in crime and punishment are often first visible in the state of New Jersey.

Crime and Punishment

New Jersey has an illustrious history in crime and punishment. Some of the greatest crimes of the 20th century took place in New Jersey. On September 14, 1922, Episcopal priest Edward Wheeler Hall and his mistress Eleanor Reinhardt Mills, a member of the church choir, were both found dead in New Brunswick, New Jersey. This case became known as the Hall-Mills case and the sensational trial that followed led to the acquittal of the priest's wife Frances Noel Stevens Hall and her brothers in 1926. This case was considered perhaps the trial of the century before the Lindbergh case because of the widespread national attention and the novels and films that were inspired by the case. Charles Augustus Lindbergh, Jr., the 20-month-old son of writer Anne Morrow Lindbergh and aviator Charles Lindbergh, was kidnapped from the couple's Hopewell, New Jersey, home on March 1, 1932. The decomposed body of Charles, Jr., was discovered on May 12, 1932 with a crushed skull. Bruno Richard Hauptman, was eventually apprehended and convicted of the crime. He was executed on April 3, 1936. Enoch Lewis "Nucky" Johnson (1883–1968), Republican Party political boss and racketeer in Atlantic City, New Jersey, has inspired several books and a television series. The infamous DeCavalcante crime family emerged in north Jersey during Prohibition. The DeCavalcante crime family in New Jersey included a Newark faction run by Gaspare D'Amico through 1937, followed by the leadership of Stefano "Steve" Badami through the 1950s. The DeCavalcante crime family maintained close ties with the La Cosa Nostra crime network based in New York, engaging in such activities as drug trafficking, extortion, fencing, fraud, gambling, and murder, among other crimes. The DeCavalcante family's New Jersey crime network in both Elizabeth and Newark was likely the inspiration for the HBO series *The Sopranos* and the more recent CNBC program *Mob Money*. Richard Biegenwald, the "Jersey Shore Thrill Killer," murdered several women in the Jersey Shore area during the early 1980s. The dismembered bodies of some of his victims were found in shallow graves located on his mother's property in Staten Island. Biegenwald was convicted and subsequently died in prison of liver disease in 2008.

The September 11, 2001, attacks orchestrated by the radical terrorist organization Al Qaeda are also associated with crime in New Jersey. United Airlines Flight 93 to San Francisco departed from Newark International Airport the morning of September 11, 2001, and crashed in a field in Shanksville, Pennsylvania, killing all passengers on board after being hijacked by four Al Qaeda terrorists under instructions from Osama bin Laden. Newark International Airport was renamed Newark Liberty International Airport after the attacks.

New Jersey has 14 state correctional facilities run by the New Jersey Department of Corrections. These facilities are designated for adults, youths, and women and currently house more than 24,000 women, youth, and adult inmates in total. The state has both minimum- and maximum-security prisons, such as East Jersey State Prison, located in Rahway, New Jersey. The first major prison built in the state was Trenton State Prison, created in 1799 and organized according to the congregate system (mixing all types of prisoners in one building regardless of sex, age, or mental condition). The inmates in Trenton State, regardless of type of crime, mingled liberally during the day and were housed in cells during the evening until the mid-1800s when the prison was remodeled. The East Jersey State Prison (formerly known as Rahway State Prison) was built in 1896, and women once imprisoned at Trenton (now known as New Jersey State Prison) were eventually relocated to the Edna Mahan Correctional Facility located in Clinton, New Jersey, in 1913.

There have been several New Jersey cities that have been listed as "most violent" cities in the United States in the past decade. Camden has ranked number one on the list of most violent cities in the United States more than once, and Newark has been labeled "the carjacking capital of the world" several times. In 2001, an estimated 63 percent of the prisoners in New Jersey state prisons were African American, while roughly 19 percent were white and 18 percent were Hispanic. The New Jersey State Prison is located in Trenton, Northern State Prison is located in Newark. The Edna Mahan Correctional Facility for Women is in Clinton, New Jersey. These are three of the major correctional facilities in the state.

Ironically, New Jersey contains both the most violent city in the United States and the safest city in the United States: The town of Brick, New Jersey, has been listed as the safest city in the country. This helps to illustrate the fact that New Jersey serves as a microcosm of the larger trends across the nation in terms of crime and punishment.

Newark Riots

The civil rights era brought major rebellions to the state of New Jersey within and outside the prison system. There was a serious prison uprising in the New Jersey State Prison located in Trenton in 1952. Prisoners, citing overcrowding and poor conditions, destroyed property, took hostages, and refused to surrender in what has been classified by some as the most violent year in prison rebellion that took place before the events at Attica.

Major cities such as Newark were also engulfed by rebellion in the 1960s. Poverty, diminishing purchasing power, and deteriorating living conditions in the Central Ward (where most of the expanding black population resided) led to the conflagration that was the Newark riots in 1967. On July 12, 1967, an African American taxi driver named John Smith was beaten by Newark police officers for allegedly resisting arrest. Before the riots that followed the beating of Smith, through July (amid rumors that the police had killed him), then Mayor Hugh Addonizio had offered to condemn sections of the Central ward to make way for the building of the University of Medicine and Dentistry. The Newark riots ended with 26 killed, 1,500 wounded, 1,600 arrested, and the destruction of an estimated 167 retail stores (many of which never rebuilt in the city). Middle-class communities of all races fled the city in the 1970s and 1980s, along with vital industries, leaving behind a city increasingly marred by political corruption, crime, and urban decay.

Trends in Crime and Punishment

New Jersey has at times had lower numbers than the national average in crime and punishment, although in some instances, the state has surpassed the national average. The boom in crime in the United States took place roughly between 1963 and 1974. This was an era of civil unrest, urban rebellion, and political assassinations. There was a slight hiatus in the crime "boom" in the mid- to late 1970s but the national crime rate spiked once again through the 1980s, reaching dramatic proportions. The New Jersey incarceration rate was lower than the national average through the 1980s. New Jersey exceeded the national incarceration rate in the early 1990s but has since experienced a decrease through the 2000s.

New Jersey, between 2005 and 2008, was ranked at either 27th or 30th on the list of states with the highest crime rates. Residents have a one in 308 chance of becoming a victim of violent crime. The chances of a New Jersey resident becoming a victim of property crime are far greater at one in 43. The national crime rate has been steadily declining since the 2000s, along with New Jersey's crime rate.

Hettie V. Williams
Monmouth University

See Also: Camden, New Jersey; Lindbergh Law; Newark, New Jersey.

Further Readings
Blackwell, J. *Notorious New Jersey: 100 True Tales of Murders and Mobsters, Scandals, and Scoundrels.* New Brunswick, NJ: Rutgers University Press, 2007.

Ingle, Bob and Sandy McClure. *The Soprano State: New Jersey's Culture of Corruption.* New York: St. Martin's Press, 2008.

Johnson, Nelson. *Boardwalk Empire: The Birth, High Times, and Corruption of Atlantic City.* New York: Plexus Publishing, 2010.

Salmore, Barbara G. *New Jersey Politics and Government.* New Brunswick, NJ: Rutgers University Press, 2008.

New Mexico

New Mexico's justice system began with colonization of the region by the Spanish. The earliest record of arrest and punishment begins with Don Juan de Oñate y Salazar (1550–1626). The son of a conquistador, Oñate was ordered in 1595 by King Philip II to colonize the northern frontier of New Spain. He began the expedition in 1598, and on April 30 claimed all of New Mexico beyond the Rio Grande for Spain. He and his party continued up the Rio Grande, where he founded Santa Fé de Nuevo México. Oñate served as the province's first governor. Oñate reportedly wielded a stern hand on both Spanish colonists and indigenous peoples. In October 1598, a skirmish erupted when Oñate's occupying Spanish military demanded supplies from the Acoma Indians—supplies essential to the Acoma's winter survival. The Acoma resisted, and 13 Spaniards were killed, including Oñate's nephew. In 1599, Oñate retaliated; his soldiers killed 800 villagers, enslaved the remaining 500 women and children. After a trial overseen by Oñate, he ordered the left foot of every Acoma man over 25 amputated. The reported number of men mutilated ranged between 24 and 80.

In 1614, Oñate was accused and convicted of a variety of crimes and excesses committed during his governorship, including adultery and violating the Order on New Discoveries of 1573, which declared that pacification should be carried out charitably and without force against the natives. The Order on New Discoveries was written by the Council of the Indies, created by the king of Spain in 1524 as an authoritative governing body for Spanish colonies in America. Oñate was fined and exiled from New Mexico.

On August 10, 1680, Pueblo peoples staged an uprising, laying siege to the city of Santa Fe, forcing the Spanish to retreat. On August 20, the colonists fled south to El Paso del Norte. In 1688, Capitan General y Governador Don Diego de Vargas was appointed governor of New Mexico. He assumed his position on February 22, 1691. In July 1692, de Vargas and a small contingent of soldiers returned to Santa Fe, surrounded the city, and called on the Pueblo people to surrender, promising clemency if they would swear allegiance to the king of Spain and return to Christianity. After meeting with de Vargas, the Pueblo leaders agreed. The returning settlers also founded the old town of Albuquerque in 1706. Following the recapture, the Spanish issued substantial land grants to the Pueblos and appointed a public defender to protect the rights of the Indians and argue their cases in Spanish courts.

At the outset of the Mexican–American War (1846–48), General Stephen Watts Kearny marched his 2,500-man Army of the West to Santa Fe. The Mexican military forces retreated to Mexico, and Kearny's forces took control. In 1846, Kearny set up a provisional government using a system of laws known as the Kearny Code. The judicial branch consisted of a three-man Superior Court. Each served as a trial judge, presiding over a judicial district; together, they

The gas chamber at the old New Mexico Penitentiary site in Santa Fe, New Mexico. The facility was closed in 1998 after two riots resulting in the death of 35 inmates.

constituted an appellate court that reviewed each judge's decisions. At the new American court's first session in Taos in April 1847, 17 men were tried for murder, five for high treason, and 17 for larceny. Fifteen were convicted of murder, one of treason, and six of larceny. Those convicted of homicide were hanged.

During New Mexico's mid-19th century, a series of internecine battles called range wars raged across the state. Usually, the conflicts were about economic issues, such as supplying cattle to Indian reservations and disputes over land titles, borders, or grants. Many of these battles turned into personal or familial vendettas; they included the Colfax County War and the Horrell War. The most famous, the Lincoln County War, was best known because of the involvement of William Bonney—"Billy the Kid."

It is generally accepted that the conflict began with the murder of wealthy Englishman John H. Tunstall on February 18, 1978. Tunstall sought to challenge the banking and cattle monopoly run by Lawrence Gustave Murphy. While Murphy owned no cattle, he was supplied and challenged by John Chisum, owner of the largest herds in the state. When Tunstall arrived in Lincoln County, he joined with Chisum and his political and economic compatriots. The dispute turned into an armed conflict resulting in the deaths of two men and the eventual issuance of a warrant for the arrest of Bonney.

Bonney was one of many "regulators"—essentially hired guns with negligible enforcement duties often employed to protect herds from rustlers. During this period, sheriffs such as Pat Garrett were the primary law enforcement officers in the state's counties. As more municipalities were created, police departments took on policing of the cities. One of the first police departments was established in Santa Fe.

Law Enforcement

During New Mexico's early history, there was an attempt to establish a statewide law enforcement agency. The New Mexico Mounted Police was the result. It was established in 1905 by the New Mexico Territorial Legislature.

The popularity and increased use of automobiles highlighted the need for a statewide law enforcement agency. In 1933, the New Mexico Motor Patrol was established, primarily to enforce traffic laws. In 1935 the Twelfth State Legislature changed the name of the organization to the New Mexico State Police and gave officers powers to enforce state laws.

The state police force responded to riots at New Mexico Penitentiary. On July 19, 1922, prisoners rioted against overcrowding, poor food, and excessive force by prison authorities. When the inmates refused to return to their cells, tower guards opened fire, killing an inmate and injuring five others.

A second riot occurred June 15, 1953. Inmates protesting the use of excessive force seized Deputy Warden Ralph Tahash and 12 guards and held them hostage. In the resulting melee, guards killed two inmates and wounded several others. This second riot led to the abandonment of the original facility as a prison and the construction in 1956 of what was called "the main unit." In 1980, the main unit was the scene of one of the most violent riots in the correctional history of America. Over two days, 33 inmates were killed and 12 officers were held hostage by escaped prisoners. The main unit was closed in 1998.

Uniform crime reports for New Mexico indicate that while the population has risen steadily since 1960, the level of crimes has remained consistent, placing New Mexico 36th out of the 50 states with the first owning the highest crime rate.

Teresa I. Francis
Central Washington University
Theodore O. Francis
Independent Scholar

See Also: Automobile and the Police; Billy the Kid; Border Patrol; Frontier Crime; Native American Tribal Police; Native Americans.

Further Readings
Bolton, Herbert Eugene, ed. *Spanish Exploration in the Southwest, 1542–1706*. New York: Charles Scribner's Sons, 1916.
Hammond, George P. and Agapito Rey. *Don Juan de Oñate, Colonizer of New Mexico*. Albuquerque: University of New Mexico Press, 1953.
Fulton, M. G., et al. *History of the Lincoln County War*. Tucson: University of Arizona Press, 1980.
Laylander, Don. "Geographies of Fact and Fantasy: Oñate on the Lower Colorado River, 1604–1605." *Southern California Quarterly*, v.86/4 (2004).

Simmons, Marc. *The Last Conquistador: Juan de Oñate and the Settling of the Far Southwest.* Norman: University of Oklahoma Press, 1991.

New Orleans, Louisiana

Today, as in the past, New Orleans enjoys its reputation as a colorful, zestful, unique, and slightly racy tourist destination. "The city that care forgot," despite its laissez-faire repute, antique buildings, musical traditions, and wonderful cuisine, has endured a series of blows that has left it staggering to regain its foothold as the onetime Queen City of the south. Before the Civil War, it was the site of great ethnic and political upheaval: Rival Irish and Anglo-French gangs warred, and some groups reached the status of private political armies. Corruption and a very obvious spoils system in local government were established well before secession. When the city was at its height, the Civil War and postwar occupation reduced its white inhabitants to often incoherent rage and, on more than one occasion, to insurrectionary violence. Shortly after Reconstruction, Italian American crime syndicates began to dominate the organized crime scene, and underworld figures became ensconced in urban politics well into the 1980s. The very word *mafia* entered the American lexicon in the Crescent City in the 1880s with the influx of poor Sicilians in that decade. Civil rights struggles damaged the city's reputation and sense of community in the 1950s and 1960s, and inner-city crime, always an issue in this highly congested residential area, when conflated with racial issues, did incalculable damage to New Orleans's repute within the region from the 1960s to the present. Moreover, the city's importance as an entry port for Latin America gave way to Miami in the 1970s.

The near-mortal blow delivered by Hurricane Katrina seems like a cruel anticlimax to those who have watched the city decline for 50 years. Entire vital neighborhood were left in shambles; a weather-based genocide of sorts occurred, and many New Orleaneans began an outmigration with no apparent end in sight. The disgraceful desertion of their posts by the city's infamously brutal and corrupt police added no luster to the reputation of law enforcement or of the city itself. The 2010 oil spill in the Gulf of Mexico has added to the misfortune and fatalism that plagues the damaged city. The city that in the 1800s was once the second-largest port in the nation is at present primarily a tourist-oriented backwater.

The ongoing and largely accurate perception that violent crime is pervasive throughout the region discourages many Louisianans from visiting the city. Tourists are strongly advised to stay in the French Quarter and, above all, not to wander in the quaint cemeteries that adjoin that colorful district, as they are magnets for predatory criminals. But that was true long before the storm; in the 1850s, in fact, when rural planters expressed anxiety about being victims of crime while conducting business there, predatory gangs of footpads were a matter of concern. It has often been said that Louisiana is two states: the French Catholic south and the "redneck" Protestant north. In truth, Louisiana is three mini-states: those mentioned formerly and New Orleans, which has more in common with a failed and anarchic third-world postcolonial city-state than with the rest of the state. Much of the chaos that seems to characterize the city stems from its history of crime, corruption, and civic disorder.

Early History

Jean Baptiste Le Moyne, Sieur de Bienville, founded New Orleans in 1718. It was soon noted that the city, situated surrounded by swamps, was cold and wet in the winter and hot and humid in the summer. The settlement flooded the following year when the Mississippi escaped its banks. Levees were begun, and drainage activities made the city somewhat more habitable. Colonists were obtained for this bleak outpost from jails and hospitals; prostitutes, paupers, and peasants were rounded up in France and shipped to the fledgling city. Petty criminals and vagabonds were in the majority of the first ships to arrive from the mother country. Women were in short supply. Accordingly, 88 prostitutes were shipped from a house of correction in Paris. Some were quickly married off upon arrival but the majority proved problematic and antisocial. Other, more respectable women were sent in 1728, and further shipments were sent until 1751. This had the effect of making the city a more settled and sedate place. Further contributing to the civilizing of the area was the arrival of nuns in 1727. Their charge was to aid in the care for respectable women sent by the king to find husbands, and to effect the salvation of loose women and girls of bad conduct. One historian describes the early settlers as a "motley rabble" who had little inclination to work but preferred a life of indolence and crime. Thus, the pattern of the New Orleans criminal lifestyle was set quite early.

The importation of slaves in the same decade only added to the confusion, though it relieved some whites of the necessity of manual labor. Almost all the slaves had come directly from Africa and were thought to be dangerous. Consequently, in 1724, a Black Code was written to regulate their behavior. Successive royal governors proved to be inefficient and corrupt; this contributed to a pattern that would become quite familiar in the city and, indeed, in the future state.

Colonial Period Ends: American Ascendancy

Louisiana passed to Spain at the end of the French and Indian War (1762) but the Spanish governor was driven from the city in 1768 by a revolt of French aristocrats. The following year, a Spanish fleet imposed a new governor in impressive style, but in 1800, Spain returned the state to France and shortly thereafter, in 1803, Napoleon sold the colony to the United States. Initially there was resentment toward the new American masters. Traders and uncouth backwoodsman from upriver flooded in to the city, which only increased French resentment. Many were particularly colorful and violent flatboatmen who were also prodigious drinkers. Violent confrontations ensued in river districts when these boatmen landed with their cargoes. Piracy in the Gulf of Mexico and along the river was common. Pirates such as Jean Lafitte made New Orleans a home base and a regular port of call. Another disruptive group, filibusterers—armed groups of American adventurers

A scene of the bustling New Orleans riverfront at night in 1883, crowded with people and steamboats and featuring electric lighting. A citywide electric lighting system was introduced in the city in 1886, somewhat alleviating the city's rampant crime; the riverfront was one of the few areas where the use of electric lights had been introduced a few years earlier.

trying to foment revolution in Latin American for their own gain—made New Orleans a final stop before venturing south of the border.

In order to deal with these disruptive and drunken rowdies, New Orleans created a *garde de ville* in 1806 and two years later adopted constables. They were specially detailed to patrol and keep order in the Swamp, the district of vice favored by the flatboatmen. Prostitution, gambling, and violent crime flourished in this area. In the 1820s, gangs of criminals operated with impunity from the Swamp. The Swamp, also known as Girod Street, remained a vice district into the 1890s. Duels were not uncommon in New Orleans, though they were not nearly so normal as movies and fiction might suggest. In the colonial period, swords were preferred, and fencing masters and schools were a feature of city life. Americans would fight with anything from axes to more prosaic pistols. After 1848, dueling was strictly forbidden under the state constitution, though it continued until the Civil War. The most common site for duels was the Oaks, a site outside the city proper where many an affair of honor was resolved.

Political Violence
Politically oriented gang violence began to flourish, as it did elsewhere in the nation, in New Orleans in the 1840s. In the election of 1856, the American, or Know-Nothing, Party elected a slate of city officials after seizing polling places and shooting a police officer and the chief of police. Immigrants and Democratic officials were attacked in their homes and on the street thereafter. Ultimately, a mob of Know-Nothings attacked the registrar of election's home. This led to the formation of a vigilance committee consisting of French Creoles and immigrants. On June 3, 1858, armed members of this group occupied the French Quarter. Led by a U.S. Army officer, they seized arms and strategic buildings and called for an overthrow of the corrupt American Party regime. After negotiations failed to resolve the situation and a large, threatening Know-Nothing mob assembled nearby, the vigilance committee evacuated the area. No investigation of this movement was ever made, and little is known of the leader's motivations. After the war, extremely violent incidents occurred in 1866 and 1874, both involving large-scale conflict between white supremacists and Reconstruction supporters. Cannons and Gatling guns were used in the disorders of the latter year.

Storyville
Violent crime continued to plague the city, fueled by cheap bars and prostitutes. The Gallatin Street area was the most abandoned and dangerous location in New Orleans. Burglars operated out of local bars, and gangs of toughs beat up and robbed drunks who frequented bars and houses of ill repute. Cockfights, dogfights, rat killings, and indecent exhibitions were featured in the area until the 1890s. By 1898, 36 square blocks of the French Quarter were devoted to the infamous Storyville vice district by act of the city council. Like the red-light district of contemporary Amsterdam, Storyville seen as a tourist attraction of the city. In 1900, there were at least 230 houses of prostitution and 2,000 prostitutes in the district. The bordellos were closed in 1917 by order of the U.S. secretary of the navy, but underground prostitution continued to flourish in the city's neighborhoods. The tawdry hoopla and tourist attractions of Bourbon Street are a pale evocation of the vice that flourished there in the not-too-distant past.

The Mafia
Sicilian criminal gangs were noted in New Orleans by 1861, earlier than is commonly thought, and they were well organized. New Orleans—not Chicago or New York City—was, in fact, the center of Mafia organization in the country. Criminals from Italy entered the port in large numbers in the 1880s and inaugurated a reign of terror within the Italian immigrant community. These criminals assassinated citizens and police alike, often using a "Mafia gun," a sawed-off double-barrel 12-gauge shotgun. Two Italian families, the Provenzanos and the Matrangas, began a fight for domination of the docks in the mid-1880s. On October 15, 1890, the chief of police, Pat Hennessy, who unwisely had gotten involved in the feud, was killed in the streets of the city, probably by the Matrangas. Identifying his killers as "Dagoes" with his last breath, the chief collapsed and died. This led to an outpouring of anger, and 21 Italians were arrested. After a trial replete with jury tampering, most were acquitted outright, after which a group of Sicilians reportedly tore

down an American flag and hoisted the Italian banner. This series of events further enraged the riot-prone citizens of the city, who called a mass meeting, then adjourned to gun stores and, finally, stormed the parish prison. Seven of the principals in the case were shot out of hand, and several others were shot while cowering in a doghouse; two others were hanged after being caught trying to escape. Public officials were quietly supportive, and no investigation was ever conducted. This incident precipitated a diplomatic flap between Italy and the United States. Though it broke the Mafia's overt domination of courts, organized crime figures such as Carlos Marcello have remained prominent in the city to the present.

A curious side note to Mafia involvement in New Orleans involves a theory of the assassination of President John F. Kennedy that focuses on New Orleans Mafiosi as having been involved. Curiously, Lee Harvey Oswald gave out pro-Cuba propaganda from a building shared with the naval intelligence service in early 1963. New Orleans district attorney Jim Garrison led an ill-fated investigation into the Kennedy assassination from 1965 to 1969.

Police

The New Orleans Police Department has been plagued by corruption and allegations of brutality for many years. During the 1800s, it was dominated by Democrats, then by nativists, then by different factions of the Democratic Party. During Reconstruction, it came under fire as overly protective of the newly freed slaves. This contributed to the mob violence of the period. The department continued to be famously corrupt as it protected prostitution in the late 1800s and bootlegging operations following Prohibition. In recent years, it has been dogged by controversy and allegations of brutality and corruption. One officer killed another while robbing a restaurant. Another put out a contract on a witness. During Hurricane Katrina, some 200 officers deserted their posts while others looked on while looters sacked businesses. Other officers shot innocent citizens fleeing the flood. Presently, the city is trying to rebuild the department—the latest of many attempts.

Francis Frederick Hawley
Western Carolina University

See Also: 1801 to 1850 Primary Documents; 1851 to 1900 Primary Documents; Gangs, History of; Louisiana.

Further Readings
Asbury, H. *The French Quarter: An Informal History of the New Orleans Underworld.* New York: Knopf, 1936.
"The Assassination: Did the Mob Kill J.F.K.?" *Time.* http://www.time.com/time/magazine/article/0,9171,956397-1,00.html (Accessed August 2010).
Kendall, J. "History of New Orleans, 1922." http://penelope.uchicago.edu/Thayer/E/Gazetteer/Places/America/United_States/Louisiana/New_Orleans/_Texts/KENHNO/home.html (Accessed August 2010).
Mulrine, A. "When the Cops Turn Into the Bad Guys: The New Orleans Police Department Hits Its Nadir." *US News and World Report* (October 10, 2005). http://www.usnews.com/usnews/news/articles/051010/10cops.htm (Accessed August 2010).

"New Punitiveness"

Rehabilitation remained the dominant philosophy of punishment until the 1970s. Skyrocketing crime rates coupled with the belief that treatment did not work led policy makers to reject a rehabilitative approach to dealing with crime and instead to adopt a "get tough" perspective under the premise that increased penalties would lead to reductions in offending. Strict sanctions such as mandatory minimum sentences, three strikes laws, and truth-in-sentencing legislation became commonplace in criminal justice practice. In addition, the nature of confinement and community supervision evolved from a focus on meeting the individual needs of offenders to a system that centered on surveillance and control. As such policies were implemented, research began to document the hidden consequences of the tough-on-crime movement that included housing, employment, public benefits, and voting restrictions that limited the likelihood of offenders successfully reintegrating into society post-release. Crime became a hot-button issue in which politicians campaigned

Supermax prisons (super-maximum security) were developed in the late 20th century to house violent prisoners, often in solitary confinement, in an attempt to achieve "behavior modification." The penitentiary on Alcatraz Island, off San Francisco, California, was opened as a federal prison in 1934 and is considered an early example of a supermax prison. It operated as a federal prison until 1963. Today it is a national recreation area and a National Historic Landmark.

on the promise to "get tough" in order to secure support from an increasingly fearful public who appeared to favor harsh sanctions. Research suggests, however, that the American public is not as punitive as is widely perceived. More importantly, empirical studies have overwhelmingly concluded that "get tough" policies have had little effect on recidivism rates. Despite scientific evidence, mixed public support of harsh criminal sanctions, and an overly burdened criminal justice system, policy makers continue to support and rely on punitiveness as an approach to addressing crime.

Early penal practices in the United States focused on the role of the penitentiary as a means to change the offender. Theoretically, the use of solitary confinement was viewed as a way to provide the offender with the opportunity to reflect on his actions, to repent for his misdeeds, and to reform his behavior. When, in the mid-1800s, the use of the penitentiary failed to succeed in reforming individuals as hoped, significant changes were made to these penal policies and practices. The focus continued to be on reforming the individual, and policies such as indeterminate sentences, rehabilitation programs, offender classification, and the use of early release as an incentive to reform were introduced. By the late 1800s, penal experts suggested that society's ills, and not the individual, were the cause of criminal behavior. Beginning in the 1930s, penal experts argued that criminal behavior was caused by social, psychological, and biological deficiencies that required medical treatment. Until the late 1960s, penal philosophy in the United States continued to focus primarily on the treatment and rehabilitation of the individual offender, whether while incarcerated or in the community.

Get Tough Movement

Two major turning points gave birth to the "get tough" movement in the 1970s. First, in 1974, Robert Martinson published his large-scale evaluation of prior studies of correctional treatment programs in which he concluded that existing attempts at rehabilitation had little effect on recidivism rates. Although Martinson acknowledged that these findings may reflect flawed research designs used in carrying out the original studies, as well as poor implementation of the treatment programs themselves, politicians and the public interpreted these results as "nothing works" regarding correctional treatment. Second, Americans were growing increasingly fearful as crime rates continued to increase and this in turn sparked political debate on how to address this social issue.

In general, both liberals and conservatives questioned the broad discretionary power (which was at the heart of the rehabilitative ideal) given to judges and to correctional and parole authorities. Liberals contended that the use of discretion (e.g., indeterminate sentencing strategies and parole decisions) was applied in a discriminatory and coercive fashion. They pointed to the way in which class and race influenced sentencing outcomes, with poor racial minorities receiving disproportionately longer prison sentences. Conservatives, on the other hand, argued that the rehabilitative philosophy was too lenient in its approach to punishment, which threatened public safety and therefore was ineffective at controlling crime. They argued that crime would be better controlled through increased prison sentences and stricter supervision.

While liberals and conservatives differed in their reasoning for their waning support of rehabilitation, both sides agreed that policy changes were needed. Arguably, the most significant policy change was the implementation of determinate sentencing strategies. This satisfied both liberals and conservatives by removing discretion from the sentencing process. Liberals hoped that a standardized sentencing framework would result in a fairer, more equitable sentencing process; conservatives hoped this change in policy would remove the reliance on rehabilitation as a goal of corrections and produce consistently longer prison sentences.

Growing public concerns about rising crime rates and the increasing distrust of the effectiveness of rehabilitation also resulted in a change in political rhetoric. A far less optimistic, less forgiving view of offenders and the ability of the criminal justice system to change them developed. Accordingly, politicians initiated additional get tough policies intended to curb judicial and correctional discretion and to reduce crime by increasing the severity of punishment. The newly implemented tough-on-crime policies included mandatory minimum sentences, truth-in-sentencing laws that required all prisoners to serve at least 85 percent of their prison terms, three strikes legislation that mandated life sentences for repeat felony offenders, as well as lengthy increases in sentences across a broad array of offense types, most notably for drug crimes. Strict intermediate sanctions, such as intensive probation and boot camps, were implemented as a means to punish and control offenders in the community. Interestingly, new correctional terminology evolved reflecting this more punitive approach. For instance, "supermax" prisons sprouted across the nation and phrases such as "shock" incarceration and "three strikes and you're out" were coined in an effort to deter first-time as well as repeat offenders. New "get tough" initiatives also targeted specific groups of offenders such as gang members and sex offenders in an effort to extend the scope of punishment by increasing sentences and heightening surveillance of these offenders in the community.

Confinement and Parole Changes

Changes in conditions of confinement and parole supervision also emerged to reflect the philosophical shift away from rehabilitation toward an increasingly punitive model of crime control. The incarceration of inmates in tents and the use of chain gangs became commonplace in certain regions of the country. As a means to promote a harsher correctional environment, policies were implemented that restricted prisoners' access to visits and phone calls from family and friends. Amenities such as television, coffee, cigarettes, personal hygiene items, exercise equipment, free writing supplies to mail letters, and the use of small personal appliances were restricted and/or prohibited. While correctional budgets and the safety concerns of inmates and staff led to some of these restrictions, the get tough movement was influential in the changing nature of confinement in prisons and jails.

Parole was revamped in order to diminish or eliminate a prior focus on individualized reintegration and treatment and was replaced with a system of detection and control. In other words, the job of a parole officer changed from providing assistance to recently released prisoners (securing housing, employment, healthcare, or other needed services) to one of supervision and control (monitoring parolee compliance with the conditions of community supervision). Sex offender policies are a prime example of the way in which the goals of community corrections were transformed during this tough-on-crime era. For instance, parole officers who work with this specialized population are no longer charged with the primary task of ensuring that the treatment needs of these offenders are met, but rather they are required to tighten security to enhance crime control.

Some examples include restricting computer use and the time of day in which sex offenders can run personal errands, in order to lessen contact with potential victims (e.g., grocery shopping late at night). Broader policies also were implemented to monitor and control sex offenders in the community, such as requiring sex offenders to register their address with the state, making public personal identifying information, requiring police departments to notify neighbors of the location of sex offenders, enforcing rigid residential restrictions, and, in some states, allowing for the civil commitment of those convicted of a sex crime. Community corrections experienced a fundamental philosophical change in that it began to focus less on "changing" offender behavior through treatment and services and focused more on "catching" offender behavior through the use of heightened supervision and control.

Equally important are the less visible consequences of punitive policies directed toward offenders. A growing number of studies have emerged in recent decades that have examined consequences of the tough-on-crime movement that affect prisoners in ways often not visible to the public. For example, once a prisoner is released, he or she is often banned from residing in certain locations and denied public assistance (e.g., food stamps, healthcare, and housing assistance) and access to college loans. In many states, individuals with a felony record are unable to vote, are disqualified from various forms of employment, and are restricted from obtaining a driver's license. Some states also have implemented policies that define incarceration as a form of parental abandonment, resulting in the limitation or termination of parental rights of prisoners with children. Regardless of whether the intent of such policies is punitive in nature, they create challenges for recently released offenders in their attempts to successfully reintegrate back into society.

Increased Prison Populations

Today, many politicians continue to rely on the political rhetoric of increased punishment as a means of crime control and promise to get tough on crime. However, studies on public attitudes toward punishment reveal that Americans tend to have a fairly complex set of beliefs surrounding tough-on-crime policies. Studies have found that support of such initiatives often depends on how the question is posed to respondents. For example, if individuals are asked general questions regarding their opinion on criminal sanctions, such as the death penalty or three strikes legislation, results overwhelmingly suggest that the public is in favor of such punitive policies. Yet, if respondents are presented with specific situations in which these policies may be used, support for tough-on-crime initiatives is dramatically reduced and rehabilitation for offenders is viewed by respondents as an important goal of the criminal justice system. In light of such inconsistencies in the research on public perceptions of punishment, painting the American public with the broad brush of favoring punitive criminal justice policies is misleading.

Tough-on-crime policies initiated during the 1970s continue to dominate the criminal justice system today. This philosophical shift toward increased punitiveness has placed enormous pressure on the courts and the correctional system as the prison population has expanded sixfold in the last three decades. Comparatively, it has been estimated that the United States incarcerates its citizens at rates of up to 15 times higher than other Western nations. Despite surges in incarceration rates, little evidence supports the notion that increased punishment reduces crime. In contrast, much of the research suggests that lengthier prison terms are associated with increased criminal behavior and that intermediate sanctions such as intensive supervision, boot camps, and shock incarceration have not been shown to reduce rates of recidivism. Faced with the fiscal crisis of the past few years, however, some states have begun to reexamine many of the punitive policies that are representative of this crime control philosophy and have resulted in an increasingly large and expensive prison population.

Melinda Tasca
Marie L. Griffin
Arizona State University

See Also: History of Crime and Punishment in America: 1970–Present; Incapacitation, Theory of; Rehabilitation.

Further Readings
Clear, Todd. *Harm in American Penology: Offenders, Victims, and Their Communities*. Albany: State University of New York Press, 1994.
Cullen, Francis T. "Assessing the Penal Harm Movement." *Journal of Research in Crime and Delinquency*, v.32 (1995).
Cullen, Francis T. and Paul Gendreau. "Assessing Correctional Rehabilitation: Policy, Practice, and Prospects." *Criminal Justice*, v.3 (2000).
Hepburn, John R. and Marie L. Griffin. "Jail Recidivism in Maricopa County." Final report to the Maricopa County Sheriff's Office, 1998.
Lynch, Mona. *Sunbelt Justice: Arizona and the Transformation of American Punishment*. Stanford, CA: Stanford Law Books, 2010.
Martinson, Robert. "What Works? Questions and Answers About Prison Reform." *Public Interest*, v.35 (1974).

New York

The history of crime, police, and punishment in New York can be traced back to its early colonial roots. Early encounters with French and Dutch explorers left footprints on the frontier's wilderness that paled in comparison to the influence that Britain cast over this early colony and the colonists that remained. During the years between 1620 and 1640, a great migration from England was occurring. Families were fleeing England in search of a new life and an opportunity to create a deeply religious society with a political system that gave a voice to the people.

English common law provided the framework for handling criminal offenders in the colonies. Although English common law was employed in adjudicating offenders, religion served as the foundation for determining what would be a crime and what the punishment would be. An early book written in 1648 provided a foundation of legal codes for determining what conduct would constitute a crime. The book *The General Lawes and Libertyes of the Massachusetts Bay Colony* contained very strong biblical references, much harsher than common law. This first legal code established by the colonists provided one of the earliest documents of individual rights in America.

Early crimes in the colony were as simple as lying, idleness, drunkenness, and even just plain bad behavior. The colonists held individual liberty in high regard, and crimes against moral behavior were seen as sins and punishable. Early efforts to control crime were the responsibility of the colonists themselves. Rattle watches were established to conduct citizen patrols during hours of darkness. The early watches were designed to alert the sleeping colonists and send out a hue and cry for assistance. The rattle aspect of these watches came from the citizens banging their wooden rattles together to create a loud, alarming sound that could be heard by the sleeping citizens.

Punishment and Policing
When offenders were apprehended, they were detained until a court proceeding could be held. Early detention areas, what we refer to as jails, were not used for punishment, only for detention. Once an offender was adjudicated, punishment was swift and public. Punishment was employed as a general deterrence for all to see and take the warning that behavior against the moral codes was not tolerated. However, it is worth noting that citizens of higher status were afforded lesser penalties by the courts and seldom were punished publicly. Fines were imposed and paid by citizens of a higher social class.

One of the most common methods of public punishment was the use of a wooden framed object called a stock. The convicted subject would stand before the stock and place his head in the center hole and place his hands at the wrist in the adjacent right and left holes. Citizens of the community were encouraged to insult and throw items at the stocked offender. This process was designed to change the moral behavior through embarrassment. Early reports do not support the ideology of the stock reforming characteristics. Recidivism was alive and revolving even back in the early 1600s.

Trial by ordeal was a judicial practice that was commonly used to determine guilt or innocence of the accused. Hanging and burning at the stake were punishments often used by the courts when the accused had been found guilty of the offense.

Early forms of policing were conducted by the citizens. With the continued growth in population, the need for a regulated police force was realized. England had employed the use of sheriffs to preserve the king's peace. The New York City Sheriff's Office was established in the early 1600s and was designed with a sheriff in each of the five boroughs to enforce laws under a wide jurisdiction. In 1845, the New York Police Department (NYPD) was created, transferring the responsibility of maintaining jails to the city's sheriff's departments. Today's sheriff's department can be found in all 62 counties, and they currently house 84,209 prisoners (state and local), either serving their time for a class A misdemeanor or awaiting trial.

As the state of New York continued to grow, the need for additional law enforcement capabilities also grew. On April 11, 1917, the New York State Police Department was created by New York's legislature. The department's first superintendent, George Fletcher Chandler, was responsible for the department's early organization and development. Mr. Chandler coined the term *New York State Trooper* and was an early advocate of officers carrying their service weapons exposed on a belt, which was not a common practice at the time. Today, recruits must complete a 26-week training program prior to being appointed as a trooper. At the present time, there are approximately 5,000 troopers serving New York State.

New York's Prison History

The New York State prison system is one of the oldest systems in the country. The first structure in New York built to hold offenders was a cold, damp, dim-lit stone structure built in Fort Amsterdam in 1625. The purpose of this prison was to house soldiers who disobeyed orders, native peoples, disorderly people, and debtors. Confinement was not commonly used, and for the most part, it served as a jail until offenders could be adjudicated. Executions were used for many offenses, and public punishment such as whipping and pillorying were commonly employed for lesser offenses.

In 1759, the first jail was built primarily to house civilian lawbreakers, but a space was set aside for debtors and paupers. Bridewell Prison, located at City Hall, was constructed to be a debtor prison, more commonly referred to as a workhouse. Although not prisons or penitentiaries, the first New York institutions for mass incarceration were 25 British ships anchored in the Hudson and East rivers during the American Revolution. Greenwich State Prison was built in 1797 and was New York's first prison built after becoming a state. When they were sent "up the river," convicted offenders were taken from the courthouse down to Wall Street, put on a boat, and sailed up the Hudson River to the Christopher Street docks—one block north stood the prison. Greenwich State Prison was built at the foot of the present-day 10th Street in Greenwich Village. The prison operated for 30 years until it was overshadowed by another institution, Sing-Sing Prison, constructed in Ossining, New York. Officially designated the state prison, Greenwich Village Institution soon became known as Newgate, which was the name for Great Britain's citadel of incarceration.

Newgate Prison, built in 1797, was considered a model of reform at the time, rehabilitating inmates by teaching them trades and allowing them to bathe in an indoor pool. Newgate was built on open farmland, but within a 20-year period, development of this area grew at a much faster rate than anyone could imagine. Prisoners could no longer be marched over the Washington Square to be hanged at the hanging elm tree. In 1828, Newgate was officially closed, and all prisoners were transferred to Sing Sing.

Newgate Prison differed greatly from the British system. Instead of death sentences or crippling corporal punishment, prisoners got lengthy prison sentences. That meant building facilities

Colonial punishment in New York included having one's head and hands locked into a stock similar to this structure. Passersby would try to shame the offenders by attacking them verbally and by throwing objects at them.

to house felons who, under prior laws, would have been executed or severely maimed. These early reforms were premised on the idea that each human possessed a capacity for redemption. Credit for these early reformations was given to the Society of Friends, or the Quakers, and members of the Christian churches. Their belief, which became known as the Pennsylvania system, was that sinners needed to recognize their wrongness and take responsibility for their conduct, do penance for it, and resolve to sin no more. In part, the offender who sinned must become penitent to be saved. Thus, the place set aside for such potential and perhaps actual penitents came to be called a penitentiary. Although it was a noble idea, its serious flaws were soon identified.

On September 10, 1828, construction was started on Blackwell's Island. The penitentiary was the first public institution erected on the island. It was described as "a gloomy and massive edifice, constructed of hewn stone and rubble masonry." Blackwell's Island is now known as Roosevelt Island. In 1884, New York City purchased Riker's Island from the Riker family and used the island as a jail farm. In 1932, the city opened a jail for men on the island to replace its dilapidated jail on Blackwell's Island. Today, the jail is operated by the New York City Department of Corrections with a staff of 7,000 officers and 1,500 civilians to control an inmate population of 14,000.

In 1816, New York constructed Auburn Prison. Auburn was founded as a model for the contemporary ideas about treating prisoners, known as the Auburn system. The Auburn system was in contrast to the earlier ideologies employed by the Quakers, who employed the Pennsylvania system, which was based on solitude, penance, and prayer. The Auburn system replaced prayers with hard labor. Inmates were compelled to work during the day, and the profit from their labor helped to support the prison. Inmates were segregated by type of criminality into different locations within the institution and were identified through the use of special clothing. The traditional American prison uniform, consisting of horizontal black and white stripes, originated at Auburn. Inmates had their hair cut off to prevent head lice and moved from one location to another in lockstep, keeping their heads bowed and their mouths shut. Each prisoner placed a hand on the shoulder of the man in front of him to maintain a rigid separation. Meals were conducted in communal dining halls, but a code of silence was strictly enforced by the guards. For 30 years, this system was adopted by other jurisdictions. The Auburn system was also known as the Congregate system.

The largest prison in New York was often referred to by people from New York City who were sentenced to do their time there as "New York's Siberia" because of the cold climate and isolated location. Dannemora State Prison was named after the village in which it is located in Clinton County. Built in 1844 with prison labor, Dannemora has a unique feature built inside. After the 1929 riot at Dannemora and riots that took place at other prisons, it was necessary for prison reform. The reformation brought about the construction of schools in the prison, and the renovation and restructuring of buildings within the prison creating a more modern appearance. The unique structure found behind the 60-foot walls of Dannemora is the quaint little church of St. Dismas, the Good Thief, begun in 1939 and completed two years later.

In 1899, a mental health facility known as the Dannemora State Hospital was constructed.

Sing-Sing prison, was the third prison constructed in New York State and began operation in 1826 in Ossining, New York, about 30 miles north of New York City. The prison is still in operation, although the original cellblock is no longer in use. A museum housing two historic cells, an electric chair, artifacts, and confiscated weapons is located in Ossining.

Inmates with tuberculosis noticed that their illness was cured during their time of incarceration. Upon closer review, it was determined that the clean Adirondack air was the contributing factor for curing these inmates. Currently, there are approximately 3,000 inmates housed at what is now known as Clinton Correctional Facility.

Elmira Correctional Facility, originally known as Elmira Prison or by the locals as "the Hill," began as a prisoner-of-war camp constructed by the Union army during the American Civil War to house captive Confederate soldiers. The legislature approved the building of a new prison on the site, which housed offenders between the ages of 16 and 30. In July 1876, the prison began receiving prisoners from Auburn. The opening of Elmira became a third new methodology of dealing with incarcerated offenders. Unlike the Pennsylvania system or the Auburn system, under the direction of warden Zebulon Brockway, incarceration was designed to reform each inmate by an individualized program. Brockway rejected the earlier draconian system that was grounded on hard labor, silence, and religious and moral lectures enforced by barbaric brutality. Instead, he favored the mark system, developed in Australia by Alexander Maconochie, which rewarded inmates for good behavior with early release.

The Elmira system was influential in prison reform. Two central ideas emerged from the system: Juvenile and adult offenders need to be handled differently, and prisoner rehabilitation is possible. Inmates were classified into three categories or grades. Newly arriving prisoners were graded with a 2 for the first six months of incarceration; inmates who were institutionalized were graded with a number 1 classification; and inmates who resisted institutional life, were less responsive to rehabilitation, and had behavioral problems received a grade of 3. The Elmira system ultimately influenced the construction of 25 reformatories in 12 states across the country.

Upon Brockway's resignation, the reformatory style of life succumbed to the more traditional standard of custody and treatment methods.

As the offender population continued to grow, the need for more cell space and construction of new prisons increased. Again, new lands were sought to construct another prison. In 1905, a large tract of land was purchased in Comstock. By 1909, construction had begun on what would come to be known as Great Meadow Correctional Facility. On February 11, 1911, inmates started arriving at Great Meadow, and construction continued to enlarge its holding capacity. In the beginning, Great Meadow was home to first-time offenders, and there did not seem to be a need for a wall around the institution. But as population at the prison continued to increase, and the inmate population began to change from first-time offenders to multiple offenders, the need for a wall was evident. In 1924, construction of the wall around Great Meadow began, and four years later, the inmates had walled themselves in. Great Meadow is a maximum-security facility today.

Female Prisons in New York State
New York presently has five women's prisons. Bedford Hills, the largest women's maximum-security prison, which was the old Westfield State Farm, originated with an 1892 law (Chapter 637) providing for a reformatory for women. The reformatory opened in 1901 under the jurisdiction of the State Board of Charities. Admitted were women 16 to 30 years of age who were convicted of a misdemeanor. Bedford Hills functions as a general confinement facility, reception center, detention center, and diagnostic treatment center. Approximately 800 females are housed there.

Bayview Women's Correctional Institution, known as the Vertical Institution, is an eight-story building in downtown Manhattan's West Chelsea District. It was constructed in 1931 as the Seamen's House YMCA, a place for merchant sailors to stay while their ships were docked. In 1967, the Narcotic Addiction Control Commission (NACC) was created to direct the state's efforts that were ongoing since the early 1950s to combat the rising inner-city drug problems. This program had a short life span with the introduction of Rockefeller drug laws in 1973. Addicts who formerly were committed to NACC instead received long prison sentences, and the state began to phase out its drug rehabilitation centers. Bayview's capacity today is 183 general confinement beds, plus 140 work release beds.

Taconic Correctional Facility is a medium-security women's prison that is associated with Bedford Hills. In 1973, Taconic began to operate as an autonomous medium-security prison.

Albion Correction Facility is the world's first institution for female "defective delinquents." Credit for creating the Albion institution belongs primarily to Josephine Shaw Lowell, the "Queen Victoria of New York." In 1876, she was appointed the first female commissioner on the New York State Board of Charities, an umbrella organization overseeing a multitude of agencies serving the poor, sick, blind, insane, alcoholic, orphaned, and otherwise needy. Lowell assumed a leadership role in development in New York's correctional history and reformatories for women and institutions for the mentally retarded. New York's first women's reformatory opened in Hudson in 1887. Within two years, Hudson reached its capacity of 234 inmates. Lowell pressed the legislature for two additional female houses of refuge—one in Bedford Hills, and the other in the western sector of the state. In April 1892 on an old farm site in the town of Albion, construction began on the Western House of Refuge for Women. Albion officially opened December 8, 1893. The Albion mission was to "give such moral and religious training as will induce the inmates to form a good character and such training in domestic work as will eventually enable them to find employment, secure good homes, and be self-supporting." In the beginning, Albion counseled domesticity; today, it counters domestic abuse. Once, it instilled ladylike graces; today, programs deal with aggressive behavior control, anger management, and alternatives to violence. The female population turned in their kitchen utilities for welder's helmets and sheet metal fabricating tools. Little remains of Lowell's ideology of creating ladies out of these wayward souls.

Conclusion
The history of crime, police, and punishment in New York is vast, dating back to the 1600s. The French, Dutch, and English have left notable footprints on the current judicial system. Early legal

codes, English common law, and religion shape much of the historical landscape. Colonization and crime go hand in hand, especially when social mores and moral ideologies collide. Enforcement of moral rules and social laws has its roots with colonial Americans on their rattle watches, patrolling the streets in search of violators, to paid law enforcement officers as colonies grew into cities and the need for regulated policing of streets grew with the population. Once violators were apprehended and found guilty of their crime, the need for punishment was created. Methods of punishment itself have a long, rich history.

In early New York, many of these earlier forms of punishment were used. Stocks, pillory, dunking stocks, and branding were commonly used as punishment. Hanging, beheading, and burning at the stake were used in the more serious crimes that were punishable by death. The use of incarceration for punishment became a popular way of dealing with less serious violators. Today's prison system has its roots in New York. New York has the most prisons in the United States, ranging from work camps to maximum "A" high-security institutions. Crime, police, and punishment in New York are deep and rich with history, which in turn offers scholars the opportunity to explore many fascinating areas of New York's jurisprudence system.

William T. Jones
State University of New York, Canton

See Also: 1600 to 1776 Primary Documents; Auburn State Prison; Bedford Hills Correctional Facility; Brockway, Zebulon; Elmira Prison; New York City; Sing Sing Correctional Facility.

Further Readings
"Crime in New York 1850–1950." John Jay College. http://www.lib.jjay.cuny.edu/crimeinny (Accessed December 2010).
Federal Bureau of Investigation Uniform Crime Reports. "New York Crime Rates 1960–2009." http://www.disastercenter.com/crime/nycrime.htm (Accessed December 2010).
McCarthy, Thomas C. *Penitentiary Origins in the City of New York*. New York Correction History Society. http://correctionhistory.org/html/chronicl/nycdoc/html/penitentiary2.html (Accessed December 2010).

Sullivan, Dennis. *The Punishment of Crime in Colonial New York: The Dutch Experience in Albany During the Seventeenth Century*. New York: Peter Lang, 1998.

New York City

From its earliest days as a Dutch trading post to its present-day incarnation as one of the world's centers of cultural and economic power, commerce has been at the center of New York City's raison d'être. Positioned strategically at the nexus of evolving flows of money, goods, and people between North America, Europe, and around the world, the city's shifting position in a global economy has driven its transformation from vital seaport to industrial powerhouse to world financial capital. While New York's role as a conduit for material resources has historically fueled the city's physical growth, its corresponding role as the point of origin for much of the country's news, culture, and entertainment has ensured that New York remains a symbol and a bellwether for the United States at large, as much in the realm of the illicit as in other areas of social life. Over time, the city's vast mélange of economic activity has provided myriad opportunities for gain outside the boundaries of the strictly legal.

A Hub of Trade
Initially colonized by the Dutch during the early 17th century, New Amsterdam, as it was called, began life as a trading post dealing in furs acquired from local Native American peoples. In 1626, construction began on Fort Amsterdam, and during the Dutch period, crime seems to have largely revolved around offenses committed by the soldiers stationed there—drunkenness, desertion, insubordination, destruction of civilian property, and petty larceny. When the English seized the colony from the Dutch in 1664, they quickly began to integrate the growing city into the transatlantic commercial networks that nourished Britain's expanding empire. Prior to the American Revolution, New York served as one node of a triangle that connected the North American agricultural hinterland with West Indian sugar plantations and

British manufacturers supplying finished goods to the colonies. Along with the opportunities for piracy and smuggling engendered by the booming trade—smuggling may have accounted for as much as one-third of all northern commerce during this time—came a vast increase in population that included thousands of transient laborers and an increasing number of slaves, many of whom congregated in waterfront taverns that served as sanctuaries for prostitution and the blossoming trade in stolen goods. In a city that contained the highest concentration of slaves north of Virginia, fears of both slave insurrection and class-based interracial solidarity haunted the well-to-do. Ordinances and slave codes designed to limit the ability of servants and slaves to congregate proved ineffective, and the city's thin, disorganized police apparatus was relatively powerless to prevent the development of a vibrant interracial underworld centered in and around the city's "disorderly houses," taverns often run by widows or unmarried women unable to support themselves by legal means. A bloody slave revolt in 1712, in which slaves set fires and ambushed residents who rushed out to quell them, provoked a brutal crackdown, but in 1741, New Yorkers discovered what they believed to have been a larger-scale conspiracy on the part of slaves and poor whites to burn the city, murder its inhabitants, and govern it themselves. Whether or not the "Negro Plot," as it was called, represented an actual conspiracy or simply a manifestation of panic and paranoia among the city's elite continues to provoke debate among historians to this day.

The outbreak of the long imperial crisis that resulted in the American Revolution initially brought great prosperity to New York City, as merchants amassed ever-greater fortunes supplying the influx of troops required to fight King George's and the French and Indian Wars, as well as outfitting the numerous privateering vessels that preyed upon French and Spanish ships in the Atlantic. The newfound plenitude, combined with a massive influx of soldiers, sailors, and fortune-seekers, brought new opportunities for plunder. The increasingly bold and organized trade in commercial sex flourished, as did assaults and property crimes like burglary. City authorities, who still relied on an unpaid municipal watch, were initially powerless to prevent the outbreaks of malfeasance and responded to the public outrage by constructing a new city jail, creating a paid watch, and installing whale-oil lamps along the city's streets, to be maintained by a new corps of municipal lamplighters. The jail soon proved inadequate, however, and by 1772, in the middle of economic depression, political crisis, and an unprecedented population surge, authorities constructed a new prison, which they named Bridewell after London's notorious institution of the same name. During the struggle for independence, the British quickly reoccupied New York and imposed martial law for the duration of the conflict. Imperial authorities promptly freed all slaves who would pledge allegiance to the Crown, while the outrageous behavior of British troops and their leaders, who looted and vandalized private homes and public buildings alike, extorted provisions from surrounding farmers, embezzled money from city coffers, and ran protection rackets, shocked and angered the city's cowed populace.

Upon independence, New York resumed its role as a thriving mercantile city. Improvements

A 19th-century illustration of "murderers' row" in "The Tombs," showing the cells of condemned prisoners. The Manhattan Detention Complex city jail, built in 1835 in downtown Manhattan, was referred to as "The Tombs."

in transportation and communications, especially the Erie Canal, which in 1825 connected the east coast to the agricultural interior, bolstered the city's status as the country's most important seaport, while new waves of immigration set the stage for the class and interethnic conflict that riled the city during the first part of the 19th century. Moreover, as the city's politics began to organize themselves into a recognizably modern form, the line between politics and vice became so blurred as to render the two virtually indistinguishable. The first organized street gangs in New York had appeared toward the end of the 18th century, but the arrival of large numbers of immigrants, especially from Ireland, restructured the city's criminal landscape. During the 1830s and 1840s, nativist gangs like the Bowery Boys squared off in bloody turf battles against their Irish counterparts throughout New York's notorious Five Points neighborhood, a state of affairs later chronicled in Herbert Asbury's popular book *The Gangs of New York* and Martin Scorcese's 2002 film of the same name. The gangs frequently doubled as volunteer fire companies, there being no professional force in the city at this time, and found themselves enlisted on election days to steal or stuff ballot boxes and to intimidate the supporters of rival candidates. Office-seekers elected in this manner, many of whom doubled as proprietors of the saloons where the gangs congregated, then arranged protection for the city's proliferating saloons, brothels, and "hells," or gambling dens. After the Civil War, many of the gangs transformed into quasi-legitimate "political clubs" run by district leaders from Tammany Hall, the city's notorious Democratic machine, which reached its corrupt apotheosis under the leadership of William "Boss" Tweed, the legendary manipulator of city patronage who died in the Ludlow Street Jail after stealing an estimated $25 to $45 million from the city, a figure that easily exceeds a billion dollars in today's money.

Prostitution flourished as well during this time, as the low wages afforded to the increasing numbers of single young women streaming into the city from rural areas induced many to turn to the illicit sex trade as a means to survive. They found ready clients among the crowds of single men who had entered the city, often as immigrants. Prostitution was often tolerated by authorities and encouraged by landlords, many of whom believed that prostitutes, with their relative stability of income, made for especially good tenants. In 1836, the grisly murder of young prostitute Helen Jewett in a Fifth Ward brothel sent newspaper circulations soaring and revealed the trade's allure to men of all classes. By 1860, New York City contained just over 800,000 people—and 500 brothels.

In response to the uncontrolled growth of illicit activity, officials established in 1845 a full-time, paid, professional police force roughly on the model of London's Metropolitan Police, although the decentralized nature of New York's force ensured that officers remained beholden to local politicians and retained plenty of opportunities for profit. Indeed, bribe-taking remained a routine feature of police life until at least the 1970s. The city's correctional institutions multiplied as well during this time, with penitentiaries established at Bellevue in 1816 and on Blackwell's Island (now Roosevelt Island) in 1836, and the erection of the Halls of Justice, nicknamed "The Tombs" for its distinctive Egyptian Revival architecture, in 1838. In 1884, New York City acquired Riker's Island, which from that point served as the city's main jail complex. Today, the facility houses approximately 14,000 prisoners per day, making it by most measures the largest jail facility in the United States.

Parallel Growth

The late 19th and early 20th centuries witnessed the parallel professionalization of both criminals and their ostensible nemeses on the police force. Gangs continued to run protection rackets, plunder ships docked at the city's many wharves, commit bank frauds when not robbing the banks themselves, and serve as muscle for the city's political machines. The dynamic relationship between criminals and the police was crystallized in the words of police captain Alexander "Clubber" Williams, who rejoiced upon his reassignment to the Tenderloin, one of the city's most notorious red-light districts, located in the vicinity of today's Empire State Building. Williams, who became known as the "Czar of the Tenderloin," described the opportunities for personal enrichment available to enterprising officers. "I've been having chuck steak ever since I've been on the force," he quipped, "and now I'm going to have a bit of tenderloin." Later, the city's red-light district migrated uptown to the emerging black ghetto of Harlem, where rigid racial segregation and discrimination forced many residents into the illicit economy and where police brutality was the norm. Major riots in 1935 and 1943 highlighted the crises in Harlem and foreshadowed the urban ghetto revolts of the 1960s, which were directed mainly against the police.

The first half of the 20th century proved to be a golden age for organized crime in New York, especially as Prohibition, which never enjoyed great popularity in the city, vastly increased the opportunities for illicit profiteering and spurred a greater degree of organization on the part of criminal gangs that controlled the bootlegging trade. New York functioned as a source of both supply and demand for alcohol, serving as a distribution point for much of the country and housing an estimated 32,000 speakeasies. A new generation of leaders, including "Dutch" Schultz, "Lucky" Luciano, Meyer Lansky, and Frank Costello, adopted the businesslike model set by the infamous gambler Arnold Rothstein, who allegedly rigged the 1919 World Series, and the unique "five families" structure of the city's Italian Mafia emerged. The five families, whose exploits were fictionalized in the hit book *The Godfather* and the later films of the same name, rationalized and systematized the business of crime in the city, dividing up turf and raking in cash from gambling, loan-sharking, prostitution, labor racketeering, illegal drug sales, and the usual protection rackets, now extended to New York's vegetable and garment industries.

During the latter half of the 20th century, New York, like many northern cities, experienced the related ills of depopulation, deindustrialization, increasingly rigid racial segregation, and rising crime rates. Reversing a steady decline that had commenced in the late 19th century, the number of annual murders in the city reached 1,000 for the first time in 1969, surged abruptly during the 1970s and again during the 1980s, and peaked at 2,245 in 1990. While traditional organized crime was weakened through the application of the Racketeer Influenced and Corrupt Organizations Act (RICO) and corruption on the police force was exposed in the Knapp Commission hearings, most notably by officer Frank Serpico, whose lonely crusade against graft was depicted in the 1973 film

An uncropped version of the photograph printed in a 1963 edition of the World-Telegram & Sun *reveals blood on the streets during the police brutality linked to the Harlem riots.*

Serpico, police and politicians found themselves bewildered and grasped for responses. Rioting during the 1977 citywide blackout and the panic over the Son of Sam serial killer in the same year helped make New York a nationwide symbol of the country's urban ills. Drug crime enforcement was stiffened with the passage of the Rockefeller drug laws in 1973, which imposed harsh mandatory minimum sentences on offenders, while the police department reintroduced foot patrols, part of a national trend toward "community policing."

In 1994, former prosecutor Rudolph Giuliani conducted a successful mayoral campaign largely on promises to reduce crime. While crime did indeed drop during Giuliani's tenure, controversy remains over whether his endorsement of aggressive policing tactics and "broken windows" approach, which focused on quality-of-life crimes, were active factors in the decline, which occurred nationwide. Moreover, during the Giuliani era, the police department became embroiled in a series of high-profile brutality cases, most famously when officers shot unarmed Bronx resident Amadou Diallo 41 times in the hallway of his apartment building.

The terrorist attacks of September 11, 2001, killed 23 police officers and prompted the creation of new deputy commissioners for intelligence and counterterrorism. On the whole, however, by the beginning of the 21st century, the Federal Bureau of Investigation (FBI) would report that crime had declined in New York to the point where it had become statistically one of the country's safest large cities.

Andrew Battle
City University of New York Graduate Center

See Also: 1851 to 1900 Primary Documents; 1901 to 1920 Primary Documents; 1961 to 1980 Primary Documents; 1981 to 2000 Primary Documents; 2001 to 2012 Primary Documents; Genovese, Vito; Giuliani, Rudolph; Gotti, John; Hays, Jacob; Knapp Commission; LaGuardia, Fiorello; Luciano, "Lucky"; New York; Organized Crime, History of; Rothstein, Arnold; Schultz, Dutch; Wilson, James Q.

Further Readings
Burrows, Edwin and Mike Wallace. *Gotham: A History of New York City to 1898.* New York: Oxford University Press, 1998.
Jackson, Kenneth T., ed. *The Encyclopedia of New York City,* 2nd ed. New Haven, CT: Yale University Press, 2010.
Johnson, Marilynn S. *Street Justice: A History of Police Brutality in New York City.* Boston: Beacon Press, 2003.
Lardner, James and Thomas Repetto. *NYPD: A City and Its Police.* New York: Henry Holt, 2000.

Newark, New Jersey

Newark is a city located near the Passaic River and Newark Bay in northern New Jersey within the county of Essex with a current population of 277,140. Newark is the largest city in New Jersey and one of the most ethnically diverse cities in the state. Newark was founded as a result of a land purchase by New Haven colony Puritans led by surveyor, tax collector, appraiser, and magistrate Robert Treat (1624–1710) in 1666; Treat eventually served as governor of the colony of Connecticut from 1683 to 1698. The land was purchased by the Puritans from the Hackensack Indians.

The name *Milford* was first applied to what is today Newark but later abandoned for the term *New Ark* or *New Work*, a phrase eventually abbreviated to *Newark*. Newark at its inception was essentially a settlement in which church and state were one. The phrase *city of churches* has often been applied to Newark, given the proliferation of religious structures that are prominent throughout the city. The city was incorporated in 1713 as one of New Jersey's collections of townships. Newark began to attract new immigrants through the 1700s and early 1800s, when the city began to become an industrial center.

Newark began to emerge as an industrial city in the 19th century, given its proximity to key waterways, including the Passaic River, Newark Bay, and the Atlantic Ocean.

Economics and Industry

Newark experienced dramatic changes in industry, business, commerce, and population through the late 19th century and into the 20th century. John Wesley Hyatt created the first commercially successful plastic (celluloid) from a factory on Mechanic Street in Newark. This was a product used in carriages made in Newark, billiard balls, and dentures. Edward Weston developed an improved process of zinc electroplating and the making of an arc lamp in Newark while Thomas Edison perfected the process of automatic telegraphing in a Newark lab in the 1870s before moving to Menlo Park.

The Gold and Stock Telegraph Company paid Edison thousands of dollars for his improved version of the stock ticker (a telegraph printing instrument). Newark became a center of the insurance industry with the establishment of Mutual Benefit in 1845 and Prudential in 1873. By the 1880s, Newark-based insurance companies were second only to Hartford, Connecticut–based firms in the selling of insurance. The population of Newark increased by 200,000 from 1880 to 1910, reach-

The Newark Police headquarters building on Orange Street. The Newark Police Department is the largest in New Jersey and has been in operation since 1856, when the city council approved a budget of $7,462.00 to create a daytime police department and $14,458.00 to maintain a night watch department. The departments merged in 1857 to become the Newark Police Department.

ing 347,000 including increasing numbers of immigrants from Ireland, Germany, and Italy at the turn of the century.

Newark was a thriving industrial city with one of the busiest intersections in the United States at Market and Broad streets in the first decades of the 20th century but experienced a sharp decline following World War II. By the 1920s, the population approached the 500,000 mark but began to decline with industry and white flight after 1945. Postwar practices of the U.S. federal government such as redlining helped to facilitate the decline of a once thriving city. The Federal Housing Administration (FHA) redlined nearly all of Newark, backing loans in the emerging suburbs as opposed to the city regions. This made it virtually impossible to secure a mortgage or home improvement loan in a city marked by aging buildings and declining industry. This led many manufacturers to build enterprises in outlying areas as opposed to within the city. The rise of new roadway systems such as Interstate 280, the New Jersey Turnpike, and Interstate 78 made it easier for upwardly mobile working and middle-class families to access the city from outlying suburbs as commuters. A majority of the citizens moving out of the city were white, while through the 1950s large numbers of nonwhites made their way in to the city to become permanent residents. The Great Migration of African Americans in the first few decades of the 20th century to cities in the north, such as Newark, helped to change the racial composition of the city in dramatic ways. By 1966, the majority of people living in Newark were African American. The decline of industrial jobs, the rise of unemployment, poverty, and the white flight out of the city compounded by political corruption in the second half of the 20th century help explain why Newark has been listed among one of the "crime capitals" of America.

Society and Politics

In the 1950s, Newark's white population decreased by 25 percent, from roughly 363,000 to 266,000; this decline continued into the 1960s as racial tensions increased. While Newark was becoming increasingly African American, African Americans remained out of power, such as with the police force (only 150 of 1,400 police officers in Newark were African American by 1967). Many white-owned businesses remained, but increasing poverty, diminishing purchasing power, and deteriorating living conditions in the Central Ward (where most of the black population resided) led to the Newark riots in 1967. On July 12, 1967, an African American taxi driver named John Smith was beaten by Newark police officers for allegedly resisting arrest. Before the riots that followed the beating of Smith through July (amid rumors that the police had killed him), then Mayor Hugh Addonizio had offered to condemn sections of the Central Ward to make way for the building of the University of Medicine and Dentistry. The Newark riots ended with 26 killed, 1,500 wounded, 1,600 arrested, and the destruction of an estimated 167 grocery stores (many of these establishments never returned to the city). Middle-class communities of all races fled the city in the 1970s and 1980s, along with vital industries, leaving behind a city increasingly marred by political corruption, crime, and urban decay.

Newark is currently divided into five political wards with the North, Central, and West wards containing the residential neighborhoods while the industrial area, airport, and seaport are part of the East and South wards. Governance of Newark is divided between the mayor and city council. Since 1962, five mayors of Newark have been indicted for crimes while in office, including Hugh Addonizio, Kenneth Gibson, and Sharpe James. This is every mayor elected since 1962 with the exception of the current (2012) mayor, Cory Booker. Addonizio, mayor of Newark from 1962 to 1970, was convicted of extortion for taking kickbacks from city contractors in 1967. Gibson, successor to Addonizio and the first black mayor of the city, was tried and acquitted while in office and was later convicted of tax evasion in 2002. Sharpe James, who defeated Gibson in 1986, was found guilty of fraud in 2008 and was forced to spend several months in prison following his conviction.

Crime and Punishment

Newark has an illustrious history in crime and punishment from the building of the Old Essex Jail in 1837 (recently transformed into a $24 million office complex) to Northern State Prison, which currently holds more than 2,000 inmates. "Dutch" Schultz was killed at the Palace Chophouse Bar along with members of his infamous Schultz Gang on October 23, 1935, at the height of organized crime in the city. The DeCavalcante crime family in New Jersey included a Newark faction run by Gaspare D'Amico through 1937 followed by the leadership of Stefano "Steve" Badami through the 1950s. The DeCavalcante family's New Jersey crime network in both Elizabeth and Newark was likely the inspiration for the HBO series *The Sopranos*.

Newark has had a history that is attached to both organized crime and the crime of the century with the September 11, 2001, attacks orchestrated by the radical terrorist organization Al Qaeda. United Airlines Flight 93 to San Francisco departed from Newark International Airport the

The stereotype of Newark as a crime-ridden city full of dilapidated buildings is being replaced as the area undergoes improvements to business, industry, and entertainment.

morning of September 11 and crashed in a field in Shanksville, Pennsylvania, killing all passengers on board after being hijacked by four Al Qaeda terrorists under instructions from Osama bin Laden. Newark International Airport was renamed Newark Liberty International Airport after the attacks.

In the 1990s and through the early decades of the 21st century, Newark has been identified by several sources as a high-crime city. Newark was identified by *Time* magazine as "the most dangerous city in the nation" in 1996. The causes of Newark's high crime rate are directly linked to elevated levels of unemployment, poverty, urban decay, and political corruption. In the 2003 Federal Bureau of Investigation (FBI) *Report of Offenses Known to Law Enforcement* Newark's violent crime rating was high in several categories. In this same report, murder in Newark was listed at 3.8 times the national average, and robbery in Newark was recorded at 2.14 times the national average, and aggravated assault at 1.2 times the national average. This 2003 report also recorded property crimes such as car theft and arson. In the category of car theft, Newark ranked 3.6 times higher than the national average and has been dubbed by some in the mass media as the "car jack capital of the world." Newark was rated in the Morgan Quinto list of dangerous cities in the top 25 more than once during the mid-2000s. In recent years, Newark has experienced a dramatic decrease in the murder rate, such as with the 30 percent decline that took place between 2007 and 2008. March 2010 was the first month since 1966 that not one murder occurred in the city.

Crime Trends

During the 1960s, Newark was at the center of violent unrest in 1967 as illustrated in the Newark riots that left the city economically devastated. This was compounded by the decline of manufacturing, white flight, and urban decay. There were an estimated 500 urban disturbances in the United States during the 1960s, and the post-1960s violent crime rate into the early 1970s was astronomically high. The 1980s were also a violent decade. The peak in violent crime in the United States occurred roughly in the year 1993. The 2000s indicate a significant decline in crime rates in the United States, and 2009 has been identified as the "safest year" in 40 years.

Newark has experienced trends in crime that are higher than both the state and national averages. The FBI Uniform Crime Report indicated that in 2008 Newark had a rate of 951 violent crimes per 100,000 persons. The New Jersey state average was 342 per 100,000, while the national average was 676 per 100,000 persons. Only 3 percent of the cities in America at the time had a higher crime rate than Newark. The 2000s have remained violent in Newark despite the national trend of declining crime since the 1990s. From 2001 to 2002, more than 1,000 violent crimes per 100,000 persons occurred, and from 2004 to 2006, the trend was similar and above 1,000. Crimes of property in Newark have remained high in the past decade, remaining at 3,000 to 5,000 property crimes per 100,000 since 2001. Newark was classified as "safer" than only 12 percent of the cities in the United States between 2006 and 2008.

Newark's Renaissance

Newark continues to serve as an important center of business, commerce, and entertainment while at the same time the city is undergoing a much-needed renaissance in these arenas. Prudential, one of the world's largest insurance companies, remains headquartered in Newark. The Newark airport, one of the busiest in the nation, Rutgers University, the University of Medicine and Dentistry of New Jersey, the New Jersey Institute of Technology, and PSE&G constitute vital aspects of business, industry, and entertainment in Newark today. The New Jersey Performing Arts Center (NJPAC) is a $180-million entertainment center that opened in 1997 and is home to the New Jersey Symphony Orchestra.

The center features a diverse contingent of performances from opera to gospel to hip hop. Riverfront Stadium is home to the minor league baseball team the Newark Bears, and the Prudential Center recently opened in 2007 for the New Jersey Devils hockey team. Newark has endured a cycle of industrialization, deindustrialization, and renewal not unlike other cities in the United States such as Detroit, Chicago, and Camden, New Jersey.

Hettie V. Williams
Monmouth University

See Also: Camden, New Jersey; New Jersey; Riots; Terrorism; Urbanization.

Further Readings

Immerso, Michael. *Newark's Little Italy: The Vanished First Ward*. New Brunswick, NJ: Rutgers University Press, 1999.

Ingle, Bob and Sandy McClure. *The Soprano State: New Jersey's Culture of Corruption*. New York: St. Martin's Press, 2008.

Mumford, Kevin. *Newark: A History of Race, Rights, and Riots in America*. New York: New York University Press, 2008.

Porambo, Ronald. *No Cause for Indictment: An Autopsy of Newark*. New York: Melville Publishing, 2007.

Rudolph, Robert. *The Boys From New Jersey: How the Mob Beat the Feds*. New Brunswick, NJ: Rutgers University Press, 1995.

Tuttle, Brad R. *How Newark Became Newark: The Rise, Fall, and Rebirth of an American City*. New Brunswick, NJ: Rutgers University Press, 2009.

News Media, Crime in

The news media spends much time reporting on crime and criminal justice in America and is a primary source of information about these topics for the general public.

People now have easy access to the news at their fingertips, with online news sources and the sharing of information through social media. They also have the ability to discuss the articles through forums on many news Websites. Citizens must discern which information is accurate and which information is inaccurate, and may come to conclusions about a suspect's guilt or innocence or make judgments about a crime victim's actions based on what they read. Citizens will also draw conclusions about how the criminal justice system operates and whether or not it does so fairly. In other words, our collective knowledge about the causes, amount, and types of crime in our society—as well as the workings of criminal law, the police, courts, corrections, and other aspects of the criminal justice system—is heavily influenced by the news media.

Early Crime News

Crime stories often lead the evening news and are given prime spots in newspapers and online news sources, though this was not always the case. While crime has been with us for millennia, crime news is a much more recent development, though by no means solely a modern phenomenon. Indeed, the Roman Senator Cicero is said to have lamented the too frequent reports of criminal violence that filled the "newspaper" of ancient Rome—the *acta diurnal populi Romani*. However, for most of human history, technological limitations and low levels of literacy meant that these presentations of crime were restricted primarily to oral accounts, with some augmentation through written text and artistic renderings such as sketches, wood etchings, and paintings. While actual accounts of crime in early news were relatively rare, some attention was devoted to issues of "justice"—that is, the state's retributive response to wrongdoing. Newspaper-like accounts of executions can be found in the historical records of many African, Asian, and European nations. These stories were frequently devoted to the "spiritual" consequences of crime, though they were occasionally paired with notions of the state's retributive responsibility. Tales of executions were recounted in gruesome detail for the news audience, serving both the functions of vicarious titillation as well as general deterrence.

An early incarnation of broadsheet newspapers, the English "newsbooks" of the 17th century began to include sensational and bizarre accounts of crime and misadventure. In the United States, the publication of criminal narratives goes back to the colonial era. Strict morality and religiosity in colonial America curbed crime, but also created ample opportunity for news accounts of transgression and punishment. News accounts of colonists convicted of using profanity, displaying public drunkenness, or inappropriate behavior occurring between men and women and sentenced to lashings, the stock, or pillory were a common fixture. For example, in 1656 a newspaper in Boston reported that a naval officer, Captain Kemble, was placed in the stocks for having engaged in lewd behavior on the Sabbath, while a Salem paper recounted the fines imposed on John Smith and Mrs. John Kitchin for their frequent absences from church. In addition to other strategies for shaming

As crime news became more prominent in the 19th century, papers like the New York Herald *and the* Sun *captivated their readers with detailed accounts of crime. The coverage of the murders of high-class New York prostitute Helen Jewett in 1836 (left) and Mary Rogers, a New York tobacco shop worker in 1841 were the beginnings of sensationalized news coverage.*

offenders (such as clipping ears, branding, or forcing them to wear signs—such as "A" for adultery) crime news coverage heavily emphasized specific and general deterrence.

In keeping with the punitive orientation of American justice, the harsh punishment of offenders was a common theme in colonial accounts of crime. Stories recounting public lashings, scalding, and executions were among newspapers' staple offering, even for what we would today consider relatively minor offenses. For example, in 1752, the *Pennsylvania Gazette* reported that John Broughton had the letter "R" branded on his hand and was sentenced to a lifetime of servitude for the crime of pickpocketing.

As early American cities grew, the general populace's fear of crime increased. In 1744, a newspaper in New York reported that the city's streets were becoming very dangerous at night and that only the "sufficiently strong or well armed" were safe. Indeed, according to the press, it was not simply growing urban areas that were dangerous, but small communities as well. Many colonial newspapers featured editorial content condemning the English for transporting some of Britain's criminals, particularly counterfeiters, pickpockets, and highwaymen to America.

Nineteenth-Century Crime News

Growing populations, increased literacy, and technological advancements in the early decades of the 19th century made news accounts of crime a more prominent component of the general public's knowledge of crime and criminal justice. By the 1830s bizarre and fear-laden crime news coverage under the auspices of the "astonishingly real" became standard fare. James Bennett's fledgling paper, the *New York Herald*, vastly increased its circulation with long, drawn-out crime stories, such as that of the murder of Helen Jewett, an upscale New York City prostitute in 1836. The paper titillated readers with details from the trial and of Jewett's death and championed the innocence of her accused murderer Richard Robinson. Other New York City newspapers, such as Benjamin Day's *The Sun,* condemned Robinson and editorialized that he used his family's prominent wealth to buy an acquittal from a corrupt criminal justice system.

By the mid-1840s the penny presses in the United States began to publish lurid accounts and photos of the dead and dying, frequently related to street crime, but also included those resulting from what the media frequently termed *industrial accidents.* While this decade began with a clear distinction on the treatment of crime between the "exploitative" newspapers and their more "serious" counterparts, it was not long before all the papers were including sensationalized accounts and photographs of heinous crimes among their staple offerings. Coverage of the death of Mary Rogers, a tobacco store employee from a New York City in the summer of 1841, exemplified the news media's approach to crime news coverage during this time period. Dubbed the "Beautiful Cigar Girl," she was missing for three days before her body was found floating in the Hudson River. The New York press transformed her death into a national story with sensationalized coverage—alternately speculating suicide and several different murder scenarios and reporting a confession that Rogers died as a result of a failed abortion. Drawn out for months, these stories also served as a venue for criticism of the police, debates over abortion, and gang activity.

By the mid-19th century newspapers were regularly covering a host of crime and criminal justice issues in connection with city politics, industry, labor movements, and immigration. Anti-Irish immigrant sentiment in the 1860s resulted in newspapers from all political stripes running stories about crimes and disturbances linked to Irish immigrants. This period also saw newspapers addressing the role of government authority in crime news stories ranging from the New York City Draft Riots through police discretion and the use of firearms.

Twentieth-Century Crime News

By the turn of the 20th century, crime took on the character of the saleable news commodity we know it to be today. This epoch saw the rise of yellow journalism, exemplified by Joseph Pulitzer's *New York World.* These periodicals ran features on atrocious, though statistically rare criminal violence, including cannibalism, human sacrifice, kidnapping, white slavery, and gangland murder. William Randolph Hearst's *San Francisco Examiner* similarly entertained readers, devoting a quarter of the paper to coverage of crime. Stories about transgressive (typically, lascivious) behavior and humorous coverage of arrestees brought into lower courts were standard fare.

By the 1920s crime news coverage took on an increasingly lurid, sensational flavor. A growing number of mediated depictions of crime, particularly visual representations of dead and dying crime victims, became the standard fare in newspapers. News audiences were inundated with photographs of spectacular death moments, brought on by criminal violence on the streets of urban cities. During this decade, news coverage of crime also harkened back to a zeitgeist of an earlier age—the punishment of criminals. News accounts of trials abounded, as did exposes on hard labor in prison and executions of convicted felons. In 1928, newspaper photographer Tom Howard smuggled a small camera into the press viewing gallery of New York's Sing Sing Prison during the execution of convicted murderer Ruth Snyder. Howard snapped a photo as the electricity surged through Snyder's body. The blurry, full-page photo of Snyder's jolting body captioned "DEAD!" appeared on the front of New York's *Daily News* the following morning. By the end of the day, the paper sold more than 1.5 million copies—the highest sale of any newpaper in history at that time.

The general public's social desire to consume crime through the news coalesced with newspaper visuals and media loops by the 1930s. From fatal bar brawls and car chases through brothel raids to mobster warfare, the visual record of crime swelled in the 1930s and 1940s. One of the most famous contributors was New York photojournalist Arthur Fellig. Fellig built his early career on capturing images of crime, which he sold to newspapers and magazines. As one of only a few journalists who had a license, Fellig used a police-band shortwave radio to listen in on police radio calls. As a result, he frequently arrived at crime scenes before the police or ambulance personnel. Nicknamed "Weegee the Famous," Fellig shocked and delighted news audiences with his detailed accounts and explicit photos of crime scenes. The work of Fellig and journalists like him not only generated substantial profits for newspapers and magazines but perhaps more importantly cemented the relationships among crime, spectacle, and the news media.

In the early 20th century, large police departments hosted crime reporters whose focus it was to report on the major activities of the department. The fascination with crime was in part fueled by a media campaign organized by J. Edgar Hoover, who wished to make the Federal Bureau of Investigation the premier law enforcement agency in the nation. To generate public support, he strategically portrayed his agents as crime fighters, and the suspects as hardened criminals who were dangerous and difficult to apprehend.

By the mid-1950s, higher standards of living and economies of abundance resulted in lower crime rates but, ironically, greater news coverage of crime. In fact, the mid-20th century was a watershed moment for crime in the news media, with increasingly aggressive marketing of crime news through specialized "crime beat reporting." The result was more sensationalistic coverage of crime that relied ever more heavily upon the police, prosecuting attorneys, and other criminal justice officials for commentary and analysis.

In the final decades of the 20th century, the news media was quickly ascending to a position of unchallenged dominance for producing and filtering popular portrayals of crime. Now there are several types of news media that provide the public with information about crime and justice in America. Television, newspapers, the radio, and the Internet are all popular sources of news coverage. Local media outlets tend to focus on events occurring within a certain geographic area and national outlets choose to cover events that either have implications for the entire nation, or those that will capture national attention.

Crime Suspects

The news media provides considerable information about the suspects who are accused of having committed crimes. After they are arrested, suspects can expect to have their mug shots, criminal histories, and even mental health history reported in news coverage. This information can be gathered from a variety of places, including the police, public court records, attorneys, friends, and family members. This information can also include whether the suspect and victim knew each other.

In cases where the suspect is unknown, the news circulates information provided by the police in the hope that someone will know the suspect and report him or her to the police. Sometimes this includes a sketch of the suspect provided to a police sketch artist by the victim. In the cases of crimes committed in public places, such as banks or retail stores, there is often video of suspects, which is aired to the public. Some news coverage is specifically directed at the apprehension of people who are suspected of committing crimes. For example, *America's Most Wanted* focuses on encouraging citizens to provide information about suspected criminals so they can stand trial. This TV show was the first of its kind, developed by John Walsh, whose son Adam was murdered in 1981. Walsh has been a figurehead in the news not only because of this show but because of his efforts to create stricter laws for sex offenders and his leadership in searching for missing children.

Crime Victims

The news also reports information about crime victims, but is usually more selective in what it shares. Some information about victims is not provided to the public. For example, the names of child victims or rape victims are usually not published to assist the victims in keeping their experiences private and possibly protecting them from further violence. Sometimes information about victims is shared that casts them in a negative light. For example, a good deal of private information about the woman who accused Kobe Bryant of raping her was made public, including mental health problems she experienced when she was younger. Her name quickly spread across the Internet, and after she filed a civil lawsuit against Bryant, some news media made the decision to publish her name. The charges were dropped and Bryant was never tried for, nor convicted of, committing any crime.

Sometimes victims of crimes are portrayed by the media as deserving of what happened to them, or at least, as being partly at fault for what happened to them. Researchers have found that gender is a significant ingredient in the news media's

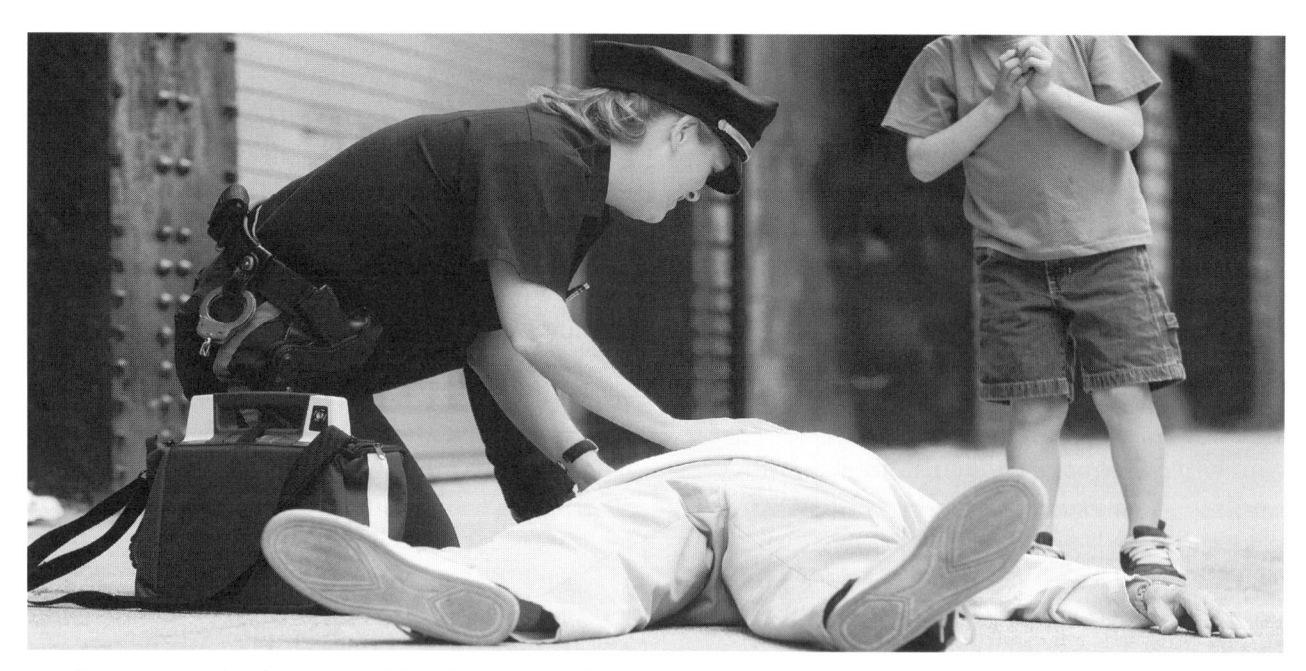

A policewoman renders first aid to a citizen. Since the late 20th century, television shows have been developed that blur the line between news and fiction by filming police officers while they perform their duties. These shows include COPS, Alaska State Troopers, Border Wars, *and the* Police Women *series in locales such as Broward County, Florida and Maricopa County, Arizona.*

coverage of crime victims. For example, while men are the most common victims of violence, it is women who are overrepresented as victims of violent crime in the news media. While female victims may be more newsworthy than their male counterparts, they must be deemed innocent (i.e., virtuous and honorable) as opposed to blameworthy (i.e., shameful and unscrupulous) if they are to warrant sympathetic media coverage.

The Police

Crime reporting has largely focused on the police since their development in the mid-1800s. Reporters were stationed at police departments, where they received firsthand accounts of any activity or crime. The police are portrayed in the news media largely as crime fighters and law enforcers. This image is only partly based on reality. While the police are responsible for enforcing laws, their shifts are often filled with other duties. The police are responsible for assisting citizens with noncriminal matters, maintaining order, investigating traffic accidents, and providing service to the community. Officers often engage in activities designed to bridge the gap between them and citizens, such as the DARE program or citizen police academies.

Police misconduct and abuse are frequently covered by the news media. The public normally has little knowledge of police activities; however, personal recording devices and video recording capabilities on cell phones have made it easier for police activity to become more publicized. The publicity surrounding the altercation between Rodney King and the Los Angeles Police Department (LAPD) marks one of the earliest and most controversial instances of private citizens secretly videotaping police officers on duty. In 1991, four LAPD police officers were accused of using excessive force against King. These officers were tried in a court of law, and were subsequently acquitted of any criminal wrongdoing at the state level, resulting in violent rioting in Los Angeles. This case was widely covered by the news media and analyzed by reporters.

The news media played the videotape of Rodney King's experience with these officers multiple times. The officers were subsequently indicted on federal criminal charges and two were convicted of violating King's constitutional rights.

There are several shows on television that blur the line between news and fiction. Born in the late 1980s and truly taking form in the decade of the 1990s, this "tele-visual" medium is sometimes referred to as "crime vérité." First aired in 1989, *COPS* and similar shows follow police officers while they are on duty, often showing either the most exciting events or the strangest events. This depiction of police work does not always accurately reflect reality. It takes many hours of filming officers to fill a half-hour segment of the show. Officers also have other duties aside from enforcing the law, but because these duties might be perceived as uninteresting, they are not covered by such shows. More recently, developed shows such as *Police Women* (e.g., with several different series set in Broward County, Florida, Cincinnati, Ohio, and Memphis, Tennessee) focus solely on women police officers on patrol.

Trial Coverage

The majority of the general public has not been inside a courtroom or taken part in a criminal trial and instead relies upon news coverage of trial events reported after the fact. Now, more than ever, people have access to information about what occurs in the courtroom. Most national news stations devote coverage to high-profile trials. There are also entire television networks dedicated to trial coverage. The first of these was Court TV (now truTV). Though the network began broadcasting in 1991, it was the coverage of the murder trials of Lyle and Erik Menendez in 1993 and O. J. Simpson in 1994 that truly propelled it into a national sensation. Originally featuring continuous live trial coverage, with commentary by a team of anchors and legal analysts, it later began airing more stylized and fictional programming such as *Forensic Files* and *Homicide: Life on the Street*.

With the Internet, reporters can now blog live coverage of trials. In Warren County, Ohio, reporters from the major news stations blogged trial coverage during the Ryan Widmer murder trial, allowing the public to follow the trial and make comments as the trial progressed.

Corrections

The corrections field (jail, prison, probation, and parole) is not covered in the news media as much as other components of the criminal justice system. The field of corrections is covered largely in the form of serial television documentaries with an investigative or exploratory focus. The shows tend to document life in prisons and provide information about how inmates adjust to life without freedom. Some of the coverage features interviews with inmates who reflect upon their lives in jail or prison, and who sometimes speak about the crime of which they were convicted. The shows also emphasize the manner in which corrections officers must conduct business.

Moral Panics

A moral panic occurs when the public believes an event or a series of events is a threat to the public order and well-being. The media contributes to moral panics by continuous coverage of crime events and other issues that could be construed as related to crime. One example of a moral panic, created in part by the media, is school shootings. Since the 1990s, there have been several dozen shootings in American schools. The news media reported extensively on these events, with a focus on the perpetrators of these crimes. The media described these school shooters as loners and outcasts who were angry and depressed. In reality, although there may be warning signs that a student may resort to violence, school shooters do not fit a single profile that allows them to be identified. Sometimes moral panics are localized and occur in only one geographic area.

Special interest groups sometimes use moral panics to put pressure on the criminal justice system to respond to the relevant issue, usually by creating or changing laws and their enforcement. Often the result is legislation designed to punish or monitor offenders that sometimes has unintended consequences.

One such example is the proliferation of news coverage of gang and drug activity in the inner cities in the 1980s. Public fear of drug crimes and an outcry over the ensuing violence prompted legislators to draft sentencing laws that mandated prison time for certain offenses, such as possession of crack cocaine. Other legislation mandated prison time after a certain number of offenses had been committed (i.e., the Three Strikes Laws). The unintended consequence of these laws is prison overcrowding, which has created fiscal and public relations problems for prisons in such circumstances.

Conclusion

Crime is central to the production of news. It grips the collective imagination of a diverse audience of viewers, readers, and listeners. Indeed, the ubiquity of the news media has resulted in these narratives becoming the overwhelmingly dominant forum for the social depiction of crime. The portrayal of crime in the news media is largely piecemeal and is sometimes not reflective of the actuality of crime and criminal justice.

Stephen L. Muzzatti
Ryerson University

See Also: 1921 to 1940 Primary Documents; Famous Trials; Fear of Crime; Film, Crime in; Literature and Theater, Crime in; News Media, Police in; News Media, Punishment in; Television, Crime in.

Further Readings

Barak, Gregg, ed. *Media, Process, and the Social Construction of Crime*. New York: Garland Publishing, 1994.

Cohen, Stanley and Jock Young, eds. *The Manufacture of News*. Beverley Hills, CA: Sage, 1973.

Fishman, Mark. "Crime Waves as Ideology." *Social Problems*, v.25/5 (1978).

Hanusch, Folker. *Presenting Death in the News: Journalism, Media and Mortality*. New York: Palgrave Macmillan, 2010.

Jewkes, Yvonne. *Media and Crime*, 2nd ed. London: Sage, 2010.

Miller, Wilbur R. "Police Authority in London and New York City 1830–1870." *Journal of Social History*, v.8/2 (1975).

Surette, Ray. *Media, Crime and Criminal Justice: Images, Realities, and Policies*, 4th ed. Belmont, CA: Wadsworth, 2011.

News Media, Police in

Forms of news media vary from the traditional printed newspapers, radio, and television news programs to Internet news and infotainment. Modern technology has allowed individuals to more easily obtain information. In addition to television news, news programs have extended their coverage to news Websites such as MSNBC.com, ABCnews.com, and even Google News. Add to this the public addiction to YouTube, blogging, and tweeting, and many people mistakenly identify anything posted on the Internet as accurate news. In all, news today tends to provide situational coverage without added context, which tends to distort larger issues and support stereotypes.

Police are the gatekeepers to the public's source of crime information presented in the news media. As much as 25 percent of news is dedicated to crime coverage. While most people do not experience crime firsthand, they are exposed to news media in some form or another. As such, the media has a powerful influence in our understanding of crime and justice. Media images of the police have been found to directly affect public opinion and thus police–public relations. Police tend to be depicted as either the good cop or the bad cop and not much in between. Furthermore, the advancement of infotainment has worked to place unreasonable expectations on the police.

Historical Context

Crime has long been a focus of news media. By the end of the 1500s, it was common for notorious murders to be publicized in some media. The most common forms of early crime news were distributed as broadsheets (or broadsides) or pamphlets, or communicated in speeches or sermons. By the 1600s, England published pamphlets dedicated to crime. The most common crimes reported were murder, treason, and witchcraft. Additionally, news publications were sold as a form of entertainment. The United States adopted this same form of broadside reporting. However, early U.S. news was limited mostly to political editorials published in early newspapers. Crime reported within these papers was brief and usually focused on trials. There was widespread fear that frequent reporting of crime details would serve to encourage copycat criminals. It was not until the 1830s that the first daily city newspapers started to publish crime news as front-page stories. In 1833, the *New York Sun* was one of the first newspapers to publish daily crime news, primarily reported by the police.

In response to a growing market for crime news, the form of crime reporting changed drastically.

Newspapers started to devote more time to crime and justice. the focus was over-sensationalized, often fabricated in new mass-circulation newspapers called the "penny press." Benjamin Day was the first to practice the new style of crime reporting when he founded the *New York Sun* in 1833. Day initiated news reporting that provided many more details than previous practices. Day's reporters wrote crime stories that included gory details.

James Gordon Bennett, another famous journalist, founded the *New York Herald* in 1835. Bennett was the first to follow stories and run them for as long as they lasted. Bennett's influence revealed itself in 1836, he spent so much time chronicling the murder of a prostitute named Ellen Jewett that the murder trial had to be postponed because of the publicity his news coverage stirred. Crime reporting of the day focused on crime reports released by police courts and police stations. Newspapers within the penny press sent their reporters to the same location where police would provide reports of crime. This relationship allowed the police to partially shape the image of crime and justice. However, as the penny press was known to publish sensationalized and fabricated information, stories often became distorted. Additionally, the detail and time given to crimes resulted in criticism of the penny press as swaying public opinion in what law journals called "trial by newspaper."

There was also growing attention given to corruption within the system, especially among the police. The yellow journalism of the later 19th century developed by William R. Hearst and Joseph Pulitzer was an even more sensationalized descendant of the penny press. By the 1920s, tabloids carried on the tradition, heightening sensation by including photographs. Both were widely criticized for inaccurate and negative reporting. Criminal justice dissatisfaction with media images of justice officials as corrupt resulted in other weekly news publications to the contrary. Publications such as the *National Police Gazette* (1845–1977) were established to provide an increasingly literate population with a more favorable view of police and their crime-fighting activities.

By the end of the 1800s, social perceptions changed from viewing crime as a sin or the result of structural corruption to viewing crime as an individual deficiency. The ceremonial nature of the trial was soon replaced by the factual details provided by the police. By the 1920s, radio news became the first live reporting of crime. This practice continues today with television news, all utilizing police as the gatekeepers to crime news.

The presentation of crime news as entertainment quickly took root, and soon media forms of news entertainment sprung up around the nation. Infotainment is a media presentation that mixes news with entertainment. These news media releases tend to sensationalize, exaggerate, and skew aspects of crime and justice, blurring the line between entertainment and news information. The first infotainment in mass media was yellow journalism. Currently, well-known forms of infotainment include tabloids such as the *Inquirer* and television programs such as *60 Minutes*, the *Today* show, *COPS*, and *America's Most Wanted*.

Police Image and Image Management

Early crime reporting by the penny press was dedicated to presenting crime as a social malady. With the changed focus on crime as an individual deficiency, the media started to rely heavily on police reporting of the facts of crime. The adaptation of a structured format for reporting all crime stories also made relying on police accounts of the crimes more desirable. Furthermore, reliance on police accounts reflected the official police standpoint and eliminated the need to retract stories. This reliance on police for crime information is referred to as front-end reporting. Front-end reporting focuses on the causes, investigations, and solutions to crime.

Today, police departments assign officers to deal directly with the news media in order to control the flow of information and images of the police. These officers are commonly known as public information officers or public relations officers. They also determine most of what is presented to the public about the extent and nature of crimes. Along with this, police provide media with a specific orientation toward crime. This orientation, depending on the era, may be law and order, a war on crime, or a crime epidemic. In any presentation, the concern maintains that crime is an individual deficiency that can only be eradicated by the police.

Even with the public relations officers working closely with the media, two contradictory images of the police tend to be present at the same time. The first is the positive "good" cop who is a highly moral and concerned expert in fighting crime using the latest technology and fighting for the safety of the citizens. The good cop image is a soldier in the war against crime who usually quickly captures the criminal and is a very competent professional. Crimes fought by the good cop tend overwhelmingly to be of a violent nature. The second image is the negative "bad" cop, who is either incompetent or corrupt. This cop does not care and is often criminal and violent. If the police do care, then they are simply bumbling idiots, and crime can only be eradicated by private citizens, either private enforcement agents or vigilantes.

These two images are both wrong. The reality of police work involves mostly noncrime service calls. These tend to involve crisis management (traffic accidents or fires), community education (workshops and school visits), or administrative work. Crimes typically addressed by the police tend to be minor violent or nonviolent crimes. In fact, more than 80 percent of all crimes reported to the police are nonviolent crimes. However, when consistently working so closely with public relations officers, media images depict a society ridden with violence.

According to the media, when police investigate crimes, they tend to be forensics and computer experts when, in fact, nationally most police officials do not have this expertise. Among departments that widely use these technologies, only a few officers are trained in such skills. Hence, even with the good cops around the nation, the competence tends to be overstated. Media overreliance on police accounts of crimes tends to focus on the crime details and the immediacy of the situation and has come to be known as forensic journalism. The facts provided by the police are brief and identified as factual. Forensic journalism tends to present a form of media investigation similar to forensic science. Since forensic journalism relies on the police, it also reinforces the image of police as competent and as forensics experts. The details provided go unquestioned until police reports specify otherwise.

Unfortunately, the bad cop image can be very damaging to crime fighting. Even with public relations officers, reporters are able to uncover some of the police corruption that occurs. Stories of police murder for hire occasionally hit the nation or instances of police brutality, such as in the Rodney King or Abner Louima beatings. To further push the bad cop image is the increased possession and use of cell phones with videotaping and Internet capacity. The use of the Internet and such sites as Facebook and YouTube allow everyday people to post police abuse of authority for national consumption.

Media researchers have also found that looping works to push the bad cop image. Looping is when stories are repeatedly recycled throughout the daily news reporting and can last for weeks. A video recording of police brutality may be placed on the Internet for public consumption. Newspapers and television and radio news media then report on the video recording.

Next, an infotainment program may use the clip in a public interest piece. The video will find its way onto the news organization's Website and even be used as evidence in a court case. Looping allows the media to keep ratings up but it also serves as an alarm to public consumers. Though the incident is one instance of police brutality, the constant barrage of the story gives the appearance of widespread police brutality. Research has revealed that an instance of police corruption in one department can negatively affect the public opinion of local police on the other side of the nation.

Police Corruption and Violence

Public image of the police from the 1960s through the 1980s reflected waves of public distrust in the government. The 1960s and 1970s experienced civil unrest. As a result, members of society led the civil rights movement, the student rights movement, and the Vietnam War protest. Police were often shown in the news as the primary oppressors of the people. Initially, public outrage and distrust was found primarily in African American communities. Television news captured numerous occasions of police brutality during peaceful civil rights protests. The famous 1963 news footage of the Birmingham, Alabama, police hosing down civil rights activists with high-powered fire hoses and letting loose attack dogs was further memorialized by the PBS documentary *Eyes on the Prize*. The Birmingham

On day 14 of the Occupy Wall Street protests in 2011, the Granny Peace Brigade and other citizens marched against police brutality from Zuccotti Park to the headquarters of the New York Police Department. The media often rely on law enforcement for crime information, which generally portrays the police in a positive light; however, coverage of corrupt police and police brutality is growing with the increased usage of cell phone videotaping and the ease of posting videos online.

police chief reported to the news cameras that he would do it again.

The 1968 Chicago Democratic National Convention resulted in what was termed a police *riot*. The 1968 convention was overridden by nearly 10,000 yippies who were viewed to be a threat to the city. Chicago police were said to have started the riot by beating a young boy who pulled an American flag down from a flagpole. The Democratic National Convention is nationally covered by the media. During the riots, famous news anchor Dan Rather was beaten by police. The National Guard shooting of four Kent State University student war protesters on May 4, 1970 was preceded by student–police conflict. While the National Guard and not the Kent city police were the shooters, national outcry opened the gates. Media coverage of the brutalization of white, middle-class citizens worked to extend public distrust in the white American community.

The 1960s and 1970s also uncovered widespread economic corruption among police in parts of the nation. Public trust and confidence reached one of its lowest points. News stories uncovered numerous occasions of police taking bribes from organized crime syndicates. These bribes resulted in police shielding criminals and their crimes, ranging from prostitution to gambling to murder. The news presented organization-wide police corruption in Kansas City, Missouri, Chicago, and New York City in the 1960s. The famous case of New York City police detective Frank Serpico was widely covered in the news in the late 1960s and early 1970s. Serpico's initial attempts to report witnessed corruption went unaddressed by his superiors. Finally, he turned to the media and told his story to the *New York Times*. As a result of the in-depth media coverage of Serpico's whistle-blowing, the Knapp Commission was formed in New York

City and worked to document police corruption and reform.

On the tail end of these events and with a drastic increase in drug and violent crime, the public voiced dissatisfaction with police ability to protect the people. The popularity of vigilante justice flourished. The media were at the forefront of this image. While movie and television entertainment media played a larger role, the news media frequently presented the need, or the public's desire, for vigilante justice. Frequent news coverage of the establishment and activities of the Guardian Angels (a civilian nonviolent vigilante group) often emphasized the need of private citizens to protect themselves. The Guardian Angels identified themselves as community safety patrols and first patrolled the streets of New York City in 1979. By 1981, Guardian Angels patrols were established nationwide. The establishment of the Guardian Angels was meant to provide protection that the people felt they were not receiving from the police. News media uncovered a relationship between the Guardian Angels and the police, which on the surface appeared to be civil but actually was plagued by distrust on either part. As the decade unraveled, news media presented increasingly negative images of the civilian patrol group that often resulted in arrests and the police having to restore public order.

As the 1980s came to a close, much of public sentiment shifted from incompetent police to corrupt police but with a racial divide. The looping of the 1991 video recording of Rodney King being brutally beaten by four Los Angeles Police Department (LAPD) resulted in increased African American mistrust nationwide. The television news media presented the beating on a daily basis and then covered the case through the criminal trial. News stories of the acquittal of the police officers resulted in major riots in New York and Los Angeles. In 1994, the Los Angeles police investigation of O. J. Simpson as a suspect in the murder of his ex-wife and her friend received media attention worldwide. While on the one hand, the media tended to present O. J. Simpson as guilty, they also presented the Los Angeles police corruption as a detrimental factor in the case. Media coverage of the case paid close attention to the prejudicial and discriminatory history of Detective Mark Fuhrman and Simpson's claims that he planted evidence. The distrust in the LAPD helped O. J. Simpson to gain an acquittal.

Other cases attesting to police brutality have been presented in the media. In the 1990s, the two most famous cases were the 1997 beating and forcible sodomization of Abner Louima by New York City police officers in the 70th Brooklyn precinct house. The attack resulted in a protest of 7,000 marchers. Media coverage stressed that the case was one of torture, prejudice, and discrimination. In 1999, news media presented yet another insistance of police violence against a black immigrant. Four New York City police officers, of the Street Crime Unit, fired 41 shots at the unarmed West African immigrant Amadou Diallo.

With the increasing tough-on-crime sentiment of the 2000s, aided by heroic police response on September 11, 2001, public trust in the competence and morality of the police increased. However, the 2006 shooting of unarmed Sean Bell on the eve of his wedding by New York City police officers continues to present police as trigger-happy cops who hold prejudicial views of black males, seeing them as immediate threats. The Innocence Project has worked since 1992 to exonerate more than 260 convicts, most in the 2000s. Media coverage has focused on incompetent police or corrupt police who falsify evidence or force confessions. However, as discussed earlier, media reliance on police as their primary source for crime information helps to provide a positive image of the police.

Good Cops in the Media

While news reporters never gave up the practice of demonizing police, the move toward relying on police accounts of crime worked in giving police a level of control over crime information and how this information was to be presented. Police tend to provide situational facts of crime and emphasize their expertise in being able to fight crime. The emphasis is on the need to treat crime as an attack on the public and allows police to maintain their war on crime. Further, the tendency of the media and the police to focus on the less frequent violent crimes paints police as soldiers.

News coverage of crime has always sold crime as entertainment; however, this particular practice increased substantially in the 1990s with the introduction of criminal profiling and televised infotainment news. Though infotainment programs such as *60 Minutes* have been on the air for decades, infotainment took a new entertainment approach when television first aired *COPS* in 1989. While the program is purely entertainment, the public tends to interpret the televised police activities as real police work and real police personalities in response to real crimes of violence that are at epidemic proportions. Unfortunately, viewers do not understand that the producers work very closely with the police, allowing them to edit out footage that is unfavorable to positive police images. Other programs such as *America's Most Wanted*, *American Justice*, *Criminal Minds*, *Forensic Files*, *Fugitive Chronicles*, and *The First 48* have chronicled police expertise and response to violent crimes.

Though the stories chronicled in these television shows may be true, the details tend to be dramatized. Furthermore, viewers are not informed that most crimes go unsolved and most criminals are not caught. The programs also do not inform viewers that most police are not highly trained crime scene investigators, nor are they trained in the latest technological and forensic sciences. These very positive images of police are further reinforced when the viewer is made to interpret these shows as crime news that should be generalized to all police.

Fortunately, infotainment is not the only source of media images of the good cop. There is no shortage of good police in the United States. Heroic and prompt police responses to heinous violent crimes have often been looped through the news media. The 1966 University of Texas at Austin shooting in which 16 people were shot and killed by Charles Whitman from the university's landmark tower prompted the image of police courageous enough to charge the tower in the face of adversity. This image of charging the tower was further stressed during the more recent heroic and unselfish police responses when many charged the World Trade Center as it was attacked on September 11, 2001. Many police officers and firefighters were so concerned with the safety of others that they charged the tower, even to their own peril. These stories have been continuously looped through the various forms of news media memorializing the sacrifices that police are willing to make in order to fight crime and protect the public.

Other well-known police responses that have been looped through the media include the response to the 1997 Columbine school massacre; the 2006 Amish school shooting in Nickel Mines, Pennsylvania; and the 2009 Binghamton, New York, massacre. While there are always questions and critiques as to how police responded to the crimes and what they could have done to save all victims, media coverage stressed the timely response and training of the police. For example, 14 people were killed in the Binghamton shooting; however, media stressed that it took police only two minutes to arrive at the scene following the 911 call and that no hostages were shot once police arrived. Police took six minutes to arrive at the scene of the Nickel Mines attack, where a heavily armed man killed four young school girls. Most recently, news coverage

The badge of officer number 1012, a Port Authority of New York and New Jersey police officer and 9/11 attack victim named George Howard. The selfless actions of police and firefighters were well documented during the 9/11 attacks.

of retired police officer Mike Jones stressed the heroic nature of police even after leaving the job. Mike Jones overtook a man shooting at a Panama City, Florida, school board at its January 3, 2011, meeting. Looping of this crime incident focused on the heroics and strong characters of police, stressing "once a cop, always a cop."

As with all people in society, there are good and bad to be found. The news media has been at the forefront of bringing out the best and the worst in policing throughout United States history. The unfortunate fact is that news has not paid close attention to the more typical officer or the more typical crime. Focusing on positives and negatives as well as placing focus on these day-to-day activities may provide us with a more accurate understanding of policing and may minimize unreasonable expectations of police. The police have aided news media in their images via their public relations officers, so the blame cannot be placed solely on the media. However, examining the media through an organizational perspective, media researchers have learned that focusing on the mundane does not sell.

Venessa Garcia
Kean University

See Also: News Media, Crime in; News Media, Punishment in; Police Abuse; Television, Police in.

Further Readings
Altheide, David L. *Creating Fear: News and the Construction of Crisis*. New York: Aldine De Gruyter, 2002.
Bailey, Frankie Y. and Donna C. Hale, eds. *Popular Culture, Crime and Justice*. Belmont, CA: Wadsworth, 1998.
Barlow, David E. and Melissa H. Barlow. *Police in a Multicultural Society: An American Story*. Prospect Heights, IL: Waveland Press, 2000.
Lawrence, Regina G. *The Politics of Police Force: Media and the Construction of Police Brutality*. Berkeley: University of California Press, 2000.
Marsh, Ian and Gaynor Melville. *Crime, Justice and the Media*. New York: Routledge, 2009.
Spencer, David Ralph. *The Yellow Journalism: The Press and America's Emergence as a World Power*. Evanston, IL.: Northwestern University Press, 2007.

News Media, Punishment in

Current research has found that the media has the greatest influence on the public's perception of crime, justice, and punishment today. Further, the media is responsible for the production and reproduction of cultural images of crime and justice and the construction of the social reality of crime that affects perceptions of crime and justice. Many criminologists have studied the impact of the portrayal of crime in the media on the public. Criminologists have found that the depiction of crime, criminality, and the seriousness of crime does not correspond to actual crime statistics.

Various types of media serve as sources of information about crime and justice. Newspapers and magazines are significant sources of crime information. Further, film and television are also important types of media because they are sources of entertainment and utilize audiovisual technology that overcomes the obstacle of literacy that the other forms of media have to contend with. In addition, with the advent of videotape technology, film now joins with television, and has become more readily accessible to home audiences. This means that individuals can watch these films and television programs at their leisure within the comfort of their own homes, making the messages that are transmitted through television and film accessible to a large number of people around the world. Television has become the primary source for socialization and information received by the public.

Learning About Crime and Punishment
Several theories have been posited about the process through which the public learns about crime, justice, and punishment issues. Albert Bandura's social learning theory states that individuals learn through the process of observation. Individuals frame conceptual ideas regarding behavior and ultimately translate these conceptual models into actual behavior. Social learning is a complex process through which behavior is based on the modeling of symbolic verbal cues and observational inputs. These obervationally learned inputs can either be behavior learned from parents and teachers or representational symbolic events.

These representational symbolic events can be presented through televsion and film.

In addition to learning theory, cultivation theory has been used to explain the learning process that takes place through the media. George Gerbner, originator of cultivation theory, focused his research within the medium of television. He studied the extent to which television viewing contributed to viewer beliefs about gender, minority, and age-role stereotypes; health; science; the family; educational acheivment and aspirations; politics; religion; the environment; and other topics. He also examined the way that television viewing contributed to viewer behaviors. Cultivation theory is based on the notion that television "cultivates" or contributes to attitudes and beliefs of audiences over time. Those who spend more time watching television are more likely to see the world in relation to the constructed images, depictions, values, mores, and ideologies that are presented on television. Regardless of specific theoretical beliefs about how the media impacts perception and behavior, we know that the media does influence the public's perception of crime in the United States.

The production and reproduction of the social reality of crime by the media is potentially hazardous if it often distorts the reality of crime, justice, and punishment. Richard Quinney noted the mass media's influence on the social reality of crime. He states that the media of mass communication are among the most influential agents in the diffusion of the conception of criminals. The mass media is preoccupied with the topic of crime. Consequently, the conceptions of crime and punishment by the public are created, to a certain extent, by the images presented by the mass media. Additionally, the mass media is selective in the presentation of images of crime to the public, choosing to present the most sensational aspects of crime, serving to distort the everyday reality of crime, justice, and punishment.

It is almost impossible to isolate oneself from the reach of the mass media and the information it relays. The mass media industry and its by-products are significant because the messages that get translated through it reach an extraordinarily large number of individuals. Recently, there have been some significant historical changes to the mass media industry that have repercussions in regard to who controls the production and reproduction of knowledge of crime, justice, and punishment in today's society.

Media Industry Shifts

As recently as the past two decades, there has been a dramatic and telling change in the mass media industry. The number and variety of media choices available to most Americans has changed significantly. In the late 1970s, there were only a few television stations from which to choose, and only 20 percent of the American public had access to paid cable systems comprised of only a dozen more stations. Three national television networks (ABC, NBC, and CBS) dominated prime-time viewing, attracting 90 percent of the viewing audience. Today, television networks not only have to compete with a variety of cable television stations but also with the Internet for their audience.

During the 1970s, typical Americans could choose from between 10 and 15 radio stations. They could also see a movie at a downtown or suburban movie theater. Americans would often read one daily newspaper, although some larger towns and cities had two daily papers, and they could choose from an assortment of magazines that they could buy at a local newsstand or bookstore.

Today, the number of daily newspapers continues to decline while television, radio stations, and magazine outlets continue to expand. While the public has seen significant changes in the amount of production by these media industries, what is more significant is that two decades ago, one could speak of these media industries as separate entities. Now, however, these industries are merging both technologically and economically. Since the 1980s, the mass media industries have become subject to an emerging phenomenon—the global commercial system that is dominated by a small number of extremely powerful corporations based in the United States.

Mass Media Oligopoly

For-profit corporations control almost all of the mass media in the United States. As an aspect of large-scale mergers, fewer and fewer corporations own the majority of the mass communications in the country. Furthermore, these controlling corporations have reached into the international market. Changes in the political and economic landscape, such as pressure to deregulate and privatize the mass media from the International Monetary Fund, the World Bank, and the U.S. government, have helped fuel the rise of the few global media giants.

As of 2010, five media conglomerates control the majority of the mass media industry in the United States. Listed in descending order by 2009 revenues, these corporations are Walt Disney ($36.1 billion), News Corporation ($30.4 billion), Time Warner ($28.8 billion), Viacom ($13.6 billion), and CBS ($13 billion). These media corporations are among the top 500 largest corporations in the world. Listed by top 500 rank in 2009 they are Walt Disney (57), News Corporation (76), Time Warner (82), Viacom (170), and CBS (177).

Although these five large media conglomerates are separate entities, they all are remarkably similar. Currently, they control the majority of the mass media in the United States, and they are reaching into international domains. The United States has not always been a country dominated by the corporatization of the mass media. Expansion of most mass media by corporate domination is the result of an important change in the relation of the government and the media. Recently, Federal Communication Commission (FCC) regulations have been relaxed or in some instances eliminated. One of the areas of the media to be affected by these recent historical changes is the motion picture industry.

Social Constructionist Perspective

It is important to understand the context in which media images are produced. In order to examine this context further, researchers have begun to examine the ownership of media organizations from a social constructionist perspective. This perspective contends that media-generated images are used to create meaning about political and social issues. The lens through which images are focused is not impartial but is influenced by the political agenda set forth by the privileged few who construct these images. The brilliance of this system is to make the process seamless so as to not raise questions.

The oligopolistic structure of the media industry means only five very wealthy and powerful corporations are controlling the majority of American media construction. Ben Bagdikian, a leading researcher in the field of media studies, compares the few media corporations to the Organization of Petroleum Exporting Countries (OPEC) in that while each corporation is technically competing with the others, they all share a common cause, as does OPEC in its interest in oil. The lack of diversification results in highly duplicative manufactured media content. These repetitive media images account for a lack of representation of multiple viewpoints. This shared ideology and values results in the homogenization of imagery that replicates corporate power interests effortlessly. While the media industry is not the only oligopolistic industry, it is unique because it is in the business of manufacturing images that affect the social and political world. The concern is that a few corporations own the majority of the media and are determining what is socially and politically acceptable for the majority of American consumers to believe.

How then does this process apply to crime and punishment? The media is the platform through which Americans learn about social and political issues. Several scholars have examined the mechanism by which crime, the criminal justice system, and punishment are chosen among other relevant topics of interest by the media. Scholars have outlined a three-step process. First, crime is chosen from among various issues and elevated in status in a process known as "agenda setting." Second, once selected, the crime issue is narrowed in scope to street crime, and finally, the solution to the

The social constructionist viewpoint posits that the media industry is unique because it manufactures images that affect the public's view of social and political issues.

crime problem is seen as one that can be addressed by investing more money into the criminal justice system. News organizations and governmental leaders help to produce popular images of crime, justice, and punishment by identifying what is socially thought provoking about crime. This argument can also be extended to encompass not just news media but also the entertainment industry. Edward Herman and Noam Chomsky show that in this way, the media in all of its forms serves a particular function, to operate as propaganda for the state's ideological machinery by communicating specific messages to the general public.

Other scholars have added to this discourse on the media and crime. In 1988, Gregg Barak introduced the concept of newsmaking criminology to the field. Newsmaking criminology refers to the process through which criminologists use mass communication to interpret, inform, and alter images of crime, criminals, and victims. Barak's newsmaking criminology primarily focuses on such mass communication as newspapers, magazines, and television. His work serves as a call to arms as he advises criminologists, as the experts on crime, to redefine and realign the focus that is perpetuated in the media. One way that criminologists can counter the perpetuation of the media bias is to alert the public to the realities of crime and the processes that take place within the criminal justice system. However, researchers must first be able to speak to the biases that are being perpetuated by the media to the public. In order to do this, academics must evaluate the media's perspective on crime and punishment and assess whether it reflects reality.

Representation of Crime and Punishment

The representation of crime and punishment is a complex process. J. Ferrell et al. discuss the process by emphasizing that this is more than a simple reporting of criminal events by news organizations. While the population of prisoners in the United States is increasing, the average American is more likely to read about or view the prison experience than they are to have knowledge of it firsthand. The literature addressing the representation of prison by the media has focused on film and television depictions. The general public gets much of its information about the institution of prison from film. In the United States, there has been little representation of prison on television except for two recent television dramas, *OZ* and *Prison Break*.

Today, prison films purport to depict the difficulties of life behind bars, which offers the audience a fantasy and an escape from the monotony of everyday life. Stock plots, characters, and themes have surrounded the prison film. Prisons in film often portray stereotypical depictions of a young "fish" arriving at an institution only to be given guidance about the prison experience from an older, wiser, seasoned convict. The theme of injustice that is met with rebellion by the main characters is a stock theme depicted in prison films. As the film develops and as the audience grows to know the characters in the film, the heroes who are originally presented as hardened criminals change to soft-hearted characters with whom the audience can sympathize. Additionally, the bulk of prison films present stock characters such as the sadistic warden, malicious correction officers, the young hero, and the unlikely friendships between convicts. The majority of prison films focus on all-male institutions. The rare film that depicts female inmates is typically a low-budget, sexual exploitative production. Prisons in film are depicted as maximum-security institutions that house hardened criminals. However, the majority of prisons in the United States are medium security.

The highly ordered structure of the prison institution in real life allows the prison film to embrace an immediate rhythm and repetition. While for most prisoners daily life is filled with the monotony and boredom associated with waiting for time to pass, prison films do not show this process, as it does not make for an exciting, captivating film. Prison films are often applauded by the public for their "realism." However, research has shown that the penal institutions and daily life of convicts depicted on film are far from realistic. For example, B. Jarvis points out that in 55 episodes of the television show *OZ*, which depicts the maximum-security Oswald State Penitentiary, there are almost 100 deaths. However, the majority of the violence depicted was nonfatal, such as stabbing, mutilation, and self-mutilation. The U.S. Department of Justice reports 8,000–9,000 violent incidents per year along with 50–60 murders throughout

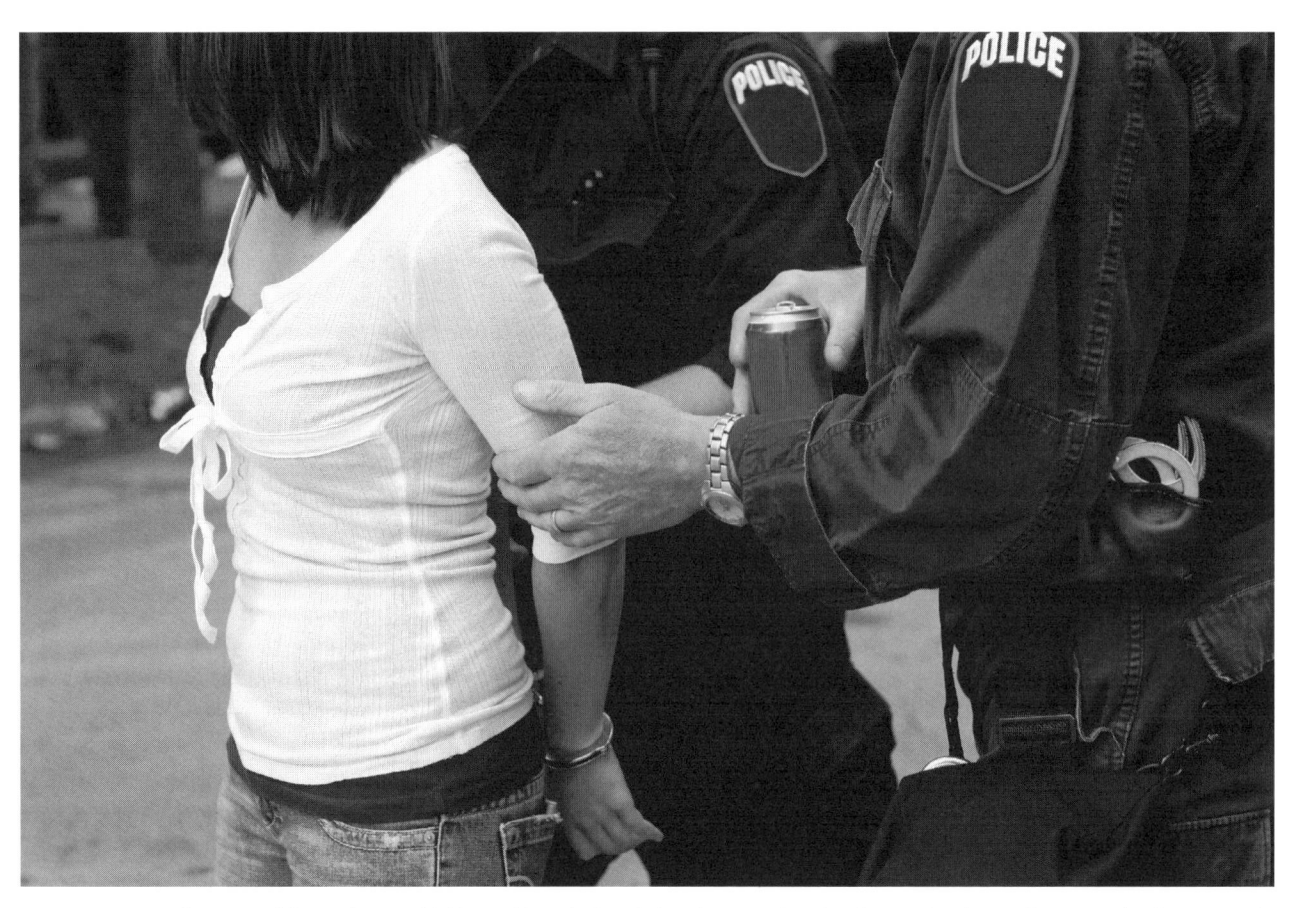

A young woman is arrested for underage drinking. Although female involvement in crime is growing (according to Federal Bureau of Investigation research, arrests for males increased 0.6 percent while arrests for females increased 5.1 percent from 2004 to 2008), news reports show stories involving mainly nonwhite males as suspects and criminals.

all the penitentiaries within the United States. Clearly, the representation of violence in prisons on television is overrepresented compared to the national statistics. Even though most research has concluded that the representation of penal institutions and the daily life of convicts as seen by the media in prison films (and the occasional television program) do not reflect what is known about these institutions as reported in the criminological literature, this visual media does give viewers a glimpse inside an institution often shrouded in mystery. In addition, recent research has just begun to address the public opinion shift toward punitiveness and the intersection between the consumption and interpretation of media depictions of punishment.

Furthermore, research has examined the portrayal of criminals by the media. It has been found that news programs influence audiences about the picture of crime in the United States. One of the public's primary sources of crime information is local news reports. Crime stories dominate these nightly news programs. Investigations have found that new stories overrepresent violent street crime. They also primarily depict perpetrators of these crimes as nonwhite males. Crime stories are presented as small sound bites where images of individual violent crimes are presented, a prime suspect is named, and information about this prime suspect is presented by a demographic profile that includes the race and/or ethnicity of the suspect. Because of this limited presentation of crime by television news, the public views criminals in a similar vein. Because crime news is framed in this manner, it is not surprising that increases in the viewing of local television news stories have been positively associated with public support for punitive crime policies.

In addition to research on the portrayal of crime and criminal offenders by the media, scholars have also examined the death penalty and the depiction of capital cases in the news and in crime dramas. When executions moved from the public square to behind prison walls, punishment became an abstract concept for the majority of the public. While few television dramas depict the prison institution itself, crime dramas do often focus on executions and the death penalty as a sanction. Interestingly, general support for the death penalty was found among viewers of crime drama programs. Further, research has attempted to explore whether media depiction of executions has a deterrent or brutalizing effect on homicides. Other research has examined the effect of news reporting of executions on public opinion. Historically, media coverage of the death penalty has emphasized questions of constitutionality, morality, deterrence, equity of application, and cost-effectiveness. However, recently, the media has raised questions about the guilt or innocence of offenders. In a study of 3,692 abstracts from the *New York Times* crime stories about the death penalty, researchers found that the reporting of the death penalty issue has grown in importance in recent years, peaking in the year 2000. In addition to the amount of news media coverage of the death penalty issue, the type of media coverage has changed.

Media focus has shifted from pro–death penalty coverage after the constitutional moratorium on the death penalty (1972–76) and into the early 1990s, to an anti–death penalty agenda by 1997. Since 2000, the focus of the media on the death penalty has been on fairness. An increasing number of exonerations of death row inmates, highlighted by such groups as the Innocence Project, have fueled this media representation. The focus of the media on the innocence of death row inmates has the potential to sway current public opinion away from the current pro–death penalty feelings in the United States. The repetition of exonerated and innocent death row inmate media coverage increases this potential.

Scholars have also addressed the extent to which media representations are related to fear of crime and, consequently, public policy decisions about crime and punishment. Media studies have found that homicide stories reported by newspapers showed the strongest relationship to fear of crime. Further, homicide stories reporting local cases increased fear, while stories about crime outside an individual's local area deceased fear. In effect, newspaper coverage of crime in other places makes people feel significantly better about crime in their own city or town. In addition, researchers have argued that the depiction of prisoners as violent and aggressive criminals both by the entertainment media and by news reporting has had an impact on public perception of punishment. Consequently, these negative images have allowed the public to turn a blind eye to the growing prison population in the United States. The representations of crime and punishment in film, on television, and by the news media have become an important cultural artifact that influences perception and ultimately public policy.

Conclusion

It has become nearly impossible to isolate oneself from the overreaching influence of the mass media industry. Television, film, magazines, newspapers, books, radio, and most recently the Internet surround Americans. Research has shown that the public relies upon the mass media for information. Crime news stories represent more than one-quarter of total news stories. The media is responsible for the production and reproduction of cultural images of crime, justice, and punishment, and the construction of the social reality of crime, which affects these perceptions. The depiction of crime, criminality, and the seriousness of crime are not accurately represented in the media compared to actual crime statistics.

Researchers have started to study the owners of the mass media in the United States, as these corporations are responsible for the construction of the social reality of crime. In recent years, the mass media industry has become an oligopoly. Five large conglomerates own the majority of all media outlets in the United States. This shift in media ownership likely has a major influence on the information that is being relayed to the public. Unless the American public seeks out alternative media outlets, citizens are left without much choice but to accept the information that is presented to them by the mainstream media.

Because the media is the stage through which Americans learn about social and political issues, the way crime and punishment are presented by the media is extremely important. Some say that the media, including the motion picture industry and television, magazine, and newspaper conglomerates, reproduces the dominant ideology set forth by its corporate owners. In this way, the mass media industry and a few corporate conglomerates decide what is socially acceptable about crime and punishment in the United States.

Melissa E. Fenwick
Western Connecticut State University

See Also: Death Row; Film, Crime in; News Media, Crime in; News Media, Police in; Television, Crime in.

Further Readings
Bagdikian, B. *The New Media Monopoly.* Boston: Beacon Press, 2004.
Bandura, A. *Social Learning Theory.* Upper Saddle River, NJ: Prentice Hall, 1977.
Barak, G. "Newsmaking Criminology: Reflections of the Media, Intellectuals, and Crime." *Justice Quarterly*, v.5 (1988).
Gerbner, G., L. Gross, M. Morgan, and N. Signorelli. "Growing Up With Television: The Cultivation Perpective." In *Media Effects: Advances in Theory and Research*, 2nd ed., J. Bryant and D. Zillmann, eds. Hillsdale, NJ: Lawrence Erlbaum, 2001.
Herman, E. H. and N. Chomsky. *Manufacturing Consent: The Political Economy of the Mass Media.* New York: Pantheon, 2002.
Jarvis, B. "The Violence of Images: Inside the Prison TV Drama OZ." In *Captured by the Media: Prison Discourse in Popular Culture*, P. Mason, ed. Portland, OR: Willan Publishing, 2006.
Potter, G. and V. Kappeler. *Constructing Crime: Perspectives on Making News and Social Problems.* Long Grove, IL: Waveland Press, 2006.
Quinney, R. *The Social Reality of Crime.* Piscataway, NJ: Transaction Publishers, 2001.
Rafter, N. *Shots in the Mirror: Crime Films and Society*, 2nd ed. New York: Oxford University Press, 2006.
Welch, M., M. E. Fenwick, and M. Roberts. "State Managers, Intellectualism and the Media: A Content Analysis of Ideology in Experts' Quotes in Feature Newspaper Articles on Crime." *Justice Quarterly*, v.15/2 (1998).

Nitti, Frank

"The Enforcer," Capone underboss and bodyguard, reputed leader of the Chicago "Outfit" after Al Capone's fall from power, Frank Nitti was born Francesco Raffaele Nitto in Italy. Details of Nitti's early life are sketchy. He was born either in 1881, 1884, or 1886 near Salerno, Sicily, or the town of Angri, near Naples, where his father died when Nitti was 2 years old. He was brought to America in either 1891 or 1893 by his mother, Rosina, and his stepfather, Francesco Dolendo, whom his mother had married shortly after his father's death. Dolendo immigrated to America, finding work and saving enough money to send for Rosina, stepdaughter Giovannina, and young Francesco. Nitti grew up in New York, taking his criminal apprenticeship with the street gangs of the time. In 1907, Nitti headed up a Brooklyn gang of juveniles, the Navy Street Boys, who were reported to have had an 8-year-old mascot by the name of Alphonse Capone. From there, Nitti moved on to become a member of New York's notorious Five Points gang, who, besides Capone, also claimed the likes of Johnny Torrio, Frankie Yale, Charles "Lucky" Luciano, and Meyer Lansky as alumni. As a young man, Nitti worked at several legitimate jobs and eventually became a barber. Unable to get along with his stepfather, Nitti left home and moved to Chicago around the time of World War I, where he also entered a new trade—fencing stolen jewelry. Through this endeavor, he became reacquainted with Torrio, Capone, and other gangsters.

By the 1920s, Nitti was solidly entrenched as a member of the Torrio-Capone organization, which Capone took complete charge of after Torrio's "retirement." Serving in various capacities, reputedly as Capone's bodyguard, counselor, second-in-command, and go-to guy when Capone needed someone to "apply some muscle," Nitti earned the nickname "the Enforcer." Nitti also learned the ins and outs of Capone's operations in vice, prostitution, and bootlegging during this time. Nitti's role in the post-Capone organization (called "the Outfit" in Chicago) is also sometimes murky and often in dispute. According to some, after Capone reported to the federal penitentiary in Atlanta to serve his sentence on income tax evasion charges in 1932, Nitti was the one running the Outfit, having the experience from his many years working with Capone, and, despite the nickname of the Enforcer, had an aptitude for business and efficiency. Other sources, however, claim that Nitti was no more than a "front man" for the likes of Outfit notables like Paul "the Waiter" Ricca, Anthony "Big Tuna" Accardo, and others, who were the real brains of the organization.

In December 1932, two Chicago detectives entered Nitti's office on North LaSalle Street. The two detectives shot Nitti, one of them inflicting a minor gunshot wound to himself so as to claim self-defense. The origin of the plot is in dispute, but reportedly the attempt on Nitti's life was ordered by Chicago Mayor Anton Cermak to try to rid Chicago of the vestiges of the Capone organization and leave room for other gangsters—and allies of Cermak's—to move in. Nitti was seriously wounded in the attack but eventually recovered. Although unproven, Nitti was later allegedly behind the assassination of Cermak in Miami in retaliation for the attempt on Nitti's life.

In the mid-1930s, Nitti became involved in a shakedown scheme run by Willie Bioff and George Browne, in which money was extorted from several major Hollywood studios that were forced to pay or have their theaters shut down with "labor problems." The scheme lasted until 1941, when the brother of a Twentieth Century Fox executive, indicted for income tax evasion, provided information on the Browne/Bioff scheme to authorities in exchange for leniency. Nitti was indicted along with Browne, Bioff, Tony Accardo, and others. On March 19, 1943, employees at a railroad yard watched from a distance as Nitti put a gun to his head and pulled the trigger. According to some reports, Nitti committed suicide rather than face a long prison term on the labor racketeering charges.

Paul A. Magro
Ball State University

See Also: Bootlegging; Capone, Al; Chicago, Illinois; Illinois; Italian Americans; Organized Crime, History of; Organized Crime, Sociology of; Prohibition.

Further Readings

Abadinsky, Howard. *Organized Crime*. Belmont, CA: Wadsworth, 2010.

Eghigian, Mars, Jr. *After Capone: The Life and World of Chicago Mob Boss Frank "The Enforcer" Nitti*. Nashville, TN: Cumberland House, 2006.

Humble, Ronald D. *Frank Nitti: The True Story of Chicago's Notorious "Enforcer."* Fort Lee, NJ: Barricade Books, 2007.

Ness, Eliot and Oscar Fraley. *The Untouchables*. New York: Popular Library, 1960.

Roth, Mitchell P. *Organized Crime*. Upper Saddle River, NJ: Pearson Education, 2010.

Sifakis, Carl. *The Mafia Encyclopedia*. New York: Checkmark Books, 1999.

Nixon, Richard (Administration of)

In part because of the social turmoil that had come to characterize aspects of the 1960s, Richard Nixon (1913–94) found a receptive audience among U.S. voters when he established law and order as a centerpiece of his campaign for the presidency in 1968. After soliciting advice from Republican lawmakers and party leaders as to the future direction of his campaign and which issues to prioritize, Nixon announced in July 1968 that the country's top priority should be to address crime and disorder. The message proved popular with the public as rates of violent crime, property crime, and the incidence of drug use increased markedly during the 1960s. The public was also weary of civil unrest such as riots related to the Vietnam War or the civil rights movement. With regard to the latter, Nixon did not equate civil disobedience and pro–civil rights demonstrations to criminal acts, and as a result, he avoided alienating minorities and civil rights leaders.

During the presidential campaign, Americans rated crime as their principal concern. Nixon's "tough on crime" platform became politically popular, and many other politicians at the national level began to adopt the stance. Specifically, Nixon advocated a multipronged assault on the problem via the introduction of new federal legislation, the creation of a congressional subcommittee focused upon countermeasures against crime, and the allocation of additional funding and manpower resources at the federal, state, and local levels to bolster law enforcement and prosecution efforts and to facilitate improvements in the penal system and the rehabilitation of incarcerated persons.

Drug Policies

Upon assuming the presidency in 1969, Nixon began implementing his law-and-order platform and fulfilling promises of new anticrime legislation. In an address to Congress in 1969, he identified the increasingly widespread abuse of drugs as not just a threat but a national emergency and a major root cause of the broader problems of crime and social instability. He advocated a formalized and comprehensive antidrug policy to be coordinated at all levels of government. This materialized in the Comprehensive Drug Abuse Prevention and Control Act of 1970. Among other things, the act created classifications of controlled substances and established higher standards for the pharmaceutical industry in terms of monitoring production and sales records of certain types of drugs such as opiates.

A key component element of the latter act, the Controlled Substances Act of 1970, served as the cornerstone of the government's increased efforts at combating the abuse of narcotics. To better facilitate enforcement of the Controlled Substances Act and coordinate interagency efforts, the Nixon administration created the Drug Enforcement Administration in 1973 as an expansion and consolidation of several preexisting agencies such as the Department of Justice's Bureau of Narcotics and Dangerous Drugs. Such federal antinarcotics initiatives were not entirely new, but rather were a continuation and widening of early-20th-century federal regulations designed to combat the abuse of illicit drugs. The Nixon administration is credited for the escalation of governmental efforts to address the distribution and use of illegal narcotics and for coining the term *war on drugs* in 1971. His administration was also the first in U.S. history to invest significant effort in diplomatic cooperation aimed at combating the international trade in illicit drugs. Contemporary federal statutes and law enforcement programs aimed at antinarcotics efforts are largely a continuation of policies established during the Nixon administration.

The federal initiative to combat illegal drugs both during and after the Nixon administra-

Singer Johnny Cash (left) met with President Richard Nixon in 1972 to discuss prison reform. In a 1968 speech, Nixon stated that the U.S. prison system was "a crime university," graduating more than 200,000 hardened criminals a year.

tion has garnered criticism from some circles. In 1972, citing lack of precedent in the U.S. Constitution, the National Commission on Marijuana and Drug Abuse, to the surprise of Congress and the White House, recommended decriminalization of marijuana for personal use and advocated educational and other means of discouraging its use rather than codified punitive measures. The Nixon administration responded by ignoring the recommendations. More broadly, critics argue that the increased effort to criminalize drug use, and the associated increase in financial and logistical commitment to combat drug use, has been ineffectual and has consumed a disproportionate amount of law enforcement, judicial, and penal resources.

Organized Crime

The anticrime initiatives of the Nixon administration were not focused exclusively on narcotics. One of the principal accomplishments of the Nixon presidency was the passage of the Organized Crime Control Act of 1970, a culmination of a long-standing desire to bring organized crime more directly under the scrutiny of federal law. Historically, state and local prosecutors had often struggled to bring organized crime figures to justice for their activities under their jurisdictions, with acquittals, mistrials, and witness tampering being commonplace. The Organized Crime Control Act (OCCA) was designed to better enable

U.S. authorities to bring crime syndicates to justice under federal law and to establish criminal prosecution of organized crime as a high national priority. In keeping with the broader law-and-order strategy of his administration, the ultimate goal of the program in Nixon's words was to "launch an all-out war against organized crime" and eradicate its influence in the United States.

Although the goal of complete eradication was not achieved, significant strides were made by federal law enforcement against organized crime stemming from the new initiative. The OCCA has 13 component elements, each of which addresses specific aspects of investigating or prosecuting organized crime, including rules that allow for the prosecution of witnesses or jurors for noncompliance or failure to be forthcoming with facts. One element of the OCCA was the successful Racketeer Influenced and Corrupt Organizations Act, better known by its acronym, RICO. The OCCA also led to creation of the federal witness protection program. Critics of the OCCA and the RICO have described both as potentially encroaching upon civil liberties, noting that federal agencies were granted more investigative powers in certain instances than they had previously possessed and that the rights of individuals to choose whether to testify as witnesses or to assert Fifth Amendment protection in certain criminal proceedings were restricted. It is somewhat ironic that the Nixon administration, which would have otherwise perhaps been best remembered for its anticrime initiatives, is instead remembered chiefly for the illegal activity related to the Watergate scandal in which the president was implicated, ultimately culminating in his resignation.

Barry D. Mowell
Broward College

See Also: 1961 to 1980 Primary Documents; Drug Enforcement Administration; Organized Crime, History of; Watergate.

Further Readings
Black, Conrad. *Richard M. Nixon: A Life in Full.* New York: Public Affairs, 2008.
Flamm, Michael. *Law and Order: Street Crime, Civil Unrest, and the Crisis of Liberalism in the 1960s.* New York: Columbia University Press, 2005.

Small, Melvin. *The Presidency of Richard Nixon.* Lawrence: University Press of Kansas, 2003.

North Carolina

North Carolina was first inhabited by European settlers in 1584 under a charter given to Walter Raleigh. With successful settlements in the early 1600s, a loose legal structure was established based on English common law. Final judicial authority, however, remained largely in the hands of the colonial governor. The state of North Carolina has had three different constitutions—the first ratified in 1776, a second in 1868, and a third in 1971. Today, North Carolina retains a tri-level court system, with crimes tried in local districts, an intermediate court of appeals with statewide jurisdiction, and a state supreme court. North Carolina's current population exceeds 9 million people and the state's crime rate has seen recent declines, with 2010 levels reported to be the lowest in over two decades.

Crime

In colonial times, the developed towns in the eastern part of the state effectively punished criminal activity, but the criminal justice system was poorly implemented in frontier areas. Juries possessed considerable power in determining verdicts and punishments, with little uniformity across different courts or cases. Drawing heavily from the Declaration of Independence and the English legal tradition, the 1776 North Carolina constitution included traditional protections such as the right to be informed of the accusations, to confront the accusers and witnesses with other testimony, and protections from self-incrimination. The constitution also provided for "unanimous verdict[s] of a jury of good and lawful men, in open court." By 1817, 28 crimes were considered felonies, all of which were punishable by death. These crimes included murder, burglary, arson, highway robbery, sodomy, prison escape, concealing childbirth, and stealing slaves. The constitution of 1868 retained all existing rights but also limited the number of crimes subject to capital punishment and added the right to a writ of habeas corpus, which was not explicitly enumerated in the 1776 constitution.

Today, Chapter 14 of North Carolina General Statutes contains a full list of crimes, while Chapter 15 codifies criminal procedures. Recent developments include a "habitual felon" classification, which greatly increases sentences for those with three or more prior felony convictions. As its population grew in the 20th century, North Carolinians witnessed a general increase in crime. The highest crime rates in the state, based on crimes per 100,000 people, occurred in the 1990s. At its peak in 1991, 5,888 crimes were reported per 100,000 people, up from 1,179 in 1960. In 1960, the murder rate was 10.6 per 100,000 people, 11.7 in 1970, 10.6 in 1980 and 10.7 in 1990. However, in the past decade the state has seen a significant drop in all crimes, as the number of total crimes per 100,000 dropped to 3,956 in 2010. The murder rate is half that of 1960, at 5.1 murders per 100,000 people in 2010.

According to 2010 North Carolina Department of Corrections data, drug-related crimes represent the most frequent violations, with nearly one out of every five new prisoners (18 percent) and probationers (21 percent) being convicted of drug possession. Statistics also show that 11 percent of newly admitted prisoners were convicted for assault, another 11 percent for larceny, 10 percent for driving while impaired, and 10 percent for breaking and entering. Concerning those who received a non-drug-related probationary sentence in 2010, 16 percent were convicted of driving while intoxicated (DWI), 13 percent for larceny, and 12 percent for other traffic violations.

As in many states, law enforcement remains a largely local activity. In 1738, an early colonial law established local sheriffs for each county, but private citizen groups often served as the chief law enforcers. The 1776 constitution also included a provision that each county should have a sheriff. Today, sheriffs are popularly elected in each county and have the duties of law enforcement, administering the local jails, and providing courthouse security. North Carolina statutes as provide municipalities the ability to create city police forces and state agencies with statewide law enforcement powers. Statewide organizations include the North Carolina Highway Patrol, the State Bureau of Investigation, and Wildlife Enforcement officers.

Punishment

As with decisions of guilt, punishments during colonial rule were largely under the control of the juries. This led to inconsistent punishments throughout the colony, including crimes going unpunished when juries failed to show up at court. With the constitution of 1776, provisions on punishment were codified, including restrictions on excessive bail, excessive fines, and cruel or unusual punishments. North Carolina continued to practice capital punishment as well as hard labor and imprisonment sentences. The ratification of the North Carolina constitution in 1868 created several changes in criminal law, including a specific provision enumerating that punishment should include reforming the offender.

Historically, the presiding judge in each case possessed wide discretion to dictate punishments for criminal activities. This, too, led to inconsistent and sometimes arbitrary punishments. However, in 1981, the legislature passed a statute setting presumptive prison terms for every crime. The 1994 Structured Sentencing Act created a more formal sentencing rubric. This framework created a detailed presumptive range of punishments based on the class of crime committed and the prior criminal record of the defendant. Punishments may

In 2008, the police department in Leland, North Carolina, began a program to collect expired or unused prescription drugs to remove them from circulation. A press conference was held in 2010 to display the pounds of narcotics collected.

vary from the presumptive range based on mitigating or aggravating factors. Penalties include death, imprisonment, fines, restitution, community service, restraints on liberty, and work programs.

The 1868 constitution provided for the first state penitentiary, known as Central Prison in Raleigh. Originally, inmates worked on state projects or could be leased out to private employers. Many inmates currently work on state projects or through work release, a practice started in 1957 that allows inmates to work in the private sector during the day and return to confinement at night. As of 2010, the state maintains 70 prisons and work farms across the state, with an inmate population of more than 40,000 and nearly 112,000 probationers. In 2010, the vast majority of new prisoners (93 percent) and new probationers (76 percent) were male. A majority of new prisoners and probationers (57 percent) were African American while 35 percent were white.

Concerning the death penalty, by 1663, the colony could legally carry out capital punishment under the Charter of the Carolinas. The 1868 constitution limited the number of crimes punishable by execution to rape, murder, arson, and burglary. In addition, the 1868 constitution prohibited public executions and created first- and second-degree murder categories. In 1909, the North Carolina General Assembly outlawed hanging and limited executions to electrocution. In 1935, the North Carolina General Assembly again changed its prescribed mode of execution from electrocution to lethal gas. Under the current structured sentencing format, first-degree murder is the only crime for which one can receive the death penalty. Since 1984, 43 prisoners have been executed, the most recent occurring in 2006.

Todd Collins
Priscilla Warren
Western Carolina University

See Also: Capital Punishment; Executions; Felonies; Hanging.

Further Readings
Johnson, Guinn. *Ante-Bellum North Carolina: A Social History.* Chapel Hill: University of North Carolina Press, 1937.

Nelson, William E. "Politicizing the Courts and Undermining the Law: A Legal History of Colonial North Carolina, 1660–1775." *North Carolina Law Review,* v.88 (2010).

North Carolina Department of Corrections. http://www.doc.state.nc.us (Accessed December 2010).

North Carolina History Project. http://www.northcarolinahistory.org/commentary/23/category (Accessed December 2010).

Orth, John V. "'The Law of the Land': The North Carolina Constitution and State Constitutional Law." *North Carolina Law Review,* v.70 (1992).

University of North Carolina. "NC Capital Punishment Timeline." http://www.lib.unc.edu/mss/exhibits/penalty/timeline.html (Accessed December 2010).

North Dakota

One of the least populous states, North Dakota lies along the Canadian border. It was admitted to the union in 1889, when the Dakota Territory was divided into North and South Dakota. During the territorial period, many settlements were military forts and important posts in the Indian wars of the 19th century. As the area became more populous, more forts and infantry posts were established to protect railroads and early settlers from Indian attacks. Many settlements in this period had mixed populations of military, white settlers, and Indians. The territory attracted its share of banditry and outlaw activity, particularly targeting railroads and stagecoaches.

In 1883, shortly before statehood, the territorial government appropriated $50,000 to construct the Bismarck Penitentiary, which would become the North Dakota State Penitentiary. It was built two miles east of Bismarck's business district, along the Northern Pacific Railroad line. The first inmates were admitted in 1885, and by the next year the concern was that the transfer of 60 inmates from territorial jails would overcrowd the prison. In order to offset prison expenses, beginning in 1892, inmates were contracted out as laborers to the private sector, a practice abolished after five years after criticism of the treatment of the prisoners.

Crime

North Dakota's violent crime rate, 225 crimes per 100,000 inhabitants in 2010, is a little more than half of the national average, and is made up mostly of aggravated assaults. However, the crime rate is considerably higher than it used to be. Though the crime rate grew from the 1960s to the 1990s, it still remained very low (below 100) even when the national crime rate was peaking at more than 700. Since 2001, while the national crime rate has gradually declined, the North Dakota crime rate has steeply increased, peaking at 266.4 in 2009.

One notable incident occurred in 1969, when the "Zip to Zap" college spring break event degenerated into the only official riot in North Dakota history to require the intervention of the National Guard. Chuck Stroup, a North Dakota State University student who couldn't afford to travel to Florida for spring break (the traditional spring break destination at the time), proposed a North Dakota spring break celebration called Zip to Zap, to take place in the town of Zap in Mercer County. His advertisement in the student paper led to local news coverage, which was picked up by the Associated Press, and students as far away as Texas—and, ironically, Florida—became interested in attending.

North Dakota students were aware of the transformations in student culture on the coasts and the hippie movement and other elements of youth culture that were the subject of popular entertainment, but none of it had yet made its way to the remote state. Somehow, because of both student interest in participating in those nationwide phenomena and local papers hungry for news, what originated as a spring break party was portrayed and discussed more and more as—in the words of the student paper—"a full program of orgies, brawls, freak-outs, and arrests." None of the organizers were prepared for the scale of the event.

The price of beer was doubled almost as soon as students arrived in town, because demand was so high, and students quickly outnumbered townspeople in Zap by about 10:1. When nighttime temperatures fell, drunken students started a bonfire in the center of town. When they were asked to leave, a drunken riot broke out, destroying one of the two bars in town and the local café. The National Guard arrived at dawn to disperse the hungover students in full view of the national media that had expected a hippie freak-out and protest.

In the 21st century, the most significant crime problem in North Dakota is the rise of methamphetamine abuse. Although local production has increased (despite laws limiting purchases of precursor drugs), most meth used in North Dakota is produced in Mexico or California by Mexican criminal organizations and arrives in the state either via distribution channels in Minnesota and Washington, or is distributed locally by the Sons of Silence motorcycle gang and their associates. Meth-related crimes include not only possession and distribution but meth-driven violence and assaults and addiction-motivated burglaries and thefts. At least 80 percent of the inmates in the North Dakota women's penitentiary are incarcerated for meth-related crimes, and one in five high school students has reported trying the drug.

Punishment

In 1883, shortly before it was granted statehood, the territorial government appropriated $50,000 to construct the Bismarck Penitentiary, which became the North Dakota State Penitentiary. It was built two miles east of Bismarck's business district, along the Northern Pacific Railroad line. The first inmates were admitted in 1885, and by the next year, the warden was already expressing his concern that with the transfer of 60 inmates from territorial jails, the prison would soon face overcrowding. He also wrote to the governor of his worries over finding sufficient work for the prisoners to keep them busy and to offset the cost of their care and asked for funding to install electric lighting in the facility because of the safety concerns over the kerosene lamps the prison was then using. Other early requests included a prison library, a prison hospital, and cells for female prisoners. These requests were repeated in following years. In order to offset prison expenses, beginning in 1892, inmates were contracted out as laborers to the private sector, a practice abolished after five years as a result of criticism of the treatment of the prisoners.

The prison library was soon established through charitable donations, and the board of trustees continued to request funds to expand the library and hire a librarian who could double as a teacher of arithmetic and reading. Parole, first mentioned in an 1888 report to the governor, was introduced in the 1890s in the form of an early release program for prisoners with short sentences, who were released to the custody of an employer (nearly always a local farmer). The number of parole violators who were turned in shortly after harvest—and therefore returned to prison once their labor was no longer necessary—indicates that this form of "parole" was in many cases just another form of convict leasing. The North Dakota Pardon Board assumed duties of parole in 1939, when the system was modernized to resemble parole systems as we know them today.

Although the death penalty was historically used in North Dakota—and, in the Dakota Territory period and early years of statehood, lynchings outnumbered legal executions because of the vigilante justice that developed from residents' frustrations with the sparse distribution of law enforcement—the last execution in the state was in 1905. The death penalty was abolished in 1975 after 70 years without an execution, and attempts to revive it have failed.

Bill Kte'pi
Independent Scholar

See Also: Convict Lease System; Penitentiaries; South Dakota.

Further Readings
Brovald, Ken. *Silent Towns on the Prairie*. Missoula, MT: Pictorial Histories, 1999.
Robinson, Elwyn B. *History of North Dakota*. Lincoln: University of Nebraska Press, 1966.
State Historical Society of North Dakota. http://history.nd.gov (Accessed September 2011).

PIONEER SETTLERS BUILDING ADVENTURE GALLEY ON THE YOUGHIOGHENY

An image from the 1927 publication, History of the Ordinance of 1787 and the Old Northwest Territory, *depitcting pioneers who had gone west over the mountains and settled in Pennsylvania on the Youghiogheny River.*

Northwest Ordinance of 1787

The Northwest Ordinance of July 13, 1787, was the most important achievement of the U.S. Congress under the Articles of Confederation, America's first attempt at a national government. The law was passed during the same summer that the Constitutional Convention was meeting in Philadelphia to create the Confederation's successor. The Northwest Ordinance established the machinery of territorial self-government with eventual statehood, letting the territory grow until its population was large enough to be represented along with the original states in the Congress. The ordinance was the blueprint for the western expansion of the new nation. Thirty-one states were admitted into the United States through procedures first laid out in this law. The ordinance also created a "compact" of six articles that protected the civil liberties of its residents. These key civil liberties were later incorporated into the Constitution and in its first 10 amendments, the Bill of Rights.

The young republic was troubled by several political and economic afflictions. It had incurred massive debt during the Revolutionary War. The United States faced the threat of war with the Native Americans in the western lands it had acquired from Great Britain. British troops still occupied some of those lands and would not evacuate from the area until 1794. Land speculators and squatters were already settling the frontier. There was no orderly process for selling land or establishing legal title. Some political leaders feared that the frontier economy might fall under the control of European powers, given the most convenient trade outlets for the west were in the hands of Britain and Spain. Many states were reluctant to cede their land claims to the national government.

Thomas Jefferson first sought to deal with these problems in a proposal drafted in 1784. It never passed. There followed a three-year struggle to find an accommodation that respected the competing needs of the nation. Some believed that the development of western lands required the establishment of law and order. Others sought to pay off the national debt by selling the vast western lands. The Northwest Ordinance was prompted by this tangled web of lofty principles, economic interests, and pragmatism.

Five new states were created by the Northwest Ordinance in the frontier bounded on the east by the Appalachian Mountains, on the west by the Mississippi River, on the south by the Ohio River, and on the north by the Great Lakes. These states were Indiana, Ohio, Illinois, Michigan, and Wisconsin.

The ordinance protected essential liberties such as religious freedom, the guarantee of the due process of law, such as the right to bail and a trial by jury, a prohibition against cruel or unusual punishment, the protection of contracts (the first such guarantee in any government's charter), and a ban on ex post facto laws. It also established a written guarantee of the writ of habeas corpus and the right to just compensation for government confiscation of private property.

Three features of the law had long-term implications. It sought to protect Native Americans, prompting the first official U.S. Indian policy. It encouraged public education by setting aside land for the construction and funding of public schools, setting a precedent for federal funding of public education and the ideal of public education. The ordinance also declared that no one could be born a slave in the territory.

The antislavery provisions were the most idealistic and problem ridden. Slavery was already well established in some portions of the region. No slaves in the territory were immediately freed. Moreover, the ordinance contained a fugitive slave clause protecting slaveholders whose property escaped into the territory, and there was no enforcement clause to root out existing pockets of slavery. Two to three thousand slaves remained in the area until 1848.

Nonetheless, the ordinance discouraged slave owners from moving into the region, guaranteeing the emergence of free states. Practically, it created a region of free states that would balance the south's clout in Congress. Finally, it was the only act passed by the national government indicating public disapproval of slavery until the Missouri Compromise of 1820.

Timothy J. O'Neill
Southwestern University

See Also: African Americans; Slavery; Slavery, Law of.

Further Readings
Onuf, Peter S. *Statehood and Union*. Bloomington: Indiana University Press, 1987.
Williams, Frederick, ed. *The Northwest Ordinance*. East Lansing: Michigan State University Press, 1989.

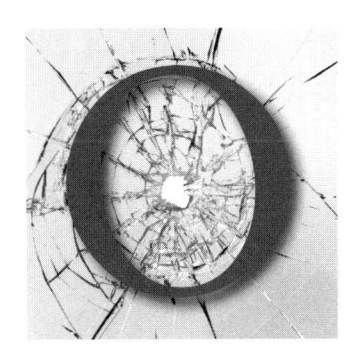

Oakland, California

Founded in 1852 and located in California's East Bay, Oakland is one of several cities incorporated in Alameda County. From the beginning, Oakland has been the dominant city in the area, serving as the county seat since 1873. With a police department established in 1853, crime in early Oakland was not a major issue; though influenced by the leavings of California gold rush lawlessness, Oakland in its formative years was not atypically criminal. Despite a decrease in felony arrests in the latter part of the 19th century, the size of the police force grew. The primary policing concerns during the early decades of Oakland's history were maintaining order and discipline, as evidenced by a majority of arrests for public disturbances such as brawls, drunkenness, and vagrancy. The first drug arrests in Oakland arose in the 1880s with the formation of drugs laws that made the sale or use of opium a misdemeanor. Reflecting the beginnings of a history of racial tensions, many of these arrests targeted Chinese immigrants. The primary mode of punishment for crime in early Oakland was incarceration in county jails or federal prisons, with the majority of petty criminals placed in jails for short sentences. Unlike other emerging cities in California at the time, less emphasis was placed on levying fines as punishment, and incarceration functioned as the main form of punishment.

Oakland in the Twentieth Century

Oakland was designated the terminus station for the transcontinental railroad in 1869, laying the foundation for a transportation hub that would continue to grow into the 20th century. Oakland's economy and population grew rapidly in the first decades of the 20th century. By 1920, the population exceeded 200,000, more than 90 percent of whom were white. Notions of nativism were amplified by the simultaneous growth of this white middle class and the influx of southern European and Irish Catholic immigrants with socialist politics. As a result, racial and ethnic tensions permeated debates over the role of police, Prohibition enforcement, court appointments, and other crime issues. Additionally, Oakland became one of the main centers for African American settlement in California. In conjunction with the rise in nativist politics, Oakland saw the rise of an active and large branch of the Ku Klux Klan with elected members across the city government in the 1920s.

Policing concerns during the Great Depression were impacted by domestic migration and labor unrest. Like many other California cities, Oakland saw increased domestic migration during the Great Depression as white migrant workers were displaced from their farms by droughts and new farming mechanization. As was the case across California, migrants were persecuted by residents who saw them as economic competition

Members of the Black Panther Party marked their 40th anniversary in Oakland, California, in 2006. The organization was founded in Oakland by Huey Newton and Bobby Seale in1966, who believed that racism was rampant in the United States. The group sought to empower African Americans, fight police brutality, and organize urban activists.

and cultural threats. Additionally, labor unrest in the 1930s was a primary concern for police and the courts. This concern was epitomized in May 1934 when local maritime workers went on an 83-day strike at city docks, and Oakland police opened fire on striking union members.

The ethnic makeup of Oakland shifted significantly during World War II, as migrant workers from across the country traveled to the East Bay to find work in the city's booming defense industry. A significant number of these migrants were African American. During the World War II era, the African American population in Oakland increased more than 150 percent. This arrival of African American citizens transformed the racial makeup of Oakland as African Americans outnumbered Asians as the largest minority group. Housing became scarce and placed heavy strain on Oakland police, who struggled to maintain order and discipline in a city plagued with homeless migrants. Several landlords were prosecuted during the housing crisis for profiteering and health violations.

The arrival of African American migrants in the Bay Area for defense industry employment in the 1940s evolved over the following decades and fed into the Black Power generation. The Black Panthers transformed the city of Oakland, not just in terms of demographics, but in education, labor, politics, and policing and prisons. The Black Panthers' sudden growth in the 1960s was based on the group's ability to address the concerns of black migrants, with police brutality topping the list. Famed for their armed patrols in which members followed police on patrol to document any violation of rights while openly carrying guns, the

Panthers challenged an increasingly discriminatory and violent police force, as well as prosecutorial bias and unjust incarcerations.

Through the end of the 20th century, high homicide rates along with gang violence and activity became and remain a primary concern for law enforcement and the court system. Oakland gangs differ from those in other major California cities because they are less formal and instead function as loose-knit neighborhood associations. Latino and African American gangs have a significant presence, but given the lack of formal structure, many of these affiliations and corresponding crimes are not classified as gang-related under state law. Regardless, the African American neighborhood gang associations in Oakland are highly affiliated with the drug trade and drug violence. The majority of drug trade is neighborhood based and occurs throughout the day in the open air on street corners.

Oakland began operating drug courts in the 1990s in an attempt to reduce the strain placed on the court system by drug-related offenses. Oakland drug courts focus on reviving the generation of people of color who have been disproportionately affected by failed drug policies. During the 1990s, police emphasis included not only the drug trade but also "soft crimes" of public disturbances in order to promote a more positive image of the Oakland community, which was quickly becoming known for its drug crimes and high homicide rates.

Currently, Oakland is rated the fifth most dangerous city in America. From 2000 to 2005, Oakland's total homicides accounted for more than 70 percent of the total homicides in Alameda County. The victims of these homicides were primarily African American or Hispanic minorities between the ages of 18 and 34. Given the informal structure of Oakland gang activity, gang affiliations among victims are difficult to track. Similar statistics exist for those convicted of crimes. Educational outreach programs informing young minorities of the impacts of crime and the drug trade are being implemented across the East Bay in an attempt to mitigate these high rates of crime and victimization.

Amy N. Cole
Washington State University

See Also: Black Panthers; California; Federal Prisons; Ku Klux Klan; Strikes.

Further Readings
Friedman, Lawrence M. and Robert V. Percival. *The Roots of Justice: Crime and Punishment in Alameda County, California, 1870–1910.* Chapel Hill: University of North Carolina Press, 1981.
Murch, Donna Jean. *Living for the City: Migration, Education, and the Rise of the Black Panther Party in Oakland, California.* Chapel Hill: University of North Carolina Press, 2010.
Rhomberg, Chris. *No There There: Race, Class, and Political Community in Oakland.* Berkeley: University of California Press, 2004.

Obama, Barack (Administration of)

Barack Obama became the 44th president of the United States on January 20, 2009. During his first two years in office, Obama signed several significant pieces of criminal justice legislation, including an expansion of existing hate crimes legislation and the Fair Sentencing Act.

His administration also released a statement in 2009 indicating that federal authorities would not raid medical marijuana dispensaries, a very different stance than the two previous presidential administrations had taken. Still, other domestic issues, such as the economy and healthcare, took the front seat during the first two years of his administration.

While Obama served in the Illinois State Senate (1997–2004), he successfully passed legislation requiring police officers to record the race of automobile drivers they detained in order to monitor racial profiling. He also advocated legislation that required the videotaping of interrogations of suspects in capital cases; Illinois was the first state in the United States to do so. A highlight of his Senate career was his legislation that called for the state to place a moratorium on executions in order to study problems with the death penalty system.

Presidential Election Politics

Obama defeated Senator John McCain (R-AZ) in the general election. During the presidential campaign, crime was not a central issue, although Republican strategists attempted to paint Obama as soft on crime. They released an ad attacking Obama for his opposition to a bill while in the Illinois State Senate that would have extended the death penalty to gang-related murders. The ad was quickly criticized for its drastic misrepresentation of the bill and Obama's position, squelching any momentum for making crime a central campaign issue. A crime-related issue that drew attention during the campaign was illegal immigration, on which the candidates had differing positions. Obama's position included a pathway toward citizenship for immigrants who entered the United States illegally. McCain opposed this approach (even though he previously sponsored such legislation in the U.S. Senate) and emphasized a stricter anti-immigration stance that included more law enforcement and strengthening of the borders.

Guantanamo Bay

One of the first policies that President Obama focused on was the closing of detention facilities at Guantanamo Bay naval base in Cuba. Established under the Bush administration in 2002 for the purpose of holding detainees from the wars in Afghanistan and Iraq, the facilities had been criticized for not providing ordinary protections to foreign prisoners established by the Geneva Conventions. Obama signed an executive order on January 22, 2009, that ordered the closure of the detention facilities "as soon as practicable, and no later than one year from the date of this order." The executive order also specified that any individuals would be returned to their home country if not transferred elsewhere before the closure. Congress, however, has so far prevented the transfer of all of the detainees through amendments to defense spending bills. As of February 2011, 172 detainees remained at Guantanamo.

Hate Crimes Prevention Act

On October 28, 2009, President Obama signed into law the Matthew Shepherd and James Byrd, Jr., Hate Crimes Prevention Act, an expansion of the existing hate crimes legislation to include acts of violence motivated by a victim's sexual orientation, gender, disability, or gender identity. The existing legislation, as part of the 1968 Civil Rights Act, had only considered hate crimes to be those motivated by a victim's religion, race, color, or national origin. The law also allows judges to impose harsher penalties for hate crimes and permits the Justice Department to help local police departments investigate alleged hate crimes. The bill is named for Matthew Shepherd, a 21-year-old gay man who was brutally beaten and murdered by two men in Wyoming in 1998; Shepherd's sexual orientation was the motive for the murder. The other named individual in the bill, James Byrd, Jr., was a 49-year-old African American man who was beaten and murdered by three white men in Jasper, Texas. The murderers chained and dragged Byrd behind a pickup truck for several miles, dumping his dead body in front of an African American cemetery.

Drug Laws

Obama made several remarks during the presidential campaign that the sentencing disparities between possession of crack and powder cocaine should be eliminated and that Congress should lift the ban on federal funding for needle exchange programs; both were eventually changed. In December 2009, Obama signed into law an end to the long-standing ban on federal funding for

President Barack Obama greets James Byrd, Jr.'s sisters and Matthew Shepard's mother at a reception commemorating the enactment of the Matthew Shepard and James Byrd, Jr., Hate Crimes Prevention Act in 2009.

needle exchange programs. Eight months later, President Obama signed into law the Fair Sentencing Act, which reduced the disparity in sentencing between crack and powder cocaine from a 100:1 to an 18:1 ratio. The law also eliminated the mandatory five-year sentence for simple possession of crack cocaine. The 100:1 disparity, established by the 1986 Anti-Drug Abuse Act, meant that somebody had to possess 500 grams of powder cocaine to trigger the same mandatory five-year prison sentence that one would get for possession of five grams of crack cocaine. The initial disparity reflected largely unscientific notions that crack cocaine was more harmful and violence-provoking than powder cocaine. The policy has also been criticized for being racially biased and contributing to the disproportionate imprisonment of African Americans.

Obama has also relaxed the use of federal authorities to raid medical marijuana dispensaries. Since 1996, 15 states and the District of Columbia have approved the use of marijuana for medicinal purposes. During the Clinton and Bush administrations, federal authorities frequently raided marijuana dispensaries, citing violations of federal drug laws. The Obama administration has appeared to take a different approach in this area, and made a public statement in October 2009 that federal resources would not be used to prosecute patients or those running marijuana dispensaries that were complying with state laws.

There are several other crime- and punishment-related policies that Obama has mentioned that he would like to focus on in the future, especially concerning prisoner re-entry. He also wants to revive former President Clinton's Community Oriented Policing Services (COPS) program in order to fund thousands of new police officers. Although Obama's primary focus during his first two years in office has not been crime related, he still believes there are problems with the criminal justice system that need to be addressed.

Jennifer Murphy
Elizabeth Rae Pierson
California State University, Sacramento

See Also: Bush, George W. (Administration of); Clinton, William (Administration of); Drug Abuse and Addiction, Contemporary; Sentencing.

Further Readings
Bacon, Perry, Jr. "After 10-Year Dispute, Expansion of Hate Crimes Law to Gays Signed." *Washington Post* (October 29, 2009).
Stout, David and Solomon Moore. "U.S. Won't Prosecute in States that Allow Medical Marijuana." *New York Times* (October 20, 2009).
The White House. "Issues." http://www.whitehouse.gov/issues (Accessed February 2011).

Obscenity

Obscenity refers to expressions, actions, or ideas, particularly of a sexual nature, that cross the boundary between the acceptable and the unacceptable in a community. The idea of obscenity is associated with the ideas of sacrilege, taboo, blasphemy, or heresy in matters of religious faith or political beliefs; each challenges norms or "morality" in a severe or fundamental way. By definition, that which by consensus is obscene does not need to be tolerated by a community, because that which is obscene is whatever a community does not believe it can tolerate. As such, American law has long assumed that obscenity falls outside the protections guaranteed to individuals by the U.S. Constitution, such as the rights of free speech and free press. Obscenity is often contrasted with indecency, a less serious category of expression that is offensive to some observers but has been given greater protection.

The central problem in the concept of obscenity is that its definition depends on the individual, or, as Supreme Court Justice Potter Stewart famously defined it, "I know it when I see it." Because individuals always live within a social setting, the nature of obscene material or actions varies widely across communities, cultures, and over time. Not all societies have labeled depictions of sexual activity as obscene. Written and artistic depictions of human sexuality can be found in Greek, Roman, and ancient Eastern cultures. Anthropologists have noted cultures in which sex in public places has been acceptable. Thus, even after obscenity emerged as a significant "social problem" in the United States, the large and diverse country displayed significant disagreement about obscenity.

Early Obscenity Laws

Though the regulation of obscenity is sometimes criticized as "puritanical"—referring to the strict moral standards of the early settlers of colonial New England, the Puritans—through the first half of the 19th century, obscenity prosecutions were relatively rare, with one court finding just three per year. After the Civil War, however, obscenity prosecutions surged. Within the moral climate of the Victorian era and the fear of a breakdown in the social order, crusader Anthony Comstock, leader of the New York Society for the Suppression of Vice and long-time U.S. Postal Inspector, drove the passage of the Comstock Law of 1873. This amendment to the 1865 Postal Act criminalized mailing or receiving "obscene," "lewd," or "lascivious" publications, which in Comstock's vision included not only pornographic texts and pictures but also materials referring to contraceptives and abortion.

Mae West, photographed in 1933 riding in a carriage, was arrested in 1927 on a morals charge for the content of her Broadway play Sex. West used the publicity and her sex symbol image to her advantage throughout her career.

Though Comstock objected to nudity in art and even in medical anatomy books, many materials declared "obscene" in the 19th century qualify as literature today. The prevailing definition given to obscenity by courts drew on an 1868 English case, *Regina v. Hicklin*, which deemed materials obscene based on whether they displayed a "tendency" to "deprave and corrupt those whose minds are open to such immoral influences, and into whose hands a publication of this sort may fall." By this standard, only select words or passages needed to be obscene, or for the work to thematically address matters of sexuality, for the work as a whole to be considered obscene.

Under this legal regime, antipornography groups and prosecutors focused on the protection of youth from corruption. In the late 19th century and first half of the 20th century, works that were banned or subjected to obscenity trials included Henry Miller's *Tropic of Cancer*, Theodore Dreiser's *An American Tragedy*, and D. H. Lawrence's *Lady Chatterley's Lover*. Other books and magazines were forced off the market under pressure from antiobscenity activists, who also urged police raiding and otherwise suppressing works and merchants who sold those works. Among the most notable, Victoria Woodhull, a prominent suffragette, was arrested in 1872 (along with her husband and sister) at Comstock's instigation for publishing a newspaper advocating free love, sex education, and licensed prostitution. In 1927, the famed actress and sex symbol, Mae West, was tried and imprisoned for 10 days for the raunchy dialogue and subject matter of the Broadway play *Sex*, which she wrote, directed, and produced.

Obscenity often attracts readers precisely because it challenges social conventions and norms, piquing the already strong interest in matters of sexuality. One side effect of efforts to condemn obscenity has been to provide publicity to the work being banned. For example, criticism by Comstock and others of *September Morn*, an unremarkable 1912 painting by French artist Paul Chabas featuring a nude woman with a backdrop of a lake and mountains, generated enough of a scandal to drive the sale of reproductions for years. Over the 20th century, artists in many media have become more proficient in using shock value and the specter of oppression to generate attention and sympathy.

Censorship in the Twentieth Century

What is "shocking" and obscene in one era has tended to become commonplace and absorbed into the mainstream, and with that process the American understanding of obscenity changed greatly over the course of the 20th century. Because obscenity law depends on society's sense of the tolerable limits, changes in opinion have resulted in changes in the law. The significant departure from the Victorian era of obscenity regulation can be seen in the response to James Joyce's monumental *Ulysses*. The classic novel was banned in the United States in 1921, following its partial serialization in a magazine. The New York Society for the Suppression of Vice objected to the book following publication of a passage concerning masturbation. However, the book was judged not obscene in 1933 by a federal district court judge in New York City who, two years earlier, had protected works containing information on birth control and marital sexual relations. His decision on *Ulysses* was upheld on appeal to the Second Circuit Court of Appeals, at the time the most important appellate court below the Supreme Court.

In 1957, the U.S. Supreme Court rejected the *Hicklin* standard and in *Roth v. United States* moved to consider the view of the "average person," rather than the most vulnerable, and the work "taken as a whole." In stating that obscenity should be judged by "contemporary community standards," the court recognized that judgments about obscene material depend on values that change with time. Though the Supreme Court under Earl Warren was eager to adapt the law to changing times, the primary shift was the dramatic changes to American society that were becoming clear by 1960, with increasing openness to discussions of sexuality. Though the 1950s are idealistically portrayed with the purity of the American nuclear family and growing suburbia, efforts to restrict as obscenity works such as Allen Ginsberg's *Howl and Other Poems* suggest the rising current of challenge to traditional norms. New forms of media also contributed to changing social values, with the national distribution of Hollywood movies in particular disseminating new ideas about romance and youthful rebellion.

Still, efforts to restrict literature of a sexual nature continued. The English novel, *Memoirs of a Woman of Pleasure* by John Cleland, first published in 1748 and circulated thereafter with the better known title *Fanny Hill*, had been banned in the United States since 1821. Using the *Roth* standard, the Supreme Court decided that the erotic work—telling the story of a girl who falls into prostitution—was not "utterly without redeeming social value," a heightened standard that made prosecution difficult. *Fanny Hill*, though focused on explicit depictions of sex and often accompanied in various editions by explicit illustrations, had begun receiving attention for its historic and literary value. In the wake of this decision, courts began to hear expert witness testimony from famous authors and scholars speaking to the artistic value of questioned works.

It has been insufficient for proponents of obscenity regulations to assert a mere desire for moral standards. A common strain in Victorian-era obscenity regulation had been to emphasize the capacity of such material to corrupt people by encouraging sexual activity in general and "improper" forms of sex in particular. The changing views about divorce, infidelity, and homosexuality—the latter often dated to the 1969 Stonewall riots in New York—that were reflected in the decisions of the Warren Court made it difficult to

Paul Émile Chabas's painting September Morn *caused a scandal when it was first displayed in the window of a Chicago art gallery in 1912. The mayor charged the gallery owner with indecency, leading to a demand for reproductions.*

limit material that advocated openness in matters of sex and relationships.

An alternative approach to obscenity in the second half of the 20th century was to emphasize the harms of "hard-core" pornography to the observer, the participants, or communities in which it was distributed. In the 1969 decision of *Stanley v. Georgia,* the Supreme Court ruled that a man could not be prosecuted for possessing obscene material in his own home, suggesting that obscenity would be protected by an individual's right to privacy. Nevertheless, the conservative court under Chief Justice Warren Burger retained room for the community's interest in its rulings. In *Miller v. California* (1973), the court rejected the "utterly without redeeming social value" standard and instead asked whether the work as a whole "lacks serious literary, artistic, political, or scientific value." Emphasizing the depiction or description of sexual conduct in a "patently offensive" way that "appeals to the prurient interest," Burger, joined by other new appointees of President Richard Nixon, tried to exclude "hard-core" pornography from constitutional protection.

Widespread Availability of Obscene Materials

Even though government regulation remains, since 1970, the social backdrop for the legal battles has featured increasing availability and diversity of the market for obscenity of all stripes. Commercial purveyors of pornographic material commonly have been at the cutting edge of new technologies, from home video recording and mail-order video to Internet-based dissemination of photographs, streaming video, and online chat. As the Supreme Court considered, in later years, whether the mythical "average person" or some form of "reasonable person" should be the judge of obscenity, the challenge is that any such person is likely to have had increasing awareness of the significant market for pornography, making either formulation a very permissive test.

Seeking to ground obscenity regulations on the harm caused, rather than the visual content itself, in the 1980s, some feminists allied with social conservatives in a campaign against pornography on the basis that it degraded women and encouraged sex crimes. They were successful in getting ordinances passed in a small number of U.S. cities, but these were struck down in court.

The regulation of child pornography has seemed on stronger ground, given the overwhelming social consensus for classifying it as obscenity and the direct harm to children involved in producing it. In 1982, the Supreme Court ruled that pornographic materials made using children constitute obscenity. However, with the ability of computers to generate realistic, "virtual" children, and the literary potential for such "actors" to be portrayed in sexual situations—such as in Vladimir Nabokov's classic, *Lolita*—the "direct harm" rationale for regulating such obscene material had been undercut. In 2002, the court ruled unconstitutional the section of the federal Child Pornography Prevention Act of 1996 banning "virtual" child pornography on the basis that the law was too broad in scope.

Recent information technologies, like printing presses and film before it, have markedly shaped the ambition of limiting obscenity. Even if technologically feasible to control it, congressional efforts to prohibit dissemination of obscene material over the Internet have proven unsuccessful. Congress first attempted to do so in the 1990s, first with the Communications Decency Act of 1996 and then, in 1998, the Child Online Protection Act. The Supreme Court ultimately rejected both attempts to restrict sexually obscene and indecent material from the Internet, even though the latter act was carefully tailored to follow the *Miller* guidelines. Even without the court's protections, the Internet has freed from the scrutiny of communities and neighbors sexually oriented materials about a wide range of sexual practices.

Yet, the idea that some forms of expression are "obscene" in society remains, at least in the judgments of some individuals or communities. Even if virtual sexual activity—including "sexting" and the distribution of obscene photos via Twitter—is difficult to regulate, social norms may shame or punish those whose activity becomes public. And where sexual activity moves from the virtual to the physical, such as in nude dancing, communities have continued to use their regulatory powers to limit or shun the activity.

Further, even "indecent" communications and activity can generate intense social and governmental responses when it is delivered in ways that make it difficult for unwilling audiences to avoid it. The Federal Communications Commission retains authority over broadcasters that use offensive language (famously, certain "dirty words") on the radio, and the brief, partial nudity of performer Janet Jackson at the 2004 Super Bowl made clear that there remains an active debate about the acceptability of public nudity in the United States.

In comparative perspective, the United States has a peculiar relationship with obscenity. To much of the world, the United States is among the most permissive societies for producing and consuming both sexualized and genuinely pornographic material. Yet, to critics, especially European audiences, the United States is still relatively puritanical about nudity and sexual content in mainstream television. Still, obscenity depends on culture rather than consistency: Europe's relative tolerance of sexuality in the broadcast media does not extend as generously to the depictions of violence in American television.

Patrick Schmidt
Macalester College
Hopi Costello
Davis Polk & Wardwell LLP

See Also: 1921 to 1940 Primary Documents; 1941 to 1960 Primary Documents; Comstock Law; Obscenity Laws; Pornography.

Further Readings
de Grazia, Edward. *Girls Lean Back Everywhere: The Law of Obscenity and the Assault on Genius*. New York: Random House, 1992.
Gillers, Stephan. "A Tendency to Deprave and Corrupt: The Transformation of American Obscenity Law From *Hicklin* to Ulysses II." *Washington University Law Review* (v.85/2, 2007).
Saunders, Kevin. *Degradation: What the History of Obscenity Tells Us About Hate Speech*. New York: New York University Press, 2011.

Obscenity Laws

The U.S. Supreme Court had great difficulty reaching a consensus on the legal standard for what is or is not obscene. This was the critical issue, as once it was determined that something was obscene, it was no longer protected by the First Amendment to the Constitution of the United States. Freedom of speech and press are guaranteed by the First Amendment. The words of the amendment are simple and seemingly absolute. The amendment states, in pertinent part, "Congress shall make no law ... abridging the freedom of speech, or of the press." Obscenity litigation exemplifies the difficulties the court has encountered in giving meaning to these words. These words have been interpreted by the Supreme Court as neither simple nor absolute. The general standard for obscenity was established in 1973. However, the court continues to deal with this issue as the views of society have changed and new forms of disseminating information have been created; in 1973, personal computers, the Internet, cell phones, cable television, and all that goes with them did not exist.

Roth v. United States

The Supreme Court did not squarely address the issue of obscenity until 1957, in the case *Roth v. United States*. Roth had been convicted of mailing advertisements for a book many considered obscene. He challenged his conviction, stating that it violated the First Amendment. The Supreme Court was faced with the need to develop a legal standard to determine obscenity. Once a work was determined to be obscene, it no longer was protected by the First Amendment. The legal standard developed in *Roth v. United States* for determining whether a specific item is obscene is "whether to the average person, applying contemporary community standards, the dominant theme of the material taken as a whole appeals to the prurient interest." The *Roth* test of obscenity is based on obscenity's presumed effect on an individual's psychological state. Implicit in this presumption of changes in a person's psychological state because of exposure to obscene materials is a further assumption that this psychological effect will result in deleterious behavioral changes such as antisocial conduct, primarily sexual.

The *Roth* standard received harsh criticism in the dissenting opinions from the majority opinion in *Roth*. One criticism was that the court failed to articulate the governmental interest in the regulation or proscription of obscenity, making it inconsistent with the main body of First Amendment jurisprudence. Justice William J. Douglas's dissenting opinion cited the difficulty inherent in defining obscenity by means of focusing on the subjective responses assumedly evoked by exposure to obscene materials, rather than focusing on the prohibited conduct precipitated by such exposure. In essence, Justice Douglas argued, the standards punished thoughts rather than antisocial conduct, and that surely freedom of thought is protected by the First Amendment.

The legal standard for obscenity enunciated in *Roth v. United States* did not end the controversy surrounding the legal definition of obscenity. Rather than leading to a convergence of views and the development of a uniform standard that the lower courts could follow, the views of the justices became more divergent. Review by the Supreme Court of obscenity cases increased dramatically. Given this divergence of opinion, the court began the tedious and confusing practice of deciding obscenity cases not on the basis of a uniform standard but rather by each justice applying his individual standard to the allegedly obscene materials.

Miller v. California

In 1973, a majority of the court was able to agree on a new legal test for obscenity, one that was intended to end this approach. In *Miller v. California*, the Supreme Court set the following as the new obscenity standard: (1) whether the average person applying contemporary community standards would find the work, taken as a whole, appeals to the prurient interest; (2) whether the work depicts or describes, in a patently offensive way, sexual conduct specifically defined by the applicable state law; and (3) whether the work, taken as a whole, lacks serious literary, artistic, political, or scientific value.

Although longer and arguably more protective of free speech, this test is open to some of the same criticisms leveled at the standard enunciated in *Roth v. United States*. Unlike the analysis presented in *Roth*, *Miller v. California* addressed the issue of what important state interests would be supported by the proscription of pornography. Specifically, the court identified the state's interests in protecting the quality of life of its citizens, the "tone of commerce in the great city centers, and possibly, the public safety itself." As support for this last important state interest, the court cited the Hill-Link Minority Report of the 1970 Commission on Obscenity and Pornography that concluded that there was at least arguable support for the contention that there is a causal link between pornography and criminal behavior. The 1970 Report of the Commission on Obscenity and Pornography stated that there was insufficient evidence to conclude that exposure to pornography was causally related to antisocial or criminal behavior.

The three justices who dissented in *Miller v. California*, Justices William Brennan, Potter Stewart, and Thurgood Marshall, criticized the court for upholding legislation, the true purpose of which is the regulation of thought and morality. Their second major criticism focused on the court's failure to sufficiently scrutinize the state's purported interests in support of legislation that prohibits the publication, distribution, or viewing of obscene materials. Citing one of the court's recent opinions, the dissenters noted that in that case the court had ruled that the idea that there is a legitimate state interest in controlling the moral content of the thoughts of American citizens was inconsistent with the philosophy of the First Amendment. The dissenters concluded that instead of encroaching upon rights protected by the First Amendment, the state should use the deterrents ordinarily applied to prevent crime, education and punishment for the violation of the law. The dissent identified two interests that it deemed to be sufficiently compelling to support a state's right to regulate pornographic materials. These were the prevention of the distribution of pornographic materials to juveniles, and the prevention of the exposure of such materials to consenting adults.

New York v. Ferber

With regard to pornography and juveniles, the court, in *New York v. Ferber* (1982), held that states have a self-evident compelling interest in "safeguarding the physical and psychological well-being of a minor." The breadth and importance of this interest is not only a sufficient basis for states to make the distribution of pornography to minors illegal, it is recognized as such a sufficiently compelling interest that states can criminalize the production, distribution, and possession of photographs and films depicting sexual activity by children. Such material is not subject to the obscenity standard the court announced

Obscenity has proliferated almost uncontrollably on the Internet. The definition of whether a work was "obscene" was determined in Roth v. United States *based on the work's presumed effect on the viewer's psychological state and the assumption that these psychological changes will result in antisocial and possibly sexual behavior. Without the protection of the First Amendment of the U.S. Constitution, the government can criminalize the production, distribution, and possession of materials ruled to be obscene.*

in *Miller v. California*. The fact that children are depicted engaged in sexual activity is sufficient for a state to criminalize the production, distribution, and possession of such photographs and films.

The court provided several bases for the latitude given states in prohibiting and punishing anyone involved in the production, distribution, and possession of photographs and films depicting sexual activity by children. First, photographs and films of sexual activity by children necessarily require the sexual exploitation and abuse of those children. In addition, they reasoned that banning such materials was justified as a means of countering the powerful economic motives that fuel the child pornography industry. The justices commented that the purveyors of this form of entertainment could use models that appeared younger than their actual ages, a practice that would allow the conveyance of the same intended effect.

Thus, *New York v. Ferber* created a dual standard for the regulation of specific sexually explicit materials, one for materials aimed at and using adults, and another for materials aimed at or using children. The latter category of materials could be proscribed, without violating the Constitution, without the prerequisite that these materials first be proven to meet the constitutional standard for obscenity established by the court in *Miller v. California* and *New York v. Ferber*. These cases continue to be the constitutional standards for obscenity and pornography using or distributed to minors.

The development of new technologies has raised additional issues. For example, computer animation makes it possible to make very realistic animations of children having sex with adults and each other. *Ferber* makes it clear that images of actual children engaged in any sexual activity can be prohibited in accord with the Constitution. In fact, this standard has been adopted into federal law. Since the technology did not exist in 1982, *Ferber* did not address the issue of producing, distributing, and possessing lifelike computer-generated animation of children engaged in sexual activity. Congress passed a law criminalizing this, stating that this encouraged pedophiles and thus threatened children. The Supreme Court ruled that this law was unconstitutional. The essential difference between computer-generated animation, regardless of its lifelike qualities, and photographs and videos of actual children engaged in sexual activity is that fact that actual children are involved. Without this, computer-generated, animated child pornography must be judged by the standards announced by the court in *Miller v. California*. If they were found to be obscene, these materials would fall outside of the protection of the First Amendment, and their production and distribution could be prohibited.

The *Miller* standard, at least in part, is based on the assumption that exposure to sexually explicit material results in violent behavior, predominantly involving sex. If true, this provides a rationale for upholding the constitutionality of laws restricting sexually explicit material. The First Amendment has been consistently interpreted to exclude from its protection speech that creates a "clear and present danger," as held in the 1919 Supreme Court decision in *Schenck v. United States*, and speech "directed to inciting or producing imminent lawless action," as held in the 1969 *Brandenburg v. Ohio* Supreme Court decision.

A substantial body of research exists that has examined whether exposure to pornography leads to aggressive or violent behavior. This research has examined the effects of exposure to both nonviolent and violent pornography. The findings from this research arguably provide support for those who wish to see pornography banned and for those who contend that it should receive full First Amendment protection. The presence of violence in some pornography confounds the effects of exposure to sexually explicit material. Some research, such as that done by Edward Donnerstein, suggests that it is the combination of violence and sexually explicit material that results in increased aggressiveness. In an experiment comparing the aggressiveness of groups exposed to either violent sexually explicit material, nonviolent sexually explicit material, or violent material with no explicit sexual content, violence was found to be a potent variable. Violent material with no explicit sexual content resulted in slightly less aggression than when violence was combined with sexually explicit material. The least aggressive group was the one that was exposed to sexually explicit material that contained no violence.

In sum, after struggling for decades, the Supreme Court has defined obscenity using a standard that excludes sexually explicit material that has serious literary, artistic, political, or scientific value. Material that is determined to be obscene is not protected by the First Amendment. Sexually explicit films and photographs that show minors involved in sexual activity are not protected by the First Amendment and do not have to be found to meet the standards for obscenity. With no constitutional protection, the government can criminalize the production, distribution, and possession of such materials. The obscenity standard developed by the court assumes that exposure to sexually explicit material leads to deleterious effects, particularly sexual violence. While research has yet to provide a definitive answer, there is good evidence that violent material, with or without sexually explicit components, plays a major role in aggressive behavior.

Allen J. Brown
Anna Maria College

See Also: 1921 to 1940 Primary Documents; 1941 to 1960 Primary Documents; *Brandenburg v. Ohio*; Computer Crime; Obscenity; *Roth v. United States*; *Schenck v. United States*; Sex Offenders.

Further Readings
Epstein, L. and T. G. Walker. *Constitutional Law for a Changing America: Rights, Liberties, and Justice*. Washington, DC: CQ Press, 2010.
Malamuth, N. and M. Huppin. "Drawing the Line on Virtual Child Pornography: Bringing the Law in Line With the Research Evidence." *New York University Review of Law and Social Change*, v.31 (2007).
Miller v. California, 413 U.S. 15 (1973).
New York v. Ferber, 458 U.S. 747 (1082).

Ohio

Formerly part of the Northwest Territory, Ohio has been a state since 1803 and shares aspects of many of the regions surrounding it: the northeast, the south, and the midwest. It is one of the most densely populated states, with seven metropolitan areas with populations of at least 500,000.

Crime

Akron, Ohio, was one of the first midwestern cities to attract the Mafia. Before the spread of organized crime during Prohibition, Don Rosario Borgio had headquartered his crime family in Akron's north side in the early 1900s. His general goods store was both a legitimate business and a front for the criminal operations he conducted from the store's two back rooms, and the property was protected by alarms on both sets of stairs, spiked pits beneath the stairs, solid steel doors, and an arsenal of weapons. His gambling and prostitution revenues gave him ample money to bribe politicians, but he had difficulty getting any of the Akron police force to take a bribe, and raids on his operations began in 1918. He brazenly declared war on the police, offering a $250 bounty for any police officer. Several were killed in the winter of 1918, and the head of the New York City Police Department's "Italian Squad" (as the anti-Mafia unit was called at the time) was called upon for assistance. A case was built against Borgio fairly quickly, and he was sentenced to 20 years in prison—but was secretly paroled in 1934, at which time he returned to Italy.

Ohio has been home to a number of high-profile or otherwise notable murders, including Anna Marie Hahn, a German-born serial killer. Claiming to have been sent to America by her scandalized parents after her affair with a doctor, Hahn began poisoning elderly men and women in Cincinnati's German community in 1933. All in all, she had five known victims over the next four years. Her motive was her gambling habit: She would befriend an elderly person in the hope of being named in his/her will, or in order to borrow money, and then kill him in order to collect the inheritance or avoid paying the debt.

Another Ohio serial killer was Donald Harvey, who claims to have killed 73 people between 1970 and 1987 and is known to have killed at least 26. An orderly working in several Cincinnati-area hospitals, Harvey claims his first killings were to put suffering patients out of their misery but has admitted anger at victims, and a sadistic pleasure from the act of killing. His killings transpired over at least 17 years, and his methods included multiple poisons, suffocation, turning off or sabotaging medical equipment, and overdoses of morphine. Because his methods varied, it was difficult for the pattern of deaths to be detected. He was eventually sentenced to three consecutive life sentences.

Alton Coleman, at the time of his execution in 2002, was the first and only person to receive the death sentence in three states: Illinois, Indiana, and Ohio (twice). A middle-school dropout, at the age of 28 he and his borderline mentally retarded 21-year-old girlfriend, Debra Brown, killed multiple people in six states, including numerous children. The U.S. attorney chose Ohio as the first state to try the killers, because it was believed the death sentence would be achieved fastest there. Coleman was eventually given two death sentences and was executed in 2002. Brown's sentence was eventually commuted on the grounds of her low intelligence.

Wilford Berry, Jr., was convicted in 1999 for the 1989 aggravated murder of his boss, the owner of a Cleveland bakery. Berry was inconsistent in explaining his motives, and after his direct appeal in 1997, he became the first defendant since Ohio reinstated the death penalty in 1981 to waive his right to further appeal. A competency hearing was scheduled, and he was found to have a mixed personality disorder but was considered competent enough to waive his rights. Berry was assaulted repeatedly during a prison riot by death row inmates who felt that his "volunteering" to be executed would somehow impact their own appeals.

Christopher Newton was executed in 2007 for the aggravated murder of his cellmate while serving a sentence for the burglary of his father's home. Newton had previously been incarcerated, and in fact stated that the only purpose of the burglary was to return to prison, where he intended to die—and that killing his cellmate (for the putative offense of being a poor chess player) was motivated by this wish to die in prison. Despite this and the violence of the murder, the court denied Newton's defense team funds to conduct neuropsychiatric tests to determine Newton's mental fitness, which might have justified exempting him from the death penalty. Further controversy arose because Newton's overweight condition resulted in the execution taking so long—10 attempts to find a vein—that Newton was given a bathroom break in the middle of the two-hour ordeal, six times longer than is considered reasonable.

Ohio's crime rate is slightly lower than the national average, at 315 violent crimes—mostly aggravated assaults and robberies—per 100,000 inhabitants in 2010. Robberies are a larger portion of the violent crime than in most states. The crime rate has not changed greatly, though it is lower in the 21st century than at its height from the late 1970s to 1990s (peaking at 561 in 1991), and the murder rate has fallen to half of its 1979–80 peak.

Police
Early Ohio law enforcement included constables, night watchmen, and property guards, and the duties of local law enforcement officials were often limited to specific types of crimes. The City Marshal's Office of Lancaster, for instance, was established when Lancaster was incorporated in 1831, and the marshal was tasked with dealing with horse thieves, drunkards, problems in the saloons, and clashes with local Native American tribes. Like many young small towns, Lancaster lacked a jail, and more serious problems were deferred to county or federal authorities. City marshals were typically elected positions, and night watchmen often worked on a volunteer basis, much like early firefighters. The creation of organized police departments was gradual in Ohio, as the constabulary and night watch first grew in numbers and were assigned more duties, until local populations reached the critical mass that resulted in professional police forces emerging. In the more urban areas like Cincinnati, professional city police forces were preceded by private police funded by merchants to supplement the work of the night watch.

Cincinnati established its police department in 1850, a few years after a private police force had been formed to safeguard the merchants of Pearl Street. The city council appointed a police chief and six lieutenants to whom day and night watchmen answered. The positions of sergeant and captain were created the following year. In 1855, Cincinnati hired its first police detectives, and the police department began to become more formalized and professional, with uniforms, training, and certification. Cleveland's police department followed in the 1860s, and other cities thereafter.

Punishment
Early prisoners were kept in town or county jails, typically for short periods of time. The Ohio State Penitentiary was built in Columbus in 1834, with a separate women's building added in 1837, and operated until 1983, when the Southern Ohio Correctional Facility in Lucasville replaced it. The "Ohio Pen" is perhaps most famous for the escape of General John Morgan during the Civil War and for housing Dr. Sam Sheppard, the inspiration for the TV series and movie *The Fugitive*.

Correctional facilities in Ohio vary in size from this small cell in an eight-bed prison in the Brecksville Police Department to the Southern Ohio Correctional Facility, housing more than 1,400 and the inspiration for the movie The Fugitive.

Ohio is a capital punishment state, and 388 executions have been carried out since 1885. After the 1970s Supreme Court rulings rendered unconstitutional all extant death penalty statutes, Ohio's death penalty was reinstated with a new law in 1981. Under the new law, the jury decides the sentence, choosing from the death penalty, life without parole, life without parole in the first 30 years, or life without parole in the first 25 years. Capital murder includes aggravated murder with at least one of the following aggravating factors: murder for financial gain, murder committed by a person incarcerated or on probation, a murder that put someone other than the victim at grave risk of death, the calculated murder of a victim under the age of 13, political assassination, murder of a witness in a criminal proceeding, murder in the commission or attempted commission of terrorism.

From 1885 until 1897, executions were carried out by hanging at the Ohio Penitentiary in Columbus. Hanging was replaced by the electric chair in 1897 (Ohio was the second state to adopt electrocution) and by lethal injection in 1963. In 2009, Ohio announced that it would begin lethal injection executions by a single drug, sodium thiopental, a drug in use in other states as one of several drugs used in the injection. In 2011, this was changed to pentobarbital, because Hospira, the manufacturer of sodium thiopental, discontinued the drug.

Like many states, Ohio faces a prison overpopulation problem and has considered sentencing reforms as a remedy. In mid-2011, a bill that would expand the role of mandatory drug treatment in lieu of sentencing for nonviolent drug offenders, and would increase parole, passed the House of Representatives with widespread support. It also eliminated the disparity between crack and cocaine sentences, the former of which was more harshly dealt with, a disparity considered racist because of the demographics of the users of these two different forms of the same drug. At the same time, because prison overpopulation also exacerbates budget problems, another remedy that gained in popularity was prison privatization, which began to gain traction among Ohio lawmakers.

Bill Kte'pi
Independent Scholar

See Also: Cincinnati, Ohio; Cleveland, Ohio; Sheppard, Sam.

Further Readings
Cayton, Andrew R. L. *Ohio: The History of a People.* Columbus: Ohio State University Press, 2002.
Franklin, Diana Britt. *The Good-Bye Door.* Kent, OH: Kent State University Press, 2006.
Stimson, George. *The Cincinnati Crime Book.* Cincinnati, OH: Peasenhall Press, 1998.

Oklahoma

Formed by the union of the Oklahoma Territory and Indian Territory in 1907, Oklahoma was one of the last states to enter the Union. At a time when most of the country was formalizing its police departments, requiring professional training and certification of its new officers, much of Oklahoma was still functionally lawless. Town and county jails were used to hold prisoners for brief periods, and federal marshals were in many cases the only form of law enforcement. Other towns had elected town marshals or constables, and night watchmen who doubled as the fire watch. In the early decades of the 20th century, Oklahoma's police departments began to catch up to those in the east.

In the territorial days, convicted felons were incarcerated in the Kansas State Penitentiary in Lansing, Kansas. In 1908, shortly after statehood, Kate Barnard, the new Oklahoma commissioner of charities and corrections, made an unannounced visit to the Kansas facility to investigate complaints about the mistreatment of Oklahoma inmates (and perhaps others, though it was the Oklahomans she was there to see) and discovered systematic torture of inmates, prompting an immediate recommendation to the governor that Oklahoma inmates be returned to the state. They were temporarily housed in a federal jail and were put to work building the new Oklahoma State Penitentiary, which opened later in the year. The prison was later the site of one of the worst prison riots in American history, in July 1973. Overcrowding, in part because of the governor's refusal to approve parole recommendations for drug offenders and violent offenders, had reached the point that the prison was housing more than twice its capacity.

Early Crime

Oklahoma has been home both to Wild West outlaws and Depression-era gangsters and bandits. In the Indian Territory era, the Rufus Buck Gang was an outlaw gang whose members were primarily multiracial, each of them part African American and part Creek. Operating in 1895 and 1896, they held up various stores and ranches and succeeded in resisting capture until the summer of 1896, when a combined American and Creek force captured them and brought them before "Hanging Judge" Isaac Parker, who lived up to his name.

Indian Territory was also home to the Dalton Gang, relatives of the Younger brothers, who were part of the James-Younger Gang in Missouri from 1890 to 1892. Grat, Bob, and Emmett Dalton had moved to the Indian Territory from Missouri, and were originally lawmen, having become marshals after the death of brother Frank Dalton, who had tracked a horse thief into the Oklahoma Territory and been shot to death by the suspect. Their life as lawmen didn't last long, and they were soon robbing gambling houses and numerous trains. They were eventually apprehended in Kansas, while trying to increase their reputation by robbing two banks at once in broad daylight.

Another Dalton brother, Bill Dalton, was one of the leaders of the Wild Bunch gang. Having originally been a California legislator, he grew bored with politics, assisted the Dalton Gang with a Los Angeles train robbery, and relocated to Oklahoma after the Dalton Gang's 1892 defeat in Kansas. He had inherited the Dalton obsession with fame and was determined to be more famous than his brothers. With Bill Doolin, he formed the Wild Bunch and robbed banks, stagecoaches, and trains throughout Oklahoma, Texas, Arkansas, and Kansas during the 1890s. (Butch Cassidy's Wild Bunch was a separate gang, operating at the turn of the century in Wyoming.)

One of the most wanted criminals in Oklahoma during the 1920s and 1930s was Wilbur "Mad Dog" Underhill, Jr. Beginning his life of crime as a teenager, he was repeatedly arrested for burglaries and armed robberies throughout his 20s, and

Residents of the Indian Territory in Oklahoma, most of the members of the Dalton Gang were killed following a botched bank robbery. Pictured after their deaths, from left, are Bill Power, Bob Dalton, and Grat Dalton.

escaped from prison several times. After a mass jail escape from Lansing state prison, where he was incarcerated in 1931 for the murder of a police officer, Underhill and his fellow escapees formed the Bailey-Underhill Gang, named for Underhill and Harvey Bailey, the millionaire bank robber who was one of the most successful thieves of the 1920s. The gang proceeded to rob several banks, and Underhill took control of the gang when Bailey was erroneously sentenced to life for a kidnapping (having been passed money that had been used to pay the ransom). A federal task force was formed to stop the gang, which by then was attracting considerable media attention, and Underhill was killed on his honeymoon when a 24-man strike force of federal, state, and local police surrounded his rented cottage and he opened fire on them. He died of his wounds in a prison hospital. The gang shot up the town of Vian in revenge for Underhill's capture, which succeeded only in motivating the strike force to apprehend them all the quicker, and within months, most of the members had been killed or captured.

Contemporary Crime

Oklahoma was one of the states where a surge of methamphetamine use in rural and suburban areas began in the late 20th and early 21st centuries. From 1994 to 2003, the Oklahoma Bureau of Narcotics and Dangerous Drugs estimated that meth labs skyrocketed from about 10 to more than 1,200. In 2002, there were 1,300 lab seizures in Oklahoma, more than 10 percent of the total meth lab seizures in the country, at a time when in much of the rest of the country, methamphetamine supply still came from organized crime, particularly Mexican criminal organizations. In 2004, Oklahoma was one of the first states to limit the sale of pseudoephedrine, the key precursor in meth cooking, by requiring that the ingredient be sold behind the counter, with limits imposed on purchase amounts. Purchasers were also required to show identification and sign a log. The subsequent drop in Oklahoma meth crime inspired other states to follow suit.

In 2010, one-pot meth labs soared in popularity in Oklahoma. While the meth labs in use only a few years earlier entailed a setup fee of roughly $1,000, one-pot labs can use a two-liter soda bottle and a handful of items from a hardware store to begin cooking meth using recipes widely circulated online. While the risk of fire and explosion is much greater, the development seems inevitable in retrospect: Law enforcement efforts had focused most heavily on disrupting the commercial meth trade, and one-pot cooking, with its low start-up cost, is a method well-suited to producing small amounts of meth for personal use, turning customers into their own dealers, whose activity won't necessarily be affected by pseudoephedrine purchase limits so long as the drug remains available in some quantity.

A further development in Oklahoma's meth crisis came in 2011, when the federal government cut off funds previously available to states for chemical disposal and other cleanup expenses in dealing with seized meth labs. The state's Bureau of Narcotics warned that health complaints throughout the state, blamed on pollen or molds, could actually be caused by contaminants in air ducts and air conditioners in places where the residence or motel room had previously been used as a meth lab—and that without federal funding, the state would not be able to clean sites as quickly as it would like.

Oklahoma lags behind only Texas and Virginia in modern executions (executions performed after the death penalty reforms required by the 1970s Supreme Court case *Furman v. Georgia*). It was the first jurisdiction in the world to adopt lethal injection as the method of execution and the first state in the country to use pentobarbital as the drug of execution after Hospira ceased manufacture of sodium thiopental, the drug previously used.

Crime rates in Oklahoma are slightly higher than the national average, at 479.5 violent crimes per 100,000 inhabitants in 2010. Having peaked at 664 in 1995, the crime rate has always been high, with aggravated assaults constituting a large share.

Bill Kte'pi
Independent Scholar

See Also: Frontier Crime; Gangs, History of; Oklahoma City Bombing; Parker, Isaac.

Further Readings
Kinney, John. *Captain Jack and the Dalton Gang: The Life and Times of a Railroad Detective.* Lawrence: University Press of Kansas, 2005.

Morgan, R. D. *Taming the Sooner State.* Stillwater, OK: New Forums Press, 2007.

Morgan, R. D. *The Tri-State Terror.* Stillwater, OK: New Forums Press, 2005.

Oklahoma City Bombing

On April 19, 1995, an explosion tore through the Alfred P. Murrah Federal Building in Oklahoma City, Oklahoma. The blast occurred with such force that much of the north side of the Murrah Building was simply vaporized; hundreds more buildings within a 16-block radius were damaged. The bombing killed 168 people and injured nearly 600 more; 19 of the dead were children. Until September 11, 2001, the event was the single most lethal terrorist attack ever committed on American soil, eclipsing its nearest rival—the 1927 Bath School Bombing committed by Andrew Kehoe in Michigan—by over 100 fatalities.

In the early days following the bombing, media speculation focused on international terrorists as the likely culprits behind the act, specifically, Arab terrorists with an anti-Western or Islamic fundamentalist agenda, such as those behind the first World Trade Center bombing on February 26, 1993, or the bombing of Pan Am Flight 103 over Lockerbie, Scotland, on December 21, 1988. Some in the media, however, began looking in a different direction, noting that the event took place on the two-year anniversary of the disastrous Federal Bureau of Investigation/Alcohol Tobacco and Firearms (FBI/ATF) raid on the Branch Davidian compound near Waco, Texas, over the course of which 86 people, including 20 children and four government agents, lost their lives. Vocal leaders in the burgeoning patriot militia movement had for two years been using Waco as a rallying cry, a powerful symbol of federal government tyranny and excess, memorialized by such figures as Carl Klang in his song "Seventeen Little Children," and Linda Thompson in her video "Waco: The Big Lie." These figures, and the militias they inspired, believed strongly in Second Amendment rights; some advocated armed resistance to government overreach.

Investigation of Timothy McVeigh and His Co-Conspirators
Media speculation surrounding the significance of the Waco anniversary was confirmed two days after the attack, when Timothy McVeigh was taken into federal custody. He had originally been arrested 90 minutes after the explosion for driving without a license plate and carrying a concealed weapon. When arrested, McVeigh had been wearing a T-shirt with two slogans printed on it: On the front, the shirt read, *sic semper tyrannis*, Latin for "thus always to tyrants," the motto of the state of Virginia and the words shouted by John Wilkes Booth upon his assassination of Abraham Lincoln; and on the back, a phrase attributed to Thomas Jefferson: "The tree of liberty must be refreshed from time to time with the blood of patriots and tyrants."

Among McVeigh's other possessions were an unlicensed 9mm handgun and a copy of *The Turner Diaries*, William Luther Pierce's fictional account of a terrorist bombing sparking a race war in an alternative future America; first published in 1978, the novel had long been a fundamental text of the white separatist militia movement, inspiring the assassinations, bank robberies, and other criminal activities of Robert Matthews's group The Order in the early 1980s.

After McVeigh's arrest, the investigation of the incident and the trials of those involved proceeded briskly, backed by the federal government. McVeigh's accomplice, Terry Nichols, was arrested April 21, turning himself in the same day McVeigh was taken into federal custody. Also arrested were Michael and Lori Fortier. Evidence about the planning and execution of the bombing came to light, developing into an overall narrative of a deliberately and carefully planned terrorist act designed to enact the highest possible toll in human lives and destruction.

McVeigh and Nichols began stockpiling weapons and supplies some eight months before the event and scouted their target, selected because it contained offices of both the ATF (Alcohol, Tobacco, and Firearms) and DEA (Drug Enforcement Agency), at least twice as part of their planning process. In the end, the two packed 7,000 pounds of explosives into a rented Ryder truck. The primary explosive component was ammonium nitrate fertilizer, but the conspirators also used race-car fuel and the industrial explosive Tovex, mixed, packed into 55-gallon drums, and arranged within the truck's storage compartment to form a shaped charge that would maximize casualties. On the day of the attack, McVeigh drove the truck to the Murrah Building himself, lighting two fuses and parking the truck on the building's north side before fleeing on foot to his car, parked several blocks away. McVeigh was in fact only some three blocks distant when the bomb exploded.

On Trial
Of the co-conspirators, only Nichols and McVeigh were tried for direct participation in the bombing. The Fortiers—who knew about the planning of the attack to the extent that Michael aided McVeigh and Nichols in scouting the Murrah Building, and Lori laminated the fake ID McVeigh used to rent the Ryder truck—both agreed to testify against the two central conspirators. Lori received full immunity for her testimony, and Michael was sentenced to 12 years in prison; both entered the Witness Protection Program. Nichols, who turned himself in and consented to the search of his property, was convicted of federal crimes and 161 counts of murder in the state of Oklahoma; he escaped the death

Search and rescue workers from the Federal Emergency Management Agency (FEMA) gather at the scene of the Oklahoma City bombing. The blast caused a partial collapse of all nine floors of the 20-year-old building, killing 168.

penalty as the result of a jury deadlock on the issue, instead receiving life in prison without the possibility of parole. On June 13, 1997, Timothy McVeigh became the first person since 1963 to receive the death penalty in a federal trial.

Throughout his trial and subsequent interviews and media communications, McVeigh never expressed remorse for his actions, instead presenting them consistently as a justified act of war against the American federal government. He wrote a number of essays during his incarceration that further explained his motives for the attack and connected his actions to world events and government activity, including an April 26, 2001, letter to Fox News with the subject line, "I Explain Herein Why I Bombed the Murrah Federal Building in Oklahoma City." In the letter, he compares federal actions such as the siege at Waco to the actions of the Chinese government in the Tiananmen Square crackdown, and compares his bombing of the Murrah Federal Building to the bombing of Serbian government buildings by the U.S. Air Force. McVeigh was executed on June 11, 2001, at the federal penitentiary in Terre Haute, Indiana. He chose "Invictus," a defiant poem by William Ernest Henley, as his final statement.

Political Rhetoric and Violence
In the immediate wake of the Oklahoma City bombing, President Bill Clinton gave a powerful speech decrying political rhetoric, popularized at the time through the talk-radio format, that might tacitly or explicitly condone violent action or terrorism as an acceptable form of political expression; this speech was echoed by President Barack Obama in his own remarks at a memorial for the victims of a 2011 shooting in Tucson, Arizona, that critically injured U.S. Representative Gabrielle Giffords and killed six others. Both presidents received criticism for implying connections between political rhetoric and violent action that cannot readily be proven; however, the membership and media visibility of American patriot militia organizations dropped sharply after the Oklahoma City bombing, not returning to the levels reached before the event until the election of Barack Obama as president in 2008. A memorial to the victims of the bombing was completed and dedicated by President Clinton on April 19, 2000, at the former site of the Murrah Federal Building.

Daniel Stageman
John Jay College of Criminal Justice

See Also: McVeigh, Timothy; Oklahoma; Terrorism.

Further Readings
Kifner, J. "Terror in Oklahoma City." *New York Times* (April 20, 1995).
McVeigh, T. "McVeigh's Apr. 26 Letter to Fox News." Fox News. http://www.foxnews.com/

story/0,2933,17500,00.html (Accessed February 2011).

Michel, L. and D. Herbeck. *American Terrorist: Timothy McVeigh & the Tragedy at Oklahoma City.* New York: HarperCollins, 2001.

Neiwert, D. *The Eliminationists: How Hate Talk Radicalized the American Right.* Sausalito, CA: PoliPointPress, 2009.

Neiwert, D. *In God's Country: The Patriot Movement and the Pacific Northwest.* Pullman: Washington State University Press, 1999.

Parkin, W., G. Cavender, A. Kupchik, D. Altheide, and R. Hanson. "Timothy McVeigh: The Social Construction of an American Terrorist." In *Terrorism and the International Community,* Shlomo G. Shoham and P. Knepper, eds. Toronto: de Sitter, 2005.

Southern Poverty Law Center. "Meet the 'Patriots.'" *Intelligence Report* (Summer 2010).

Olmstead v. United States

In 1928, the U.S. Supreme Court decided *Olmstead v. United States,* concluding that the government's interception of telephone communications did not constitute a search or seizure under the Fourth Amendment. This decision launched a national debate on law enforcement wiretapping. It served as the key precedent for when law enforcement activities constituted a search for nearly 40 years, until it was overruled. Justice Louis Brandeis's dissent, invoking the right to privacy, serves as the rationale for current Fourth Amendment jurisprudence. *Olmstead* involved the prosecution of a 91-person, alcohol-distribution conspiracy. The conspiracy, headed by Roy Olmstead, imported large amounts of alcohol from British Columbia, Canada, through Puget Sound to various ports. Conspirators took the alcohol to a farm outside Seattle and then distributed it. To oversee his $250,000 a year business, Olmstead used telephones, having three lines in his office alone. Law enforcement tapped these lines to obtain their evidence.

Before the district court, Olmstead sought to suppress the wiretap evidence, arguing that the taps violated the Fourth Amendment. The district court denied the motion. The 9th Circuit Court of Appeals affirmed the judgment, reasoning that the Fourth Amendment only applied to entering homes and offices to obtain documents. Wiretapping was like looking through open windows or listening at doors. Supreme Court Chief Justice William Taft wrote the majority opinion. He described the court's prior decisions on the exclusion of evidence seized in violation of the Fourth Amendment. Then, Taft examined what the Fourth Amendment protected, stating that the amendment's original intent was to prevent the government from forcibly intruding upon a person's house or body to obtain papers or effects. To Taft, this meant that the Fourth Amendment only protected tangible items, not phone conversations.

After denying the Fourth Amendment claim, Taft discussed the admissibility of evidence obtained by federal agents in violation of state law. Washington law prohibited intercepting telephone communications, making violations a misdemeanor. Taft concluded that there was no authority for excluding constitutionally obtained evidence, regardless of the ethics of seizure. He compared wiretaps to law enforcement's undercover involvement in criminal conspiracies. Excluding wiretap evidence would also require the exclusion of evidence obtained in undercover operations. Noting that Congress could pass a wiretap law if it so desired, Taft stated that the court would not do it.

While Taft's opinion carried the majority, four justices led by Louis Brandeis dissented. Brandeis began the movement recognizing that the Fourth Amendment protects people and their privacy, rather than places. He asserted that the Constitution must adapt to technological innovation; the Constitution's drafters could not have possibly foreseen using wiretapping to collect evidence. Therefore, Brandeis reasoned, constitutional interpretation should be based on its principles, namely, liberty and security. Because tapping telephone wires invades privacy and infringes on liberty and security, seizing telephone calls was unjustified, and the fruits should be suppressed. Both Taft's and Brandeis's opinions have had lasting and influential repercussions—Taft's in the short term, and Brandeis's in the long term. The U.S. Congress soon accepted Taft's invitation and prohibited wiretapping by federal law enforcement as part of the

Federal Communications Act in 1933. *Olmstead* also set the standard for when law enforcement required a search warrant prior to performing intrusive investigatory techniques. Law enforcement officers only had to consider whether the place searched was private or not. If it was exposed to the public or for public use, they did not need a warrant, even to conduct a wiretap.

The public/private distinction formed the foundation of the government's case in *Katz v. United States*, the U.S. Supreme Court case that adopted the rationale of Brandeis's opinion from the *Olmstead* case. *Katz* involved a government wiretap of a public telephone booth. Before the Supreme Court, the government argued that the Fourth Amendment was not violated because there was no trespass on private property. The court rejected the argument, reasoning that the Fourth Amendment protected people, not places. Katz, therefore, had an expectation of privacy upon stepping into the phone booth. This meant that the government needed some type of judicial order prior to conducting the wire tap. The *Olmstead* case served as the foundation for search and seizure law for nearly 40 years. It also touched off the debate about the propriety of the government's use of wiretapping to gain evidence in criminal cases. Finally, the case became the starting point for a fundamental change in how courts interpreted the Fourth Amendment.

Scott Ingram
High Point University

See Also: Defendant's Rights; Electronic Surveillance; *Katz v. United States*; Prohibition; Supreme Court, U.S.

Further Readings
Katz v. United States, 389 U.S. 347 (1967).
Olmstead et al v. United States, 19 F.2d 842 (1927).
Olmstead v. United States, 277 U.S. 438 (1928).
Pringle, Henry F. *The Life and Times of William Howard Taft*, Vol. 2. New York: Farrar & Rinehart, 1939.
Steiker, Carol S. "Brandeis in Olmstead: 'Our Government is the Potent, The Omnipresent Teacher.'" *Mississippi Law Journal*, v.79 (2009).
Urovsky, Melvin I. *Louis D. Brandeis: A Life*. New York: Pantheon Books, 2009.

Omnibus Crime Control and Safe Streets Act of 1968

Public concern over high crime rates throughout the 1960s led President Lyndon Johnson's administration to authorize federal funds for the improvement of state and local police. The Omnibus Crime Control and Safe Streets Act (OCCSSA) of 1968 assisted state and local governments in reducing the incidence of crime, and it increased the effectiveness, fairness, and coordination of law enforcement and criminal justice systems at all levels of government. The act focused on regulating firearm sales, established the Bureau of Justice Statistics, and created grants for construction and renovation of courtrooms, correctional facilities, treatment centers, and other criminal justice–related structures. The act contained 11 titles, including sections on wiretapping and electronic surveillance, admission of confessions, and the formation of the Law Enforcement Assistance Administration (LEAA).

Titles

Title I of the OCCSSA dealt with the formation of the LEAA. Congress realized crime was a local problem and that it had to be dealt with by state and local governments if it was to be effectively controlled. The LEAA supported crime control efforts through aid to state and local authorities, targeting street crime, riots, and organized crime. Funding started in 1968 with $60 million; by 1982, the agency had spent more than $8 billion on grants to law enforcement agencies around the country. Grants from the act were used to purchase devices, facilities, and equipment designed to improve and strengthen law enforcement, and to recruit and train law enforcement personnel; for public education on crime prevention and respect for law and order; for constructing buildings or other physical facilities; for the development, education, and training of special law enforcement units to combat organized crime and control riots; and for recruiting and training community service officers to assist local and state law enforcement agencies in improving police–community relations.

Part D of Title I dealt with the formation of the National Institute of Law Enforcement and Criminal Justice, which encouraged research to improve and strengthen law enforcement. The institute was authorized to fund grants and enter into contracts with public agencies, institutions of higher education, or private organizations to conduct research, demonstrations, and special projects. The institute also carried out programs of behavioral research to provide more accurate information on the causes of crime and the effectiveness of various means of controlling and preventing it. The institute also evaluated correctional procedures and made recommendations for action to be taken by federal, state, and local governments.

Title II of the OCCSSA dealt with the admissibility of confessions and eyewitness testimony. This provision aimed to overturn Supreme Court decisions as to the admissibility of evidence obtained in violation of the constitutional rights of the people under the Fourth Amendment. Title II of the act allowed the admission of voluntary confessions, even if the police failed to inform the suspect of his/her rights.

Title III of the OCCSSA focused on wiretapping and electronic surveillance. Because people involved with organized crime made use of oral communications in their criminal activities, the interception of such communications via wiretapping to obtain evidence of the commission of crimes or to prevent their commission was an aid to law enforcement and to the administration of justice. This provision addressed privacy issues in wiretaps and the potential methods of ensuring privacy while providing for effective law enforcement.

Title IV addressed trafficking of firearms. This provision made it unlawful for anyone other than a licensed importer, manufacturer, or dealer to engage in importing, manufacturing, or dealing firearms or ammunition. This included shipping, transporting, or receiving any firearm or ammunition in interstate or foreign commerce. Title IV was expanded upon in Title VII, which established who and what constituted an unlawful possession or receipt of a firearm. Title VII declared illegal the receipt, possession, or transportation of firearms by felons, veterans who are other than honorably discharged, mental incompetents, aliens who are illegally in the country, and former citizens who have renounced their citizenship.

Title V of the OCCSSA dealt with riots and civil disorders. It declared an individual inciting a riot or civil disorder, organizing or promoting a riot, or aiding and abetting persons involved in a riot or civil disorder would be ineligible to hold any position in the government of the United States for five years following the date on which the conviction became final. Any person holding a position in the government and found guilty of rioting or civil disorder would be immediately removed from such position.

The final five titles addressed smaller or more administrative issues. Title VI set forth the procedure for the president of the United States to appoint and have confirmed by the Senate a director of the Federal Bureau of Investigation. Title VIII provided for a process of appeal by the

The Omnibus Crime Control and Safe Streets Act (OCCSSA) has drawn criticism regarding the rights of citizens, particularly over Title III, which set guidelines for obtaining orders to wiretap phone lines in the United States.

United States from decisions sustaining motions to suppress evidence. Title IX focused on additional grounds for issuing warrants: It stated that a warrant could be issued to search for and seize any property that constituted evidence of a criminal offense in violation of the law. Title X dealt with prohibiting extortion and threats in the District of Columbia: It made illegal any threat of kidnapping; any ransom demand for a kidnapping; and any threat to injure the property or reputation of a person in the District of Columbia. Title XI concluded the act with general provisions, which held that if a certain section of the act were deemed invalid, then the rest of the act remained unaltered.

Criticism

Criticisms of the OCCSSA include the LEAA's lack of clear objectives and control of funding dispersed to law enforcement agencies. The program failed to monitor its expenditures and did not establish procedures to evaluate the impact of funded programs on crime. The declared objectives of the organization were diverse, ambiguous, and conflicting with the scope of the program; many were exceedingly broad and ill defined. Failing to clarify its objectives resulted in the LEAA allocating a disproportionate amount of funds to the police and caused great confusion in the operation and understanding of certain programs. Little attention was paid to the underlying social and economic problems that led to crime and incarceration, and serious crime continued to grow into the 1980s. Another criticism of the OCCSSA is with Title III: Citizens were concerned with their privacy while using telephonic communications. Title III allowed the suppression of evidence obtained through the use of police wiretapping but declared that evidence received from private surveillance turned over to law enforcement was obtained with "clean hands." The vague language made suppression a discretionary act of the judiciary, which led to difficulties in attempting to apply the title's exclusionary rule to law enforcement officials using wiretap evidence obtained with clean hands.

The Omnibus Crime Control and Safe Streets Act was approved June 19, 1968. This act served to initiate a nationalization of crime policy. In the early years, it gave money through the LEAA to police for hardware (e.g., helicopters, tanks, riot gear), but in later years, the LEAA emphasized community corrections and diversion programs. The existence of a central grant-producing presence in Washington, D.C., increased the flow of information between jurisdictions and fostered a sense of common participation.

Kyle A. Burgason
University of Arkansas at Little Rock

See Also: Johnson, Lyndon B. (Administration of); Law Enforcement Assistance Administration.

Further Readings

Omnibus Crime Control and Safe Streets Act of 1968. Public Law 90-351, 82 Stat. 197, 42 U.S.C. § 3711 (1968).

Roth, Mitchel P. *Crime and Punishment: A History of the Criminal Justice System*. Belmont, CA: Thomson Wadsworth, 2005.

Oregon

A large state in the Pacific northwest, Oregon was admitted to the union in 1859. Beginning in the territorial era, early Oregon saw frequent anti-Chinese violence. Portland had one of the country's first Chinatowns, home to many of the Chinese workers who had been brought in to work on railroads and mines. Throughout the Pacific northwest in the late 19th century, mobs drove or attempted to drive Chinese workers out of town, motivated by racist distrust and fear. The National Guard armory near Portland's Chinatown was even built, in 1888, out of fear of a Chinese uprising.

Police and Punishment

Early law enforcement was handled by night watchmen, constables (often elected officials, often working part-time), or federal marshals. The Portland Metropolitan Police Force, one of the state's first organized police departments, was established in 1870 and modeled after well-established police departments in other states. While in the east law enforcement had evolved toward the

Portland police officers on bicycle patrol gather in front of the City Police Bureau on day one of Occupy Portland, a protest movement that began "in peaceful solidarity with Occupy Wall Street" on October 6, 2011. The Portland police reported that more than 4,000 people began the march, increasing to 10,000 by midday and filling city streets.

modern police department gradually, with a transitional period in which a town or city marshal oversaw "day watch" or police workers, Portland's police department was essentially modern from its inception, with a chief of police overseeing a force of six patrolmen and a lieutenant. In 1908, the department hired the first female police officer in the country, Lola Baldwin, as the head of the Women's Protective Division. The department adopted its current name, the Portland Police Bureau, in 1915, and in 1919, it became the first American police department to use radios.

The first state prison in Oregon was built in Portland in 1851. It was replaced by a new facility in Salem in 1866, which has remained Oregon's only maximum-security facility. Today, most of the cellblocks have been converted to double-occupancy cells in order to maximize capacity, and there are special housing units for death row, inmates with psychiatric problems, and disciplinary solitary confinement.

Oregon is a capital punishment state. Executions were conducted by the territorial government and made explicitly legal in 1864. Since 1904, executions have been carried out exclusively at the state penitentiary in Salem. The death penalty has been repeatedly outlawed and revived in Oregon, having first been repealed in 1914 by a ballot measure to amend the state constitution; the repeal effort won by a margin of 0.04 percent. A new amendment restoring the death penalty passed only six years later. In 1931, lethal gas replaced hanging as the method of execution.

A ballot measure outlawed the death penalty again in 1964, this time with 60 percent of the vote. It was again revived in 1978 by ballot measure, but the measure was overturned in 1981 by the Oregon Supreme Court because it denied defendants the right to a trial by jury. A new ballot measure in 1984 successfully restored the death penalty by requiring a separate sentencing hearing, decided by a jury, in cases of aggravated murder, that is, murder accompanied by aggravating factors such as a contract killing, a victim who is a child, or the killing of a witness or a police officer. Oregon's death penalty statute is substantially similar to those of other states.

Throughout the 1990s and early 21st century, ballot measures have reformed Oregon's criminal sentencing guidelines. A 1994 ballot measure, part of a nationwide call for stricter sentencing, established mandatory minimum sentences for violent crimes: murder, manslaughter, assault, kidnapping, rape, robbery, sexual abuse, unlawful sexual penetration, and sodomy. (Oregon's sodomy laws are applicable only if the sex is nonconsensual or if one party is under the age of 16.) Several 1999 ballot measures were enacted that limited parole and excluded people convicted of specific crimes from serving on criminal trial juries or grand juries. A 2008 measure further increased sentences for drug trafficking, theft against the elderly, and certain other crimes of theft, while requiring addiction treatment for some drug offenders. The measure came at a time when many states, faced with prison overpopulation, were rolling back or proposing the rollback of mandatory sentences enacted in the 1980s and 1990s; Oregon, instead, continued on the path laid out in the previous century. As a result, while it has seen a greater decrease in crime than the country as a whole, it spends the highest percentage of its state budget on prison and parole of any state, and since the 1994 establishment of mandatory minimum sentences it has seen the prison population increase from about 4,000 to nearly 15,000.

Crime

In 1994, the neo-Nazi group Volksfront was founded by inmates in the Oregon State Penitentiary. Since then, chapters have been opened in 10 countries and throughout the United States. Volksfront's stated goal, the Northwest Territorial Imperative, is to establish a partially autonomous, exclusively white community in the Pacific northwest, which will be home to a European American community center with a museum, library, and the headquarters for Volksfront. Officially opposed to lawbreaking, Volksfront includes many members who have been arrested for racially motivated crimes, both before and after their joining the group. In 1998, the European Kindred white supremacist gang was formed in the Snake River Correctional Institution in eastern Oregon. More secretive and ritualistic than Volksfront or the California-based Nazi Lowriders (also popular in the Oregon prison system), the European Kindred seem primarily interested in controlling the crime in the prison system, running dogfights, and making and selling methamphetamines.

Oregon is also the headquarters of two major outlaw motorcycle clubs and is home to local chapters of several others, including the Gypsy Jokers, the Vagos, and the Outsiders. The Brother Speed Motorcycle Club was founded in Boise, Idaho, but relocated to Portland. The Free Souls Motorcycle Club is a one-percenter gang formed in Eugene, with multiple chapters throughout Oregon and an affiliated chapter in Washington State. The motorcycle gangs in Oregon are generally involved in the methamphetamine, marijuana, and hash trade in the state, and in the trafficking of stolen firearms.

The crime rate in Oregon has long been considerably lower than the national average and has followed the national trend of rising in the decades leading up to a peak and then declining. While the national crime rate peaked in the 1990s, as it did in most states, in Oregon, the peak was reached in 1985, with a violent crime rate of 551 crimes per 100,000 inhabitants. Decline was slow, but by 2010, the rate had fallen by half and was at 252 per 100,000.

Bill Kte'pi
Independent Scholar

See Also: Crime Rates; Penitentiaries; Race-Based Crimes.

Further Readings
Donnelly, Robert. *Dark Rose: Organized Crime and Corruption in Portland*. Seattle: University of Washington Press, 2011.
Goeres-Gardner, Diane. *Necktie Parties: A History of Legal Executions in Oregon, 1851–1905*. Caldwell, ID: Caxton Press, 2005.
Oregon Historical Society. http://www.ohs.org (Accessed September 2011).

Organized Crime, Contemporary

To the general public, notions of organized crime often carry stereotypical images associated with Hollywood productions, such as *The Godfather*, *The Sons of Anarchy*, *The Sopranos,* and *The Departed*. While these portrayals may enlighten the public about the mere existence of organized crime, they inadequately capture and represent the historical and present-day facts concerning criminal organizations. Unfortunately, because of their misconstrued portrayal in movies and television series, individuals have developed misperceptions about organized crime, especially as it relates to the 21st century.

Historical Development

The origin of organized crime in the United States dates as far back as 1890 when the Italian American Mafia (i.e., La Cosa Nostra or American Mafia) murdered the New Orleans chief of police. Following this event, many Italian immigrants living in the surrounding area were targeted by mobs of retributive residents and were subsequently forced to flee New Orleans and seek shelter in other major cities throughout the United States, such as Chicago, New York, Kansas City, and Las Vegas. Mafia families operating in these (and other) cities continued to expand—enjoying the high levels of secrecy and solidarity produced by their ethnic homogeneity and traditional Sicilian ideologies—and became heavily involved in an assortment of criminal activities.

American Mafia families gained an influential position in the criminal underworld by exploiting business opportunities and corrupt government officials. For example, the Chicago families that operated during the 1920s gained high levels of prestige by capitalizing on the illicit liquor market produced by Prohibition. During this era, Mafia families cultivated useful relations with local law enforcement and government officials and became prominent suppliers of bootlegged liquor. Additionally, the American Mafia developed a presence in licit enterprises by gaining control of labor unions during the 1920s and the gambling ring in Las Vegas during the 1940s. Other criminal activities utilized by the American Mafia included drug trafficking, gambling, loan-sharking, and "protective" services. While maintaining an influential role during the early and mid-1900s, the American Mafia faced a rapid decline resulting from antiorganized crime legislation and the cultivation of other criminal organizations, which led to their replacement in the transnational drug market (by an assortment of drug distribution networks). However, even after experiencing such a dramatic reduction in the number of active members, recent law enforcement operations targeting the American Mafia show that they are still present and evolving today.

As one of the first criminal organizations operating in the United States, the American Mafia created an illusion that criminal organizations follow a strict structure with stern recruiting guidelines, which focus heavily on ethnic similarity. The reality, however, could not be further from that stereotype. As many criminal organizations have demonstrated throughout the 20th and 21st centuries, organized crime is more versatile and opportunistic than rudimentary descriptions would lead one to believe. Thus, rather than being hindered by an inextensible, vertically configured, and ethnically homogeneous structure (e.g., Sicilian Mafia, 'Ndrangheta, Chinese triads, and Japanese Yakuza), modernized crime syndicates have, for the most part, adopted a flexible, decentralized, and ethnically diverse composition with relaxed recruiting guidelines. As a result, many contemporary criminal organizations have ignored inalterable characteristics (e.g., race, gender, and ethnicity) and recruited/formed alliances with people possessing a desired skill set, position of authority, or equally useful quality.

Contemporary Organized Crime

By altering their original structure of vertical hierarchy, clearly defined leadership positions, and centralization, many contemporary organized crime groups appear more subtle and loosely connected, without a traditional pyramid structure. Taking this approach was very useful because groups that did not fit the stereotypical "Mafia" description were largely overlooked (e.g., the Russian Mafia). Yet as law enforcement developed a comprehensive understanding of criminal organizations and criminal networks, it became exceedingly more difficult for criminals to evade their attacks. In response to the government's changing tactics, some organized crime groups altered their criminal activity (e.g., the Russian Mafia withdrew from international drug trafficking and began providing security for Mexican drug cartels, and the Mexican drug cartels began kidnapping in addition to drug trafficking), while others modified and/or advanced their structure and methods of operation (e.g., Asian and Russian organized crime).

American crime syndicates, such as the Chinese and Russian Mafia, benefit from their involvement in a variety of criminal activities. The Russian Mafia, for example, engages in a list of financially motivated crimes, which include theft, prostitution, gambling, fraud, and international drug, person, firearm, and vehicle trafficking. To remain authoritative in its respective markets, while simultaneously evading attacks by law enforcement officials, the Russian Mafia is thought to operate under two different structures. The first consists of a loosely connected and ethnically heterogeneous network that recruits members and forms ties based on an individual's skill set, rather than kinship. This type of organization often forms with a specific purpose (e.g., committing varying types of fraud and racketeering) and has both short-term and long-lasting operations, depending on the network's interest(s). The second structure has its roots in foreign-based affairs and often operates internationally in the trafficking of people, drugs, firearms, and vehicles. Under each of these functions, communication is conducted on an as-needed basis, and ties are formed only long enough to complete a task—similar to licit enterprises.

Like the Russians, Asian criminal organizations have varying structures and methods of operation. Some traditional Asian groups (e.g., Chinese triads from Hong Kong and Taiwan and the Japanese Yakuza) enjoy a fixed vertical hierarchy, while others (especially in the United States) have shifted to a loosely connected and ethnically diverse structure, making them more opportunistic in nature. Because of these attributes, the latter group recruits people from a variety of ethnic backgrounds, generally forms only long enough to complete a task, and is often involved in transnational criminal activities. The fact that each of these criminal organizations operates under multiple structures makes identifying and combating them difficult for law enforcement officials, who must differentiate and categorize groups as conforming to one structure or the other.

Accompanying their involvement in legitimate enterprises (e.g., the stock market, construction, waste disposal, and wholesale markets) and illicit domestic activities (e.g., gambling, prostitution, loan-sharking, violence, and providing protective services), Chinese American criminal organizations also participate heavily in transnational human and drug trafficking. Despite having a lower frequency than many Asian countries, the high number of Chinese women working in the sex trade throughout the United States has brought a considerable amount of attention to the international trafficking of women. Additionally, because large quantities of heroin and amphetamines are produced in the Burmese part of the Golden Triangle, international drug trafficking from Asian countries poses a grave threat to the United States. In recent years, many drug cartels located south of the United States border have started infiltrating the international drug market by exploiting their access to drugs (e.g., cocaine, marijuana, and heroin) and transnational trade routes. This fact has alternated the nature of international drug trafficking by increasing competition (among organized crime groups) and the need for international law enforcement tactics.

Other Forms of Modern Organized Crime

While the term *organized crime* is often held synonymous with the Italian Mafia, the shift toward viewing organized crime as loosely connected, ethnically heterogeneous, and flexible has led to the discovery of criminal organizations that differ from traditional Mafia-type groups. In addition to the Italian, Russian, and Asian Mafias operating in the United States, refined descriptions of organized crime have been expanded to include American outlaw motorcycle gangs (OMGs), organized street gangs (e.g., Mara Salvatrucha, or MS-13), criminal networks (e.g., drug cartels and "men for hire"), and alliances between terrorist and organized crime groups (i.e., narcoterrorism). These recently discovered gangs and criminal networks have convoluted the understanding of organized crime by forming unconventional alliances (e.g., the business alliances between terrorist and organized crime groups) and borrowing traditional tactics utilized by criminal organizations (e.g., kidnapping and international drug trafficking).

Originating in the 1930s, most OMGs formed between the late 1940s and 1960s. Initially, these gangs were not seen as a threat to others; rather, they functioned as small, nonviolent, counterculture groups known as motorcycle clubs (MCs). During the latter part of the 20th century, however, several of these motorcycle clubs began displaying elements of criminal organizations, which included implementing requirements for inclusion (e.g., riding a particular type of motorcycle), a formal vertical structure (similar to the Italian Mafia's) and dress code, solidarity through subcultural beliefs, and a propensity toward violent and criminal behavior.

To date, there are more than 300 American OMGs, several of which operate transnationally with both domestic and international alliances. For example, one of the most notorious American OMGs—the Outlaws—expanded its organization in the early 21st century to include a "supported club" known as the Black Pistons. After receiving Outlaws support, the Black Pistons expanded rapidly and developed a presence in the United States, Canada, and Europe, which enhanced the organization's manpower and territorial control. Similar to other criminal organizations, OMGs are involved in a variety of criminal activities, which include assault, homicide, weapons trafficking, theft, and drug manufacturing and distribution (primarily methamphetamines and marijuana). In addition, OMGs also use legitimate business operations to cover their clandestine enterprises (e.g., running strip clubs), violence (or threat of violence) and murder to protect their fellow members, and tactical alliances to enhance their business opportunities (e.g., the Hells Angels have formed alliances with Colombian drug cartels and the American Mafia). Although the American OMGs appear structurally and operationally similar to traditional criminal organizations, their tactically developed alliances and business operations make them some of the most dangerous, long-standing, and successful contemporary criminal organizations.

Whether a street gang is considered criminally organized typically depends on the gang's

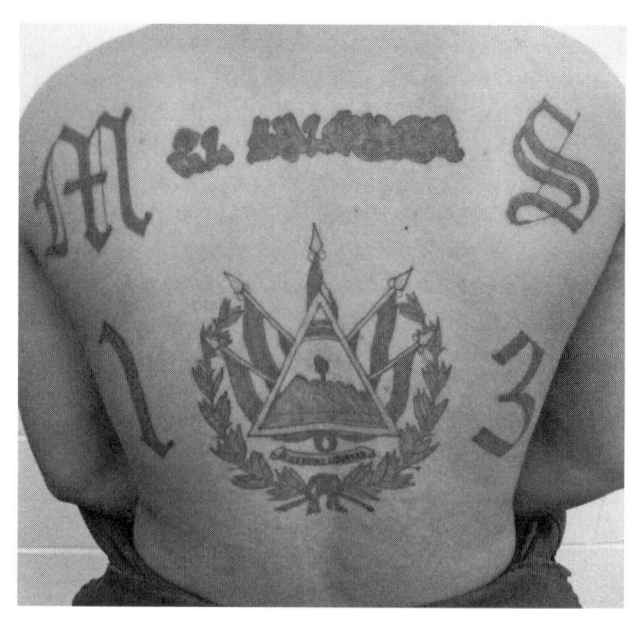

This Mara Salvatrucha (MS-13) gang member bears a tattoo showing his membership in the original Salvadorian MS-13. The gang is now represented in at least 13 U.S. states and has spread to Canada, Mexico, and Central America.

characteristics. Although it can be argued that many are not, some gangs, such as the Mara Salvatrucha (MS-13), clearly possess elements akin to traditional criminal organizations. At the time of its origin (during the 1980s), MS-13 restricted its membership to Salvadorians. This is likely because Salvadorians formed MS-13 in Los Angeles, California, in order to provide a unified defense against well-established rival gangs. During the 21st century, however, MS-13 expanded its membership to include people from Ecuador, Guatemala, Honduras, Mexico, and African American communities within the United States. Additionally, MS-13 demonstrated its high levels of organization and sophistication when it started to mobilize in response to heightened attacks by law enforcement. Because of their violent demeanor, willingness to commit a variety of crimes, and high levels of organization and mobility, MS-13 now has a presence in approximately 13 states and three countries. Ultimately, MS-13 has gained a reputation for borrowing organized crime tactics such as assassinations, kidnapping, auto theft, human and contraband trafficking, extortion, and other forms of racketeering. As a result, they are considered one of the most violent and ruthless contemporary criminal organizations.

Drug distribution networks located along the United States-Mexico border (i.e., "Mexican drug cartels") have adopted a powerful position in the transnational drug market since the Colombian drug cartel demise in the 1990s. Initially trafficking small amounts of marijuana and opiates during the 1960s, these Mexican drug cartels have enhanced their operations to include a variety of tactics and criminal activities. Using weapons (that are usually) trafficked from the United States, the various cartels fight among one another—in addition to the constant conflict they maintain with U.S. and Mexican law enforcement officials—over territory and popular trafficking routes into California, Arizona, New Mexico, and Texas (e.g., the crossing near Tijuana). For example, the Sinaloa and Gulf cartels have been fighting one another since 2001 for control of Nuevo Laredo—a Mexico city with access to the most efficient international trafficking route on the 2,000-mile border. Because of their widely used violence and success as international drug traffickers, the Mexican drug cartels became a salient target for Mexican and U.S. law enforcement agencies. As a response to the heightened attention from law enforcement, Mexican cartels expanded their criminal involvement to include kidnapping and weapons and human trafficking. Because of their tactful shift between various criminal activities and their relentless use of violence and murder, they are now, like MS-13, considered one of the biggest organized crime threats to the United States.

Until recently, the lines separating criminal organizations from terrorist groups appeared clear. However, since the 1990s, terrorist groups have been forming alliances with criminal organizations and utilizing their tactics more frequently than they had in previous years. Examples of this crossover include the Revolutionary Armed Forces of Colombia (FARC), which uses drug trafficking and kidnapping to finance terrorist operations in Colombia, and Al Qaeda, who often exchange opium trafficking for funding by criminal organizations. In exchange for their funding, terrorist groups often perform violent and public acts, while the organized crime groups operate clandestinely. Although this terrorist–organized crime link may not specifically occur in the United States, it does demonstrate a potential threat, especially when one considers the attacks of 9/11 and questions where funding for similar terrorist attacks originated.

Conclusion

Many modern criminal organizations appear strikingly more advanced than traditional organized crime groups. While earlier groups, such as the Italian American Mafia, operated under a stern vertical hierarchy with membership thresholds and restricted methods of operation, most contemporary organized crime groups possess a flexible and loosely connected structure with an opportunistic modus operandi. As this entry illustrates, some contemporary organized crime groups are more restricted by their fixed structure and membership requirements (e.g., the Hells Angels) than other opportunistic groups (e.g., drug cartels); however, it is also arguable that these rigorously controlled groups remain active because solidarity, secrecy, and sense of belonging reinforce commitment to the group's ideologies and practices. Accounting for enhanced law enforcement tactics, technological advancements, and the increasing number of opportunistic crime syndicates, contemporary organized crime groups must be adaptable, flexible, and willing to take advantage of opportunities to make money. In sum, to understand contemporary organized crime, one must account for its constantly evolving nature rather than focusing on incipient definitions synonymous with the original Italian Mafia.

Nick C. Athey
Simon Fraser University
Weston Morrow
Arizona State University

See Also: 1961 to 1980 Primary Documents; 2001 to 2012 Primary Documents; Italian Americans; Organized Crime, History of; Organized Crime, Sociology of; Terrorism.

Further Readings
Baker, T. "American Based Biker Gangs: International Organized Crime." *American Journal of Criminal Justice*, v.36 (2011).
Cheloukhine, S. "The Roots of Russian Organized Crime." *Crime, Law & Social Change*, v.50 (2008).

Finckenauer, J. O. and K. L. Chinm. "Asian Transnational Organized Crime and Its Impact on the United States: Developing a Transnational Crime Research Agenda." National Institute of Justice. https://www.ncjrs.gov/pdffiles1/nij/grants/213310.pdf (Accessed September 2011).

Roth, M. P. *Global Organized Crime: A Reference Handbook*. Santa Barbara, CA: ABC-CLIO, 2010.

Siegel, D., H. van de Bunt, and D. Zaitch, eds. *Global Organized Crime Trends and Developments*. Norwell, MA: Kluwer Academic Publishers, 2003.

Varese, F. *Organized Crime: Critical Concepts in Criminology*. New York: Routledge, 2010.

Organized Crime, History of

The history of organized crime necessarily begins with a definition of organized crime, something that has perplexed law enforcement officials, government leaders, and scholars for years. There is no universally accepted definition of exactly what organized crime is. Two robbers who plan their roles, one who acts as a lookout and drives the getaway car while the other brandishes a gun and demands "Give me all your money!" have organized their crime, yet few would label such an action organized crime in the sense that one would label an act street crime, property crime, or hate crime.

There have been numerous attempts by various people to construct a definition; some criminologists feel that attempting to define whether criminal activity is or is not "organized" is less helpful than identifying the degree of organization on a continuum. Others argue that organized crime cannot be adequately defined, but that characteristics can be assigned to organized crime that sufficiently describe activities or enterprises that are organized or not. Still others turn to legal statutes for a definition. The Organized Crime Control Act of 1970 defines racketeering as participation in one of several different criminal acts, including murder, counterfeiting, theft from interstate transit, mail or wire fraud, extortion, illegal gambling, and many others.

Some point out, however, that the definition of what is today called organized crime is fluid, changing throughout the years as society has changed along with various forms of criminal activity. Further, a definition of organized crime can vary according to who is doing the defining. From the standpoint of law enforcement, the government, and the big-business industrialists, for example, the Molly Maguires were members of a group of Irish criminals belonging to a secret organization bent on destroying the anthracite coal mines of eastern Pennsylvania in the years following the Civil War. From the point of view of the coal miners, the citizens of the region, however, the Mollies were a group of latter-day Robin Hoods who came to the aid of the exploited workers and organized labor, attempting to unionize workers and eradicate dangerous and unsafe working conditions.

There are, however, a number of groups throughout history that can be singled out as precursors to organized crime. While many would agree that these were organized crime groups or groups that led into the development of other groups, there is no single universal definition of organized crime since there is no single unified group of organized criminals, nor is there any single monolithic history or evolution of organized crime.

For most people, the term *organized crime* equates with terms like *Mafia, La Cosa Nostra*, and the negative stereotypes of Italian Americans. No ethnic group, however, holds a monopoly on criminal activity, although gangs have frequently been organized with ethnicity at their core. Long before the mass migration of Italians to America's shores, several gangs operated organized and profit-oriented criminal enterprises—among the most prominent, the Irish and Jewish gangsters. What all three groups had in common was their oppression in their homeland, their immigration to America, and the difficulties arriving out of their ethnic background with isolation from mainstream American culture upon their arrival.

Pirates

For most, piracy conjures up the images popularized by picaresque novels or the swashbuckler romantic movie roles of Errol Flynn, not those of the Corleone family or today's drug cartels

The Molly Maguires were viewed as both heroes aiding exploited mine workers and as criminals determined to destroy the eastern Pennsylvanian anthracite coal mines after the Civil War. Above is an example of a coffin notice sent to mine bosses.

that dominate the news. Although the differences between modern-day organized crime and the maritime piracy of the so-called golden age of piracy are apparent, there are also several similarities that cause many to see maritime piracy as an earlier form of organized crime. The most active era of maritime piracy lasted from about the middle of the 1600s to the early decades of the 1700s and dominated the areas of the West Indies, colonial North America, and Africa; for the most part, ethnicity played little role among pirates.

England's Navigation Acts, a series of laws enacted from about 1650 to 1700, regulated the importation and transportation of certain goods between England and its colonies. Essentially, the laws stated that goods could not be brought to England or its colonies unless they were transported by British ships manned by British citizens. The laws further stipulated that goods exported by the British colonies could only be transported and sold to England. The laws had the intended effect of strengthening England by restricting colonial commerce with other European countries, but the restrictiveness of the Navigation Acts also had the effect of creating a black market and a higher demand for certain products, giving rise to maritime piracy much as Prohibition and the Volstead Act did for the Irish, Jewish, and Italian gangsters of the early 20th century.

Corruption of the police, prosecutors, judges, and politicians is often cited as one of the major reasons that Prohibition failed in 1920s America, and corruption was also common as a means of getting around the Navigation Acts. Merchants, faced with the prospect of paying exorbitantly high prices, provided an outlet for pirates to sell their plunder taken from merchant ships on the high seas. Representatives of the Crown used to enforce the laws were scarce, and evidence suggests that pirates freely bribed local colonial officials, and the colonists themselves, to abet their criminal enterprises. In cities like Boston, New York, and Philadelphia, pirate collusion with local citizens and officials to have their plunder unloaded and distributed for sale was common.

Just as the use of violence in obtaining their objectives is used by modern-day gangsters, pirates of the golden age used violence for the same ends. Accounts of pirate violence and brutality were well known, and the use of the skull and crossbones image had the intended effect of striking terror into the hearts of potential victims. As with modern-day gangsters, sometimes only the reputation of violent and brutal acts was enough to gain the compliance and surrender of their enemies.

As with their later gangster counterparts, poverty and social conditions often played a role in influencing young men to pursue a life of crime as a pirate. Poor, unemployed, and uneducated, many of them barely literate, many young men of the 17th and 18th centuries left home and chose an occupation that was open to them—going to sea. Many sailors opted to join up with pirates as a means of obtaining the luxurious and exotic items they saw there for themselves. While the life of a pirate may have been more dangerous, it could also be more lucrative, and for many it won out over the prospect of working for wages as an ordinary seaman. The spoils that the pirates reaped were pooled and divided up among the men according to rank, with everyone getting their previously agreed-upon share. Among modern criminal groups, a similar dividing of profits occurs, although the lowest-ranking pirates were usually not able to be as entrepreneurial as the lowest-ranking soldiers of modern groups.

Since most pirates had once been navy men, pirate ships were organized similarly to naval vessels. As with naval vessels, pirate ships had codes of conduct, rules that organized operations so that things would run smoothly, usually agreed upon by all involved prior to setting sail, with ritualistic oath-taking ceremonies as have been described in some organized crime group initiations.

As with modern groups, pirates often had to swear to codes of silence to their activities when ashore. Pirates, too, had their "colors" to swear their loyalty to, just as modern street gangs and outlaw motorcycle gangs have theirs, the most commonly known being the skull and crossed bones of the "Jolly Roger," although many variations of this existed.

Pirate captains held their positions at the behest of their crews. While some could be violent or cruel, if they were effective and made things profitable, they were tolerated by the group. If not, the crew could turn the tables on the captain and refuse to serve. The quartermaster was elected by the crew and served as the check on the captain's power. Other ranks below the quartermaster usually depended on their skills and standing for status with the rest of the crew, and included gunners, bosuns, mates, and carpenters. Like modern-day criminal groups, individuals served by their rank and by distinguishing themselves individually in their criminal enterprises. While there are some differences between maritime pirates of old and modern forms of organized crime, some of the similarities are striking, especially considering the differences between time periods in which both have flourished.

Irish American Organized Crime in New York

The Irish had long been the victims of oppression by the English, generally Protestant versus Catholic. By the 1840s, this oppression, along with the failure of the potato crop and the subsequent famine, had pushed a large segment of the Irish population to seek better opportunities elsewhere. The first large-scale immigration of peasants to the

An 1896 lithograph depicts "a pirate's ruse, luring a merchantman in the olden days." Pirates attacked ships in North America and the Caribbean as late as the 1870s. Twenty-first-century pirates prefer to target small boats or modern cargo vessels with relatively small crews, yet they still cause international losses of up to $16 billion per year.

United States, the Irish settled primarily in urban areas and primarily in the northeast. Although able to speak English, the Irish were isolated and ostracized in America because of their different culture and their Catholic religion.

Youth gangs had flourished in urban neighborhoods in America since the turn of the 19th century. With no social safety nets, gangs made up of orphans, dropouts, and antisocial boys roamed the streets of the cities, defending their neighborhoods. The rise of the city bosses and political machines in the 19th century also characterized urban life at the time. Saloons were the center of urban neighborhoods, a place of respite for urban residents and a place for local gatherings and meetings when needed, such as labor unions and electioneering for local politicians. Saloon keepers and tavern owners often worked for the political machines and city bosses and were often looked up to and trusted by both the machines and the local residents. The value of the youth gangs was not lost on the saloon keepers or local politicians as a means of getting out—and sometimes coercing—the vote. Corrupt political machines and city bosses existed throughout America, but perhaps none are as well known as New York's Tammany Hall and William "Boss" Tweed. Neighborhood gangs benefited from their associations in several ways, not least among them the alliances and loyalties formed between them and the political bosses. They also learned how the bosses operated their organizations, the networks and contacts that could be made, the how and who that could be bribed, and to whom and when threats or violence could be used to gain another's compliance. Through the political bosses and machines, ethnic groups also learned the way they could redress their grievances, since most ethnic groups coming to the United States from Europe in the 19th and early 20th centuries were met with more and more anti-immigrant nativist sentiment.

The most prominent of the 19-century Irish gangs in New York was probably the Five Points gang, so named because of the convergence of five streets in that neighborhood; this was depicted in the 2002 Martin Scorsese film *Gangs of New York*. The ethnic makeup of the Five Pointers later changed as the Irish were supplanted by other groups, most notably the Jews and Italians. In addition to the Five Points gang, other prominent Irish gangs of the times included the Whyos, the Forty Thieves, the Dead Rabbits, the Kerryonians, and the Plug Uglies. Although not organized crime per se, these gangs were precursors to organized crime where politics and political corruption were learned that would later serve a large part of the success of ethnically organized crime groups. They were also important training grounds for teaching the workings of the urban environment to those from groups that were largely rural peasants when they first emigrated, such as the Italians and the Irish.

Irish Crime in Other Cities

Similar situations existed between gangs and political bosses in other cities, such as Chicago, Boston, Philadelphia, and others. A popular misconception exists that Irish crime groups and gangsters faded away in the 20th century, but this is not so. Jack "Legs" Diamond and "Big Bill" Dwyer were two of New York's famed bootleggers of the Prohibition era, while the Westies from the west side of Manhattan figured prominently in the news well into the late 20th century. In Chicago, several Irish gangs dominated the city's streets well into the Prohibition years. The North Side Gang, a combination of Irish and Polish gangsters that had evolved out the earlier Market Street Gang, went to war with the Torrio-Capone organization in the 1920s and was led by the infamous Dion O'Banion and later by George "Bugs" Moran. It was seven members of the North Side Gang that were gunned down in a north side garage in what has come to be known as the St. Valentine's Day Massacre, an attempted but failed hit on Moran.

Boston's several Irish neighborhoods have spawned many such gangs throughout the years. Most famous is The Winter Hill Gang from Somerville and Boston's Charlestown Mob, who opposed each other in the Irish Mob Wars of the 1960s. The Winter Hill Gang was later led by James "Whitey" Bulger, who became embroiled in a corruption scandal with the Boston Federal Bureau of Investigation (FBI) office and who for years became a fugitive from justice until his 2011 capture. The decline of Irish organized crime came with the decline of the purely Irish urban neighborhood and the transformation of ethnic identity. Although some Irish neighborhoods can still be found in America, after World War II, several things contributed to their decline and the transformation of ethnic identity: the move from the urban areas to the suburbs, the invasion and succession of other ethnic groups, and then the supplanting of the older, European immigrants by newer groups from Asia and Central America, and acculturation/assimilation of the Irish as a group that accompanied higher rates of exogamy.

Jewish American Organized Crime
Jewish gangsters began to grow in strength in the late 19th century as waves of Jewish immigrants began succeeding the Irish. As with the Irish before them, mostly eastern European Jews had endured prejudice and discrimination in their homelands and upon their arrival were the objects of anti-immigrant and nativist sentiment, as well as anti-Semitism. Unlike the Irish, or the Italians who were shortly to follow, Jews came from many different countries. While there is some convergence in the evolution of Jewish organized crime with their Italian and Irish counterparts, there are, generally speaking, several differences.

Jewish groups arose from youth gangs as well, and Jewish extortion gangs similar to the Italian Black Hand gangs plagued New York in the early 20th century. Jewish gangs tended to specialize in property crime and labor issues and, perhaps because the Jewish immigrants as a group were better educated than most other immigrants, tended to approach criminal activities with less crudity and more businesslike operations. With only a couple of exceptions, Jewish gangs did not rise to prominence as much as individual Jewish gangsters did, the list being long and infamous. The Jewish underworld can be characterized more as a complex cooperation with other criminal ethnic groups than as a homogeneous organization.

Jewish organized crime was centered primarily in New York, which has a large Jewish population. Probably the best-known exception was Detroit's Jewish criminal group, the Purple Gang, although they are usually described more as a loose confederation than a unified organization. The Purple Gang, or the Purples as they were sometimes called, especially prospered during Prohibition with their geographic location just across the Detroit River from Canada. The gang held a monopoly on what was transported across the river from Canada and at one time had made a business deal with Chicago's Al Capone to furnish him with Canadian whiskey. Capone had also hired Purple Gang hit men to use in the St. Valentine's Day Massacre. The Purples also enjoyed a reputation as hijackers, much of their hijacking being shipments of liquor from other criminals trying to take advantage of their geographic location. In the 1920s, the Purple Gang was hired by the Wholesale Cleaners and Dyers Association to enforce a trade restriction that the association had placed upon its members. When a dry cleaning shop failed to comply, the Purples were sent in to force them to comply by means of arson, with stink bombs that would ruin the clothing in the shop or with real bombs that would destroy it.

Eventually, gang leader Abe Bernstein took over the association, and the same tactics were used for shops that did not pay their dues or refused to go along with the association agenda. The Purple Gang eventually went into decline after the repeal of Prohibition, with the source of their revenue gone and the successful prosecution and the imprisonment of various gang leaders. Italian criminals eventually supplanted them as the Detroit edition of organized crime.

Jewish organized crime today has not been replaced as much as it has been transformed. Today, most Jews emigrate from Russia and the other former Soviet countries, and are focused in the Jewish community of Brighton Beach in Brooklyn; much of their criminal activity is centered in the northeast. They are usually identified, though, by their Russian nationality, rather than as Jewish.

Italian Organized Crime
Organized crime in Italy began in the south of Italy and in Sicily among the oppressed peasantry residing in a region that had been occupied by foreign governments and their armies for thousands of years. Jutting out into the middle of the Mediterranean Sea, this region, dubbed the *mezzogiorno*, was coveted for its strategic location for commercial and military purposes and throughout the millennia had been controlled and occupied by the Greeks, Romans, Spanish, Arabs, Normans, and Carthaginians, among others. The end of feudalism in the early 19th century resulted in the establishment of large private

Smiling convicted New York mobsters Emanuel "Mendy" Weiss (right) and Louis Capone, surrounded by detectives, ride a train "up the river" to the Sing Sing prison death row after receiving their sentences. Capone was not related to the Chicago criminal Al Capone but was a supervisor for Murder, Inc.—a group of mainly Jewish and Italian American hit men from Brooklyn.

estates owned by the aristocracy, many of whom left their land and became absentee landowners, leaving the day-to-day management of their land to overseers. The peasants were forced to curry favor from these overseers in order to lease parcels of land from them or to make arrangements to work the land and share the crops. This enabled the overseers to gain an enormous amount of power, as they controlled the food source for the peasants and the crops that were to be sold in the cities. Commonly, the overseers began to hire henchmen to help them protect their interests, as many took unfair advantage of the peasants that farmed their land.

The effect of hundreds of years of oppression and maltreatment, along with the system that arose after the decline of feudalism, was to make the local populace distrustful of those in authority, whose favor they needed to farm the land and earn a living. With the unification of the kingdoms of Italy in the 1860s, the peasants were hopeful of gaining equality and ending the discrimination against them, but it was not to be. Instead, they were left to their own devices to find ways to achieve what they needed to survive. What evolved was a patronage system of getting and receiving favors from the powerful overseers, a complex network of alliances and enemies. The word *mafia* originally meant "to be bold or daring" in the local dialect, a term that was applied to the overseers as men who were bold, daring, and commanded the respect of others, sometimes cruelly. It eventually evolved to equate with the patronage system that had grown up around them; thus, *mafia* became a method, or a way of doing things, not a criminal organization. It was *mafia* as a method that came to America when mass immigration of Italians to America began in the late 19th and early 20th centuries, not a formal criminal group that members brought with them. The word *mafia*, however, has come to mean any tightly knit and unified group in the vernacular of the 21st century.

The peasants who came were for the most part from small villages and rural areas of the *mezzogiorno*, but there were no strong ties to farming. Thus, they settled in urban areas in America where they could find work. Children were sometimes left to play in the streets, and playgroups often grew into youth gangs, much as what had occurred earlier with the Irish and Jewish immigrants. Petty youth crimes such as stealing from apple carts often turned into more serious crimes such as burglary, extortion, and violence. Black Hand gangs arose, and although often erroneously associated with the Mafia, they were, in fact, independent gangs whose only business was extortion.

The coming of age of Italian gangsters coincided with the passage of the Eighteenth Amendment and the Volstead Act, or Prohibition. Prohibition afforded them as well as other gangsters the opportunity to reap huge financial profits and build large-scale organizations out of what had previously been little more than street gangs. Competition for power between the two top Italian gangs in New York erupted into a gang war in the late 1920s. Known as the Castellamarese War, the conflict eventually culminated in the killing of the leaders of both factions and the organization of the five-family structure in New York. Many historians and criminologists point to this as the formal organization of the Mafia.

From the 1930s through the 1980s, the Italian American Mafia followed no specific progression or chronology as an organization. Instead it followed a catalog of names and events that have occurred throughout the years that have become part of the lexicon of popular culture in America: Luciano, Giancana, Columbo, Bonanno, Ricca, Gravano, Gigante, and Gotti are all surnames of people who have been involved in repeated patterns of power struggles to the ascendency of various families and control of the Mafia. Historical events such as the establishment of Murder, Inc., in the 1920s; the incident at Appalachin, New York in 1957; the Kefauver hearings in the early 1950s and the McClellan hearings in the late 1950s, along with the testimony of Joseph Valachi in 1963; the Pizza Connection, which began in 1985; and organized crime involvement in gambling and labor unions have all become a part of the storied and infamous history of organized crime, sometimes intertwined with works of fiction or semi-fiction such as *On the Waterfront* (1954), *The Godfather* (1972), *The Untouchables* (1987), *Goodfellas* (1990), and *Casino* (1995). Today, while Italian American organized crime is not dead, it is a far cry from the strength it once had.

Modern Organized Crime

Changing social conditions of the last half of the 20th century contributed to the decline of the gangs that were once common in American cities and to the transformation of ethnic identities. The second and subsequent generations no longer identified with the oppression felt by the first generation or with the attitudes and methods originally spawned in the *mezzogiorno* of the late 19th and early 20th centuries.

There was a concerted effort by law enforcement and legislators to reduce or eliminate the problem of organized crime. For years, FBI director J. Edgar Hoover refused to admit even to the existence of the Mafia or organized crime. The reasons for the denial have been speculated about for years, but the real reasons died with Hoover in 1972. At any rate, federal efforts to combat organized crime were minimal until they began to change in the 1960s under the direction of Attorney General Robert Kennedy. A few attempts had been made at legislation targeting organized crime prior to the 1960s, but all were flawed and largely ineffective. Title III of the Omnibus Crime Control and Safe Streets Act of 1968 made wiretaps more effective in the fight, and the Organized Crime Control Act of 1970 established two important tools in the fight against organized crime. One was the Witness Protection Program, which provided a safe haven for potential witnesses to be able to come forward and testify against bosses and other organized crime figures, and the other was Racketeer Influenced and Corrupt Organizations (RICO), a law that, although not used extensively until the 1980s, made it easier to prosecute those in leadership positions by establishing a pattern of racketeering. By the late 1980s, these tools were invaluable in combating organized crime.

Another factor to consider is the globalization of organized crime. For example, while the Mafia had long been in cooperative ventures with other crime groups throughout the world, particularly in Italy and Sicily, organized criminal enterprises went global in the waning years of the 20th century, far beyond the boundaries of declining neighborhoods. Once relatively unchallenged by other groups, the Mafia found itself being outpaced by drug cartels capable of producing and transporting their own product, and by more sophisticated scams that relied on technology and international cooperation that the Mafia did not have. Today, only vestiges remain of the 26 families that existed nationally on the flow charts and diagrams of the Justice Department, with the only real Mafia presence remaining in Chicago and New York, albeit in a much smaller and more weakened state.

Conclusion

The Irish, Jews, and Italians are not the only ethnic groups that have participated in criminal organizations, nor has shared ethnic background been the only focal point. In the United States, the history of organized crime is littered with examples of interethnic cooperation between groups, and although multiculturalism was not a value shared by many of the early gangsters, ethnic differences were often set aside in pursuit of riches and profit. And while many countries each have their own history of organized crime, organized crime today is a global phenomenon that knows no boundaries. Organized crime in the United States, for the most part, had its origins in the complex relationship between ethnicity, nationality, immigration, and the sociohistorical context of the time and the countries from which each group emerged. No ethnic group is inherently criminal, and the vast majorities of all ethnic groups that have come to America have taken their place as upstanding and law-abiding citizens. While there still may be an ethnic component among the various organized crime groups of today, most organized crime groups of the modern era are now strictly driven by profit and opportunity and not by ethnic background.

Paul Magro
Ball State University

See Also: 1921 to 1940 Primary Documents; 1941 to 1960 Primary Documents; 1961 to 1980 Primary Documents; Chicago, Illinois; Irish Americans; Italian Americans; Jewish Americans; New York City; Organized Crime, Contemporary.

Further Readings
Albini, J. L. *The American Mafia: Genesis of a Legend*. New York: Appleton-Century-Crofts, 1971.
English, T. J. *Paddy Whacked: The Untold Story of the Irish American Gangster*. New York: Regan Books, 2005.
Nelli, Humbert S. *The Business of Crime: Italians and Syndicate Crime in the United States*. Chicago: University of Chicago Press, 1976.
Roth, Mitchell P. *Organized Crime*. Upper Saddle River, NJ: Pearson Education, 2010.
Sifakis, Carl. *The Mafia Encyclopedia*. New York: Checkmark Books, 1999.

Organized Crime, Sociology of

Establishing a concrete definition of organized crime is rather difficult given the multidimensionality of scholarship surrounding criminal organizations. Because working definitions of organized crime have been offered by disciplines such as economics, criminology, political science, international affairs, and anthropology, determining the precise elements of a criminal organization and organized crime itself becomes difficult. Additionally, creating a comprehensive definition is further complicated by the changing and adaptive nature of organized crime and the cultivation of new groups (e.g., terrorist organizations, criminal networks, and street gangs).

Because organized crime groups adapt to their environment, their criminal activity, structure, and methods of operation fluctuate—this, in turn, alters the definition. Therefore, rather than ascertaining a concrete definition, it is best to incorporate the most frequently cited elements and causes of organized crime.

Current definitions frequently include elements of a formal structure, longevity, use of crime and violence to obtain money and power, and use of corruption to ensure immunity. A great deal of research suggests that a criminal organization's structure varies depending on its membership requirements, size, and hierarchy. There is also some overlap regarding structure when discussing a criminal organization's longevity, because a group's structure may reflect a need to be opportunistic and short-lived or protected and durable. Finally, when discussing the use of crime for financial profit, it is necessary to identify the services and goods being provided, because the type of goods and services provided by criminal organizations generally reflect the demands of the local community.

Formal Structure

The structure of organized crime generally follows three different models. Some groups are structured hierarchically with a formal division of labor and identifiable leaders, a few are based on ethnicity and often have ties to cultural ideologies, and most have a flexible structure, which they alter to meet changing economic opportunities. Although most criminal organizations fit under only one of the three models, it is important to note that some groups comprise elements from multiple models. For example, the Italian American Mafia recruits exclusively from the pool of Italian Americans; emphasizes the Sicilian ideologies of secrecy, respect, honor, and family ties; and maintains a strict, vertically tiered structure with known leaders. This is similar to the Hells Angels motorcycle club, which recruits primarily Caucasian males—who drive American-made motorcycles (e.g., Harley-Davidson)—and operates under a strict vertical hierarchy. With such a wide variety of structures, a comprehensive understanding of organized crime requires a review of the elements affecting its makeup.

The selective recruitment of members is an essential component for most definitions of organized crime because organizations vary in their requirements for membership. For example, some criminal organizations select members based primarily on ethnic ties and familial association (e.g., the American Mafia), others recruit based on location (e.g., prison gangs) or means of transportation (e.g., outlaw motorcycle clubs), and most recruit based on an individual's skill set or connections (e.g., Russian Mafia, drug cartels, etc.). The justification for choosing one form of recruitment over another is predicated on a desired outcome, but it is important to note that most contemporary organized crime groups have relaxed their membership requirements regarding fixed attributes (e.g., ethnicity or gender) and focused heavily on dexterity and networking.

The basic premise underlying organized crime is the desire to achieve monetary gain. However, in addition to being profit oriented, organized crime values secrecy, immunity, efficiency, and, in many cases, cohesion. Therefore, criminal organizations must find a balance that allows them to complete their desired tasks in a clandestine fashion. To achieve this, some groups recruit based on ethnicity, because the solidarity and shared values produced by ethnic homogeneity are thought to enhance group cohesion and a sense of belonging, which often result in higher levels of trust and secrecy. Yet, placing ethnic limitations on membership hinders an organization's ability to recruit the best people for a particular task, which further inhibits its ability to operate opportunistically. Thus, while some groups benefit from the high levels of secrecy and solidarity produced by their ethnic similarity, they are simultaneously limited by the type of people they may recruit. This likely explains why the American Mafia was replaced in the international drug market by an assortment of multiethnic criminal networks.

Charlie "Lucky" Luciano became known as the father of U.S. organized crime after he split the New York City area into five Mafia crime families, established the first commission, and was the first official boss of the Genovese crime family.

While it is widely accepted that some criminal organizations maintain an ethnic requirement for full membership in their group/family/organization, criminologist J. Albanese cautions that generalizing this element to all groups would lead one to fall into an "ethnic trap." To this point, modern research acknowledges that while some groups are ethnically similar, it is a more appropriate description of organized crime during the late 19th and early 20th centuries, when Italian organized crime was supreme. Thus, rather than maintain the fallacious view that all organized crime is akin to the Italian Mafia, researchers and law enforcement officials have acknowledged the transnational and opportunistic nature of most contemporary criminal organizations, which requires high levels of dexterity and intergroup cooperation. For a crime group to remain influential and competitive in light of these advancements, it must be willing to cooperate with the most skilled individuals, irrespective of their ethnic origin. In this respect, contemporary organized crime functions more like a crime syndicate and less like a rigorously governed "family."

Organization Size
Identifying a criminal organization's size can be an extremely daunting task, especially for groups that operate transnationally and under a code of silence. To this end, it is necessary to consider how the size of a criminal organization fluctuates depending on the environment in which it is situated, its prestige, and its criminal involvement. For example, criminal enterprises that operate in communities characterized by a weak and corruptible governing body are more likely to expand in size, while communities possessing strong, authoritative governments are not. In addition to its immediate environment, a criminal organization's size is shaped by the nature of its criminal involvement. Specifically, the size of a criminal enterprise may reflect a need to be covert, opportunistic, or undoubtedly present. For crimes such as international drug, human, and vehicle trafficking, where the need to be unnoticed is high, criminal organizations alter their size to be no larger or more pronounced than is necessary. Additionally, because the number of criminal enterprises has increased in the past two decades, the need to be opportunistic and competitive is more important now than it was in previous years. This point is illustrated by the assortment of constantly expanding Mexican drug cartels.

Attempting to meet the high U.S. demand for illicit narcotics (e.g., cocaine and methamphetamines), Mexican drug cartels have been engaged in violent turf wars over the best trafficking routes to California, New Mexico, Arizona, and Texas, which has expanded their violent presence to several cities in the United States as well. As a result, they have been purposively targeted by competitive crime syndicates, as well as both U.S. and Mexican law enforcement agencies, which only seems to perpetuate their growth and propensity toward violence. Thus, despite law enforcement officials' ability to hinder their operations in the past, the lucrative and prestigious nature of drug trafficking in Mexico seems to outweigh the fear of potentially being apprehended by law enforcement officials, as is evident by their continued growth in the international drug market. In addition to the above-mentioned factors, a discussion of the strengths and weaknesses for small and large criminal organizations is warranted.

Most crime groups are small, unsophisticated in both operation and structure, and have little to no reputation; however, because of their simplicity, they also tend to be highly mobilized, opportunistic, and lucrative. In contrast, J. Finckenauer and E. Waring illustrate the value of large criminal organizations by arguing that they are more sophisticated in both operation and structure, better able to participate in multiple criminal enterprises, and comprise members that tend to see themselves as belonging to an accredited group. Additionally, M. Bouchard and F. Ouellet suggest that large criminal organizations are valuable because of their inherent access to more resources (e.g., social capital). Despite each of these desired attributes, large criminal organizations are negatively impacted by their heightened exposure to attacks by law enforcement and their inability to mobilize quickly. Although each of the aforementioned sizes has strengths and weaknesses, determining which one to operate under is usually contingent on the type of crime being committed and the multiplicity of craft required to be successful.

As Albanese demonstrates, international drug trafficking networks must be larger and more sophisticated than street-level drug dealers because of the intricacy involved in (1) obtaining the raw substance, (2) processing the end product, (3) transporting the end product to consumer nations, and (4) "laundering" or transporting the illicitly obtained funds back to the original source. Given the elaborate and demanding process described by Albanese, it is easy to see why transnational organized crime groups recruit and/ or cooperate based on an individual's skill sct and/ or position (e.g., geographically or politically) rather than ethnicity. Moreover, beyond demonstrating the salience of dexterity, it also illustrates why an organization needs to be large enough to handle the intricacies of transnational crime while accounting for the increased likelihood of obstruction by law enforcement officials.

To the contrary, while international drug trafficking is necessary when the raw substances are located in other part of the world (e.g., coca and opioids), drugs such as marijuana and methamphetamines tend to be grown/manufactured locally and, consequently, require less manpower and sophisticated trafficking methods. As a result, their organizations tend to be smaller in size and more simplistic in their operations. Despite the inherent weaknesses of being small (e.g., less social capital, less opportunity to expand, etc.), these criminal organizations benefit from their ability to mobilize quickly and operate clandestinely. A criminal organization's size can fluctuate quite dramatically, depending on the current task; thus, law enforcement officials are able to combat a criminal enterprise most efficiently only after identifying its environment, type and complexity of criminal involvement, and level of prestige.

Hierarchy

The hierarchy of organized crime varies dramatically depending on its division of labor, ethnic makeup, and desire to be opportunistic. The American Mafia, Hells Angels motorcycle club, and other large organizations maintain a strict vertical hierarchy with a strong central governing body, which usually comprises identifiable leaders and homogeneous members. Under this structure, assignments/tasks are generated at the top and distributed to the lower entourage. Because groups operating under this structure are complex, large, have a division of labor, and are therefore easier to manage, a vertical hierarchy is often the preferred structure. However, while they benefit from the organizational element, groups operating under this structure are simultaneously weakened by their exposure (i.e., ease of identification) to outsiders, such as law enforcement officials. During the notorious years of the American Mafia (i.e., preceding the 1970s), this stern structure allowed leaders of the various Italian American families to maintain an influential role (by allocating tasks and scheduling "hits") without falling victim to attacks by law enforcement. However, after the United States passed the Racketeer Influenced and Corrupt Organizations Act (RICO) in 1970, federal prosecutors were able to arrest influential mobsters and apply long prison sentences for charges that were previously unavailable to them. In response to legal developments such as this, criminal organizations began operating under a different hierarchical structure, or refrained from acquiring one at all.

This second, and more popular, hierarchy is horizontal, meaning that it does not have a top-down structure but rather operates without a clearly identified leader. An organization with this structure includes a decentralized and flexible network and no (or very few) identifiable leaders. Organized crime groups structured by horizontal hierarchy are problematic for law enforcement officials because they make it extremely difficult to identify individuals occupying leadership positions. The types of criminal organizations most likely to use this hierarchy are often opportunistic, well protected, ethnically heterogeneous, and well equipped to handle adversity. Moreover, specific groups that would fit this structure include most drug cartels, the Russian Mafia, the Chinese Mafia, and profit-oriented criminal networks comprising individuals with or without allegiance to another organization.

Longevity

The longevity of criminal organizations such as the Hells Angels, Outlaws, and the American, Chinese, and Russian Mafia reflect the ability of organized crime groups to react and adapt to changing environments. While criminal organizations utilize tactics such as secrecy and decentralization to combat attacks by law enforcement, they also

A 1988 press conference of the Soviet Public Prosecution Office's team investigating the existence of an official Russian Mafia look at gold coins, jewelry, and other valuables confiscated from high-ranking bribetakers.

face advances in technology (e.g., tracing credit cards and Internet portals, wiretapping, etc.) and globalization that challenge their ability to remain intact. Contemporary organized crime groups must overcome the traditional obstacle of evading attacks by law enforcement officials while simultaneously remaining competitive in their respective markets; however, because of the recent advances in technology, this requires that they update their methods of operation in conjunction with the latest innovations.

Throughout the early and mid-1900s, the American Mafia exploited the public's demand for illicit goods and services. For American Mafia families residing in Chicago during Prohibition (1920–33), this involved trafficking and distributing bootleg liquor; for the Las Vegas–based families operating during the 1940s, it included providing illicit gambling services. Moreover, for the Russian Mafia located in Pennsylvania, fraud was seen as the quintessential method of obtaining funds. For example, during the early 1990s members of the Russian Mafia created an automobile insurance ring that appeared legitimate to the outside world but eventually claimed more than $1 million in fraudulent claims. Since that time, the Russian Mafia has advanced its involvement in fraud to include the production of counterfeit credit cards, checks, Immigration and Naturalization Service documents, and passports. Additionally, various other organized crime groups have expanded their criminal involvement to include diamond smuggling, counterfeiting, and cybercrime, which includes, among many others, online pornography and hacking (e.g., into a victim's bank account). What is interesting about the level of evolution for these and other criminal organizations is their use of innovative techniques to stay modern. Without such practices, it is unlikely that they would continue their longevity.

For contemporary organized crime groups to successfully maintain both business operations and defense strategies, they must use and/or threaten to use violence. Whether it is because of lack of payment for drug transactions, refusal to pay gambling debts, potential testimony against a fellow member, or any assortment of acts in opposition to the criminal organization's wishes, the use or threat of violence is considered a valuable method for reaching a desired end. In support of this fact, two members of the American Mafia—Al Capone of Chicago and John Gotti of New York—gained more popularity in their respective communities than many politicians because of the fear they instilled in others. Additionally, the Mara Salvatrucha (MS-13)—a multiethnic gang that originated in a California prison—is known to have increased rapidly in size and reputation because of its propensity toward violent behavior. After consideration of the nature of organized criminal behavior, which relies on fear as a method of coercion and policing, it is logical that the use or threat of violence would be considered a necessary element to remain influential in the criminal underworld. Understandably, the criminal underworld cannot rely on law enforcement officials to reconcile their differences; thus, utilizing violence and fear as a form of retaliation is an imaginable alternative.

Given the ubiquitous nature of law enforcement, it is not plausible for many criminal organizations to remain authoritative in their respective markets without ensuring immunity from the state. Unfortunately, the corrupting and coercing of politicians, law enforcement officials, and prosecutors occurs throughout the world, including the United States. However, documenting the occurrence of corruption is extremely difficult because (1) politicians, law enforcement officials, and prosecutors are not likely to admit having engaged in corruption irrespective of its voluntary or coerced nature; and (2) the people generally conducting research on corruption (i.e., the government) are the ones who would be involved in it. Nevertheless, there are several well-known occurrences of it in the United States. For example, the Chicago families that operated during the 1920s pursued higher levels of prestige by capitalizing on the illicit liquor market produced by Prohibition. During this era, Mafia families had to cultivate useful relations with local police and government officials if they wanted to remain prominent suppliers of bootleg liquor. Had they not done so, it is more likely that they would have been apprehended or, at the very least, had their operations interrupted.

Causes of Organized Crime
It is widely accepted that most criminal organizations form because of an opportunity for financial gain. Therefore, organized crime groups are most likely to prosper in communities that have a weak and/or corruptible government and a population that demands illicit goods and services. Additionally, organized crime is often caused by immigration, the globalized economy, easy transnational travel and communication, political change, and other criminal organizations meeting their demise. The Colombian drug cartels, for example, were successful because of Colombia's weak government and the cartels' ties to criminal organizations in other parts of the world.

For these drug cartels, collecting and manufacturing cocaine was simple, because their government was weak and incapable of disrupting their operations; however, because of the unflattering state of their economy, the cartels were unable to sell their finished product locally and therefore needed to reach consumer markets in other parts of the world. Given that the two largest consumers of illicit substances are North America and Europe, the drug cartels were forced to form business alliances with criminal organizations in these countries. In the United States, the drug cartels have been known to cooperate with the Hells Angels, the American Mafia, and the Russian Mafia. In this example, the drug cartels were successful because of a weak governing body, the ease of transnational trafficking, and the presence of a consumer market. Additional occurrences of organized crime being cultivated are the result of increases in immigration and the changing nature of organized crime—usually in response to heightened attacks by law enforcement officials.

The development of organized crime is often the result of increases in immigration to a particular country. In the United States, this was most evident during the late 1800s and early 1900s when Italian, Irish, German, and Russian immigration increased. What is most fascinating about this link between immigration and organized crime is the behaviors and ideologies many of the mobsters transferred from their homeland. For the Sicilians settling in the United States, this involved the ideologies of secrecy, solidarity, and distrust for authority, which developed after being negatively affected by years of suppressive and treacherous dictators. Similarly, individuals who immigrated to the United States from the former Soviet Union were reluctant to trust government officials and, resulting from their experiences with corrupt governing bodies, carried little remorse about stealing from those dissimilar to themselves.

This fact may explain why the Russian Mafia prefers fraud as its primary means of income. Each of these causes of organized crime brings attention to the salience of an evolving society that is both positively and negatively affected by advances in technology. Because of advances in the ease of travel and communication (e.g., the Internet), countries like the United States are influenced by the ideologies of other countries. While this influence is considered a positive when the ideologies are beneficial, it is often not the case regarding individuals interested in criminal involvement. It is therefore helpful to review the causes of organized crime in other parts of the world in order to better understand the causes and influences of organized crime in the United States.

Conclusion
The sociology of organized crime is often concerned with the causes, structure, historical development, and criminal involvement of varying groups. Regarding the causes, it is generally agreed that organized crime is most likely to

exist in communities that desire illicit goods and services and lack a strong governing body. Moreover, because of technological advances in travel and communication, people studying organized crime are forced to consider its presence in cyberspace and parts of the world containing copious amounts of illicit substances (e.g., opium and coca), thus illuminating the unbounded nature of crime. Considering the transnational nature of crime, it is imperative that criminal organizations be described in reference to the social forces likely to alter their structure and criminal involvement because, as this entry suggests, the nature of organized crime is constantly changing and adapting to the rest of the world.

Nick C. Athey
Simon Fraser University
Weston Morrow
Arizona State University

See Also: 1941 to 1960 Primary Documents; 1961 to 1980 Primary Documents; 2001 to 2012 Primary Documents; Organized Crime, Contemporary; Organized Crime, History of; Terrorism.

Further Readings
Albanese, J. S. *Organized Crime in Our Times*, 5th ed. Newark, NJ: Matthew Bender & Co., 2007.
Bouchard, M. and F. Ouellet. "Is Small Beautiful? The Link Between Risks and Size in Illegal Drug Markets." *Global Crime*, v.12/1 (2011).
Finckenauer, J. O. and E. J. Waring. *Russian Mafia in America: Immigration, Culture, and Crime*. Lebanon, NH: Northeastern University Press, 1998.
Reuter, P. "The Decline of the American Mafia." *Public Interest*, v.120 (1995).
Roth, M. P. *Global Organized Crime: A Reference Handbook*. Santa Barbara, CA: ABC-CLIO, 2010.
Siegel, D., H. van de Bunt, and D. Zaitch, eds. *Global Organized Crime Trends and Developments*. Norwell, MA: Kluwer Academic, 2003.

Oswald, Lee Harvey

Born in Slidell, Louisiana, Lee Harvey Oswald (1939–63) was raised by a single mother and two older brothers. The family moved several times within the Louisiana and Texas area, living in 22 different homes throughout his childhood. Oswald was never one for traditional schooling, skipping most of his classes starting in the eighth grade, leaving him to roam the streets of whatever city he may have lived in at the time. He was caught by a truant officer at one time and was sent to a youth detention center for three weeks. There, he received a psychiatric evaluation and was found to be nonemotional and introverted, possessing the feeling that no one cared about him. As a child, Oswald was deeply interested in politics and socialism, joining the Young People's Socialist League when he was 16 years of age. He has stated that his interest in politics stemmed from the reading of a political pamphlet announcing the execution of Ethel and Julius Rosenberg (who were accused of selling secrets to the Soviet Union).

Military Service
Oswald attempted to sign up for service with the Marine Corps in 1955 but was rejected because of his age. He instead joined the Civil Air Patrol, a youth auxiliary of the Air Force. A year later, in October 1956, he entered the U.S. Marine Corps, only a week after he turned 17. While in the Marine Corps, Oswald received extensive marksmanship training, making him a skilled shooter. During his training and service, Oswald discussed with his fellow recruits his radical political views and pro-Soviet tendencies. Only a year into his enlistment, Oswald accidentally shot himself with an illegally obtained pistol. He was court-martialed for the incident and later attacked the sergeant he believed was responsible for his punishment. He was court-martialed a second time for the assault. Around this time, he began to learn the Russian language and follow Marxism.

Based on a hardship plea by Oswald, the Marine Corps released him in September 1959. Just nine days after his release, Oswald left the country to travel through France and England, ending in the Soviet Union to attempt to relocate and to obtain citizenship. Deeply dissatisfied with the American way of life and values, Oswald wanted to become a citizen of the Soviet Union; however, he was denied asylum. Upon receipt of this news, Oswald attempted suicide for the first time. He was later recruited by the KGB (Soviet Union national security agency) for a short time, but never joined their ranks.

Assassination of President Kennedy

In 1961, Oswald's love affair with the Soviet Union came to a halt, leaving him to appear at the U.S. Embassy to request his return to the United States. Eighteen months later, the newly married Oswald and his wife, Marina Prusakova, moved to America to begin their life together. Upon arrival, Oswald was questioned by the Federal Bureau of Investigation (FBI) and was found to be aggressive and evasive. The couple moved to Dallas, Texas, where Oswald created his first alias: Alek J. Hidell. While living in Dallas, Oswald showed signs of losing control of his rage and temper, picking fights with family and with his wife. He became a supporter of Fidel Castro, and became even more critical of U.S. policies under the Kennedy administration. He traveled to New Orleans and Mexico City to promote his pro-Castro sentiments. Again, Oswald tried to return to the Soviet Union, but after his application for residency was denied, he returned to Dallas and got a job at the Texas School Book Depository.

On November 22, 1963, President John F. Kennedy was traveling via chauffeured car through the streets of Dallas. When the car the president was traveling in reached Dealey Plaza at 12:30 p.m., three shots were fired at Kennedy, striking him in the head and causing his death. The majority of witnesses stated that they believed the shots came from the Texas School Book Depository. An investigation by the Warren Commission, headed by U.S. Supreme Court Chief Justice Earl Warren, followed the assassination.

The commission determined that Lee Harvey Oswald committed the assassination of President John F. Kennedy. According to the report, Oswald woke up that morning and left his wife, Marina, with his wedding ring and cash. When he left his home, he was carrying an oblong package that was wrapped in brown paper; he told his neighbor it was a curtain rod. Oswald spent the morning filling book orders at the School Book Depository and stated that he spent his lunchtime with two coworkers. However, his coworkers denied this fact; it is thought that Oswald remained on the sixth floor of the building.

Three minutes after the assassination took place, Oswald was seen walking out the front door of the Book Depository. He then boarded a bus but hastily disembarked and got into a taxi after the bus hit traffic. He was dropped off a couple of blocks away from a rooming house he had in Oak Cliff. He acquired a .38 revolver and left the house. Soon after he left the rooming house, Oswald encountered Dallas police officer J. D. Tippit, whom he then shot with his revolver. An eyewitness stated that Oswald was the shooter, and that after the shooting, he ran to the Texas Theater; Oswald was apprehended there by police. The FBI crime lab collected the bullets and cartridges from the scene, and they were matched to Oswald's revolver; although the bullet recovered from Tippit was fired from a

Jack Beers, Jr., a Dallas Morning News photographer, captured the moment when Lee Harvey Oswald was shot by Jack Ruby (in foreground) as Oswald was being moved by police in 1963.

barrel that was bored out, the hammer markings matched. After Oswald was questioned by police for murdering Tippit, he was declared a suspect in the Kennedy assassination. Oswald was charged with the murder of President Kennedy and was scheduled to be transferred for interrogation. In route, he was shot and killed by Jack Ruby, a Dallas nightclub owner.

To this day, there is much debate by the public and political officials alike concerning the assassination of President Kennedy. Many conspiracy theories have circulated throughout the years concerning how the assassination took place and who "really" committed the act. Many believe that there were actually four shots fired that fateful day, and that there had to have been two different gunmen to pull off the assassination. Some believe the shooting was a part of a large conspiracy fashioned by the mob, the Central Intelligence Agency (CIA), and/or Castro extremists.

Melissa J. Mauck
Sam Houston State University

See Also: 1961 to 1980 Primary Documents; Ballistics; Federal Bureau of Investigation; Guns and Violent Crime; Kennedy, John F. (Administration of); Secret Service.

Further Readings
Cardinale, Krysta. "Lee Harvey Oswald Biography." *Encyclomedia.* http://www.encyclomedia.com/lee_harvey_oswald.html (Accessed September 2011).
"Lee Harvey Oswald." *Biography.* http://www.biography.com/articles/Lee-Harvey-Oswald-9430309 (Accessed September 2011).
McAdams, John. "The Kennedy Assassination." http://mcadams.posc.mu.edu/home.htm (Accessed September 2011).
Public Broadcasting System. "Who Was Lee Harvey Oswald?" *Frontline.* http://www.pbs.org/wgbh/pages/frontline/shows/oswald/cron (Accessed September 2011).
Simon, Jonathan. "Ghosts of the Disciplinary Machine: Lee Harvey Oswald, Life-History, and the Truth of Crime." *Yale Journal of Law & the Humanities,* v.10/75 (1998).

Padilla v. Kentucky

Padilla v. Kentucky is a 2010 U.S. Supreme Court ruling that stipulates under the Sixth Amendment that the attorney and/or defense counsel of a noncitizen client charged with a crime is required to advise the client about the risk of deportation from the United States upon entering a guilty plea.

Jose Padilla was born and spent his early formative years in Honduras. Immigrating to the United States in the 1960s, he became a lawful permanent resident. Padilla later served honorably in the U.S. military and fought in the Vietnam War. For over 40 years, he was a legal resident of the United States, where he later became a licensed commercial truck driver. In September 2001, a Kentucky law enforcement officer conducted a traffic stop on Padilla in order to perform a routine document check on his truck. During the traffic stop, the officer obtained consent from Padilla to conduct a search of his vehicle, where he located 23 separately wrapped Styrofoam boxes in the trailer area that did not appear on the truck's manifest. The officer reported that he asked Padilla if he knew the content of the boxes and Padilla replied "maybe drugs." A subsequent search revealed the boxes contained nearly half a ton of marijuana. Padilla was arrested and later indicted by a Hardin County grand jury on drug trafficking and other related charges. Padilla was appointed state-funded legal counsel and was unsuccessful in his motion to suppress the key evidence in the case (the consent to search the vehicle and his confession). Subsequently, in 2002, Padilla pled guilty to trafficking more than five pounds of marijuana, possession of marijuana, and possession of drug paraphernalia.

Based upon Padilla's plea agreement, he would serve a five-year prison sentence and serve the remaining five years on probation. During his conversations regarding a plea agreement, Padilla claimed that his defense counsel never advised him that under federal criminal codes his drug conviction was considered an "aggravated offense," making it a deportable crime. Padilla also claimed he was instructed by his defense counsel that, based on his long residency in the United States (over 40 years), he would not have to worry about deportation.

In August 2004, fearing deportation from the United States, Padilla filed a motion for post-conviction relief with the Hardin County Circuit Court. Post-conviction relief is a generic term referring to the formal appeal of a criminal conviction, which if granted by the court may include a new trial, modification of a sentence, or even release. Padilla claimed that his constitutional rights under the Sixth Amendment, specifically regarding effective counsel, had been violated. Padilla claimed that he would have never accepted a plea agreement had his attorney advised him of the deportation consequences. Under *Padilla*, 253 S.W.3d at 483, the court denied the motion for relief, finding that defense counsel is not required to inform a client of the "collateral consequences" of a guilty plea in order for the plea to be valid. The Kentucky Court of Appeals later reversed the decision (*Padilla*, 253 S.W.3d at 483-84), remanding the case for an evidentiary hearing. The Court of Appeals ruled that although the Sixth Amendment does not require full disclosure of all collateral consequences of criminal convictions by legal counsel, such as deportation, to validate a guilty plea, the affirmative act of grossly misadvising a client can justify post-conviction relief. In January 2008, The Kentucky Supreme Court later reversed this decision (*Padilla*, 253 S.W.3d at 483-84), ruling that a defense counsel's failure to advise a client of collateral consequences or misadvising regarding collateral consequences does not provide a basis for post-conviction relief.

In March 2010, the Supreme Court of the United States heard the case and reversed the Kentucky Supreme Court, ruling that under the Sixth Amendment, defense counsel of a noncitizen client charged with crime is required to advise the client about the risk of deportation upon entering a guilty plea. The court supported the ruling by confirming that recent changes to immigration laws have dramatically raised the stakes of a noncitizen's criminal conviction, including reforms that have expanded the class of deportable offenses, for which deportation is now virtually inevitable for a vast number of noncitizens convicted of crimes. The U.S. Supreme Court added that accurate legal advice for noncitizens accused of crimes has never been more important thus, as a matter of federal law, deportation is an integral part of the penalty that may be imposed on noncitizen defendants who plead guilty to specified crimes.

Tony Gaskew
University of Pittsburgh at Bradford

See Also: Customs Service as Police; Defendant's Rights; Homeland Security.

Further Readings
Baum, Lawrence. *American Courts: Process and Policy*. Belmont, CA: Wadsworth, 2012.

Hails, Judy. *Criminal Evidence*. Belmont, CA: Wadsworth, 2011.
Hartzler, Kara. *Surviving* Padilla. Raleigh, NC: Lulu, 2011.

Paine, Thomas

Thomas Paine (1737–1809) was born in Thetford, England, and began his life as a corseter's son. At birth, has name was Pain, and the change is spelling is somewhat disputed. Evidence shows that he spelled it "Paine" by 1769, while he was still living in England. At 13, he began working as his father's apprentice, but this trade did not initially suit him. At 19, he enlisted and briefly served in the navy. After returning to Britain, he set up a business in Kent, and shortly after, he married Mary Lambert. His wife died in childbirth, along with their child, and Paine drifted afterward. He briefly served as an excise officer. After being deposed of his post twice in four years, he had brief stints as a minister, a schoolteacher, and a tobacco shop owner.

In 1768, Paine moved to Lewes, where he lived above the tobacco shop of Samuel and Esther Ollive. Samuel Ollive introduced him to the Society of Twelve, an elite intellectual group that discussed town politics. While living here, Paine married Elizabeth Ollive. In the midst of a new marriage and finding a place within society, Paine joined local excise officers in asking Parliament for better pay and working conditions. In 1772, he published a 21-page article, "The Case of the Officers of Excise," arguing for the cause. Over the next two years, he lost his job and business because of extended absences brought on by his travel and writings, and in April 1774, he sold his household possessions to avoid debtor's prison. In June 1774, he formally separated from his wife and moved to London. By happenstance, that September a friend introduced him to Benjamin Franklin. By this point, Paine had developed a sense of political fervor, and in his conversations with Franklin, the two discussed the fate of the colonies. Franklin encouraged Paine to move to Philadelphia, and he gave him a letter of recommendation. In October, Paine left Great Britain; he arrived in Philadelphia in November.

American Political Writing

After spending nearly six weeks recovering from the voyage, Paine became the editor of the *Pennsylvania Magazine* in January 1775. He held the post ably, and shortly after arriving in Philadelphia, Paine began joining local democratic groups discussing the rising protests and royal taxes. In 1776, taken up with the colonial cause, he published *Common Sense*. *Common Sense* appeared after the revolution began, but it was widely recognized as important and was immediately popular. Individuals read it aloud in taverns, and his use of plain language and concise writing, and his call for immediate separation from Britain helped solidify the work as part of the popular rhetoric. Most significantly, since the Continental Congress was more concerned with how independence would affect the war effort, *Common Sense* did more for the general public as a rally cry and call for support. The core of the argument rested on the belief that monarchies ruled by force, making them an illegitimate form of government.

In late 1776, Paine published *The Crisis* to inspire the revolutionaries on the battlefront. He described Americans as devoted to civic virtue and opposing the selfish provincial man, and the pamphlet proved extremely popular among the troops. George Washington even had it read aloud to troops. Paine became a hero during the Revolutionary War, but shortly after, he left America to return to Europe. He felt the need to continue to write for social and political reform there. He published *The Rights of Man* in 1792—his anti-monarchy stance in support of the French

A statue of Thomas Paine stands in Thetford, Norfolk, England, where he was born. He moved to the British American colonies in 1774 in time for the American Revolution. His main contributions were Common Sense *and the widely read* The American Crisis, *a prorevolutionary pamphlet series written between 1776 and 1783.*

Revolution. He fled England for France, where in 1793, he was imprisoned because he refused to support the execution of Louis XVI. James Monroe worked to prevent his execution, and Paine left France in 1802 when Thomas Jefferson invited him back to the United States. During this period in England and France, Paine published *The Age of Reason*, an antichurch text, and he learned upon his arrival in the states that he was held in disregard by most of the public for his religious stance. He died in New York City in 1809.

Paine's political writings reflected revolutionary fervor, but they also called upon the individual to engage in acts of civil disobedience. Refusal to pay taxes, boycotting, and taking up arms for a revolution were considered treasonous to supporters of the king. After the American Revolution, Paine's continual calls for a revolution in government every generation threatened the newly formed government. Although Paine ended his days amid public rejection, his ideas have inspired many people in later generations.

Annessa A. Babic
New York Institute of Technology

See Also: American Revolution and Criminal Justice; Colonial Courts; Political Dissidents.

Further Readings
Loughran, Trish. *The Republic in Print: Print Culture in the Age of U.S. Nation Building, 1770–1870.* New York: Columbia University Press, 2009.
Paine, Thomas. *Common Sense.* New York: Tribeca Books, 2011.
Paine, Thomas. *Writings of Thomas Paine—Volume 1 (1774–1779): The American Crisis.* Memphis, TN: General Books, 2010.

Paretsky, Sara

Sara Paretsky is a novelist and editor of more than 20 books. She is best known for her crime and detective fiction and as the creator of the female private eye Victoria Iphigenia (V. I.) Warshawski. Paretsky was born in Ames, Iowa, on June 8, 1947, the daughter of physicist David Paretsky and librarian Mary E. Edwards Paretsky. Paretsky and her family moved to Lawrence, Kansas, in 1951. After receiving her bachelor's degree in political science from the University of Kansas in 1967, Paretsky moved to Chicago. She briefly worked as a secretary at the University of Chicago before earning a university fellowship and going on to complete a Ph.D. in American history in 1977. Her dissertation "Words, Works, and Ways of Knowing: The Breakdown of Moral Philosophy in New England Before the Civil War" examined 19th-century Calvinists, or "Christian scholars," at Andover Seminary in Massachusetts.

The poor employment market in higher education convinced Paretsky to study for a business degree. The same year she earned her Ph.D., she also received an M.B.A. from the University of Chicago. From 1977 to 1986, Paretsky managed the advertising and direct mail marketing programs at CNA Insurance Company, observing the insurance industry firsthand. The experience proved invaluable in developing the various white-collar crimes V. I. Warshawski later investigated.

Paretsky began writing fiction when she was not bust working at CNA. She was critical of the way women were traditionally portrayed as powerless victims or evil femme fatales in crime and hard-boiled detective novels. Paretsky envisioned a lady private eye with a feminist sensibility. Thus was born V. I. Warshawski, the multiethnic offspring of a Polish American policeman and an Italian-Jewish mother.

V. I. Warshawski is a product of the women's movement and a new kind of private investigator. Warshawksi's sexual independence and tough intelligence departs from the persona of the elderly Miss Marple in Agatha Christie novels, as well as the social anomie characteristic of Dashiell Hammett's Sam Spade or Raymond Chandler's Philip Marlowe. Rather, Warshawski identifies with the underdog and downtrodden while maintaining emotional connections to family, friends, and community.

Paretsky's mysteries are geographically and socially rooted in Chicago. In the early novels, V. I. Warshawski resides in the Lakeview neighborhood along Halsted Street, just north of Belmont Avenue. In *Indemnity Only* (1982), her protagonists include a North Shore banker, a union leader, University of Chicago students, and insurance agents. Warshawski tackles Chicago's shipping business in *Deadlock* (1984). *Killing Orders* (1985) examines Roman Catholicism as Warshawski investigates a Chicago monastery with missing funds and eventually exposes church corruption. The flooding of Chicago's underground tunnels in the central business district in 1992 is relived in *Tunnel Vision* (1994). *Burn Marks* (1989) investigates corruption and murder in Chicago's construction industry.

Paretsky's vivid renderings of Chicago have generated comparisons with prominent authors such as Nelson Algren. But her fiction also epitomizes the Chicago-based urban realism associated with Theodore Dreiser, Frank Norris, Carl Sandberg, Gwendolyn Brooks, and Studs Terkel. Just as Brooks's *In the Mecca* (1968) transformed a single South Side apartment building into a paradoxical emblem of African American life and urban renewal, and Terkel's *Division Street* (1967) made that local thoroughfare a symbolic divide in Chicago and the entire United States, Paretsky's V. I. Warshawski evokes a gritty, pragmatic feminism confronting the raw, unrefined, and violent elements of the late-20th-century, deindustrialized metropolis.

The popularity of the Warshawski series generated multiple awards for Paretsky. In 1987, *Ms. Magazine* named Paretsky Woman of the Year. In 1996, she received the Mark Twain Award for distinguished contribution to Midwest literature. The British Crime Writers Association honored Paretsky with the Cartier Diamond Dagger Award for lifetime achievement in 2002 (the first non-British writer to receive the award) and the best novel of 2004 (*Blacklist*). Her 2007 memoir, *Writing in an Age of Silence*, was a National Book Critics Circle Award finalist.

Timothy J. Gilfoyle
Loyola University Chicago

See Also: Chicago, Illinois; Christie, Agatha; Literature and Theater, Crime in; Private Detectives.

Further Readings
Gilfoyle, Timothy J. "A Writing Crime in Chicago: An Interview With Sara Paretsky." *Chicago History*, v.31/3 (2003).

Paretsky, Sara. *Breakdown*. New York: Penguin Books, 2012.
Paretsky, Sara. *Indemnity Only*. New York: Random House, 1991.

Parker, Isaac

Isaac Charles Parker (1838–96) was born in Ohio. Much has been written about his life and legal career, and he is one of the best-known judicial figures in American history. He is known as "the Hanging Judge" because of his willingness to sentence offenders to the gallows. This readiness to employ capital punishment makes him a somewhat divisive figure in American history.

Early Career
At age 17, Parker began studying law. After studying for the bar exam largely on his own, he was admitted to the Ohio Bar Association in 1859. Shortly thereafter, he moved west and began practicing law in St. Louis, Missouri. Initially a Democrat, Parker was elected to the office of city attorney, but within days, the Civil War broke out and he reexamined his political views. He ended up fighting vigorously to keep Missouri in the Union and was an enlisted member of the 61st Missouri Emergency Regiment, a guard for Union forces.

Parker was elected to the office of prosecutor (on the Republican ticket) in Buchanan County, Missouri, and by the age of 30, he had been elected to the bench of the 13th Judicial District in Missouri. In 1870, Parker resigned his bench and served two consecutive terms in Congress as a representative from Missouri. After Parker made an unsuccessful bid for the U.S. Senate, President Ulysses S. Grant nominated him to be the chief justice to the Utah Territory. Before the nomination was finalized, Parker requested that the nomination be changed so that he could be a judge in the U.S. District Court for the state of Arkansas and the Indian Territories. It is largely unknown why he requested this change, though Mary Stolberg speculates that he might have desired the lifetime appointment that came with the Arkansas bench. His nomination was confirmed, and he was sworn into office on March 25, 1875.

Isaac Charles Parker served as a U.S. district judge for 21 years. He is remembered today as the "Hanging Judge" of the American Old West, sentencing 160 people to death.

An Earned Reputation

When Parker arrived in Fort Smith, Arkansas, he found a court that was rife with corruption and that was essentially in chaos. Several clerks were accused of embezzlement, and the previous judge had stepped down amid allegations that he mismanaged court funds. In addition to corruption, there was a pervasive feeling among Fort Smith residents that Arkansas and the Indian Territories were simply out of control. In order to do his job, Parker had to fix the issues of the court, as well as win over the residents in the area. In an effort to do to the latter, it is said that he helped found a library and hospital in Fort Smith, as well as organize the county fair.

During his first term on the bench, Parker found eight men guilty of murder; six of them were hanged on September 3, 1875. It is important to note that during the first 14 years of his tenure, all of Parker's decisions were final. There was no appeal either by error or by writ of certiorari because the court operated largely as a circuit court. The situation changed on February 6, 1889, when Congress stipulated that death penalty cases could be reviewed—and possibly reversed—by the U.S. Supreme Court. Nearly two-thirds of Parker's cases were reversed and remanded back to Fort Smith for new trials.

In an effort to hear as many cases as possible, Parker would often hold court six days a week for at least 10 hours a day. During Parker's 21 years on the bench, he tried 13,490 cases (most of them criminal cases); 9,454 resulted in guilty verdicts. While he is often referred to as "the Hanging Judge," it was ultimately a jury that made the decision between guilt and innocence, and in Parker's view, he was upholding the law by passing down death sentences. All told, he sentenced 160 people to death (four of them were women), and of those, 79 were hanged on the gallows. Some notorious outlaws were among the 160 people sentenced to death by Parker. One such group was the Rufus Buck Gang, a five-member group comprising four Native Americans (Sam Sampson, Maoma July, and brothers Lewis and Lucky Davis) and led by Rufus Buck. During the summer of 1895, they went on a crime spree in which they raped, murdered, robbed, and generally terrorized citizens in the Indian Territory.

Parker's last term on the bench began in the summer of 1896, but he was too ill to hold court, and he passed away on November 17, 1896. He is buried in the Fort Smith National Cemetery.

Laurie A. Gould
Georgia Southern University

See Also: Arkansas; Capital Punishment; Judges and Magistrates.

Further Readings

Brodhead, Michael. *Isaac C. Parker: Federal Justice on the Frontier*. Norman: University of Oklahoma Press, 2003.

Miller, John. "Isaac C. Parker." *Arkansas Historical Quarterly*, v.31 (1972).

Radcliff, Miranda. "Isaac Charles Parker." *Encyclopedia of Arkansas History and Culture*. http://encyclopediaofarkansas.net/encyclopedia/entry-detail.aspx?entryID=1732 (Accessed September 2011).

Stolberg, Mary. "Politician, Populist, Reformer: A Reexamination of 'Hanging Judge' Isaac C. Parker." *Arkansas Historical Quarterly*, v.47 (1988).

Parker, William

William H. Parker (June 21, 1905–July 16, 1966) rose through the ranks to become chief of the Los Angeles Police Department (LAPD). A member of the LAPD for 39 years (1927–66), he is the longest serving chief in the department's history (1950–66). Following his death, the Police Administration Building (which was replaced in 2009) was renamed in his honor.

Parker was born in Deadwood, South Dakota. His parents were William and Mary Katherine Moore Parker. His family moved from Lead, South Dakota, to Los Angeles in 1922. Parker, who was an attorney, joined the Los Angeles Police Department on August 8, 1927. As a police officer advancing through the ranks, Parker avoided the corrupt police culture where officers routinely beat suspects and engaged in graft in alcohol, prostitution, and vice. He served as an LAPD officer for 15 years before taking a leave to serve in World War II. He received a Purple Heart after being wounded during the Normandy invasion, and an Italian Star and a Silver Star. He later helped "de-Nazify" local police forces in Germany and Italy as the Allies advanced. When he returned to the LAPD after the war, he was reassigned to basic patrol status in the LAPD. He became deputy chief and the first head of the bureau of internal affairs. The Brenda Allen scandal rocked the department in 1949, when it was revealed that members of the LAPD's vice squad had offered "protection" to gambling and prostitution operations and that they had attempted "shake down" organized crime figures (including Allen, who was known as the "Queen Bee of Vice") in the city. Chief Clemence B. Horrall and Assistant Chief Joe Reed resigned.

Parker became permanent police chief on August 9, 1950, and is credited with transforming the LAPD into a professional law enforcement agency. The department that he took over in 1950 was notoriously corrupt and was heavily influenced by politicians. Parker embarked on a campaign to reform the LAPD by introducing professionalism while making the department autonomous from civilian control. This effort was threatened by the "Bloody Christmas" incident, when five young Latino and two Anglo men were beaten by more than 50 police officers while they were in police custody on Christmas Day, 1951. The men had been arrested after fighting with some officers in a bar. Latin American leaders demanded greater police accountability to civilian authority. Eight officers were indicted for assault in the scandal. Five of the eight were eventually convicted, but only one was sentenced to more than a year in prison. By limiting the damage of the scandal, Parker ensured the independence of the department. Parker's efforts to root out corruption included the establishment of an "intelligence division," and the resurrection of the vice squad, designated "administrative vice." These two divisions were referred to as the "palace guards," and they reported directly to the office of the chief.

Parker's experience with military public relations in World War II was used to develop an effective media relations strategy for the police department. Following the Bloody Christmas scandal, Parker created a television program, *The Thin Blue Line*, to broadcast a favorable image of the LAPD. Through television shows such as *Dragnet*, and a steady stream of good publicity from local newspapers, he was highly admired nationwide. He introduced the motto "To Protect and to Serve" in 1955. Among the changes made by Parker were the introduction of more proactive policing methods and less use of violence but more use of force in securing areas, practices very similar to military peacekeeping methods that he was exposed to during the war.

Another change initiated by Parker was to transform the police force from one with officers on foot patrol into a force that relied on automobiles. He also reduced the size of the force. He believed that a smaller force would mean less corruption. This required a shift to more mobile policing, which allowed for faster response times from a smaller force. This also had the effect of isolating his officers from the neighborhoods they patrolled, further reducing the potential for corruption.

Parker was accused of being hostile toward African Americans and Latinos and of creating a departmental culture that tolerated brutality against minorities. Parker's police force protected white neighborhoods from "invasion" by the city's minorities, ensuring the support of whites for Parker's style of policing. Ultimately, the department's attitude toward minorities culminated in the Watts Riots of August 1965. Over six days, 34 people were killed, 1,032 injured, and 3,438 arrested. Parker's explanation of the Watts riots underscored just how disconnected the department seemed from the moment. "One person," Parker is reported to have said, "had thrown a rock, and then like monkeys in a zoo, others had started throwing rocks."

On July 16, 1966, Parker died of a heart attack. Following his death, the Los Angeles city council voted to name the police administration building the Parker Center, in honor of the chief. When a new $437 million police headquarters complex was nearing completion in 2009, a proposal to name the building for Parker was opposed by a number of political and civic leaders who blamed him for police officers' discrimination against minorities—especially blacks and Latinos—and brutality. At the building's dedication in October 2009, Mayor Antonio Ramon Villaraigosa acknowledged the controversy, stating "Our department has emerged from that dark cloud. The weight of the past instead has transformed this department into the strongest, most well-equipped, most respectful force this city has ever seen."

Jeffrey Kraus
Wagner College

See Also: 1961 to 1980 Primary Documents; Los Angeles, California; Police, Contemporary; Police, History of.

Further Readings
Buntin, John. *L.A. Noir. The Struggle for the Soul of America's Most Seductive City.* New York: Harmony Books, 2009.
Gooch, John C. "Imagining the Law and the Constitution of Societal Order in Los Angeles Police Chief William Parker's 1965 'Crime and the Great Society' Address." http://ssrn.com/abstract=1391668 (Accessed February 2011).
Kramer, Sarah Alisa. "William H. Parker and the Thin Blue Line: Politics, Public Relations and Policing in Postwar Los Angeles." Ph.D. diss., American University, 2007.
"L.A.P.D. Blues: Race, Rap and the L.A.P.D." PBS. http://www.pbs.org/wgbh/pages/frontline/shows/lapd/race/racerap.html (Accessed February 2011).

Vives, Ruben. "With New Police Headquarters, LAPD Ends an Era." *Los Angeles Times* (October 25, 2009). http://articles.latimes.com/2009/oct/25/local/me-lapd-opening25 (Accessed February 2011).
Yang, Mina. "A Thin Blue Line Down Central Avenue: The LAPD and the Demise of a Musical Hub." *Black Music Research Journal*, v.22 (2002).

Parole

Parole is the portion of state correctional systems in which convicted individuals are supervised after they have been released from prison. Parole serves two purposes: (1) to assist former prisoners in their transition from prison into the community and (2) to provide a means of early detection and sanction of potentially deviant behavior. Parole differs from probation in that probation is often used as a diversion from prison time, and parole is used as a means of supervising reentry into society. The term comes from the French word *parole,* which means "word," as in giving one's word. The U.S. parole system was based on the Irish system and introduced in 1876. Though parole is historically defined as discretionary release, many states have eliminated their parole board but maintained some form of parole or post-release supervision. Today, only Maine and Minnesota do not have either a parole board or some form of post-release supervision; the U.S. Parole Commission is in charge of parolees in Washington, D.C. As of 2008, one in 45 adults is on parole or probation, and more than 800,000 adults are on parole.

Development of the Parole System
The concept of parole first appeared in the 1600s; it was used as a way to expand the labor pool in English colonies. Children (indentured poor and delinquents) and pardoned convicts (individuals granted reprieves or stays of execution) were shipped to American colonies and became indentured servants. Initially, no conditions were placed on those pardoned to the colonies. After some convicts returned to England early, conditions were attached, the chief of which was a

specified number of marks that eventually led to freedom. Bad behavior resulted in a move back to an earlier stage.

Maconochie's mark system had five stages. First, prisoners were subject to strict imprisonment. Second, prisoners were allowed to work in work gangs. Third, prisoners were allowed freedom in a restricted area. Fourth, prisoners earned a ticket-of-leave onto parole. During this stage, prisoners earned a partial pardon and were expected to live by certain conditions of release. In the fifth and final stage, prisoners earned a complete restoration of liberty and were completely released from their sentence.

Maconochie first implemented his mark system in 1840 on Norfolk Island with much success. Colonial administrators in Australia, however, found his system to be too lenient on the prisoners, and he was relieved of his duties in 1844. In 1849, he was placed in charge of two English prisons, but criticism of his approach once again led to his dismissal. He then began advocating for penal reform and became the inspiration for a new system of leave in Ireland.

The Irish parole system was first implemented in 1853. Walter Crofton, who was appointed administrator of the Irish prison system in 1854, adopted Maconochie's mark system and created the Irish ticket-of-leave. The Irish ticket-of-leave had four stages. First, prisoners were subject to three months of reduced rations and no employment followed by six months of full rations, employment, and religious teachings. These first nine months occurred in solitary confinement. Second, inmates were moved to a congregate prison system where they worked together in groups. After earning a specified number of marks, inmates moved to the third stage, which allowed them to earn tickets-of-leave. Unlike the English and Australian systems, however, the Irish ticket-of-leave was not a permanent leave. Rather, it allowed for periodic release from the institution. In the fourth and final stage, those who had earned a ticket-of-leave could then be placed on conditional release. While on conditional release, local police officers were required to supervise these individuals, help them secure employment, verify employment, and perform periodic home visits. The individual on release was required to report to the police officer at set intervals. The role of the police officer in

The main cellblock of Dublin Prison in Dublin, Ireland. The Irish ticket-of-leave system included periodic release from prison, with the final stage allowing conditional release with supervision from local police officers.

promise not to return to England until the expiration of the sentence.

This system of parole expanded with the transportation of prisoners to Australia. In Australia, under Alexander Maconochie, who was superintendent of the penal colony at Norfolk Island off the coast of Australia, a system similar to the present-day parole system was developed. Indeed, Maconochie's system is credited as the origin of the modern-day parole system. Maconochie was critical of definitive prison sentences. He argued that sentences should not only punish individuals for their past behavior but also prepare them for life after the prison sentence. Because he believed the time necessary to prepare an individual for the future varied, he developed a system similar to modern-day indeterminate sentences. Under Maconochie's "mark" system, prisoners were rewarded for good conduct and labor. The mark system allowed prisoners to progress through stages of increased responsibility by earning a supervising those on conditional release was the precursor to the modern-day parole officer.

Parole in the United States

In 1870, Zebulon Brockway, a penologist and warden at various U.S. institutions, presented a paper based on the Irish system that described the usefulness of an indeterminate sentencing structure and a parole system at the very first meeting of the American Prison Association. Those in attendance urged New York to adopt Brockway's proposal at the recently approved Elmira Reformatory. In 1876, Brockway was appointed superintendent of the newly opened Elmira Reformatory, where he implemented his version of the Irish marks system. Once enough marks were earned, parole from Elmira required six months of supervision by reformatory authorities. It was at this time that the modern-day version of parole was first established in America.

It was not until 1907, however, that the first formalized system of parole was established. Although many states had systems of early release, New York was the first to establish a statewide parole system that required specialized agents to supervise parolees. Throughout the early 1900s, parole grew in popularity. By 1927, all but three states had a parole system. In 1942, all states and the federal government had formally established parole systems.

As David Rothman points out, however, parole had many weaknesses. Not only did it suffer from massive public criticism, but it was also blamed for the failures of other societal institutions (including prisons) to stop a paroled individual from committing another crime. Furthermore, parole systems nationwide failed to competently determine release dates or supervise those on parole. The parole board, in particular, suffered from a number of inadequacies. Members of the parole board often lacked the expertise needed to make an informed decision. Board members were politically appointed and, in many cases, were government officials with other responsibilities. Even if board members had full-time appointments, they still lacked adequate information as to how to make release decisions. Specifically, the information provided in a prisoner's file was not useful in predicting future behavior, and legislatures rarely provided specific criteria by which to judge the information. As a result, board members focused on the conviction offense and prior criminal behavior. This resulted in privileging first-time offenders over repeat offenders or in making wholesale decisions to release or not release everyone. When release decisions were made, they were often based on capricious factors such as appearance. In terms of supervision, the parole system faced the same failures as probation and prisons in delivering rehabilitation. Part of this was related to the fact that agents were inadequately trained and were poorly qualified to assist parolees. Agents were also overburdened, which means they were not able to properly follow up on a parolee's monthly report to determine compliance or begin the revocation process when necessary.

Despite these problems, systems of parole became a key component of correctional systems nationwide from the 1940s through the 1970s. During this time, correctional systems operated under the medical model, which viewed prisoners as sick and in need of a cure and utilized scientifically supported treatment programs. It was also believed that individualized treatment was necessary to address a prisoner's weaknesses, prepare him/her for a law-abiding life, and reduce recidivism. Conditional release onto parole became the part of this individualized treatment that continued in the community and provided a way to determine whether the individual was "cured" and could live a law-abiding life outside prison or needed to be returned for additional treatment. Parole boards also gained power as they became the sole authority to determine who could be released and when.

Challenges to the Parole System

The power of parole boards was challenged in *Morrissey v. Brewer* (1972). John J. Morrissey and G. Donald Booher were released from prison in Iowa, placed on parole, and then had their parole revoked after they violated their conditions of release. The two sued, challenging the revocation procedures, which did not provide a hearing, and arguing that the procedures violated their due process rights. The U.S. Supreme Court held that because parole revocation is not a part of criminal procedures, parolees were not entitled to full due process rights. Some rights, however, were required. These rights included notice of the evidence against the parolee and the right to confront witnesses.

The parole system was further challenged in the early 1970s when criticisms of the medical model began to grow. These criticisms included little evidence that parole reduced recidivism rates, a belief that indeterminate sentencing structures were unjust and inhumane, and increased signs of inconsistent and discriminatory release decisions. Because of these criticisms, both liberals and conservatives called for a move away from indeterminate sentencing systems and toward determinate sentencing systems. As a result of these changes, many states abandoned discretionary release and eliminated their parole boards.

Parole Process

Today, release on parole can occur through either discretionary or mandatory release. Most individuals released on parole are released through discretionary release. This means that individuals in prison who are eligible for parole go before a parole board and make a case for their release. The parole board then determines whether or not to release the individual based on numerous criteria. These criteria vary by state, but often include items such as employment and residence upon release. Individuals released discretionarily then serve the remainder of their prison sentence on parole. If they violate their parole supervision, they are returned to prison where they complete the remainder of the sentence. Under a discretionary release system, state laws may limit parole eligibility. For instance, many states bar those sentenced to life, life without parole, or those convicted of certain crimes (e.g., first-degree murder or drug trafficking) from early release on parole.

Individuals released through mandatory release do not have their release determined by a parole board. Rather, their release is determined by legislation, that is, sentencing guidelines. These guidelines determine who is eligible for supervision and how much time must be spent in prison prior to release. Unlike discretionary release, mandatory release is not the continuation of a prison sentence in the community. It is an additional phase of the sentence that occurs after the prison sentence is served. For instance, individuals sentenced to time in prison in California must serve three years on parole after they have completed their prison sentence. Under the mandatory release system, state laws may dictate who must be placed on parole. For instance, in some states, individuals convicted of a violent crime serve time on parole, but those convicted of a nonviolent crime do not.

Regardless of how an individual is released, systems of parole and post-release supervision are usually set up in the same manner. State parole systems are divided into regions or divisions, which are then divided into parole offices. Administrative positions usually include those in charge of parole offices, regional or district administrators, the head of the parole system, and parole board members if such a board exists.

On the most basic level, supervision is carried out by two individuals: the parole agent and the parolee. The parole agent is directly responsible for supervising and assisting parolees. Agents provide assistance to parolees with regard to housing, employment, and substance abuse (among other possible avenues for assistance) and ensure parolees follow the conditions of parole supervision set forth by the agent. A parole agent's caseload may include parolees with a variety of backgrounds and criminal offenses. Specialized caseloads may include high-risk sex offenders or those with a mental illness. Parole agents perform many roles, including visiting parolees at their homes, collecting samples for drug tests, preparing cases for parole revocations, and filling out paperwork regarding the activities and actions relating to a particular case.

Those on parole typically share the same characteristics as those in prison. The majority of parolees are male (88 percent) and are white (41 percent), African American (38 percent), or Hispanic (19 percent). Parolees are most likely to have served time for a drug offense, followed by property offenses and violent offenses. About half of all parolees are 35 or younger, and only 7 percent have attended some college or higher-level education. Upon release, parolees tend to live in geographically concentrated areas. These areas often lack the services needed by parolees. Where services do exist, they tend to be too small to meet the need for the service. Parolees are required to follow certain rules put in place by their parole agents. These rules, known as conditions of parole, place restrictions on what parolees can do. These conditions range from prohibiting parolees from drinking alcohol or using drugs to restricting where a parolee may go. Failure to follow these conditions may be grounds for revoking parole and sending the individual back to prison.

There have been mixed reviews as to the effectiveness of parole and post-release supervision. Some studies found that those released on parole adjusted to living in the community better than convicts who did not go through the parole system. Other studies, however, found that parolees were more likely to be rearrested than nonparolees. One additional study focused on noncriminal justice–related outcomes and found that parole has no effect on housing stability, minimal effect on family stability, and a strong effect on employment.

Rita Shah
University of California, Irvine

See Also: Corrections; Probation; Rehabilitation; Sentencing: Indeterminate Versus Fixed.

Further Readings

Bottomley, A. K. "Parole in Transition: A Comparative Study of Origins, Developments, and Prospects for the 1990s." *Crime and Justice*, v.12 (1990).

Bureau of Justice Statistics. "Probation and Parole in the United States, 2008." http://bjs.ojp.usdoj.gov/content/pub/pdf/ppus08.pdf (Accessed September 2011).

Gottfredson, Michael. R., Susan D. Mitchel-Herzfeld, and Timothy Flanagan. "Another Look at the Effectiveness of Parole Supervision." *Journal of Research in Crime and Delinquency*, v.19/2 (1982).

Rothman, David J. *Conscience and Convenience: The Asylum and Its Alternatives in Progressive America*. New York: Aldine de Gruyter, 2002.

Schlager, Melinda. D. and Kelly Robbins. "Does Parole Work?—Revisited: Reframing the Discussion of the Impact of Postprison Supervision on Offender Outcome." *Prison Journal*, v.88/2 (2008).

Travis, Jeremy, Amy L. Solomon, and Michelle Waul. *From Prison to Home: The Dimensions and Consequences of Prisoner Reentry*. Washington, DC: Urban Institute, 2001.

Yaher, J., C. Visher, and Amy Solomon. *Returning Home on Parole: Former Prisoners' Experiences in Illinois, Ohio, and Texas*. Washington, DC: Urban Institute, 2008.

Peltier, Leonard

Leonard James Peltier (1944–) is a Native American political activist who is incarcerated for murder and has become a symbol for political prisoners. Peltier was born on the Chippewa reservation in North Dakota. His father, Leo Peltier, was three-quarters Chippewa and died in 1990; his mother, Alvina Showers, who died September 9, 2002, had a Chippewa father and a Lakota Sioux mother. Peltier attended Flandreau Indian School in Flandreau, South Dakota, but did not graduate. Peltier had some involvement with the criminal justice system prior to the incident at the Pine Ridge Reservation that brought him national recognition. In March 1970, Peltier was convicted of trespassing in Fort Lawton, Washington. On November 22, 1972, he was acquitted of the attempted murder of an off-duty policeman in Milwaukee, Wisconsin.

Pine Ridge Reservation

At the Lakota Sioux Pine Ridge Reservation in South Dakota, Tribal president Richard "Dick" Wilson was elected in 1972 by a slim margin. Wilson's administration was marked by accusations of corruption and patronage. As president, Wilson controlled a tribal ranger group funded by a $67,000 grant from the U.S. Bureau of Indian Affairs (BIA); this group referred to itself as the GOON Squad, an acronym purportedly standing for "Guardians of the Oglala Nation." Many of the Pine Ridge BIA tribal police officers were moonlighting on the GOON Squad, along with hundreds of other individuals who cycled in and out of the group. The GOON Squad was accused of terrorizing leaders of a group that opposed Wilson in a land claims struggle. Part of this issue involved the holding by the federal government of a parcel of the northwestern portion of the Pine Ridge Reservation, known as the Sheep Mountain Gunnery Range, which amounted to about one-eighth of the total area of the reservation. At the beginning of World War II, the Department of War had borrowed the land for use as a training field for aerial gunners. The federal government had promised that this area would be returned to the Oglala Lakotas at the end of the war, but it never was. This occupation was contrary to the 1868 Treaty of Fort Laramie. Further, in 1970, the National Uranium Resource Evaluation Project in

A sign demanding Leonard Peltier be released is posted outside Detroit, Michigan. Peltier was charged with the murders of two Federal Bureau of Investigation (FBI) agents in the Pine Ridge Reservation incident. He was placed on the FBI's 10 Most Wanted list and was ultimately found guilty and sentenced to two consecutive life terms in prison.

collaboration with the National Aeronautics and Space Administration had determined that there were substantial uranium deposits near Sheep Mountain, and governmental efforts appeared to be directed at permanently holding onto the parcel of land.

The GOON Squad and others used the tactic of political violence to intimidate those who were opposed to allowing the federal government to continue holding the Sheep Mountain Gunnery Range. In response to this, the Oglala Sioux Civil Rights Organization was formed to solicit the U.S. Justice Department to intervene. A petition for removal of Dick Wilson, who was in favor of the continuation, was circulated by the Oglala Sioux Civil Rights Organization; there were more names on the petition than people who had voted for Wilson as tribal president. In February 1973, a meeting for the impeachment of Wilson was held, but the BIA named Wilson to preside over his own impeachment; U.S. marshals were dispatched to the meeting to keep order. Wilson, not surprisingly, was not impeached at this meeting, and he immediately issued a ban on any further meetings on the reservation by opponents.

Wounded Knee Occupation

Leaders of the American Indian Movement (AIM), including Russell Means, supported traditional Oglala Lakota Sioux in their positions. Means attempted to meet with Wilson to come to an agreement over their differences and resolve tribal tensions, but his efforts were unsuccessful. In protest, AIM members occupied the small town of Wounded Knee on the Pine Ridge Reservation for 71 days, during which time they were under siege by federal authorities from the Federal Bureau of Investigation (FBI), the BIA, and, of course, the GOON Squad. Leonard Peltier was a member of AIM, and supported the traditional Oglala Lakota Sioux in the standoff.

Federal authorities arrested 562 individuals who participated in the Wounded Knee siege, of whom 185 were subsequently indicted by federal grand juries based on evidence supplied by the FBI. Only 15 were ever convicted, most for minor offenses like trespassing or interference with a postal inspector.

Brutal repercussions continued against opposition supporters on the Pine Ridge Reservation. From March 1973 to March 1976, there were at least 342 serious physical assaults of AIM members and supporters, and 69 persons were killed. Unfortunately, none of these homicides was ever solved by the FBI, who had preeminent jurisdiction over these incidents. As a member of AIM, Peltier became involved in efforts to address the pattern of violence at Pine Ridge.

On June 26, 1975, a firefight broke out between an AIM enclave and the GOON Squad, BIA tribal police, FBI agents, and a contingent of white vigilantes from off the reservation. Two FBI agents, Jack R. Coler and Ronald A. Williams, were killed during this melee. Leonard Peltier, who was then 32 years old, was charged with the murders of Coler and Williams. On December 22, 1975, Peltier was placed on the FBI's Ten Most Wanted list. On February 6, 1976, he was extradited from Canada based on an affidavit by Myrtle Poor Bear, which she later claimed had been made as a result of intimidation by FBI agents. Peltier was found guilty on April 18, 1977, and was sentenced on June 1, 1977, to two consecutive life terms. In January 1976, the U.S. Congress passed Public Law 90-468, which codified the transfer of the Sheep Mountain Gunnery Range to the U.S. Department of the Interior. Peltier conducted hunger strikes in April and May 1984 in protest of his incarceration; numerous unsuccessful appeals have been filed on his behalf. He is currently incarcerated at the U.S. Penitentiary in Lewisburg, Pennsylvania. His projected date of release is October 11, 2040. However, there is a large, highly visible, and active movement of concerned individuals interested in working to free Leonard Peltier from what they feel is an unjust incarceration.

Victor B. Stolberg
Essex County College

See Also: Federal Bureau of Investigation; Leavenworth Federal Penitentiary; Native American Tribal Police; Native Americans.

Further Readings
Arden, Harvey. *Have You Thought of Leonard Peltier Lately?* Houston, TX: HWT Publishing, 2004.
Messerschmidt, James W. *The Trial of Leonard Peltier*. Cambridge, MA: South End Press, 1983.
Peltier, Leonard. *Prison Writings: My Life Is My Sun Dance*. New York: St. Martin's Press, 1999.

Pendleton Act of 1883

The Pendleton Act of 1883, also known as the Civil Service Act, was the first major piece of legislation that regulated elements of a federal bureaucracy plagued with a history of patronage, graft, and corruption. In the decades following the American Civil War, reformers advocated a system of government administration that was more responsive to the public and less beholden to political parties and their machines. Despite attempts in the early 1870s to establish a civil service commission with the power to control the hiring and dismissal of employees, meaningful change at the national level only came after the assassination of Republican President James Garfield.

The legislation, originally proposed by Democratic Senator George H. Pendleton from Ohio, authorized the establishment of a three-person bipartisan commission with the power to assist the president in creating rules that regulated the federal workforce. The legislation outlined eight guidelines to direct the work of the president and the commission that included the use of competitive exams to determine the qualifications of applicants. The legislation also required that all new employees be subject to a probationary period before an offer of permanent employment was tendered, and eliminated the requirement that employees contribute to the political campaigns of elected officials. The overarching purpose of the law was to establish a system based on merit that ended the practice of removing individuals from federal positions for purely partisan motives.

Although the bill passed both the House of Representatives and the Senate rather handily during the lame-duck legislative session of 1882 and 1883, the reform proposal likely would have been defeated if not for the death of President Garfield. Garfield's election to the presidency came as a result of a compromise between two competing factions in the Republican Party. The Stalwarts supported the nomination of Ulysses S. Grant for a third term in large measure because Grant opposed civil service reform. The moderate wing of the party, the Half-Breeds, advocated the candidacy of James Blaine of Maine, who supported the elimination of political patronage. Garfield represented an acceptable middle ground, although the Stalwarts were able to strengthen their position with the selection of Chester Arthur as Garfield's running mate.

Despite Garfield's ostensible moderation, he surprised many by calling for significant reform to the federal bureaucracy in his inaugural address—a proposal met with resistance from Republicans who controlled Congress. On July 2, 1881, only four months into his tenure as president, Garfield was shot and gravely wounded by Charles Guiteau. Guiteau, who was likely mentally ill, was active in Republican Party politics and had supported the nomination of Grant for president. He fancied himself a political insider and attempted to curry favor with a number of party leaders. After the election of Garfield, he moved to Washington, D.C., expecting to be awarded a patronage position with the federal government as a reward for his efforts during the election. Guiteau became well known in Washington as a nuisance, and was eventually banned from entering the White House. Angered over being rebuffed, he purchased a revolver that he used to shoot Garfield in a Washington train station.

Guiteau was arrested and tried for the assassination of the president, who died from his wounds on September 19, 1881. At trial, the defense raised the insanity defense, a strategy that seemed to be buttressed by the odd behavior of Guiteau at a trial that included five days of rambling testimony. The jury, not persuaded, found him guilty, and Guiteau was executed in June 1882. The public and the press alike believed that Garfield's death was a direct result of the corrupting effects of the patronage system that allowed political parties to abuse the system of employment at the federal level. Arthur, who assumed the presidency after Garfield's death, pursued civil service reform as a memorial to his predecessor's efforts, signing the bill into law in January 1883. Although the legislation was an important first step in eliminating influence of partisanship on the bureaucracy, the law only regulated approximately 10 percent of the federal workforce. As a result of amendments to the original Pendleton Act, more than 90 percent of all government employees at the national level are covered by civil service protections today.

Charles F. Jacobs
St. Norbert College

See Also: Arthur, Chester (Administration of); Garfield, James (Administration of); Guiteau, Charles; Insanity Defense.

Further Readings
Howe, George Frederick. *Chester A. Arthur: A Quarter-Century of Machine Politics*. New York: Frederick Ungar, 1957.

Chester Arthur assumed the presidency in 1881 after President James Garfield's death. He pursued civil service reform as a memorial to his predecessor.

Reeves, Thomas C. *Gentleman Boss*. New York: Alfred A. Knopf, 1975.

Van Riper, Paul P. "The Pendleton Act of 1883 and Professionalism in the U.S. Public Service." In *Modern Systems of Government: Exploring the Role of Bureaucrats and Politicians*, Ali Farazmand, ed. Thousand Oaks, CA: Sage, 1997.

Penitentiaries

The term *penitentiary* refers to a specific type of prison popular in the early to mid-19th century. The word can be traced to the 15th century and was originally used to describe institutions for punishing crimes against the Roman Catholic Church. Penitentiaries in the 18th and 19th centuries were designed to reform inmates, usually through extensive religious education, sometimes accompanied by elaborate architectural designs and rigorous monitoring of inmates' interactions. By the first quarter of the 19th century, two models of penitentiary construction and operation vied with one another for dominance: the Pennsylvania or Separate system, most closely associated with Philadelphia's Eastern State Penitentiary, and the New York or Auburn system, most closely associated with New York's Auburn and Sing Sing penitentiaries. Though the word *penitentiary* became synonymous with "prison" by the last part of the 19th century, most penitentiaries had abandoned or heavily scaled back their religious orientation following the Civil War, opting instead for the more "scientific" rehabilitative methods of the reformatory system pioneered by Zebulon Brockway at the Elmira Reformatory.

Walnut Street Jail

The first institution to be called a penitentiary was Philadelphia's Walnut Street Jail. This institution was constructed in 1776 and functioned as both Philadelphia's city jail and Pennsylvania's state prison. Originally designed as a U-shaped building surrounded by a high wall, the jail was designed to confine groups of inmates in large rooms. Inmates were not differentiated by age or crime, which made keeping the peace at the facility extremely difficult. Worse, the accommodations were (like most jails of the time) squalid, which facilitated the transmission of disease, and the building was often not secure, which allowed inmates to escape. Finally, jail administrators often extorted money from inmates in exchange for better food and accommodations, which only encouraged inmates to prey upon one another.

Unfortunately, none of these issues was unique to the Walnut Street Jail; many jails and workhouses around the world faced similar challenges. In response, by the middle of the 18th century, a group of English, French, and American reformers began agitating for corrections to the issues prisons faced. The most famous prison reformer of this period was an Englishman named John Howard who, in 1777, published an exposé of prison conditions titled *The State of the Prisons in England and Wales*. Howard's book decried many of the worst conditions prevailing in jails and prisons of the time, including unsanitary conditions and administrative corruption. He furthermore recommended that inmates be separated from one another and be housed according to age so that younger inmates (who were presumably being held for lesser crimes) would not become "hardened criminals" through their association with older prisoners.

Inspired by Howard's example and appalled by conditions at the Walnut Street Jail, a group of prominent Philadelphians organized the Philadelphia Society for Alleviating the Miseries of Public Prisons (PSAMPP) in 1787. Their goal was to reform the Walnut Street Jail by introducing some of the reforms suggested in *The State of the Prisons*. In particular, the PSAMPP's members hoped to make the Walnut Street Jail a place where inmates could be reformed by separating convicts from one another and introducing labor and religious programming; these three things formed the basis of penitentiary discipline for the next century.

Because the Walnut Street Jail's design was not conducive to separating inmates from one another, in 1790, the Pennsylvania legislature (after extensive lobbying by the politically prominent members of the PSAMPP) built an addition to the institution. Called the "penitentiary house," it was designed to separate inmates from each other by housing each in a single cell. Moreover, inmates received piecework and had access to local ministers who volunteered to provide the convicts with religious counsel. The new innovation proved very popular, and within a short time, similar institutions were constructed in New York (Newgate) and New Jersey (Trenton).

Eastern State Penitentiary

Unfortunately, the Walnut Street Jail's new penitentiary house quickly became overcrowded, making strict separation of inmates nearly impossible. Moreover, the expanding prison population in Pennsylvania exacerbated the Walnut Street Jail's problems. In response, by the second decade of the 19th century, the PSAMPP began advocating the construction of replacement penitentiaries, specifically built to practice the Pennsylvania system. Western State Penitentiary, the first of these, opened in Pittsburgh in 1826, but the administration was unable to fully implement the Pennsylvania system because the cells were not large enough for inmates to practice their newly acquired trades. As a result, Philadelphia's Eastern State Penitentiary, which was built between 1821 and 1836, was specifically designed to implement all aspects of the Pennsylvania system; this institution became one of the archetypes of a Pennsylvania system penitentiary. Eastern State was constructed on a radial plan, with the seven original cellblocks meeting at a central location like the spokes of a wheel; the cellblocks were surrounded by a massive wall designed to resemble a medieval castle. All of the cells opened to a small, walled exercise yard where prisoners were allowed one hour of recreation daily. Because inmates were expected to spend most of their time in their cells, each cell had indoor plumbing and running water, and Eastern State Penitentiary was the largest and most expensive public works project of its time as a result of these amenities.

Eastern State Penitentiary in Philadelphia, Pennsylvania, was built between 1821 and 1836. This 2003 aerial view reveals the radial plan it was constructed with, showing the seven original cellblocks meeting at a central location like the spokes of a wheel. Around the cellblocks, a massive wall was erected resembling a medieval castle.

Auburn State Prison

Yet, the Pennsylvania system was not the only model of penitentiary administration popular in antebellum America. Many Americans, most notably the Prison Discipline Society of Boston, advocated the New York or Auburn system of penitential discipline. On first glance, there appeared little difference between the Pennsylvania and New York systems: both called for the rigorous separation of inmates, and partisans of both systems demanded that inmates labor while incarcerated. The difference was that, while inmates at a Pennsylvania system penitentiary slept and labored in their cells, inmates of New York system penitentiaries only slept in theirs; during the day, they labored in large, factory-like workrooms attached to the cellblocks. In both systems, however, inmates were expected to remain silent and not communicate with each other in any way.

The New York system was first practiced in New York's Auburn Prison, which opened in 1816. Though the prison was initially overseen by William Brittin, the man most commonly associated with the New York system was Auburn's second warden, Elam Lynds, who became infamous for his brutality. Though Lynds did not design the New York system, he methodically and ruthlessly enforced it through floggings and other forms of physical punishment. Despite his fearsome reputation, Lynds enjoyed the support of some New York legislators due to the fact that Sing Sing's factory system consistently produced a profit; this was in marked contrast to the prison's ideological rival, Eastern State Penitentiary, which never turned a profit.

Reformatory Movement

Ultimately, the New York and Pennsylvania systems were both eclipsed by the reformatory movement pioneered by Zebulon Brockway in the 1870s, and both systems' distinctive features slowly disappeared. Partially, this was due to the pervasive overcrowding that affected most American penitentiaries after the Civil War, and partially it was due to the substitution of religious solutions to crime for scientific ones. Moreover, because reformatories required no elaborate (and expensive) architectural forms, these institutions were more attractive to cost-conscious legislators. As a result, few new Pennsylvania or New York system penitentiaries were built in the United States after the Civil War, and many penitentiaries formerly conducted along the New York or Pennsylvania systems were transitioned into reformatories.

Paul Kahan
Montgomery County Community College

See Also: Auburn State Prison; Eastern State Penitentiary; Pennsylvania System of Reform; Rehabilitation; Sing Sing Correctional Facility; Walnut Street Jail.

Further Readings

Ignatieff, Michael. *A Just Measure of Pain: The Pententiary in the Industrial Revolution*. New York: Pantheon Books, 1978.
Kahan, Paul. *Eastern State Penitentiary: A History*. Charleston, SC: History Press, 2008.
Morris, Norval and David J. Rotman. *The Oxford History of the Prison: The Practice of Punishment in Western Society*. New York: Oxford University Press, 1997.

Penitentiary Study Commission

The Arkansas Penitentiary Study Commission was established in 1967 to investigate the increasingly poor conditions within the Arkansas penitentiary system. The report it generated following its investigation was the leading catalyst in penal reform in the state. The commission was established by then-Governor Winthrop Rockefeller in response to a report by the Criminal Investigation Division of the Arkansas State Police that described deplorable conditions within the two prison farms of the Arkansas penitentiary system. Because of the political atmosphere of the time and the public opinion that criminals should be locked away and forgotten, reform of the penal system was projected to take many years. Dissatisfied with the proposed timeline the reforms, Rockefeller requested that the state legislature establish the Penitentiary Study Commission to conduct further investigations, and it was officially organized in January 1967.

Upon the conclusion of the first round of investigations, the commission released its first report in February 1967, which addressed present problems within the penal system and suggested three recommendations in response to the findings. First, it suggested that more paid personnel be hired to run the administration and guard the prison. It also recommended that control of hiring and firing of personnel be turned over from the governor to the Penitentiary Board. And lastly, it recommended that the prison no longer be required to pay its own operating fees. Because this report only addressed current administrative concerns rather than the actual conditions within the prison, a further study was conducted and its results published in January 1968. This two-volume document detailed the deplorable conditions within the prison farms and reported that the Arkansas penal system differed from other national institutions in a number of ways. First, it found that the Arkansas prison farms had very few paid employees but rather used low-risk prisoners as guards over other inmates. It also found that inmates were confined in open barracks where violence, sexual assault, and alcohol and drug use were rampant. Third, the commission found that the prison farms lacked rehabilitative programming.

More specifically, the commission found that the operations of the prison farms were well in violation of the Thirteenth and Fourteenth Amendments, which protect against involuntary servitude and require due process and equal protection, respectively. As part of the Thirteenth Amendment violation, the commission found that inmates were required to work long hours in the prison fields regardless of weather conditions, without proper clothing, and without compensation. In addition, workers were almost entirely supervised by other inmates armed with high-powered weapons, and murder, bribery, and extortion were a way of life.

Claims of violations of the Fourteenth Amendment were also numerous. Of primary concern were the cruel and unusual living conditions within the prisons. During the course of the commission's investigation, they also found a variety of torture devices used on inmates, including whips, electrocution, and humiliation. To address these issues, the commission recommended that the prison-guard system be phased out in its entirety. Also in violation of the Fourteenth Amendment were the living conditions within the barracks. These barracks were filthy, with discolored mattresses, overflowing toilets, and bug-infested beds. In addition, the dormitories were segregated by race but not by violence of the offender, and sexual assault and violence were commonplace. The conditions in the kitchen also left much to be desired, and bug debris was found to cover many of its surfaces. Lastly, the lack of rehabilitative programming was found to be in violation of the Fourteenth Amendment. In response to this finding, the legislature adopted Act 50, which identified education and rehabilitation as essential programs within any penal system.

To address the remaining findings of the commission, the act proposed by the legislature also called for the creation of the Department of Corrections to replace the outdated and inefficient Penitentiary Board. In addition, the previously separate Board of Pardons and Paroles was integrated into this new department, the Youthful Offenders Facility was built, a new maximum security facility was designed, the number of civilian employees was significantly increased, and the system of using low-risk prisoners as guards was eliminated. The commission's findings also had lasting effects on the operation of other Arkansas prisons and invited widespread reform and modernization throughout the penal system.

Kathrin Ritter
Todd Moore
University of Tennessee, Knoxville

See Also: Arkansas; Corrections; Penitentiaries.

Further Readings
Chaneles, Sol. *Prisons and Prisoners; Historical Documents*. New York: Haworth Press, 1985.
Friedman, Lawrence. *Crime and Punishment in American History*. New York: Basic Books, 1994.
National Council on Crime and Delinquency (NCCD). "Probation and Parole in Arkansas: A Survey for the Arkansas Penitentiary Study Commission." New York: NCCD, 1967.
Wines, Frederick Howard. *Punishment and Reformation: A Study of the Penitentiary System*. Charleston, SC: Nabu Press, 2010.

Penn, William

An early American colonist, Quaker writer, and minister, William Penn was born in London, England, in 1644 to Sir William Penn and Margaret Jasper. As an exalted admiral in the English Navy, Sir William Penn provided his son with a life of luxury, often attending royal events. Shortly after enrolling in Christ Church College, University of Oxford, Penn was exposed to Quakerism for the first time. He noted the peaceful nature of the religion and the Quakers' emphasis on nonviolence and humanism. Penn was expelled from Oxford for refusing to participate in daily Anglican services. By 1668, he had converted to Quakerism against the wishes of his father and was repeatedly imprisoned for his beliefs. Throughout such persecutions, he wrote several pamphlets including *Truth Exalted* and *No Cross, No Crown* espousing religious tolerance and criticizing discriminatory religious laws in England. Upon his father's death in 1670, Penn inherited an annual income. As his father's final wish, the king and the duke of York appointed Penn a royal counselor in honor of the elder Penn's service to the Crown. Utilizing his position and seeking to escape religious intolerance, William Penn set up the colony of Pennsylvania using progressive notions regarding religion and the penal system.

Penn was continually arrested in England for his religious beliefs and ministry. With thousands of Quakers imprisoned and their land confiscated due to the Conventicle Act, Penn held public meetings to protest the law. He was arrested, and authorities refused to show him a copy of his charges. The judge further dictated the jury to come to a verdict without hearing Penn's defense. The jury acquitted Penn and his fellow defendants; the jurors were placed in jail and levied with fines. Eventually, the jury was released per a writ of habeas corpus and it was ruled that juries could not be coerced or punished for their verdicts. This experience was a key precedent influencing Penn's later constitutional provision in Pennsylvania, outlining the right to a trial by jury. Following his imprisonment, Penn petitioned for legislation outlining religious liberty. He was rebuffed and became convinced that religious toleration could not be achieved in England and called for a mass exodus of Quakers from England to America.

William Penn was arrested many times in England for his religious beliefs, along with thousands of other Quakers, and was ultimately arrested, jailed, and acquitted.

Beginning in 1677, Quakers slowly began to leave England for the provinces of West and East Jersey in America. Seeking to extend the area, Penn petitioned King Charles II for a charter of land, which was officially signed on March 4, 1681. With the territory, Penn was made the largest private (nonroyal) landowner and officially formed the colony of Pennsylvania.

In the spring of 1682, Penn wrote the first Frame of Government of Pennsylvania. This document was to serve as a constitution for the colony. Inspired by the nonviolent and humanistic nature of the Quakers, Penn strove to create a society based on religious toleration and individual liberties in his "Holy Experiment," the new province of Pennsylvania. The first frame, while only enacted for a short period of time, was considered progressive. It would also later serve as the basis for the U.S. Constitution and the Bill of Rights.

Penn's constitution included religious liberty, an assembly elected by the people to make the laws, freedom of the press, and trial by jury and was the first to provide for peaceful change through amendments. Additionally, Penn is considered one of the early initiators of correctional reform in the United States. Whereas the English penal code outlined over 200 offenses that could be punished by the death penalty, Penn reduced this number to two in Pennsylvania—treason and murder. Pennsylvania's criminal code also forbade torture and other forms of cruel punishment. His penal system, inspired by Quakerism, was designed to reform, not merely punish. Jails and prisons, which replaced corporal punishment, were to correct delinquent individuals through the use of workshops and labor. Although these reforms were reversed after Penn's death, the Quakers would petition for their return years later. The frame went through several revisions, until Penn wrote the fourth frame, the Pennsylvania Charter of Privileges, which remained in place until the American Revolution. William Penn died in 1718 and was buried in England.

Katie A. Farina
University of Delaware

See Also: Pennsylvania; Pennsylvania System of Reform; Quakers.

Further Readings
Endy, Melvin B. *William Penn and Early Quakerism.* Princeton, NJ: Princeton University Press, 1973.
Moretta, John A. *William Penn and the Quaker Legacy.* New York: Longman, 2006.
Penn, William, et al. *The Papers of William Penn.* Philadelphia: University of Pennsylvania Press, 1981.

Pennsylvania

Founded as a colony in 1682 by William Penn and granted statehood in 1787, Pennsylvania has been a pioneer in criminal punishment reform. The state was home to Eastern State Penitentiary in Philadelphia and developed the Pennsylvania system of reform. Pennsylvania was active in prison and capital punishment reform and was the first state to make only first-degree murder a capital offense in 1794, as well as the first to abolish public executions in 1834. While the state still allows capital punishment, efforts by reform groups to end executions and improve conditions for prisoners continue.

Crime

In early Pennsylvania, policing morals and protecting the public order shaped the types of crimes that were on the books; fornication, bastardy, adultery, and operating tippling houses were criminal acts. During the 17th and 18th centuries, there was a slow but steady increase in homicide rates. In 1800, the murder rate in Pennsylvania was 1.5 per 100,000 people; by contrast, today's rate is 5.2 per 100,000. Burglary and robbery also increased at an alarming rate in the 18th century. During the 19th century, property crime patterns followed residential and business expansion, particularly in cities. Sometimes necessity motivated acts of larceny, but in growing cities with larger populations and more businesses, larceny also became a crime of opportunity. Property crime currently occurs at a rate of 24.07 per 100,000 people. Riots became conspicuous after the American Revolution and increased during the antebellum decades. Philadelphia had several race and ethnic riots in the 1830s and 1840s, the most notable being the Nativist Riots in 1844. Fugitive slave riots also occurred in southern Pennsylvania leading up to the Civil War.

Pennsylvania dealt with numerous occasions of labor violence and unrest. The Molly Maguires, a group of Irish American coal workers in northeastern Pennsylvania, became tired of poor and unsafe working conditions. After a failed strike in the late 1870s, some of the Mollies continued the fight with violent killings of local mine authorities. After trials in which an undercover Pinkerton agent provided much of the testimony, 20 Mollies were executed between 1877 and 1879. In 1902, another coal strike in the same region provoked threats of violence and required federal intervention to end the strike. In western Pennsylvania, steel strikes were common. The 1892 Homestead Strike began on June 30 with workers from various steel plants around Pittsburgh striking; the strike conditions resulted in a violent battle on July 6, 1892, between strikers and private police. The mill owners used strikebreakers to continue production in mid-July, and a failed assassination attempt on the mill owner caused the downfall of the strike. In 1919, steelworkers in Pittsburgh went on strike again in order to force local officials to allow the American Federation of Labor to hold union meetings in the city. In September of that year, a general steelworker strike began, halting half of the nation's steel production—in Pennsylvania and other states. Companies used violence, threats, and strikebreakers to demoralize the strikers. In early January 1920, the strike fell apart, resulting in little union organizing for steelworkers for the next 15 years.

Police

From Pennsylvania's inception, law enforcement occurred at the local level with appointed sheriffs. They attended all court sessions, oversaw arrests of people committing infractions, and oversaw the local prisoners. In 1701, the office of sheriff became an elected office with three-year terms. Currently, the sheriffs of each county are elected to four-year terms, and role of sheriff is usually limited to court security and transporting prisoners. Many boroughs, cities, and townships have their own police departments that deal with the local law enforcement duties. Cities like Philadelphia and Pittsburgh established professional police forces in the 1850s. In the mid-1860s, the Pennsylvania legislature established a private police force, the Coal and Iron Police, in order to protect coal and iron production sites. This police force was also used by companies in a strikebreaking capacity. After the Coal and Iron Police failed to stop the Anthracite Coal Strike in 1902 in northeastern Pennsylvania, and because of growing frustration with the refusal or inability of the local police to enforce the law, Governor Samuel W. Pennypacker created the Pennsylvania State Police in 1905.

Punishment

The colony of Pennsylvania modeled its legal system after that of England, utilizing trials and public physical punishments for wrongdoers. While England had several hundred capital crimes on the books, in 1682, Pennsylvania had only murder as a capital offense. Other criminal punishments in Pennsylvania included fines, whippings, time in the stocks, or branding. This mild penal code, when compared to that of England and other colonies, illustrates the Quaker influence of benevolence and pacifism on colonial institutions such as criminal punishments. Between 1718 and 1794, the number of capital crimes fluctuated but by 1794, only first-degree murder warranted the death penalty.

Penal reformers in Pennsylvania worked to find a better way to punish offenders because it was believed that public punishments were degrading and left no room for character reform. In 1787, the Philadelphia Society for Alleviating the Miseries of Public Prisons was established to improve prison conditions. The organization moved to create a penitentiary system in Pennsylvania that would allow offenders to reform their behavior. The group continues its work today as the Pennsylvania Prison Society. In 1790, Walnut Street Jail in Philadelphia became a penitentiary, with Western State Penitentiary in Pittsburgh opening in 1826 and Eastern State Penitentiary in Philadelphia in 1829. In these penitentiaries, inmates underwent the Pennsylvania system of reform. Inmates were placed in individual cells and were kept in total silence to allow for reflection and reform. Inmates were not exposed to physical punishment and worked at artisanal crafts in their cells. While critics of the Pennsylvania system suggested that the solitary confinement would produce insanity, Pennsylvania reformers stood by their system, utilizing it at Eastern State until 1913. Today, there are 26 state correctional institutions in Pennsylvania.

Reformers also worked against capital punishment in Pennsylvania. The 1794 law was an early success. Executions, however, continued to be public spectacles. In 1834, Pennsylvania declared public executions illegal, moving them to the county jail yards to avoid such scenes. In 1913, the electric chair became the mode of execution, and in 1990, lethal injection replaced the electric chair. In the 1970s, the state declared capital punishment to be unconstitutional, but it was reenacted in 1974 and is still on the books today. Only three executions have taken place in the state since 1976, and as of 2011, more than 200 inmates are on death row.

Erica Rhodes Hayden
Vanderbilt University

See Also: 1777 to 1800 Primary Documents; Eastern State Penitentiary; Penn, William; Pennsylvania System of Reform; Quakers.

Further Readings

Johnson, Donald R. *Policing the Urban Underworld: The Impact of Crime on the Development of the American Police, 1800–1887*. Philadelphia: Temple University Press, 1979.

Marietta, Jack D. and G. S. Rowe. *Troubled Experiment: Crime and Justice in Pennsylvania, 1682–1800*. Philadelphia: University of Pennsylvania Press, 2006.

Meranze, Michael. *Laboratories of Virtue: Punishment, Revolution, and Authority in Philadelphia, 1760–1835*. Chapel Hill: University of North Carolina Press, 1996.

Pennsylvania System of Reform

The term *Pennsylvania system* refers to a regimen of inmate reform most commonly associated with Philadelphia's Eastern State Penitentiary during the 19th and early 20th centuries. Also known as the separate system, the Pennsylvania system called for inmates to be completely and totally separated from one another, to learn and practice a trade while incarcerated, and to receive religious instruction. Because of the complexity of these requirements, successfully implementing the Pennsylvania system was nearly impossible and required elaborate and expensive physical plants, making the Pennsylvania system far less competitive when compared with the congregate, or New York, system. The Pennsylvania system is often misconstrued to have meant that prisoners were kept in strict solitary confinement; in fact, though separated from one another, inmates at both the Walnut Street Jail and Eastern State Penitentiary had regular interactions with staff, administrators, prison inspectors, and selected visitors, which is why it was also known as the separate system.

The first attempt at implementing what came to be known as the Pennsylvania system occurred in 1790 at Philadelphia's Walnut Street Jail. Under heavy pressure from a group of local notables who comprised the Philadelphia Society for the Alleviation of Public Prisons (PSAMPP), the Pennsylvania legislature mandated the construction of a special "penitentiary house" on the grounds of the already extant Walnut Street Jail. This addition held state prisoners one to a cell in the hope that the inmates could be reformed by strictly controlling their environment (e.g., visitors, books).

Eventually, overcrowding frustrated this plan, as did the inability to implement various other aspects of the evolving ideology, such as teaching inmates a trade. Thus, the PSAMPP began advocating the construction of two state penitentiaries—one in Pittsburgh and one in Philadelphia—that would be specifically designed to implement the Pennsylvania system by guaranteeing inmates individual cells large enough for sleeping, eating, and working.

The PSAMPP's efforts bore fruit in the opening of Pittsburgh's Western State Penitentiary (1826)

Also known as the separate system, the Pennsylvania system called for inmates to be completely separated from one another and to learn a trade while incarcerated.

and Philadelphia's Eastern State Penitentiary (1829). As a result of poor architecture, Western State Penitentiary was never able to fully implement the Pennsylvania system, so the building was razed in the mid-1830s and rebuilt to mirror Eastern State Penitentiary's design; thus, Eastern State Penitentiary became *the* model of a Pennsylvania system penitentiary, including its physical design. Originally, Eastern State Penitentiary contained seven cellblocks that radiated, like spokes on a wheel, from a central hub. This design minimized the need for a large guard force, because one individual could survey all of the cellblocks from a single location. Because inmates were expected to spend all of their time in their cells or in the attached exercise yards, each cell contained running water and plumbing (in an era when the president of the United States still used an outhouse!), making Eastern State Penitentiary the largest and most expensive public works project in the United States up to that point.

Alexis de Tocqueville, who visited Eastern State Penitentiary in 1831, called the Pennsylvania system a "powerful" tool in the reformation of inmates. Charles Dickens, who visited a decade later, disagreed; he called the Pennsylvania system "immeasurably worse" than physical torture. Despite the controversy, prisons that were designed and/or administered at least partially according to the Pennsylvania system proliferated before the U.S. Civil War and included the State Prison of New Jersey at Trenton, the city prison of Manhattan, and jails and prisons throughout the United Kingdom and France.

Unfortunately, the exorbitant cost of constructing and maintaining Pennsylvania system institutions doomed the system. Even at Eastern State Penitentiary, the system was never practiced as intended because prisoners were routinely employed around the institution as a cost-cutting measure. Moreover, pervasive overcrowding of these institutions following the Civil War meant that most prisons could not adequately separate inmates, many of whom were housed two or even three to a cell. Finally, the growing conviction that penitentiaries had failed to actually rehabilitate inmates made alternative models, such as the reformatory system, more attractive to reformers and cost-conscious legislators alike. By the 1870s, many formerly Pennsylvania system institutions had abandoned the system in favor of the cheaper and more "scientific" reformatory model pioneered by Zebulon Brockway at the Elmira Reformatory. Though Eastern State Penitentiary would continue the Pennsylvania system (in name at least) until 1913, Pittsburgh's Western State Penitentiary adopted the congregate (New York) system in 1869.

Paul Kahan
Montgomery County Community College

See Also: Brockway, Zebulon; Eastern State Penitentiary; Penitentiaries.

Further Readings
Johnston, Norman. *Eastern State Penitentiary: Crucible of Good Intentions*. Philadelphia: Philadelphia Museum of Art, 1994.
Kahan, Paul. *Eastern State Penitentiary: A History*. Charleston, SC: History Press, 2008.
Kahan, Paul. *Seminary of Virtue: The Ideology and Practice of Inmate Reform at Eastern State Penitentiary, 1829–1971*. New York: Peter Lang, 2012.
Rothman, David J. *The Discovery of the Asylum: Social Order and Disorder in the New Republic*. Boston: Little, Brown, 1971.
Teeters, Negley K. *The Prison at Philadelphia: Cherry Hill*. New York: Columbia University Press, 1957.

People v. Pinnell

People v. Pinnell is a 1974 California case concerned with equal protection under the Fourteenth Amendment in the selection method of grand jurors, secret proceedings wherein each juror's oath is to maintain that secrecy. Targets of the grand jury and suspects and their attorneys are not permitted to testify or be present during the presentation of testimony. Only the prosecutor, key staff members, and witnesses are allowed inside, and deliberations are completely secret. The rationale for the secrecy is to encourage witnesses to testify free from the fear of retribution or retaliation from the criminal element; however, secrecy breeds distrust. Typically, trial court judges administer the selection of those who serve on the grand jury pursuant to statutory authority establishing the method of selection, thus evidence of any discriminatory practice therein lies with the selecting judges.

In this case, the judges asked 79 different groups to submit names of prospective jurors and received 75 names; the judges themselves submitted an additional 30 names. Those 105 people were sent questionnaires from which the judges unanimously selected 30 people to serve on the jury panel. Those 30 people were placed in a jury wheel from which the 19 jurors who served were randomly selected, a selection method not previously used in Marin County but pursuant to statutory authority in California Penal Code Section 903.4.

The California Supreme Court had previously found California Penal Code Section 903.4 to be constitutional in its selection of grand jurors under the Fourteenth Amendment, in *In re Wells*, (1971) and *People v. Newton* (1971). However, *Pinnell* presented a different issue, whether the selection process "as applied" singled out for different treatment any of the classes to which Pinnell might belong. He alleged that the opportunity for discrimination in the process was sufficient to make the process applied in his case unconstitutional despite the constitutionality of the statute itself. Four cognizable groups were statistically underrepresented in his grand jury; therefore, he alleged he had met the burden of establishing the opportunity for discrimination, which, under his theory, resulted in an unconstitutional application of the statute. The selecting judges testified in an evidentiary hearing that they sought a fair cross-section of the community and that no group was intentionally excluded. The trial judge agreed with Pinnell's position and found the method of selection failed to ensure a fair representation of those groups, thus the method as applied violated the Fourteenth Amendment.

The California Court of Appeals reversed and held that because this selection method had never been used before, no statistical history existed from which an inference of intentional and systematic exclusion could be drawn, nor was there any direct evidence of purposeful exclusion of a class. In fact, the only direct evidence, the testimony of the selecting judges that they sought a fair cross-section of the community and that no group was intentionally excluded, directly contradicted Pinnell's assertion. The decision followed long-established U.S. Supreme Court precedent. In *Hernandez v. Texas* (1954), the U.S. Supreme Court held that whether a group constitutes a distinct class in a community is a question of fact and that a method of selecting jurors violates equal protection when it intentionally and systematically excludes or underrepresents a cognizable or distinct class. Further, the court ruled that while direct proof of this sort of discrimination is very rare, purpose may be inferred from a substantial history or inadequate representation by the distinct classes. *Hernandez* therefore provides two methods of proof in a case of alleged discrimination in jury selection: either through direct evidence or a substantial historical record of systematic and intentional exclusion, neither of which was supported by the evidence in *Pinnell*. Prior to *Hernandez* in *Akins v. Texas* (1949), the Supreme Court held that the mere fact of inequality in the number selected does not in itself show discrimination, and in fact, the proportional limitation necessary to achieve equality in numbers is forbidden per the ruling in *Cassell v. Texas* (1949). Based on these precedents, the court held a statistical imbalance in one grand jury insufficient to sustain a showing of systematic intentional exclusion. Even if the opportunity for discrimination existed, absent evidence of the exercise of that opportunity, no Fourteenth Amendment violation is shown. *Pinnell*'s importance lies in its successful extension of the rule of law under the Fourteenth Amendment, which says equal protection is denied when a method of selection "intentionally and systematically" excludes or underrepresents a cognizable class to the grand jury setting. The court established that in jury selection, either petit or grand, it is the manner of selection, not the result, that determines constitutionality.

Karen S. Price
Stephen F. Austin State University

See Also: Juries; Racism; Supreme Court, U.S.

Further Readings

Epps, Garrett. *Democracy Reborn: The Fourteenth Amendment and the Fight for Equal Rights* in *Post–Civil War America*. New York: Holt Paperbacks, 2007.

Lewis, Tracey McCants. "*Campbell v. Louisiana*." *Duquesne Law Review*, v.37/407 (1999).

Washburn, Kevin K. "Restoring the Grand Jury." *Fordham Law Review*, v.76 (2008).

People v. Superior Court of Santa Clara County

People v. Superior Court of Santa Clara County, a 1982 California Supreme Court case, is representative of the enduring struggle in the United States with the appropriateness of execution as punishment. Enthusiasm for imposition of the death penalty was at one of its lowest points in the 1970s, not only in California but across the nation.

In the 1972 case *Furman v. Georgia*, the U.S. Supreme Court held Georgia's death penalty statute unconstitutional, along with all death penalty statutes in use. It did not hold the death penalty per se unconstitutional. Widely split, the court agreed that the statutes established a cruel and unusual punishment under the Eighth and Fourteenth amendments to the Constitution but agreed on little else. In the wake of *Furman*, states amended their death penalty statutes to comply with the prescribed rules of the court. With this precedent in hand, those favoring abolition of capital punishment believed their goal to be an eventual certainty. However, four years later, in *Gregg v. Georgia*, the Supreme Court held the death penalty to be a permissible form of punishment for carefully defined categories of murder with limited discretion allowed the sentencing authority and abolishing mandatory death in any case. Sociologically, the development of the law in this area reflects the responsiveness of courts to social and political realities; as those dynamics shift, so must the law. Put another way, the law evolves to meet the evolving standards of society.

Death Penalty in California

California believed that its statute assigning the death penalty to homicides "especially heinous, atrocious, cruel, [and] manifesting exceptional depravity," defined as "a conscienceless or pitiless crime or one unnecessarily torturous" to the victim, was in compliance with *Furman* and *Gregg*. In *People v. Superior Court of Santa Clara County*, however, the defendants challenged the California statute, arguing that as it was sufficiently broad as to include all murders, the *Gregg* requirement for capital punishment was not met, and so the statute was void because of vagueness.

Defending the statute, the state of California asserted two arguments: that *Proffitt v. Florida*, having successfully withstood a federal constitutional challenge containing the exact language of the California statute, was binding precedent, and that the special circumstances finding was only a sentencing function. The California Supreme Court in distinguishing *Proffitt* held that the statute violated the fundamental principles of due process, pointing out that the challenge in *Proffitt* was on Eighth Amendment grounds. In rejecting California's second argument, the court found the pejoratives therein were too imprecise and lacked the requisite certainty for punishment as either an element of an offense or a special circumstance. According to the court, due process under California's constitution requires the same specificity in defining special circumstances or aggravating factors as required in the definition of the crime itself.

Vagueness has its roots in the common law, where courts refused to pass judgment on legislation found to be too uncertain to enforce. At the country's founding, the concept of certainty regarding the precise nature of the violations charged was established as a necessary precedent to enforcement in the Fifth Amendment to the U.S. Constitution. Certainty as to whom a statute seeks to punish, the specific prohibited conduct, and the resulting punishment is required in order to prevent one whose liberty is at stake from having to speculate as to the meaning of the statute under which he is charged. Difficulty in meeting those demands arises as words commonly have multiple meanings in the English language. On the other end of the spectrum, too much specificity in a statute creates gaps in prohibited conduct.

Twenty years after *People v. Superior Court of Santa Clara County*, in *Ring v. Arizona* (2002), the U.S. Supreme Court in interpreting the same language applied *Santa Clara*'s rationale but

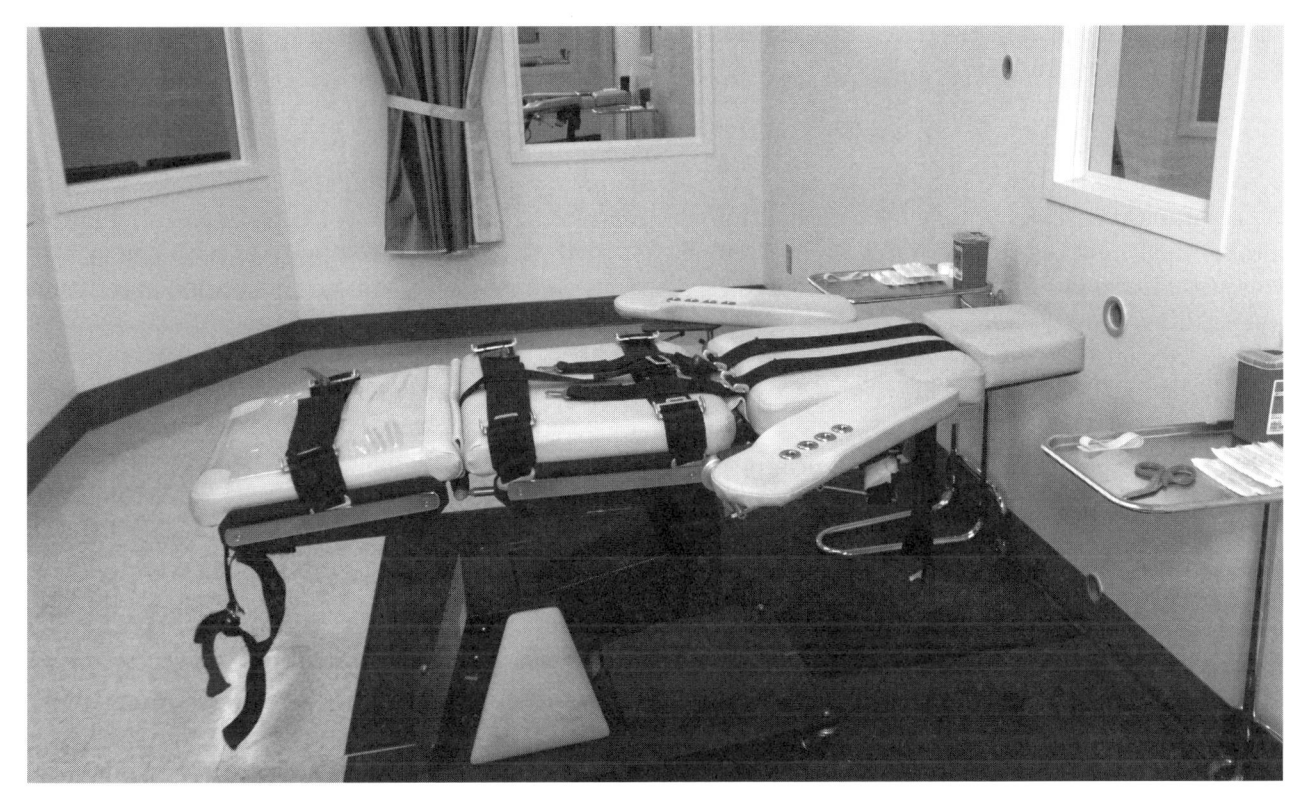

The lethal injection room at San Quentin State Prison in California was completed in 2010. Although the constitutionality of the death penalty is settled, the struggle with the appropriateness and delivery still remains an issue and continues to evolve. It is an enduring struggle in the United States. In November 2011, California state attorneys and death row prisoners agreed to review new lethal injection procedures by September 2012, postponing any lethal executions until then.

decided the case on Sixth Amendment trial by jury grounds rather than on due process. While the constitutionality of death as punishment is settled, the struggle with appropriateness and due process in adjudication and delivery continues to evolve.

Karen S. Price
Stephen F. Austin State University

See Also: Capital Punishment; *Furman v. Georgia*; *Gregg v. Georgia*.

Further Readings
Cochran, Jill. "Courting Death: 30 Years Since *Furman*, Is the Death Penalty Any Less Discriminatory?" *Valparaiso University Law Review*, v.38 (2004).
Jeffries, John Calvin. "Legality, Vagueness and the Construction of Penal Statutes." *Virginia Law Review*, v.71/189 (1985).
Shatz, Steven F. and Nina Rivkin. "The California Death Penalty Scheme: Requiem for *Furman*?" *New York University Law Review*, v.72 (1997).

Percival, Robert V.

Robert V. Percival is professor of environmental law at the University of Maryland, where he has been on faculty since 1987. He has been visiting professor at Harvard and Georgetown and in Slovakia and China and has presented environmental law workshops around the world. He is also a world authority on global environmental law and a member of the International Union on Conservation of Nature (IUCN) Commission on Environmental Law and editor and/or board member of several governmental environmental organizations. He earned a B.A. from Macalester College in 1972 and both an M.A. and a J.D. from Stanford in 1978. At Stanford, he edited the law review and graduated first in his class. After graduation, he clerked for a justice of the Ninth Circuit Court, then for Justice Byron R. White, and was special assistant to the first secretary of education. Prior to joining the University of Maryland, he was senior attorney for the Environmental Defense Fund.

His *Environmental Regulation: Law, Science and Policy* is the leading casebook in environmental law in the United States. *Law and the Environment*, which he coedited with Dorothy C. Alezizatos, was the first work to collect major cross-disciplinary environmental works, including material by philosophers, scientists economists, historians, ecologists, and legal scholars. It attempted to treat environmental concerns as a public policy issue. The combination of history, society's response, and future implications in a global context make this work unique. He also writes on federalism, presidential power, legal history, and regulatory policy. In the aftermath of 9/11, President George W. Bush assumed great power, leading Percival to write in the *Duke Law Journal* in opposition to unitary theory, the assumption that presidents can order agency heads to make certain decisions. Percival concludes that the unitary theory that conservatives refer to in attempting to give the president total control over administrative agencies is constitutionally flawed. Rather, agency heads have a relative degree of autonomy and the Bush administration overstepped its constitutional authority in blocking the release of Reagan presidential papers and more notably in authorizing military tribunals for noncitizens. Percival addresses presidential directive authority again in 2011 in an article for the *Fordham Law Review* and again finds unitary theory invalid; presidents violate constitutional limits if they mandate agency decisions.

The Roots of Justice: Crime and Punishment in Alameda County, California, 1870–1910, coauthored with his mentor Lawrence M. Friedman in 1981, won prizes in Western and legal history. Friedman had seven years earlier called for scholars to leave the study of court cases and actually take a look at how the criminal justice system operated. It was time to look at the system in its private moments, inside the jails, rather than just in the public setting of the courtroom. The work was a landmark in legal and criminal justice studies. The work was the first to deal with the entire system, rather than one institution or one part, over time. The study of Alameda noted that the county was atypical because of the proximity of San Francisco but typical in its rapid population growth and industrialization. Thus, it was a reasonable case study for the groundbreaking study of the total criminal justice system. With his mentor, Friedman, Percival examined victims, accused, police, and other actors as they worked through the criminal justice system from crime and arrest to indictment and jury selection, pretrial and trial maneuvering, sentencing, parole and probation, appeal, and jail. The study used 73 tables and figures to display the multitude of records that the system generated, from police blotters to court records to prison and jail reports. Newspaper coverage was also a valuable source. The study found that serious crime rates declined over the period of the study, freeing citizens from fear and allowing them to use the criminal justice system for enforcing the community moral values and discipline. Crimes such as brawling and drunkenness were the norm, and the Alameda justice system emphasized order rather than law. A class bias was obvious in the types of crime prosecuted, as well as in the sorts of people brought into the system. The study also demonstrated how the professionals took over and manipulated the system with the acquiescence, if not admiration, of those whose morality the system came to represent.

The study remains a landmark examination of how the legal system actually works at the ground level, a clear departure from the traditional view from above, the theoretical operation of the legal system. They were criticized for somewhat simplistic methodology, overreliance on traditional sources such as newspapers, and neglect of the political aspect, but they were praised for achieving their stated goals of exploring from the ground up and the outside in.

John H. Barnhill
Independent Scholar

See Also: California; Crime and Arrest Statistics Analysis; Criminology; History of Crime and Punishment in America: 1850–1900; History of Crime and Punishment in America: 1900–1950.

Further Readings

Hall, Kermit L. "Review of Lawrence M. Friedman and Robert V. Percival, *The Roots of Justice: Crime and Punishment in Alameda County, California, 1870–1910*." *American Journal of Legal History*, v.27/3 (1983).

Percival, Robert V. "Who's in Charge? Does the President Have Directive Authority Over Agency Regulatory Decisions?" *Fordham Law Review*, v.79/6 (2011).

Percival, Robert V. and Dorothy C. Alevizatos, eds. *Law and the Environment: A Multidisciplinary Reader*. Philadelphia: Temple University Press, 1997.

University of Maryland. "Robert Percival" http://www.law.umaryland.edu/faculty/profiles/faculty.html?facultynum=091 (Accessed June 2011).

Walker, Samuel. "Review: Exploring the Roots of Our Criminal Justice Systems." *Michigan Law Review*, v.81/4 (1983).

Peterson, Scott

Scott Peterson was born on October 25, 1972, in San Diego, California, to Lee Peterson and Jacqueline Latham. Growing up, Scott was described as a well-behaved child who was praised for his golf skills and accomplishments. For his golf achievements, Peterson was awarded a partial athletic scholarship to play golf at Arizona State University (ASU). After one semester, Peterson left ASU and moved back in with his parents. In 1994, Peterson enrolled in California Polytechnic State University, where he met his future wife, Laci Rocha. The couple later married in August 1997 and moved to Modesto, California.

On December 24, 2002, Laci Peterson, who was eight months pregnant with the couple's first child, disappeared from the couple's Modesto home. On the day of his wife's disappearance, Scott reported that he had spent the day fishing on his boat in San Francisco Bay. Initially, the Rocha family was supportive of Scott as he coped with the disappearance of his wife. As a result of this support, Scott was not identified as a suspect in Laci's disappearance. However, investigators later discovered that Scott had extramarital affairs. One of his affairs was with Amber Frey, whom Scott was seeing at the time of Laci's disappearance. The discovery of this affair, in addition to discrepancies in Scott's reports of his wife's disappearance, ultimately prompted investigators to focus on Scott as the prime suspect in his wife's disappearance. On April 14, 2003, the partial remains of Laci Peterson and her unborn son were discovered in San Francisco Bay, which led to Scott's arrest for these murders on April 18. When he was arrested, Peterson claimed that he was meeting his father and brother to play golf. However, at the time of his arrest, Peterson was in possession of various suspicious items, including $15,000 in cash and camping equipment, which investigators believed to be evidence that Peterson had planned to flee.

On June 1, 2004, the trial of *People of the State of California v. Scott Peterson* commenced. Peterson was charged with the double homicides of his wife, Laci, and unborn child, with a guilty conviction carrying with it the possibility of death. Due to the media attention surrounding the trial, the presiding judge, Al Girolami, ordered that the trial be moved from Modesto, California, to Redwood City, and he enacted a gag order prohibiting everyone involved in the case from speaking to the media.

The prosecution focused its case on forensic evidence, Peterson's affair with Amber Frey, and on Peterson's actions throughout the investigation into Laci's disappearance. Lead prosecutor Rick Disatso argued that a hair found in a pair of pliers on Peterson's boat provided forensic evidence that Peterson used his boat to discard Laci's body. According to Disatso, prior to her death, Laci had never been on Peterson's boat, thus indicating that the hair must have been transferred on the day of her death. In addition, the prosecution argued that Peterson's actions prior to Laci's disappearance, namely, his affair with Amber Frey, further established Peterson's guilt. Frey testified at the trial that throughout the affair Peterson claimed to be a widower. Frey further reported that she did not learn that Peterson was married until news of Laci's disappearance reached the media. Disatso used this testimony as well as taped conversations between Frey and Peterson to establish that Peterson had a motive to kill his wife in order to continue his affair with Frey. Peterson's selling of Laci's car and his desire to sell the couple's

Modesto home were also presented as evidence of Peterson's motive.

The defense, led by Mark Geragos, focused on trying to prove that the prosecution's forensic evidence was circumstantial and that Peterson's affair with Amber Frey indicated that he "was a cad" but did not prove that he was a murderer. In addition, Geragos argued that the discovered remains of the fetus were full-grown, which he claimed suggested that Laci was likely kidnapped, held for an extended period of time, and later murdered by an unknown individual or group. On November 12, 2004, Scott Peterson was found guilty of one count of first-degree murder in the death of his wife, Laci, and one count of second-degree murder in the death of his unborn son. On March 26, 2005, following the jurors' recommendation, Judge Alfred Delucchi sentenced Scott Peterson to death by lethal injection and ordered that Peterson help pay for Laci's funeral. On March 17, 2005, Peterson was moved to San Quentin State Prison where he awaits the death penalty.

JoAnna Elmquist
Andrew Ninnemann
Butler Hospital and Brown University
Gregory L. Stuart
University of Tennessee, Knoxville

See Also: Capital Punishment; News Media, Crime in; San Quentin State Prison.

Further Readings
Ablow, Keith. *Inside the Mind of Scott Peterson*. New York: St. Martin's Press, 2005.
Crier, Catherine. *A Deadly Game: The Untold Story of the Scott Peterson Investigation*. New York: HarperCollins, 2005.
Fleeman, Michael. *Laci: Inside the Laci Peterson Murder*. New York: St. Martin's Press, 2003.

Petty Courts

Petty courts are known by various names: city or municipal courts, mayor's courts, magistrate's courts, or justice of the peace courts. They occupy the lowest level of courts and are courts of limited jurisdiction. Their jurisdiction is most often limited by subject matter and by geography. These courts may vary significantly in organization and practice from jurisdiction to jurisdiction.

Petty courts have been used as local arbiters of justice in the United States since colonial times. They are deeply rooted in the local context from which they emerged, and each court's practices have been shaped by local needs and customs. In early petty courts, proceedings focused more on dispute resolution than on crime control per se. Proceedings were initiated by private citizens rather than by agents of the state and were overseen by local authorities (e.g., squires and aldermen) who rarely had formal legal training. The high degree of local control caused concern among progressive reformers as many petty courts were susceptible to undue and inappropriate local political influence. Mayors and other local political figures enjoyed broad discretion in using the local courts to advance their own agendas, for example, using court appointments to reward loyal supporters. Though modern petty courts continue to be locally funded and managed, they are being brought under greater levels of state control. Increasingly, state legislation subjects local courts to regulations that seek to minimize vulnerability to local political whims and to ensure uniform legal procedures and standards across jurisdictions. Though still separate from most state court systems, decisions made in the petty courts may be subject to review by courts in the state-administered court system should a petty court defendant wish to appeal a case.

Cases

Types of cases typically heard in petty courts include traffic offenses, local ordinance violations, minor criminal cases (i.e., misdemeanors), and low-value civil cases. In some cases, petty courts may conduct the preliminary proceedings in felony cases (e.g., the entering of a plea). In addition, some jurisdictions allow for proceedings of more serious motor vehicle offenses to be heard in the petty courts if the defendant agrees to such an arrangement.

Misdemeanors that are commonly addressed by petty courts include petty theft, disorderly conduct, public drunkenness, curfew violations, loitering, resisting arrest, simple assault, underage possession of alcohol, and minor controlled substance and paraphernalia offenses. Petty courts may also hear some civil cases—these cases are typically limited by the amount of money involved. A growing trend in localities across the United States is the creation of specialized petty courts focused on processing distinct types of cases (e.g., truancy or drug cases) or on resolving cases involving unique populations (e.g., the homeless, or enlisted military personnel and veterans of war).

Caseloads in urban and suburban petty courts are often staggering, far outweighing the number of cases processed in all other types of courts. Even with heavy caseloads, petty courts must process every case in a reasonable amount of time—usually within two years of when the case was originally filed.

Cases enter the petty court system in a variety of ways: as a result of an indictment, a complaint made by a member of the public, or a citation or violation notice issued by a public official or law enforcement officer. Like defendants in other courts, defendants in petty courts may plead not guilty, guilty, or, in some cases, nolo contendere, or "no contest." A no contest plea means that the defendant is claiming neither guilt nor innocence. No contest pleas are treated the same as a guilty plea (or a guilty ruling) in sentencing decisions. Unlike other courts, defendants may not be required to appear in court or to meet with a judge in order to enter a plea and resolve their case; many jurisdictions allow defendants to plead guilty through the mail or, increasingly, online. Like other courts, a guilty (or no contest) plea is the most common plea made in petty courts. If a defendant does not appear when required by the court, a warrant may be issued for the individual's arrest.

Sanctions

Petty courts most commonly rely on two forms of sanctions: the assessment of fines and fees or short-term incarceration in a local jail. They may also have the authority to require individuals to participate in counseling, community service, or other types of rehabilitative or educational programming.

In the past, many local jurisdictions allowed the presiding judge in the petty courts to take a percentage of the proceeds obtained from any fees and fines collected. This practice encouraged judicial corruption and has since been outlawed. In contemporary times, some of the revenues generated by fines and fees are used to pay local court and criminal justice administration costs. Increasingly common is the allocation of revenues generated by the petty courts into the general funds of the local and state governments. Petty courts tend to be the only component of a state's criminal justice system that generates a profit. In some states, millions of dollars of revenue are generated each year by the local petty courts; for this reason, some legal scholars are concerned that political figures may deemphasize the role of the courts in justice seeking and order maintenance and, instead, utilize the petty courts as a "cash cow" that can be used to generate discretionary revenue for the government.

Petty courts may also order guilty parties to serve time in a local jail. Generally, jail terms are

Petty court cases are typically traffic offenses, ordinance violations, minor criminal cases, and low-value civil cases, taking place without the involvement of a defense attorney.

less than one year. Noncompliance with court requirements may result in additional charges, for which defendants can be sentenced with more strenuous requirements or with additional jail time. Many courts may also restrict individual access to a driver's or professional license. In addition, charges in petty court may have significant hidden civil consequences for defendants. Criminal records may result in social stigma or limit the ability of an individual to retain or obtain certain forms of employment. Many jurisdictions have provisions for the expunging (i.e., erasing or sealing) of a criminal record. Which charges and how many charges can be expunged vary depending on the jurisdiction.

Procedures

Most petty court processes take place without the involvement of a defense attorney. For much of their history, petty courts were not required to provide attorneys for defendants who could not afford counsel. In 1972, the U.S. Supreme Court ruled that legal counsel must be provided in any case where there is a possibility of deprivation of liberty (i.e., incarceration) no matter how brief the deprivation. In jurisdictions where punishments may include jail time, legal counsel may be provided for those who prove themselves to be indigent (i.e., poor). Courts that provide defense counsel may require an application and an application fee from defendants who seek appointed counsel. Indigent defense attorneys often have heavy caseloads and little time to prepare for each of their cases. In addition, indigent defense programs are often underfunded and lack access to the necessary resources to mount a rigorous defense of clients, including funds for additional investigations or expert witnesses. As with other types of courts, defendants have the option to hire their own representation, but most do not.

Given the high volume of cases and the expectation that legal cases be processed quickly, there is significant institutional pressure exerted on petty court personnel to minimize challenges posed by defendants to the charges they face. Trials are infrequent, and court processes are rarely recorded. Multiple defendants are scheduled to be seen at one time, and their legal rights are often told to them en masse. Without a trial, defendants in the petty courts rarely have the opportunity to exercise many of the rights considered fundamental to the American justice system, including the right to review evidence against them, to present evidence in their defense, to confront witnesses, and to have their case heard by a jury of their peers.

Depending on the jurisdiction, judges in petty courts are either appointed by the local government (e.g., the city council) or elected by local residents. As with judges in other types of courts, petty court judges are predominantly white and male. Not all jurisdictions require a serving petty court judge to have a law degree, or in some cases, a college degree. Judges may not have any support staff (i.e., clerks, bailiffs) and may only work part time, especially in small or in rural jurisdictions.

Conclusion

Though petty courts receive little media or scholarly attention compared to other types of courts, these courts are the most likely and most frequent point of contact between members of the public and the justice system. Experiences in petty courts may have significant impact on public trust and confidence in the larger justice system and on the perception that American courts are unbiased, efficient, and accessible.

Elyshia D. Aseltine
Lycoming College

See Also: Courts; Defendant's Rights; Due Process; Traffic Crimes.

Further Readings
Feeley, Malcolm. *The Process Is the Punishment: Handling Cases in a Lower Criminal Court*. New York: Russell Sage Foundation, 1979.
Jacob, Herbert. *Urban Justice: Law and Order in American Cities*. Upper Saddle River, NJ: Prentice Hall, 1973.
Meyer, Jon'a and Paul Jesilow. *"Doing Justice" in the People's Court*. Albany: State University of New York Press, 1997.
Mileski, Maureen. "Courtroom Encounters: An Observation Study of a Lower Criminal Court." *Law & Society Review*, v.5/5 (1971).
Steinberg, Allen. *The Transformation of Criminal Justice, Philadelphia, 1800–1880*. Chapel Hill: University of North Carolina Press, 1989.

Philadelphia, Pennsylvania

The largest city in the Commonwealth of Pennsylvania, Philadelphia was established as the first settlement in the colony of Pennsylvania in 1682 by William Penn. It was incorporated as a city in 1701. Philadelphia was an important trading and cultural center in the British Empire during the 17th and 18th centuries and became a center for revolutionary activities. Philadelphia has, since the 18th century, been active in prison reform activism and is home to the internationally renowned Eastern State Penitentiary.

Crime is always an issue in urban centers, and Philadelphia is no exception. In the 18th century, homicide indictment rates ranged from 1 to 6 per 100,000 people, with a spike of 11.6 per 100,000 during the period of 1765–75. Rates of property crime ranged between 150 and 200 incidents per 100,000 people during the late 18th century. During the 19th century, rates of homicide indictments ranged from 2.2 to 4 per 100,000. Crime in 19th-century Philadelphia also involved violent rioting, particularly in the 1830s and 1840s, stemming from ethnic and racial tensions in the city. The most notable of the riots were the Philadelphia Nativist Riots, which took place in May and July 1844. These riots occurred between Irish Catholics and American nativists as a result of growing anti-Catholic sentiment and frustration over the rising Irish population in Philadelphia. Catholic churches were burned, and there were more than 100 casualties.

By the turn of the 20th century, Philadelphia's homicide rate had dropped to 2.1 per 100,000. Over the course of the 20th century, crime rates increased steadily, and drug-related and Mafia crime became serious issues in the 1970s and 1980s. In 1990, the violent crime rate was 1,348.8 per 100,000; the property crime rate was 5,843 per 100,000. By 2005, violent crime had increased to a rate of 1,467.1 per 100,000, while the property crime rate had dropped to 4,102.0 per 100,000. In 2007, the homicide rate was 27 per 100,000.

Law Enforcement

Law enforcement in early Philadelphia consisted of a night watch, which was organized in 1751.

Moyamensing Prison, or the Philadelphia County Jail, opened in 1835 in the southern part of the city to deal with the growing number of offenders committing lesser crimes.

Without much of a police force, private prosecution was the mainstay of criminal justice for Philadelphia's lower classes. Individuals had the ability to take others to court without police intervention in the first half of the 19th century, and the courts acted as a means to settle disputes. The system changed when a professional police force was established, and other criminal justice officials such as district attorneys became salaried employees of the state.

Philadelphians realized the need to create a unified police department in the 1830s with the rise of racial and ethnic violence. In 1833, an initial preventive police department was established. Trouble over police jurisdiction arose between the city and surrounding independent boroughs in the 1830s and 1840s. In 1854, when Philadelphia incorporated these boroughs into the city proper, a centralized police department was also established, splitting the larger city into separate police districts, all part of the Philadelphia Police Department. The Philadelphia police have received national attention from several cases in the 20th century, notably those dealing with the communal black liberation group MOVE during a raid in 1978 and the bombing of their compound in 1985. The case of Mumia Abu-Jamal, who was convicted of killing Philadelphia police officer Daniel Faulkner in 1981, also received national recognition. Abu-Jamal is currently incarcerated, while appeals trials determine whether his death sentence will be upheld or commuted to a life sentence.

Prison Reform

During the colonial era, punishments in the city were public, including hangings, work gangs, whippings, and the use of stocks and pillories. In 1776, the city opened a new prison, later known as Walnut Street Jail, in downtown Philadelphia. Prisoners were held in large rooms, and little effort was made to help inmates rehabilitate. During the Revolutionary War, some citizens became active in trying to improve the conditions for prisoners, initiating some of the earliest prison reform work for which the city later became known. In 1787, the Philadelphia Society for Alleviating the Miseries of Public Prisons was established. Three years later, Walnut Street Jail was expanded to become the nation's first penitentiary, utilizing individual cells to halt prisoner corruption and to attempt to produce character reform in the inmates.

Prison reform efforts continued into the 19th century. Eastern State Penitentiary opened in 1829 on the northwestern outskirts of the city. The penitentiary used the Pennsylvania system of reform, in which inmates served their entire incarceration term in total silence and isolation. Each prisoner had his or her own cell and worked at artisanal crafts. Prison reformers from the Philadelphia Society visited the penitentiary regularly to ensure that attempts at rehabilitating inmates were being made. In 1835, Moyamensing Prison, or the Philadelphia County Jail, opened in the southern part of the city to deal with the growing number of offenders committing lesser crimes. With the opening of this county jail, Walnut Street was closed. Moyamensing Prison was destroyed in the 1960s.

In 1971, Eastern State closed its doors, and most of its inmates and employees moved to Graterford Prison outside the city. Even though the historical prisons are now closed, prison reform efforts still emanate from Philadelphia. The Philadelphia Society was later renamed the Pennsylvania Prison Society, and the organization still has its headquarters in the city.

Erica Rhodes Hayden
Vanderbilt University

See Also: 1801 to 1850 Primary Documents; 1851 to 1900 Primary Documents; Eastern State Penitentiary; MOVE; Pennsylvania; Pennsylvania System of Reform; Quakers.

Further Readings

Abu-Jamal, Mumia. *Live From Death Row.* New York: Avon Books, 1996.
Meranze, Michael. *Laboratories of Virtue: Punishment, Revolution, and Authority in Philadelphia, 1760–1835.* Chapel Hill: University of North Carolina Press, 1996.
Scharf, J. Thomas, et al. *History of Philadelphia, 1609–1884.* Philadelphia: L. H. Everts, 1884.
Steinberg, Allen. *The Transformation of Criminal Justice, Philadelphia, 1800–1880.* Chapel Hill: University of North Carolina Press, 1989.

Pickpockets

The word *pickpocket* first emerged in the late 1500s to describe a person who steals wallets, money, and other valuables from the pockets of other people. Pickpockets have a lengthy history throughout the world and have likely existed as long as people have carried valuables with them. Edwin Sutherland placed pickpockets in a class of skilled criminals that includes shoplifters, confidence men, and check writers. He described these types of criminals as professional thieves who have great acting skills and principally depend on their wits and talking ability. While pickpocketing could conceivably be committed by just about anyone of any age, race, or gender, it was not uncommon for children to engage in the "trade" in early American cities. This topic is an important one to explore because many societal factors coalesced to allow pickpocketing, and juvenile pickpockets in particular, to flourish in large American cities in the 1800s.

Ample references to pickpockets in the United States can be found in newspapers dating back to at least the 1800s. A *New York Times* article from 1865 describes a "swell mob" of pickpockets who would rush toward city cars in the evening and go about emptying the pockets of the crowd. Pocket picking persists to this day, and the method has remained largely unchanged. John Young, a former criminal investigator with the Amtrak Police Department, states that contemporary pickpockets tend to operate in places where large crowds of people congregate (e.g., cities or train stations) and will typically bump into their intended victim in an effort to distract him/her long enough to steal his/her wallet or other valuables.

Pickpockets have oft been romanticized in classic literature through colorful characters like Charles Dickens's controversial character Fagin, who teaches children the finer points of pocket picking in his veritable school for crime. Fictional accounts aside, historical examinations of pickpocketing reveal an entire subculture that existed in the 1800s; many well-known American pickpockets began their criminal careers as children. Understanding the history of pickpocketing is no easy task because of the deeply secretive nature of the pickpocketing subculture that existed primarily in larger American cities during the 1800s. Timothy Gilfoyle, who has written extensively on juvenile pickpockets, notes that records are scarce, as the subculture of juvenile pickpockets was largely organized around an oral culture that left little written evidence. Gilfoyle goes on to state that the lack of written records coupled with the fact that pickpocketing was, for the most part, an invisible crime makes historical analysis of the subject very difficult. However, historians have been very clear on the factors that precipitated and allowed juvenile pickpockets to flourish. With industrialization in the United States came an infusion of people into large cities, and large-scale factories (or sweatshops) largely replaced craftsmen and skilled laborers. As a consequence, many children who might previously have been engaged in an apprenticeship were largely left to their own devices. All of these factors converged, along with the fact that school attendance was not compulsory in the 1800s, to result in an abundance of juvenile pickpockets. The newsboy profession often overlapped with pickpocketing. George Appo, who is perhaps the most famous American pickpocket, revealed that he and a fellow newsboy were able to pickpocket for a full two years before police apprehended them. Another pickpocket and newsboy, Larry Caulfield, is quoted as saying, "I made a great deal of money at picking pockets, without getting into difficulties with the police." The "newspaper dodge" was a favored tactic among newsboy pocket pickers. This strategy involved waving a newspaper in the

Pickpockets like Fagin in Charles Dickens's Oliver Twist *(depicted above) have often been romanticized in literature. Historical research of pickpocketing reveals that an entire subculture existing during the 1800s shared their techniques by word of mouth, leaving little documentation. Many well-known American pickpockets started their careers at a young age.*

face of a potential victim and while he/she was distracted, the newsboy would reach into the victim's pocket and remove any valuables. Larry Caulfield would often board crowded streetcars and shove a newspaper in the face of male passengers and yell "News, boss?" in an effort to divert the attention of his intended victim. Caulfield bragged, "If you will stand for a newspaper under your chin, I can get even your socks." So many of these children posed as newsboys that it was vitually impossible to tell a real newsboy from a thief.

Use of the newspaper dodge was certainly not the only pickpocketing technique employed. Numerous tactics were (and still are) used by pickpockets. For example, "the sandwich" involves a team of two pickpockets. One pickpocket bumps into the victim as a distraction, while the accomplice steals the person's valuables.

The Case of George Appo

George Appo, who began his criminal career as a pickpocket in New York City, is regarded as a compelling and significant criminal of the 19th century. Appo, the son of immigrants, never went to school and largely supported himself as a child by working as a newsboy, pickpocket, and confidence man. His father was convicted of murder and spent most of Appo's life in and out of prison. Appo's mother and younger sister died in a shipwreck when he was just 6 years old, effectively making him an orphan. By the age of 12, with his father back in jail, George fell in with a gang of pickpockets and took up the trade to support himself. He worked the streets for two years, until he was arrested and sentenced to the School Ship Mercury, a floating prison of sorts that was designed to teach young delinquents nautical skills. Appo served more than one year on the vessel, but accounts differ about the nature of his release. Tyler Anbinder reports that he jumped ship in New York Harbor in 1873, but according to Appo himself, he was released on good behavior after he saved a fellow shipmate from drowning. Debates about his release notwithstanding, it appears that his time on the ship did little to alter his behavior, as he very quickly returned to his previous environment and associates and began pickpocketing again in earnest. By age 16, Appo was once again arrested for pickpocketing and was sentenced to two and one-half years' imprisonment with hard labor.

By all accounts, Appo was a skilled pickpocket, and on a good night, he would earn about as much as a skilled laborer's salary. Throughout his career as a pickpocket and confidence man, he likely earned thousands. The money he earned through his criminal enterprises did not come without a steep cost, however, as he served decades behind bars and suffered numerous injuries. At various points, Appo had his teeth knocked out, and once released, he was assaulted nine times, shot twice, and stabbed in the throat once. The physical cost of criminality did not deter Appo, and his career transitioned from pickpocket to confidence man. Of course, young men were not the only ones engaged in pickpocketing, though it was a predominantly masculine trade. Men and women would often work in teams, with the woman largely serving as a distraction for the intended victim. This technique (which is still employed by pickpockets today) typically involved a beautiful woman distracting the victim while the accomplice stole from the victim. Sophie Lyons was one such female pickpocket. She would go on to become one of the most skilled confidence women in early American history. Gilfoyle notes that Lyons was an extremely successful pickpocket who would occassionaly use knives to cut open bags and steal valuable contents.

The pickpocketing problem did not go unnoticed by the criminal justice system. By the latter part of the 1800s, rates of arrest and conviction were quite high. Gilfoyle reports that proscutions of pickpockets nearly tripled between 1869 and 1876. During the period, juries became much more likely to convict juveniles for pickpocketing. Evidence suggests that punishments also became quite harsh in the 1870s. A number of juveniles were sent to penitentiaries, with some serving sentences of several years. Despite the availablility of juvenile facilities, almost 85 percent of male pickpockets aged 16–17 were sentenced to Sing Sing Penitentary at Ossining, New York. In summary, the history of pickpocketing is largely a history of juvenile crime, exacerbated by the Industrial Revolution. As Gilfoyle notes, many of the children who engaged in this practice were children who lacked parental supervision and used pickpocketing as one of many strategies to survive on the streets.

Laurie A. Gould
Georgia Southern University

See Also: Juvenile Delinquency, History of; Juvenile Delinquency, Sociology of; Juvenile Justice, History of.

Further Readings

Anbinder, Tyler. *Five Points: The 19th Century New York City Neighborhood That Invented Tap Dance, Stole Elections, and Became the World's Most Notorious Slum.* New York: Free Press, 2001.

Gilfoyle, Timothy. *A Pickpocket's Tale: The Underworld of Nineteenth Century New York.* New York: W. W. Norton, 2007.

Gilfoyle, Timothy. "Street-Rats and Gutter-Snipes: Child Pickpockets and Street Culture in New York City, 1850–1900." *Journal of Social History* (Summer 2004).

Moss, Frank. *The American Metropolis From Knickerbocker Days to the Present Time: New York City Life in All Its Various Phases.* London: Author's Syndicate, 1897.

Young, John. "Pickpockets, Their Victims, and the Transit Police." *FBI Law Enforcement Bulletin* (2003).

Pierce, Franklin (Administration of)

Democrat Franklin Pierce (1804–69) served one term as the 14th president of the United States from 1853 to 1857. Although Pierce was from New Hampshire, he was largely viewed as a southern sympathizer who desired to protect the legality of slavery and the Fugitive Slave Act of 1850. Pierce was most noted for his signing of the Kansas-Nebraska Act of 1854, granting the voters of those territories the right to decide slavery's legal status through the doctrine of popular sovereignty. His administration was unable to stem the widespread election fraud and violence in "Bleeding Kansas" that resulted. The Pierce administration's expansionist foreign policies were overall more successful.

Franklin Pierce served as a postmaster and lawyer upon his graduation from Bowdoin College. He had a lengthy on-and-off political career as a Democrat before running for president, serving in the New Hampshire legislature from 1828 to 1832 and in the U.S. Congress from 1832 to 1842 before resigning for personal reasons. Pierce was a supporter of President Andrew Jackson and his Democratic principles. He also served as a general during the Mexican–American War (1846–48). Pierce was nominated to the Democratic ticket in 1852 as a compromise candidate on the 49th ballot of the nominating convention because of his northern origins and southern political leanings. Franklin Pierce defeated Whig Party nominee General Winfield Scott in the general election.

Slavery Under the Pierce Administration

Many historians view Pierce as an ineffective president who allowed sectional divisions to worsen during his administration. Pierce had been an outspoken critic of the abolitionist movement and was seen as a southern sympathizer, or "doughface," despite his northern origins. Pierce sought to maintain national unity by composing his cabinet of both northerners and southerners and through his rigid enforcement of the earlier Compromise of 1850, including the Fugitive Slave Act, which allowed slave catchers to pursue escaped slaves into free states. A noted case involved fugitive slave Anthony Burns, who was captured and held in Boston, Massachusetts. Pierce supported the attorney general's refusal to allow Burns's friends to purchase his freedom and deployed federal troops to ensure his return to slavery.

Anthony Burns, a slave owned by Virginia merchant Charles Suttle, escaped to Boston as a shipboard stowaway. Suttle later determined the location of the fugitive through a letter Burns sent to his brother, who was also Suttle's slave. In 1854, Suttle traveled to Boston to reclaim Burns under the Fugitive Slave Law of 1850. Burns was arrested and held at the federal courthouse. Boston area abolitionists converged on the courthouse to protest and free Burns, leading to a riot that attracted national attention. Pierce ordered U.S. marines to protect the courthouse and ensure that the Fugitive Slave Law would be executed. Under the Fugitive Slave Law, a commissioner rather than a jury heard the case. Although renowned Boston lawyer Richard Henry Dana represented Burns, Judge Edward G. Loring convicted him as a fugitive slave, and Suttle was named his rightful owner. An African American church purchased

Burns's freedom soon after his return to Virginia aboard a federal ship.

Domestic and Foreign Policy

Pierce's commitment to national unity was most tested when the territories of Kansas and Nebraska began the path to statehood. Pierce signed the Kansas-Nebraska Act of 1854, repealing the old Missouri Compromise line restricting slavery to south of 36°30' north latitude and implementing the concept of popular sovereignty in the territories of Kansas and Nebraska. Popular sovereignty would allow the people of a territory to vote to determine the legality of slavery when that territory applied for statehood. There was election fraud as Missouri voters crossed into Kansas to illegally vote it a slave state, and a violent struggle between pro-slavery and abolitionist factions erupted in what became known as "Bleeding Kansas."

The Pierce administration did little to address the violence and illegal elections even after John Brown's Pottawatomie Massacre left five dead, and Kansas had competing pro- and antislavery governments appealing to Washington for legitimacy. The divisiveness over popular sovereignty and the subsequent violence in Kansas resulted in deepening sectional divisions within the Democratic Party, the demise of the Whig Party over sectional differences, and the creation of the Republican Party in the north.

The Pierce administration's foreign policy aims were more successful and expansionist in character. Successes included U.S. ships' gaining limited access to Japanese ports under Commodore Matthew Perry, the Gadsden Purchase of land near the Mexican border, and the negotiations of treaties with Canada settling fishing rights and Great Britain settling Central American conflicts. More controversial were the recognition of American William Walker's regime in Nicaragua and a failed attempt to acquire Cuba from Spain revealed in the Ostend Manifesto, which damaged Pierce's reputation when it was publicly revealed. The Cuba plot also furthered northern criticisms, as many felt southerners desired Cuba as a potential new slave territory.

When the Democratic Party failed to nominate Pierce for a second term in 1856 because of his unpopularity in the north, he left politics and returned to the practice of law in Concord, New Hampshire. His criticisms of President Abraham Lincoln and his Emancipation Proclamation freeing slaves in rebellious territories during the Civil War led to further accusations of his southern sympathies. Franklin Pierce died in Concord on October 8, 1869.

Marcella Bush Trevino
Barry University

See Also: Fugitive Slave Act of 1850; Lincoln, Abraham (Administration of); Slavery, Law of.

Further Readings

Gara, Larry. *The Presidency of Franklin Pierce.* Lawrence: University Press of Kansas, 1991.

Nichols, Roy F. *Franklin Pierce: Young Hickory of the Granite Hills.* Newtown, CT: American Political Biography Press, 1998.

Wallner, Peter. *Franklin Pierce: Martyr for the Union.* Concord, NH: Plaidswede, 2009.

Pittsburgh, Pennsylvania

Pittsburgh, Pennsylvania, located at the confluence of the Monongahela and Allegheny rivers, forming the Ohio River in western Pennsylvania, developed in the 18th century as a site for trading between Native Americans and Europeans and became a battleground for control between colonial powers. Pittsburgh was home to Western State Penitentiary, one of the earliest penitentiaries in the United States, which opened in 1826. In the 19th century, the city became known for its steel industry, which led to violent labor unrest.

Early History

Because of its location on the colonial frontier, much of Pittsburgh's early crime and violence stemmed from hostilities between European settlers and Native Americans. Each group perpetrated violent attacks on the other. Other minor offenses such as dishonesty or ill fame were punished internally through a system of ostracism. The offender was ostracized from the community until his or her behavior was reformed. After the

American Revolution, Pittsburgh was still considered the American frontier. In the early 1790s, more resistance occurred during the Whiskey Rebellion, when frontiersmen in western Pennsylvania used violence and intimidation to prevent government officials from collecting a tax on whiskey. The violence culminated in 1794 when more than 500 protesters attacked the home of a tax inspector. The federal government responded by sending troops to quell the violence. Approximately 20 leaders were arrested and tried for their participation, but all were later acquitted or pardoned.

When the city was incorporated in 1816, Pittsburgh established a Mayor's Court, which tried assaults and batteries, riots, and all other offenses that were normally tried in a county Court of Quarter Sessions. Pittsburgh's Mayor's Court sat four times a year, just like the traditional Court of Quarter Sessions. While there had been a night watch patrol in Pittsburgh since 1794, in 1816, the order of incorporation for the city provided for a high constable and four other constables, a watch captain, and 12 watchmen. The day and night patrols dealt with the common urban crimes such as burglary, prostitution, murder, and gambling. The Pittsburgh Bureau of Police, founded in 1857, became the unified police force for the city. Currently, it is the third-largest law enforcement agency in the state.

In 1826, the state opened Western State Penitentiary in what is now West Park, Pittsburgh. This first Western State Penitentiary remained in operation until 1880. Its original design resembled Jeremy Bentham's Panopticon, which ideally would provide constant surveillance of every cell. When it was determined that the design presented security issues, the building plans were modified to resemble the hub-and-spoke plan that the builders of Eastern State Penitentiary were following in Philadelphia. The first Western State Penitentiary housed more than 100 Confederate soldiers captured in Morgan's Raid in 1863. In 1882, the current Western State Penitentiary opened. In its early days, it housed some maximum-security inmates. It closed from 2005 to 2007 for maintenance purposes. It currently houses low- and medium-security inmates who require substance abuse treatment. Pittsburgh is also home to Allegheny County Jail. An early jail attached to the county courthouse was built in 1886, and the building now houses the county's Family Court Division. The current Allegheny County Jail is still located in downtown Pittsburgh.

The Nineteenth Century and Beyond

Pittsburgh grew in the 19th century because of booming industries, which fostered a great deal of labor unrest and violence in the late 19th and early 20th centuries. On July 14, 1877, a railroad strike began in Martinsburg, West Virginia, as a result of the railroad company's reducing wages for a second time in one year. The strike quickly spread to other railroad workers across the region. Pittsburgh became the site of the worst violence that occurred during the strike. On July 21, 1877, militiamen attacked strikers with bayonets and gunfire, killing 20 and wounding dozens more. In retaliation, strikers caused the militia

The steel business, along with other booming industries, fostered much labor unrest and violence in Pittsburgh, Pennsylvania, in the late 19th and early 20th centuries.

to take cover in a roundhouse and set fire to the railroad yards. The next day, the militia fought its way out of the roundhouse, killing 20 more people. President Rutherford B. Hayes was forced to send federal troops to end the strikes after a month of rioting and violence.

In 1892, skilled union members who worked for Carnegie Steel went on strike at the Homestead Steel Works to protect their jobs from being taken by unskilled workers. The company locked union members out of the plant, and the strike began on June 30, 1892. Workers from other nearby steel plants joined the strike in sympathy. The company tried to continue production with strikebreakers and attempted to get Pinkerton agents to the plant to protect the strikebreakers. The strikers anticipated the plan, and a bloody battle erupted between the strikers and the Pinkerton agents, resulting in several deaths on both sides. The Homestead Strike eventually failed after an assassination attempt on the company executive. The strikers lost public support for their cause, and workers returned to the plant. In 1919, steelworkers in Pittsburgh went on strike again in order to force local officials to allow the American Federation of Labor to hold union meetings in the city. In September, a general steelworker strike began, halting half of the nation's steel production in Pennsylvania and other states. Companies used violence, threats, and strikebreakers to demoralize the strikers. By early January 1920, the strike fell apart.

In the 20th century, Pittsburgh dealt with organized crime and high crime rates. The LaRocca family held control over politicians, police officers, and labor unions. The group was involved with bootlegging and ammunition trading during the early and mid-20th century, and turned to gambling and illegal drug rackets in the 1980s. Top members were convicted in the 1990s, greatly weakening the family's power. Crime rates for the past 25 years have shown a steady decrease in property crimes, dropping from 6,129.7 incidents per 100,000 people in 1985 to 3,771.2 per 100,000 in 2009. Violent crime rates have averaged 1,065.1 incidents per 100,000 since 1985. In 2003, statistics indicated that Pittsburgh had a murder rate 2.61 times higher than the national average.

Erica Rhodes Hayden
Vanderbilt University

See Also: Court of Quarter Sessions; Penitentiaries; Pennsylvania; Strikes.

Further Readings
Hays, Samuel P., ed. *City at the Point: Essays on the Social History of Pittsburgh*. Pittsburgh, PA: University of Pittsburgh Press, 1989.
Krause, Paul. *The Battle for Homestead, 1880–1892: Politics, Culture, and Steel*. Pittsburgh, PA: University of Pittsburgh Press, 1992.
Slaughter, Thomas P. *The Whiskey Rebellion: Frontier Epilogue to the American Revolution*. New York: Oxford University Press, 1986.

Plea

A plea is an agreement reached by the prosecution and defense in a criminal case in which the defendant admits guilt rather than pursuing a trial in exchange for a reduction in charges (charge bargaining) or a recommendation for a lesser sentence (sentence bargaining). Many scholars believe that pleas originated as a means to deal with burgeoning caseloads in the 19th and 20th centuries in order to increase efficiency. However, there is evidence to suggest that this is not the case. Rather, plea practices appear in isolated examples in the 1700s in England and in the colonial American courts. Just after the Civil War, the practice of offering pleas started to become more commonplace. Many scholars point to increased industrialization, immigration, and corruption in urban criminal justice systems among the many causes for the plea trend. Others have drawn a parallel between the emergence of plea negotiations with the advent of public prosecution, increased rights for defendants that created lengthier trials, and even the creation of a public defender system.

There is no consensus about whether pleas grew in usage as a means of increasing efficiency or if other underlying factors led to the increased use. Nonetheless, it seems clear that the volume of cases entering the system during the 1920s as a result of federal Prohibition laws was the driving force behind the institutionalization of plea bargaining. From that point forward, in many cities across the country, the plea became the most

Attorneys approach the bench to speak with the judge. A plea offer may include a reduction in the number of counts, a reduction in the level of offense, or offering to make recommendations regarding the sanction. Taking a plea is often thought to represent a better deal than taking the chance of a trial in which sanctions could be much higher.

prevalent means by which cases were disposed. By the end of the 20th century, pleas had become entrenched as a permanent fixture of the modern criminal justice system, and as of 2006 (the most recent year for which data were available), more than 95 percent of all criminal cases nationwide were disposed by guilty plea.

Definition of Plea Bargaining

The practice of plea bargaining is highly controversial and viewed by many legal scholars as an affront to moral, legal, and ethical conceptualizations of justice. Other scholars are staunch advocates of the use of pleas, citing numerous benefits to the state, the defendant, and the criminal justice system overall. Although the critics are vocal and many, there is little support in the courts for eliminating plea bargaining. In fact, the practice has survived numerous court challenges and the constitutionality of plea bargaining was upheld by the U.S. Supreme Court in 1970 in *Brady v. United States* and in *Santobello v. New York*.

Pleas can take many forms and serve several different purposes, most of which are seen in terms of benefit to the state rather than to defendants. Specifically, pleas can be used (1) in exchange for testimony against another defendant, (2) to encourage the timely resolution of a case and the avoidance of a lengthy and costly trial, and (3) to promote public safety by securing a conviction of a defendant. There are no national guidelines or case law as to when a plea can or should be offered or what the terms of a plea should be. (In individual prosecutors' offices, however, there are specific policies on plea negotiations.) Nevertheless, the common practice generally involves a determination on the part of the prosecutor during screening, charging, or even pretrial preparations, in which the prosecutor exercises his or her discretion about whether to make a plea offer to the defendant. The decision whether to accept the plea in this instance lies with the defense. In situations where the plea negotiation is initiated by the defense, the decision about whether to negotiate lies solely with the prosecutor.

The plea offer may include a reduction in the number of counts (i.e., an offer to plea to one count of bad checks in exchange for dropping the other five counts); a reduction in the level of offense (for example, reducing an aggravated assault to an assault charge); or offering to make recommendations regarding the sanction. The practice of including charges in the plea negotiation process has become known as "charge bargaining." When the focus is on the sanctions, or the sentencing options, the negotiation has become known as "sentencing bargaining." In recent years, the practice of charge bargaining has become particularly important. With many states legislating determinate or mandatory sentencing as a means for limiting judicial discretion, the practice of charge bargaining then effectively moves the discretionary power over sentencing to prosecutors. By negotiating which charges to file, the prosecutor is in part also negotiating which sentencing guidelines will apply.

Whether it is the charges or the sentence being "bargained," the plea represents a means for certainty about the sanctions for defendants rather than the uncertainty of trial—in other words, taking the plea is often thought to represent a better deal than taking the chance of a trial in which the sanctions could be much higher. A plea offer is usually made with the caveat that if the defendant opts to go to trial, it is likely that the maximum sanction will be levied against him or her if convicted. Some critics point to this very notion as the epitome of what is wrong about the use of pleas, arguing that the plea is used by the state to obtain a conviction in what would otherwise be a weak case that would be unlikely to result in conviction at trial. Part of the concern here stems from the fact that during the negotiation stage, the prosecutor typically has a significant advantage over the defense in that he or she generally has a better sense about the strength of the case than the defense counsel does, particularly when plea negotiations begin before discovery. Moreover, the prosecutor has unparalleled bargaining strength—a defendant is forced to deal only with the prosecutor who is handling the case for the state and cannot "shop" for better deals with other prosecutors who may be seen as more lenient or who offer better deals. As a result, critics claim, defendants feel coerced into accepting plea offers. On the other hand, from the state's perspective, the plea represents the certainty of a conviction, some sanction for an offender, and no chance of an appellate reversal.

Rules of Pleas

Because of concerns that pleas not violate defendants' rights, there are a number of rules regarding guilty pleas designed to protect these rights. Pleas must be entered into by the defendant voluntarily, without coercion from either the prosecution or the defense. Defendants must plead openly in court, informing the court that the plea was entered into voluntarily, without coercion, and acknowledging the right to a trial if he or she so chooses. The plea agreement reached by the prosecution and the defense is only a recommendation to the judge, who ultimately has the authority to decide whether or not to accept the plea in whole or in part, and what the appropriate sanction should be. More often than not, the plea is accepted by the court with little or no modification to the terms. Once the court has accepted it, a guilty plea cannot be revoked, which eliminates the possibility of appeal and transparency in the system. Here again, critics find fault with the "rules," arguing that they are symbolic only and afford no real protection against coercion or injustice.

Despite the fact that there are very specific rules with regard to the entering of a guilty plea that stem from long-seeded concerns about self-incrimination and self-conviction, there is a continuous debate about the appropriateness of the plea as a tool for disposing criminal cases. Much of the debate stems from the question of whether the practice of plea bargaining is morally justified and the extent to which such practices may invalidate the concept of justice. Proponents of pleas focus on the efficiency gains created by guilty plea case disposition, which allow the system to process a greater volume of cases than it would otherwise be able to handle. Proponents also argue that pleas create certainty of punishment, thereby maximizing the public good through deterrence and ensuring public safety—in essence, bargaining for the public good.

Criticisms of Pleas

The list of criticisms of pleas runs long. Opponents raise concerns about the subversion of due process through the use of pleas, noting that plea bargaining is inherently unfair and coercive. There is no opportunity for defenses to be presented before a judge or jury, rather in pleas, these defenses become the mitigating factors by which the defense hopes to achieve a more beneficial plea offer for his or her client.

The strongest critics of plea bargaining point to disparities in sentences between those defendants that decide to plead guilty and those who prefer to have a trial. There is evidence to suggest that defendants who plead receive more lenient sentences than those who go to trial, thus raising questions about fairness—how can two defendants who share similar characteristics and have committed the same crimes be sentenced differently because one decided to plead and one decided to exercise his or her right to a trial? The idea that a defendant can be "rewarded" with a more lenient sentence for pleading guilty is particularly troublesome.

Part of the rationales for leniency for defendants who plead guilty is born out of the idea that by pleading guilty, defendants are demonstrating a certain amount of remorse and a willingness to accept responsibility for their crimes. It is the defendant's frame of mind regarding the crime and his willingness to "own up" for what he has done that deserves reward. A defendant who knows the evidence against her but fails to accept responsibility for her actions or demonstrate repentance does not deserve such a reward but rather should receive the maximum punishments allowable. Critics believe, however, that such a rationale is fundamentally flawed—that a person guilty of committing a crime receives less punishment than he or she deserves in a plea bargain or, conversely, if a person is not guilty, then he or she may receive more punishment than they deserve. Both instances, then, are seen by critics as potential sources of injustice.

Defendants are also thought to be pressured into accepting plea offers by prosecutors and even defense counsel because of caseload constraints—both sides want cases resolved quickly. There are no universal rules guiding which pleas will be offered to which defendants and under which circumstances. Although many prosecutors' offices have their own policies that guide plea negotiations, there is wide variation in the application of these policies among line attorneys, who exercise a great deal of individual discretion. Moreover, because pleas are negotiated outside the court and generally accepted by the court, there is no further review of the case, creating the potential for prosecutorial misconduct and wrongful conviction. More recently, the extent to which pleas are used in criminal cases has been analogized with "bargain" justice that ultimately weakens public trust and confidence in the criminal justice system.

Benefits to the Justice System

Despite the vast and, in many instances, strong criticisms of plea bargaining, the practice is pervasive and institutionalized. The Supreme Court has upheld the practice of pleas and there is little incentive within the courts to eliminate pleas. Proponents, however, offer a systemic perspective that points to additional benefits of pleas—plea bargains can help to bolster public trust and confidence in the system because of the certainty of conviction, thereby eliminating the potential for juries to get easy cases wrong. In this vein, plea bargaining is seen as a tool for disposing of the "easy" cases and ensuring that only those cases that are most difficult go to trial.

Both proponents and critics of pleas make strong arguments supporting their position. As such, a more productive debate (and possible solution) stems not from a dichotomous argument of plea/no plea but rather focuses on creating checks and balances on the plea process. At the heart of all the debate around plea bargaining lie concerns about the enormous power afforded to the prosecutor and the fact that this power is virtually unchecked in a system dominated by pleas. Thus, demands for reform are more likely to be realized when the focus shifts from elimination of the plea practice altogether to one that limits the opportunities for increased and unchecked prosecutorial discretion.

M. Elaine Nugent-Borakove
Justice Management Institute

See Also: Defendant's Rights; Discretionary Decision Making; District Attorney; Due Process; Mandatory Minimum Sentencing; Prohibition.

Further Readings

Alschuler, Albert W. "Plea Bargaining and Its History." *Law & Society Review*, v.13/2 (1979).

Fisher, George. *Plea Bargaining's Truimph: A History of Plea Bargaining in America*. Palo Alto, CA: Stanford University Press, 2003.

Kipnis, Kenneth. "Plea Bargaining: A Critic's Rejoinder." *Law & Society Review*, v.13/2 (1979).

Vogel, Mary E. "The Social Origins of Plea Bargaining: Conflict and the Law in the Process of State Formation, 1830–1860." *Law & Society Review*, v.33/1 (1999).

Plessy v. Ferguson

In 1896, the U.S. Supreme Court, in a 7–1 decision, ruled that the separate but equal provision of private services was constitutional under the equal protection clause. State laws requiring segregation based solely on race in private businesses were entirely legal based on the court's ruling. This standard would allow continued de jure discrimination against racial minorities through legalized segregation until *Brown v. Board of Education* was decided in 1954, which overturned the separate but equal doctrine.

In July 1892, the New Orleans Comité des Citoyens arranged for Homer Plessy to board a whites only car of the East Louisiana Railroad in New Orleans. The car was designated for only white patrons in accordance with Louisiana state law. The Comité des Citoyens planned the act of civil disobedience in hope of having the court (at any level) rule that separate but equal was not an acceptable policy when considering segregation.

To show how difficult it can be to enforce racial segregation, the Comité des Citoyens chose Plessy, who was born free and only one-eighth black. Under a state law from 1890, he was still considered to be black and was not supposed to sit in that car. After the conductor was made aware of Plessy's race, Plessy was asked to move to the proper car. When he refused, he was removed and arrested.

The arguments in the case were clear. Louisiana argued that conditions in the two cars were equal and consequently there was no issue. Further, the state claimed there were neither constitutional provisions nor national laws that prevented them from enacting and utilizing a separate but equal policy. Plessy and the Comité des Citoyens, on the other hand, believed the forced segregation denied him his rights under due process and the Thirteenth and Fourteenth Amendments of the Constitution. Both the district court and Supreme Court of Louisiana held that the state had the right to regulate any type of transportation operating within state boundaries. In 1896, the Supreme Court of the United States granted a writ of certiorari for Plessy's case.

The Supreme Court was ultimately no more sympathetic to Plessy than either state court had been, ruling 7–1 that the Louisiana law did not in any way violate the Fourteenth Amendment. Going even further, the court found that the law did not suggest the inferiority of blacks but instead asked for the races to be separated as a matter of public policy. Justice Henry B. Brown, writing for the majority of the court, stated "We consider the underlying fallacy of the plaintiff's argument to consist in the assumption that the enforced separation of the two races stamps the colored race with a badge of inferiority. If this be so, it is not by reason of anything found in the act, but solely because the colored race chooses to put that construction upon it." If anyone felt inferior as a result of the law's presence, it was due to their perceptions, rather than what the letter of the law asked for and mandated.

Justice John M. Harlan, who had owned slaves in his life and was formerly a member of the Ku Klux Klan, vehemently disagreed with the majority and believed the decision of the court would become infamous for its negative effects on minorities in America. Harlan believed that the court had made a sweeping judgment based solely on a cursory examination in the quality differences between railway cars. While railway cars were admittedly close to equal, public restrooms, restaurants, and schools were not. With the court's ruling, separate but equal became a foundation of American law and public policy for decades—particularly throughout the south. For many states, *Plessy* provided the ability to separate races and ensure differences in quality without fear of remand from state or national authorities. For the Comité des Citoyens, they were left to state, "We, as freemen, still believe that we were right and our cause is sacred."

Rather than working to assure fairness throughout the country, the *Plessy* decision was instead used to further segregation laws. Hard-earned victories for African Americans throughout Reconstruction were undone immediately through the use of separate but equal. Worried about how states could potentially use this national precedent to create unfair conditions for minorities in their states, Justice Harlan wrote in his dissent that "we shall enter upon an era of constitutional law, when the rights of freedom and American citizenship cannot receive from the nation that efficient protection which heretofore has unhesitatingly accorded to slavery and the rights of the master." His fears were well-founded as the Jim Crow south took significant steps to assure that states could limit the rights of certain individuals.

Plessy did more than simply allow segregationists to see that society remained segregated. States and localities that had previously begun working toward integration reverted to their former ways under the blessing of *Plessy*. It would take until 1954, when a mother grew tired of watching her daughter ride by a white-only school seconds from her home to drive miles away to the school for African Americans in Topeka, for the Supreme Court to return to the question of separate but equal. In *Brown v. Board of Education of Topeka, Kansas*, the Supreme Court deemed separate but equal was no longer an acceptable doctrine and set out to ensure greater equality.

William J. Miller
Southeast Missouri State University

See Also: 1851 to 1900 Primary Documents; Constitution of the United States of America; Racism; Supreme Court, U.S.

Further Readings
Brook, Thomas. Plessy v. Ferguson: *A Brief History With Documents*. Boston: Bedford Books, 1997.
Fireside, Harvey. *Separate and Unequal: Homer Plessy and the Supreme Court Decision That Legalized Racism*. New York: Carroll & Graf, 2004.
Lofgren, Charles. *The* Plessy *Case: A Legal-Historical Interpretation*. New York: Oxford University Press, 1987.

Poe, Edgar Allan

One of America's foremost writers and men of letters, Edgar Allan Poe (1809–49) wrote in a variety of genres: poetry, short story, novel, book review, and essay. His works include classic tales of horror, crime stories, lyrical love poems, and even science fiction. He was an innovative contributor to the gothic tradition and helped to develop a philosophy of literary aesthetics; he is often credited with inventing modern detective fiction.

One of three children of itinerant actors, he was born on January 19, 1809, in Boston, Massachusetts. After the early death of his parents, he was raised by a wealthy tobacco merchant, John Allan, with whom he had a tempestuous relationship. He attended the University of Virginia, joined the army briefly, and even gained a short appointment at West Point.

In 1836, he married his cousin, Virginia Clemm, when she was only 13 years old, and lived with her until her early death in 1847. He lived in Richmond, Philadelphia, New York, and Baltimore. From his adolescence on, Poe was primarily devoted to his writing, and this remained the central calling of his life.

Poe published five collections of works within his lifetime, beginning with *Tamerlane and Other Poems* in 1827. His works appeared extensively in the contemporary press and in literary magazines, including *Godey's Lady's Book*, *The Southern Literary Messenger*, *Graham's Magazine,* and the *Broadway Journal*. He also served as editor of a newspaper and several literary magazines, including the *Messenger* and *Graham's*. Poe's most important works include the stories "The Fall of the House of Usher" (1839), "The Murders in the Rue Morgue" (1841), "The Masque of the Red Death" (1842), "The Tell-Tale Heart" (1843), "The Cask of Amontillado" (1847), and the poem "The Raven" (1845).

Poe's contributions to crime and detective fiction include his trilogy of mystery tales, all crafted in the 1840s and set in Paris: "The Murders in the Rue Morgue" (1841), "The Mystery of Marie Roget" (1842–45), and "The Purloined Letter" (1844). Closely identified with these works is his urban story of the same period, "The Man of the Crowd" (1840). Poe referred to the first three of these as "tales of ratiocination," stories about mysterious crimes whose solutions are reasoned by the elusive C. August Dupin, his brilliant detective hero, a stand-in for Poe. These works echo Poe's preoccupation with death, violence, loss, and decay, just as they reiterate his time period's obsession with death and mourning. They also reflect the rise of the modern city and its growing problems with crime and urban policing.

With the exception of "The Purloined Letter," which takes place indoors, these stories use the architecture and the culture of the city to unfold their narratives. Here, the traditional countryside gothic motif is replaced by urban ones, and the references within the works reflect the emerging urban mystery novels (made most famous by Eugene Sue's *The Mysteries of Paris*, published in 1842), the pamphleteers of Grub Street, the Newgate Calendar, and the Penny Dreadfuls. These new forms of popular culture often featured sensational events, including murder, told in the vernacular language of urban popular culture.

Both "The Murders in the Rue Morgue" and "The Mystery of Marie Roget" have the death of a woman (or women) as their primary subject, and project Poe's belief that female death, especially the death of a beautiful woman, was a primary literary subject. In "Murders" the detective Dupin solves the bloody murder of a mother and daughter, two withdrawn characters whose brutalized bodies are found in their Paris apartment. Even though the rooms are in total disarray, the door has remained locked, there is no sign of entry or exit, and no clues are found in what is nothing less than a grotesque and bloody murder scene, Dupin solves the murder. He concludes, through ratiocination, that only an orangutan coming through the chimney could have committed the crime.

In "The Mystery of Marie Roget," the first detective story to attempt to solve a real crime, the city as a social and intellectual space displaces the city as an architectural space as in "Rue Morgue" and "Man of the Crowd." The tale is based around the real disappearance and mysterious death of Mary Cecelia Rogers, the "tobacco girl," who was found dead in the Hudson River in 1841. Poe gave Mary the name "Marie" and transposed the events to Paris.

A celebrated event that led to the criminalization of abortion in New York State in 1845 and contributed to the reform of the police department that same year, the death of Rogers was made famous by the penny press, which used the case to express a series of contemporary concerns about sex, women, and crime in the quickly growing city. Poe attempted to solve the murder by using the available newspaper stories or what he called the "public prints," thus making the new penny press, and even reading itself, the subject of the tale.

With "The Purloined Letter," a story about blackmail over a stolen letter containing compromising information, these tales form the basis for the works of Conan Doyle, Robert Louis Stevenson, G. K. Chesterton, and modern detective fiction generally. Dupin and the unnamed narrator anticipate the similarly isolated but brilliant detective Sherlock Holmes and his companion Watson. Holmes, like Dupin, solves puzzling crimes though the use of reason and intellect and, again like Dupin, is able to outwit the often bumbling, or at least inefficient, police, who in real life would become a topic of concern throughout the century. Poe died in 1849 of unknown causes in Baltimore, where he is buried.

Amy Gilman Srebnick
Montclair State University

See Also: Detection and Detectives; Literature and Theater, Crime in; Literature and Theater, Police in.

Further Readings
Kennedy, J. Gerald. *Poe, Death and the Life of Writing*. New Haven, CT: Yale University Press, 1987.
Mabott, Thomas Ollive, ed. *The Collected Works of Edgar Allan Poe*. Cambridge, MA: Belknap Press of Harvard University Press, 1969–1978.
Pearl, Matthew. *The Murders in the Rue Morgue: The Dupin Tales by Edgar Allan Poe*. New York: Modern Library, 2006.

Police, Contemporary

During the 20th century, contemporary police departments sought to enhance both their images and their abilities. Ways of accomplishing these goals included the adoption of professionalism, community policing, the science of policing, and the endorsement of new technologies.

For much of American history, the emphasis in policing was simply to place officers in neighborhoods on the theory that their very presence would serve to deter criminal activity. However, in the post–World War II environment of the 1950s, police departments began to believe that they should be more like the military, and they began initiating what came to be known as "professionalism." The three major elements of professionalism were focusing on suppressing crime, acting with objectivity according to the principles of police science rather than yielding to political pressure, and centralizing police departments.

By the 1980s, enthusiasm for professionalism began to wane. During the 1990s, it was replaced with community policing, in which the police cooperated with civilians in combating crime. The idea originated with Herman Goldstein, a law professor at the University of Wisconsin. Most cities began putting police officers back on neighborhood beats to give them firsthand knowledge of where crimes were likely to occur and who the criminals were. Community policing was not popular with everyone. Critics claimed that it was too expensive and that it tended to expect police officers to serve as "social workers with guns." Supporters cited the many successes of community policing in cities of various sizes. One common example was New Haven, Connecticut, which was identified as the city with the sixth-highest rate of violent crime per capita, even though it was 140th in population. New Haven turned to community policing in 1991 and witnessed an immediate decline in violent crimes over the following year. A survey conducted by the National Institute of Justice in 1990 revealed that 71 percent of officers polled believed they needed more training in community relations.

At the federal level, officials began to promote the notion of intelligence-led policing, which focused on basing policy decisions and implementation on data that had been scientifically generated using the latest technology. Another method that received a good deal of attention was predictive policing, which had been implemented in New York, Boston, and Los Angeles under the guidance of Police Chief William Bratton, the creator of CompStat. The central idea of predictive policing was using scientific analysis of crimes and criminals to place police officers in those areas where crimes were likely to occur before the crimes took place.

Battling Crime

Violence was ubiquitous in American cities in the 1970s. Drugs were sold on street corners throughout the United States, and people were afraid to walk in their own neighborhoods. Crime rates soared even higher in the 1980s as a crack cocaine epidemic spread. Responding to this environment, James Q. Wilson and George L. Kelling of Harvard's John F. Kennedy School of Government authored an article that appeared in *The Atlantic* in March 1982 in which they set the stage for a major transformation in the way that police departments viewed their roles in preventing crime. Wilson and Kelling reminded the police and the public that "if a window in a building is broken and is left unrepaired, all the rest of the windows will soon be broken," regardless of the type of neighborhood involved. The "broken windows" theory became a major element of community policing, with police officers working with local communities to fight crime through maintaining individual neighborhoods and working with young people to steer them away from gangs.

More aggressive measures include controversial practices such as "stop and frisk," which involves officers detaining potential suspects long enough to search for possible weapons by lightly patting them down. In *Terry v. Ohio* (1968), the Supreme Court held that officers must have probable cause before engaging in "stop and frisk." The police often arrest suspected criminals for minor offenses on the principle that it deters them from committing major crimes. Racial profiling is another controversial practice that has been used as a deterrent. In such cases, suspects are targeted on the basis of race, ethnicity, religion, or national origin on the assumption that certain groups are more likely to commit crimes. The practice of stopping people of color for minor traffic violations in order to search for possible contraband became so common that it became known as "driving while black or brown." After the terrorist attacks of 9/11, racial profiling extended to targeting Arabs, Muslims, and south Asians as potential terrorists.

In a survey conducted by the Police Executive Forum in 2007, two-thirds of police officers questioned stated that they operate on the principle that monitoring "hot spots" is the most effective way to reduce the incidence of violent crimes. Police chiefs and sheriffs contend that the easy availability of firearms is the chief cause of high rates of violent crime in America. New York City has frequently been cited as clear evidence of that fact. In 1990, 2,245 murders occurred in the Big Apple. When officials began focusing on gun crimes between 1988 and 1998, the rate for gun-related crimes dropped from 1,220 to 376.

Policing Environment

In the federal system of the United States, each state, city, and township has its own system of choosing those who exercise authority over police forces at its particular level. In the heyday of political machines, police chiefs were answerable to party bosses. Even now, political pressure may force contemporary police administrators to operate in an environment that makes it difficult to enact the best policies. Some qualified candidates elect to remain in lower-level positions rather than battle politicians for control. The International Association of Chiefs of Police has identified five major entities that affect the environment in which police forces function: the police department as a cooperative entity, the public, the media, public and private agencies, and politicians. Successful police chiefs must be successful in working with all of these groups.

Police officers risk their lives for relatively little money. They are required to respond correctly to any situation that arises. Basic training for most police officers includes amassing knowledge about how the criminal justice system works, laws and methods governing search and seizure, correct behavior concerning the use of force, police procedure, professional ethics, and elementary first aid. Training time varies greatly among jurisdictions. In Texas, a hairdresser is required to train for 1,500 hours, but only 618 hours of training is mandated for police officers. Much of police training is accomplished through lectures rather than hands-on training. As more women enter police work and as the pool of candidates has declined, physical requirements for becoming a police officer have become more lenient. Officers may be as short as 5'5" and weigh as little as 100 pounds. The hands of some police officers are perceived as too small to operate high-capacity semiautomatic guns.

Much attention is now being paid to the use of force by police officers because of the large number of shootings of unarmed suspects in cities throughout the United States. In 1985, in *Tennessee v. Garner*, the Supreme Court held that officers may use force only in cases where an officer is threatened with a weapon or where there is probable cause to believe that a suspect has committed a crime that involved serious physical harm. Even under those circumstances, officers are required to issue a warning to the suspect. In the case in question, Tennessee officers shot and killed a suspect simply to prevent his escape after a minor robbery at a private residence.

While early histories were often characterized by internal corruption, it is less likely among contemporary departments because of tighter recruiting standards, better internal monitoring, improved psychological testing of officers, and greater leadership accountability.

Throughout American history, police departments have been forced to deal with crises of

The Los Angeles Police Academy's 21-acre complex graduated its first recruit class in 1936. The facility has classrooms, a gymnasium, athletic field, obstacle course, and a firing range.

both major and minor proportions. Those challenges have ranged from draft raids during the Civil War to curtailing lawlessness on the frontier to battling organized crime during Prohibition to the civil rights violence of the 1960s to modern battles against drugs and gangs. Police departments in most large cities have repeatedly come under attack. As the largest cities, New York and Los Angeles have perhaps been criticized more harshly than others. Both cities have experienced scandals that have generated public outrage over police brutality, planted evidence, and the shooting of unarmed suspects. Southern cities have also come in for their share of blame. In New Orleans, for instance, a Department of Justice investigation revealed endemic racism and repeated use of excessive force. On the other hand, police departments have also demonstrated unprecedented courage, as was the case with the New York Police Department on September 11, 2001, when terrorists hijacked jetliners and crashed them into the Twin Towers.

Elizabeth Rholetter Purdy
Independent Scholar

See Also: Boston, Massachusetts; Los Angeles, California; New York City.

Further Readings
Aveni, T. J. "Critical Analysis of Contemporary Police Training." http://www.theppsc.org/Staff_Views/Aveni/Police-Training.pdf (Accessed March 2012).
COPS. "Contemporary Issues in Community Policing." http://www.cops.usdoj.gov/default.asp?Item=881 (Accessed October 2011).
Lardner, James and Thomas Repetto. *NYPD: A City and Its Police*. New York: Henry Holt, 2000.
Slansky, David Alan. *New Perspectives in Policing*. Cambridge, MA: Harvard Kennedy School of Government, 2011.
Wilson, James Q. and George L. Kelling. "Broken Windows." *Atlantic*, v.249 (March 1982).

Police, History of

From the colonies in the early 1600s to the present time, America has depended on some type of police force to protect citizens and to help maintain order. From the earliest watchmen to today's policemen surrounded by computers and other technology, their work has both changed and stayed the same.

In the beginning, the early colonies of the 17th century brought with them the police system used in England at that time. This system involved members of each community looking out for each other and taking turns standing watch at night. Since the early colonists lived in rather archaic conditions and were busy building shelters and planting crops, crime was not much of a problem. The system was used more to protect and keep order in the community, not necessarily to fight crime.

Most of the problems came about from individuals who either broke a moral code or did not live up to their community obligations. Disorderly behaviors such as loitering, panhandling, and public intoxication were targeted because it was believed that these behaviors would lead to more serious crimes. Volunteer constables usually heard court cases of colonists who found themselves in trouble after committing these activities or actions such as working on the Sabbath, cursing in public places, not having animals properly restrained, or giving birth to a baby without first being married. However, since the colonists generally conformed to accepted community ideals, they gave little thought to establishing formal policing institutions. As settlers established larger villages such as seaports Philadelphia, Boston, and other areas where strangers and sailors traveled through more often, volunteer watch did not work as well any longer. Populations increased, crime became more abundant, keeping watch turned into a more active duty, and volunteers had trouble staying awake at night after working all day at their paying jobs. As settlers complained about this mandatory volunteer duty, colony governments began to threaten them with fines if they refused their obligations.

Formal Systems Development
By the middle of the 18th century, as these villages grew more economically affluent with significant increases in population, colonists were better able to pay fines and did so instead of standing watch. However, since the growth of cities brought in more jobless outsiders trying

to find employment, crime increased, and there were not enough watchmen or constables to handle the problems.

Therefore, in 1749, Philadelphia provided tax monies to hire officials called "wardens" who could employ the watchmen they needed. If someone wanted to work all day and still stand watch at night, he was permitted to do so. However, the wardens were authorized to fire anyone who did not perform their duties well. Law enforcement improved under this plan, and other cities began to make similar changes in their own communities to provide for a paid police force. Into the mid-1800s, police officers still spent much of their time preserving order in their communities and keeping the streets clear of drunks and those who became too unruly. Records in Boston and New York City around this period showed that a large percentage of arrests were for intoxication.

As the agrarian society was decreasing in rural communities, industrialization was growing in the urban areas. People moved around more, immigration increased, ethnicity changed in the neighborhoods, and citizens no longer were as familiar with their neighbors as they had been in the past. These changes made self-policing more difficult, and people began to depend more often on the official police force provided by the governments.

The Boss System
By the late 1800s, more men from various immigrant groups were being hired into large city police forces, with the Irish dominating in numbers. As these groups began to fill more police jobs, they began to take on new responsibilities in various immigrant neighborhoods. This new population in America did not know where to turn for much-needed social services. Therefore, they would often rely on the police officers who lived in their neighborhoods, those whom they saw as a connection to the political network that seemed unreachable. They may have seen the police officer as one who protects them and keeps order in society, but they also saw him as the one person who could help them find assistance when in need. As waves of immigration and poverty added to the duties of the policemen, elements of corruption also appeared. Law enforcement personnel grew into a part of both the ethnic communities and the political machines of local governments.

This combination not only made the delivery of social services easier, but bribery for money and favors also became more prevalent.

Police departments were now powered by the governments and heavily influenced by the politicians of their community. These smaller neighborhoods were critical to what became known as the community "boss" system. Individuals in these communities started their leadership quest by joining important neighborhood institutions, such as the volunteer fire department. After being elected leaders by their peers, they pledged their followers' votes to certain politicians. Once votes were delivered as promised, bosses could expect more favors to come their way. Party leaders rewarded these bosses with jobs, contracts for city services, and other opportunities to make money for themselves, their friends, and others in their neighborhood. During a time when civil service was nonexistent, everyone working for governments owed their job to a politician.

Neighborhood bosses made sure that only those most loyal to them earned a job on the police force. Employment as a policeman who regularly patrolled the neighborhood was a highly sought-after job. The wages were fairly high, and the position offered steady employment, two attributes that lower-income workers seldom found. Citizens often pleaded with their community's bosses for a job, and politicians could insist on their loyalty before hiring them as patrolmen.

Politicians were often elected with promises of keeping down prostitution, gambling, and the sale of alcohol, for politicians and police were considered guardians of a society's virtue. However, having laws in place to suppress such activities opened up another avenue for entrepreneurship and bribery. Those who offered the services did so illegally and considered bribery just another business expense (which was often easier and cheaper than campaigning against moral advocates). Policemen on the street, as well as politicians, took monetary bribes or used of one of the services to stay quiet. Eventually, the bribery system was used to protect thieves as well. The job of a policeman became so lucrative that many not only begged for a job, they began to pay large sums of money to get such a job. Not all policemen fell into corruption, but many did.

More law enforcement changes appeared in larger cities during the mid-19th century. New York City combined day and night shifts in 1845, and Boston began consolidating day and night shifts in the 1850s. It was also during this time that police forces moved to a more preventive policing method instead of focusing on punishment after the fact. The state of New York passed legislation in 1844 to establish a preventive police force in New York City, followed by New Orleans, Cincinnati, Boston, Philadelphia, and finally Chicago and Baltimore.

It was during this time that cities also began requiring policemen to wear uniforms. This decision was controversial, with many policemen complaining that uniforms represented subordination and made them appear less masculine. Others were afraid that criminals would flee the scene of a crime more quickly once they saw the uniform, yet some believed a victim could find help more quickly if policemen were more recognizable.

The idea of arming a policeman with a gun was even more contentious. Some believed that guns would provide the police too much power, but a number of policemen felt they needed a gun when they came in contact with an armed criminal. Many citizens owned guns, and law enforcement wanted weapons as powerful as the ones being used by the criminals.

Migration

People began to leave the populated areas of the east and migrate into the American west but the need for police protection stayed with them. Towns were often separated from each other by many miles and they could not depend on people outside their own communities to come in and help should trouble arise. During the mid-1820s, several of these isolated communities produced small militias, and a few of the units were utilized to patrol the frontier. These men were called "Rangers."

In many small villages, however, a single marshal or county sheriff could usually provide the legal services within the community. The first village law enforcement created by settlers in the American west was in Texas. By 1831 the town of San Felipe de Austin had established a community patrol under the command of Captain Thomas Gay. The village governing council established formal regulations, reflecting the basic need for law enforcement in the sparsely populated west. As more towns developed, the same procedure ensued: A mayor or town council during the early years would most often appoint a *marshal* or *constable*, terms preferred over *chief of police*.

African American Police

As for African Americans in the police force, "people of color" served in New Orleans as early as 1805. By the 1870s, African Americans were fulfilling police positions in almost every major city in the south, and two black policemen, Ovid Grefory of Mobile and Bryan Lunn of Raleigh, were serving as assistant chiefs of police. However, by 1877 and the beginning of a period known as the Redemption (when most federal troops that had been stationed in the south at the end of the U.S. Civil War were removed), most all southern black policemen were forced to leave their positions. The U.S. census of 1910 reported that there were only 576 African Americans working as policemen in the country, which amounted to less than 0.5 percent of the total 61,980 employed. By 2009, their numbers had increased to 100,700, or more than 14 percent of the total employed.

Samuel Battle was the first African American to be hired as a policeman in New York City after consolidation of the five boroughs. Battle was born in Newbern, North Carolina, to parents who had both been born into slavery. His application had previously been rejected three times after a physician had reported a heart murmur. However, in 1911, with the help of an African American politician and a medical examination by a physician outside the police department who found no heart murmur, Battle was appointed to the police force.

He did not sleep in the same barracks as the white men but instead stayed separated in another room. Many of the white officers would not speak to him, though according to his captain, he never complained about the silence. By 1913, he was assigned to a Harlem precinct, and a few years later he protected a white officer (who had killed an African American) from an angry Harlem mob. Battle served for 35 years as a police officer and became the New York Police Department's first black police sergeant and lieutenant.

Police and the Community

The community focus of a police force became more apparent with the passing in 1919 of the National Prohibition Act (41 Stat. 305). Rural populations often supported this law and police were encouraged to make arrests when finding violations. City communities were more apt to enjoy alcoholic beverages and did not support this new law. Therefore, to continue a positive public image of policemen in the city, there were fewer arrests.

During the 1930s and a few years preceding, violent criminals and gangs committing robberies and murders made sensational names for themselves. J. Edgar Hoover, director of the Bureau of Investigation (predecessor to the Federal Bureau of Investigation) began to refer to John Dillinger, "Baby Face" Nelson, Bonnie and Clyde, and other criminals by the term *public enemy*. The general public became very familiar with this term public enemy and the sensational stories being told in the news, and the public image of the police became even more important. With communities hearing more about crimes and criminals than they did about the community work being done by their local police, it became important for the community police forces to now be known as crime fighters.

Technology improved: More policemen began driving squad cars instead of walking on the streets. They carried radios and stayed in touch with headquarters. The science of fingerprinting was improving, and more states began to use this technology in the solving of crimes.

With so many people out of work during these financially hard times, applications for police jobs increased. The large number of applicants meant more competition for each position and higher standards set for each hire. College-level training programs were being offered, and the first complete police curriculum put in place in 1930 at San Jose College in California. The higher standards and availability of increased education led to a more efficient and professional police force.

Civil Unrest

Urban areas continued to grow, and troubled race relations, poverty, and the Vietnam War caused tension and unrest in several heavily populated cities. In the 1960s, there was the civil rights movement, the student activist movement, the anti–Vietnam War movement, and the ghetto riots in Los Angeles, Detroit, and other cities. Sometimes different races joined together to fight the establishment. Riots broke out in major cities such as Los Angeles, Detroit, and Newark, New Jersey. There were separate incidents in each that set off the anger, but problems such as deteriorating housing, economic inequality, and reports of police abuse kept the riots going for several days. The National Guard was called in to police the streets of these cities until peace returned.

In 1967 President Lyndon B. Johnson appointed the National Advisory Commission on Civil Disorders. One major problem they reported was the tense and difficult relationship between police and those they monitor and protect in the ghettos. There were complaints that police did not spend enough time in the ghettos for crime prevention. Yet when police patrols increased, their presence caused increased hostilities between the two groups. During this time of increased violence, in September 1968, in Indianapolis, Indiana, Liz Coffal and Betty Blankenship also made history as the first two female policewomen ever to go out in a police car on street patrol. Since the early 20th century, policewomen had held jobs in police departments performing safer duties, such as those in housekeeping, food service, and clerical. However, Coffal and Blankenship were the first two to take on the more dangerous job of patrolling the streets.

As the United States has progressed from the first colonies of the 17th century, so has the job of law enforcement. There have been changes in society such as immigration, population growth, urbanization, poverty, technology, and criminal activity. The police force has addressed these changes by moving forward with the newest technologies and well-educated men and women of various backgrounds. However, even with changes in society and in the world of law enforcement, the police are still required to interact with people, protect their communities, continue in the role of service, and take the lead in maintaining a safe society.

Antoinette W. Satterfield
U.S. Naval Academy

See Also: 1851 to 1900 Primary Documents; Boston, Massachusetts; Civil Disobedience; Philadelphia, Pennsylvania; Urbanization.

Further Readings

Dulaney, W. Marvin. *Black Police in America*. Indianapolis: Indiana University Press, 1996

Hahn, Harlan and Judson L. Jeffries. *Urban America and Its Police Force*. Boulder: University Press of Colorado, 2003.

Prassel, Frank R. *The Western Police Officer: A Legacy of Law and Order*. Norman: University of Oklahoma Press, 1972.

Snow, Robert L. *Policewomen Who Made History*. Lanham, MD: Rowman & Littlefield, 2010.

Police, Sociology of

Since the early 1960s, sociology has examined the construct of "police" and "policing." As a result, sociology has probed the forms and institutions in which policing has occurred and the concealments and symbols that it uses to forge its identity. This examination has been intertwined with the history of police and seeks to determine what policing means, has meant, and can mean. This focus has bedeviled sociologists for five decades and differs significantly from concurrent research that has taken place in the related fields of criminology, law, police administration, and police science. Some sociologists have argued that police and policing have little to do with law enforcement, assertions that have proven highly controversial.

Police as an instrument of social control have existed since ancient times. In the United States, the U.S. Marshals Service was established in 1791, and city police forces were formed in Philadelphia, Pennsylvania, in 1751; in Boston, Massachusetts, in 1838; and in New York City in 1845. Much of the policing in small towns was of very poor quality for much of the 19th century. As national organizations such as the Federal Bureau of Investigation began to provide training and support services to local law enforcement agencies during the first half of the 20th century, however, the quality of policing improved. During the 1920s, the Berkeley, California, police department began to adopt new technologies, emphasize professionalism among members of the force, and make available extensive training so that police could improve their skills. O. W. Wilson, the chief of police of Wichita, Kansas, and, later, Chicago, introduced strategies that came to be known as police science. Wilson regularly rotated police from a beat in one community to another to reduce the threat of corruption, established a nonpartisan police board to advise and regulate the force, and raised salaries to attract a more educated and professional officer. For most of the first half of the 20th century, academic notice of police occurred only in history departments, law schools, or police science programs that were designed to provide practitioners with training. Only during the latter half of the 20th century did sociologists begin to study police, and their findings and theories changed how many viewed that occupation and those who practiced it.

Police Role and Functions

Early studies of police focused primarily upon requests for police service and the levels of discretion exercised by officers in fulfilling their duties. Scholars such as Frank J. Remington and Herman Goldstein, both of the University of Wisconsin Law School, undertook major studies that examined policing and criminal law. These examinations of police practices cast doubt upon the generally perceived notion that these individuals were fighting crime or enforcing the peace. Indeed, early studies suggested that the majority of police duties had little to do with enforcing the law, keeping the peace, or otherwise acting as agents of social control. Instead, it was proposed that police engaged in functions so varied, and sometimes contradictory, that any attempt to define police by the functions they are alleged to perform and the ends they are theoretically to achieve is misguided and ill-fated.

Sociologically, policing is best defined in terms of its means rather than in terms of its ends. Some have suggested that individuals join the police not as a form of employment, as a way to obtain stable economic benefits, training in criminology, or even to achieve a generous pension, but instead as an authorized way to use coercive force against others. While this supposition was highly controversial, its adherents maintained that while other variables regarding police varied greatly as a result of history or geography, no entity ever termed *police* had ever existed that did not have the authorization to use coercive force. This assertion had the elegance of being universal and was applicable across time and boundaries. It also proved morally and politically neutral, insofar as it was applicable to subjects that were engaged in either exemplary or loathsome behavior. Finally, it opened a new series of queries regarding police: Why do all modern societies have police? What does having police provide to those societies, regardless of their political leanings? Which duties are best assigned to police and which to other societal institutions?

Sociologists grappling with these questions have suggested that societies require that certain duties be done, be done quickly, and be done by whatever means necessary. Situations that call for police meet all three of these criteria. Time becomes a crucial element here, as some situations cannot be put aside for a later resolution. Situations dealing with an escaped murderer, vandalism affecting city lights, keeping the curious away from an accident scene, or interrupting a domestic dispute call for immediate action, and most individuals would approve of the use of coercive force to protect the greater good in these situations. These arguments overturn traditional conceptions about why police join the force. Rather than acquiring the right of coercive force to assist in their duty to enforce the law, sociologists suggest that many police enforce the law because doing so allows them to engage in coercive force.

David H. Bayley, of the State University of New York at Albany, examined the role of police discretion in a series of studies begun during the 1970s and 1980s. Bayley suggested that police work can be summarized as having guidelines that explicitly define its realities. These guidelines include that most police work is done by a single officer or two partners, that officers must make many decisions outside of the control of a supervisor, and that officers make decisions based upon internalized knowledge and skill. These guidelines influence the development of policing standards, and the preparation and training of officers. Emphasizing that officers adhere to a process, and making these officers accountable for adhering to that process, is one of the more significant ways that policing outcomes are consistent with public values. James Q. Wilson, who taught at Boston College, developed the "broken widows" theory, which suggested that accepting vandalism and urban disorder created an environment in which crime was tolerated and that cleaning up environments stopped further vandalism and an escalation in crime. Wilson also suggested that different types of policing were more effective in different areas, building support for differentiated policing practices for disparate communities. Wilson's theories affected policy choices in such disparate settings as New York City, Albuquerque, New Mexico, and Lowell, Massachusetts, all of which implemented "zero tolerance" programs intended to reduce crime rates.

Sociological studies of police were most popular during the 1960s and 1970s. Scholarship in that area continues but now often extends to ancillary areas such as judicial, occupational, organizational, and political aspects of police. The law-and-order sentiments expressed by many voters during the 1980s and thereafter may have played a role in this shift. The growing fields of criminology and police science, with their emphasis on training students to assume positions as police, may also have reduced interest in the field. Despite this, sociology of police remains a vital part of many sociology programs and presents an important and diverse perspective on how we define "police."

Stephen T. Schroth
Jason A. Helfer
Knox College

See Also: Crime Prevention; Defendant's Rights; Interrogation Practices; Police, History of; Prisoner's Rights; Reform, Police and Enforcement.

Further Readings
Bayley, D. H. *Police for the Future.* New York: Oxford University Press, 1994.
Levey, S. R. and M. Killen, eds. *Intergroup Attitudes and Relations in Childhood Through Adulthood.* New York: Oxford University Press, 2010.
Reiner, R. *The Blue-Coated Worker: A Sociological Study of Police Unionism.* New York: Cambridge University Press, 1978.

Police, Women as

When considering women's impact on the history of policing, it is necessary to address the limited opportunities in the field for women. For most of U.S. history, women were tasked with the maintenance of the household. Women, serving as the primary caretakers of most households, were considered subservient to men despite their disproportionate contributions to the preservation of the family unit. Prospects for employment outside the household were bleak, thereby confining women to the private sphere. The social roles fulfilled, and broken, by women are mirrored by women's experiences in law enforcement.

The history of women in policing is roughly categorized into three major periods: women as police matrons, later as policewomen, and finally as police officers (who happen to be women). As women comprise approximately 50 percent of the population, but only about 12 percent of state and local law enforcement agencies, an understanding of their historical struggles is crucial in efforts to address problems they still face today.

Police Matrons

Women initially entered the field of law enforcement through their work in correctional institutions as police matrons, with Maryland becoming the first state to officially hire a woman for jail duties in 1822. In jails and prisons, matrons ensured that men and women would be kept separate from one another and that adequate food and clothing were provided to the prisoners. This work was done on a volunteer basis but soon became paid as prison administrators began to appreciate the unique contributions of women in this role. The early 19th century marked the beginning of women's work in policing but they were not treated on an equal basis until the 1960s.

The volunteers, many from advantaged backgrounds and many of them Quakers, harnessed the stereotype of women as moral entrepreneurs in order to justify their work in early prisons. They viewed themselves as agents of transformation to the indigent, immigrant, and otherwise "fallen" women they supervised. Appalled at the abhorrent conditions found in the early-19th-century prisons, these women were part of a larger social movement that pushed for more government intervention in the affairs of the less fortunate. Many sought inspiration from reformers abroad. One of the more famous influences was found in Britain: Quaker minister Elizabeth Fry publicly promoted the better treatment of female prisoners.

In working with the less fortunate, women reinforced gender roles while simultaneously altering them. For example, Eliza Farnham, working out of the Sing Sing prison, helped fuel the larger feminist movement under way because she questioned the double standards inherent in the legal system. Even conservative reformers like those belonging to the 1845 Women's Prison Association (WPA) in New York advocated training for women prisoners so that they could support themselves once released. Of course, the training they embraced only reinforced the stereotypical roles of women in this period by preparing them for positions as housekeepers, nannies, and seamstresses. These occupations were not meant to supplant wifedom; rather, they dealt with the reality of women's economic predicament. The Civil War had left many women impoverished,

Women police officers being trained to inspect and aim handguns sometime between 1910 and 1920. During the early 1900s, women began to be hired in law enforcement.

and rapidly expanding cities further contributed to the number of families plunged into poverty. To these police matrons, it made sense to train women to be self-sufficient.

Even though police matrons showed no interest in challenging the long-accepted mores of the time, women gained a presence in police departments, where they were responsible for the custodial maintenance of incarcerated juveniles and women. This reflected a combination of the biblical and social values that were dominant at the time, relegating women to more domestic tasks.

Women excelled in these roles; nevertheless, the resistance to their employment in law enforcement remained unaffected. With any internal advancement that was made by women, challenges ensued claiming that their femininity, as well as their safety, was at risk. Women's ability to handle the more dangerous criminals underwent extreme scrutiny because they were seen as being more fragile. To some extent, the men of these early departments were resentful of the matrons' presence because these women were considerably more educated and of a higher socioeconomic standing than many of the men. When police matrons began to advocate for separate prisons staffed by women, stressing the immorality of male supervision of incarcerated women, their efforts were met with resounding disapproval.

Policewomen

It had been generally accepted that women possessed a restricted public role in society, which was used to rationalize their exclusion in most public workplaces. Regardless of their qualifications, this common perception created an environment within law enforcement where women were paid less, worked longer hours, and were confined to working only with juveniles and women. This inequity in treatment angered potential activists and inspired the "policewoman" movement. Early reformers of this movement lobbied for better pay and fought against the limited functions that women performed in law enforcement. In order not to threaten the status quo, however, women's domestic role was embraced rather than rejected and focus was placed on expanding women's legal authority rather than their roles in society. The policewoman movement thus began.

Mary Owens, the first woman to have the power to arrest, was hired in 1893 by the Chicago Police Department in order to financially compensate her for her husband's death. This was not entirely uncommon because in many departments, widows fulfilled the roles of police matrons. In 1905, Lola Baldwin was tasked with the protection of young women's virtues in Portland, Oregon. Though given some police powers, she could not arrest men. As seen in Owens's and Baldwin's cases, policewomen can be identified as an outgrowth of police matrons; indeed, the roles had considerable similarities. Nevertheless, at the time, the public saw them as revolutionaries.

The early 1900s brought sporadic successes for the inclusion of women in law enforcement. Among these was the hiring of the first official policewoman in 1910 by the Los Angeles Police Department, Alice Stebbins Wells. After petitioning the city, Wells received full arrest powers, setting her apart from all of her female predecessors. Though Wells worked primarily with women and juveniles and was not issued a gun, she was still considered a trailblazer. Among her achievements, she helped establish the International Policewomen's Association and was indirectly responsible for the hiring of women in police departments across the United States.

Throughout her career, Alice Stebbins Wells advocated for women police officers while maintaining that women's social role should inform their role in law enforcement. Arguments of women's superiority in moral matters, as well as their advanced training and prior background in social work, were used to reinforce their inclusion in the profession. Still, many policewomen felt it necessary to push further, advocating initiatives that would help prevent crime through their social services and actual arrest powers. Through their increased duties, the professionalization of law enforcement, and the consequent endorsement from the International Association of Chiefs of Police, they inadvertently subjugated the value of existing police matrons.

Police Officers

It was not until the 1950s that serious questions were raised in regard to the limitations placed on women's responsibilities in police work. No longer satisfied with their allotted place in police departments, many women began to see themselves as police officers. In some respects, the movement to professionalize law enforcement, which began in the 1930s, also helped spur women's desire to be officers. The two world wars also contributed to a changing sentiment toward women's abilities in this realm by acclimating the public to women in uniform. Even when qualified male police officers were scarce, women were not given the same responsibilities. Despite this, women made considerable advancements in the 1950s, both in numbers and in the professionalism of their position in law enforcement agencies.

In the 1960s, women began to enter police work on equal footing with men, even though there were still obstacles to their equality. The work remained heavily dominated by men and was generally seen as antithetical to the feminine qualities women possessed. In addition, women commonly faced isolation, ridicule, sexual harassment, and outright hostility by their colleagues. These issues led to numerous lawsuits, which broke many legal and organizational barriers but did little to change individual attitudes toward women in policing. The 1972 revision of Title VII of the 1964 Civil Rights Act prohibited discrimination in public agencies, thus providing some important inroads for many women as it affected hiring, promotion, and the general working environment in police departments.

The environment and police culture remained stubbornly masculine, but after time and a number of experiences, attitudes began changing. On September 20, 1974, Officer Gail Cobb became the first female police officer to be killed in the line of duty. This dubious distinction elevated the view of women as police officers, but academics continued to document an unwelcome working environment irrespective of women's demonstrated competence.

In 1985, Penny Harrington became the country's first female chief of police in a major U.S. city and founded the National Center for Women and Policing Advisory Board. Her 21-year rise to the top of the Portland, Oregon, police department was no easy accomplishment; she had to file 40 sexual discrimination lawsuits along the way. She has since become known as a crusader for women in policing and, not unlike Alice Stebbins Wells, has significantly raised awareness of the problems women face in the field and the many benefits of increasing women's representation in police agencies.

The 1991 Christopher Commission, tasked with the investigation of the Rodney King beating, stimulated, albeit briefly, a renewed interest in women's competence in policing. Expert testimony corroborated the prior academic research demonstrating women's strengths in policing. Still, stereotypes of law enforcement as a masculine occupation remained resilient and women continued to struggle for acceptance in the field. Sexual harassment suits would last well into the 21st century.

In law enforcement today, women still face gender-specific discrimination. Policies that undermine family life and, more importantly, the lack of policies that accommodate women's disproportionate share of caretaking responsibilities, continue to plague efforts at recruiting and retaining women police officers. Though studies demonstrate women's viability in this line of work, particularly in their contributions to community policing efforts, the percentage of women in local and state law enforcement agencies hovers around 12 percent.

Conclusion

The legal barriers erected to keep women out of law enforcement are gone and many law enforcement agencies actively recruit women. The National Center for Women and Policing (NCWP), created in 1995, collects data pertinent to women's representation and informs the profession of women's status and current treatment. Organizations such as this are critical to the lasting success of women as they document instances of discrimination and policies that undermine their presence in law enforcement. The last obstacle for women to overcome may be the persistent distinctions created by a culture that has delegated men and women to very different employment opportunities based on gender role stereotypes.

Corina Schulze
University of South Alabama

See Also: Gender and Criminal Law; Police, Contemporary; Women in Prison.

Further Readings

Appier, Janis. *Policing Women: The Sexual Politics of Law Enforcement and the LAPD*. Philadelphia: Temple University Press, 1998.

Freedman, Estelle B. "Their Sisters' Keepers: An Historical Perspective on Female Correctional Institutions in the United States: 1870–1900." *Feminist Studies*, v.2/1 (1974).

Horne, Peter. *Women in Law Enforcement*, 2nd ed. Springfield, IL: Charles C. Thomas, 1980.

National Center for Women and Policing. "Under Scrutiny: The Effect of Consent Decrees on the Representation of Women in Sworn Law Enforcement." http://womenandpolicing.com/pdf/Fullconsentdecreestudy.pdf (Accessed September 2011).

Price, B. R. "Female Police Officers in the United States." In *Policing in Central and Eastern Europe: Comparing Firsthand Knowledge With Experience From the West*, Milan Pagon, ed. Ljubljana, Slovenia: College of Police and Security Services, 1996.

Schulz, Dorothy M. *Breaking the Brass Ceiling: Women Police Chiefs and Their Paths to the Top*. Westport, CT: Praeger, 2004.

Schulz, Dorothy M. "The Police Matron Movement: Paving the Way for Policewomen." *Police Studies*, v.115 (1989).

Seklecki, Richard and R. Paynich. "A National Survey of Female Police Officers: An Overview of Findings. *Police Practice and Research*, v.8 (2007).

Warren, Christopher, et al. "Report of the Independent Commission on the Los Angeles Police Department (LAPD)." Los Angeles, CA: Independent Commission on the LAPD, 1991.

Police Abuse

The police in America are charged with keeping peace and maintaining order in society. In order for them to achieve these goals, they need power and authority to force those who do not comply to do so. Police have been defined as institutions or individuals given the general right by the state to use coercive force within the state's domestic territory. There are two important ideas in this definition. First is the right to use coercive force. This means that the police have the right to use force to overcome any citizen resistance and to compel citizens to do that which they may not wish to do. Further, this right is given to the police by the state, which confers legal legitimacy upon the use of force. The police are the only people in society who are legally authorized to use force against others. The coercive power of the government as envisioned by the social contract has been given to the police to fulfill their duties. The granting of legal legitimacy to the police use of force does not necessarily equate to moral legitimacy. This means that the police may use their legally granted right to use coercive force for ends that may not be morally justifiable but are nevertheless legitimate.

Along with the right to use coercive force, the police have the power and authority to carry out their mission. Authority refers to the unquestioned entitlement to be obeyed and that comes from their fulfillment of a specific role. People obey these commands because it is both right and necessary to do so. Power is similar to authority in that both are found in the role of police and both are forms of social control. Power differs from authority, however, in that it is recognized that there might be resistance to police authority and if such resistance exists, it will be overcome. The police may not always have to resort to use of coercive force because they may use persuasion to overcome resistance to their authority. Persuasion means an attempt to encourage people to comply with the police by means of words, argument, or symbols so as to avoid the use of force.

While the police have a great deal of power to carry out their mission, there are restrictions on its use. The police have vast discretion in their exercise of power and authority but remain accountable to the public. The proper exercise of police power is of great concern to a society that considers itself free and democratic. Police in the United States are bound by the restrictions of the Constitution, state statutes, and local policies and procedures in the application of their powers. The public not only expects the police to use their power and authority responsibly; they also expect to be treated with courtesy and respect and to have their rights recognized. When the police do apply coercive force, it is expected that it is done so reasonably and that its application does not exceed what

Issues surrounding police abuse of minorities persist. A protest of the shooting death by an officer of a young African American; the officer was found guilty of involuntary manslaughter.

is necessary to accomplish the mission. In every country, there is a desire and an expectation that the police respect the fundamental human rights and dignity of the person as stated in the United Nations Declaration of Human Rights.

History of Police Abuse

While it is hoped that police respect the rights and dignity of persons, this has not always been so. Historically, and through present day, there have been issues of police abuse. Often, this has taken place with police harassment of minorities with the consent of the community. During the "political era" of policing, the police were controlled by politicians who used the police as a means to solidify their power. Immigrants, slaves, and Native Americans were seen as threats to the community because they threatened the status quo. Police used their powers to keep these various groups in line. There was little public outcry since the harassed minorities had little power and prevailing public attitudes, enforced and shared by the police, were against them. This abuse lasted well into the 20th century. For example, police mistreatment of African Americans continued in many states until the 1960s and beyond as police in many states enforced the Jim Crow laws used to keep segregation in place.

There was little official recognition of the problem of police abuse until 1929, when the National Commission on Law Observance and Enforcement, also known as the Wickersham Commission, published its report, "Lawlessness in Law Enforcement." The report documented abuses by police that included the use of pain in interrogations, as well as corruption and other abuses. While this report spawned outrage and calls for reform, little materialized. The law-abiding public wanted crime and undesirables dealt with and cared little about how this was accomplished as long as they didn't bear the brunt of police abuse. Public opinion in recent times has shifted in regard to police abuse for a variety of reasons, including citizen awareness and growing willingness to speak out, Supreme Court decisions governing police powers, greater citizen oversight of the police, federal government intervention through the Department of Justice, and more transparency regarding police operations.

Types of Abuse

There are many forms and definitions of police corruption, misconduct, and deviance. Police abuse is a form of occupational deviance because it is an improper use and application of police power and authority. It differs from corruption in that corruption involves a misuse of one's official position for financial gain. Police abuse is a form of police misconduct that may not, and often does not, involve financial gain. It is misconduct in which there is a misuse of official position in acts other than for financial gain. With this definition, for an act to be considered misconduct, there are two important elements to consider. First, there must be an act that is a misuse of an officer's power and authority and a contradiction of the Constitution, law, or policy. Second, it must be an "official" misuse of power and authority: The police officer must be acting in an official capacity as a police officer.

Police abuse has been called both abuse of power and abuse of authority. Both have the same meaning. Abuse of power/authority was defined by Thomas Barker and David Carter in 1985 as any action by a police officer without regard to motive, intent, or malice that tends to injure, insult, trespass upon human dignity, manifest feelings of inferiority, and/or violate an inherent legal right of a member of the public in the course of performing police work. Police abuse can be broken down into three specific areas: physical, psychological, and legal abuse.

Physical abuse is the use of excessive force or physical harassment. This can be further broken down into two categories: extralegal and unnecessary police violence. Extralegal force, also called brutality, is the application of intentional physical abuse inflicted maliciously and for no legitimate police purpose. It is often used against persons who challenge the police authority. When used in this manner, extralegal force is considered a form of punishment and is intended to teach those who have challenged the police not to do it again. Unnecessary force is usually not the product of malice but rather arises from incompetence. It occurs either as a result of poor training or because officers have placed themselves into what they perceive to be a vulnerable position because they may have misjudged a situation. It might be that the officer is afraid of being hurt since he/she lacks the confidence to handle the situation. Once this occurs, the officer may use more force than is necessary for the situation, not out of malice, but to compensate for the inadequacies already stated. Whatever the reason, it is still unnecessary force and will be seen as such by the recipient as well as by others.

Psychological abuse takes place when a police officer verbally assaults, ridicules, discriminates, or harasses persons. It is also when an officer places an individual who is under the control of the police in a position where the person's conception of him/herself as a person is devalued. Psychological abuse can also occur when an officer treats a person with disrespect, for example, by the use of profanity or demeaning language. It may also take the form of intimidation through threatening words or bodily language intended to place the person in fear. Additionally, it may be seen in intimidation such as excessively stopping and searching someone without sufficient reason. Using degrading language toward someone based on their race, ethnicity, gender, age, or sexual identity also falls into this category of abuse. It is possible that psychological and physical abuse may happen together and may be used to complement each other.

Legal abuse can transpire with or without physical or psychological abuse. It is identified as the violation of a person's rights, either constitutional or those defined by statute. Examples include detentions without reasonable suspicion, searches without probable cause, and lying by officers to ensure conviction. Other examples might include planting of evidence or the making up of informants in order to arrest persons suspected of criminal activity. Legal abuse may be involved in noble cause corruption. Police officers who engage in these acts often do so for what they consider to be a noble cause or in the belief that the end justifies the means. Officers assume that the person being arresting is guilty and that their actions will ensure a conviction, thereby getting the guilty party off the street. Therefore, the actions are noble because even if the means to achieve them are bad, the outcome is good. Unlike traditional corruption, there is usually no personal gain for the officer, and the intended good is for the organization or society at large.

Factors in Abuse

There are many reasons police officers engage in abuse. Policing is largely a discretionary activity and is conducted in a low-visibility environment. Police have a great deal of discretion in how to perform their duties. In policing, this means that officers can decide which laws will be enforced, as well as when and how. It also means that officers can decide whom to arrest as well as which means of maintaining order and keeping the peace they will use. While there are laws and policies guiding police discretion, it is often the officer on the street making decisions as to how discretion will be used.

Policing is low-visibility work. This means that the police often make their decisions in an environment in which they are not observed either by their supervisors or by citizens. Police are spread out temporally and geographically in such a manner that makes it difficult to constantly supervise them. Consequently, many of the actions and decisions that they make are free of direct supervisory scrutiny, and reporting is based on their own word. In addition, police work in areas and at times of day where there may not be many, if any, civilian witnesses to their actions. This gives officers who are so inclined the freedom to do as they please. The existence of the code of silence, or blue wall of silence, should also be noted here. It has been documented that many police officers are reluctant to report other officers who may abuse their powers, and some may go as far as to lie about what they may have witnessed. Often, officers may tolerate some behaviors like abuse while reporting more serious actions such as corruption. Because abuse is often looked at as a means to a noble cause or as necessary to achieve organizational goals or to ensure respect for the law and police, it may often be overlooked. These factors lead to an environment in which some officers believe that they may engage in abuse without fear of repercussion.

There are other reasons police may engage in abuse. It has been argued that police work in a culture of violence. Police officers are often injured and sometimes killed in the performance of their duties. This violence comes at the hands of the citizens they are charged with protecting. Further, police work is often framed in metaphors of war, such as a "war on crime" or a "war on drugs." Policing in this fashion takes on a paramilitary tone with an "us against them" mind-set. The police adopt a military philosophy using military-type uniforms, equipment, and strategies. In this philosophy, members of the public are viewed as symbolic assailants and as the enemy. This can be seen in some types of zero tolerance or broken windows policing in which citizen complaints against the police increased dramatically.

One other reason for police abuse is that it is seen as street justice and as a way to correct a bad attitude, or disrespect for the police. When police officers believe that a citizen has a bad attitude because he/she is openly defiant or disrespectful, they may resort to some form of abuse in order to "correct" the attitude problem. It is a way for the police to take control of the situation, to show that they are in charge, and to ensure that the citizen will act "respectfully" toward the police in future encounters. The police are trained to believe that they must always be in control and that they must win in every encounter. Therefore, disrespect cannot be tolerated and must be rectified. Another aspect of street justice is that it is often perceived that criminals never get their just punishment from the justice system; consequently, the police must ensure that "justice" is delivered on the street.

Whatever the reason for abuse, police departments must take steps to ensure that it does not occur. There are several ways to go about this. First, and perhaps most important, the right people must be recruited and selected for police work. Persons must be selected for their good character and integrity above all else. Ethics and integrity training, focusing on human rights and the dignity of the person, must begin in the police academy and continue throughout an officer's career. The importance of adherence to the Constitution, use of force training, the use of courtesy, and recognition of cultural diversity are topics that must also be emphasized.

Leadership must set the tone for integrity in the department and create a climate in which abuse and other forms of misconduct cannot survive. An open citizen complaint procedure must be set up in which every complaint is thoroughly investigated, and there must be a fair system of discipline in place to ensure that abusive behavior is rooted out and stopped, and good policing must also be recognized. Abuse by police officers is incompatible with good policing, and police administrators must make every effort to keep it from occurring.

Marcel F. Beausoleil
Fitchburg State University

See Also: Code of Silence; Interrogation Practices; Police, Contemporary.

Further Readings
Barker, Thomas and David L. Carter. *Police Deviance*, 3rd ed. Cincinnati, OH: Anderson Publishing, 1994.
Fyfe, James J. and Robert Kane. *Bad Cops: A Study of Career-Ending Misconduct Among New York City Police Officers*. Washington, DC: United States Department of Justice, 2005.
Palmiotto, Michael J., ed. *Police Misconduct: A Reader for the 21st Century*. Upper Saddle River, NJ: Prentice Hall, 2001.
Pollock, Jocelyn. *Ethical Dilemmas & Decisions in Criminal Justice*, 7th ed. Belmont, CA: Wadsworth Publishing, 2012.
Prenzler, Tim. *Police Corruption: Preventing Misconduct and Maintaining Integrity*. Oxfordshire, UK: Taylor & Francis, 2009.

Political Crimes, Contemporary

Although numerous definitions of political crime exist, one of the most useful is the one developed by P. Beirne and J. Messerschmidt in 1991. They define political crimes as the following:

> ... crimes against the state (violations of law for the purpose of modifying or changing social conditions) ... [and] crimes by the state, both domestic (violations of law and unethical acts by state officials and agencies whose victimization occurs inside [a particular country]) and international (violations of domestic and international law by state officials and agencies whose victimization occurs outside the U.S.).

Subsumed under this broad rubric are numerous actions. On one end of the continuum are nonviolent oppositional political crimes that include dissent, sedition, treason, espionage, and spying, as well as violent actions such as sabotage, assassination, and terrorism. On the other end of the spectrum are state crimes that include corruption, illegal domestic surveillance, police and correctional officer use of excessive force, civil and human rights violations, and state corporate crimes.

Both oppositional and state crimes do not exist in a vacuum. More often than not, there is an intimate relationship between the two illegal activities, where one often type of crime leads to the other. Likewise categorizing political crimes into separate decades (as follows) is in many respects arbitrary as political crimes do not stop and start every 10 years and grievances and dispositions to engage in organizational malfeasance, deviance, and crimes can persist over numerous years and across changes in government and leadership.

The 1960s

During the 1960s and the early 1970s, several race riots and violent antiwar student demonstrations (opposing the Vietnam War) took place in the United States. In addition to this mass political violence were a number of assassinations of prominent politicians, including President John F. Kennedy (1963), his brother Senator Robert Kennedy (1968), and civil rights leader Martin Luther King, Jr. (1968). These actions, in part, set the conditions for the growth of a number of terrorist groups with different ideological leanings. While the Ku Klux Klan (which can trace its origins back to the Reconstruction period of American history) increased its violent tactics against African Americans, as well as against individuals and groups that were in favor of expanded civil rights guarantees for minorities in the United States, some of the terrorist groups that operated during this period were affiliated with émigré or nationalist-separatist movements such as the anti-Castro Cubans, Croatian Separatists, and Puerto Rican and Armenian nationalists.

In 1969, radical elements of the left-wing Students for a Democratic Society (SDS) formed the Weather Underground to commit terrorist actions against the U.S. government. They bombed government (including police and military) and corporate buildings, offices, and vehicles across the country. In reaction to these incidents, federal, state, and local law enforcement agencies, in addition to other federal agencies, including the Internal Revenue Service, increased their monitoring of dissident groups—especially the SDS and the Black Panther Party—and radical rightwing organizations such as the Ku Klux Klan. Collectively known as Operation CHAOS, some of these actions bordered on state crimes as various government organizations engaged in illegal domestic surveillance and used excessive force.

The 1970s

During the 1970s, as domestic terrorism declined, incidents of state crime started coming to public attention. In May 1970, for example, members of the Ohio National Guard shot and killed four students and injured nine others after a series of student protests at Kent State University in Ohio against the U.S.-orchestrated bombings in Cambodia. Additionally in May 1970, a similar incident took place at Jackson State University where two students were killed by police. Shortly after this incident, in 1971, Daniel Ellsberg, an analyst working for the Rand Corporation, provided the *New York Times* with top-secret documents about U.S. involvement in Vietnam. These items, collectively referred to as the Pentagon Papers, provided a comprehensive official history of the U.S. involvement in Vietnam, including official documentation of efforts to extend the war to Cambodia and Laos.

Other incidents related directly to domestic issues. In 1971, prisoners at the Attica Correctional Facility in New York rioted. Four days later, Governor Nelson Rockefeller called in the National Guard, which retook the prison. The ensuing melee resulted in a death toll of 43, including 11 prison employees. Most of the individuals died at the hands of state troopers and the National Guard.

One year later, a state crime of profound political impact took place. In 1972, during a routine patrol, a security guard stumbled upon "the Plumbers," a secret team assembled by President Richard Nixon. This group was in the process of burglarizing and wiretapping the Democratic National Committee headquarters, located in the Watergate Building in Washington, D.C. When investigations into the Plumbers were conducted, it was found that they "ultimately handled such tasks as forging diplomatic cables and hiring thugs to disrupt peace rallies."

The Federal Bureau of Investigation's (FBI) ongoing illegal surveillance of American citizens (1925–72) was an agencywide operation that was conducted with the guidance of top FBI officials and involved almost every field office in the United States. Even though a federal court order has long been necessary for any law enforcement agency to open private mail, between 1959 and 1966, the FBI illegally examined 42 million pieces of mail in New York City alone. Furthermore, the Central Intelligence Agency (CIA), prohibited by legislation from engaging in domestic surveillance, read private mail sent to and from the United States and the Soviet Union during the height of the cold war. It has been determined that CIA agents opened 216,000 pieces of mail and compiled a list of 1.5 million names of individuals from these mailings alone.

Even though dissident groups in the United States had suspected for some time that they were being spied on, infiltrated, and, to some extent, destabilized by the FBI, it was not until March 8, 1971, that their suspicions were confirmed. On that date, a group identifying itself as the Citizens' Commission burgled a regional FBI office in Media, Pennsylvania. The Citizens' Commission stole about 1,000 Counter-Intelligence Program (COINTELPRO) documents that indicated that the FBI had,

for years, operated a national, organizational, and illegal operation against several dissident groups. The FBI actions included spying, infiltration, and disruption of the Black Panther Party, the American Indian Movement (AIM), SDS, and the Communist Party of the U.S.A. (CPUSA).

In 1978, several congressmen were charged with and convicted of accepting bribes from FBI undercover agents. In an operation known as ABSCAM, federal agents posed as wealthy Arab businessmen desiring political and business favors from Congress members in exchange for bribes, some of which were as high as $100,000. In all, five congressmen were convicted and sentenced to prison terms ranging from 18 months to three years. State and local officials were also indicted for and convicted of corruption. In addition to ABSCAM, under almost each new president, there have been political scandals, most involving some form of corruption in the executive, legislative, and judicial branches of government.

The 1980s

In 1983, the FBI began an investigation of the organization Committee in Solidarity with the People of El Salvador (CISPES), which opposed the U.S. involvement in that country. At this time, many U.S. citizens had grown concerned about the federal government's continued financial support and military training of the El Salvadoran government, a regime that most human rights watch groups considered repressive; CISPES sought to increase public awareness of this issue. When the FBI investigation of CISPES garnered a negative public reaction, Director William Sessions ignored the organizational nature of the surveillance program and imposed disciplinary sanctions against six agents. Nonetheless, a Senate Select Committee criticized the FBI and its continuing surveillance of people and groups involved in dissident political activities. In response, the FBI claimed that all domestic surveillance had been discontinued.

Some incidents of state-corporate crime have resulted in national tragedies remembered by millions of Americans. The 1986 explosion of the space shuttle *Challenger* technically resulted from faulty seals; however, a deeper analysis points to the "hurry-up" agenda of the National

Aeronautics and Space Administration (NASA), which is a federal agency, and to the mismanagement of Morton Thiokol, the company that manufactured the seals. Although corporate engineers voiced misgivings over the scheduled flight of the shuttle, their concerns were overridden by both NASA and Morton Thiokol's management—which yielded to state-corporate pressures to produce a series of space shuttle flights in a set time. The fatal consequences—the death of seven astronauts and the loss of millions of dollars of equipment—were the result of both private producers and state managers whose concerns for production, flight schedules, and a financially self-sufficient space shuttle program overshadowed those for human life.

In 1989, as the result of a detailed investigation, Oliver North, a Marine Corps colonel and a national security adviser to President Ronald Reagan, received public attention because of his activities in the Iran-Contra scandal. In sum, starting in 1985, North was responsible for managing and (depending on which source one believes) orchestrating a deal whereby Nicaraguan Contras were provided financial aid and allowed to secretly sell and/or transport illegal drugs, the profits from which were channeled to Israel to pay for antiaircraft missiles that were later shipped to Iran. During this time, the congressionally mandated Boland Amendment placed an embargo not only on the types of aid that the Contras could receive but also on the goods the West could supply to Iran. North was charged with lying under oath, obstructing a congressional inquiry, taking money and not declaring it to the Internal Revenue Service (IRS), and destroying government documents. He had also accepted an illegal gratuity: a home security system worth $13,800. North was convicted of these charges in 1989, but the conviction was subsequently overturned because his testimony at the trial had been "immunized." This outcome was predictable because the appellate panel was primarily composed of Republican appointees. Similar outcomes befell North's accomplices, Robert McFarlane, Richard R. Miller, and Carl ("Spitz") Channel.

The 1990s

The 1990s witnessed further prosecutions of government employees in various intelligence agencies. In 1994, Aldrich H. Ames, a veteran CIA official and his wife, Rosario, were convicted of espionage. Ames was given life in prison, and his wife served five years. In 1996, Earl Edwin Pitts, an FBI agent for 13 years, was arrested, and a year later, he pleaded guilty to espionage. In 1996, Harold J. Nicholson, a CIA station chief, was arrested and convicted of espionage two years later. In October 1998, a retired army intelligence analyst, David Shelton Boone, was convicted of selling secrets to the KGB (the Russian national security agency until 1991). For almost a decade prior to his arrest, Boone had passed on information concerning the U.S. nuclear arsenal.

Although there have been numerous incidents of police corruption and violence in the United States, in March 3, 1991, four white Los Angeles policemen were caught on videotape severely beating African American motorist Rodney King. This led to their suspension and the filing of criminal charges. On April 29, 1992, when an all-white jury in neighboring Simi Valley acquitted the officers, Los Angeles became the scene of a major riot that lasted nearly a week. Also in August 1992, in Ruby Ridge, Idaho, federal agents tried to arrest avowed white supremacist Randy Weaver on weapons charges. The armed standoff resulted in the government sniper killings of Weaver's wife and son. Both the beating of Rodney King and the shooting of Weaver's wife and child are examples of how excessive state violence can violate the civil rights of an individual and call into question government procedures for armed standoffs.

Although numerous incidents of state-corporate crime have occurred in the United States, one of the most notable events took place in an Imperial Chicken processing plant fire in September 1991 in Hamlet, North Carolina, in which 25 people were killed. In particular, the state of North Carolina's history of regulatory failure as perpetrated by various state and federal agencies contributed to the tragedy in Hamlet. During this period, North Carolina failed to fund (and to use available federal funds toward) its own state Occupational Safety and Health Administration (OSHA)—a program designed to protect worker safety on the job. At the national level, federal funding for OSHA had decreased in the pro-business, antilabor political climate of the 1980s. In turn, North Carolina had promoted a social climate friendly to business

An aerial view of the Pentagon showing emergency crews responding to the destruction caused when a hijacked commercial jetliner crashed into the building during the September 11, 2001, terrorist attacks. It is debated whether such acts of terror should be considered and prosecuted as criminal (political crimes) or deemed acts of war.

and hostile to labor and corporate regulation. The state's right-to-work laws weakened the little power organized labor had previously held. Workers at Imperial, paid slightly more than minimum wage, were nonunion and likely would have remained that way had events not taken the course they did. State regulatory inspectors knew that Imperial kept the Hamlet plant's fire exit doors locked to prevent workers from stealing chicken parts. Because they could not escape the building when the fire started, 25 workers died. Clearly, the state had shirked its responsibility for protecting workers (which in this case amounted to to a failure to properly enforce the existing law) and allowed a corporation to engage in illegal and, ultimately, deadly actions.

As one final example of state-corporate crime in the 1990s, one must mention ValuJet Flight 592, which crashed in the Florida Everglades in May 1996, killing all 109 people on board. During the investigation into the incident, it was discovered that the government inspectors from the Federal Aviation Administration who were supposed to inspect the safety operations of the ValuJet and Sabre (a contractor for the airline company) technologies had failed to perform their full duties; thus, this incident is considered an act of state-corporate crime.

Governmental misconduct was not limited to the corporate world during this period. In February 1993 in Waco, Texas, the Bureau of Alcohol, Tobacco, and Firearms (a division of the U.S. Department of Treasury) tried to arrest David Koresh, the charismatic leader of a Christian millenarian sect called the Branch Davidians. The situation led to an armed standoff at the Branch Davidian compound. After 51 days, the final assault, at this point managed by the FBI, resulted in the compound becoming a veritable inferno. Eighty-six cult members, including children, died in the flames. This incident, along with the one at Ruby Ridge, helped to bolster the fledgling militia movement in the rural west over the next decade.

In addition, arguably the best-known type of political crime—terrorism—also increased in many countries during the 1990s. On February 26, 1993, members of Al Qaeda placed a truck bomb in the underground parking garage of the World Trade Center in New York City. Although the original intent of the bombers was to fell one of buildings, the resultant blast only killed six people, although it injured 1,042 individuals. On April 19, 1995, in Oklahoma City, decorated Gulf War military veteran Timothy McVeigh, along with Terry L. Nichols, detonated a Ryder truck bomb that destroyed the Alfred P. Murrah Federal Building. The death toll reached 186, including several children in the building's second-floor day care center. McVeigh, who was later apprehended and given the death penalty, said that he committed the action because of his disillusionment with the federal government's actions in the Ruby Ridge and Branch Davidian incidents. On April 3, 1996, Theodore (Ted) Kaczynski (popularly known as the Unabomber) was arrested and charged with a series of mail bombings he had perpetrated, which were ostensibly directed against supporters of technology and those whom he perceived as hurting the environment. In January 2001, President Bill Clinton left office under a shroud of controversy because of a number of scandals in which he (and sometimes, his wife) was alleged to have been involved in (e.g., Whitewater, abuse of power, and romantic or sexual involvements). Additional tension was produced by President Clinton's unsuccessful impeachment.

The 2000s

The early 2000s witnessed a highly publicized espionage case. In the spring of 2001, Robert P. Hanssen, a senior FBI agent, was convicted of having illegally transferred sensitive documents to Soviet and then Russian intelligence agents and their organizations starting in 1985. Hanssen was in a unique position to collect sensitive information because of his contacts with the CIA and the State Department. Why and how he managed to evade detection for a decade and a half were matters of grave concern to U.S. intelligence officials.

On September 11, 2001, one of the most infamous cases of political crime occurred. Four planes were hijacked by members of Osama bin Laden's Al Qaeda network. These planes were crashed into the World Trade Center, the Pentagon, and a rural field in Pennsylvania, causing close to 3,000 deaths and more than 6,300 injuries. Although not nearly as dramatic or deadly, several anthrax-filled letters were sent through the U.S. mail in late 2001, some addressed to well-known television broadcasters and politicians. The attacks led to the deaths of three people, the hospitalization of others, and the slowdown and virtual shutdown of the U.S. postal system. In 2008, following a series of U.S. law enforcement failures and multiple interpretations, the FBI conceded that Bruce Ivans was the likely culprit. Ivans, a disgruntled federal government biodefense researcher who had experienced psychological problems. committed suicide before formal criminal charges could be filed. In the wake of the attacks, Congress passed the USA PATRIOT Act, which has given state and federal law enforcement agencies increased powers in investigating and charging individuals suspected of or engaging in terrorism. Some of the more important highlights include so-called roving wiretaps (tied to certain people rather than to particular telephone lines); nationwide search warrants, instead of those limited to specific jurisdictions; searches of electronic mail; and the power to detain foreigners for extended periods of time. The bill gives "authorities the ability to hold immigrants suspected of terrorist acts for seven days without filing charges." The PATRIOT Act also permits longer and more severe sentences and the extension of the statute of limitations on terrorism cases. Few literate Americans, including some of the members of Congress who passed the bill, have read the full text of this rather draconian antiterrorism legislation.

In 2006, Jack Abramoff, a former businessman and Republican lobbyist, was convicted of mail fraud and conspiracy. He, along with several White House officials, had engaged in corruption through the "selling" of political influence to a number of individuals and organizations, which included various Native American tribes that were trying to obtain concessions for their gambling operations.

Conclusion

In each new decade, the full panoply of political crimes has occurred, although the number of occurrences has obviously varied. Despite this continuity, the passing years have resulted in a greater appreciation that political crime is not simply limited to actions directed against the state, but that the government (through its criminogenic agencies—national security/intelligence, military, and law enforcement) is capable of and has carried out numerous actions that should be labeled as state crimes. Although this may seem unfathomable to many Americans who may see this statement as somewhat un-American, the veracity of the claims cannot be denied.

Jeffrey Ian Ross
University of Baltimore

See Also: Black Panthers; Federal Bureau of Investigation; Kent State Massacre; King, Rodney; Ruby Ridge Standoff; Terrorism; Waco Siege.

Further Readings
Aulette, J. R. and R. Michalowski. "Fire in Hamlet: A Case Study of State-Corporate Crime." In *Political Crime in Contemporary America: A Critical Approach*, Kenneth D. Tunnell, ed. New York: Garland, 1993.
Beirne, P. and J. Messerschmidt. *Criminology*. New York: Harcourt Brace Jovanovich, 1991.
Churchill, W. and J. Vander Wall. *The COINTELPRO Papers: Documents From the FBI's Secret Wars Against Domestic Dissent*. Boston: South End, 1990.
Havill, A. *The Spy Who Stayed Out in the Cold: The Secret Life of FBI Double Agent Robert Hanssen*. New York: St. Martin's Press, 2001.
Kappeler, V. E., et al. *Forces of Deviance*. Prospect Heights, IL: Waveland, 1994.
Matthews, R. and D. Kauzlarich. "The Crash of ValuJet Flight 592: A Case Study in State-Corporate Crime." *Sociological Focus*, v.3 (2000).
Wright, J. P., F. T. Cullen, and M. B. Blankenship. "The Social Construction of Corporate Violence: Media Coverage of the Imperial Food Products Fire." *Crime and Delinquency*, v.41 (1995).

Political Crimes, History of

When examining the history of any phenomenon, one typically talks about periods of change and stagnation. When drilling deeper into the history of a controversial action like crime, it is important to see that the frequency and types of occurrences vary as a reflection of different processes at work (e.g., the growth of technology, introduction of new laws, diffusion of ideas, and social change).

It is also necessary to keep in mind that the dialectical nature of political crime as oppositional (actions against the government and its allies) may cause the state to overreact and engage in state crimes. Political crime, an increasingly important scholarly subject that is often mentioned in passing in introductory textbooks on criminology, is no different. Part of the initial problem in tracing the history of political crime in any country is a lack of widespread agreement on what constitutes political crime. Some of this confusion results from a lack of consensus over broad definitions of crime in general. In the current state of criminology, crime covers not only violations of existing laws but also violations related to social harm, moral transgression, and civil and human rights. This "social justice" perspective acknowledges that some behaviors are not traditionally labeled criminal, but should be, and that certain activities that do not violate the existing law, yet fall under the previously mentioned characteristics, should be considered crimes. A definition of political crime is provided by P. Beirne and J. Messerschmidt:

… crimes against the state (violations of law for the purpose of modifying or changing social conditions) … [and] crimes by the state, both domestic (violations of law and unethical acts by state officials and agencies whose victimization occurs inside [a particular country]) and international (violations of domestic and international law by state officials and agencies whose victimization occurs outside the U.S.).

The purpose of this entry is not to examine definitional, conceptual, or theoretical debates but to provide a rather straightforward chronological history of political crime in the United States in seven different periods, from the country's founding to the contemporary era. This includes such acts as oppositional political terrorism, sabotage, sedition, espionage, corruption, illegal domestic surveillance, human rights violations, and state-corporate crime.

Founding Period
The founding period covers a large swath of history that predates the passage of the U.S. Constitution. Some scholars and many leftist political activists argue that the creation of the United

States as an independent country was not simply a rebellion against Great Britain, the interpretation that is common in most popular textbooks. The revolution was, rather, part of the natural progression of colonialism on the North American continent, a series of events that included genocide against Native Americans and the practice of slavery, both different types of political crimes. The American Revolutionary War (1775–83) itself was an act of sedition and treason against the British monarch. Shortly after America gained independence (1783), small rebellions took place throughout the country. One of the most notable was the Whiskey Rebellion. In 1794, farmers in western Pennsylvania believed they were being unfairly charged for the grain they grew that was later converted to whiskey, and they used intimidation and violent tactics to keep the tax from being collected. Shortly after America's separation from Great Britain, it was necessary for the new government to provide a legal structure with which its inhabitants could live. Numerous laws, both civil and criminal, were passed. Thus, Congress passed the Sedition Act of 1798, which criminalized any scandalous article written about the president or Congress. In general, the act made it a crime to say, write, or publish anything "false, scandalous, or malicious." Later federal law defined seditious conspiracy as follows:

> If two or more persons in any State or Territory, or in any place subject to the jurisdiction of the United States, conspire to overthrow, put down, or destroy by force the Government of the United States, or to levy war against them, or to oppose by force the authority thereof, or by force to prevent, hinder, or delay the execution of any law of the United States, or by force to seize, take, or possess any property of the United States contrary to the authority thereof.

The Nineteenth Century

During the greater part of the 19th century, as the country expanded westward and new territories, states, and municipalities were acquired and/or created, there were ample opportunities for lawbreaking by those in political leadership positions. Numerous land scandals through which local elites profited at the expense of ignorant homesteaders, farmers, and native peoples had the semblance of corruption and other similar political crimes. During the War of 1812, the U.S. government, as a security precaution, arrested numerous British citizens who were living in east coast cities. Some were deported to England while others voluntarily relocated to Canada (and became known as the Upper Canada Loyalists). The Seminole War of 1818, instigated and led by then general and later President Andrew Jackson, included numerous instances of human rights violations and genocide. Until recently, few history books would have—as Howard Zinn did—described Jackson as "slaveholder, land speculator, executioner of dissident solders, exterminator of Indians." These actions were followed by other acts of political crime: the assassination of President Abraham Lincoln (1865); attempts by the Ku Klux Klan and others to thwart Reconstruction (1865–77); the assassination of President James A. Garfield (1881); and the assassination of William McKinley (1901). As factory workers, miners, and those working in the context of the rapid U.S. industrialization began to demonstrate, police, the state patrol, and the military were used by mayors, governors, and presidents to quell labor unrest, sometimes resorting to excessive force and violence.

World War I

In 1918, in an effort to shore up support for the entrance of the United States into World War I and to reduce criticism of the war, the Sedition Act of 1786 was amended. The act was made more specific and was popularly referred to as the Sedition Act. During this time, close to 1,000 individuals were incarcerated under state or federal sedition laws because they opposed U.S. involvement in World War I or because of their "controversial" union activities or religious and political beliefs. During the U.S. involvement in World War I (1917–18), the Department of Justice also interned 6,000 German and other European-born civilians and merchant seamen in military barracks in Georgia and Utah. These seizures were motivated by both justifiable and unfounded suspicions of espionage and subterfuge in North America.

Interwar Period

One of today's most widely used spying techniques is wiretapping, which was, ironically, declared illegal in the United States in 1934.

Although the FBI continued using this technology in subsequent years, agents did discontinue its use briefly after a Supreme Court ruling in 1937 that applied the law to the Federal Bureau of Investigation (FBI) and its operations. Two years later, in opposition to the Supreme Court's decision, President Franklin Roosevelt claimed the FBI had the authority and right to wiretap in "national security" cases.

World War II

Normally, the offense of treason needs to be committed inside the United States, but during this period, the jurisdiction was expanded to include actions by Americans in other countries. For example, several persons were prosecuted for their broadcasts that aired in foreign countries during World War II. One of the most famous cases was against the rather eccentric, pro-Fascist American writer Ezra Pound. During World War II, Mussolini's Fascist government allowed Pound to broadcast in English from Rome. Pound was arrested and charged with treason. During the trial, he claimed that his actions were patriotic. The trial resulted in a verdict of "unsound mind," and Pound was committed to the mental ward at St. Elizabeth's Hospital in Washington, D.C., from 1945 to 1948, when he was released with the diagnosis that he was "incurably insane, but not dangerous." During World War II (1941–45), 120,000 Japanese American citizens (born in the United States) and 8,000 Japanese nationals were interned in prison camps located in Utah, Colorado, Idaho, and Washington. Besides these individuals, 3,500 Germans and 1,000 Italians (American citizens and foreign nationals) were incarcerated. The internment included women and children and lasted through the declaration of peace. These innocent people lost their jobs and homes and suffered great hardships that continued into the years that followed the war.

The 1950s

In the post–World War II era, America, facing the threat of communism, passed an array of laws pertaining to sedition and treason, including the McCarran Act (1950), the Internal Security Act (1952), and the Communist Control Act (1954). Many state and local governments enacted similar or even more sweeping laws.

One of the best-known cases of espionage during this time period concerned the activities of Julius and Ethel Rosenberg. In 1950, at the height of the cold war, this couple, along with a handful of coconspirators, were arrested, tried, and convicted. On June 19, 1953, despite considerable public protest, the Rosenbergs were executed for leaking classified information on the highly secret atomic bomb to authorities in the Soviet Union.

The 1960s to the Present

During the 1960s, public protests against the war in Vietnam, the draft, and civil rights often placed the public at odds with law enforcement and national security agencies. Numerous instances of police use of excessive force occurred. On several notable occasions, the police clashed with student demonstrators against the Vietnam War and with civil rights protesters. Other public protests were organized as reactions to police brutality. These confrontations were largely centered in big cities like New York, Chicago, and Los Angeles. Other incidents took place on college campuses, including Jackson State in Mississippi and Kent State in Ohio (both of which occurred in May 1970).

Some of the more salient oppositional political crimes that occurred during the 1960s included the assassinations of three notable public figures: President John F. Kennedy, Martin Luther King, Jr., and Senator Robert Kennedy.

Domestic Surveillance

In an attempt to monitor dissent, local, state, and federal law enforcement agencies increased their domestic surveillance activities. Most major urban police agencies (e.g., Chicago, New York, Los Angeles, and Philadelphia) spied on American citizens during this time. Each police department had special units whose responsibilities focused on information gathering and the infiltration and destabilization of citizen groups defined as threatening to social order. While engaging in their own surveillance operations, the city police departments often acted in tandem with national law enforcement agencies, most typically the FBI.

For example, the Chicago Police Department's political surveillance operation claimed in 1960 that it "had accumulated information on some 117,000 local individuals, 141,000 out-of-town subjects, and 14,000 organizations." Until 1968,

Some of the most notable political crimes occurred during the 1960s, including the assassinations of John F. Kennedy, Robert Kennedy, and Martin Luther King, Jr. (above).

most of the department's spying had been limited to ideologically threatening groups—the Communist Party and the Socialist Workers' Party. However, with the Democratic National Convention scheduled for Chicago in 1968, surveillance increased to include a wide variety of "civic groups and prominent citizens," linking them, as best the authorities could, to communism and communist subversion, although very little substantiation ever materialized.

New York City opened a separate spy unit, the Bureau of Special Services (BOSS), and Philadelphia, under Mayor Frank Rizzo, the son of a police sergeant and a career police officer himself, established a surveillance unit known as the Civil Defense Squad. The New York, Philadelphia, and later, the Los Angeles police departments operated similarly to the surveillance squad of Chicago—clearly violating laws and spying on citizens. Each department now claims that its spy operations have long been shut down, although just after former Los Angeles Police Chief Darryl Gates retired in 1993, evidence emerged indicating that he had used a special Los Angeles Police Department surveillance force to spy on various leftist sympathizers and political enemies, including actor Robert Redford and former Mayor Tom Bradley.

Wiretapping remained illegal until 1968, when it was ruled legal if authorized by court order based on sufficient probable cause. Despite this judicial intervention, illegal domestic surveillance continues unabated. Also, criminal justice personnel often have to go "judge shopping" in order to gain the trust or confidence of a sympathetic judge. Illegally planting listening devices, or bugs, is possible mainly through burglaries. While the rate of using these devices has varied, FBI director J. Edgar Hoover continued condoning illegal burglaries and the planting of bugs throughout his career.

In 1978, the U.S. government passed the Foreign Intelligence Surveillance Act (FISA). Its passage was a response to the perceived excesses of the Nixon administration in connection with spying against political groups that engaged in legitimate political dissent; it also arose because of the revelations of the Church Committee, which investigated illegal domestic surveillance engaged in by both the Federal Bureau of Investigation and the Central Intelligence Agency (CIA). FISA was designed to monitor communications between foreigners outside the United States and was not intended to record domestic communications.

Since 1986, the FBI has been using Carnivore, a program that intercepts all e-mail traffic coming in and out of the United States. News reports periodically allege real or purported bugging incidents. For example, in February 2002, it was revealed that the CIA had planted listening devices in the rooms of Japanese officials during the most recent round of trade negotiations between the United States and Japan.

FISA was amended in 2001 because of the USA PATRIOT Act. The legislation was once again changed in 2007 through the Protect America Act. This new act expired one year after its implementation and was seriously flawed thus a new FISA bill was passed in 2008.

One of the most pervasive intelligence operations bears the name *Echelon*. Although its existence was originally denied by the U.S. National Security Agency, the operation monitors every electronic transmission related to U.S. interests, including cell phone calls and e-mail messages. A scandal broke out in Europe in February 2001 when it was discovered that the CIA was spying on behalf of American businesses. Numerous contemporary cases have explicitly been labeled as state-corporate crimes and include the following: the January 1986 *Challenger* explosion; the September 1991 deadly Imperial Chicken processing plant fire in Hamlet, North Carolina; and the U.S. Department of Energy's role in nuclear weapons production (1960s to present).

Additional contemporary examples of state-corporate crime in the United States have included the work by Wedtech, a defense contractor that was charged with fraud in its dealings with the government in 1987, and the crash of ValuJet Flight 592 in May 1996. In the former case, under the pretense of helping disadvantaged minority businesses, the Small Business Administration, White House aides, a number of members of Congress, and Attorney General Edwin Meese III were implicated in corruption charges. In the latter case, it was discovered that Federal Aviation Administration inspectors who were supposed to inspect the safety operations of ValuJet and Sabre Technologies (which had a contract with the airline company) were negligent in their affairs. This omission led to the deaths of all 109 individuals on board when the plane crashed in the Florida Everglades.

Undoubtedly, some of the most notable instances of political crime in the United States over the past four decades have been instances of both domestic and international political terrorism. On February 26, 1993, members of Al Qaeda placed a truck bomb in the underground parking garage of the World Trade Center (WTC) in New York City. Although the original intention of the bombers was to fell one of the buildings, the resultant blast killed five people and injured 1,000. Similar incidents included the 1995 Oklahoma City bombing by Timothy McVeigh, which killed 186 and injured 680 people. On September 11, 2001, 19 Al Qaeda members hijacked four planes, two of which were flown into the WTC, one into the Pentagon in Washington, D.C., and one headed for another location in Washington, D.C., which was intentionally crashed into a field in Pennsylvania when passengers took action against the terrorists. This coordinated act killed 3,000 people and injured approximately 6,300 people.

Conclusion

The terrorist incidents of the past decade, both in the United States and abroad, should not force the reader into thinking that either terrorism or political crimes are things of the past. For as long as we have states and as long as we have individuals and groups vying for political power, political crime will exist. In order to better appreciate the progression of political crime in the United States, more scholarship needs to be produced. Future research should include not only case studies but also an accounting of sorts that would place this issue into a quantitative format that is easily understandable.

Jeffrey Ian Ross
University of Baltimore

See Also: 1600 to 1776 Primary Documents; 1851 to 1900 Primary Documents; 1941 to 1960 Primary Documents; Federal Bureau of Investigation; Homeland Security; King, Martin Luther, Jr.; Ku Klux Klan; McVeigh, Timothy; Oklahoma City Bombing; Political Crimes, Contemporary; Terrorism; USA PATRIOT Act of 2001.

Further Readings

Aulette, J. R. and R. Michalowski. "Fire in Hamlet: A Case Study of State-Corporate Crime. In *Political Crime in Contemporary America: A Critical Approach*, Kenneth D. Tunnell, ed. New York: Garland, 1993.

Churchill, W. *A Little Matter of Genocide: Holocaust and Denial in the Americas, 1492 to the Present*. San Francisco: City Lights Books, 1997.

Donner, F. J. *Protectors of Privilege: Red Squads and Police Repression in Urban America*. Berkeley: University of California Press, 1990.

Friedrichs, D. O. *Trusted Criminals: White Collar Crime in Contemporary Society*. New York: Wadsworth, 1996.

Hagan, F. *Political Crime: Ideology & Criminality*. Boston: Allyn & Bacon, 1997.

Neville, J. F. *Press, the Rosenbergs & the Cold War*. Westport, CT: Greenwood, 1995.

Ross, Jeffrey Ian. *The Dynamics of Political Crime*. Thousand Oaks, CA: Sage, 2003.

Zinn, Howard. *A Peoples History of the United States*. New York: HarperPerrenial, [1980] 2010.

Political Crimes, Sociology of

Political crime is rarely examined when studying the dynamics of crime, justice, and law. Yet understanding political offenses or illegalities is fundamental to comprehending the workings of a criminal justice system that selectively defines, enforces, and adjudicates who is defined as criminal. As a variety of scholars, jurists, policy makers, legislators, and activists have argued, the law and, by extension, crime qualify as political acts. Hence, interpreting law, crime, and criminals requires a political focus. Various criminal acts are explicitly political. For example, sedition and treason have traditionally been viewed by states as political offenses because of their real or alleged threats to order (public, social, or otherwise) or national security. As a result, these behaviors have been codified in law. However, some state reactions to dissent are almost or actually criminal. This is the case when governments occasionally engage in repressive actions during which law-abiding individuals are placed under surveillance and/or harassed or groups are infiltrated and/or destabilized.

These escalating state responses are rarely recognized in domestic criminal law. Both actions, oppositional and state-initiated, are increasingly understood by many scholars and activists as political crimes. Likewise, and according to recent theoretical advances in criminology, sociology, political science, and law, many controversial behaviors are considered politically and socially harmful, yet are not presently classified in legal codes as criminal. Legal definitions of crime are often too narrow, and the law is frequently too dynamic to be helpful. In other words, we cannot impose the kind of neutrality upon the law that might be implicit in the philosophy of "equal justice under the law."

Thus, an alternative, more contemporary, and inclusive definition and conceptualization of crime is needed. One definition that is gaining increasing legitimacy recognizes that crime is not only a type of deviance that has been codified or has been conceptualized as a violation of a criminal law but can be interpreted by the wider body politic as a social harm, moral transgression, and/or civil or human rights violation. This "social justice" perspective acknowledges that some behaviors are not traditionally labeled criminal but should be and that certain activities that do not violate the existing law yet fall under the previously mentioned characteristics should be considered crimes. This notion would accommodate not only the actions of individuals and organizations, but also those of states, their employees, and contractors. Thus, political crime is a more far-ranging label than previously considered.

Understanding and Interpreting Political Crime

It is difficult to come to terms with political crime. Several reasons contribute to this state of affairs. In general, there is often a lack of consensus with respect to a definition, availability of good information, rigorous analysis, and/or interest in political crimes. Undoubtedly, considerable confusion exists about what constitutes a political offense. Experts are often divided over how to define political illegalities, and many seem to purposefully define political crime differently. Moreover, information presented by the mass media and news media minimizes the ability of citizens to understand political crimes properly.

Although this is less the case with oppositional political crimes such as terrorism, the media construction of state crimes such as genocide often presents them as unavoidable illegalities, the "just deserts" inflicted upon "irrational" dissidents, or the collateral damages of war. Perhaps more importantly, the identification of crimes by the state is not popular. Many people do not criticize the legitimacy of their own political system because of high levels of trust, deference to authority, apathy, or repeated experiences of powerlessness.

P. Beirne and J. Messerschmitt define political crime as follows:

> ... crimes against the state (violations of law for the purpose of modifying or changing social conditions) ... [and] crimes by the state, both domestic (violations of law and unethical acts by state officials and agencies whose victimization occurs inside [a particular country]) and international (violations of domestic and international law by state officials and agencies whose victimization occurs outside the U.S.).

Given this categorization, a political crime in the United States could involve a correctional officer violating a prisoner's civil, human, or constitutional rights. On the other hand, an international political crime could include the destabilization of a foreign government, as the United States was accused of attempting in Salvador Allende's Chile in 1970. Alternatively, the 1998 bombing of the U.S. embassies in Kenya and Tanzania, allegedly committed by the Al Qaeda terrorist organization, would also qualify as an international criminal action.

Jurists usually distinguish a crime by referring to the existing criminal code, and if this is insufficient, they examine the context. The context includes the perpetrators' motives, affiliations, targets/victims, and the effects of the action. Although democratic governments and their employees are bound by specific laws and statutes forbidding them to engage in illegalities (typically embedded in criminal and administrative law), they periodically violate these rules for particular purposes.

Crimes committed by the state are somewhat unique because they include illegalities committed by the government as a whole, by organizational units of the state, and by individual officials who break the law for their own personal or their agency's gain. These types of crimes differ because the former two categories are organizationally based, whereas the latter is regarded as individual crimes of occupational corruption. Just as some types of white-collar crime are organizationally based (e.g., the Ford Pinto case of violence against consumers), some specific political state crimes are also considered organizational. For instance, the Federal Bureau of Investigation's (FBI) ongoing illegal surveillance of American citizens (1925–72) was an agencywide operation conducted with the guidance of top FBI officials and involving almost every field office in the United States.

Theories of Political Crime

No widely accepted causal theories of crime, including political crime, exist. Though this hinders the ability to specify an appropriate explanation for political crime, we can examine relevant theories. Robert Merton (1938; 1964, 1966) provided one of the earliest explanations that, in part, touches on political crime. According to his anomic theory of deviance (i.e., strain theory), individuals live in societies that have a considerable amount of structural dysfunctionalism. This leads people to experience an ends/means discrepancy. These processes combined together create stress. In order to minimize the discomfort, individuals have five options, one of which is rebellion (nominally a type of political crime). Unfortunately, Merton's theory, regardless of who uses it, is too limited for a more encompassing understanding of political crime.

Similarly, R. Moran (1974) describes "sequential stages which in successive combination might account for the development of a political criminal." The first are what he calls "predisposing conditions or background factors, the conjunction of which forms a pool of potential political criminals. These conditions exist prior to an individual's decision to commit a political crime and by themselves do not account for his behavior." The aforementioned conditions include the concept of strain and "a political problem solving perspective." The latter consists of "situational contingencies which lead to the commission of political crimes by predisposed individuals." Moran advocates a five-stage developmental model consisting of the following steps: (1) strain, (2) political problem-solving perspective, (3) a turning-point event, (4) commitment to act, and (5) engaging in the political crime. Although he recognizes many of the limitations of his idea, the cases upon which Moran builds his model may be too ideographic to legitimately support the kinds of generalizations he made.

An alternative perspective has been offered by Austin Turk (1982). His structural conflict theory posits that although power and inequality are important factors in explaining political crime, the cultural gap between offenders and authorities is the primary factor that leads to the commission of political crime. Turk's theory is interesting, but it is limited in its explanatory power.

Merton's, Moran's, and Turk's theories are useful in describing, and in some cases explaining, various types of political crime, but they are not very helpful in accounting for all types of this phenomenon. The dynamic nature of such activities needs to be more thoroughly explored, and furthermore, the macro- and micro-level processes in political crime should be linked.

The Sociological Interpretation

Often, research about political crime has taken a static perspective or has maintained that political crime primarily results from either state or oppositional activities. Like many other phenomena in the social and natural sciences, the process of political crime follows an interactive, iterative, or dynamic pattern. In short, building on Newtonian physics, nothing in nature is static, and neither is political crime. One of the central hypotheses underlying political crime is grounded in the interaction between anti-systemic crime and state crime.

In an effort to illustrate how dynamic political crime can be, numerous historical examples offer a perspective whereby state crimes can cause oppositional crimes and vice versa. In other words, political crime does not exist in a vacuum. Rather, as previously mentioned, it is affected by a series of factors that are endemic to the people who commit the crimes, the occupations they hold, the organizations that employ them (or of which they are members), and more generally, the context in which a particular crime exists. Thus, political crime is a response to a variety of subtle, ongoing, interacting, and changing psychological and structural factors manifested by perpetrators, victims, state agencies, and audiences.

A vast array of theories may shed light on the nature of political crime. Moreover, one must accept the fact that each type of political crime may have a different cause. The relative cause of a particular political crime, therefore, depends on the situational dynamics. One category of theories are micro in focus because they explain phenomena pertinent to people, their differences, their mental states, and their interactions. The micro theories typically explain individual-level behavior and encompass explanations subsumed by psychology. On the other hand, macro theories are relevant because they clarify how environmental factors (including institutions, economics, political systems, and cultures) affect individuals and groups. Among the macro theories are sociological explanations, sometimes called structural explanations.

In general, structural theories posit that the causes of terrorism can be found in the environment and/or the political, cultural, social, and economic structure of societies. Social-psychological theories specify and explain group dynamics and explore why individuals join organizations and how participants (perpetrators, victims, and audiences) affect the commission of acts. Finally, rational choice theories explain the participation in organizations and the choice of actions because of participants' cost-benefit cognitive calculations.

Structural theories explain human behavior by focusing on the social structures within which individuals must function and on the organizational dictates that affect varieties of behavior. Despite their diversity, these theories share a main concern in explaining societal organization and the ways that people are affected by institutions, culture, economies, and conflict.

Although several structural theories may be relevant to a discussion of political crime, many scholars regard conflict theory as the most valuable or useful explanation. To make matters more complicated, a variety of different conflict theories have been formulated. They range from conservative to radical perspectives, but they all agree that conflict is a naturally occurring social phenomenon. Special attention should be given to the variety of radical and critical theories including but not limited to Marxist, neo-Marxist, and conflict approaches. Radical conflict theory, some theorists suggest, explains the roots of much political crime that is situated in and emanates from social, political, and economic processes.

Conflict theories differ specifically in their origins, their persistence, their ability to create change, and their contribution to criminal behavior. Many theories that have emanated from the radical/conflict tradition are parsimonious, have considerable explanatory power over other efforts, and are widely accepted by many criminologists, as evidenced by their inclusion in a large body of literature pertaining to political, white-collar, and state crime research. Nonetheless, these theories are difficult to apply to practical policy concerns.

Radical conflict theory traces its origins to the work of Karl Marx (1818–83). He (along with Friedrich Engels) suggested that conflict in society is the result of a scarcity of resources (i.e., property, wealth, power, and jobs). This creates inequalities among individuals and constituencies that in turn lead to a struggle between those who possess these resources and those who do not. During the 1960s, a number of theorists applied these theories to crime. These Neo-Marxist or "radical" conflict theorists suggested that class struggle affects crime.

R. Quinney, a leading radical conflict theorist, argued that all crime in capitalist societies (which stress individualism and competitiveness) should be considered a manifestation of the class struggle, whereby people strive for wealth, power, money, status, and property. In countries dominated by a capitalist mode of production, a culture of competition arises. This is seen as normal and desirable and takes many forms, including criminality. Traditional neo-Marxists can be criticized for the disproportionate emphasis they place on the working class and the poor (what Marx calls the "dynamite") as a catalyst of change. The working class and the poor levels of society rarely participate in the political process. Furthermore, the types of activities that are legislated as criminal, and that are responded to by the crime control industry, are often those behaviors most often engaged in by the poor and the powerless.

Conclusion

Although many political crimes are committed by groups that are formally or loosely structured, whether oppositional in nature or organized by state organizations, these activities are, in the final analysis, committed by individuals. These people are working within the structural confines of both informal and complex organizations, political systems, political economies, and different cultures. They make decisions and act, while often denying that any wrongdoing has occurred. In sum, political crime is the result of a complex interplay among individuals (I), situations/opportunities (S), organizations (O), and resource adequacy (R). These combined factors have been identified as the ISOR explanation. In general, governmental response to political crime ranges from apathy to policy advocacy to organizational or political change. In general, anti-systemic political crimes are met with state resistance or change, whereas state crimes are met with apathy, resistance, or demand for change from the public or its elected representatives. Apathy and resistance are the most disconcerting responses to state crime because they prevent its control and encourage future commission. For example, a state that is the victim of espionage can simply ignore that a threat to national security has taken place. Alternatively, a state can analyze the event or can engage in counterespionage. In this context, the ISOR relationship is not simply a resource mobilization theory or a crime prevention method brought into alignment with environmental design theories.

Even though conflict and differential association theories were developed to further the understanding of nonpolitical crime, they can easily explain political lawbreaking and, as a result, help us to understand the dynamics of political crime. Conflict in general, rather than that specifically motivated by economic factors alone, is the most important reason why people engage in political crime. Groups and in-group socialization are equally important and powerful motivators.

Jeffrey Ian Ross
University of Baltimore

See Also: 1600 to 1776 Primary Documents; 1921 to 1940 Primary Documents; Political Crimes, Contemporary; Political Crimes, History of; Political Dissidents.

Further Readings

Allen, F. A. *The Crime of Politics: Political Dimensions of Criminal Justice.* Cambridge, MA: Harvard University Press, 1974.

Barak, G., ed. *Media, Process, and the Social Construction of Crime.* New York: Garland, 1994.

Beirne, P. and J. Messerschmidt. *Criminology.* New York: Harcourt Brace Jovanovich, 1991.

Political Dissidents

Political dissidents are individuals who disagree with the establishment, policies, or cultural, social, and economic practices of their time. They act, either as individuals or in tandem with like-minded groups, to effect change in the social, economic, political, or cultural arenas. They can be severely persecuted or punished by their government or law-enforcing groups because they pose a threat to the established order. Because of their new ideas or new ways of thinking, dissidents make important contributions to the society in all areas, instigating necessary shifts and forging new ground for multifaceted changes. Contemporary American political dissidents, usually being controversial figures, have been present and influential in the American public discourses because of political stances or intellectual differences.

Political dissidents are dissatisfied with or in opposition to the practices of the ruling class. They can convey their opinions in peaceful discussions, civil disobedience, or demonstration with force. While repressive regimes have been known for persecuting their political dissidents, pro-democracy governments like the one in the United States have been more tolerant of them.

In spite of the diverse areas in which dissent has been expressed in the United States, the term *political dissident* has been used as the common term. Since the impetus for the dissidents' defiance of the current system is their dissatisfaction with the establishment, their ultimate goal is to change the existing paradigm. Political dissidents, therefore, assume a form of authority and establish a kind of polity via their acts and thoughts. While the term *political dissident* was widely used first in the mid-20th century, it is also applicable to figures living before this time with similar orientations and public reputations.

The Risk of Dissent
It is noteworthy that a substantial number of political dissidents from other countries have sought refuge in the United States. This fact, together with the freedom that American political dissidents have, as found in the cases of Michael Moore and Noam Chomsky, shows that political dissent is tolerated, and with time, celebrated. American political dissidents do not have the need to use a pseudonym for the sake of their safety and life. While the American political dissidents might not be able to effect change in the system, be it governmental or social or cultural, at the time of their engagement, they do contribute to change by transforming the public thoughts and discourses over time. However, a dissident deemed a threat to the government will not be tolerated. If the dissent demonstrates nationwide influence with a movement behind it, then the dissidents' lives will be at risk.

Critics of politicians and policies can be labeled dissidents and persecuted for treason against the authorities. In 1919–20, for instance, an estimate of 10,000 members of labor organizations and socialist-communist groups were arrested in raids led by U.S. Attorney General Alexander Mitchell Palmer. In like manner, in the late 1940s through the mid-1950s, hundreds of leftist civilians were investigated or blacklisted from selected jobs. During the civil rights movement in the 1950s and 1960s, several opponents of racial segregation and political exclusion were arrested and assaulted by the governing body.

An early case of political dissent involved the trial of John Peter Zenger. During the early 1730s, William Cosby was the governor of the colony of New York. The *New York Weekly Journal*, America's first independent political paper, criticized the governor for replacing Lewis Morris, the chief justice of New York, who decided against the governor in a lawsuit. The founder and editor of the *Weekly*, James Alexander, had authored the critical articles. John Peter Zenger was in charge of the printing. The governor then sued Zenger "for printing and publishing several seditious libels dispersed throughout his journals or newspapers, titled the *New York Weekly Journal*; as having in them many things tending to raise factions and tumults among the people of this Province, inflaming their minds with contempt of His Majesty's government, and greatly disturbing the peace thereof."

Andrew Hamilton, a Philadelphia attorney, defended Zenger, arguing that the published statements could not be considered libelous if they were true. According to the English law of the time, truth was not a defense to libel. The jury acquitted Zenger nonetheless and by so doing established a central tenet of defamation law—that truth is an absolute defense. The decision redefined the law of libel and slander during the era of the trial and set the ground for the freedom of the press that the United States celebrates today. Gouverneur Morris wrote this of the Zenger case: "The trial of Zenger in 1735 was the germ of American freedom, the morning star of that liberty which subsequently revolutionized America."

Prominent Dissidents
While several political dissidents have been male, an early female figure changed the world of politics, exerting a bicontinental, if not global, influence during the first decades of the 20th century. Emma Goldman, native of Kovno, present-day Lithuania's Kaunas, was born in the Russian Empire in 1869 and moved to the United States in 1885. Her interest in anarchism developed after the Haymarket affair, and blossomed into great writings and lectures on anarchist philosophy,

women's rights, and social issues. Goldman joined her lover and lifelong friend, anarchist writer Alexander Berkman, in planning the assassination of industrialist and financier Henry Clay Frick as an act of propaganda. Although the assassination failed, Berkman was sentenced to 22 years in prison. Goldman was incarcerated multiple times the following years, having incited riots and illegally distributing information about birth control. Goldman left a substantial legacy of political activism and writings in various areas, such as prisons, atheism, freedom of speech, militarism, capitalism, marriage, free love, and homosexuality.

A political dissident of the early 20th century—who participated in politics—was Eugene Victor Debs. He was known for his commitment to political activism, social justice, union organizing, women's rights, children's rights, and pacifism. He is also known for epitomized progressivism, humanitarianism, and social criticism. Born in Terre Haute, Indiana, in 1855 to French immigrant parents, Debs left school and worked as a painter for the railroad yards when he was only 14. A year later, he worked as a railroad fireman, and engaged in the trade union movement.

In 1884, Debs was elected to the Indiana legislature as a Democratic candidate. He was elected the first president of the American Railway Union (ARU) in 1893. The ARU called for a strike in 1894 when the Pullman Palace Car Company reduced workers' wages and refused arbitration. The strike spread to 27 states, with Debs being recognized as an orator comparable to Abraham Lincoln. Nonetheless, Debs was arrested and imprisoned as a result of Richard Olney, the attorney general, filing an injunction under the Sherman Anti-Trust Act against the Pullman Strike. The Supreme Court heard the case in 1895, where David Brewer refused the ARU's appeal. This hearing adversely pushed back the initial efforts of the trade union movement.

During his incarceration in Woodstock Prison, Debs engaged in the writings of Karl Marx and became a socialist, convinced that a new cooperative system should replace capitalism. Remaining on the moderate and balanced stance, Debs rejected the revolutionary violence endorsed by some left-wing groups. He cofounded the Social Democratic Party (SDP) with Victor Berger and Ella Reeve Bloor in 1897.

Debs ran for presidency in 1900 under the endorsement of the SDP, but lost. In 1901, the SDP and Socialist Labor Party merged into the Socialist Party of America (SPA). Debs also contributed to the weekly *Appeal to Reason*, whose circulation was among the highest in the United States. In 1904, Debs ran again as an SPA presidential candidate and was rather close to winning, only third to Theodore Roosevelt's first.

Debs was also against some wars, opposing World War I because of its roots in the imperialist competitive system. In 1917, the U.S. declared war on the Central Powers. In 1918, Debs gave a speech in Ohio criticizing the Espionage Act, was arrested, convicted, and sentence for 10 years. While in prison, Debs commenced his fifth attempt at the U.S. presidency under the Socialist Party in 1920. Lincoln Steffens paid Debs a visit during his incarceration, and later campaigned for Debs' release on the ground that Debs rejected Bolshevism and violence. In 1921, President Warren G. Harding pardoned Debs, but the socialist activist died five years later in Elmhurst.

Contemporary American Dissidents

It is useful to examine the discourses of some leading political dissidents in contemporary American history. Dr. Martin Luther King, Jr., though celebrated as a renowned civil rights leader in the 21st century, was a political dissident of his time. He was born on January 15, 1929, and grew up during the turbulent era of the Great Depression and World War II. Though a religious leader because of his role as a Baptist minister, King worked tirelessly and fearlessly for a color-blind society and civil rights. He received threats from the Federal Bureau of Investigation (FBI), challenged the establishment in racial injustice, called for economic equality, and organized marches for the working poor. Though King's activism is celebrated worldwide today, his work was not accepted by the establishment at that time. King was opposed to the U.S. involvement in Vietnam. He criticized the government for spending too much money and resources on the war in Vietnam and not enough on the needy at home. He accused the United States for the loss of civilian lives in the war. His antiwar stance had severed support from his white allies, including President Lyndon Johnson, prominent publishers, and union leaders.

Nonetheless, King called for change in the political and economic structures of the nation. He urged a redistribution of resources to remedy racial and economic injustices.

The benefit of hindsight proves that King contributed tremendously to the development of the United States as a nation in the areas of civil rights, racial justice, and economic equalities. Nonetheless, as in the case of most dissidents, he suffered resentment, violence, threats, and assassination. He was clandestinely persecuted by the FBI because of his influence and his message. Yet in 1964, King was the youngest person to ever have received the Nobel Peace Prize for his activism to end racism through nonviolent means. As American society evolved, King was acknowledged at home as well. He was posthumously accorded the Presidential Medal of Freedom in 1977 and Congressional Gold Medal in 2004. In 1986, Martin Luther King Jr. Day was established as a U.S. federal holiday in honor of his contributions.

Another prominent political dissident in American contemporary history is Avram Noam Chomsky. Born on December 7, 1928, he is an American linguist, philosopher, cognitive scientist, and social activist. In the 1960s, Chomsky started to emerge as a political dissident and anarchist, opposing the Vietnam War with his 1967 essay, "The Responsibility of Intellectuals." Two years later, he expanded this essay into a book titled *American Power and the New Mandarins,* detailing his opposition to the Vietnam War.

These publications, together with Chomsky's provocative commentaries about U.S. foreign and domestic policies, helped establish him as a prominent political dissident. He has since been consistently outspoken against U.S. foreign policies, declaring himself anarcho-syndicalist and a libertarian socialist. Chomsky is also critical of certain aspects of American life, culture, and society. His 1988 *Manufacturing Consent: The Political Economy of the Mass Media,* coauthored with Edward S. Herman, analyzed how propaganda model theory worked in the mainstream media. Chomsky argued that the U.S. government and mega-media corporate companies conspired to manipulate the opinions of the American public.

Chomsky's influence is widespread and steady, making him the most cited living author and the eighth most cited source of all time. The 1992 Arts and Humanities Citation Index listed Chomsky as the most cited scholar from 1980 to 1992. Like most political dissidents, he has a controversial status, particularly because of his criticism of U.S. foreign policies. Nonetheless, Chomsky has authored more than 150 books and gained global awareness of his stance.

Another popular political dissident, closely connected to the entertainment industry, is Michael Moore. An author, filmmaker, and political activist, Moore has engaged with pressing issues in contemporary America through documentaries with an edge. A highly controversial figure, Moore has produced and directed numerous films that are critical of American political, social, and cultural practices. His 2009 *Capitalism: A Love Story* documentary sought to see why the American government is still subsidizing the financial institutions that are responsible for the loss of jobs and homes of millions of Americans. In 2007, Moore released *Sicko,* raising debates about the millions of Americans without health coverage and treatment. His numerous other documentaries tackle issues such as gun violence, the chasm between the first and third worlds, terrorism, and corporate America.

Trangdai Glassey-Tranguyen
Stanford University

See Also: 1600 to 1776 Primary Documents; 1777 to 1800 Primary Documents; 1801 to 1850 Primary Documents; 1851 to 1900 Primary Documents; 1901 to 1920 Primary Documents; 1941 to 1960 Primary Documents; Federal Bureau of Investigation; King, Martin Luther, Jr.; National Association for the Advancement of Colored People; Political Policing.

Further Readings
Carson, Clayborne, Tenisha H. Armstrong, Susan A. Carson, Erin K. Cook, and Susan Englander. *The Martin Luther King, Jr. Encyclopedia.* Westport, CT: Greenwood Press, 2008.
Chomsky, Noam. *American Power and the New Mandarins.* New York: Pantheon Books, 1969.
King, Martin Luther, Jr. *A Call to Conscience: The Landmark Speeches of Martin Luther King Jr.* Clayborne Carson, ed. New York: IPM/Warner Books, 2001.
Moore, Michael. *Dude, Where's My Country?* New York: Warner, 2003.

Moore, Michael. *Stupid White Men: And Other Sorry Excuses for the State of the Nation!* New York: HarperCollins, 2001.

Political Policing

Political policing, though it might have had its genesis in previous American and European history, is seen as a 20th-century phenomenon. Political policing is defined as the police's curbing of political expressions and activities of the people, which can be in the form of protests, demonstrations, sit-ins, town hall meetings, walks, and others. In very few cases, political policing can be seen in investigations of corrupt political practices. Political policing can involve coerced force, beating of civilians, use of weapons, arrests, incarceration, and persecution. Today, political policing takes place worldwide and is documented by bloggers or demonstrators across the Web. The multimedia outlets also feature news and editorials pertaining to political policing incidents.

The root of political policing can be traced back to the 18th and 19th centuries, when states increasingly employed the political police to enforce codes of behaviors and to suppress internal opposition. When the people organized and pushed for social and political changes, as seen in the French Revolution, the government and its neighbors were concerned about the spread of such movements and uprisings. Better means of communicating helped political organizers amass supporters and followers, leading to an organic growth and far-reaching effects.

While some political police forces were set up to suppress a particular event, these forces remained in place even after the conclusion of such event. This helps explain why political policing accumulates, continuing through regime changes and transitions in the form of structural continuities, common targets, or other characteristics and methods. Though the American people enjoy a great deal of democratic processes, political policing is also present and prevalent. In recent years, political policing has focused on immigration issues, targeting immigrants and activists alike. While political policing can target corrupt elected officials and shady governmental administrators, it is most often seen in oppressing civil demonstrations and protests.

Political policing touches upon various governing and law-enforcing aspects. Though the police force is projected as defender of the public in a democratic society like the United States, it can be said that such effort is made because federal leaders know how much they need public support. Therefore, politicians can use double speech in order to uphold the police force and cover up ambiguities or abuses. Furthermore, the police force is essentially a law enforcement agency, working primarily to endorse a dominant ideology and to protect the ruling classes.

Historical Context

The earliest incident of political policing might have been the Alien and Sedition Acts of 1798, an effort by Congress to strengthen the federal government as it faced the threat of war with France. The four laws collectively named the Alien and Sedition Acts and sponsored by the Federalists were intended to repress possible political opposition from the Republicans under the leadership of Thomas Jefferson. On June 18, Congress passed the first law, the Naturalization Act, which required that aliens be residents for 14 years instead of five years before they became eligible for U.S. citizenship. On June 25, Congress passed the Alien Act, authorizing the president to deport aliens deemed "dangerous to the peace and safety of the United States" during peacetime. On July 6, Congress enacted the third law, the Alien Enemies Act, allowing the wartime arrest, imprisonment, and deportation of any alien subject to an enemy power.

On July 14, the fourth and final law, the Sedition Act, was passed, declaring that any treasonable activity—including the publication of "any false, scandalous and malicious writing"—was a high misdemeanor, punishable by fine and imprisonment. This legislation was responsible for the arrest of 25 men, most of them editors of Republican newspapers, and the forced closure of their respective newspapers. Among the 25 arrested was Benjamin Franklin's grandson, Benjamin Franklin Bache, editor of the *Philadelphia Democrat-Republican Aurora*. He was charged with libeling President John Adams, and his arrest

U.S. Army soldiers of the 130th Military Police Company, Tennessee Army National Guard role-play as rioters during training for their upcoming deployment. Political policing is the police's curbing of political expressions and activities of the people, which can be in the form of protests, demonstrations, sit-ins, town hall meetings, walks, and others.

resulted in a public outcry against all of the Alien and Sedition Acts.

At the time, several Americans challenged the constitutionality of these laws. Public opposition put tremendous pressure on the government and helped elect the Republican candidate Thomas Jefferson to the presidency in 1800. The new president pardoned all those convicted under the Sedition Act, and Congress refunded all fines including interest.

Party line is not the only factor that prompts political policing. For various reasons, political policing can be closely linked to racial profiling in that certain racial groups are targeted as a result of criminal stereotypes or discriminations. The establishment or expansion of a particular political police force can also be sustained even after the cause, such as a moment of crisis, has dissipated. In 1917, the Federal Bureau of Investigation (FBI) developed a political mission to monitor the activities of radicals opposing U.S. entry into the war and to surveil large groups of German immigrants. At the conclusion of World War I, the force was maintained because of the rise in left-wing radicalism.

Governmental Justifications

The government can argue that political policing is used to gather information about the public in order to aid in better governing. This can be a pretext in that in a democracy, other channels of communications, such as newspapers and online forums, can accomplish this task. It is important to note that in democratic regimes, the targeted groups are focused, whereas in dictatorships, the extremist approach can be the case and therefore the targeted groups can mean anyone.

It can be said that the police structures are most specialized in the political arena, where secrecy shields policing activities from public view. Techniques used in political surveillance include collection of information, intercepting correspondences, listening to conversations, using informants and agents, and manufacturing evidence should such become unprocurable by force. When using force, the police are aware that they will be held accountable by the public, and abuse always takes place in secret.

The U.S. government is also alleged to have trained police forces in Latin America and elsewhere on political policing, and hence partaking in this process beyond its geographical territories. The U.S. training programs are preferred for penetrating police structures, starting with basic coaching in traffic control techniques and technologies. Then the training moves to large-scale operations and manipulations.

The United States spends a large budget on police assistance to third world countries, exceeding $337 million in the years 1962 through 1974 alone. During these 12 years, the United States sponsored almost 1 million foreign police officers to receive instruction in their own countries and more than 5,000 trained at the International Police Academy based in Washington, D.C. The training program covered surveillance techniques, interrogation procedures, methods of conducting raids, crowd-control procedures, and intelligence gathering. Participants in these training programs also watched films with policemen using violent techniques in suppression procedures. In their final writing assignments, the participants claimed that the programs had prompted them to use physical coercion and torture.

In the World War II era, with the fight against communism and fascism, the U.S. police assumed a dominant and implicit role in Central America. Presidents Harry Truman, Dwight Eisenhower, and John F. Kennedy expanded the policy on political policing in these countries, giving it a less intimidating look than direct military intervention. When the policy was at its peak in the 1960s and 1970s, Latin American countries experienced state-led brutality and inhumanity. This has been seen as the United States ensuring its own security by asserting its agenda, rather than delivering what it claimed, which was to democratize the police forces in its southern neighbors.

During the first decade of the 21st century, the American public has scrutinized its law enforcement for political policing of people with Muslim backgrounds, such as through raids at mosques, arrests, imprisonments, and home searches. After the September 11, 2001, attacks on the World Trade Center in New York and the Pentagon in Washington, D.C., and the Iraq War in 2003, law enforcement had shown increased interference with the civil liberties of Muslim Americans.

Trangdai Glassey-Tranguyen
Stanford University

See Also: American Civil Liberties Union; Political Dissidents; Terrorism.

Further Readings
Calvan, B. C. "New Surveillance Guidelines Fuel Debate in California: Concerns Raised on Civil Liberties." *Boston Globe* (November 30, 2003).
Greenberg, Ivan. *The Dangers of Dissent: The FBI and Civil Liberties Since 1965*. Lanham, MD: Lexington Books, 2010.
"House Un-American Activities Committee (1950) Report on the National Lawyers Guild: Legal Bulwark of the Communist Party." Report 3123. Washington, DC: U.S. Congress, 1950.
Whitaker, Reg. *The End of Privacy: How Total Surveillance is Becoming a Reality*. New York: New Press, 2000.

Polk, James K. (Administration of)

Often referred to by the American press as "Young Hickory," James Knox Polk (1795–1849) served one term as the president of the United States, 1845–49, but is most remembered for acquiring Oregon, California, and Texas, which established the United States as a continental power, united from coast to coast. Polk was born to Samuel and

Jane Polk in Mecklenburg County, North Carolina; he was the first of nine children. Soon after Tennessee entered the Union in 1796, Samuel Polk moved his family there to settle along the Duck River in the newly formed Maury County. Faced with the hardships of frontier life, young James Polk suffered from chronic illness caused by a urinary bladder stone that had to be removed surgically at age 17. In 1818, Polk graduated from the University of North Carolina with honors in mathematics and the classics he subsequently studied law in Tennessee at the office of Felix Grundy. Admitted to the Tennessee bar in 1820, Polk began practicing law in Columbia, Tennessee. While a member of the Tennessee state legislature, in 1823, Polk kindled a friendship with Andrew Jackson and soon became a great proponent of the Jacksonian ideas of westward expansion and Manifest Destiny, which he maintained as a congressman, as the governor of Tennessee, and later as the 11th U.S. president.

As president, Polk sought the annexation of Texas and reclaimed the American rights to the Oregon Territory, which were disputed by Great Britain. His aim was to gain vast lands to the west that would provide the United States with vital resources and ports, especially San Francisco Bay. Ultimately, his goals led America into its first successful invasion of a foreign country and its first occupation of a foreign capital.

The Texas Revolution of 1836 was sparked by the Battle of the Alamo, which later led to the defeat of Mexico's General Antonio Lopez de Santa Anna at the Battle of San Jacinto. The newly independent Republic of Texas was recognized by Britain, France, and the United States. However, efforts by Texans to join the United States offended the Mexican government, which in turn threatened military action if the United States attempted to annex the territory. The 1845 annexation of Texas subsequently resulted in President Polk mobilizing U.S. troops at the Rio Grande boundary, whereby this provocation swiftly initiated the U.S.–Mexican War when U.S. cavalrymen were killed and wounded at the Rio Grande in May 1846. Polk proclaimed the incident as the shedding of American blood on American soil, which resulted in a declaration of war from Congress. Outmatched and outnumbered, the resource-depleted Mexican army was decimated by the much larger American forces. The 1848 Treaty of Guadalupe Hidalgo ended the war and coerced Mexico to surrender the territories that make up the current American southwest, including Arizona, California, New Mexico, Nevada, and Utah. However, the treaty also entailed the payment of $15 million to the Mexican government. Approximately 75,000 to 100,000 Mexicans living in these areas instantaneously became American citizens by default and were consequently subjected to harsh property taxes that many were unable to pay, leading to numerous land seizures and many dispossessed people.

In the midst of the war with Mexico, President Polk accepted a compromise with Britain that led to the Oregon Treaty, whereby the 49th parallel was set as a boundary between the United States and Canada, with rights of free navigation for both countries. The resulting land acquisition included the modern-day states of Idaho, Oregon, and Washington. These new lands presented the opportunity for the expansion of the institution of slavery to western America, since the soil of southern cotton plantations had become depleted of nutrients, an issue later addressed by the Civil War. Polk retired in 1849 and died four months later in Nashville at age 53. His remains rest at the state Capitol grounds in Nashville.

Brian G. Sellers
University of South Florida

See Also: California; Oregon; Presidential Proclamations; Texas.

Further Readings
Farrell, John J. *James K. Polk, 1795–1849*. New York: Oceana Publications, 1970.
Fernandez-Kelly, P. and D. S. Massey. "Borders for Whom? The Role of NAFTA in Mexico-U.S. Migration." *Annals of the American Academy*, v.610 (2007).
Haynes, Sam W. *James K. Polk and the Expansionist Impulse*, 3rd ed. New York: Pearson Education, Inc., 2006.
Pinheiro, John C. *Manifest Ambition: James K. Polk and Civil-Military Relations During the Mexican War*. Westport, CT: Praeger Security International, 2007.

Pornography

Obscenity is one of the only types of speech not protected under the First Amendment free speech clause of the Constitution of the United States. As pornography has been characterized as obscenity over the years, this has resulted in an often tumultuous history between pornography and crime. The definition of obscenity, and what sexually explicit materials qualify as obscene, has been the topic of some of the primary debates at the center of the issue of pornography and crime.

Pornography typically refers to erotic or sexual representations designed to arouse and/or pleasure those who read, hear, see, or handle them. More broadly, the actual definition of "pornographic" is always shifting between two equally ambiguous concepts, the erotic and the obscene. In the United States, representations considered erotic are often considered socially acceptable, as they are associated with aesthetics, good taste, or considered artistic. In contrast, obscenity represents criminality and vulgarity. In the United States, obscene material can be prosecuted because of its offensiveness, demeaning quality, or inhumanness. However, pornography is considered to be legal. Thus, pornography is legal, but only within certain limits that are defined by ever-changing definitions of obscenity.

The difficulty in officially defining "obscenity" resides in the words of former Supreme Court Justice Potter Stewart, who said of obscenity: "I know it when I see it." Because Stewart was essentially blind at the time of his comment, he exhibits the difficulty of deciding what is obscene rather than pornographic. The U.S. justice system has been equally vague when coming to a definitive statement defining obscenity. Sexual norms are always changing, thus representations of what might be considered obscene are constantly changing. When a representation once considered obscene or criminal becomes so commonplace that stigma against it weakens, it eventually moves into the pornographic, then into the erotic.

Obscenity laws were first established in the mid-19th century. The first laws were put in place after the Civil War in response to lewd postcards sent via the mail by members of the Union army. Soon after, in the early 1870s, Anthony Comstock began organizing the first antipornography campaign in the United States. These efforts culminated with the passage by Congress in 1873 of the Comstock Act. This law forbade sending any sexual content through the mail, including not just explicit pictures but also any information about birth control, sexual health, and abortion. Anthony Comstock was also empowered to enforce this law as a special agent of the U.S. Post Office Department. Comstock devoted his career of 40-plus years to personally arresting those he found guilty of violating the law, claiming great success.

The U.S. Supreme Court first addressed the issue of obscenity after World War II in an effort to allow literature with sexual content such as the works of William Faulkner to be published while excluding pornography. In 1957, the court formally stated that obscenity was not protected as free speech. At the same time, the standard of what counted as obscene was shifted from consideration of isolated passages to the work as a whole. Then, in 1969, the Supreme Court first legalized possession of pornography.

The first determination of obscenity established by the courts was the Hicklin test. This was part of the decision of the 1868 case *Regina v. Benjamin Hicklin*. The test of obscenity was ruled to be "whether the tendency of the matter charged as obscenity is to deprave and corrupt those whose minds are open to such immoral influences, and into whose hands a publication of this sort might fall." The Hicklin test was replaced by the Roth test. The Roth test was part of the 1957 decision in *Roth v. United States*. The Roth test was intended to set a national standard for defining obscenity. The Roth test argued that a text was obscene if the "dominant theme taken as a whole appeals to the prurient interest" of an "average person, applying contemporary community standards." This would be again disputed and revised in 1966 in *Memoirs v. Massachusetts,* where obscenity was defined to be that which is "patently offensive" and "utterly without redeeming social value." These criteria would be altered and compiled into the current legal definition of obscenity.

The current definition of obscenity was established by the Supreme Court in its ruling on the 1973 case *Miller v. California*. This ruling establishes that states can establish their own standards of obscenity as long as they also meet the criteria that "as a whole, they appeal to a prurient interest in sex," that sexual behavior is portrayed in a way that is "patently offensive" and that the works in question "as a whole, do not have serious literary, artistic, political or scientific value." If a work is found to meet all three of these criteria, it may be deemed obscene and regulated or censored. These criteria still remain open to interpretation.

The regulation of obscene material has also impacted the study of sexuality. As early as 1950, when in *United States v. 31 Photographs* Alfred Kinsey's Institute for Sex Research was accused by the federal government of illegally importing obscene material. Ultimately, the Institute for Sex Research prevailed in 1957 when a federal court ruled in its favor. However, concern about obtaining and considering the impacts of pornographic content has remained a concern for sexuality researchers. This is particularly true for research on adolescent sexuality, as viewing pornographic content by a minor or showing a minor pornographic content is illegal and severely punished in the United States.

There is also a long-standing debate as to whether viewing pornography encourages violence, particularly sexual violence. Two separate presidential commissions have been convened to explore these questions, as well as considerable psychological and sociological research. The first President's Commission on Obscenity and Pornography was appointed by Lyndon Johnson and reported to Richard Nixon. The conclusion of this commission was that pornography had no discernible effects on encouraging crime. The commission further advocated that most obscenity laws should be repealed. President Nixon rejected the recommendations of the commission, yet sexually explicit movies, books, and magazines thrived in popularity during the 1970s.

The second presidential commission was convened by Ronald Reagan. The Attorney General's Commission on Pornography, better known as the Meese Commission, was specifically tasked with finding a causal relationships between pornography and social problems. The Meese Commission, comprised of 11 members, six of whom were antipornography activists, concluded that pornography did contribute to social problems. This included the conclusion that pornography encourages sexual violence and abuse. Several members of the commission formally dissented. Psychological and sociological research has not come to a consensus regarding any relationship between pornography and crime. Nonetheless, in response to the Meese Commission's report, the National Obscenity Enforcement Unit was created. It was employed by Presidents Ronald Reagan and George H. W. Bush to indict hundreds of manufacturers and distributors of sexually explicit movies. They employed tactics such as filing charges in conservative districts to capitalize on the community standards component of the definition of obscenity. While many companies were successfully prosecuted, this did not prevent a significant rise in the popularity and production of pornography from the mid-1980s through the 1990s. One company in particular, PHE, which produced the Adam & Eve catalogs of products, fought the indictments and successfully defended itself against the charges.

Larry Flynt, pictured here at an adult film event, is the head of Larry Flynt Publications. In 2003, *Arena* magazine listed him as number one on the "50 Powerful People in Porn" list.

After George H. W. Bush's presidency, the focus of the Department of Justice was shifted away from prosecuting video manufacturers and distributors. In 1996, the Communications Decency Act was passed that regulated the transmission of obscenity over the Internet. This was still not a priority of the federal government during the second term of Bill Clinton. However, George W. Bush and Attorneys Generals John Ashcroft and Alberto Gonzalez returned to a concerted effort to charge and prosecute a number of pornography companies and individuals with obscenity. Most of the people and companies charged by these attorneys general were ultimately dismissed by courts or unsuccessfully prosecuted.

Organized Crime

Although the connection between pornography and organized crime has diminished over the last two decades, the association still exists in certain facets of the pornographic industry. For the first half of the 20th century, profits in the pornographic industry were minimal and attracted little attention from organized crime. However, the growing popularity of pornographic magazines and films in the 1960s and 1970s led to Mafia control over distribution and production of a variety of pornographic materials. During this time, the Mafia moved forcefully into peep shows, arcades, and adult movie houses where porn could be exhibited and sold, and competing organized crime syndicates fought, scammed, and murdered one another for various pornographic enterprises. For example, in New York, organized crime organizations leased or purchased real estate in slum neighborhoods, then subleased the building to sex businesses for inflated rent, operated protection rackets, and used such businesses to launder money.

The Attorney General's Commission on Pornography and the Justice Department both cited criminal organizations' heavy involvement in the pornography industry during the 1970s. Organized crime is contingent on providing goods and services that are forbidden and illicit but also in high demand. For example, in the late 1960s, organized crime possessed or controlled practically all homosexual meeting places in New York City. However, once homosexuality began to lose its taboo in the United States and hold the rights of heterosexual citizens, the Mafia's profits began to falter. Similarly, as the distribution of sexual representations gradually became decriminalized and legalized, organized crime began to retreat from pornographic enterprises.

However, even into the 1980s, organized crime controlled various conduits into the pornographic industry, such as magazines, films, videos, and sexual accessories; owned book distributorships; and laundered money through strip clubs and bars. Since the 1980s, the influence of organized crime within the porn industry has waned. The reasons are many: continued convictions of pornographers tied to the Mob, the relentless prosecution of crime syndicates by the Justice Department, the decline of porn theaters due to DVD sales, and the Internet, which distributes a massive amount of pornography and is unable to be controlled by organized crime. Currently established communications and cable corporations earn the largest profits from pornography, primarily through selling it via cable services in hotel rooms. Aside from prostitution, only the connection between organized crime enterprises and strip clubs or bars remains as significant as in the past. Some experts suggest that strip clubs and bars may be the last of the pornographic enterprises tied to organized crime syndicates because they provide opportunities for skimming profits and laundering money.

Child Pornography

In the United States, child pornography refers to pornographic material that includes sexual depictions of anyone under the age of 18. Producing or owning child pornography carries severe penalties. It is also a serious crime to show anything pornographic to anyone under the age of 18. Given the cultural taboo and the ongoing investigation and prosecution of child pornography production and viewing, it is limited to a very small segment of the population. The issue was brought to widespread attention with the cases of Traci Lords in the early 1980s and Alexandra Quinn in the early 1990s. These two actresses were discovered to have used false identification to enter the pornography business and appeared in numerous pornographic films while under the age of 18. Popular media reported on the threat and spread of child pornography, largely on the Internet. While most scholars agree that these threats were inflated, they took hold in the popular imagination and the federal government responded. This led to the passage of 1995 laws that required producers of any pornographic images to keep evidence of the age of all participants. The 1996 Communications Decency Act was passed soon after to further regulate pornography on the Internet and establish harsh penalties, in particular for child pornography.

Patrick O'Brien
Marshall Smith
University of Colorado Boulder

See Also: Comstock Law; Indecent Exposure; Morality; Obscenity; Organized Crime, Contemporary; Sodomy.

Further Readings
Elias, James, Veronica Diehl Elias, Vern L. Bullough, Gwen Brewer, Jeffrey Douglas, and Will Jarvis, eds. *Porn 101: Eroticism, Pornography, and the First Amendment.* Amherst, NY: Prometheus Books, 1999.
Kipnis, Laura. *Bound and Gagged: Pornography and the Politics of Fantasy in America.* Durham, NC: Duke University Press, 1996.
Slade, J. W. *Pornography in America: A Reference Handbook.* Santa Barbara, CA: ABC-CLIO, 2000.

Posses

The term *posse*, from the medieval Latin *posse comitatus*, generally refers to the power associated with a group of men. Posse comitatus is defined as "A group of citizens who are called together to help the sheriff keep the peace or conduct rescue operations—Often shortened to *posse*."

Legal Basis of the Posse
As a part of the compromise reached between northern and southern politicians at the end of Reconstruction, Congress agreed to limit future use of federal troops in local law enforcement matters by passing the Posse Comitatus Act of 1878. It stated that it would be unlawful to use any members of the army as a posse, except in exceptional situations authorized by the Constitution or by an act of Congress. The act also prohibited the appropriation of funding for any such use of troops if in violation of the act. At the state level, the authority for a county sheriff or other law enforcement officer to conscript any able-bodied males to assist him in keeping the peace or to pursue and arrest a fugitive originates in what is known as common or de facto law. Initially, law enforcement officers were authorized to form posses without any structured authority, but over time and with the misuse of the practice, many states imposed statutory requirements on the deputization of civilians. In the 20th century, most states have statutes that diminish the role of sheriff's posses, except for rare instances, such as in Arizona. Recently, a number of sheriff departments have formed civilian groups, appropriately also known as posses, to assist with the organizational and communal needs of their communities but without the legal authority to arrest fugitives.

Posses in the American Old West
The more popular use of the word is most often associated with the American Old West, even though law enforcement officers have used the practice throughout Europe and the United States for several hundred years. Also known as a sheriff's posse, civilians were deputized for a limited time frame in order to accompany the sheriff in apprehending fugitives and outlaws. The posses of the Old West were made up mostly of men on horseback in order to travel as quickly as possible. The use of posses in the Old West also exhibited a form of justice identified by Michel Foucault as "popular justice." By legally deputizing citizens to assist in the apprehension of criminals, local law enforcement officers were also, at times, attempting to limit the growth and popularity of vigilantism. The largest of the early posses was formed by the sheriff of Northfield, Minnesota, to apprehend the James Gang after a failed robbery attempt at the First National Bank of Northfield. Three gang members were killed in town and the other six fled, pursued by a posse of well over 1,000 men. Only Frank and Jesse James managed to escape the posse and return to their home in Missouri.

The conflict that resulted in the Lincoln County War provided one of the most compelling examples of an Old West posse. The difference between an officer of the law and an outlaw in the Old West was often dependent on political power. In 1876, Jon Tunstall and his business partner Alexander McSween opened a store in Lincoln County in direct competition with an existing store owned by Lawrence Murphy and James Dolan. As the competition built, Murphy and Dolan turned to local sheriff William J. Brady to support their business, while Tunstall and McSween in turn called in the town constable Richard Brewer and a posse of armed men, known as the Regulators, to protect them. Through their contacts in the local government, Murphy and Dolan obtained court orders against McSween and Tunstall. As the conflict grew, both lawmen turned to known outlaws to form their posses. Although posses were originally formed to apprehend fugitives, local business interests often turned to the men they employed as law enforcement officers to legitimize their control over their economic and financial empires. Sheriff Brady's posse drew first blood with the murder of Jon Tunstall. Several of Tunstall's men, including Billy the Kid, witnessed the murder, but were too far away to prevent it. However, they saw the men who killed their employer, and the death of Sheriff Brady followed soon after.

Even though both sides initially employed legally formed posses, Murphy and Dolan's associates controlled the justice system in the Arizona Territory, thus the posses formed by Sheriff Brady and later Sheriff Pat Garrett had the support of state officials. Ultimately, Samuel B. Axtell, territorial governor, revoked John Wilson's appointment as justice of the peace in Lincoln County, claiming that the Lincoln County commissioners had no legal status to appoint him. Since Wilson deputized the Regulators and issued the warrants

The jail and courthouse in Lincoln, New Mexico, where Billy the Kid was tried, still stands today. The Lincoln County War was a feud that became famous because of the participation of a number of notable figures of the Old West, including Billy the Kid, John Chisum, and Sheriffs William Brady and Pat Garrett and the Old West posses that tracked them.

for Tunstall's murderers, Axtell's decree resulted in the Regulators losing their right to serve as deputies. Stripped of their legal protection, Tunstall's men were labeled outlaws and were left to face the Lincoln County sheriff and his posse as criminals. Sheriff Pat Garrett, appointed sheriff of Lincoln County in 1880, took quick advantage of his position, formed well-armed and tenacious posses, and ultimately hunted down each of the Regulators, including the infamous Billy the Kid. Once the regulators were gone, the sheriff's posses were disbanded and the men simply went on their way.

The last significant use of a deputized sheriff's posse resulted in the Latimer Massacre. In 1897, the Latimer mine owners near Hazelton, Pennsylvania, in an attempt to force striking workers to return to work, turned to the Luzerne County Sheriff's Office for assistance. The sheriff, recognizing the advantage of manipulating racial overtones, intentionally deputized a posse consisting of 100 English and Irish citizens to stand against the mine workers, who were Slavs and Germans.

On September 10, the sheriff and 150 armed deputies confronted nearly 400 unarmed strikers. The violence resulted in the deaths of 19 miners and as many as 49 men wounded. Public outrage over the deaths resulted in criminal charges against Sheriff James Martin, and 73 of the deputies who made up the posse were arrested. Although medical testimony provided evidence at the trial that nearly all the strikers had been shot in the back, the sheriff and his posse were acquitted. In response, and to limit any future similar altercations, many state legislators voted to restrain the use of posses and the arbitrary deputization of citizens.

Modern Day

Starting during the middle of the 20th century, local sheriff departments, depending on the state, employed community policing strategies where people helped the sheriff but without the legal protection afforded by being deputized as a member of a posse, and their services focused more on administrative and public relations duties. Yet, civilians are still called upon to serve in sheriff's posses as deputies in states where the legislature provides for their use, on rare occasions.

In June 1977, the sheriff of Aspen, Colorado, called for a posse to search for Ted Bundy when he escaped captivity. In the state of Arizona, many sheriff's offices allow for community policing units, known as posses, which work in a reserve status assisting the sheriff's staff in a number of situations. The posse members are considered part of the community policing corps and are not sworn deputies and have no legal rights to arrest offenders.

Phoenix, Arizona's sheriff, Joe Arpaio, created a group of civilian members known informally as the Immigration Posse. Sheriff Arpaio formed the posse, which includes nearly 3,000 members, in response to growing concerns over illegal immigration. Members of the posse are sworn in by the sheriff as "illegal immigration fighters" and function in the same manner as the earlier Old West posse members tasked with assisting the sheriff in apprehending fugitives—specifically, illegal immigrants crossing the U.S. boundary with Mexico. The Maricopa County Sheriff's Office defends the use of the posses by providing evidence of their effectiveness. Between 2007 and 2010, the sheriff's office, including its deputized posse members, investigated, arrested, or detained more than 42,000 illegal immigrants. Amid growing public debate about the use of the posses and the focus on apprehending illegal immigrants, the Arizona legislature passed a state law in April 2010 making it a crime if an immigrant is found not carrying immigration documentation, and authorizing police officers to detain or arrest anyone they suspect of being an illegal immigrant.

The U.S. Justice Department, facing pressure from Latino American and Human Rights groups, as well as the governments of Mexico and Central and South America, filed lawsuits against the State of Arizona and against the Maricopa County Sheriff's Office, charging that the state of Arizona violated the rights of the individuals stopped for suspicion of being illegal immigrants, and that the sheriff's office practiced discrimination, unconstitutional searches and seizures, and English-only policies in the Phoenix jails. The future use of sheriff's posses is dependent upon the outcome of the pending court cases.

Robin Annette Hanson
St. Louis University

See Also: 1851 to 1900 Primary Documents; 1901 to 1920 Primary Documents; Adversarial Justice; Arizona; Billy the Kid; Dime Novels, Pulps, Thrillers; Justice, Department of; Sheriffs; Vigilantism.

Further Readings

Arizona Revised Statutes, Section 11-1051.

Athearn, Robert G., *The Mythic West in Twentieth-Century America*. Lawrence: University of Kansas Press, 1988.

Foucault, Michel, *Discipline & Punish: The Birth of the Prison*. New York: Random House, 1977.

Presidential Proclamations

Mother's Day, Easter, World War II Veterans Remembrance, Crime Victims Recognition, Crime Prevention Week, Stalking Awareness, Sexual Assault Awareness, and hundreds more—these are the common occasions for presidential proclamations. Presidential proclamations can be an aspect of constituent services when they are largely ceremonial recognition of special events, days, weeks, months, or groups. Proclamations can be extremely controversial as in Gerald Ford's proclamation pardoning Richard Nixon or Jimmy Carter's amnesty for draft evaders. Traditionally, presidents in the closing days of their administrations issue proclamations pardoning wrongdoers, and sometimes these pardons generate controversy as well. Presidential proclamations are also a vehicle for setting aside land for parks and other uses. Presidents from Teddy Roosevelt to Bill Clinton and Barack Obama have used proclamations to designate public land for national forests and monuments.

George Washington established American neutrality, and Abraham Lincoln emancipated slaves through presidential proclamation. Lincoln also pardoned deserters, ordered the arrest of individuals who armed hostile Indians, and closed and opened southern ports. Andrew Johnson ordered the arrest of Jefferson Davis and other members of the Confederate government and blocked insurgent vessels while also lifting blockades of southern ports, amnestying rebels, ending martial law, and recognizing reconstituted southern governments.

Powers and Limits

A presidential proclamation can implement a law or declare one. The presidential powers in event of crisis, emergency, or exigency other than war or natural disaster are derived from the Constitution and 200 years of congressional delegation. The powers are extensive, but they are not absolute. Since 1976, with enactment of the National Emergencies Act, the president has to declare formally the existence of a national emergency and specify what authorities he intends to use. Proclaimed emergencies have termination dates, and extension when the emergency persists requires the issuance of a new proclamation.

Legally, a presidential proclamation is equal in weight to an executive order (EO), but the EO targets those inside government while the proclamation affects those outside government. While less powerful than laws, they can have the same effect on trade, foreign affairs, travel, war, and peace. Usually, Congress delegates the powers exercised through EO or proclamation. The president may not suspend the Constitution, other than habeas corpus, regardless of the nature of the emergency, but the judiciary as well as the Congress have the right and obligation to restrain presidential use of emergency powers. The U.S. president can declare emergencies for rebellion or invasion and can suspend habeas corpus. He can also exempt military cases from the grand jury requirement during public emergencies.

The Eighteenth Century

In the summer of 1792, western Pennsylvanians, Virginians, and Carolinians began using force in protest of the imposition of the federal whiskey excise tax enacted in 1791. Given the limited means of transport, whiskey was the only product that farmers could ship at a profit. The tariff took what little profit the farmers made. Farmers in western Pennsylvania attacked federal excise agents. By 1794, the attacks had increased to include rioting and an attack on a federal marshal and the home of a regional inspector. Mobs of several hundred roamed the area, and Pittsburgh was in disarray. Congress authorized the calling up of the militia in the event of rebellion

Some proclamations can be extremely controversial, as was Gerald Ford's proclamation to pardon Richard Nixon. President Ford is shown here in the Oval Office in 1976.

and mandated that the president issue a presidential proclamation warning rebels to stand down. Were they to continue, the militia would go after them. On August 7, 1794, George Washington issued a presidential proclamation calling on the mobs to return home and calling out the militia into an army as large as the one that defeated the British—13,000 men. By issuing the proclamation, Washington assumed extraordinary powers, a great leeway granted by Congress for the emergency. Washington for the first time used the 1792 militia law and established a precedent that it could be used to suppress insurrections and execute the laws of the land and that the federal government could use troops from one state to deal with problems in another. The federal government was superior to the individual states. Washington also pardoned the leaders after their trials.

The Nineteenth Century

For 100 years after the Whiskey Rebellion, Congress granted presidents standby or permanent powers in emergencies. Permanent powers are inherent in the presidency because they are specified in the Constitution or laws, and the president can act without further authorization. Standby powers are available only within limits, and the president must activate them by issuing a proclamation of labor, economic, or military emergency. Through the first half of the century, presidents were largely free to act without restraints. The first challenge to the president's authority came in the early days of the administration of Abraham Lincoln.

With Congress not in session and the south seceding in 1861, Lincoln issued a proclamation blockading secessionist ports. He subsequently enlarged the navy, expanded the blockade, and called up an army by proclamation. Lincoln also suspended habeas corpus on April 27, 1861, in part of Maryland and the midwest, including southern Indiana, in response to requests by his generals for the establishment of military courts to control Copperheads (sympathizers with the Confederacy). Congress retroactively authorized his emergency acts, and the court exercised no oversight. When Lincoln imposed martial law under congressional authorization on September 15, 1863, he regularized the suspension of habeas corpus that he had proclaimed on his own authority on April 27, 1861.

Imposition of martial law is a controversial use of the presidential proclamation. Martial law occurs when the military assumes emergency control because civilian authorities are not functioning well enough to preserve order and security and to provide essential services. In extreme cases, the highest-ranking military officer becomes de facto governor and suspends the Constitution. Martial law is associated with suspension of habeas corpus, civil rights, and civil law. Habeas corpus is the right to a hearing about whether imprisonment is lawful, a means of judicial oversight of law enforcement. The Constitution allows suspension of habeas corpus in cases of rebellion or invasion if necessary to preserve public safety.

Under martial law, curfews are put in place. Military law and justice apply to civilians. Checks on presidential power are in the hands of the judiciary. In the major habeas corpus case of the Civil War, Lambdin P. Milligan and four other Indiana Copperheads were sentenced to be hanged in 1864 for treason against the Union. Because the executions had not occurred by the end of the war, they had time to appeal to the Supreme Court, which declared the suspension unconstitutional because the civilian courts were in operation at the time of their trials. In *Ex parte Milligan,* the Supreme Court ruled that Lincoln exceeded his Constitutional authority when he suspended habeas corpus where civilian law was still in operation.

In the United States, the most extensive use of martial law came during Reconstruction after the Civil War. Ulysses S. Grant used proclamations frequently. In May 1870, he issued a proclamation against the Fenian Brotherhood's attempts to harm relations between the United States and Britain. The Fenian Army of Vermont responded by attempting to invade Canada. The effort failed, and the United States compensated Canada.

That same month, Grant received Congressional authority against the Ku Klux Klan. The first Klan Act made deprivation of civil or political rights by interference with voting a federal offense and allowed federal action in such cases. The third act, the Ku Klux Klan Act, passed in April 1871, enforced the Fourteenth Amendment by banning wearing disguises, intimidating officials, and creating conspiracies. Grant used the act in the election of 1872. Before then, in October 1871, he issued a proclamation against the South Carolina Klan. In September 1874, Grant's proclamation demanding the dispersal of the White League rebellion in Louisiana eventuated in the sending of three gunboats and 5,000 troops to New Orleans. The uprising ended in two days, but Grant and the Republicans were roundly criticized for sending troops to interfere in a local matter.

Presidents also proclaimed *posse comitatus.* The 1878 Posse Comitatus Act banned military involvement in domestic law enforcement unless authorized by Congress. After the Civil War, federal troops at southern polls helped to ensure blacks the vote and to keep out former Confederate officers, who were stripped of citizenship rights, including voting. In the west, there was also a need for more law than the sparsely populated areas could provide, so military commanders exercised civilian police powers against criminals and Indians. When Congress enacted the Posse Comitatus Act, it seemed to infringe on the right to use troops in civilian police roles when no alternative existed. Although Rutherford Hayes vetoed the 1880 Army Appropriations Act because it seemingly blocked *posse comitatus,* he failed to notice that on congressional approval, the president could still activate a *posse comitatus* through proclamation.

World War I and Beyond
World War I and its aftermath saw the expansion of standby emergency authorities that the president could activate by proclamation of a national emergency. Proclamations ranged from the limited single event to the virtually unlimited ongoing state of emergency. Standbys remained a major source of presidential authority until the Vietnam War era, when in 1976, Congress revoked presidential use of standby authorities and required specific statutory authorization for proclaimed emergencies.

Woodrow Wilson, having proclaimed a state of war after Congress's declaration of war, used the presidential proclamation vigorously in 1918 for such war-related functions as registering men for the draft, licensing commercial activities, setting commodity prices, restricting diversion of foodstuffs to alcoholic beverages, taking of land and other resources for military purposes, calling up the coast artillery and other units, nationalizing American Railway Express and other transport activities, and expanding the coverage of the Trading With the Enemy Act.

In 1919, Wilson used the *posse comitatus* proclamation against rioters in Chicago. He sent the army into West Virginia's coal mining areas between 1917 and 1921. The army routinely intervened in labor disagreements in the coal mines of West Virginia between 1877 and 1920. By 1917, it was routine army duty because the process was clearly spelled out by the law and the Constitution, including the Posse Comitatus Act, and there was little chance that state and local authorities could abuse military power. Army efforts were perceived as equitable and fair, unlike those of the state National Guard called up by the state in similar disputes. Then, in 1917, Wilson abdicated the presidential role in labor disputes. In federalizing the National Guard for wartime service, Secretary of War Newton Baker suspended the legal procedures that involved state legislatures, the president, and the war department. Power to call out federal troops devolved to state and local officials sympathetic to local business and patriotic groups. Between 1917 and 1921, without the restrictions of the presidential proclamation process, the use of federal troops to crush protest and organized labor was without precedent

In 1932, Herbert Hoover proclaimed an emergency and used the military against the World War I veterans of the Bonus Expeditionary Force. Franklin Roosevelt issued his national emergency proclamation within 48 hours of taking office in 1933, using the 1917 Trading With the Enemy Act to declare a bank holiday. When Congress passed validating legislation, he issued a second bank holiday proclamation based on the law. In September 1939, Roosevelt proclaimed a limited national emergency, and in May 1941, he proclaimed an unlimited national emergency. The two remained in effect until 1947 when certain provisions were rescinded. Peace with Germany in 1951 and Japan in 1952 ended World War II, and presidents used the Emergency Powers Interim Continuation Act and the Emergency Powers Continuation Act to justify subsequent emergency proclamations after Harry Truman proclaimed in April 1952 that the 1939 and 1941 proclamations were terminated.

Hawai'i was under martial law from December 7, 1941, until October 24, 1944. During the Korean War, on December 16, 1950, Truman proclaimed a state of national emergency. Under the emergency proclamation, Truman nationalized the railroads and put them under the command of the Army Corps of Engineers. In 1952, the court ruled in *Youngstown Sheet & Tube v. Sawyer* that Truman had exceeded his authority because presidential actions during an emergency still had to conform to congressional acts.

When nationalized by proclamation in the 1950s and 1960s, the National Guard served in civil rights disturbances such as that Little Rock, Arkansas, and in the disarray surrounding the Democratic National Convention of 1968 in Chicago. Proclamations of emergency sent federal forces into Watts in Los Angeles, California, and other riot-torn cities.

Not all emergencies proclaimed by the presidents require the use of troops. Under the International Emergency Economic Powers Act of 1977, presidents can proclaim an emergency and freeze assets, confiscate property, and limit trade. Nixon also used emergency proclamations to declare the 1970 postal strike an emergency and for tariff adjustments. When a federal emergency is declared, the Federal Emergency Management Agency (FEMA) is empowered and federal assistance becomes available. Unlike in normal disasters (hurricanes and floods), in a federal emergency, FEMA can ignore administrative processes, and the federal government appoints those who oversee dealing with the emergency.

As a result of several presidential proclamations, the United States is currently in a state of emergency because of terrorism. In January 1995, Bill Clinton signed an executive order declaring a state of emergency and establishing an embargo on trade with terrorists interfering with the Middle East peace process.

Other emergencies that triggered presidential proclamations include the Sierra Leone diamond trade and the Iran hostage crisis of the Carter administration, which continued under new declarations in 1995 and 2001. In July 2011, Barack Obama issued a proclamation to fight transnational organized crime. The proclamation established antiterrorist measures, restricted travel to the United States by those involved, provided for seizure and blocking of assets, and established domestic and foreign activities to destroy terrorist networks by reducing the drug and money trade both at home and abroad. Assistance to foreign governments in implementing domestic antiterrorist networks and sharing information were also authorized.

Oversight

The power of presidential proclamation is extensive, particularly when Congress and the courts decline to check presidential actions. The Insurrection Act of 1807 gives the president authority to deploy troops domestically to put down insurrection, rebellion, and lawlessness. The applicable laws seek to give state and local governments the first chance to control unrest, and the idea is to delay and limit presidential involvement. In the aftermath of the terrorist attacks of September

11, 2001, and Hurricane Katrina in 2005, neither Congress nor the Supreme Court seemed inclined to intervene against the president. Rather, the restraining forces tended to be enablers.

In 2006, after George W. Bush requested expanded national powers after Hurricane Katrina, Congress modified the act to give the president wider leeway, authorizing the deployment of troops in natural disaster, public health emergency, terrorist attack, and other conditions when the president determines the states are unable to act effectively. Opponents decried the easing of the restrictions on presidents declaring martial law and the expansion of the uses of the military in civilian matters. Martial law was not declared after Hurricane Katrina; rather, New Orleans was in a state of emergency. The mayor said that officers could ignore civil rights and Miranda rights of looters, and up to 15,000 federal troops and guardsmen patrolled the city. Proclamations may occur at the state or local level when a governor or mayor issues a declaration of emergency, usually the result of a natural disaster. The Bush-requested law expanding the use of the military in civilian disasters passed, but the changes generated controversy and protest and were removed from the insurrection legislation two years later.

Some emergencies were forgotten, and emergency powers and penalties remained in effect long after the need ended. Gerald Ford revoked the executive order interning Japanese during World War II by proclamation in 1976. The 1950 proclamation of an emergency in Korea continued in effect into the Vietnam years. The Korean War emergency ended on September 14, 1978. Courts continue to uphold harder-than-normal penalties, including deportation, authorized because of and levied during the period of emergency. When Nixon authorized various illegal actions during Watergate, Congress realized that the Truman state of emergency was still in effect. The 1976 National Emergencies Act established a two-year limit on emergency declarations unless the president explicitly extended them and specified in advance which provisions he was invoking. In 1998, Bill Clinton issued a proclamation expanding the 1995 Middle East state of emergency to cover Osama bin Laden and other targets, and President George W. Bush extended it. The Bush declaration of emergency on terrorism was renewed by Obama in 2009 and 2010.

John H. Barnhill
Independent Scholar

See Also: 1777 to 1800 Primary Documents; 1961 to 1980 Primary Documents; Ku Klux Klan; Military Courts; Rule of Law.

Further Readings

Baker, Bonnie. "The Origins of the *Posse Comitatus*." *Air & Space Power Journal*. http://www.airpower.au.af.mil/AIRCHRONICLES/cc/baker1.html (Accessed October 2011).

Laurie, Clayton D. "The United States Army and the Return to Normalcy in Labor Dispute Interventions: The Case of the West Virginia Coal Mine Wars, 1920–1921." *West Virginia Culture*. http://www.wvculture.org/history/journal_wvh/wvh50-1.html (Accessed October 2011).

Miller Center. "Key Events in the Presidency of Ulysses S. Grant." http://millercenter.org/president/keyevents/grant (Accessed October 2011).

Relyea, Harold C. "CRS Report for Congress: National Emergency Powers." http://fpc.state.gov/documents/organization/6216.pdf (Accessed October 2011).

President's Commission on Law Enforcement and the Administration of Justice

The President's Commission on Law Enforcement and the Administration of Justice was assembled during the presidential administration of Lyndon B. Johnson. Following the social unrest of the 1960s, President Johnson established this commission to study specific social issues that were plaguing America—crime and deviance.

The task delegated to the commission was to conduct a critical and thorough evaluation of the entire American criminal justice system. The objective of this enormous effort was to make

Antiwar protesters march against the U.S. involvement in the Vietnam War in Washington, D.C. on April 24, 1971. The President's Commission on Law Enforcement and the Administration of Justice was convened during a time of social unrest in the United States, which arose out of the civil rights movement and the demonstrations against the Vietnam War.

recommendations that would reduce or eliminate crime in the United States of America. The commission had a significant impact on policing tactics, techniques, and procedures across the United States. The work of the commission was vital to the criminal justice field because it was the first large-scale official attempt to examine all parts of the criminal justice system systematically since the Wickersham Commission.

During the era when the President's Commission on Law Enforcement and the Administration of Justice was convened, the United States was recovering from the social unrest that arose out of the civil rights movement and the Vietnam War. The social change that came about from these historical events fueled changing ideologies in many aspects of American life. President Johnson used the changing American social arena as a platform to acknowledge crime as a social problem and subsequently used the commission as an instrument to combat this social problem—crime and deviance.

The Challenge of Crime in a Free Society

The 19-member panel, led by Attorney General Nicholas Katzenbach, relied on multiple field research efforts conducted at local and national levels in order to examine crime and deviance within the changing American society. In addition, the commission relied on feedback from federal, state, and local criminal justice officials in order to draw conclusions concerning the status of the criminal justice system. After 18 months, the panel published what has since been recognized as one most significant reports ever published within the American criminal justice system—*The Challenge of Crime in a Free Society*. This 342-page report outlined the massive efforts of the commission. Soon after being published, the report became widely recognized as being critical of various criminal justice strategies. For example, the commission condoned the unilateral efforts of local, state, and federal law enforcement agencies and noted that interagency cooperation would be essential for combating crime in the coming decades.

Although critical of certain aspects of the criminal justice system, the commission made more than 200 individual recommendations that supported the positive control of crime and deviance in America. The President's Commission on Law Enforcement and the Administration of Justice called for the criminal justice system as a whole to enact numerous efforts that would enable the system to develop into one that would be capable of handling the crime dilemma for centuries to come.

Within their general recommendations, the commissioners noted that crime can only be reduced and controlled, never eradicated. The recommendations of the commission were sociological in nature in that many acknowledge the social nature of crime and deviance. In addition, the commission broadly stressed the importance of integrating the community into crime prevention and reduction strategies. With this, the commission stressed that police agencies needed to adapt a proactive ideology that would encourage preventive policing rather than reactive policing. Another general theme noted in the findings of the commission that was emphasized as being essential to the reduction and prevention of crime was the establishment of a broad range of tactics, techniques, and procedures to handle the dynamic situations that police officers often face while policing the community. The intent behind this recommendation was to have departments establish uniform policies and practices that would standardize and professionalize policing. Considering the historical time frame when the commission was conducting its research, the members and staff recognized that police agencies needed to eliminate injustices that existed within law enforcement agencies at all levels. The intent behind this recommendation was to counter many of the biased ideologies that flourished within the unique social arena of the era. More generally, the commission noted that agencies should recruit better-qualified candidates into the field of policing.

The proposals put forth by the commission that are credited as having the most significant impact on crime and deviance today include the recommendation to conduct more research on crime and deviance; the recommendation to invest significantly more money into all areas of the system; the proposal that practitioners and citizens must view the issue of crime and deviance as a communal problem; and the recommendation that criminal justice agencies embrace and leverage technology in the fight against crime. Other areas of the criminal justice system such as courts and corrections were not scrutinized to the same degree as the policing sector, but they were evaluated. The recommendations that were relevant to those sectors have significantly impacted the contemporary criminal justice system. For example, some practitioners might posit that the commission played a role in advances such as 911, community policing, and the establishment of national policing standards, certification, and accreditation.

Conclusion

Despite often being criticized as overly ambitious in its efforts and recommendations, the commission laid the foundation for criminal justice policies for centuries to come. The work of the commission has helped practitioners answer the challenge of combating crime by positing that the government and citizens are ultimately responsible for the control and prevention of crime. To justify this stance, the commission argued that official statistics concerning crime were ultimately misleading and that crime would never be eradicated. Consequently, according to the commission, criminal justice officials would face a monumental task for centuries to come. To tackle this monumental feat, the commission recommended that the government establish an agency to assist but not usurp state and local law enforcement agencies as they combat crime.

Although some of the recommendations of the commission have yet to come to fruition, many of its recommendations are now common policies and practices that assist law enforcement agencies in accomplishing the monumental task of preventing and controlling crime in the United States.

Michael J. Reed
Mississippi State University

See Also: Johnson, Lyndon B. (Administration of); Police, History of; Technology, Police.

Further Readings
Feucht, Thomas and Edwin Zedlewski. "The 40th Anniversary of the Crime Report." *NIJ Journal*, v.257 (2007).
Scott, Michael. "Progress in American Policing: Reviewing the National Reviews." *Law & Social Inquiry*, v.34/1 (2008).
U.S. Department of Justice. The Challenge of Crime in a Free Society." http://www.ncjrs.gov/pdffiles1/nij/42.pdf (Accessed January 2011).

Prison Privatization

States have been turning to privatization as a way to deal with a burgeoning and increasingly costly prison system. In corrections, privatization is the transference of the construction, operation, or specific functions of a prison facility from the public to the private sector. Proponents argue that there are many benefits to privatization. Construction of new prison facilities will occur faster and for less money when done by private companies. Operation costs will be lower, while correctional officers will receive higher salaries, and inmates better services and programming.

However, private prisons have not always turned out to be the panacea that proponents hoped. Due to lower wages and less benefits, the personnel in private prisons often lack the necessary experience and training. For this reason, staff turnover rates are high. Many private prisons have also been plagued with incidents of violence and abuse. Opponents of privatization are also concerned that private facilities are often more driven by making a profit than with safety and security. Currently, there are over 100,000 inmates housed in private facilities across the United States. Given that the recent trend toward privatization does not appear to be waning, many researchers have suggested that steps need to be taken to ensure that private prisons are regulated and held accountable to the same standards as prisons in the public sector.

History of Privatization

While prison privatization has received renewed attention over the past 20 years, its origins date back to the early 1800s with the lease system. As part of this system, states, which were often in financial debt, would shift control of an institution to a private contractor as a way to deal with the rising cost of a growing prison population. This system is known to have first occurred in the Frankfort, Kentucky, state prison in 1825.

The state, which was suffering from a financial crisis, entered into an agreement with businessman Joel Scott, wherein the state would receive $1,000 per year for the work of the inmates in the prison in return for allowing Mr. Scott to operate the prison for five years. As a way to reduce their debt after the Civil War, southern states also turned to the practice of leasing inmate labor. The abolition of slavery after the war deprived southern states of their cheap labor force. As a result, states turned to leasing out inmate labor as a way to replace slave labor and to help rebuild their economy.

Initially, the primary reason for turning to privatization was to offset the costs of an increasing

Prison privatization's origins date back to the 1800s. States would shift control to a private contractor as a means of dealing with the rising cost of a growing prison population.

prison population. However, states quickly found that there was a downside to privatization. For example, in 1871, the first Texas prison lease was awarded to a private company. While initial reactions to this arrangement were positive, the state ended up having to regain control over certain aspects of the facility in 1876 because of reports of 382 escapes and 62 deaths, in addition to concerns over the treatment of inmates. The state eventually assumed complete control over the facility in 1883 after continued reports of inmate deaths and abuse. States continued to contract with private companies until the early 1900s, despite concerns about corruption and abuse. The stabilization of prison populations after 1930 reduced the need for states to turn to privatization. The privatization of prisons did not become an issue again until the early 1980s, when incarceration rates in the United States began to skyrocket.

Prior to the mid-1970s, the prison population in the United States was relatively stable, fluctuating from between 100–150 inmates per 100,000 persons. Crime rates began to increase during the late 1960s and 1970s and a shift occurred in the philosophy of punishment. Previously, the focus was on rehabilitation, with individualized sentences and a treatment approach to corrections. The increase in crime, along with research that discounted the effectiveness of rehabilitation programs in reducing recidivism, led to a tough-on-crime approach where inmates were sent to prison solely to be punished for the crime committed.

As part of this crime control model, individuals were sent to prison for a wider range of offenses and for longer periods of time. In addition, as part of truth-in-sentencing, inmates were required to serve a greater portion of their sentence before being released. As a result of these changes in policy, in addition to the weakening of parole, the incarceration rate in the United States increased rapidly. For example, between 1980 and 1990, the incarceration rate in the United States increased from 139 to 292 inmates per 100,000 persons. By the mid-1990s, the incarceration rate had grown to approximately 600 per 100,000 persons.

States, which were suffering from the economic downturn of the early 1980s, were unable to keep up with the cost of a growing prison population. There was no money to build new prisons, and the prison facilities that did exist were old and in need of repair. As a result, existing prisons became overcrowded. Conditions in many prisons across the country were getting so bad that many states were put under federal court order to limit their prison populations until they were able to increase the capacity of their facilities. Privatization offered a cost-effective solution to states. For states that were in need of new prison facilities, the private sector was able to secure funds and build prisons faster than the government. In addition, the private sector also claimed to deliver better services at a cheaper price. For example, initially, private companies boasted that they would specialize in supervising specific populations, such as inmates with acquired immune deficiency syndrome (AIDS) and maximum-security inmates, utilizing innovate programming at a lower cost. By privatizing prisons, politicians were able to still appear tough on crime, yet also fiscally conservative.

Corrections Corporations

The privatization of prisons that occurred during the late 20th century was in marked contrast to the system of privatization that occurred a century before. Previously, states would completely relinquish control of the facility, which they contracted out to a private company. This included both control over the operation and management of the prison as well as responsibility for the inmates. In contrast, in the modern system of privatization, states continue to maintain responsibility for the inmates, yet transfer control over prison functions to the private sector. In addition, one of the benefits of the lease system was that private contractors could profit from the labor of prison inmates, an aspect of privatization that no longer exists today.

The privatization movement in the United States began with the formation of the Corrections Corporation of America (CCA) in 1983. While CCA initially operated facilities for detained immigrants and juvenile offenders, in 1985 the company was contracted to operate a minimum-security facility for adults in St. Mary, Kentucky, the first private prison for adult inmates in the country. That same year, the company entered into negotiations with the state of Tennessee to take over control of its entire prison system. While there was initial support to privatize the state's prison system, eventually the contract fell through. The state did not feel confident transferring control of its prison system to a recently formed company. In addition, there were concerns that, if problems arose, the state would not be able to take back control of the system.

In 1988, a second firm, the Wackenhut Corrections Corporation (now known as the GEO Group) was developed. Over the next two decades, the number of private prisons across the country grew substantially. In 1991, over 13,000 inmates were housed in 44 private correctional facilities across the country, operated by 14 companies. The use of private prisons continued to grow rapidly during the 1990s, with Corrections Corporation of America and Wackenhut monopolizing the field. For example, in 1999, CCA supervised so many inmates that it was the ninth-largest prison system in the country, and Wackenhut the 19th-largest prison system for adults.

Early studies found that privately operated prisons function as well as publicly operated prisons and for lower costs. However, many have argued that this may have been due to the fact that initially, private prisons were only operating minimum-security prisons, which house inmates who pose little risk. Since 1992, states have begun to contract with private companies for the operation of maximum-security prisons.

Criticisms of Private Prisons

Over the years, private prisons have not escaped criticism. While proponents of privatization argue that private prisons operate more efficiently, with some suggesting a cost reduction of between 15 and 20 percent, concerns have been raised about how this is actually accomplished. Primarily, private prisons are more cost-effective due to the fact that they reduce labor costs by having less staff, lower wages, or offering fewer benefits, yet the average savings has been shown to be only about 1 percent. The reduction in costs has, however, proven to have negative implications for the prisons. As a result of cutting back on personnel costs, private prisons are more likely to hire less experienced and well-trained staff. As a result, the staff turnover rates are much higher in private prisons, with one study reporting a difference of 41 percent in private prisons compared to 15 percent in public prisons.

Many have argued that the problems with staffing, along with defective classification and security procedures, have led to an increase in violence in private prisons. In July 1998, there was a highly publicized escape of six maximum-security inmates, five of them convicted murderers, from the Northeast Ohio Correctional Center, drawing increased attention to this issue. A year later, a prison guard was killed during a riot in the Guadalupe County Correctional Facility, a Wackenhut-operated prison in New Mexico. In both cases, it was found that inexperienced staff and a lack of basic security procedures were to blame.

Whether the escapes and violence that occur in private prisons are more serious than those that occur in public prisons has been explored by several researchers. A study conducted by Judith Greene in 1999 compared the quality of services in a private prison run by the Correctional Corporation of America with those of the public prisons in Minnesota and found that the private prison exhibited a higher level of operational problems. In addition, Greene's research found that these problems, which included unreliable classification methods, high rates of staff turnover, and inadequate program services, were directly related to security and safety issues within the prison. Another study that year conducted by James Austin compared the number of assaults in public and private facilities and found that there were 49 percent more assaults on staff and 65 percent more inmate-on-inmate assaults in private prisons. Not only does cutting back on administrative and programmatic services increase problems within the prison, but it also limits the ability of a facility to adequately prepare inmates for their release back into the community.

In addition to concerns about the operation of private facilities, opponents of privatization have argued that prisons should not be driven by a profit motive, because their fundamental obligation is to increase stockholders' profits. Both CCA and the GEO Group bring in millions of dollars of revenue each year. Opponents are concerned that industry executives will continue to lobby for tougher sentencing laws to ensure the continuation of their business, regardless of whether it is in the best public interest. Because of concerns over violence in private prisons, by the turn of the century, the desire among states to privatize had decreased significantly. However, at this time, the federal prison system was experiencing unprecedented growth in its prison population, increasing by 31 percent between 1995 and 1999 alone. In turning to private companies to assist them with this increasing prison population, the federal prison system was also helping to salvage a failing industry.

Modern Facilities

Despite the fact that states were no longer seeking private contracts, private companies were continuing to build new prisons on speculation that contracts would follow. As a way to fill these empty prisons, private companies began to contract with states that had overcrowded prison systems to incarcerate their inmates on a per diem basis. This benefitted states because it allowed them to reduce overcrowding while also saving money because the per diem cost to house inmates in private prisons was less than the state's cost. For example, the state of Virginia, in 1994, had shifted to a tough-on-crime approach as a way to deal with their crime problems, as had many states at that time.

Sentence lengths were increased through truth-in-sentencing and the use of parole was abolished. As a result, it was predicted that the state's prison population was going to expand rapidly and the state built six new prisons, and contracted with a private company for a seventh in five years to prepare for this increase. By 1997, however, the growth in the state's prison population slowed and the state was left with a number of empty prison beds. The state began to charge other jurisdictions on a per diem basis to house their inmates. This enabled the state of Virginia not only to fill these prisons but also increased revenue to the state. By the end of the 1990s, from 10,000 to 15,000 inmates were being housed in prisons outside the state in which they were convicted and sentenced, and oftentimes in private prisons.

By 2005, there were 415 private facilities under contract to state and federal correctional authorities, housing 108,523 inmates. Currently, approximately 7 percent of inmates in the United States are housed in private prisons. While the majority of private facilities are still minimum security (364 facilities in 2005), there are currently 43 medium-security-level and eight maximum-security-level private facilities in operation in the United States. Although the number of inmates housed in private facilities makes up a only small percentage of the overall prison population, there is no indication that the privatization of corrections will cease to exist anytime soon. One of the reasons for this is because prisons, particularly private prisons, have become a growth industry in rural areas and provide a benefit in terms of jobs and revenue to areas that have previously experienced a collapse in their economy.

For this reason, researchers argue that steps must be taken to ensure that private facilities are appropriately regulated and held accountable. In addition, more research must be conducted to evaluate the effectiveness of private facilities. Many of the studies that have been conducted to date simply compare private and public prisons on a number of measures. However, long-term studies are needed that enable researchers to examine whether private prisons are able to provide cost savings—and a comparable quality of confinement—to states over time.

Over the past 20 years, states have turned to privatization as a way to help offset the cost of their once-growing prison population. Privatizing certain aspects of their correctional system has proven to provide some benefits to states, namely, the ability to build new prisons within a short period of time for lower cost. However, privatization did not come without its problems. Reducing operating costs oftentimes meant less-experienced staff and problematic security and classification procedures, which can lead to violence and escapes. For some types of inmates, primarily minimum security, private prisons do appear to be able to meet their goal of providing more efficient services than the public sector. Yet, this does not appear to be the case for all types of facilities.

While the rate of incarceration in the United States has slowed over the past few years, private companies have still been able to remain viable, particularly given the recent recession. States still struggling with overcrowding and a tight budget have turned to private companies to house their inmates for a lower cost. In addition, private companies have also found a niche in the rural economy by providing job opportunities and economic growth. Given the history of private prisons and the problems that have occurred, it is important that states learn from the lessons of the past and seek to develop ways to ensure that private prisons keep the safety and security of inmates—and not simply increased revenues—as their driving motivation.

Kerry M. Richmond
Lycoming College

See Also: Corrections; Federal Prisons; Penitentiaries; Prisoner's Rights.

Further Readings
Austin, James and Garry Coventry. *Emerging Issues on Privatized Prisons*. Washington, DC: Bureau of Justice Assistance, 2001.
Greene, Judith A. "Entrepreneurial Corrections: Incarceration as a Business Opportunity." In *Invisible Punishment: The Collateral Consequences of Mass Imprisonment*, Marc Mauer and Meda Chesney-Lind, eds. New York: New Press, 2002.
Harding, Richard W. "Private Prisons." In *Handbook of Crime and Punishment*, Michael Tonry, ed. New York: Oxford University Press, 1998.
Shichor, David. *Punishment for Profit: Private Prisons/Public Concerns*. Thousand Oaks, CA: Sage, 1995.

Prison Riots

Violence is an unwanted yet expected aspect of life in many prison facilities. Individual incidents of violence, however, are different from widespread prison riots, which are defined as an attempt by inmates to collectively take control of all or part of a prison facility. Prison riots can be either expressive, in that they are spontaneous events, or instrumental, meaning that they are planned with some goal in mind. Over the past century, as the prison system in the United States has grown, prison riots have become more common, ignited primarily by overcrowded and substandard living conditions.

Several theories have been put forth regarding why inmates riot. One perspective is that inmates are simply responding to poor prison conditions, while another focuses on the fact that inmates are more likely to riot when the status quo of a prison is shifted. A more common perspective is that prison riots are the result of an administrative breakdown in the prison facility. While many of the riots that have occurred over the years have been in overcrowded prisons, research has found that prison conditions alone cannot fully explain why this type of violence takes place in prisons.

There have been four waves of prison riots in the United States over the past century, each influenced by a specific set of circumstances. Prior to 1929, riots were caused by disgruntled inmates who were attempting to escape from the prison. Frustration riots were common during the late 1940s and 1950s. During this time, there was a unified inmate subculture that often clashed with prison authorities regarding "brutal and crowded" prison living conditions. The period between 1950 and 1953 had an increase in prison riots. In that three-year period alone, there were 50 prison riots, more than had occurred in the prior 25 years. One of the most significant factors that led to an increase in prison riots during this time was the enforced idleness of inmates because of a lack of prison programming available. The riots that occurred during this period reinforced the belief that rehabilitation programs were necessary in improving the behavior of inmates not only upon release from prison but also while incarcerated.

Early Riots
Escape attempts and rioting were commonplace in early penitentiaries because of overcrowding and harsh living conditions. Newgate Prison, the first penitentiary in New York state, experienced disturbances regularly as inmates challenged the conditions of their confinement. In April 1803, a riot occurred when armed guards were summoned to prevent the escape of 20 inmates. Four inmates were killed.

The riot that heralded the modern era of prison riots occurred in 1946 at the U.S. Federal Penitentiary on Alcatraz Island in 1946. This riot, which initially started over a failed escape attempt, led to a three-day uprising, which has become known as the Battle of Alcatraz. Prisoners were armed, and marines and army soldiers were called in to suppress the violence; they did so using explosives such as demolition bombs, antitank shells, and rifle grenades. By the end of the third day, three inmates and two guards had been killed, and one inmate and 14 officers were injured.

Over the next decade, the civil and political unrest that American society was experiencing, in addition to the fact that prisons were becoming more racially integrated, led to an increase in two specific types of riots. The first wave of riots that occurred during this time have been referred to as race riots. The unified inmate subculture that was seen in prisons during the 1940s and 1950s had disappeared as more distinct groups came to form. The riots that occurred during this period were primarily the result of racial conflict between various groups. However, riots were also used as attempts by specific inmate groups to push for specific rights while incarcerated. For example, inmates who associated with the Nation of Islam resorted to riots to fight for the right to practice their religion freely within the institution. The general unrest within the country and in prisons is illustrated by the fact that between 1969 and 1970, 98 prisons riots were reported.

Political Riots

The next wave of riots are known as political riots and occurred during the early 1970s. The purpose of these riots was to address many of the concerns inmates had regarding their treatment and conditions of confinement. One of the most famous political riots was the riot at upstate New York's Attica Correctional Facility in 1971.

Overcrowded prison conditions initially ignited the four-day riot at Attica, with more than 1,000 inmates rebelling and taking control of the entire prison for the first day, holding a number of guards hostage. A series of demands were made by the inmates to improve

Prison riots are acts of defiance by a group of prisoners usually to force change or express a grievance. Initially, the actions of prisoners during a riot were viewed as irrational. More recently, however, external conditions like overcrowding and cost-cutting measures in correctional facilities are considered more of an explanation of these events.

living conditions. When negotiations over these demands fell through, authorities forced the inmates to retreat to the exercise field, then shot more than 3,000 rounds of tear gas, in addition to live ammunition, into the field. The firestorm left 29 inmates and 10 hostages dead. Another three hostages, 85 inmates, and one state police trooper were wounded. In addition, one guard and three inmates had been killed by the rioting inmates. The damage to the facility cost the state tens of millions of dollars.

In the next year, 1972, there were 48 prison riots, which was more than in any other year in the history of the United States. The riots during the 1970s led to a shift in not only the way in which prison riots were carried out but also how they were viewed by the general public. The taking of hostages became a common feature of prison riots during this time. As a result of an increasing number of riots, some of which were highly publicized, the public increasingly began to associate prison riots with "violence and even organized terrorism."

Rage Riots

The final wave of riots have come to be known as rage riots. These riots were often spontaneous and resulted from guard efforts to break up altercations between inmates. At other times, rage riots were deliberate acts designed to incapacitate parts of the facility or to get revenge on an inmate or guard perceived to have started the trouble.

On February 2, 1980, inmates at the Santa Fe Penitentiary took seven guards hostage, obtained a set of keys, and embarked on a prison wide brawl. Reportedly, some inmates found blowtorches and used them on inmates who were snitches or against whom other prisoners had grudges. Inmates also assaulted and sodomized 11 guards. After 36 hours, authorities were able to restore order in the facility. In total, 33 inmates died. During negotiations, inmates cited overcrowded prison conditions (the facility was at 150 percent of its rated capacity at the time of the riot) and abuse by prison guards as some of their concerns and reasons for inciting the riot.

In recent years, two riots in particular have received national attention; however, their motivations are not as obvious. On Easter Sunday, April 11, 1993, 450 inmates rioted at the Southern Ohio Correctional Facility, a maximum-security prison in Lucasville, Ohio. The riot, primarily caused by overcrowded prison conditions (the prison population was at 150 percent capacity at the time of the riot), lasted for two weeks. It took hundreds of National Guardsmen to eventually quell the riot, after which nine inmates were allegedly beaten to death and one guard was strangled. During the riot, $40 million in damage was inflicted on the prison.

Most recently, in August 2009, inmates at the California Institution for Men in Chino rioted for 11 hours straight, leaving 250 people injured and 55 hospitalized. While it is unclear what specifically set off the riot, racial tensions between black and Latino inmates and overcrowded prison conditions have been cited as potential causes.

Causes of Riots

While the prison riots that have occurred over the past century have appeared to follow certain trends, researchers have focused more specifically on what causes inmates to riot. Two central models have been used to explain inmate behavior. The first is the importation model. Essentially, the behavior of inmates in prison is shaped by their individual characteristics; for example, offenders from lower-class backgrounds bring a set of attitudes specific to their cultural situation, including views on the acceptability of violence. Since these attitudes are specific to individuals, the importation model is not applicable to collective violence, nor does it provide any guidance on universal changes in governance that can limit or prevent such situations.

The second model is the deprivation model. This model argues that inmate behavior is shaped by the stress and oppression of living in prison. For example, overcrowded prison conditions, lack of programming, and stringency of rule enforcement have been found to be associated with levels of disorder. Much of the violence under such conditions is thought to be expressive, lacking any goal other than tension reduction.

While these are two broad explanations for inmate behavior while incarcerated, there are many specific explanations as to why prison riots occur. External social and political factors, such as what influenced the race and political riots during the 1970s, can shape the motivation of inmates. However, research has found that the conditions within the prison, mainly the role that prison management plays in controlling inmate behavior, is a stronger motivating factor than the characteristics of inmates themselves or the sociopolitical context at the time.

Two theories provide explanations as to why inmates riot. The first is the inmate-balance theory. This theory argues that the there is a tenuous balance of power that exists within a prison. Because life in prison is so austere, and privileges so few and far between, any change in the balance of those privileges can be a catalyst for violence, either personal or collective. Any administrative change such as tighter security procedures can upset this balance and potentially be stress-inducing for inmates. This may also result when prison officials abuse their positions or assert strict authority over inmates. This theory argues that the social setting of prison itself is the root of the problem. As long as the status quo is maintained, violence may be manageable, but once the balance is upset, prisoners can be motivated to riot.

The other theory is the administrative control theory. This theory argues that weak management can cause prison officials to lose control over the prison, leading to collective violence and rioting. Examples of poor prison management include high staff turnover, lack of staff discipline, lax security, and failure to search inmates or disperse crowds. Idleness among inmates, similar to what was experienced during the 1950s, can also lead to inmate riots. Essentially, this theory, which is based on the deprivation theory, argues that prison riots occur in response to the conditions at the prison; prisoners will, for example, riot when faced with overcrowding, food shortages, systemic abuse or racism, or other negative circumstances. Prison conditions, particularly overcrowding, are often noted as a cause of prison riots. However, prison conditions alone cannot fully explain why inmates riots. Instead, research, particularly that by Bert Useem and Peter Kimball, has found that prison riots are primarily the result of some form of administrative breakdown that has occurred within the prison. While prison conditions may be a motivating factor, more important is how well the administration within a facility deals with these conditions. Prisons that are poorly managed, regardless of the conditions in which inmates are housed, are most at risk for collective violence.

Conclusion

The risk of inmates rioting is always a concern for prison administrators. Yet the motivations for why inmates riot are not often clear. The prison riots over the past century have been characterized as occurring in four waves, each with its own specific causal factors. In the early part of the 20th century, prison riots resulted from an initial escape attempt or other attempt to break free from the confines of prison life. However, in the 1930s and 1940s, riots were a collective attempt by a unified inmate subculture to lash out at prison authorities over the conditions of their confinement. During the 1960s and 1970s, race and political riots were prominent, influenced by the civil and political unrest that the country was experiencing at the time. More recently, rage riots have been common within prison facilities, spontaneous events sparked by inmate frustration over what they perceive to be mistreatment. However, the motivating factors behind prison riots are often complex and not necessarily caused by one issue alone. Although there are many explanations as to what leads inmates to riot, research has found that most often some type of administrative breakdown is to blame. Despite concerns over prison conditions and the characteristics of inmates within a facility, it is imperative that prison officials maintain a safe and secure environment and take the steps necessary to reduce the likelihood of violence within their facility.

Kerry M. Richmond
Lycoming College

See Also: Attica; Corrections; Federal Prisons.

Further Readings
Adams, Robert. *Prison Riots in Britain and the US*. New York: St. Martin's Press, 1992.
Graber, Jennifer. *The Furnace of Affliction: Prisons and Religion in Antebellum America*. Chapel Hill: University of North Carolina Press, 2011.
McCorkle, Richard C., Terance D. Miethe, and Kriss A. Drass. "The Roots of Prison Violence: A Test of the Deprivation, Management and 'Not-So-Total' Institution Models." *Crime and Delinquency*, v.41/3 (1995).

Useem, Bert and Peter Kimball. *States of Siege: U.S. Prison Riots, 1971–1986*. New York: Oxford University Press, 1989.

Useem, Bert and Michael D. Reisig. "Collective Action in Prisons: Protests, Disturbances, and Riots." *Criminology*, v.37/4 (1999).

Prisoner's Rights

Prisoner's rights are those rights that individuals retain after they are found guilty of a crime and sentenced to a term of confinement in a prison or jail. In the United States, prisoner's rights include both positive rights, such as the right to challenge a criminal sentence and the right to challenge conditions of confinement within prison, and negative rights, such as the right to be free from cruel and unusual punishment and the right to be free from discrimination.

Most prisoner's rights are civil rights, meaning that a prisoner must file a lawsuit against a specific individual or agency and seek a particular remedy, such as a change in policy or a payment for damages suffered. In such cases, prisoners often represent themselves (pro se), initiating and pursuing their own legal challenges. The development of prisoner's rights in the United States can be divided chronologically into roughly three different eras of progress: limited rights in the early republic and 19th century; an expansion of rights in the mid-20th century, especially during the Warren Court, when courts broadened civil rights in general; and a contraction of rights in the late 20th century, especially after 1996.

Early Republic and the Nineteenth Century: Two Basic Prisoner's Rights

The U.S. Constitution codified one basic right of convicted criminals: habeas corpus. The right to habeas corpus originated in English common law and traditionally provides convicted criminals the right to challenge the authority of a judge or jailer to impose a particular sentence. The Bill of Rights, ratified in 1791, codified a second basic right of convicted criminals: the Eighth Amendment guarantee against the infliction of cruel and unusual punishment. These two rights became the foundation of prisoners' attempts to exercise their civil rights from within prison walls.

However, when these rights were first codified in American law, prisons as such hardly existed. Criminal sentences traditionally involved a range of punishments from warnings and fines to public whippings and the ultimate sanction: execution. A few scattered jails existed in the 18th century, but judges rarely meted out prison terms to convicted criminals. Prisoner's rights law, then, only slowly began to develop, following the establishment of the first penitentiaries and prisons in the United States in the early 1800s.

In Re Medley was one of the few 19th-century federal cases to even mention conditions of confinement in prisons—a topic that became a frequent subject of prisoner's rights litigation in the 20th century. *Medley*, an 1890 U.S. Supreme Court case, condemned the use of solitary confinement in Colorado for death-sentenced prisoners. Specifically, the court ordered that James Medley, whom a Colorado judge sentenced to death for a first-degree murder conviction in 1889, be released from solitary confinement and from prison. The court explained that at the time Medley committed his crime, Colorado did not keep death-sentenced prisoners in solitary confinement. Because Medley could not have known at the time of his crime that he would be subject to the severely punitive punishment of solitary confinement, the imposition of the punishment was unconstitutional (a violation of the ex post facto clause). The court did not, however, address the constitutionality of using solitary confinement or of imposing the death penalty.

In Re Medley foreshadowed the procedural complexity of prisoner's rights claims in the 20th century; successful challenges to the death penalty and to other conditions of confinement increasingly turned on questions not of the morality of cruelty but of the fairness of procedure. While a convicted criminal's right to challenge the judicial authorization for his sentence was well established even in English common law, and the Eighth Amendment in the U.S. Bill of Rights forbade the imposition of cruel and unusual punishments, these rights were of limited application to most prisoners in the United States until the mid-20th century.

Indeed, throughout the 19th century, and well into the 20th century, federal courts viewed prisoners as "slaves of the state," who were *civiliter*

Prisoner's rights in the United States include the right to be free from discrimination. At the state penitentiary in Canon City, Colorado, in the early 1900s, homosexuals are being punished by wearing dresses and wheeling heavy rocks.

mortuus, or civilly dead. In *Ruffin v. The Commonwealth* (1871), the Virginia Supreme Court explained the meaning of civil death: Prisoners lost the rights that non-prisoner citizens of the United States could claim, like those rights codified in the Bill of Rights. Moreover, if a prisoner had any possessions in his name when he entered prison, his estate would literally be "administered like that of a dead man."

Warren Court Era and Beyond: Expanding Prisoner's Rights

In the mid-20th century, three significant changes in federal law led to a steep rise in the number of prisoner's rights claims brought in federal courts. First, in *Miller v. Overholser* (1953), a Washington, D.C., district court case, and *Brown v. Allen* (1953), a Supreme Court case, federal courts expanded the habeas corpus remedies available to prisoners to include challenges to conditions of confinement (instead of limiting these remedies to challenges to the terms of sentences). Second, in *Robinson v. California* (1962), the Supreme Court incorporated the Eighth Amendment prohibition on cruel and unusual punishment against the states. This was part of a slow process by which the Supreme Court made most of the Bill of Rights applicable to any citizen anywhere in the United States and therefore enforceable by individual citizens against individual state actors. Third, in *Cooper v. Pate* (1963), the Supreme Court held that the Civil Rights Act gave prisoners the right to sue prison officials directly for civil rights violations suffered in prison. This kind of civil rights challenge is called a Section 1983 claim, named for the relevant section of the Civil Rights Act.

The expansion of habeas corpus rights, the extension of federal Eighth Amendment protections to state prisoners, and prisoners' new power to sue under Section 1983 together produced an explosion of prisoner lawsuits, which challenged both the conditions of confinement in prisons and the constitutionality of the death penalty. Responding to the increased attention these lawsuits brought to prisons and prisoners in the United States, Congress also stepped in, passing laws that further changed the shape of prisoner's rights.

Conditions of Confinement Litigation

In 1965, three prisoners filed a federal district court case, *Talley v. Stevens*, challenging the conditions of their confinement at Arkansas State Penitentiary. Within five years, the case had expanded to include the entire Arkansas state prison system, and in 1978, the case reached the U.S. Supreme Court, as *Hutto v. Finney*. For the first time, the court directly considered the application of the Eighth Amendment to prison conditions in a state prison system. The federal district court in Arkansas had ordered state officials to take multiple remedial actions to improve conditions in the state's prisons, including desegregating prisons, improving basic living conditions, and limiting periods of confinement in isolation cells. The Supreme Court agreed that the combination of severe deprivations documented in the Arkansas prisons constituted a violation of the Eighth Amendment prohibition on cruel and unusual punishment and upheld the district court orders.

Three years after *Hutto*, in 1981, the Supreme Court heard its second major case regarding the application of the Eighth Amendment to prison conditions: *Rhodes v. Chapman*. *Rhodes* was the first case in which the court considered the application of the Eighth Amendment to the conditions of confinement at a particular prison, as opposed to an entire prison system. In *Rhodes*, the court did not find the same interdependence of multiple deprivation conditions that had existed in Arkansas and so refused to uphold the district court's orders to improve prison conditions and to release prisoners from the Southern Ohio Correctional Facility in Lucasville.

In *Rhodes*, Justice William Brennan noted that, as of 1981, there were 8,000 pending prisoner lawsuits challenging conditions of confinement in the United States, and 24 states with either individual institutions or entire prison systems subject to orders to remedy unconstitutional conditions of confinement. In fact, the vast majority of Eighth Amendment standards governing prison conditions in the United States were set not by the Supreme Court but by lower federal courts. Throughout the 1960s and 1970s, district courts in states from Alabama to California found violations so egregious that the officials in charge of the offending prisons either did not appeal the lower court's remedial orders, or did appeal, only to be summarily dismissed by the circuit courts.

Medical Experimentation Legislation

While federal courts heard more and more claims about unconstitutional prison conditions throughout the United States, the public media also increasingly covered unconstitutional prison conditions. For instance, in the 1970s, Americans were shocked to learn of both the Heller experiments, funded by the U.S. government between 1963 and 1973, which examined the effects of radiation on the testes of Oregon prisoners, and the Tuskegee syphilis experiments, funded by the U.S. government from 1932 through 1972, which evaluated the long-term effects of untreated syphilis in African American men. In 1978, in response to public revelations about these and other experiments on prisoners and other vulnerable human subjects, Congress passed the Act for the Protection of Human Subjects. This act, codified at Title 45 of the federal register, regulates all categories of human subjects' participation in experimental research. Title 45 provides for prisoner participation in federally funded medical experimentation under very limited circumstances, subject to rigorous safeguards for obtaining prisoners' consent and ensuring that the research will benefit the prisoner subjects.

In spite of these rigid federal regulations, U.S. prisoners in the 21st century continue to participate in a variety of experimental biomedical research protocols. Prisoners in private prison facilities are particularly vulnerable to recruitment for participation in experiments that might not be clearly beneficial to the prisoner participants. In fact, as of 2008, more than 125,000 prisoners, or 8 percent of the U.S. prison population, were housed in private prison facilities. The growing use of these private facilities arguably undermines prisoner's rights because the private facilities are not subject to the same federal regulations as public facilities and because private facilities have greater incentives to engage in cost-cutting that tends to make these facilities both more profitable and less comfortable.

Death Penalty Litigation

In the same decades that U.S. federal courts received the first barrage of claims about unconstitutional prison conditions, they also received claims about the unconstitutionality of the death penalty, as implemented in various states. These claims are generally brought by prisoners, under the habeas corpus law or under the Eighth Amendment; death penalty challenges affect the kinds of punishments to which prisoners are subject generally, as well as the procedural rights of prisoners to bring challenges under habeas corpus and Eighth Amendment laws.

In a 1972 case, *Furman v. Georgia*, the Supreme Court declared a de facto moratorium on carrying out death sentences throughout the United States. The court found that Georgia's death penalty, as arbitrarily and inconsistently applied to criminal defendants, violated the Eighth Amendment prohibition on cruel and unusual punishment. However, just four years later, the court reconsidered Georgia's newly minted death penalty statute and found it to be constitutional (*Gregg v. Georgia,* 1976). Among other safeguards, *Gregg* mandated automatic federal appellate review, all the way to the Supreme Court, of death sentences. Since *Gregg*, federal courts have scrutinized death sentences much more carefully. As federal appellate courts have been required to consider dozens of death sentences annually, these courts have increasingly restricted the conditions under which the death penalty may be imposed. In 1986, in *Ford v. Wainwright*, the Supreme Court held that severely mentally ill defendants could not be executed. In 2002, in *Atkins v. Virginia*, the court held that mentally retarded defendants could not be sentenced to death. And in 2005, in *Roper v. Simmons*, the court held that defendants who were under 18 at the time they committed their capital offense could not be sentenced to death.

Roper is important not only for its holding but for its unusual references to international law. In *Roper*, Justice Anthony Kennedy noted that by executing criminals who were juveniles at the time they committed their crimes, the United States was an outlier among the developed world powers. In fact, most countries in the world, Kennedy pointed out, have signed onto international treaties pledging not to engage in such extreme punishment practices.

In addition to cases challenging the constitutionality of imposing the death penalty on particular defendants, the federal courts have also heard cases about the constitutionality of various state methods of execution. Most recently, in 2008, in *Baze v. Rees*, the Supreme Court considered a case challenging the constitutionality of Kentucky's method of execution. The court upheld Kentucky's use of lethal injection to execute death-sentenced prisoners. Indeed, since the 1970s, the U.S. Supreme Court has continued to hear a variety of cases, brought as both habeas corpus challenges and as Section 1983 Civil Rights Act challenges, regarding the imposition of the death penalty. However, in this same period, the court has heard many fewer claims about conditions of confinement.

Welfare Reform Era: Limiting Prisoners' Rights

The bipartisan welfare reforms of 1996 completely reshaped federal benefit plans and social safety nets in the United States; as such, the welfare reforms obscured attention to the passage of two lesser-known pieces of federal legislation, which would, nonetheless, have a dramatic impact on the U.S. criminal justice system. In 1996, Congress passed the Prison Litigation Reform Act (PLRA) and the Anti-Terrorism Effective Death Penalty Act (AEDPA) with the specific intention of limiting the number and kinds of lawsuits that prisoners could bring to challenge both their criminal sentences and the conditions of their confinement.

Both acts sought to accomplish their goals through complex procedural reforms. The PLRA limits the scope and duration of consent decrees issued by federal courts overseeing state prison conditions, caps the rate at which attorneys may be compensated for representing prisoner clients, requires prisoners to exhaust available in-prison administrative grievance processes before turning to the federal courts for assistance, and bars prisoners who file "frivolous" lawsuits from having their claims heard in federal court. In 2010, the Supreme Court heard oral arguments about the application of the PLRA to a class action lawsuit filed in California, challenging the provision of healthcare and the high degree of overcrowding throughout the state's prison system. This case, *Plata v. Schwarzenegger*, marked the first time the high court directly considered the PLRA's procedural provisions.

However, just two years after the passage of the PLRA, the Supreme Court held in *Pennsylvania Department of Corrections v. Yeskey* that the Americans with Disabilities Act applies to prisoners. This holding allowed prisoners with disabilities to challenge conditions of their confinement related to disability accommodations without being as constrained by the PLRA provisions limiting the scope of consent decrees and attorney compensation. Analyses of the PLRA suggest that the law has accomplished its goals of limiting prisoners' access to federal courts, although it has not necessarily increased the efficiency of prisoner litigation or facilitated the enforcement of prisoners' constitutional rights.

Like the PLRA, the AEDPA limits the situations in which federal courts may hear claims from and grant relief to prisoners sentenced to death or to prison by state courts. The AEDPA requires federal courts to find that a state court was unreasonable in its application of law or in its determination of facts before agreeing to hear a prisoner's claim for habeas corpus relief. In addition, the AEDPA enacted strict timelines within which prisoners must file state and federal appeals of death sentences. In sum, both the PLRA and the AEDPA imposed limitations on the lawsuits prisoners could bring challenging either their sentences or the conditions of their confinement.

Keramet Ann Reiter
University of California, Berkeley

See Also: 1851 to 1900 Primary Documents; 1901 to 1920 Primary Documents; Bill of Rights; Eastern State Penitentiary; Furman v. Georgia; G*regg v. Georgia*; Habeas Corpus, Writ of; Supermax Prisons; Walnut Street Jail.

Further Readings
Boston, John and Daniel E. Manville. *Prisoners' Self Help Litigation Manual,* 4th ed. New York: Oxford University Press, 2010.
Feeley, Malcolm M. and Edward L. Rubin. *Judicial Policy Making and the Modern State: How the Courts Reformed America's Prisons*. New York: Cambridge University Press, 1998.
Friedman, Lawrence M. *Crime and Punishment in American History*. New York: Basic Books, 1993.
Haney, Craig and Mona Lynch. "Regulating Prisons of the Future: A Psychological Analysis of Supermax and Solitary Confinement." *New York University Review of Law & Social Change*, v.23/4 (1997).
Reiter, Keramet. "Medical Experimentation on Prisoners: Dilemmas in Rights and Regulations." *California Law Review*, v.97 (2009).

Private Detectives

Private detectives are people who undertake police-like activities without being part of the police service but customarily work within the private sector on an individual or freelance basis, or more likely as part of a specialist company. Initially, private detectives were involved in work that supplemented activities of the state, when the reach of the latter was still insufficient to complete its various requirements. This notably included antiunion activities in industrial action in the 19th century and the search for spies and saboteurs. In the 20th century, the nature of private investigation changed as state capacity increased while more private citizens were willing to use their services to pursue their own interests, often but not always as a result of suspicion about a spouse's loyalty and activities. In the contemporary United States, much of the demand for private investigation results from possible fraud in the insurance industry as well as family-based issues. The nature of this work has been revolutionized by the arrival of modern information technology.

The Pinkerton Agency
Prior to the invention of uniformed police in the mid-19th century, all police operatives were effectively private detectives who worked for victims of crime, who paid a fee for recovery of stolen property. Taking fees became illegal for uniformed public police, and their creation coincided with the development of corporate-level private investigation, in the form of the Pinkerton Agency. The concept of organized private investigation first came to prominence with the establishment by Allan Pinkerton of his eponymous detective agency in 1850. His reputation was made by the successful foiling of a plot to assassinate Abraham Lincoln, prior to his election as president. Subsequently, the company achieved considerable commercial success undertaking work that would in many cases have been undertaken by the police or military forces if the federal or state governments involved had sufficient capacity. One strand of this work was to track down suspected criminals operating in remote locations without many state services, such as the James brothers, Butch Cassidy and the Sundance Kid, and other notorious outlaws. Pinkerton agents were paid by and worked for corporations directly. These included railroads, stagecoaches, and banks. When involved in labor disputes, agents were hired by the corporation involved and, again, worked on their behalf.

Given the absence of scrutiny and the portrayal of the wanted individuals as heavily armed and dangerous, Pinkerton's agents (predominantly if not exclusively men) would normally have had a free hand in conducting their work. The workforce included, as a result, many young men without a strong stake in society (e.g., often poor or recent migrants) who were willing to take risks to make a living. When the Pinkerton agents were brought in to break strikes, infiltrate unions, and take physical action against workers, they also were able to call upon protection from prosecution. Eyewitness reports of strikes in the second part of the 19th century describe scenes of open warfare, with the collusion of the state acting to support the hated Pinkerton men. Ultimately, this resulted in the so-called 1893 Anti-Pinkerton Act, which prevented the state from hiring companies providing quasi-military or mercenary forces for strikebreaking activities. Private detective work subsequently took a more peaceful turn, and their protection from the law was greatly diminished. However, this has changed to some extent in the wake of the 2001 terrorist attacks on the United States and the creation of the Homeland Security industry; Pinkerton has been reinvented as Pinkerton Government Services, Inc., with a much closer private-public sector arrangement than would have previously seemed possible.

The Pinkerton Agency used an eye for its logo and a slogan attesting to the fact that the agents never slept. This gave rise to the term *private eye*, which has stuck ever since. The company now competes in a marketplace that is characterized by the entry of large new companies featuring ex-military personnel and high-level contacts that offer all-encompassing, turnkey-style service provision. Smaller companies and individuals tend to position themselves as niche operators because of location or the possession of specialist skills or knowledge.

The Nature of Private Investigation Work

Private investigation in the past involved a great deal of physical activity, with physical confrontation, tracking down wanted people, and acting without state-provided infrastructure and services. The work has subsequently changed to a more sedate form in general, in part because of the need to comply with the law and to keep private investigator actions distinct from those of the official police. As demand for services switched to the personal level, work focused more on labor-intensive activities such as surveillance, checking records, and interviewing possible witnesses. This kind of work represents the common symbol of the private eye in the media of popular culture. When divorces were restricted to the demonstrable production of cause and blame, private detectives were called upon to monitor suspected philanderers to provide attested, photographic evidence in flagrante. This required a degree of physical dexterity and tradecraft that meant ex-military or security forces were attracted into the industry. To some extent, the private detective represented the force of bourgeois society into a sphere of activity that is usually considered to be private. The private detective in this case was seen as an unwanted irritant and an intruder. Even when a divorce might be mutually acceptable and the infidelity an invention for the sake of legal requirements, the private detective was still seen as an unavoidable extra.

As demand for private detective services from the insurance industry has increased, the role of the investigator has continued to focus on careful, often dull but also secretive scrutiny of possible evidence. The reduction in the need for physical requirements has broadened the employment possibilities for women and people not possessed of above-average physical abilities. However, these changes have not further endeared the private eye to the public, since few people have a positive

Allan Pinkerton along with President Lincoln and Major General McClernand in 1862. Pinkerton was head of Union Intelligence Services at the time and also formed the Pinkerton National Detective Agency.

opinion of insurance companies as a whole, and many consider insurance fraud a form of victimless crime. In recent years and partly to address these issues, some attempts have been made to professionalize the industry with the use of licenses to try to ensure proper quality assurance standards and to enhance transparency in the industry. Licenses are issued at the state level, and only five states no longer require such a license, although the requirements vary considerably. It is clear that problems of legality and jurisdiction continue to hinder investigations when cross-border issues are involved. In some cases, this issue might have an impact on the behavior of those whose actions might be investigated in one way or another. Professionalization also assists in the specialization of individual companies, branding, and enhancing services. That has implications for the nature of individuals hired and the need for qualifications and competencies. Unionization has also made a moderate impact upon the industry and will in due course raise the standards of pay and terms and conditions of employment.

The Impact of Technology

Improvements in information technology such as mobile phones, the Internet, rapid identification of individuals captured on photograph, and so forth have revolutionized the scope of private detective work and the way in which it might be conducted. For various reasons, many people have become very interested in tracing their ancestors or current family members with whom they have had little or no contact, and online tools have been developed to enable such activities to be conducted successfully. The same tools can be used by people to replicate the kind of search that private detectives, in addition of course to state officials, had access to as a monopoly. Further, urban development and the spread of intelligent personal communication devices have together acted to widen the range of occasions on which people are effectively visible and the same technology can also be used to transmit evidence of that visibility widely and very quickly. Privacy and legal issues aside, the technical ability to provide evidence of the actions of an individual has thus become easily obtainable, and so members of the public can again undertake work that once only private detectives were able to do. This is an additional reason for the professionalization of private detective work, which stresses potential dangers that members of the public are not aware of and that might affect them while also further incorporating advanced technical skills as necessary for detection but beyond the scope of ordinary citizens. Currently, the sense of fear and anxiety that has been fostered in the creation of the concept of a society under imminent terrorist threat has fueled the sense of social solidarity necessary to encourage the majority of people to accept elevated levels of surveillance.

Raymond Burr in the Ironside *television show.* Ironside *is an example of a private investigator being portrayed as a decent individual forced into isolation through unfair social forces.*

The Private Investigator in Popular Culture

The private detective has become a popular and even iconic figure in modern culture, and variations have been portrayed in print and on screen, although the representation of the individual varies from country to country. In the United States, the first manifestation of the private eye was seen in the dime novel detectives of the last decades of the

19th century. Such detectives were routinely portrayed as having great moral rectitude; they acted to restore the moral order when it was compromised by lawless persons. A second stereotype of the private eye was created in the 1920s and 1930s as part of the hard-boiled literary genre and most commonly associated with Dashiell Hammett and Raymond Chandler, who respectively created the antiheroes Sam Spade and Philip Marlowe.

These investigators are outsiders operating in a society that is almost entirely corrupt, with those hiring the detectives morally indistinguishable from the criminals to be investigated. Despite the often unappealing habits of the detectives concerned and their old-fashioned attitudes toward gender relations, the audience tends to side with them because it is made clear that the state and its representatives have not only failed to provide the police services required but might also be complicit in illegal action for financial gain. The private eye is, in this sense, the armed outsider who, from an existential perspective, demonstrates that only direct action by the individual can achieve any desirable goal. It is no surprise that this image became popular at a time of economic crisis when millions of people were becoming impoverished as a result of large-scale forces over which they had little control and the true outlines of which they could scarcely discern.

More recently, various television series have portrayed the private investigator as an inherently decent individual who has been forced into social isolation through social forces, often unfairly applied. *Ironside*, for example, was forced to retire from the police force and use a wheelchair after being shot by an assassin; he subsequently became a consultant to the police. Jim Rockford from the *Rockford Files* was falsely accused of a crime and as an ex-convict turned to righting wrongs as a private investigator. It is possible to argue that Miss Marple, an amateur private detective, suffers from prejudice against elderly women in obtaining meaningful employment and that investigators specializing in the supernatural (e.g., *Buffy the Vampire Slayer*) represent the difficulty that members of minority interests face, having to hide their true identity from the public. In just about every case, the innate decency of the private detective shines through, although she or he is often disadvantaged as a result.

Private Detectives and Society

In a heavily armed country like the United States, it is inevitable that private detectives will feel the need to be armed to go about their work, thereby intensifying the arms race and making their jobs more likely to lead to deadly violence. One result of this is to reduce trust where private detectives are concerned, and this makes their relationship with society different from what may be found in western Europe, with its general reverence for the skilled professional, or from societies under authoritarian rule where all figures wielding power, state-mandated or not, are met with more or less resentful obedience.

The demographic features of private detectives have varied through the ages. In the early days of the industry, most detectives were fit young men with a willingness to tolerate physical hardship and risk; they were often recently arrived immigrants. As the nature of the work changed, the people involved became more educated and skilled, often with access to necessary personal connections with the authorities and almost certainly an urban bias. This was a period when private detection took place in cities, according to the concept of corrupt cities and innocent countryside. In recent years, the labor market has broadened, and career paths are being opened to aspiring detectives as one of a range of competing career options.

These people are operating now in a society in which it has become increasingly accepted that the state should not and cannot in any case provide policing for all purposes. Indeed, since the 1960s, the proportion of state officials acting as police has declined considerably in comparison with private sector operators.

However, since hiring private detectives continues to require quite large amounts of money, it tends to be less likely that the poor and ethnic minorities will be confronted with them on a daily basis. Indeed, it may be the case that private detectives are the one branch of the quasi-official police services that can reach out and affect rich and settled members of society who are able to avoid unwanted interactions with the police through various means.

John Walsh
Shinawatra University

See Also: 1851 to 1900 Primary Documents; Dime Novels, Pulps, Thrillers; Hammett, Dashiell; Private Police; Strikes.

Further Readings

Geherin, David. *The American Private Eye: The Image in Fiction*. New York: F. Ungar, 1985.

Gill, M. and J. Hart. "Private Investigators in Britain and America: Perspectives on the Impact of Popular Culture." *Policing: An International Journal of Police Strategies and Management*, v.20/4 (1997).

Johnson, David Ralph. *Policing the Urban Underworld: The Impact of Crime on the Development of the American Police, 1800–87*. Philadelphia: Temple University Press, 1997.

McMahon, Rory J. *Practical Handbook for Professional Investigators*, 2nd ed. Boca Raton: CRC Press, 2007.

Morn, Frank. *The Eye That Never Sleeps: A History of the Pinkerton National Detective Agency*. Bloomington: Indiana University Press, 1982.

Private Police

Private police are members of private-sector organizations providing personnel who offer various police-related activities, usually on a contractual basis. The range and nature of the services offered has varied considerably, depending on the location and nature of the venue concerned and the changing legislative structure in force. In general, private police complement the services provided by public police officers rather than substituting for them.

Private police also have a less significant status in law and cannot perform many of the functions that public police can. While some private police may be used for personal security in locales considered vulnerable to violence, they are also widely used as security guards intending to bar entry to once public spaces now privatized on a commercial basis.

While public sector policing developed in nature over the course of centuries, the emergence of private police has arisen with dramatic speed since the 1960s, until now the relative numbers in the United States greatly favor the private over the public. Reasons for the rapid emergence of this industry include the expansion of policing services demanded (e.g., personal security, background checks, and asset surveillance), the increase in expense of the police resulting from professionalization and increases in technology, and the greater willingness of state agencies to privatize services once considered essential for the government to provide in one form or another. Consequently, private–public contracting schemes have emerged in many different parts of the country. Notable examples include the Buffalo Creek, West Virginia–Guardsmark contract in 1976 and the Kalamazoo, Michigan–Charles Services contract, when private police were sworn in as government officials in order to increase their legal status and ability to use those powers normally reserved for public police.

Privatization Issues

In many cases, private police are parts of corporations that have received outsourcing contracts determined by public-sector organizations for a mixture of operational or ideological reasons. Much effort has been expended in trying to establish whether this practice is cost-effective and/or delivers efficiency improvements. This is very difficult to resolve because direct comparative data are not available: private police may not have official powers, but they can rely upon the fact that people with whom they interact are aware of the powers of public police upon whom they can call when required. Private police rely upon a great deal of state-funded infrastructure and governance, without which they would find it much more difficult to fulfill their allocated functions.

The privatization of the police and police activities in America has represented an extension of capitalist control over all forms of social and economic life. When only public-sector police are present, the citizens had the expectation, which was of course not always met, that objective policing of democratically accountable laws would govern their daily lives. Since policing is objective and universal within the country, citizens have accepted that the same laws will apply to everyone and so contribute to the social solidarity necessary to ensure an orderly and fair society. The presence of private police changes the relationship between citizens and the authorities since it is evident that at least some police are acting on behalf of corporate interests and not for the state as a whole. Increasingly, as private police come to guard gated communities or shopping centers, those deemed "undesirable" are excluded, physically if necessary, from more and more parts of the country. The designation of who is undesirable has had plain ethnic- and gender-based components. The process has been likened to a new enclosure of the commons, in which American land, which in the public imagination at least acted as a resource anyone could use, is now reserved for the personal use of a small number of wealthy people who use their influence with politicians to ensure this arrangement is recognized in the law. Protestors and those critical of these arrangements are routinely subjected to harassment.

Relationships Between Private and Public Sector Police Services

Although it might appear clear that public and private police are funded by wholly different sources, in practice, it has become increasingly difficult to distinguish this difference. State and federal administrations that have favored market, rather than state-based means of providing services have entered into contracts with private-sector providers that necessarily include means of oversight and accountability that make the relationship between the two often very close.

However, at the operational level on the ground, cooperation between private and public has not always been straightforward. Public police in some cases understandably resent the shrinkage of their authority and workplace conditions, particularly when private police are freed from the kind of paperwork involved with documenting incidents and crimes that most police workers tend to dislike. One well-known example of this comes with university campus police. Although this form of private police has existed since the beginning of the 20th century, it has only been from the 1960s onward that campus police have had more than a custodianship role and have been increasingly empowered to investigate and deter and, in general, become a more obvious and intrusive service. This has not been universally popular, and a number of students and their representatives have questioned the legitimacy of such police to carry out activities for which they are not democratically accountable. Personal issues have also been important in the case of events of political protest, most notably during protests against the Vietnam War, as well as in the case of the physical safety of female students.

John Walsh
Shinawatra University

See Also: 1851 to 1900 Primary Documents; Police, Contemporary; Police, Sociology of; Political Policing; Private Detectives.

Further Readings
Davis, Monk and Daniel Bertrand Monk, eds. *Evil Paradises: Dreamworlds of Neoliberalism.* New York: New Press, 2008.
Forst, Brian. "The Privatization and Civilianization of Policing." In *Boundary Changes in Criminal Justice Organizations,* vol. 2. Charles M. Friel, ed. Washington, DC: National Institute of Justice, 2000.
Shearing, C. D. and P. C. Stenning, eds. *Private Policing.* Thousand Oaks, CA: Sage, 1987.
Sloan, J. J. "The Modern Campus Police: An Analysis of Their Evolution, Structure, and Function." *American Journal of Police,* v.11/2 (1992).
Spitzer, Steven and Andrew T. Scull. "Privatization and Capitalist Development: The Case of the Private Police." *Social Problems,* v.25/1 (1977).

Private Security Services

Private security is an industry responsible for the protection of life, property, and information. Definitions of the term *private security* vary. Private security can be considered any type of protective service that is typically financed through nonpublic funding sources. In 1970, the U.S. Department of Justice funded the first major study of the private security industry in the United States, which was conducted by the Rand Corporation. The Rand report defined private security as "all types of private organizations and individuals providing all types of security-related services, including investigation, guard, patrol, lie-detection, alarm, and armored transportation."

The American Society for Industrial Security (ASIS), the largest association of private security professionals in the United States, has defined private security as "an independent or proprietary commercial organization whose activities include safeguarding the employing party's assets—ranging from human lives to physical property (the premises and contents), responding to emergency incidents, performing employee background investigations, performing the functions of detection and investigation of crime and criminals, and apprehending offenders for consideration."

Private security experts affiliated with ASIS have identified core elements of the private security industry, which include physical security, personnel security, information systems security, investigations, loss prevention, risk management, legal aspects, emergency and contingency planning, fire protection, crisis management, disaster management, counterterrorism, competitive intelligence, executive protection, violence in the workplace, crime prevention, crime prevention through environmental design (CPTED), and security architecture and engineering. Annual revenue for private security firms in the United States has been on the rise in recent years and was estimated in 2012 at between $19 billion and $34 billion.

Origin

During the colonial era in America, crime control was generally the responsibility of the community. Laws were enforced by unpaid citizens who rotated service as watchmen. This loose and informal system gradually fell out of favor

Frank Leslie's Illustrated Newspaper *published this rendering in October 1884, which reads "Ohio: The mining troubles in Hocking Valley–Scene in the town of Buchtel–the striking miners' reception of "Blackleg" workmen when returning from their work escorted by a detachment of Pinkerton's detectives." Pinkerton's men were sent in lieu of the police to break strikes by coal miners.*

as homogenous and closely connected communities transformed to more fragmented societies. Private policing grew out of the early office of the constable. Early constables profited from their positions by selling protective and investigative services or by collecting fees and demanding rewards.

The growth of the private security industry in America traces its origins to the widespread industrialization in the 1850s and 1860s, along with the development of uniformed, professional policing agencies, penitentiaries, and the expansion of the criminal code and court system. Industrialization, urbanization, and rapid population growth from immigration brought about an increase in crime in urban areas. With formal policing agencies fragmented and limited by jurisdictional boundaries, private security transcended these boundaries and became the protective as well as the enforcement agents of the industrialists.

In 1850, Allan Pinkerton established the first private security and investigations company in the United States. The Pinkerton's Protective Patrol began as an agency that augmented the Chicago metropolitan police. During the U.S. Civil War, Pinkerton's agency conducted espionage for the Union army. After the Civil War, the Pinkerton National Detective Agency became the primary protective agency for the growing railroad industry and also functioned as an expanded police force to break coal miner strikes. Franklin B. Gowen, president of the Philadelphia & Reading Railroad, called upon the Pinkerton Detective Agency and his own Coal and Iron Police to infiltrate and crush labor organization and discontent with work and labor conditions.

Throughout the late 19th century and early 20th century, the Pinkertons and other private security agencies provided two general services to industries: general property protection and strike services. Pinkerton provided owners of industry with four strike services: labor espionage, strikebreakers, strike guards, and strike missionaries. Labor espionage was an infiltration of labor activities, which provided management with information about employee discontent, serving to undermine worker organization and collective bargaining. Strikebreakers were workers who replaced the striking employees in an attempt to undermine strikes and worker negotiations. Strike guards or "watchmen" protected the owner's property during strikes. Strike missionaries served to incite worker and citizen antipathy and even violence against striking employees. By the early 1900s, the Pinkerton agency had established liaisons with police organizations in Europe and was exchanging information about international crime. Their methods influenced many modern policing agencies throughout the world. Their early trademark was "The Eye That Never Sleeps," which was the origin of the informal term for private investigators, *private eyes*.

Private security employment declined between 1929 and 1939 because of the Great Depression, although there was a high level of volatility within the American populace, with at least 25 percent of the workforce unemployed or facing layoff. Despite the overall decline in private security employment, corporations still maintained a contingent of privately compensated police, spies, and strikebreakers, which led to a Senate investigation led by Senator Robert M. LaFollette, Jr. The LaFollette Committee subpoenaed the records of many private security agencies, including the Pinkerton National Detective Agency, and the William J. Burns International Detective Agency as well as documents belonging to their clients. After nearly three years of testimony, Senator LaFollette introduced the Oppressive Labor Practices Act, which prohibited the use of private policing to conduct industrial espionage and strikebreaking. The bill passed in the Senate but was defeated in the House of Representatives, ultimately lost amid the increasing turmoil in Europe.

War and Private Security

Throughout World War II, private security involved the organization of citizens to protect military installations, factories, and railroads, in addition to conducting training for civil defense and other emergency services. The private security industry grew after World War II, with many of the returning veterans working in the defense industry. In 1954, retired Federal Bureau of Investigation (FBI) agent and World War II veteran George Wackenhut founded the Wackenhut Corporation, which grew into one of the largest private security organizations in the world. In 1955, a group of security executives formed a national organization of security directors who worked on manufacturing contracts for the U.S. Department of Defense. This association became the American Society for Industrial Security (ASIS). Today, ASIS International is dedicated to professionalizing the security industry and providing educational and networking opportunities within its membership.

Throughout the 1960s, the increase in crime and social disorder fueled the federal government's interest in shifting more crime prevention responsibility to the private security industry. In 1976, the National Commission of Criminal Justice Standards and Goals issued its *Task Force Report on Private Security*. This report encouraged an improvement in the working relationships between public law enforcement and the private security industry.

The September 11, 2001, attacks on the United States further encouraged the expansion of the private security industry and an increased collaboration between private security and public policing relating to domestic security. With private security currently responsible for protecting a significant amount of the nation's critical infrastructure, partnerships between the private and public sectors will likely continue.

Services Provided

The two major types of private security are proprietary security and contract security. Proprietary security is also referred to as in-house security. Employees working under a proprietary security structure are employed by the companies where they perform their services and are not working for a private security firm. Security personnel working in a casino and loss prevention agents working in a department store are the most common examples of proprietary security services.

Contract security services are performed by a security firm that provides its services to another company on a contractual basis. The services provided typically include patrol, alarm system monitoring, investigations, and armored car delivery. Most shopping malls employ contract security to patrol the property. The largest firms providing contract security services are Securitas and Wackenhut. Companies often outsource their security needs to a private security firm because of the cost savings in maintaining an in-house security staff. Contract security firms are responsible for hiring, scheduling, supervising, and training their security staff, which provides additional benefits and savings to the client. Some of the disadvantages, however, are that contract security personnel tend to be paid less than in-house security, and therefore, the turnover rate among contract security tends to be much higher. Lack of adequate training and qualifications for the particular job site is also an ongoing problem. Because the security firm is responsible for hiring and providing security staff for the client, the client has little control over the quality of personnel the firm provides. Therefore, it is the contract security firm's responsibility to thoroughly screen individuals and perform adequate criminal background checks.

Private security functions include physical security, personnel security, and information security. Physical security includes locks, fences, building design, and alarm systems. Personnel security includes the protection of celebrities, dignitaries, corporate executives, customers, and guests. Information security includes the protection of a company or organization's intellectual property or any confidential information.

Some of the major controversies involving private security services include hiring and background check practices, licensing and regulation, adequacy of training, liability, lack of procedural safeguards, and the deployment of private security contractors in areas of conflict around the globe.

Background investigations and criminal history checks of private security applicants are now becoming standard practice within the industry. The thoroughness of the background investigations of private security employees varies based upon the particular agency and the position; checks are not standardized from state to state.

The Private Security Officer Employment Authorization Act, enacted in December 2004 as Section 6402 of the Intelligence Reform and Terrorism Prevention Act of 2004, allows states to perform fingerprint checks of state and national criminal history databases to screen prospective private security personnel. The background checks are not mandatory, however, and employees may still continue to work pending the outcome of the background check.

Licensing and regulation of private security employees vary widely from state to state. Some states require all security officers to be licensed, and others only require security personnel who carry firearms at their job site to be licensed. ASIS International has developed a code of ethics and administers several certification programs, with the Certified Protection Professional (CPP) designation being the most widely recognized in the security industry.

Criminal or civil liability is a major concern within the private security industry. Public police officers tend to have protection from personal liability, whereas private security officers acting within the scope of their employment may be held criminally liable for offenses such as false arrest, false imprisonment, assault, and trespass. Additionally, the security company can be held vicariously liable for the negligent actions of its employee who was acting within the scope of his or her employment with the security company. Private security firms must be aware of the liability involved within the industry and take appropriate measures to mitigate those risks by thoroughly screening applicants, properly training and supervising employees, and maintaining adequate liability insurance.

Future trends in private security will likely be related to innovations in security technology, threats related to globalization, and continuing concerns over domestic and international terrorism. Advances in security technology, as well as threats of cyber-related attacks, will drive the need for highly trained and educated security professionals within the area of information technology (IT).

This will likely lead to a need for closer collaboration between private security, local law enforcement, and homeland security agencies in order to address threats that transcend jurisdictional boundaries. Ironically, this takes the private security industry back to its American roots under the Pinkerton agency, which grew out of a need to protect industry from threats that transcended state and international boundaries prior to the formation of the FBI. Specialized areas involving fraud investigations and computer-related investigations will likely continue to grow.

Jonathan M. Kremser
Kutztown University of Pennsylvania

See Also: 1851 to 1900 Primary Documents; Private Detectives; Private Police; Strikes; Terrorism.

Further Readings

Hess, K. M. *Introduction to Private Security,* 5th ed. Belmont, CA: Wadsworth, 2009.

Horan, J. *The Pinkertons: The Detective Dynasty That Made History*. New York: Bonanza Books, 1967.

Maggio, E. *Private Security in the 21st Century: Concepts and Applications*. Sudbury, MA: Jones & Bartlett, 2009.

Nemeth, C. P. *Private Security and the Law,* 3rd ed. Oxford: Elsevier Butterworth-Heinemann, 2004.

Spitzer, S. and A. T. Scull. "Privatization and Capitalist Development: The Case of the Private Police." *Social Problems*, v.25/1 (1977).

Weiss, R. "The Emergence and Transformation of Private Detective Industrial Policing in the United States, 1850–1940." *Crime and Social Justice,* v.9 (1978).

Probation

Probation is the most widely used sentencing option in the United States. The term *probation* derives from the Latin word *probatio* (meaning "period of proving" or "trial and forgiveness"), thus implying that an offender must prove himself/herself through a specified period of time (the length and term of probation) by complying with the terms and conditions of probation. According to the Bureau of Justice Statistics, of the 7.2 million persons under correctional supervision (including both community-based corrections and institutional corrections) at year-end 2009, 58 percent were on probation (4.2 million). Approximately half of all persons on probation at year-end 2009 were being supervised for a conviction for a felony offense. Probation is a community-based sanction that affords the convicted offender an opportunity to remain in the community with the possibility to receive therapeutic support programs as an alternative to going to prison. Persons sentenced to probation are subject to terms and conditions ordered by the court or other governing body. Probation allows the offender to remain in the community subject to terms and conditions imposed by the court and is an alternative to incarceration. Probation can be either unsupervised (in which the offender is not monitored) or supervised (in which the offender is monitored by a probation officer or other community corrections professional).

Reasons for Probation
There are a number of advantages and disadvantages associated with probation. First and foremost, probation is more cost-effective than incarceration. Nationwide, the average cost per day to house an offender in a jail or prison is $62 per day, far more than $2 to $3 per day for probation. Probation offers a reduced criminalization of offenders as they are not subject to socialization with more hardened offenders behind bars. Community-based corrections allow the offender to maintain his/her family ties, as parents on probation are able to remain in the home to raise their children (whereas incarcerating the parent may result in the children being placed with other family members or foster care). Because probation affords an offender the opportunity to work, thereby providing for his/her family as well as paying restitution, court costs, and fees, and contributing to the tax base, probation is advantageous as the offender is contributing financially to society versus being a tax burden through the cost of incarceration, any public assistance his family may receive in his absence, and so on. Probation offers the offender a greater opportunity to receive therapeutic and professional services in the community. In prison, there are few programs available to offenders, and those that are available have limited availability based on the large numbers of offenders in prison seeking to participate in those programs.

A main disadvantage of probation is that it can be considered a lack of punishment. One of the widely held criticisms of probation is that the offender is allowed to reside in the community. That, coupled with the relatively nonrestrictive terms and conditions of probation, does not constitute a "real" punishment in the eyes of opponents, and there is no severity in the punishment.

Community-based corrections also have a social liability in that offenders remain in the community and often reoffend, sometimes committing violent acts. According to the Bureau of Justice Statistics, 35 percent of offenders recidivate, being rearrested for a subsequent offense after exiting probation (either having their probation revoked, terminated, or transferred to unsupervised probation).

Early Probation
Probation as a community-based sanction can trace its origins to the English courts in the 18th and 19th centuries. Judges had the discretion to grant what was deemed a judicial reprieve, thereby sparing the offender from incarceration by suspending his/her sentence if the judge deemed there was no purpose served by incarcerating the offender. This practice was adopted in the American colonies. In Boston, Judge Peter Oxenbridge Thatcher employed judicial leniency by allowing offenders to be released from custody on their own recognizance (their verbal or written promise to appear in court if need be) either before or after they were convicted. In 1841, John Augustus, a Boston shoemaker and a member of the temperance movement against alcohol, often visited the Boston courts to observe the daily hearings, operations, and business of the courts. There, Augustus often intervened on behalf of offenders charged with being a public drunkard; he observed that many offenders were held over for court or remained in custody because they could not afford to pay the fine or other monetary assessment ordered by the court. Augustus then decided to approach judges and asked if they would consider releasing the offender if Augustus promised to "monitor" him/her while he/she was released and ensure that he/she did not get in further trouble. Augustus also attempted to rehabilitate alcoholics and assisted those arrested for alcohol-related offenses. It is estimated that by the time of his death in 1859, Augustus supervised 2,000 offenders, both men and women, over the years, and thus Augustus is widely considered to be the "father" of modern probation.

After Augustus's death, another Boston philanthropist, Rufus R. Cook, continued Augustus's work through the Children's Aid Society and assisted juvenile offenders. Benjamin C. Clark volunteered as well to continue Augustus's work. Boston led the nation in establishing probation as a statutory sanction in that the first state law prescribing for probation was passed

Probation officers from the Anchorage Probation Enhanced Supervision Unit display a bag of cash found in a search of an offender's apartment. When the offender denied access to his apartment, the officers returned with a search warrant and found $30,000 in cash and cocaine. The offender was remanded and the case was forwarded for new criminal offenses.

in Massachusetts in 1878, granting the mayor of Boston the authority to hire the first probation officer, a retired police officer, Captain Edward Savage, who became a full-time paid probation officer. By 1925, probation was available for juveniles in every state and for every adult by 1956. The growth of probation at this time can be credited to the attitudes and beliefs held during the Progressive Era, when, in an effort to address the challenges of crime and deviance, reformers advocated strategies to rehabilitate offenders rather than house them in correctional institutions. Alternatives to incarceration such as probation, parole, and indeterminate sentencing, which afforded offenders the option to secure their freedom if they made strides in reforming their lives, proliferated.

Probation Standards

Although the terms and conditions vary from jurisdiction to jurisdiction and offender to offender (based on the offense, the offender's challenges, and other factors), there are standard conditions of probation (required of all offenders, regardless of the their offense, special needs, or previous convictions). These conditions require the offender to be gainfully employed or enrolled in a program of study; commit no criminal offense and notify the court and/or probation officer if charged with a new offense; pay a fine, cost of court, restitution, or other fees; report as directed to the court, probation official, or other community corrections professional; notify officials of any change in address and/or employment; not possess any illegal weapons; maintain family obligations (e.g., child support); and remain within the court's jurisdiction unless given permission to leave by the court and/or probation officer. Punitive conditions of probation are those that increase the punishment of the offender based on the severity of the offense. Therefore, the offender may be sentenced to complete community service hours as a condition of probation or be required to be on curfew or be placed on intensive probation (a more restrictive form of probation). Treatment conditions of probation (such as requiring the offender to participate in substance abuse treatment or mental health counseling) attempt to reverse the offender's self-destructive behavior.

There are three primary types of probation: supervised probation, unsupervised probation, and intensive supervision probation. Intensive supervision probation (ISP) is a more restrictive form of probation in which the offender is subject to additional terms and conditions and closer monitoring of his/her behavior. ISP was first implemented in Georgia in 1982 in response to the state's incarceration rate (it was the highest per capita rate of any state). The overcrowded conditions in Georgia's prisons were spilling over into the local jails, and thus the state had to develop probation programs that were effective alternatives to incarceration. While the model for ISP varies from state to state, it typically involves the use of two probation parole officers (oftentimes a probation officer and a surveillance officer) who work together to monitor the offender. Whereas an offender on regular probation has one encounter with his/her probation officer once per month (or in some instances, once every other month), an offender on ISP sees his/her offender several times per week. In addition, these offenders are typically subject to curfew, which is closely monitored by the two-person team, and are required to complete more community service hours than an offender on regular supervised probation. They are subject to searches of their person, premises, and vehicle (a condition that is typically ordered only in special circumstances for regular probation). ISP officers typically have smaller caseloads (an average of 30) than do regular supervision probation officers (the recommended average is 90), allowing ISP officers more time to dedicate to the close monitoring of offenders.

There are five models of probation (the manner to describe the relationship between the probation officer and the client). These models are the treatment model, the rehabilitation model, the due process model, the just-deserts model, and the community model. The treatment model, sometimes referred to as the medical model, makes the assumption that criminal behavior is somewhat like an illness, and if the cause of the illness is addressed, then the offender will be less likely to engage in criminal behavior again. The treatment model aims to remedy the offender's illness. The rehabilitation model stresses reforming the offender through rehabilitation. The due-process model, which is sometimes referred to as the justice model, stresses fair and equitable treatment of all offenders, regardless of extralegal factors such as race, socioeconomic status, or gender. The just-deserts model emphasizes that the punishment should be equitable with the severity of the crime and that offenders should get their "just" or rightful punishment, or the punishment that they deserve based on their offense. The idea is that the more serious the offender's crime is, the more restrictive his/her probation or level of supervision should be. Finally, the community model, sometimes referred to as the reintegration model, focuses on preparing the offender to return to the community and thereby equipping the offender with appropriate resources to reintegrate (i.e., providing resources for counseling and stable living environments). There are three conceptual models of intensive supervision probation: the justice model, the limited risk control model, and the treatment-oriented model. The justice model seeks to be punishment centered, yet fair to the offender. This model emphasizes daily or near-daily contact with the offender, community service, and if applicable, restitution or reparations to the victim. This model does not address rehabilitation for the offender. The limited risk control model is based on an offender's anticipated criminal behavior. A risk assessment is conducted to determine which level of supervision is appropriate for the offender and takes into account the offender's previous criminal history, current criminal offense, and the risk he poses to the community based on the same. Finally, the treatment-oriented model focuses on rehabilitation of the offender in an effort to reintegrate the offender into the community.

Mechanics of Probation

Probation is typically a suspended sentence. Once an offender is convicted of an offense, rather than incarcerate the offender, the judge can suspend his/her sentence and place him/her on probation. So long as the offender complies with the terms and conditions of his/her probation, he/she can remain free in the community. However, if the offender violates the terms and conditions of probation, his/her probation can be revoked, he/she can be remanded into an active sentence in jail or prison. In general, there are two types of violations of probation: technical violations and new offense violations. Technical violations are those in which the offender violates a technical condition of probation (such as maintaining full-time employment, adhering to curfew, or completing community service hours) and thus breaks the terms of probation. New offense violations involve the offender being arrested and/or convicted of a subsequent or new criminal offense. Of the offenders who have their probation revoked and are sent back to jail, it is estimated that one-third commit new offense violations while two-thirds commit technical violations. Probation officers typically have the responsibility for determining whether the offender has violated the terms and conditions of probation.

Although the U.S. Supreme Court held in *Griffin v. Wisconsin* (1987) that probationers do not have the same rights as other members of society and that the probationer's freedom is conditional contingent on his/her compliance with special restrictions, offenders do have certain due process rights, including the right to an attorney during the revocation process (*Mempa v. Rhay,* 1967). In addition, the Supreme Court, through *Morrissey v. Brewer* (1972) and *Gagnon v. Scarpelli* (1973), ruled that the probation revocation hearings must include a three-stage procedure, affording offenders limited due process rights that must be protected. Per the landmark decisions, offenders must be afforded a preliminary hearing, a probation revocation hearing, and a revocation sentencing hearing.

At the preliminary hearing, a "disinterested person" (such as a judge or an administrative hearing officer) determines if there is probable cause to revoke the probation. In other words, whether the facts and circumstances cause a reasonable person to believe that the offender likely violated the terms and conditions of his/her probation. If, at the preliminary hearing, probable cause has been found, the probation officer (or other representative of the supervising agency) presents evidence to support the contention that the offender violated the terms and conditions of probation. At this hearing, the offender has the right to know the charges being alleged against him/her, the right to present witnesses on his/her behalf, and the right to confront witnesses against him/her. At this stage, a neutral and detached body, such as a judge or an administrative hearing officer, makes a decision in favor of the probation officer or the offender. If the decision is made to revoke the offender's probation, then the judge must decide whether to remand the offender to a period of incarceration in a jail or prison and for what length of time. The judge can also decide whether to keep the offender on probation and possibly make modifications to the terms and conditions (e.g., require additional community service hours, impose additional sanctions such as a term in boot camp, sentence the offender to a weekend in jail, and so forth).

Administration of Probation

There are a number of challenges in effective administration of probation that impact the effectiveness of supervision by probation/parole officers. Sex offenders present a problem for probation and parole and require unique programming and policies. Megan's Law and other similar statutes require convicted sex offenders to register with local law enforcement; law enforcement officials are in turn required to notify the community of the offender's presence. Because many communities do not want sex offenders residing nearby, probation officers not only face the possibility of the sex offender re-offending, they also have to protect the offender from vigilante behavior by community members. Special needs offenders such as sex offenders also pose a challenge for probation in that probation agencies have created specialized caseloads and special programs to target these offenders. For example, the North Carolina Department of Correction, Division of Community Corrections created specialized caseloads in which all sex offenders were supervised by the same officer (or officers). States must also deal with a lack of access to adequate mental health facilities for these offenders, and probation officers are sometimes underprepared or undertrained to work with certain categories of offenders such as sex offenders or mentally ill offenders.

Another challenge of probation is the lack of public confidence in probation and the perception that probation is too lenient. According to the American Probation and Parole Association (APPA), between 43 percent and 65 percent of offenders sentenced to probation are either arrested during probation/parole or within three years of their probation sentence. Only 57 percent of offenders sentenced to probation successfully complete their sentences. Because of the recidivism rate and relatively low successful completion of probation, there is a perception that probation is ineffective.

Terrorism is another challenge for probation officers. While it is doubtful that most terrorist activities will warrant a probation sentence, offenders who have been convicted of funding these organizations and offenders with terrorist ties have been placed on probation, and extremist domestic terrorist organizations have members who are on probation and/or parole. Further, probation officers may be instrumental in knowing their offenders' affiliations with various organizations and other associates, which may prove useful for counterterrorism efforts.

Budget cuts have resulted in challenges for agencies. These cuts result in staffing issues and problems ensuring that officers have appropriate resources (equipment, training). Although the number of persons placed on probation has increased, funding of these agencies has not—in some places, it has declined. As such, many probation officers have caseloads that exceed the American Probation and Parole Association recommendation that regular probation supervision caseloads be no greater than 90 offenders for every officer. In some jurisdictions, there are 352 offenders for every officer. When officers have that many cases, the quality of supervision suffers, and probation officers suffer stress and burnout. This can impact the probation officer in terms of physical and emotional health and can often result in high turnover rates of probation officers, which can result in a lack of or lapse in supervision or in offenders being supervised by less experienced probation officers.

Today, many of the offenders placed on probation are violent offenders or felons and suffer from mental and behavioral health challenges, as well as substance abuse issues. As such, probation officer safety is a concern. Probation officers often go into high-crime neighborhoods to visit their offenders (often with multiple offenders residing in the same neighborhood. Supervision standards in many jurisdictions require probation officers to visit the offender in the community at night and on weekends, exposing them to risks.

In the United States, the responsibility for the administration of probation services varies from jurisdiction to jurisdiction. At the federal level, the U.S. Probation Office is responsible for administering probation in each of the U.S district courts. At the state level, probation and parole can be administered through the state's executive branch of government, state judicial agencies, or local executive or judicial agencies. In some states, probation is administered by a combination of these agencies and organizations or may even be a private function, contracted by the states to a private organization.

Conclusion

Probation officers typically have the responsibility for the supervision of offenders sentenced to probation. Depending on the jurisdiction, these officers may be sworn law enforcement officers with the power to arrest and carry firearms. These officers monitor the progress of the offender on probation and report any violations to the court or other sentencing authority, represent the probation agency in matters against the offender, and make recommendations to the court in terms of whether probation should be revoked or continued. Probation officers are responsible for conducting office visits with the offender (meeting with the offender in the office to discuss his/her compliance with the terms and conditions of probation). Probation officers are often responsible for searching an offender, his/her residence, and/or his/her vehicle per the terms and conditions of probation, conducting curfew checks and subsequent criminal record checks, searching for new arrests and convictions, and verifying an offender's employment, residence, and school enrollment. In order to do this, probation officers conduct field visits, in which they visit the offender at his residence, place of employment, or school. During a field visit, a probation officer is able to verify and assess the suitability of an offender's residence, employment, or school enrollment.

Nicola Davis Bivens
Johnson C. Smith University

See Also: Community Service; Parole; Sex Offenders; Terrorism.

Further Readings

American Probation Parole Association. "Adult Probation in the United States." http://www2.courtinfo.ca.gov/probation (Accessed February 2011).

Champion, Dean J. *Probation, Parole, and Community Corrections*, 6th ed. Upper Saddle River, NJ: Pearson Prentice Hall, 2007.

Glaze, Lauren E. *Correctional Populations in the United States 2009*. Washington, DC: Bureau of Justice Statistics, 2010.

Glaze, Lauren E. and Thomas P. Bonczar. *Probation and Parole in the United States, 2006*. Washington, DC: Bureau of Justice Statistics, 2007.

Rothman, David J. *Conscience and Convenience: The Asylum and Its Alternatives in Progressive America*. New York: Walter de Gruyter, 2002.

Schmalleger, Frank and John Ortiz Smykla. *Corrections in the 21st Century*, 5th ed. New York: McGraw-Hill Higher Education, 2009.

Siegal, Larry and Clemens Bartollas. *Corrections Today*. Belmont, CA: Cengage, 2011.

Proclamation for Suppressing Rebellion and Sedition of 1775

The Proclamation for Suppressing Rebellion and Sedition, more simply referred to as the Proclamation of Rebellion, was a formal statement issued on August 23, 1775, by King George III (1738–1820) of Great Britain that characterized as rebellious the actions of American colonists that would eventually erupt as the American Revolution. Tensions between the American colonists and the British government had been worsening for decades prior to the proclamation. Those considered patriots by the Americans were, according to the Proclamation of Rebellion, considered rebels and criminals by the British. John Hancock (1738–93), for example, was regarded as a smuggler as evidenced by the seizure by the British of his ship *Liberty*. Paul Revere (1735–1818) was considered to be a subversive by acts like his engraving of the Boston Massacre titled "The Bloody Massacre." Settlers along the frontier, beyond the Proclamation Line established by another royal decree, the Royal Proclamation of 1763, to protect Native American–held lands, were regarded as little more than squatters.

After the First Continental Congress met in September 1774 in Philadelphia to discuss what were considered oppressive actions by the British Parliament, such as the Coercive Acts, known by the colonists as the "Intolerable Acts," colonists in Massachusetts organized groups of minutemen to collect stores of weapons to prepare for armed defense to protect their rights. By early 1775, conditions in the American colonies had deteriorated to the point where many colonists felt that there were concerted efforts on the part of the British colonial government attempting to deny them their rights as Englishmen, such as those established in 1215 by the Magna Carta. Some colonials were so incensed that they chose to actively take up arms against the British authorities and troops. Notable hostile outbreaks at that time included the shots fired in April 1775 at Lexington and Concord; the seizure of cannons and ammunition at Fort Ticonderoga and Fort Crown Point on Lake Champlain by a force led by Ethan Allen (1738–89) and Benedict Arnold (1741–1801) in May 1775; and the Battle of Bunker Hill in Boston in June 1775. These sorts of military incidents led to the urging by royal advisers to have George III, king of Great Britain and Ireland, openly express his displeasure at such "disorderly acts." These sentiments resulted in the issuance of the Proclamation of Rebellion.

The Proclamation for Suppressing Rebellion and Sedition is actually a rather short statement. It consists of one page of a little over 400 words. It was printed under a copy of the royal arms. The Proclamation of Rebellion ordered that "utmost endeavours" should be used by British authorities to "withstand and suppress such rebellion." The inflammatory tone of the Proclamation of Rebellion has been considered as contributing to the full outbreak of the American Revolution.

Prior to the issuing of this Royal Proclamation, there was not much open discussion by American colonists about possible independence from Great Britain. However, after this direct statement from the very highest level of the British government, in which what many colonists considered as justified responses were regarded as "treasons and traitorous conspiracies" by the Crown, many were moved toward revolution. The directness of the Proclamation of Rebellion, in fact, left little opportunity for reconciliation, such as had been offered in July 1775 by the "Olive Branch Petition" sent by the delegates of the Second Continental Congress. This message had been proffered by the conservative delegates, such as John Dickinson (1732–1808) of Pennsylvania, proclaiming loyalty to the Crown but dissatisfaction with the actions of governmental ministers. In addition, the Second Continental Congress also sent in July 1775 a "Declaration of the Causes and Necessity of Taking Up Arms" to King George III.

In the Proclamation of Rebellion, King George III strongly stated that the leaders of resistance to his rule were "dangerous and ill designing men" who were to be considered traitors to be captured and punished as they were clearly in "open and avowed rebellion." The bluntness of the Proclamation of Rebellion helped persuade many of the formerly loyal colonists that rebellion was the only course of action left. Most of the more moderate delegates to the Second Continental Congress were persuaded by the tone of the Proclamation of Rebellion to then side with the more radical members, like John Adams (1735–1826) of Massachusetts, who were arguing for independence. This eventually led to the drafting of the Declaration of Independence and the resulting American Revolutionary War.

Victor B. Stolberg
Essex County College

See Also: 1600 to 1776 Primary Documents; American Revolution and Criminal Justice; Colonial Courts; Declaration of Independence.

Further Readings
Ferling, John. *Independence: The Struggle to Set America Free*. London: Bloomsbury Publishing, 2011.
George III. "Proclamation for Suppressing Rebellion and Sedition." http://www.lexrex.com/enlightened/laws/rebel_proc.htm (Accessed December 2010).
Tuchman, Barbara W. *The March of Folly: From Troy to Vietnam*. New York: Ballantine Books, 1985.

The bluntness of the Proclamation of Rebellion convinces many colonists to side with more radical members like John Adams (above), eventually leading to the Declaration of Independence.

Procunier v. Martinez

Procunier v. Martinez (1974) established limits on prisons' rights to censor mail to and from inmates and established prisoners' rights to meet with law students and legal paraprofessionals who are working on the prisoner's behalf. The case was a significant milestone in American law because it extended limited constitutional rights to prisoners under the First and Fourteenth Amendments.

In *Procunier*, the court ruled on the constitutionality of California Department of Corrections regulations that gave prison personnel significant powers to censor prisoners' mail. The prisoners, who were the appellees, brought a class-action suit, charging that prisons routinely used mail censorship to silence, suppress, or discourage prisoner complaints, to censor inflammatory political or social opinions, and to censor lewd or obscene communications. Prisons screened both incoming and outgoing mail under these regulations. The appellees argued that these regulations violated their First Amendment free speech rights. Prior to *Procunier*, U.S. courts had taken disparate approaches to the issue of censoring prisoners' mail. No generally accepted standard had been established to test the constitutionality of such actions. Justice Lewis Powell, writing for the majority, set out to clarify a test for constitutionality as applied to prisoner mail censorship.

The court also acknowledged the relevance in this case of the existence of First Amendment and Fourteenth Amendment rights for third parties outside the prison who wished to communicate with prisoners. The court sought to balance the needs of prisons to maintain necessary control over the inmate population with the inmate's First Amendment rights and the First Amendment rights of those who are not prisoners but who are communicating with inmates. The *Procunier* decision acknowledged that prisoners' constitutional rights are limited, compared to non-inmates. It agreed that censoring prisoners' mail could be justifiable in certain circumstances, so long as such censorship advanced penological interests that were not founded on suppressing expression. The court posited mail concerning escape plans or criminal activities as examples of mail worthy of censorship by prison authorities.

Balancing the various interests, the court set a two-pronged test for the constitutionality of prison mail censorship. First, censorship must further an important or substantial government interest in security, order, and rehabilitation. Such censorship must be unrelated to the suppression of expression. In other words, prison officials may not censor mail simply because they disagree or disapprove of the contents. Second, the censorship should be no greater than necessary to protect the particular governmental interest involved. This sets limits on the scope of censorship and restricts broad, sweeping censorship practices. Next, the court held that the decision to censor or withhold delivery of prisoner mail must be done in accordance with minimal procedural safeguards. Prisoners must be notified of such actions. The letter's author must be allowed to appeal the rejection to some official other than the one who made the initial censorship decision. The appellees also charged that California's ban on the use of law students and legal paraprofessionals to conduct attorney-client interviews with inmates violated the inmates' right to counsel. Only licensed attorneys were permitted to interview inmates. Attorneys could not even delegate basic paperwork tasks, such as obtaining a prisoner's signature on a form.

The court had held five years earlier in *Johnson v. Avery* that prisoners have the right to legal assistance from fellow inmates. The *Procunier* decision held that California's restrictions violated prisoners' rights to due process, of access to the courts, and to legal representation. In 1974, the same year the court decided *Procunier v. Martinez*, it held in *Pell v. Procunier* that prisoners do not have a right to interviews with reporters. In *Houchins v. KQED* (1978) the court extended such restrictions to include other people outside the prison. In *Jones v. North Carolina Prisoners Labor Union* (1977), the court upheld restrictions that prohibited inmates from engaging in labor organizing activities and also upheld prison censorship of mail related to labor activism. In *Bell v. Wolfish* (1979), the court upheld a New York regulation that limited prisoners to receiving hardbound books only from established publishers or book vendors. In *Turner v. Safley* (1987), the court upheld Missouri prison regulations prohibiting mail between inmates in state prisons and established a more lenient standard for testing First Amendment constitutionality of mail censorship than did *Procunier*. In *Thornburg v. Abbott* (1989), the court upheld federal prison restrictions on prisoners' mail access to books or subscriptions to periodicals.

Procunier established a high-water mark for prisoners' First Amendment rights under American constitutional jurisprudence. Since *Procunier*, the Supreme Court has gradually eroded its conception of prisoners' rights as laid out under *Procunier*.

Thomas F. Brown
Virginia Wesleyan College

See Also: *Johnson v. Avery*; Penitentiaries; Prisoner's Rights.

Further Readings

Anderson, James F., et al. *Significant Prisoner Rights Cases*. Durham, NC: Carolina Academic Press, 2010.

Easton, Susan. *Prisoners' Rights: Principles and Practice*. London: Routledge, 2011.

Hudson, David L. *Prisoners' Rights*. New York: Chelsea House, 2007.

Palmer, John W. *Constitutional Rights of Prisoners*. Cincinnati, OH: Anderson Publishing, 2010.

Procunier v. Martinez, 416 U.S. 396 (1974).

Professionalization of Police

The development of professional standards for American policing, as well as the advancement of the concept of policing as a profession, developed during the early decades of the 20th century in reaction to various problems and challenges encountered by early municipal-level police agencies during that time. Police professionalism remains an evolving, and to a certain extent subjective, concept.

Tenets of Police Professionalism

There is some debate as to whether policing constitutes a profession at all and instead might be more accurately deemed an occupation or job. Even within law enforcement, there is disagreement surrounding what precisely defines professionalism, and whether those criteria can be objectively measured or are merely subjective. Certainly, one challenge in examining the professionalization of policing is determining precisely what police professionalism entails.

The term *professional* is generally reserved for members of occupations that require an elevated level of education and training; the command of a specific, relevant skill set; and a sense of identity and fellowship among their members. Professionals possess a personal dedication to the goals, ideals, and standards of that profession and have internalized a set of principles of performance and behavior that often extend beyond the workplace into other aspects of their lives.

Development of Police Professionalism

The first municipal-level law enforcement agencies emerged during the mid- to late 19th century in the major urban centers of the northeast and midwest, and the concept of full-time police departments designed to control crime and disorder gradually spread to communities throughout the nation. Many of these fledgling police departments, however, faced major challenges as they struggled to establish themselves, define their goals and responsibilities, and earn public trust and respect.

The most significant challenge faced by emerging police departments was a complete lack of recruitment, selection, and training standards. Many departments did not have stringent criteria regarding who would make a suitable police officer. Once hired, officers were not offered any kind of systematic training regimen or much guidance in terms of how to enforce law, interact with the public, or generally conduct themselves. Compounding these problems was the disturbing reality that in many municipalities, police and politics became inextricably intertwined; policing jobs and promotions were offered as rewards for actively supporting particular candidates, and jobs could be lost for associating with a losing candidate. Officers had very little supervision while out on patrol, and their assigned beats were often too large to be able to patrol efficiently during those pre-automobile days. Officers were vulnerable to corruption, and police supervisors had few mechanisms to adequately control the problem. In addition to the instability of the job itself, many officers experienced low pay and few, if any, benefits.

Influenced by the wide-ranging efforts of the Progressives, who during the late 19th and early 20th centuries engaged in activism that addressed political corruption and numerous other social ills that impacted many aspects of American life, police reformers worked to address perceived flaws in policing. The International Association of Chiefs of Police (IACP), which formed in 1893, was one of the first established professional organizations in the field and was especially vocal in its recommendations to untangle politics and policing and develop more clear and consistent recruitment, selection, and promotion standards. Meanwhile, investigative commissions identified specific problems plaguing police departments and issued recommendations to resolve them.

The most famous of these, the Wickersham Commission, convened in 1929 and issued its *Wickersham Commission Report* in 1931. One section of the report, "The Police" (authored primarily by August Vollmer), critiqued the lack of professionalism that was epidemic in police departments during that time and recommended refining hiring standards and improving officer pay, benefits, and access to necessary equipment and other resources. Another section, "Lawlessness in Law Enforcement," discussed the serious problems of police corruption and brutality and the lack of officer supervision and discipline.

Advocates of police professionalism in the early 20th century urged major changes in many aspects of policing. They insisted upon the complete removal of political patronage from policing. They focused on numerous personnel issues: Officers should be well trained and carefully supervised, and all hiring or promotion decisions should be based on merit alone, not political affiliation or arbitrary whim. They recommended a shift in policing focus. Crime fighting should be the primary task of police, and their success at this task would serve as an objective measure of police effectiveness. Meanwhile, all laws should be enforced equally, without bias or prejudice; police discretion should be minimized. Finally, police should take advantage of all technological innovations that would aid them in their crime-fighting mission. During this period, in fact, the development and/or increased availability of patrol cars and two-way radios greatly aided law enforcement in this renewed effort to fight crime.

Influential Early Proponents

Referred to as the "father of modern police professionalism," August Vollmer is a towering figure in the evolution of the modern police department and a pioneer in the development in police professional standards. While serving as the chief of police in Berkeley, California, from 1905 to 1932 (with a brief departure to serve as chief of the Los Angeles Police Department from 1923 to 1924), Vollmer pioneered many approaches to police hiring, training, and practice that are commonplace today. He emphasized the importance of a standardized, rigorous, academy-based training regimen for all recruits; to this end, he founded the Berkeley Police School in 1908, which was one of the first police academies in the country. This academy taught recruits a variety of subjects, including criminal law and procedure, police psychology, forensics techniques, and police administration. He later advocated the creation of regional training academies throughout the nation. Furthermore, believing that police work was, in his words, the "highest calling in the world," he felt that a college education would develop the type of intellect and character that was necessary to do the job well, and he made a special effort to recruit the college educated. Vollmer was a strong believer in improving the diversity of the police force, so as to better represent the community, and was a proponent of the hiring of African American and female recruits. He was a major figure in the academic study of police science at the college level and in fact helped develop (as well as taught at) the School of Criminology at the University of California, Berkeley. Vollmer was a strong advocate of incorporating new technologies whenever they could allow police officers to do their jobs more effectively; his department was among the first to utilize radio communications, automobile and motorcycle patrols, and forensic techniques such as fingerprint analysis. Indeed, he helped found one of the nation's first crime labs.

Orlando W. (O. W.) Wilson was a criminology student and disciple of August Vollmer at University of California, Berkeley. Already an officer in the Berkeley Police Department during his student days, he devoted the remainder of his professional life to law enforcement, at various points serving as chief of police in Fullerton, California (1925–27), and Wichita, Kansas (1928–39), as well as superintendent of police in Chicago (1960–67). He was a great advocate of improved police professionalism, which to him meant creating and enforcing tougher recruitment and training standards; like August Vollmer, for example, he preferred recruits to be college educated. Also like Vollmer, he utilized technological innovations for police work, introducing at various points the use of automobile patrols, two-way radios, and a mobile crime lab that could be accessed in the field. Wilson worked to improve professionalism in long-established departments as well.

While serving as police superintendent in Chicago in the aftermath of a serious scandal that rocked the department, decimated officer morale, and undermined police-community relations, Wilson instituted more stringent hiring guidelines, initiated a nationwide recruiting drive, and offered higher salaries to attract a better standard of applicants. He also introduced numerous measures to ferret out corruption and misconduct. In order to ensure that the best-qualified people had access to supervisory positions, he launched an improved merit system for promotions. Following in the philosophical footsteps of his mentor August Vollmer, Wilson was also a major proponent of the academic study of criminology and police methodology, even serving as the dean of the School of Criminology at University of California, Berkeley (1950–60). Perhaps his most influential contribution to the profession was his insistence on the careful evaluation and assessment of entrenched policing policies and practices; he conducted, for example, the first systematic study of the effectiveness of one-officer patrol vehicles and later examined ways to enhance the efficiency of automobile patrols and improve police response times.

Consequences of Professionalism

Policing agencies witnessed a number of significant changes in the early 20th century, and many of these shifts in policing philosophy and strategy brought unexpected consequences. The biggest criticism of how the professionalism movement manifested itself in policing practice was that it emphasized the importance of officers maintaining a "professional distance" from the community they served. Officers were discouraged from interacting with the public more than necessary in order to avoid becoming too familiar with members of the community, which might lead to favoritism or unequal treatment or somehow make the officer more vulnerable to offers of bribes and other forms of corruption. It was for the same reasons that during this time, rotating shifts and beat assignments became commonplace. Meanwhile, the greater emphasis on crime fighting, prevalence of patrol cars, and improved communications in the field meant that patrol officers were expected to spend their shifts quickly responding to calls for service and making arrests, and interacting little with the community otherwise.

Over time, critics alleged, officers became so isolated from the community that they were, in essence, outsiders, and this shaped feelings of hostility and distrust among the public. Furthermore, as a result of being so removed from the people of the neighborhoods they patrolled, officers lacked awareness of their unique issues and problems, and this made responding to crime and controlling disorder a greater challenge. This became most dramatically evident beginning in the early to mid-1960s and culminating in the latter part of that decade, when police in urban areas were increasingly called upon to respond to scenes of civil unrest or disturbances stemming from civil rights or antiwar protests. Many police agencies found they had fallen into the "trap of technology," in which their reliance on patrol vehicles and central dispatch effectively removed the officers from the kinds of regular interactions with the populace that can better inform policing strategy and response.

Policing's Current Status

What are currently considered to be the defining qualities of a profession, and does policing have these qualities? There isn't a consensus on either matter. Even within law enforcement, individual police officers may disagree as to whether policing constitutes a profession, or what particular elements might define policing as such. This is a critical issue, as professionalism generally entails a near-universal agreement among members regarding the distinguishing characteristics of that profession, including a devotion to shared goals, a commitment to pursuing a particular level of training and expertise, and an adherence to a clear set of performance and conduct standards. Regardless, researchers have highlighted a number of characteristics believed to be common to professions and have debated the extent to which law enforcement possesses them.

A profession might be identified as an occupation that, while fulfilling some critical societal need and largely acting in the public interest (although it may indeed revolve around the needs of a particular client base), is also viewed as a personal calling by those within it. Indeed, members of a profession may constitute a unique subculture to which they are completely immersed and greatly devoted. Much research on policing has been devoted to exploring these issues, and the unique nature of the policing subculture has been

Regional police training academies exist throughout the United States. Recruits experience a standardized, rigorous, academy-based training regimen.

a frequent subject of interest. Policing is ostensibly devoted to the greater public good, although officers may be called upon to make very difficult decisions, which would seem to not be in the best interests of particular individuals (i.e., the use of deadly force, or employing any type of physical force to obtain suspect compliance) but which are intended to preserve society's best interests.

Professions are also expected to develop (and carefully supervise) recruitment, selection, training, and performance standards for their members. Recruitment and selection criteria within policing have become fairly consistent across agencies, with some individual variations depending on the size and unique circumstances of the agency. Academy and field training are fairly standardized as well. All of these are changes that occurred gradually during the course of the 20th century as a result of the professionalism movement. Performance standards have been more difficult to develop and universally implement but may include the evaluation of such criteria as crime rates, arrest rates, number of tickets or citations issued, citizen satisfaction surveys, supervisor or peer evaluations of officer performance, response time to calls for service, commendations or other forms of positive recognition earned by officers, number of disciplinary actions taken against officers, and/or number of formal complaints filed against a department or particular officers.

Another possible element of a profession is the existence of a unique area of expertise that is attainable through higher education. This is a separate issue from the standardized academy and field training that is near-universal for police recruits. The examination of the criminal justice system generally and police science in particular are recognized fields of academic study at the undergraduate and graduate level, but a degree—or even some college education—is not required by the vast majority of local-level law enforcement agencies. In many departments, however, recruits are encouraged to pursue higher education via the incentives of a higher starting salary and/or pay grade or enhanced opportunities for specialized assignments or advancement within the organization, and top administrators are often expected to possess at least an undergraduate degree. Related to the academic study of law enforcement is another potential element of a profession, which is the existence of a body of professional and academic literature and an active body of research examining the practices and policies of the profession. Policing certainly meets this criterion, as there are numerous publications (including professional and peer-reviewed academic journals) targeted to police officers, academics, students, and the general public that actively disseminate current research on police policy methodology. It is difficult to assess, however, the degree to which rank-and-file officers are encouraged to familiarize themselves with this existing research or the extent to which it informs police practice.

Relatedly, a profession often entails a dedication to self-improvement through ongoing coursework, training, or in the case of the police department itself, internal and/or external evaluation and/or accreditation. Police departments routinely offer various in-service training opportunities to their officers, and such training will be required for officers seeking specialized assignments or administrative positions. Departments will, however, vary in terms of the breadth and complexity of in-service training opportunities available. The pursuit of accreditation—which entails meeting a set of standards that apply to numerous aspects of the operation of the police agency—is by no means universal and is, indeed, completely voluntary. The Commission on Accreditation for Law Enforcement Agencies (CALEA) is the standard accreditation body within policing. Agencies pursuing the accreditation process must submit an application and then conduct a self-study to determine whether they meet, or can implement, CALEA's accreditation standards.

Depending on the results of the self-study, the agency will then invite a team of outside assessors to objectively assess the agency's success at satisfying CALEA's criteria. Professional accreditation through CALEA is a significant achievement for any police department, and it can serve to elevate the agency's status within the law enforcement community and even among the general public. Perhaps most importantly, the existence of an accreditation process implies the authenticity of a set of universal standards for the operation of police agencies.

Another possible element of professionalism is the existence of professional organizations intended to further the interests of, as well as develop policy and standards of conduct for those within, a particular profession. In policing, there are organizations for top administrators such as the IACP. The majority of organizations targeted to lower-ranking officers, however, are social or fraternal in nature or are devoted to legal or collective bargaining issues.

The existence of a code of ethics is another feature that tends to characterize professions. These codes of ethics address not only how individuals are expected to conduct themselves while acting in the capacity of their profession but in all areas of their lives. Although the IACP has developed a code of ethics that it proposes be universally adopted, no common code of ethics yet exists within policing.

Professionals may be expected to be able to autonomously apply their expertise to a variety of scenarios while in the field and independently address problems and generate solutions, all with relatively little direct supervision. This would seem to be consistent with the current realities of patrol work, although increased levels of supervision, the development of explicit policies designed to address a greater variety of situations, and an emphasis on reduced officer discretion were all hallmarks of the professionalism movement of the early and mid-20th century.

Future of Police Professionalism

The refinement of professional standards in policing continues. There is an ongoing debate, for example, surrounding the value of higher education for police officers and whether a college degree (or at least some college education) should be required, and departments vary insofar as the availability of in-service training and officer involvement in professional organizations. The concept of professionalism itself has changed since the adoption of the ideals and standards of the reformers of the early 20th century.

Today, there is a focus on proactively exploring seemingly unrelated incidents to discern possible linkages and navigating the delicate territory of interpersonal interactions and community relations. As success in these areas is more difficult to objectively measure than comparing crime or response rates, assessing the level of professionalism of a particular department based on these sorts of criteria will prove to be a challenge in the future.

Miriam D. Sealock
Towson University

See Also: Automobile and the Police; Corruption, History of; Crime and Arrest Statistics Analysis; Crime Prevention; International Association of Chiefs of Police; Police Abuse; Reform, Police and Enforcement; Reform Movements in Justice; Training Police; Vollmer, August; Wickersham Commission; Wilson, O. W.

Further Readings

Carter, Lycia and Mark Wilson. "Measuring Police Professionalism of Police Officers." *Police Chief* (August 2006).

Glenn, Russell W., et al. *Training the 21st Century Police Officer: Redefining Police Professionalism for the Los Angeles Police Department*. Santa Monica, CA: RAND Corporation, 2003.

Jones, Mark. *Criminal Justice Pioneers in U.S. History*. Boston: Allyn & Bacon, 2005.

Walker, Samuel. *The New World of Police Accountability*. Thousand Oaks, CA: Sage, 2005.

Prohibition

National Prohibition came into effect across the United States at midnight on January 16, 1920. Passed by Congress in December 1917 and ratified by the requisite number of states by January 1919, the Eighteenth Amendment prohibited the "manufacture, sale, and transportation" of alcohol. There was strong voter support for the amendment within the context of mobilization for World War I—as dry supporters had successfully urged wartime bans on distilling and brewing as part of the food conservation programs—and from states that had enacted their own prohibition laws. Indeed, by the end of 1917, 18 states had adopted bone-dry laws that included prohibitions on personal use of alcohol. By 1919, 33 states had either statutory or constitutional prohibition.

Congress had passed the National Prohibition Enforcement, or Volstead Act, over President Woodrow Wilson's veto in October 1919. Drawing on existing state laws, it set out the terms of the federal Prohibition code. It outlawed the manufacture, sale, transportation, and possession of any "intoxicating liquor" (defined as any beverage that contained more than 0.5 percent alcohol) "except as authorized in this act." The act set out the regulations for the production and distribution of alcohol for industrial use and established a detailed permit system, which formed the basis for the continuing legal industry. Thus, church officials, doctors, pharmacists, industrial manufacturers, and others could still obtain alcohol under a heavily regulated system. There were also exemptions for possession of alcohol for personal consumption within an individual's private home and allowing the home fermentation of fruit juices.

Some of the seeds of Prohibition's failure lay in these exemptions. For example, one federal enforcement officer estimated that Chicago physicians had issued 300,000 bogus prescriptions for alcohol within the first six months of Prohibition. Several journalists delighted in the exposure of corrupt priests and rabbis abusing the exemptions for sacramental wine. Home production of wine and beer was a booming hobby across the United States, and male and female home brewers sold their product for a tidy profit. Through their political connections, the Genna brothers gang in Chicago obtained a permit to process industrial alcohol, which they did, into bootleg whiskey.

However, the Volstead Act still contained important differences from state prohibition laws. For example, Kansas had already been a dry state for 40 years before Prohibition was enacted and had bone-dry laws in force. Thus, there was no fixed alcoholic content in its laws defining intoxicating liquor, there were no medical exemptions, state search and seizure laws were tougher, and penalties—including life sentences for a fourth conviction by 1927—for persistent violators were harsher. Scholarship on Prohibition has traditionally tended to focus on the major northeastern cities, but there are a substantial number of local and state studies.

Enforcement

The Volstead Act divided responsibility for the enforcement of Prohibition between the Justice Department and the Treasury Department. Federal revenue officers were empowered to enforce the Volstead Act and the Justice Department handled the prosecution of violators. A Bureau of Prohibition was established as a subdivision of the Bureau of Internal Revenue, and Republican prosecutor Mabel Walker Willebrandt, the first female assistant attorney general, was appointed to run it from 1921 to 1929. However, the concurrent powers section of the Eighteenth Amendment also rested on the expectation that the states would actively enforce Prohibition. Most enacted supplementary liquor laws, like New York's Mullan-Gage Enforcement Law in April 1921.

Under the terms of the Eighteenth Amendment, the liquor industry had been given a year to wind up business, but this was also an important window for those planning to circumvent the new laws. Within minutes of Prohibition coming into effect, gangs had launched successful raids on government bonded liquor warehouses and hijacked trucks carrying medicinal and industrial liquor. Many saloons remained open and continued with business as usual. Alcohol consumption in the United States did fall in the early 1920s, probably by up to 40 percent, as a result of rising costs rather than effective enforcement but gradually rose throughout the rest of the decade.

Evasion

Sources of illegal alcohol were numerous, but in the popular image of the Prohibition years, its enjoyment is associated with a new fashionable but illegal drinking establishment, the speakeasy, and its rural and small-town equivalent, the roadhouse. Many had concealed entrances staffed by doormen and required passwords to enter. Owners installed collapsible shelves and hidden cellars to stymie raids. However, every speakeasy operator had to pay protection money to local police in order to remain in business, so that officers would ignore liquor violations and provide information about raids. High-end speakeasies were often glamorous and fashionable nightclubs where jazz musicians and exotic dancers entertained wealthy patrons drinking imported brand liquor. By contrast, the "shock houses" of the Bowery and Lower East Side served noxious liquor supplied by local "alky cookers" that induced gut rot, blindness, and even death. Ordinary citizens used a variety of methods to transport alcohol, including hip flasks, ladies' muffs, and baby carriages.

Liquor flowed into the United States from Canada and Mexico. Under phony bills of lading, it crossed international borders by railroad, truck, speedboat, and airplane, often with the assistance of customs officials and shipping clerks. Efforts to blockade the Detroit River, Hudson River, and overland routes had little effect. Innovative methods of concealment such as blocks of ice, hot water bottles, and rubber tires were swiftly adopted by a booming smuggling industry. A coastal "Rum Row" stretched the length of the east coast from Newfoundland to the Keys

Prohibition was a very controversial issue, as shown in "The Great Republican Reform Party Calling on their Candidate," an 1856 political cartoon about John C. Fremont, the first Republican party candidate for president of the United States. The man on the left states, "The first thing we want is a law making the use of Tobacco, Animal food, and Lager-bier a Capital Crime."

and Bahamas. International agreements during the 1920s extended American territorial waters from three nautical miles offshore to 12. Schooners packed with branded liquor waited outside the limit for customers in speedboats.

In the early 1920s, Rum Row was dominated by small independent operators like the legendary Bill McCoy, but they were soon squeezed out by larger organized syndicates, which began to monopolize all aspects of the illegal liquor industry. John Kobler described the ascendancy of New York gang bosses such as William "Big Bill" Dwyer, whose extensive operations included hotels, nightclubs, breweries, casinos, and racetracks in many parts of the United States. By 1923–24, Dwyer's payroll included purchasing agents, customs and Coast Guard officers, police, and Prohibition agents. He had also assembled a fleet of oceangoing vessels to ensure his lines of liquor supply remained open and efficient.

Andrew Sinclair argued that in the initial years of Prohibition, criminal gangs often provided protection and ensured delivery for ordinary brewery and distillery owners who had the necessary political contacts, as in the example of the Torrio gang and Chicago brewer Joseph Stenson, who netted up to $50 million in profits. However, the election of a reform mayor in 1924, a series of brewery raids and several arrests, and an assassination attempt on Torrio disrupted this arrangement. Respectable businessmen were edged out by increasingly powerful criminal syndicates.

Criticisms
The Anti-Saloon League (ASL), the Woman's Christian Temperance Union (WCTU), and their allies promised that a new nation would emerge in January 1920 when the United States became dry. The so-called noble experiment was intended to eradicate the social problems associated with drinking—alcoholism, domestic violence, poverty, unemployment, and low work productivity. A key target was the closure of the saloon, particularly the working-class ethnic or immigrant saloon, which many native-born ASL supporters considered to be a major impediment to assimilation. Dry advocates often linked the perceived inherent criminality of ethnic and nonwhite Americans to intemperance, and in the southern states, the "liquor question" became entwined with issues of race and the maintenance of white supremacy. Despite being portrayed as a rural, native-born, white, Protestant, middle-class goal, Prohibition nonetheless garnered significant support from different ethnic, religious, and racial groups. For example, it was linked with black racial uplift in the early 20th century.

Critics charged that the poor were most frequently arrested and jailed for bootlegging, while middle- and upper-class people bought and drank behind the protection of country clubs, political connections, and homes they owned. In his study of New York City, Michael Lerner found that Prohibition agents and the federal courts did make examples of wealthy defendants on occasion, but generally, wealthy upper-class elite Volstead violations were ignored, and enforcement efforts were directed at working-class drinking establishments and lower-class violators. As most of these defendants could not afford effective legal counsel, they were more likely to employ ineffective lawyers and be convicted or enter into plea bargains for reduced sentences and fines. The result was a two-tiered legal system. Further, the dry lobby quickly scapegoated ethnic Americans, Catholics, Jews, and African Americans for their disregard of the law and the consequent failures of Prohibition. During his unsuccessful presidential campaign in 1928, New York Governor Al Smith criticized the Eighteenth Amendment as an attack on immigrant customs and traditions by intolerant nativists and xenophobes.

The rise of celebrity bootleggers who violated the Volstead Act with impunity and seemed immune from prosecution reinforced the perception that the poor were being disproportionately targeted and confirmed that Prohibition was failing. As Claire Bond Potter observed, "By 1924, reformers, the press, and many civic leaders (both wet and dry) understood Prohibition as a moral and managerial failure that had produced a cynical, crime-ridden public, a network of powerful gangsters, and hypocrisy in government."

Initially, the Prohibition Bureau employed 1,550 agents in 18 administrative districts to police the Volstead Act and arrest those citizens who were willfully flouting federal laws. There were simply never enough agents to effectively police the massive territory of the United States. From the outset, Prohibition suffered also from a spectacular failure of presidential and congressional leadership, as President Warren G. Harding regularly played poker and drank with his Ohio political associates, and bootleggers supplied members on Capitol Hill. The Republican Congresses of the 1920s never voted for enough appropriations to adequately staff or equip the bureau, particularly with regard to the salaries and training that a professional police force required. The starting salary for a Volstead agent was $1,200 in 1920, rising to $2,300 by 1930. There were honest and efficient agents, including Izzy Einstein and Moe Smith in New York, and the incorruptible Eliot Ness in Chicago, but many others took bribes to supplement their incomes and to look the other way. As there was no civil service exam requirement until the later 1920s, many agents were political appointees with no knowledge of the law or how to enforce it. A 1927 attempt to professionalize the bureau floundered when employees were required to take the federal civil service exam and more than 40 percent failed, plus nearly 100 supervisors were demoted, dismissed, and transferred.

The bureau was supposed to be supported by more than 3,000 customs agents and special officers from several other government departments, as well as state police forces, highway patrols, and local sheriffs' officers, but many of these law enforcement officials had other offenses to investigate and were never committed to enforcing Prohibition. Further, in joint operations involving federal and local police, there was often no clear chain of command. States with a dry history like that of Kansas experienced Prohibition differently when compared to wet centers like New York City, New Orleans, and Chicago, and evidently did remain drier, yet liquor "rings," corrupt law enforcement, significant moonshine production, and public disregard for the law were found everywhere. By 1927, only a third of the 48 states continued to appropriate funds for state enforcement. New York had become the first state to repeal its state enforcement legislation in 1923, which in effect left enforcement to federal officers alone.

Bootlegging

While millions of Americans clearly resented federal and state efforts to regulate their behavior and continued to purchase and consume alcohol despite its illegality, speakeasies, bootlegging, and the violence of organized crime generated profound anxieties among local and state civil leagues, church groups, and others. It also enabled more extremist groups like the Ku Klux Klan to make political capital as champions of law and order. The Klan's projected image as guardians of white, native-born, American morality drew critical local electoral support for a short period in the early 1920s. Its rhetoric linked nativism, racism, anti-Semitism, and anti-Catholicism with lax law enforcement, widespread crime and disorder, and unchecked bootlegging and vice.

Gangs and urban crime syndicates rose to power through the saloons, gambling houses, and brothels of the 19th century but Prohibition enabled their expansion and monopolization of the illegal liquor market. Contemporary criminologist John Landesco argued Prohibition enormously increased the personnel and power of organized crime: "It had opened up a new criminal occupation, with less risk of punishment, with more certainty of gain, and with less social stigma than the usual forms of crime like robbery, burglary, and larceny." Figures such as Arnold Rothstein, "Dutch" Schultz, Charles "Lucky" Luciano, and Alphonse "Scarface" Capone built extensive crime syndicates on the profits of bootlegging and through a series of deadly gang wars in the mid- to late 1920s. They bought invaluable protection from politicians, judges, and police. The perpetrators of gang murders and bombings went unpunished because juries were either bought or too fearful to convict.

Guided initially by his onetime mentor Johnny Torrio, Capone built a large, disciplined, and ethnically diverse criminal organization that expanded from its key base in Cicero to establish control over Chicago through the elimination of rival gangs, violence, various forms of intimidation, political manipulation, and corruption. By the late 1920s, the Chicago Crime Commission estimated the Capone syndicate's profits at $60 million per year. Encouraged by the patronage of many respectable Americans, Capone presented himself as a reputable businessman who was merely catering to public demand. But a bevy of bodyguards surrounded him in public streets, hotel lobbies, at the racetracks, and in nightclubs he sat in an armor-plated swivel chair when at the "office," and his car was adorned with armor plating and bulletproof glass.

The failure to prosecute Capone for numerous bombings and murders during Chicago's beer wars, his ostentatious displays of wealth, and expressions of benevolence paid for with the profits from vice and bootlegging symbolized the impotency of national government. The Chicago Crime Commission's Subcommittee for the Prevention and Punishment of Crime, known as the "Secret Six," persuaded prosecutors to send Eliot Ness's team of "Untouchables" to Chicago to take on the Capone syndicate. The infamous 1929 St. Valentine's Day Massacre, in which seven associates of Capone's rival Bugs Moran were gunned down in a warehouse on Chicago's North Clark Street by gunmen hired by the Capone organization, and the murder of Assistant State Attorney William H. McSwiggin in Capone's headquarters at Cicero were major turning points in public attitudes.

Arguments for Repeal

There were increasing public demands for more aggressive law enforcement to curb the open gang warfare and violence that periodically exploded on city streets, and the New York Police Department (NYPD) instituted a number of get-tough anticrime measures in the late 1920s, including the use of dragnets and strong-arm squads. However, this led also to charges of increased police harassment and brutality, frequent use of the "third degree," and gross violations of the Fourth Amendment, as local police and Prohibition agents broke down doors and wiretapped private telephones in their pursuit of bootleggers.

In the late 1920s, the Association Against the Prohibition Amendment (AAPA) and Women's Organization for National Prohibition Reform (WONPR) convincingly argued that alcohol consumption was just as prevalent under Prohibition as during the pre-1920 period, that the nation was in the grip of an unprecedented crime wave, and that the government was losing valuable tax revenue to the bootleggers and racketeers. Shortly after taking up presidential office, Herbert Hoover appointed a national crime commission chaired by retired federal jurist George Wickersham to evaluate Prohibition enforcement and organized bootlegging. The Hoover administration also resolved to "get" Capone, which it did on income tax evasion charges in October 1931.

The establishment of the Wickersham Commission in 1930 was the beginning of the end of Prohibition, even though commissioners voted to continue with better enforcement (only two of 11 commissioners called for repeal). Nevertheless, they concluded that as a police force, the Bureau of Prohibition had failed, and that the trade in alcohol had not diminished.

Prohibition had turned tens of millions of otherwise law-abiding Americans into willing lawbreakers, and the resulting disrespect for the law was incalculable. The Wickersham Commission called it "a serious impairment of the legal order to have a national law upon the books ... which public opinion in many important centers will not enforce." Prohibition opponents argued that opening up distilleries and breweries would create much-needed jobs during the early years of the Great Depression. The ratification of the Twenty-First Amendment was a speedy affair with a certain result as disaffected drys and long-time wet supporters joined forces to ensure repeal by the end of 1933.

Vivien Miller
University of Nottingham

See Also: 1941 to 1960 Primary Documents; Capone, Al; Ness, Eliot; Volstead Act; Wickersham Commission.

Further Readings

Comte, Julien. "'Let the Federal Men Raid.'" *Pennsylvania History*, v.77 (2010).
Kavieff, Paul R. *The Purple Gang: Organized Crime in Detroit 1910–1945*. Fort Lee, NJ: Barricade Books, 2000.
Kobler, John. *Ardent Spirits: The Rise and Fall of Prohibition*. New York: Da Capo Press, 1993.
Kobler, John. *Capone: The Life and World of Al Capone*. New York: Da Capo Press, 2003.
Landesco, John. "Prohibition and Crime." *Annals of the American Academy of Political and Social Science*, v.132 (1932).
Potter, Claire Bond. *War on Crime*. New Brunswick, NJ: Rutgers University Press, 1998.
Ruth, David E. *Inventing the Public Enemy: The Gangster in American Culture, 1918–1934*. Chicago: University of Chicago Press, 1996.

Prostitution, Contemporary

Prostitution, sometimes referred to as "sex work," is the world's oldest profession, albeit a controversial one. Prostitution involves two or more consenting adults who negotiate some form of sexual service in exchange for monetary payment or other goods; thus, there is a buyer (e.g., client, customer, or "john") and a seller (i.e., a prostitute), a service (e.g., sexual intercourse or oral sex), and a contracted price. Prostitution is a vast, growing, and lucrative industry. In the United States alone, it is estimated that there are 1 million prostitutes, thousands of whom are arrested each year. Prostitution occurs for many reasons, can take on numerous forms, and has been made more visible in recent years due to media reports and technology. Debates have ensued as to whether prostitution should be legalized, and action has been taken to reduce criminalization and stigma of prostitution, the victimization associated with it, and the demand for these services.

Characteristics and Risk Factors

Understanding the characteristics of and risk factors for prostitution is important in analyzing the behavior, examining the various legal positions taken on it, and implementing strategies to address the issue.

Prostitutes: Females are disproportionately represented among prostitutes; they make up a large portion of individuals arrested and punished for prostitution. In particular, minority females are overrepresented among prostitutes arrested and sanctioned, although they are not representative of the prostitute population. The intersection of race/ethnicity and poverty plays a powerful role in this since urban areas have a higher concentration of minority groups, and street prostitution is much more visible to police in these socially disorganized areas. Yet, these minority females are arrested and prosecuted at higher rates than other groups involved. Males are also involved in and arrested for prostitution and prostitute-related behaviors. They have been increasingly represented in the number (approximately 40 percent) of those arrested for prostitution, soliciting sex, and "pimping."

In order to understand the nature of prostitution, numerous prostitute typologies have been created representing its hierarchal structure. The typologies vary by spatial lines, working conditions, income, and other factors. Most commonly, prostitutes have been categorized as streetwalkers, bar girls, brothel workers, and escorts, although classifications vary from study to study.

Streetwalkers make up the most visible prostitutes. They may appear on the streets, at rest stops, and in other public areas, often working in poor or deteriorated neighborhoods. Street prostitutes often face or have faced a host of negative situational and personal factors that have served to contribute to their involvement in the activity; this includes financial problems, homelessness, drug addiction, prior sexual abuse, and psychological state. Street prostitutes are commonly young, work long hours and numerous days, and earn limited amount of money, sometimes less than $20 for their services. These individuals have the highest risk for victimization by those around them. They are also the group most subject to arrest, jail, and fines. Street prostitutes, however, represent only a small portion of prostitutes.

Other types of prostitutes come at a higher price, including bar girls, brothel workers, and escorts. Bar girls are individuals who sell sexual services at bars, night clubs, private clubs, or other social institutions and typically have deals with owners of these businesses. These individuals are able to conduct their services inside private buildings and establishments, evading street visibility. They earn more and work less than street-level workers, but also face problems similar to those noted among street prostitutes. Those who work in brothels, known as "sex workers" due to their choice to engage in this as an occupation, comprise another typology.

These individuals are thought to have fewer constraints around them. They gather at one house or place of service, often licensed, where customers may select a woman (or several women) with whom they engage in sexual activities. Here, a house madam is the person in charge of the business and often takes a cut of the sex workers' earnings. The conditions afforded to the prostitute are

Many people in the United States have pushed for reform of what they consider to be outdated laws regarding prostitution. They contend that the criminalization of prostitution is unjust and hurts those already at a disadvantage, namely, the street-level prostitutes who have already been victimized and experience a host of negative life circumstances.

often much safer and better than conditions for the typologies previously mentioned. Prostitutes in massage parlors represent a similar typology, working in a similarly structured setting. Lastly, escorts are the highest class of prostitutes and make the most money, some earning thousands of dollars per hour. They are selective of customers, often work on their own terms, and see prostitution as a type of work. In sum, prostitution exists in diverse forms and across diverse sites.

Clients: When discussing prostitution, attention toward clients is warranted. Clients of prostitutes are often referred to as customers or "johns." They are disproportionately male and often diverse across demographic characteristics. Clients are usually employed and in long-term, committed relationships. These characteristics have been found across numerous studies, irrespective of the type of prostitute sought.

It is estimated that approximately 20 percent of men have paid for sex. Research has suggested that there are various reasons for patronizing prostitutes, including a lack of interest in conventional relationships, a desire to engage in sexual activities with multiple individuals or individuals of desired characteristics, and a wish to engage in behavior that a partner might be reluctant to engage in. Other reasons noted include thrill, fun, and pursuit of social and interpersonal contact, particularly for those who might be physically or socially unattractive. Cultural expectations and expression of power over women have also been cited as reasons for involvement. Those who patronize prostitutes generally know where to find prostitutes and have access to funds. Further, they often evaluate the risk of getting caught and fear being identified publicly for their conduct.

Facilitators of Prostitution: In some cases, prostitutes are recruited into prostitution and controlled by pimps. Pimps are male agents who socialize prostitutes into the subculture with promises of money and live off the earnings made. They advertise sex for sale to potential clients and connect the clients to prostitutes. Pimps have been noted to be territorial, possessive, and also abusive. They most commonly operate street-level prostitution in socially disorganized neighborhoods. In some cases, intimate partners have been noted to acts as pimps, pressuring an individual into prostitution. Similar to pimps, females who act as agents in brothels are known as madams. They have similar responsibilities and also take a cut of the prostitute's earnings. Pimps and madams have both acted as facilitators to prostitution.

The Internet has also facilitated prostitution, serving as a mechanism for communication between two parties who can contract a service and price. Prostitutes increasingly use the Internet due to the ease of advertisement, a sense of autonomy, and the ability to evade law enforcement as well as the general public. A large market for prostitution exists, made evident by numerous Internet Websites, both group and self-regulated. This method of prostitution diminishes the possibility of being apprehended for engaging in the behavior and may lead to a gradual decline in street prostitution and third parties (i.e., pimps and madams).

With technology like the Internet, it is not difficult to find listings for various adult services. Individuals may advertise freely and the advent of online prostitution has acted to facilitate sexual services offered in various private locations, including massage parlors, saunas and spas, hotel rooms, and even homes. While some prostitution on the Internet may be blatantly obvious, other forms are more subtle, using coded language. Local papers have also been notorious for selling sex discreetly, but due to the widespread use of the Internet, it is becoming obsolete. The Internet is such a strong facilitator of prostitution that it makes the act virtually disappear behind the bounds of visibility. The advent of such technology has furthered the commercialization of sex in ways not previously possible.

Explanations

A proliferation of explanations as to why prostitution occurs has been offered. At the macro level, economic and cultural factors play a role in involvement. Conditions that exist in the United States and around the world promote prostitution. Prostitution is more likely to occur in countries with economic marginalization of females, which increases vulnerability for engaging in sex work, particularly when there is a lack of opportunity for income for females. Additionally, gender arrangements that exist in patriarchal societies contribute to prostitution.

Males are socialized to be dominant and aggressive, while females are expected to be passive and submissive. A double standard for sexuality exists where men are encouraged to pursue sex, while women are simultaneously shunned from the very same behavior. The Madonna-Whore duality explains this; in patriarchal societies, females who engage in sex with multiple partners are considered bad, while those who are chaste are good. Since men cannot satisfy their desires with all women due to gender role expectations, men can fulfill their desires with a certain few, which is thought to preserve the sanctity of other females. Yet, this societal-level explanation does not explain prostitution alone. The United States has achieved substantially more gender equality than in the past and in comparison to other counties, but the demand for prostitution remains high and prostitution has been diversifying in technological and social arenas.

Life interactions also influence prostitution. Although some individuals choose to participate in the activity of their own accord, many individuals involved in prostitution are pushed into it by those around them, whether a friend, an intimate partner, or a family member. Negative life circumstances can also act as a push factor toward prostitution. The most common micro-level explanation cites evidence pointing at the large percentage of prostitutes who are survivors of abuse, particularly sexual abuse and incest committed by someone they know. Such victimization might teach victims to identify with themselves as objects rather than beings, which sways them to engage in the behavior. The victimization then continues with exposure to violence and exploitation by those in higher positions with more power. This more commonly holds for lower-level prostitution but has also been found for other levels.

The Media and Prostitution

Although street prostitution has been the most studied due to the ability to identify those involved, other forms are widespread and have received great notice, courtesy of the media. In recent years, numerous political figures and officials have faced public scrutiny when the media called attention to their roles in soliciting sexual services via phone services and Internet listings. Among these cases was married New York Governor Eliot Spitzer, a well-known lawyer and politician, who resigned from his position when he was exposed in 2008 for his involvement in an international prostitution ring known as the Emperors' Club VIP. The organization was comprised of high-level escorts who provided sexual services at great costs to clients who booked appointments online or by phone. Federal investigations found Spitzer to have procured services exceeding $80,000, revealing the lucrative nature of the industry. Other politicians have also shared media attention, including Senator David Vitter, who was linked to a Washington escort service.

In 2009, the use of Internet listings in facilitating sexual services had received national attention arising from the case of the "Craigslist killer," Philip Markoff. Markoff targeted females advertising "erotic" services; the first female was robbed, but the second was murdered. Given that higher-priced prostitution is thought to be safer, the case serves as a grave reminder that violence and exploitation occur outside street-level prostitution. These cases, among many others, demonstrate the underground nature of these services.

Legal prostitution has also been popularized. Advertisements via billboards, radio, and television have attempted to attract customers. Further, television shows and series now focus on sex work in brothels. HBO's *Cathouse* features Nevada's Moonlite Bunny Ranch.

Contemporary Views

In recent years, the debate regarding whether prostitution should be seen as criminal behavior or as legitimate activity has become increasingly contentious. There are a wide range of perspectives pertaining to this issue, often guided by morals and beliefs. Contemporary views on prostitution focus on morality, social problems, gender organization and arrangements, human rights, health, and labor. While there is a general consensus that forced prostitution through kidnapping, violence, and deception is immoral and wrong, considerably less force is always subject to deliberation. Some individuals contend that all prostitution is forced, whether through violence or threats of violence, fraud, deception, or negative life circumstances. They also see prostitution as a criminal offense that contributes to the decay of morality, community well-being, and overall health. Conversely, others argue that it should be a choice, and criminalizing prostitution only serves to revictimize those already victimized by their own life circumstances.

Against Prostitution: Individuals opposed to prostitution have coalesced around the view that prostitution is rarely voluntary, is exploitative in nature, and is an extreme form of gender discrimination that prevents females from being seen as males' equal counterparts. They argue that gender inequality will remain unattainable as long as men are buying, selling, and exploiting women for sex. Moreover, they contend that decriminalizing or legalization of prostitution would contribute to violence against women since women would be viewed as a commodity or second-class citizens. Thus, to support prostitution is a method for males to maintain dominance over women and contribute to gendered violence. Further, those opposed to prostitution argue that it contributes to moral erosion. Individuals and groups on this side of the debate oppose the legitimization of prostitution and want to end the institution of prostitution to promote an idealistic society. They also work to eliminate the sex industry overall, protesting against pornography, gentleman's clubs, and so forth.

Groups like WHISPER (Women Hurt In the System of Prostitution Engaged in Revolt) and CATW (Coalition Against Trafficking in Women) reflect the views of this side of the debate. They emphasize the patriarchal environment in which prostitution occurs and argue that it contributes to the sexual objectification and degradation of women as well as the double standard in society. Moreover, given evidence of prostitution in countries with gender inequality, they argue that is difficult to estimate just how many individuals would "choose" to engage in sex work if afforded other economic opportunities.

For Prostitution: Many individuals in the United States have pushed for reform of what they consider to be outdated law and discriminatory practices regarding prostitution. They argue that prostitution offers a viable source of income where individuals can earn better-than-average pay, which they would not be able to do given any other opportunity. Further, if legalized or decriminalized, those who choose to engage in prostitution could act with agency, acting in a self-directed way rather than being forced under the wing of a pimp or madam. This side of the debate contends that the criminalization of prostitution is also unjust and hurts those already at a disadvantage, namely, the street-level prostitutes who have been victimized and experience a host of negative life circumstances. Criminal justice responses have disproportionately focused their efforts and resources on apprehending these prostitutes and served to revictimize them. If prostitutes fear apprehension, they are also less trusting of police and therefore unlikely to report victimization. Cases of police misbehavior have also called for the decriminalization/legalization of prostitution.

Prostitutes' rights organizations, social justice networks, and various coalitions on prostitution have guided the prostitutes' movement and call for decriminalization of all aspects of prostitution in which individuals are willing participants. These groups argue that one should be able to choose whether or not to engage in such behavior, and the government should not interfere with private matters involving consenting adults. These groups argue that prostitutes should not face legal repercussions or stigma and should be afforded the same rights as workers in any other occupation. COYOTE (Call Off Your Old Tired Ethics) and HIRE (Hooking Is Real Employment) are two groups that have contributed to this movement. They view prostitution as a legitimate occupation and advocate the repeal of laws against prostitution, arguing that such laws are responsible for the real victimization of prostitutes. By providing sex workers with agency, autonomy, and self-regulation, their victimization can be reduced and they may be able to better their current circumstances. The American Civil Liberties Union also takes this view, arguing that one should be able to freely choose whether to engage in the activities and be afforded the same protection and rights as any other person.

Responses to Prostitution

Prostitution has proven to be a complex issue. Government officials, criminal justice agencies, community groups, support organizations, social service agencies, and public health agencies have largely influenced law. Four legal approaches have guided responses to prostitution: prohibition, abolition, legalization, and decriminalization. Prohibition punishes anyone involved in prostitution, whether the prostitute or those who facilitate it. Abolition criminalizes individuals other than the prostitute (i.e., clients, pimps, madams, and traffickers). People supporting this approach argue that simply targeting prostitutes does not get at the source of the problem. In this approach, prostitutes are also seen as victims, disadvantaged and constrained in their opportunities to earn a living. The legalization approach is where government regulation exists; revenue is generated from taxation of services. Decriminalization deals with repealing all laws pertaining to prostitution; those who support this view believe that government should not interfere in the private lives of consenting adults. While the former two approaches focus on criminalization, the latter two focus on normalization.

The predominant policy of federal and state law has been prohibition. Federal law prohibits crossing state or international boundaries for purposes of sex; it also criminalizes the transportation of individuals for purposes of sex and forbids deception and coercion. Prostitution near military and naval bases has also been prohibited by federal law, and federal law has placed a ban on visas and admission to the United States for any foreigner who has engaged in prostitution within 10 years of the date applied. The federal government, however, has given states discretion as to which approach to take; states have primarily followed precedent set forth by the federal government.

State laws criminalize the act of soliciting sex, engaging in prostitution, and profiting from prostitution in all but one state: Nevada. Prior to 2009, Rhode Island was a state that decriminalized these acts, but in 2009, they made it a misdemeanor. States where it is criminalized have proposed various penalties for prostitutes, customers, pimps, and brothel owners. Penalties for prostitutes and customers are typically misdemeanors for first offenses, while penalties for pimps and brothel owners have been classified as felonies for first offenses. Subsequent convictions for prostitutes or clients may be upgraded to a felony charge. An examination of potential penalties for prostitutes and customers across states reveals that most states have imposed standardized, equivalent sanctions for the buyer and seller in the form of fines and/ or jail. However, some states have proposed potentially slightly higher penalties for customers (e.g., Arizona, Montana, New York, and Rhode Island) while other states have proposed higher penalties for prostitutes (e.g., Delaware and Kansas). Laws have also been enacted in recent years to enhance the penalties for prostitutes arrested and convicted for prostitution if they are aware of their human immunodeficiency virus (HIV) status and continue to engage in the activity.

There has been a desire by many to reform what is considered to be outdated law. Recognizing that simply decriminalizing prostitution might lead to problems, and that prohibition serves to victimize those already disadvantaged, some places have adopted abolition and legalization as strategies. Abolition views the prostitutes as victims and pushes for criminalizing those who solicit sex or are third parties, thereby targeting demand. Sweden has adopted this approach. Canada, the United Kingdom, and many other places have legalized prostitution but criminalized it in public places and criminalized pimping, brothel owning, and other activities. For legalization, prostitution is regulated and mandatory health checks are imposed to prevent the spread of sexually transmitted diseases. Brothels have been legally licensed and operate in order to provide protection for vulnerable women who might otherwise be exploited; these can be found in certain counties of Nevada, as well as several places abroad like the Netherlands. Nevada has 28 brothels with about 1,000 sex workers in the counties where prostitution is legal. Most brothels have female prostitutes and male clientele; there is also an establishment that employs male prostitutes for female customers, although controversy exists as to how to subject these men to health screenings.

Law enforcement policy throughout the United States has traditionally focused on arresting and prosecuting those who sell their bodies. This concentrates police on apprehension of street-level prostitutes. Prostitutes have also been arrested for public nuisance and loitering violations. Approaches to address the inequity of response and prosecution of men and women involved in prostitution or related behaviors have also been taken. Crackdowns and client arrest programs have also been used to apprehend customers of prostitution and those in control of prostitutes, their pimps. This is thought to deter the demand and often only has a short-term effect. Court orders have also even been issued prohibiting those convicted from entering certain areas. In an attempt to reach specific deterrence, methods of shaming offenders have been used; the names of those arrested for soliciting sex have been posted in newspapers, on billboards, and on various Internet sites. Additionally, collective efficacy among communities has been encouraged by local law enforcement to have community members act as a form of surveillance to reduce any street-level disorder that may exist.

New Approaches
Some places have used innovative approaches to handling prostitution by creating multiagency responses that involve police personnel collaborating with social service agents. This comprehensive approach is thought to raise sensitivity and awareness of issues surrounding prostitution to better address it. Diversion programs that include education also exist for those who come into police contact. These approaches raise public awareness and also have offered substance abuse treatment, mental health treatment, healthcare, housing, job training, and support.

Places like San Diego, California, and Indianapolis, Indiana, have also taken unique approaches in using restorative justice methods to address prostitution. This involves community justice panels comprised of various members in the neighborhood and community service sentences rather than traditional sanctions. They are based on the notion of repairing harm and having violators understand the consequences of their actions. Diversion programs that include education also exist for those who come into police contact. This attempts to reduce stigma associated with prostitution and related offenses. Current strategies include targeting prostitutes as well as targeting clients and third parties but remain heavily concentrated on street-level prostitution. Innovative methods have surfaced and hold promise for effectively addressing the problem.

Alison Marganski
Virginia Wesleyan College

See Also: Adultery; American Civil Liberties Union; Fornication Laws; Gender and Criminal Law; Las Vegas, Nevada; Mann Act; Obscenity; Obscenity Laws; Prostitution, History of; Prostitution, Sociology of; Race, Class and Criminal Law; Sex Offender Laws; Sex Offenders; Shaming and Shunning; Sin; Television, Crime in.

Further Readings
Bernstein, Elizabeth. *Temporarily Yours: Intimacy, Authenticity, and the Commerce of Sex*. Chicago: University of Chicago Press, 2007.
Outshoorn, Joyce. *The Politics of Prostitution*. New York: Cambridge University Press, 2004.
ProCon.org. "US Federal and State Prostitution Laws and Related Punishments." http://prostitution.procon.org/view.resource.php?resourceID=000119 (Accessed March 2011).
Sanders, Teela, et al. *Prostitution: Sex Work, Policy & Practice*. Thousand Oaks, CA: Sage, 2009.
Scott, M. and D. Kelly. *Street Prostitution*, 2nd ed. U.S. Department of Justice, Office of Community Oriented Policing, Center for Problem-Oriented Policing, 2006. http://www.popcenter.org/problems/street_prostitution (Accessed March 2011).

Prostitution, History of

Prostitution in the United States can be traced back to 17th-century colonial America. The overt religious nature of early North American settlers has long overshadowed the many vices that plagued their communities, one of which was prostitution. Regarding the long-standing human preoccupation with the pleasures of sex, early American colonials were no different than their counterparts throughout the world. In public fights, it was not uncommon to hear the word *whore* used as an insult. In many cases of the colonial period, the term *prostitution* was used in reference to any prohibited sexual behavior.

For example, an Indian woman who had sexual relations with a white man, or a white woman who slept with a black man, would have been called a prostitute. The term also referred to females who traded sexual acts for food, shelter, or other goods of exchange. Prostitution in the colonial era was viewed as a personal, temporary state of sinfulness rather than a commercial vice, status, or occupation.

Early History

Female slaves and indentured servants were subjected not only to forced labor but also forced prostitution at the hands of their masters. Such women sometimes gave birth to children sired by their owners. The law only highlighted the nonexistence of their rights: A slave would witness her newborn become an asset of the man who raped her, while a pregnant indentured servant received a prolonged sentence of servitude. While such actions were often referred to as "forced prostitution," these were more a form of sexual slavery different from the commercial trade of sex. While most church records of the 17th century focus primarily on fornication and adultery, two accounts suggest that prostitution was more common than church records indicate. One told of the excommunication of a woman for being a prostitute, the other told of a 12-year-old boy who received punishment for entering a brothel.

Neither English nor American common law classified prostitution as an offense, and prior to World War I, prostitution was commonly viewed and regulated as a form of vagrancy. By the mid-18th century, prostitutes were punished under laws that prohibited adultery or fornication or for "nightwalking"—strolling the streets at night with immoral intentions. A Massachusetts law against nightwalking was enacted by colonial assembly as early as 1699 and reenacted by the state legislature in 1787. An actual crime of prostitution itself, however, was not established in Massachusetts until 1917.

Benjamin Franklin recalled seeing young women "who by throwing their head to the right or left of everyone who passed by them, came out with no other design than to revive the spirit of love in disappointed bachelors and expose themselves to sale at the highest bidder." Large numbers of prostitutes followed the military camps of the Revolutionary War. While some officers worried about the strategic and sanitary problems surrounding such a presence, others welcomed the presence of prostitutes as a method of increasing troop morale. Prostitution was by this time a permanent fixture of American society.

A gradual increase in prostitution followed the changing role of women and the American family. As the deeply religious colonies transformed into a more and more secularized and commercialized country, changes in social and economic elements of family life resulted in an ever-increasing population of prostitutes. As the cash crop market replaced the self-sufficient farm, economic relations infringed upon the traditional religious values of families in ways unpredicted. Rather than bartering, men were paid in cash for their farm labor. Early manufacturing moved some of women's duties outside the home, which weakened the female's vital role in the domestic economy. Women of differing socioeconomic status were affected in different ways. Middle- and upper-class women paid cash for the household items they once made. In an effort to expand their role in the changing society, many of these women later played a role in the initiation of the 19th-century women's rights movements. Women of lower-class families entered the workforce alongside their husbands and children to earn wages for the family. Young women from agricultural families whose skills were no longer needed at home entered the workforce in early manufacturing and textile centers.

The less fortunate, single girls and women from poor families, had fewer options outside the home. Their experiences in the workforce were tainted with both wage and sexual discrimination and exploitation. In the very best of circumstances, female work provided wages barely suitable for subsistence. In addition to such hardships, women faced new sexual troubles in their interactions with men. Domestic servants were commonly subjected to sexual exploitation. False promises of love and marriage often resulted in premarital relations. This was not uncommon in rural areas, but without the support of the family and community, the women found virtually no support. In the cities, there was no family or community to enforce a proper marriage when relations resulted in pregnancy. Many women were left with little choice but to return home and face the shame of having an illegitimate child, face the near-impossible challenge of raising a child on low wages, take a risky attempt at an abortion, resort to infanticide, or take on a life of prostitution.

This circa World War II cartoon shows two prostitutes (named Gonorrhea and Syphillis) with a warning at the top stating, "Warning: These enemies are still lurking around."

Nineteenth-Century Prostitution

The rapid industrialization of the later 19th century intensified changes in American family life and further contributed to the continual increase of prostitution. Lower-class families were no longer self-sufficient cohesive units but instead subsisted on the combined earnings of individual family members. Many single women who left the home were faced with poor wages and sexual exploitation, thereby entering the ranks of potential prostitutes. Some women found no other form of employment than prostitution; for others, sex work was simply viewed as their best option. Prostitution in the United States probably peaked during the second Industrial Revolution from approximately 1880 to 1915, as heavy industry forced women out of the labor force. Not until the growth of the clerical and service demand did women attain better employment opportunities, at which time prostitution began to decline.

During the last half of the 19th century, the demand for prostitution also increased. The growth of heavy industry brought with it an influx of male workers, and increasing militarization resulted in large male populations that provided keen support for a large prostitution industry. Bars, pool halls, and gambling parlors that were frequented by working men became prime places of business for prostitutes in developing urban areas.

Prior to the Progressive Era of 1890 to the 1920s, prostitution was frowned upon, but not officially classified as criminal conduct. Disapproval of prostitution was expressed in the form of lawless, unofficial harassment. Throughout the 18th and into the early 19th century, this enforcement of punishment was carried out by gangs that served as a type of informal police force in many cities. The enforcement technique of choice was usually a mob attack, also known as "whorehouse riots." In 1734, 1793, 1799, 1823, and 1825, mobs destroyed several brothels in Boston. Also in 1825, a mob of some 2,000 people destroyed brothels and brawled with police in Lenox, Pennsylvania. In 1857, the mayor of Chicago joined citizens as they set ablaze an entire strip of brothels before claiming that order had been restored to streets of the city.

Professional police forces were being established in major cities during the mid-19th century. The police held the discretion to arrest prostitutes, madams, or johns on charges of "keeping a disorderly house," "lewdness," or vagrancy. The main intent of such policies was not to eradicate prostitution but to merely hide it from the public eye. In wealthy neighborhoods, prostitution maintained a discreet existence in upper-class houses that catered to an affluent clientele. In such neighborhoods, madams could buy immunity from police action through cash payments to the authorities, as well as silence about patrons. Aside from these discreet, wealthy brothels, prostitution was limited to lower-class neighborhoods and urban slum areas far from the view of affluent society. The creation of proper police departments also led to the creation of red-light districts in many American cities of the latter 19th century. In these districts, prostitution houses were allowed to do business given that they paid off the police. The typical sanction for prostitution was a fine rather than serving time in jail.

The 19th-century principle of silent toleration implies underlying opinions toward prostitution that were in contrast to the publicly expressed condemnation of the day. Attitudes toward prostitution were deeply intertwined with class and gender. Despite the common public depiction of prostitutes as societal outcasts, in reality they played a rather considerable role in several facets of American society. On an economic level, prostitution provided income to, among others, madams, doctors, politicians, and the police. On a political level, it supported class and gender divisions through the image of the whore. Women saw in this image a reminder of how they might be treated or what they might become if they strayed from the prescribed path of purity or sought a life outside the protection of males. Prostitution was often associated with nonwhite, immigrant, and lower-class populations. Such associations created a divide among women and served as justification for placing populations at the bottom of the social scale. The observable association of prostitution houses with urban slums and lower-class customers depicted lower-class men as having access to prostitutes, all the while implying that the upper-class men did not. Sexual indulgence was associated with poor health and waning ambition. These associations rationalized the prevalence of poverty and malady among the poor.

Early colonists passed the first law against brothels in 1672, which prohibited the keeping of "bawdy" houses, a law that was imported from England. Beyond such ordinances, prior to 1917, very little action was taken to regulate prostitution; with the exception of an Indiana statute in 1914, there were no attempts to define prostitution. Up to this time, only 14 states had signified prostitution as a statutory offense, and some 28 states had classified prostitutes as vagrants. Moreover, only two states, Indiana and South Dakota, had legislation targeted at the "johns," or male customers of prostitutes, but in Indiana and Iowa, the Supreme Court had ruled that a man could not be guilty of prostitution.

Modern Laws Against Prostitution

Given that prostitution as a crime cannot exist absent of statutes that formally define and explicitly prohibit such actions, the history of prostitution in a legal sense can generally be dated from post–World War I to the present. This timeline stands despite the fact that actions that are currently regulated under the law as prostitution were regulated under numerous laws aimed at controlling adultery or fornication at much earlier times in U.S. history.

In the late 19th century, the growing feminist movement in the United States targeted prostitution. During the 1860s and 1870s, American and British feminists focused on the issue of state attempts to regulate prostitution. The predominantly middle-class feminist movement viewed its primarily blue-collar prostitute "sisters" as victims of the sexually deviant male rather than as deviant women. Society was blamed as having forced prostitutes into their profession and then, as a form of sexual discrimination, refusing to reward them. Feminists argued that prostitutes, therefore, maintained a right to conduct their business free from harassment by law enforcement.

The New York legislature passed a bill for the regulation and legalization of prostitution in 1871, but it never became law. Four years later, another bill was introduced that was also never signed into law. The bill failed primarily because of the efforts of women's organizations, which cited the failure of similar systems that had been implemented in Europe, where some prostitutes were actually licensed and underwent medical checks. Also pointed out was the fact that male customers faced no regulation under such systems. Furthermore, they contended that policies as such promoted corruption among those charged with the regulation.

In 1870, however, St. Louis, Missouri, passed the Social Evil Ordinance, which granted the Board of Health the power to regulate prostitution. The ordinance called for the licensing of brothels, and that all prostitutes be registered and undergo medical examinations. Medical examinations were financed with dues collected from madams and prostitutes. Legalized prostitution in St. Louis was short-lived, as in 1874 the Missouri state legislature nullified the ordinance. From 1897 through 1917, New Orleans, Louisiana, was home to a red-light district nicknamed Storyville in reference to the man who wrote the legislation establishing the district. Modeled after the legal red-light districts of northern Dutch port towns, Storyville was implemented in an attempt to limit prostitution and its accompanying social ills to one area of the city, thus allowing for easier regulation. Brothels in Storyville ranged from cheap shanties to elegant mansions for the well-to-do customers. Shortly after America entered World War I, four soldiers in Storyville were murdered in a matter of weeks. At the demand of the U.S. Armed Forces, Storyville was closed in 1917, although it continued to operate underground well into the late 1920s.

As feminist organizations joined forces with social purity organizations, the economic justifications of prostitution were weakened, which was further hastened by rising concerns over the issue of foreign women and children being trafficked and forced in sex work. The prevailing view was that evil males were forcing young, innocent women into the profession. The middle-class feminist ideology of the day held females as pure and supreme on a moral level and began to support more reform of sexual customs, primarily of the lower class. Therefore, the feminist campaign against state regulation and legalization of prostitution was transformed into a campaign to repress all sexual deviance.

The morality and purity activists were worried about what they perceived as growing acts of immorality among the lower classes in the metropolitan areas. Therefore, they sought to abolish not only prostitution but also various forms of alternative sexuality from homosexuality to pornographic materials. In the early 20th century, increasing immigration and overpopulated cities struck a fear in people that bolstered the movement against prostitution. New laws that made prostitution illegal were enacted throughout the United States. Oddly enough, these state sanctions did not abolish prostitution but rather led to its institutionalization among the criminal world. Prostitution went from being controlled by madams and prostitutes to being a supplemental income for organized crime. Furthermore, prostitutes were subject to harsher working conditions as they faced brutality not only at the hands of police but also from pimps. Ironically, the implementation of vice squads, special courts, social services, and prisons aimed at prostitution solidified the institutionalization and bureaucratization of prostitution.

Conclusion

This has been the state of prostitution in the United States to the present day. Prostitution by the 1970s was completely illegal in the United States (with the exception of 13 counties in Nevada at the time). While the specific legal definitions vary between federal, state, and local levels, most of the laws define prostitution as the exchange of sex for money.

Other laws relating to prostitution are pandering and procuring laws, which target individuals who encourage people to become prostitutes, and pimping, which is defined as living or profiting off the income of a prostitute. Laws prohibiting pimping commonly make illegal any act related to the management of a prostitute. While antiprostitution legislation is generally gender neutral, the enforcement of such laws tends to be overwhelmingly biased.

Prostitution has been legalized in some counties in Nevada. In 1973, Nevada was home to 33 legal brothels. All of the counties were rural, with the largest city to have an active brothel in 1970 being Elko, population 7,621. Today, Nevada is home to 28 legal brothels, which still exist in primarily rural areas.

Ben Atkins
Sam Houston State University

See Also: Prostitution, Contemporary; Prostitution, Sociology of; Slavery.

Further Readings

Davis, Nanette. *Prostitution: An International Handbook on Trends, Problems, and Policies.* Westport, CT: Greenwood Press, 1993.

Ringdal, Nils J. *Love for Sale: A World History of Prostitution.* New York: Grove Press, 2004.

Rosen, Ruth. *The Lost Sisterhood: Prostitution in America 1900–1918.* Baltimore, MD: Johns Hopkins University Press, 1982.

Prostitution, Sociology of

At its simplest, prostitution is the sale of sexual services to a buyer for payment, goods, or services. Prostitution is illegal in the United States, with the exception of 12 Nevada counties: Churchill, Elko, Esmeralda, Eureka, Humboldt, Lander, Lyon, Mineral, Nye, Pershing, Storey, and White Pine.

Within these counties, cities may still deem prostitution illegal. In addition to 10 federal laws that address the punishment of prostitution, most of which address transportation across state lines, all 50 states and the District of Columbia have laws, albeit highly variable laws, punishing prostitution. Penalties for prostitutes and customers are generally the same, although they vary significantly from one state to another. Arizona's penalty for a prostitute's first offense is 15 days' jail time (Class I misdemeanor) while a customer's first offense is 30 days' jail time and/or $500 (Class III misdemeanor). To the other extreme, Iowa's law regarding prostitution, which is classified as an aggravated misdemeanor, carries a penalty of two years' jail time and/or up to a $5,000 fine.

While prostitution is defined as a sexual service for pay, sociologists argue that prostitution is not about the financial exchange per se. Rather, prostitution is an issue of social power (or lack thereof). Therefore, the sale of sexual services is merely a tool by which women are arguably subjugated and degraded. The sociological understanding of why prostitution occurs may be explained by the three sociological perspectives: functionalist, conflict, and symbolic interactionist.

Functionalist Perspective

According to Emile Durkheim's view of functionalism, some crime is necessary for the continuation of social life. While excessive deviance is deemed pathological, some degree of deviance, such as prostitution, contributes to the social order through manifest and latent functions. Note that functionalists view deviance as a social good, not necessarily as a moral good. A social good is an action or occurrence that serves some purpose in the functioning of society as evidenced by its recurrence over time. According to functionalist theorists, behavior or action that does not benefit society or social members will eventually become extinct. Relevant manifest or apparent functions of deviance include boundary setting, group solidarity, and tension reduction. When prostitution occurs in a society and is punished appropriately, boundaries are set for societal members. Through the action and sanctioning, social norms are established so that cultural members are reminded of which behaviors are sanctioned as opposed to condoned. If the action were not committed and condemned, cultural members would have no verification of the boundaries of society. Further, when a culture member violates the social norms, the community tends to bond together, creating a band of support. Rather than a society of individuals, group cohesion is created.

In terms of tension reduction, rather than focusing on social ills such as structural breakdowns contributing to a violent culture that encourages rampant sexuality, being able to focus on the

The U.S. Department of State estimates that between 600,000 and 800,000 people are trafficked across international borders each year, particularly from Asia and southeast Asia. Millions more are enslaved within national borders. Human trafficking is truly a worldwide phenomenon—paradoxically hidden in the shadows and out in the open for all to see.

prosecution of a deviant such as a prostitute permits society to redirect its focus from a systemic problem to an individual problem with a ready solution. As such, the population perceives that the problem is not that American culture has run amok with violent and degrading sexual images and fewer opportunities for women, but rather that some women choose to become prostitutes to better their social standing. Proponents of this logic argue that women are better paid and have more autonomy as prostitutes than they would have if they were working at a local fast food or retail establishment.

Latent function is the social good that occurs but is less seemingly apparent and clearly defined than are the manifest functions. While deviant actions such as prostitution are certainly not a moral good, in other words, it is not an action that society would deem "good," the deviance does serve a purpose in that it justifies the need for social services to reduce such crimes. For example, the services offered by deviants such as prostitutes allow men whose sexual needs are unsatisfied at home to pay for satisfaction without emotional entanglements, thus avoiding the heartbreak and home breaking of a romantic affair. Further, goes the argument, men who are able to obtain services with consenting partners, even if for pay, will not be forced to resort to rape as a means of sexual fulfillment.

Robert Merton's strain theory elaborates that deviance is the result of a discrepancy between socially engendered goals and the legitimate means to achieve those goals. Nondeviants, termed *conformists,* both accept the social goals and have at their disposal legitimate means to achieve those goals. Merton's typology contains four types of deviants, including the innovator, the retreatist, the ritualist, and the rebel. If the socially engendered goal were to make fast money and assuming free choice, a prostitute would be an example of an innovator, given the notion that women can make more money faster by engaging in prostitution than they could in more conventional pink-collar occupations. Because women are typically relegated to the lowest-paying jobs, engaging in prostitution by choice is a way for women to make more money relative to men in the same position or to other women in lower-status but legitimate occupations.

While crime generally, and prostitution specifically, are not moral goods for society, according to the functionalist perspective, their existence does provide a social good and is necessary for the maintenance of society and social order. So while prostitution is predominantly considered dysfunctional and there are overwhelming negative attributes to the action for the individual, the occurrence of deviance does retain some redeeming qualities for the continuation of society.

Conflict Perspective

According to the conflict perspective, deviance occurs as a result of an unequal society. Prostitution is the manifestation of the struggle between the powerful and the powerless. The specific application of the conflict perspective to the deviant act of prostitution varies between pluralistic conflict theorists, who view the battle of power as being a conflict over scarce resources, and radical Marxist conflict theorists, who view the struggle as a structural issue resulting from the inequality inherent in a capitalist system.

Pluralistic conflict theorists propose that deviance such as prostitution is a cultural response to particular situations or events that bring to light competition for social or economic advantage. Thus, conflict is the inevitable result of distinctions between those in authority and those subject to authority. Richard Quinney's *Social Reality of Crime* (1970) articulates the following five propositions, with a sixth proposition being a composite statement, resulting in the social reality of crime:

1. *Crime is a definition of human conduct that is created by authorized agents in a politically organized society.* Prostitution is itself a definition of behavior that is projected on some persons by others. Political agents determine which acts are available for sale versus deemed illegal such that, with the exception of 12 counties in Nevada, sexual acts are illegal while other forms of touching, such as massage, are deemed legal.
2. *Criminal definitions describe behaviors that conflict with the interests of the segments of society that have the power to shape public policy.* Those who have the power to have their interests represented in public policy, generally white upper-class males, regulate the definition of prostitution and victimization.

3. *Criminal definitions are applied by the segments of society that have the power to shape the enforcement and administration of criminal law.* Those who have the power to determine the definitions of prostitution and victimization, generally white upper-class males, also have the power to enforce the definitions (or not).
4. *Behavior patterns are structured in segmentally organized society in relation to criminal definitions, and within this context, persons engage in actions that have relative probabilities of being defined as criminal.* The acceptance and continuation of prostitution is learned in social and cultural settings. If customers of prostitutes are socialized such that customers are not prosecuted, then the perpetrator is not likely to perceive the behavior as criminal.
5. *Conceptions of crime are constructed and diffused in the segments of society by various means of communication.* Definitions of who should be labeled as prostitutes and customers are socially constructed. As such, anecdotal evidence suggests that certain segments of the population, such as high-priced call girls, are typically not persecuted to the same degree as street-level prostitutes.

Radical Marxist conflict theorists view social conflict in terms of a struggle between social classes as a result of the structural inequalities inherent in capitalist societies. Conflict is the result of ongoing social struggle between those who profit and those who suffer to the benefit of others. There are two predominant conditions of conflict. First, the more significant the behavioral difference between authorities and subjects, the more significant the conflict. Second, subject(s) are organized to the degree that authorities can be resisted. Conflict increases when legal norms reflect the cultural norms. When the culture and laws coincide, there is a greater likelihood that a prostitute will be prosecuted. If, on the other hand, the dominant culture does not see the offense as problematic, there is less likelihood that the prostitute will be prosecuted. Conflict also increases when subjects have little power; if the definition and enforcement are likely to meet with little resistance, prosecution is more likely.

If the accused is perceived as a person of importance, the likelihood of prosecution decreases.

Whether the inequality exists between groups over perceived scarcity of resources or between classes over structural inequality, conflict theorists would concur that prostitution occurs when there is an imbalance. When the individual with power seeks to maintain or gain power, the most effective way to do so is to subjugate others. When a female sells her body to or is degraded by a male, the patriarchal social order is reinforced.

Some types of feminist scholars, specifically liberal and existentialist feminists, contend that prostitution is liberating for women. In a society of unequal freedoms where women are not coerced into prostitution, prostitution empowers women, allowing them to regain some of their social rights and responsibilities. Further, female prostitutes are entrepreneurs who are conducting economic business arraignments: fees for services rendered.

Proponents of liberal and existentialist feminism argue that the way to help women is not to further victimize them through stigmatization and prosecution but rather to legalize the victimless crime of prostitution. Through such legislative action, female workers would receive greater security and health benefits as well as increasing state and federal coffers through the payment of taxes on services rendered. These theorists further argue that through decriminalization, there would be fewer resources spent to prosecute victimless crimes and, similar to the repeal of Prohibition, there would be no market for black market sex workers and thus no coercion.

In sum, whether they are opponents or proponents of prostitution, conflict theorists globally contend that prostitution is the result of inequality. The difference lies in whether prostitution reduces or further propagates the inequality.

Symbolic Interactionist Perspective

Symbolic interactionists view deviance as a matter of labeling and social construction. J. L. Simmons noted that deviance, like beauty, is in the eye of the beholder. Specifically, prostitution is only deviant and criminal where and when it is so labeled. While this may seem contrary when considering the personal devastation of prostitution, consider the treatment of prostitution in colonial times. Women who would today be considered prostitutes were more likely to be prosecuted as vagrants than sex workers. Women who were punished for selling sexual services would likely be charged with adultery or fornication.

Further, history provides examples of cases in which prostitutes, rather than being viewed as deviants, were social servants. From 1941 through 1944 in Honolulu, Hawai'i, although technically illegal, prostitutes, labeled "entertainers," were permitted to operate with a $1 annual licensing fee in an attempt to contain and curtail venereal diseases and to service the needs of military personnel and the predominantly male plantation workers.

Similarly although not related, Japan's so-called "comfort women" were utilized in military brothels to satiate the physical needs of those fighting in World War II. Of these women, some were volunteers, whether literally or due to circumstance, while others, particularly non-Japanese women, were forced to become comfort women. While comfort women were originally disavowed by the Japanese government, the Japanese parliament has since offered its apologies and compensation to the thousands of women victimized during this period.

Howard Becker suggests that labels are created as a result of powerful "moral entrepreneurs." This labeling occurs in an orderly process: initial recruitment, role imprisonment, and entrance into sustaining subcultures. Initial recruitment into the behavior in question, such as prostitution, might include coercion by peers to commit an offense. Role imprisonment occurs as the perpetrator takes on the label of prostitute, meaning that society has labeled the offender, and the perpetrator accepts and embraces the label, unable to free himself or herself of the stigma of being a prostitute. Finally, because of the social ostracism of the prostitute, the perpetrator enters into sustaining subcultures that are accepting of the prostitute in spite of, or because of, his/her label and status as social pariah. However, norms precede labels, and the progression occurs only as the labels are applied and accepted. In cases where prostitutes are not considered deviant, such as where prostitution is legalized, role imprisonment will not occur.

Conclusion
The job of the sociologist is not to pass judgment on the quality of social acts and actors but rather to offer an objective, generalized explanation for social behavior. Toward that end, the sociology of prostitution offers three explanations for prostitution as a social behavior that has occurred throughout time. The action of prostitution contributes to social stability, maintains power differentials in society, and serves as an indication of the relativity of perception of action across time and place.

Leslie Elrod
University of Cincinnati

See Also: Adultery; Criminalization and Decriminalization; Criminology; Fornication Laws; Gender and Criminal Law; Prostitution, History of; Rape, Sociology of; Victimless Crimes.

Further Readings
Armstrong, Edward. "The Sociology of Prostitution." *Sociological Spectrum*, v.1/1 (January/March 1981).
Becker, Howard S. *Outsiders: Studies in the Sociology of Deviance*. New York: Free Press, 1963.
Davis, Kingsley. "The Sociology of Prostitution." *American Sociological Review*, v.2/5 (October 1937). http://www.jstor.org.proxy.libraries.uc.edu/stable/2083827 (Accessed August 2011).
Durkheim, Emile. *The Rules of the Sociological Method*. New York: Macmillan, 1964.
Feminist Issues in Prostitution. "The Feminist Position on Prostitution." http://www.feministissues.com/chart.pdf (Accessed February 2011).
Quinney, Richard. *Social Reality of Crime*. Boston: Little, Brown, 1970.

Punishment of Crimes Act, 1790

As the Constitution of 1789 went into effect and the central government of the United States grew in power, criminal law at the federal level became necessary. The legal traditions that had developed in the colonies, together with the need for laws to regulate crime in locations of exclusive federal jurisdiction and violations unique to the federal government, led to the Punishment of Crimes

Act of 1790. Within the American colonies, two developments set New World criminal law apart from its English parent: public rather than private prosecution of crimes, and adoption of code law in place of common law. Unlike England, where victims hired private prosecutors to go after abusers, colonial governments cultivated legal systems with public prosecutors who pursued those accused of crimes in the name of the state.

Following independence, the United States moved from English common law, which depends on juries to know and implement the laws and proper punishments if violated, to a codified system of criminal law. Codification met several important objectives. It helped to ensure limits on the national government, important to those who remained skeptical of the newly powerful national government. Code law also reduced judicial and jury discretion, as both were bound by what was written. With federal law, this meant further limits on federal government powers. Finally, code law provided a way for citizens to know the law and the punishment for breaking it ahead of time; criminal statutes created a prospective rather than a retrospective legal system in which citizens could make reasoned judgments. Both the state responsibility for prosecution of criminal offenses and codification of laws contributed to the need for statutes such as the Punishment of Crimes Act, passed by the U.S. Congress in April 1790.

Geographic limits on states' jurisdiction, meaning that some parts of the United States were not subject to their police powers, together with unique violations affecting only the national government also led to the act. Though police powers—government regulations for the health, safety, welfare, and morality of citizens—were not addressed by the division of power in the Constitution of 1789, by tradition, states rather than the national government had primary responsibility here. Thus, there was little development of criminal law at the national level, as states provided the criminal codes and prosecution of violators. Exceptions, however, came from localities under exclusive federal jurisdiction—federal military installations as well as the high seas and waterways not under states' jurisdiction. Without federal criminal law, acts within these zones would not be subject to governmental regulation. Additionally, such violations as counterfeiting federal documents, bribing of federal judges, and treason did not fall under states' criminal codes. A separate federal criminal code had to police these areas of exclusive federal jurisdiction.

Punishment of Crimes Act

The First Congress wrote the Punishment of Crimes Act, the first federal criminal law, delineating specific crimes and maximum punishments for guilt. It also stipulated how federal criminal trials would be conducted. Among the federal crimes named in the act are treason, willful murder, piracy or shipboard revolt, and forgery or counterfeiting of U.S. certificates and documents. For each of these, the penalty is death. With murder, the judge has discretion to add post-execution dissection of the body. Lesser crimes are also covered by the act. Some of these crimes are related to those already named: knowing about but not reporting treason, rescuing a body from post-mortem dissection, knowing about but not reporting murder or other felony, using false documents to gain a favorable court decision, receiving goods stolen through piracy or helping those engaged in piracy, and rescuing those who have been sentenced. Other, lesser crimes stand alone. These include manslaughter, maiming, stealing (from the U.S. government or a private citizen), receiving stolen goods, committing perjury or causing others to commit perjury, bribing a judge, obstructing a U.S. officer serving a warrant, or suing a foreign minister or ambassador. Those found guilty of these crimes are subject to a variety of punishments, from a specified number of years in prison to maximum fines to whipping a maximum number of "stripes" to prohibition on holding public office.

The act also provides for how trials will be conducted. For instance, it notes a time limit for grand jury indictment after the offense (treason and murder excepted). The accused is to receive the indictment prior to trial, to have access to counsel, and to have the right to compel witnesses. If the accused remains silent, or refuses to plea, the court will proceed as if with a not guilty plea. Executions will be by hanging. With the Punishment of Crimes Act, Congress began the federal criminal code. It established federal courts' jurisdiction to punish specific serious crimes (though it left out assaults and rapes, remedied by the Assimilative Crimes Act of 1825) in locations of exclusive federal jurisdiction. It created federal courts' jurisdiction over federal crimes (e.g., bribing a federal judge, forging a federal document, or piracy). Over time, the national government has developed a significant body of law to regulate the behavior of citizens regarding federal jurisdictions and preferences. Rather than filling a vacuum, as in 1790, when the act provided law and punishment for acts outside states' jurisdiction, federal criminal code now often overlaps, and even conflicts with, that of states.

Janet Adamski
University of Mary Hardin-Baylor

See Also: Codification of Laws; Federal Common Law of Crime; History of Crime and Punishment in America: 1783–1850; Jurisdiction.

Further Readings
Beale, S. "Federalizing Crime: Assessing the Impact on the Federal Courts." *Annals of the American Academy of Political and Social Science*, v.543 (1996).
Jacoby, Joan E. "The American Prosecutor in Historical Context." *Prosecutor*, v.31/3 (1997).
Urofsky, Melvin I. and Paul Finkelman. *A March of Liberty: A Constitutional History of the United States*, Vol. 1, 2nd ed. New York: Oxford University Press, 2002.
U.S. Library of Congress. "An American Time Capsule: Three Centuries of Broadsides and Other Printed Ephemera." http://memory.loc.gov/ammem/rbpehtml (Accessed May 2011).

Punishment Within Prison

For the general public, the punishment portion of the American criminal justice system is defined by prison: criminals, because of their guilt, are isolated from the larger society in prisons; their punishment is to remain separate until their sentence has been served. Society, however, does not end at the prison gates; even within the walls, prison officials have historically used systems of punishment and reward to maintain order, enforce rules of conduct, and deter further criminality within prison societies. Since America's first prisons were built in Philadelphia and Auburn, New York, wardens grappled with two opposing realities in designing the systems of punishment necessary to maintaining the order of the societies within their walls, as well as their own authority: first, the limited circumstances of the prisoners in their charge left them with few means of punishment through further deprivation; and second, the very isolation of prison society allowed them to exercise types and degrees of punishment unthinkable in the outside world. Common punishments for prison inmates' infractions and further crimes before the reforms of the Progressive Era were characterized by their cruelty and brutality; despite successive waves of reform, even contemporary forms of in-prison punishment continue to produce criticism and controversy within the human rights community.

Nineteenth-Century U.S. Prisons
With their dueling models of individual reform, the Eastern State and Auburn Penitentiaries immediately set tremendous administrative and managerial challenges for the wardens placed in charge of their operations; chief among these difficulties was the reliance of both models on enforced inmate silence as the key to individual spiritual self-reflection, penitence, and eventual reform. Eastern State's "separate system," in which prisoners worked alone in their cells, made the task of enforcing noncommunication between inmates considerably easier than Auburn's "congregate system," in which inmates worked and ate together silently in groups, ostensibly not permitted to communicate in any way. The method by which Auburn's early administrations chose to enforce this silence was one of the very barbarous punishments that the penitentiary was originally designed to eliminate: flogging.

Exercised in various forms by the numerous American prisons that adopted the congregate model after its popularization in the 1830s, the basic mechanics of flogging were the same: The rule-breaking prisoner was beaten with a whip or a leather strap, on the back, the buttocks, the backs of the legs, or the soles of the feet. Depending on the organization of the prison in question, the punishment might be delivered at an individual guard's discretion when the infraction was discovered or upon the order of a superior at a set time; these official punishments often took place

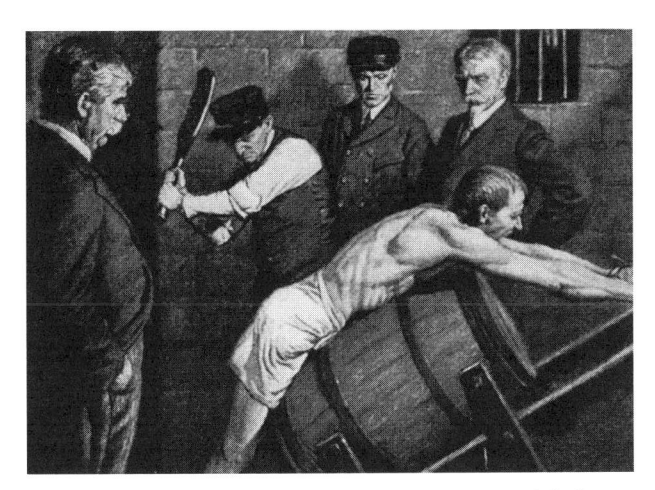

A 1912 illustration of a U.S. inmate receiving "the paddle," a form of punishment until the mid-20th century. Significant reforms were made to prisoner punishment.

in front of the rest of the prisoner population as a general deterrent to further rule breaking and would involve a set number of lashes that usually corresponded to the gravity of the infraction committed. A less formal flogging at a guard's discretion might continue for as long as the guard's strength allowed; in many 19th-century American prisons, inmate trusties wielded the whips.

During the 19th century, periodic scrutiny by government auditors, religious groups, and reformers forced prison administrators to reduce their reliance on flogging and use a more expansive and imaginative array of punishments to maintain order within their institutions. Some of these punishments, such as the iron gag (a piece of metal clamped over the tongue and secured around the jaw) and the hoods and masks used at Eastern State, were designed specifically for the purpose of enforcing the silent system; others, such as the yoke, ball and chain, cold showers, and restricted rations, were invented or adapted from more traditional punishments as sanctions for different kinds of rule breaking. A prisoner might be punished for shirking work (some 90 percent of 19th-century inmates worked, with the goal of making each prison self-sufficient), attempting escape, insubordination, possessing contraband, or engaging in sexual activity. Many of these punishments held the potential to inflict permanent disability or death upon the punished prisoner, most commonly through infection (the lacerations caused by lashes or the constant friction of a ball and chain's iron collar could lead to gangrene, staph, and fatal fevers). Many observers (often themselves proponents of Auburn's congregate system) asserted that the separate system was a dangerously cruel punishment that tended to result in mental illness for prisoners subjected to it for extended periods, a great irony given the contemporary adoption of solitary confinement as the universally accepted standard of in-prison punishment for American prisoners.

Punishment in American prisons during the 19th century varied along regional, racial, and gender lines. Female prisoners might have their heads shaved, find themselves gagged, be subjected to cold showers, or spend a period of time in a straitjacket before a warden would consider flogging, a punishment considered unseemly for women prisoners in the eastern seaboard states but increasingly acceptable as one moved west. The American south underwent a drastic change in the demographics of its prison populations after 1865, at the close of the Civil War through Reconstruction, from approximately 90 percent white in the pre-war years to 90 percent black at the close of Reconstruction. In large part, this shift was a response on the part of the southern states to the economic effects of abolition: state governments viewed the new black prisoners, themselves former slaves, as an economic resource and leased convicts out to a variety of industrial and agricultural interests as slave laborers.

Punishments for black southern prisoners in the postbellum era therefore reflected the southern traditions of African American chattel slavery, with one important difference: Now the property of the state rather than the plantation and factory owners who took advantage of their slave labor, labor overseers no longer had to treat convict laborers as capital interests. In practical terms, this often meant that overseers no longer limited punishments to a degree that preserved convicts' long-term health and labor viability. Convicts who failed to meet work quotas or attempted escape might be beaten nearly to death as a general deterrent for others; those who physically resisted guards or fought with white inmates might simply be shot, buried in an unmarked grave, and dropped from official records. Lax oversight and rampant corruption encouraged such practices.

Twentieth-Century Punishments

The onset of the Progressive Era brought with it significant reforms to official practices of prisoner punishment; beginning in the 1890s in eastern states, and spreading throughout the country through the 1930s, these reforms drastically reduced or eliminated prison administrators' recourse to corporal punishment as a means to enforce their authority. A return to the rehabilitative model pioneered by the Eastern State and Auburn penitentiaries led to a reexamination of the punitive potential of penitentiary techniques, chief among which was the solitary confinement so integral to Eastern State's separate system. Prison administrators soon found that, when coupled with various other forms of deprivation such as partial or total darkness, extreme heat or cold, cramped or confined quarters, the lack of bedding or clothing, restricted food and water rations, and limited toilet facilities, isolation cells could be highly effective tools for breaking the wills of disruptive or refractory prisoners. That this punishment could be explained and described for the benefit of government auditors, progressive reformers, journalists, and the general public in terms consistent with the rehabilitative model of the day was an added advantage, one that tended to deflect any protest at its cruelty.

Wardens who chafed at these new restrictions to corporal punishment could continue to draw upon informal and extralegal means of punishment for enforcing internal discipline and maintaining their authority. While no longer able to officially delegate flogging duties to inmate trusties, prison guards and administrators could still (depending on varying levels of public scrutiny and administrative oversight) rely on various elements of prisoner society to enforce discipline through corporal means. Official procedures, from cell and work assignments to distribution of food rations and various privileges, could serve as means of informal punishment. Gangs and individual prisoners could be unofficially authorized to discipline their fellows through beatings, torture, rape, and murder in extreme cases. Periodic prisoner protests, public outcry, and government crackdowns brought such practices to light and limited their widespread use. Contemporary examples of such abuses, however, continue to arise in periodic media accounts, guard and administrator prosecutions, and civil lawsuits brought by prisoners; such occurrences are a testament to the enduring appeal of informal systems of punishment as a disciplinary tool and retributive reaction.

Official in-prison punishment, meanwhile, remained focused on solitary confinement, a practice that continued to incorporate elements of extreme deprivation and discomfort well into the 1960s and 1970s. Such practices became a focal point for the civil rights and black nationalism movements during this era due to their disproportionate impact on African American prisoners and their targeted use to deter, discourage, and punish political agitation by black prisoners. In his autobiography, *Revolutionary Suicide* (1973), Black Panthers founder Huey P. Newton describes a solitary deprivation cell in the Alameda County Jail as the crucible of his revolutionary activism. Called the "soul breaker" by black prisoners of the day, Newton was confined to a deprivation cell as punishment for organizing a protest against inferior-quality food in 1964. Along with his vivid descriptions of the lack of light, clothing, and bedding (and the accumulation of bodily waste) that he experienced during his confinement, Newton details the techniques of resistance he used to control his physical and mental functions and maintain his sanity under such extreme circumstances. Descriptions like Newton's led to public outcry against the deprivation cell, and prisoner civil suits in the state and federal courts were successful in reforming the practice but not eliminating it.

Contemporary Prisons

The 1980s marked the end of the rehabilitative era in American penal practice and a vast increase in the scope of local, state, and federal prison systems that has continued unabated into the early decades of the 21st century. Among the engines for this approximately fivefold increase in America's prison population were the extension of sentence lengths for various offenses, the expansion of offense types for which prison was the legally mandated punishment, and the large-scale migration of severely mentally ill individuals from confinement in state mental institutions to confinement in prisons. Such massive changes in the organization of prison societies required wardens and higher level correctional administrators to revise and reconsider traditional management techniques; ultimately, however, this process led to an increased reliance on solitary confinement. In contrast to its previous use, solitary confinement under this new paradigm was not used primarily as a punishment for specific crimes and disciplinary infractions but as a widespread preemptive management technique based on administrative prisoner classifications.

The movement toward the "supermax" prison classification in the American Federal Bureau of Prisons and a number of states reflects this trend: administratively and architecturally, supermax prisons are designed around the solitary confinement model. Prisoners spend up to 23 hours a day in solitary cells and exercise alone in attached outdoor yards; in many cases, all human contact, including that with guards, lawyers, and family members, takes place through a plexiglass screen. A prisoner confined to a supermax prison might conceivably live out the remainder of his life there without further physical contact with another human being. Given the scale and historical implications of its use, solitary confinement continues to be a controversial disciplinary technique, drawing the criticism of journalists and human rights campaigners, and causing departments of correction to go to serious lengths to justify its continued use. While the relative cruelty or constitutionality of solitary confinement and its potential mental health effects continue to be debated, American prisoners at state, federal, and local levels continue to be subjected to this punishment as a matter of official disciplinary policy. The social and psychological effects of such widespread use may take years to come to light.

Daniel Stageman
John Jay College, City University of New York

See Also: Auburn State Prison; Eastern State Penitentiary; Penitentiaries; Prisoner's Rights.

Further Readings
Gawande, A. "Hellhole: The United States Holds Tens of Thousands of Inmates in Long-Term Solitary Confinement. Is This Torture?" *New Yorker* (March 30, 2009).
Mancini, M. *One Dies, Get Another: Convict Leasing in the American South.* Columbia: University of South Carolina Press, 1996.
McLennan, R. *The Crisis of Imprisonment: Protest, Politics, and the Making of the American Penal State, 1776–1941.* Cambridge, MA: Cambridge University Press, 2008.
Newton, H. P. *Revolutionary Suicide.* New York: Harcourt Brace Javonovich, 1973.
O'Keefe, M. L., et al. *One Year Longitudinal Study of the Effects of Administrative Segregation.* Colorado Springs: State of Colorado, 2010.
Rafter, N. H. *Partial Justice: Women, Prisons, and Social Control.* New Brunswick, NJ: Transaction, 1990.
Rothman, D. J. *The Discovery of the Asylum: Social Order and Disorder in the New Republic.* New York: Aldine de Gruyter, 1971.

Pure Food and Drug Act of 1906

At the turn of the century, labor unions began to take a firm hold on the American worker, and the rapid growth of factories and cities led to calls for social reforms. These social reforms varied from child labor laws to prostitution laws to sanitary reform. Grassroots efforts, primarily via women's civic organizations, made note of the dirt and filth inside American cities, and muckraking journalists made their names by providing the public with sensationalized stories of death, unsanitary conditions, and the abuse of humanity. Muckrakers also came in the form of novelists like Upton Sinclair. Sinclair wrote *The Jungle* in 1906 about the Chicago meatpacking industry. He set out to write a novel about the plight of the underpaid American worker, but the public focused more on the graphic descriptions of conditions inside meatpacking plants, the refuse on the floor, the by-products (human, refuse, and animal) ending up in the final product, and of the general condition of the American food processing industry.

Sinclair's novel caused an immediate public outcry. After reading *The Jungle,* President Theodore Roosevelt ordered an investigation of the industry. The report proved that conditions were not far off from Sinclair's telling, and in

A Food and Drug Administration (FDA) inspector gives an overview of the seafood inspection process to a restaurant processing facility in Baltimore, Maryland. The FDA existed as part of the U.S. Department of Agriculture's Division of Chemistry before 1906 but did not become a viable organization until federal legislation began forcing manufacturers to comply with sanitary and labor codes.

some cases, the plants were actually worse than expected. Roosevelt demanded that Congress take a stand on this issue, not just because canned meat sales were falling in the United States and Europe, and he threatened to release the findings of the entire report to the public if legislatures failed to respond.

Meat packing plants, while unhappy about the public outcry and the proposed encroachments on their high profit margins, initially battled the fury by supporting a reform bill. They hoped that showing support would ease the public's mind and only require minimal changes within their factories. The Meat Inspection Act of 1906 set rules for meat inspection and packing, which directly paved the way for the Pure Food and Drug Act of 1906.

The Pure Food and Drug Act of 1906 passed quickly, and easily, as the public was still fresh with horror at the meat industry and muckraker Samuel Hopkins Adams exposed many medicines as being poisons. The recently formed American Medical Association joined in the fight to reform the distribution of drugs, especially as the industry was quickly growing. The 1906 legislation required the labeling of processed foods and medicines with ingredients, and the passage of the law is considered the founding date of the Food and Drug Administration (FDA). For the first time, federal legislation put the value of the consumer before the right of profits.

The FDA existed before the 1906 legislation as part of the U.S. Department of Agriculture's Division of Chemistry, but it did not become a viable and meaningful organization until federal legislation began forcing manufacturers to comply with sanitary and labor codes. In 1911, the act was revised to prevent fraudulent labeling after the U.S. Supreme Court ruled that the 1906 law did not cover false claims for advertising. By 1938, a more forceful version of the law passed as the Food, Drug, and Cosmetic Act. The passage of the Pure Food and Drug Act created a long-standing relationship with the government and private industry in regard to consumption and sanitary production. The public's response to the FDA grew and also caused the agency to change, as in the 1911 dispute with Coca-Cola.

In 1903, Coca-Cola changed the main ingredient in its beverage from cocaine to caffeine, and in 1911, the U.S. government took claim against the company for misrepresentation in its products of high levels of caffeine. The court, in *United States v. Forty Barrels and Twenty Kegs of Coca-Cola*, ruled in favor of Coca-Cola, saying that caffeine did not violate the Pure Food and Drug Act. In 1912, Congress amended the act to include caffeine as a habit-forming and possibly harmful drug, and Coca-Cola settled out of court on reducing the caffeine in its product.

Annessa A. Babic
New York Institute of Technology

See Also: Corruption, Contemporay; Crime in America, Types; Roosevelt, Theodore (Administration of).

Further Readings
Scheindlin, Stanley. "The Food and Drug Legislation of 1906." *Molecular Interventions*, v.8/1 (2008).
Sinclair, Upton. *The Jungle*. New York: Vanguard Press, 1906.
Young, James Harvey. *Pure Food: Securing the Federal Food and Drugs Act of 1906*. Princeton, NJ: Princeton University Press, 1989.

Puritans

Puritanism, whose adherents were known as Puritans, was a radical Protestant movement that emerged in England in the middle of the 16th century in opposition to what was considered undue Catholic influence in the Church of England. Puritan ideas and activities, particularly their resistance to the Crown and the official religion it upheld, made an enduring impact on English and American culture.

Puritans in England
The rise of Puritanism was preceded by England's break from the Catholic Church and the establishment of an independent national church. These developments coincided with the rise of Protestantism in Europe, whose adherents often decried Catholicism as a pseudo-Christian cult that deviated from the pure Christianity bequeathed by the early followers of Jesus Christ. Henry VIII (r. 1509–47), who instigated England's break with Catholicism, did not intend to move the country in the Protestant direction, but he inadvertently promoted Protestantism, which many English reformers, including those who several decades later filled the Puritan ranks, wanted England to embrace.

While Protestantism made notable advances in England in the reign of Henry's successor Edward VI (r. 1547–53), some reformers complained that the Church of England retained many elements of Catholic worship. They argued that a true Christian church should be founded only on the principles mentioned in the scriptures. Therefore, they wanted to purify the Church of England of all the vestiges of Catholicism, many of which they saw as scripturally baseless. It was their hope for a "pure" church that inspired the term *Puritan*.

In their theological views, the majority of those reformers were admirers of the French theologian John Calvin (1507–64), one of the most important figures of the Protestant Reformation. His work *The Necessity of Reforming the Church* (1543) highlights the main principles of his theology. Most importantly, Calvin called upon Christians to treat the Bible as the only authority in religious matters. Consequently, he rejected many Catholic ceremonies and teachings that the Bible does not explicitly endorse. In particular, he condemned such staples of Catholicism as the veneration of saints, the use of the sacraments, and the doctrine of transubstantiation. Calvin also put much emphasis on the doctrine of predestination, according to which man's fate rests entirely in God's hands; he firmly believed that one's prospects for salvation were determined entirely by God, not one's deeds. English reformers fell under Calvin's influence during their exile in Switzerland, where many of them escaped during the brief but bloody reign of Mary I (r. 1553–58) as she forcefully tried to revert England back to Catholicism.

The succession of Elizabeth I (r. 1558–1603), who was a Protestant, allowed Puritans to return to England and begin their efforts to reform the newly resurrected Church of England, which they believed was still mired in quasi-Catholic rituals.

To their disappointment, their effort suffered some major setbacks right in the beginning of Elizabeth's reign. The new monarch, who inherited a country that was torn by Protestant radicals and their pro-Catholic opponents, was not inclined to move in either direction to avoid bloodshed. In what became known as the Elizabethan Settlement of Religion (1559), the queen attempted to find a compromise between the reformers and Catholic sympathizers by making concession to both: She allowed some Protestant rituals while preserving many elements of Catholic worship. Unsurprisingly, many Protestant reformers found this arrangement utterly unsatisfactory.

In their reaction to the Elizabethan Settlement, Protestant dissenters can be classified in two basic categories. One group was formed by those who remained members of the Church of England but continued to advocate its purification. They are called nonseparating Puritans, or simply Puritans. Another group consisted of reformers who were so dissatisfied with the Church of England that they chose to separate entirely from it. They became known as Separating Puritans, or Separatists.

Both Separatists and Puritans advocated churches' relative independence from the Crown and were persecuted for what was considered their anarchical and quasi-republican ideas. Elizabeth I reacted harshly to any criticism of the existing religious order. Her successors James I (r. 1603–25) and Charles I (r. 1625–49) were even more intolerant of religious dissent, viewing Puritanism as a threat to the monarchy. Although both kings considered themselves avowed Calvinists, they did not appreciate Puritans' open criticism of the Crown and the Church of England.

Puritans in America

The Puritan criticism of the state church was one of the chief reasons for their emigration to New England. The first to arrive, in 1620, was a group of Separatists (Pilgrims), who founded the Plymouth plantation. They were followed, in 1630, by the Great Migration of Puritans, who established a cluster of settlements in what is today Massachusetts, Connecticut, Rhode Island, and New Hampshire.

The American Puritans can be credited with creation of lasting political traditions and introducing the notion of American exceptionalism. In contrast to many other American colonies, which were primarily founded as commercial outposts, the Puritan leaders saw their mission in America in much larger terms. Many of them regarded their colonization effort as a part of a sacred—if not apocalyptic—war against Satan. Some colonists were also convinced that they were creating what John Winthrop, the leader of the Great Migration, called "a city upon a hill," a model Christian society that was to be admired (and possible replicated) by all Christendom. They even compared their escape to America to the Jewish exodus from Egypt and the conquest of the Promised Land, thus perpetrating the notion that the colonization of New England was a part of the divine plan. Traces of this vision are shared by many Americans to this day.

The Puritans' ambiguous attitude toward the relation of secular and religious institutions sparked a lasting debate in American culture. The early New England colonists nominally believed in the separation of church and state. This belief reflected their antipathy toward the Church of England, which, as a state church, combined secular and religious elements. The Puritans were convinced that the religious principles promoted by the Church of England were shaped by political concerns. This was obviously seen as a problem, because the reformers were committed to purifying Christianity. This is why they made efforts to separate religious and civil authorities.

However, while the American Puritans were afraid of tainting their religious beliefs with politics, they did not hesitate to shape their political beliefs according to their religious convictions. They wholeheartedly believed that New England should be a theocracy, a form of government designed to preserve the purity of their religious beliefs. To the extent possible, their Bible Commonwealth, as the political order of the Puritan New England was dubbed, relied on laws that were based on the Bible. Thus the *Fundamental Orders of Connecticut* (1639), the colony's constitution, was explicitly designed to "maintain and preserve the liberty and purity of the Gospel of our Lord Jesus." In the Massachusetts *Bodie of Liberties* (1641), the list of capital crimes was simply adopted from the Bible.

To protect the purity of their religious beliefs, most settlements in New England were founded on Congregational principles. The basic premise of Congregationalism is that people can form churches (congregations) and choose their ministers. Such a proto-democratic approach reflected New Englanders' desire to move away from the centralized forms of governing typical of the Catholic Church and the Church of England. As a result, Puritan settlements in New England were organized as semiautonomous religious entities, whose members participated in some functions of church governance. This approach was legitimized in the Massachusetts *Bodie of Liberties*, which gave congregations considerable freedom to conduct their affairs.

Religious Persecution
At the same time, the Puritan authorities strove to maintain a sense of religious homogeneity throughout New England. As a rule, they did not appreciate the idea of religious diversity and persecuted anyone who did not share their views. In the first decades of colonization, when they enjoyed considerable autonomy, the New England Puritans methodically combated encroachments of Anglicans, Baptists, Quakers, and other religious groups, whose adherents were forced to leave the colony or, in some cases, simply executed. In the 1620s, for example, they deported many Anglicans, including Thomas Morton, John Lyford, Samuel Brown, whose presence was deemed subversive. The authorities' religious intolerance was also apparent in their harsh treatment of the Quakers, who were regarded as religious anarchists. Massachusetts reacted to spread of Quakerism by passing several harsh laws. The first one, adopted in 1656, threatened captains of ships that brought any Quaker to New England with heavy fines and warranted punishment for the Quakers who dared to come to the commonwealth. A year later, the court adopted yet another law that allowed even more severe punishments for the Quakers; henceforth, they were to have their ears cut off and be deported. The law was modified in 1658 to require execution of those Quakers who returned to the commonwealth after being deported. Several Quakers who defied these laws, most famously Mary Dyer, were executed in 1660–61.

Religious persecution in New England was not limited to non-Puritans. Several prominent Puritans who defied the Puritan orthodoxy were expelled from New England in the 1630s through the 1650s. The first notable case, in 1635, involved Roger Williams, a radical Separatist whose views

Criticism of the church played a large part in the Pilgrims' decision to emigrate to New England. The first to arrive, in 1620, was a group of Separatists (Pilgrims), who founded the Plymouth plantation. They were followed in 1630 by the Great Migration of Puritans, who established a cluster of settlements in what is today Massachusetts, Connecticut, Rhode Island, and New Hampshire.

were considered so extreme that he was banished. He went on to establish the Providence plantation (Rhode Island), which continued to attract religious nonconformists through much of its early history. Even more scandalous was the affair of Anne Hutchinson, a Calvinist fundamentalist who took the liberty of organizing an unsanctioned Bible study group and challenged the authorities who sought to curb her activities. She was tried and expelled in 1638 after a contentious trial at the General Court. Samuel Gorton, another radical minister who was infamous for his contempt for organized religion, particularly of the sort promoted by the American Puritans, came close to being executed but was instead banished in 1644. Likewise, John Pynchon, a prominent colonist, ran into serious troubles for publishing a book in which he questioned Calvinist principles.

Crime and Punishment
The Puritan attitude toward crime and punishment was also shaped by their religious views. Since they saw the concept of original sin as a cornerstone of Christian faith, they believed that everyone was naturally predisposed toward crime. What is more, they were convinced that all crimes were related; one person's sexual proclivity, for example, was believed to be rooted in the same impulse that prompted another man to steal. It is understandable that Puritan ministers encouraged people to become aware of their criminal inclinations in order to avoid committing crimes. Punishment rituals in early New England were typically designed as occasions to promote this notion. As a rule, ministers called upon the people who attended public executions to compare themselves to condemned criminals. This was the case even when a criminal was executed for a rare crime. To quote Samuel Danforth's execution sermon, which he delivered on the occasion of a young man's punishment for bestiality, "the spectators" of executions were as sinful as "the Sufferers" on the scaffold. The authorities, likewise, routinely chastised the population for all sorts of transgressions.

Decline
The Puritan influence started to decline in the 1660s, first in Britain and then in New England. After the death of Oliver Cromwell, the Puritan dictator who ruled England in the 1650s, the monarchy and the Church of England were restored, and the Puritans lost their supremacy. Throughout the 1660s, the English parliament adopted four major laws, commonly referred to as the Clarendon Code, which were meant to promote Anglicanism and suppress religious dissent, particularly Puritanism. The New England Puritans suffered a major setback in 1684, when the king revoked the charter of the Massachusetts Bay Colony, which gave colonists considerable liberty in governing themselves, and united all English colonies from New Jersey to Maine into the new political entity called the Dominion of New England. It was governed by an appointed governor rather than an elected official. In a particularly telling sign of the Puritan decline, the Dominion's new governor, Edmund Andros, was an Anglican with little respect for the political and religious culture the Puritans had built in New England.

Puritanism's cultural impact could be felt well after its decline in the early 18th century. Several legal codes adopted in New England, particularly the *Fundamental Orders of Connecticut* and Massachusetts' *Bodie of Liberties*, created the tradition of self-governance and demonstrated the Puritan commitment to the rule of law. Equally noteworthy was their belief in the separation of church and state. In spite of their full-hearted commitment to ideological homogeneity, the Congregationalist principles that Puritans embraced can be said to promote democratic values.

Alexander Moudrov
Queens College, City University of New York

See Also: 1600 to 1776 Primary Documents; Bodie of Liberties; Massachusetts; Mayflower Compact.

Further Readings
Bremer, Francis J. *The Puritan Experiment: New England Society From Bradford to Edwards.* Hanover, NH: University Press of New England, 1996.

Haller, William. *Elizabeth I and the Puritans*. Ithaca, NY: Folger, 1964.

Knappen, M. M. *Tudor Puritanism: A Chapter in the History of Idealism.* Chicago: University of Chicago Press, 1965.

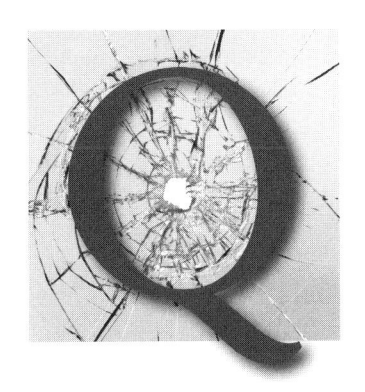

Quakers

The Religious Society of Friends, often called simply Friends or Quakers, is a Christian sect that emerged in mid-17th-century England in tandem with the religious upheavals of the English Civil War (1642–51). The sect's founder, George Fox, heavily emphasized principles of social justice, creating a strong link between Quakers and reform movements. In particular, many prominent British and American Quakers played important roles in the various prison reform movements of the 18th and 19th centuries.

The Quakers are a sect of English dissenters, or Christians who broke away from the Church of England during the 16th, 17th, and 18th centuries. George Fox, a young preacher who was disturbed by the disjuncture between many Christians' actions and their professed beliefs, founded the sect. Fox believed in the spirituality equality of all persons and thus argued that Christians required no clergy. Perhaps not surprisingly, Fox ran afoul of England's religious establishment and was jailed several times; this was a fate he shared with many other prominent Quakers (including William Penn) and one that served to galvanize the sect's commitment to social justice.

Nowhere was this clearer than in Pennsylvania's approach to criminal law. In 1682, William Penn promulgated the "Great Law or Body of Laws," which was adopted by the assembly on December 7, 1682. Though the Great Law still criminalized sexual immorality, drunkenness, and profanity, it utilized imprisonment in a house of correction and/or fines instead of public physical punishment for most offenses except murder, which was still a capital offense. William Penn was averse to jails, and the horrors he had experienced while incarcerated in London's infamous Newgate Prison pushed him to seek alternatives. Because he had been deeply impressed by Dutch workhouses (which were based on the English Bridewell system) during his tour of Holland, Penn decreed that, in Pennsylvania, all counties were to have workhouses.

Penn's control over the colonial government was extremely tenuous. Between 1682 and 1701, Pennsylvania had four different governments, and Penn lost his charter for two years beginning in 1692. By May 1718, Pennsylvania operated under the much harsher English criminal code, a system that lasted until independence. Pennsylvania's embrace of the English criminal code was rooted in the Quaker aversion to oath taking. In 1715, Parliament forbade the right of affirmation, which the Quakers had used in lieu of swearing oaths. Pennsylvania's Quakers were understandably agitated, because their refusal to swear oaths meant that they could not participate in criminal procedures, disrupting colonial justice. Pennsylvania's new governor, William Keith, offered a solution: Pennsylvania might induce Parliament to recognize the right of affirmation if the commonwealth adopted the English criminal code, which it did on May 13, 1718—in the process, repudiating Penn's vision for the colonies. By the time Pennsylvania revised its penal code following the Revolutionary War, the state's Quakers had lost much of their political power, and the new laws owed more to Enlightenment rationalism.

Influence in Social Justice

By the 19th century, English and American Quakers were at the forefront of social justice activism in fields as diverse as abolitionism, women's rights, and prison reform. For instance, in the 1680s, prominent Quakers began attacking slavery as incompatible with their belief in the spiritual equality of all people; shortly thereafter, they promulgated the first recorded protest against slavery, the 1688 Germantown Quaker Petition Against Slavery. A century later, Pennsylvania had passed the first abolition act in 1780, and three years later, English Quakers founded the first British abolitionist society.

Not surprisingly, Quakers became involved with prison reform very early. In 1777, Englishman John Howard published his seminal book *The State of Prisons in England and Wales*, which spurred the prison reform movement of the 18th and 19th centuries. English Quakers such as Elizabeth Fry (1780–1845) were at the forefront of this movement, which sought to reduce overcrowding and institutionalize humane treatment of inmates. Many prominent English Quakers joined such organizations as the Society for the Improvement of Prison Discipline and the Committee for Investigating the Alarming Increases of Juvenile Crime, which advocated increased governmental oversight of prison administration. Quaker agitation led, in part, to the passage of the Prisons Act of 1835, which created the position of inspector in order to ensure that jail keepers treated their inmates humanely.

Across the Atlantic, Howard's investigations inspired Americans to take up the cause of prison reform; many of the movement's leaders were Quakers. For instance, the Philadelphia Society for Alleviating the Miseries of Public Prisons (founded in 1787) had a large concentration of

William Penn was the founder of the English American colony of Pennsylvania. Penn received vast land holdings from the King of England, Charles II, in 1681 as a repayment of debts owed to his father, Admiral William Penn.

Quaker members. This organization was directly responsible for the creation and early administration of Philadelphia's famed Eastern State Penitentiary, the most important example of a Pennsylvania (or separate) system penitentiary. However, prominent Quakers like Thomas Eddy (called the "John Howard of America") also vigorously advocated the rival penitential system, the New York (or silent) system, which was later practiced at Auburn and Sing Sing.

In general, the influence of Quakers in American and English prison reform ebbed during the mid-19th century. As prison administration became more centralized and "scientific" during the reformatory era, many of the oversight functions performed by philanthropic organizations like the Philadelphia Society for Alleviating the Miseries of Public Prisons were absorbed by the state. Moreover, as the number of American and English Quakers declined relative to other religious sects, so too did their political influence. However, even today, Quakers continue to play a vital role in advocating prison reform in the United States and Great Britain.

Paul Kahan
Montgomery County Community College

See Also: 1801 to 1850 Primary Documents; Eastern State Penitentiary; Eddy, Thomas; Penitentiaries; Penn William.

Further Readings

Barclay, Robert. *An Apology for the True Christian Divinity: Being an Explanation and Vindication of the Principles and Doctrines of the People Called Quakers.* Charleston, SC: Nabu Press, 2011.

Hamm, Thomas D., ed. *Quaker Writings: An Anthology, 1650–1920.* New York: Penguin Classics, 2011.

Hamm, Thomas D. *The Quakers in America.* New York: Columbia University Press, 2003.